THE DIARY OF HUGH GAITSKELL 1945-1956

edited by
PHILIP M. WILLIAMS

JONATHAN CAPE
THIRTY BEDFORD SQUARE LONDON

First published 1983
Text copyright © The Estate of Hugh Gaitskell 1983
Introduction and notes © Philip M. Williams 1983
Jonathan Cape Ltd, 30 Bedford Square, London WC1

British Library Cataloguing in Publication Data
Gaitskell, Hugh
The diary of Hugh Gaitskell, 1945–1956.
1. Gaitskell, Hugh   2. statesman – Great
Britain – Biography
I. Title   II. Williams, Philip M.
941.485′5′0924   DA566.9.G3

ISBN 0-224-01911-2

Typeset by Oxford Verbatim Limited
Printed in Great Britain by
Thomson Litho Ltd,
East Kilbride, Scotland

CONTENTS

CONTENTS

INTRODUCTION

Hugh Gaitskell began his Diary as soon as he was elected to the House of Commons in 1945. His purpose, as he wrote in 1954, was to record 'what might be called "inside events" . . . of interest to future historians, or even the public generally. It is not a personal diary about my thoughts and feelings to any great extent, but a political diary, and therefore I quite ruthlessly try and restrict it to what people regard as important events'.

He kept fairly closely to that austere resolution. There are a few references in the Diary to family and social life, and some descriptions of constituency visits, State occasions, or events in the Labour calendar, like the Durham miners' gala, but for the most part he concentrates on politics at the centre. Outside the realm of public affairs, he hardly ever comments on his own emotions and feelings. (A rare exception is the passage about the death of Evan Durbin in 1948.) Thus his private warmth, so striking a feature of his personality to all his friends and many of his casual acquaintances, emerges from these pages only to a limited extent.

As his biographer, I made full use of the Diary, but for reasons of space only extracts could be quoted directly. In view of its importance as a historical source I felt that it should be published. His family have agreed to this with the exception of a few passages whose publication would cause needless offence or discourtesy to living people. The only other omissions are on legal advice. All breaks are indicated as they occur.

In the early days he scribbled the Diary in notebooks (a couple of which survive) and it was typed up afterwards. Most of it was dictated into a tape-recorder before he went to bed, and transcribed later, often much later. Occasionally he checked the transcript, usually not. A good many remaining inaccuracies – mostly in proper names, sometimes in punctuation – have simply been corrected, but amendments of words are noted (unless an obvious typing error made nonsense of a sentence).

The division into chapters is an editorial arrangement for the reader's convenience, since the original was straightforwardly chronological. (The sequence has been altered only once, to restore to their proper place in time a couple of entries concerning 1952 which were dictated in 1954). The chapters are therefore not self-contained, and their titles indicate the main but not the sole topic discussed in them. Explanations needed to understand the text are provided in the footnotes, and the editor's brief introductory notes on the context of each chapter are mainly taken from Gaitskell's biography; references to it in the footnotes specify *HG*, pp. 000–0.

Included with the text are some two dozen documents, almost all unpublished, which have been chosen to illustrate more fully Gaitskell's views as expressed, either in the Diary (where most of them are specifically referred to), or during the period in 1952 when no regular record exists, or on the Common Market. Occasionally they break the narrative, but in the great majority of cases the documents form a natural part of it.

In the Diary itself, which was not found until some time after his death, the last entry was made on 9 October 1956. It seems likely that he would then have broken off for a time, for his mother's death five days later was followed within a little over a fortnight by the frenzied activity of the early days of the Suez war. He probably recorded more subsequently, but no later transcripts or tapes have been found.

The Diary shows a good deal about the daily lives of senior politicians. Gaitskell was a back bencher only for a very short time – too short for his own good later on, for he lacked personal experience of the problems and frustrations of the majority of M.P.s. He does discuss those of junior and subordinate Ministers, in Chs. 1 and 4. It is, however, experience at the higher levels that he mainly reflects: as a Minister running his own Department in Chs. 2 and 5, as a member of the Shadow Cabinet in Chs. 6 and 7, and subsequently as Leader of the Opposition. In each of these roles he throws light on the relations with the various forces which impinge on them all – the House of Commons and the press, the civil servants and pressure groups, party colleagues and foreign statesmen; those relations have in some cases changed very little since his day. His account of the life and problems of the leader of a major party, and particularly of his dealings with his opposite number in Downing Street, are likely to arouse particular interest.

Gaitskell was keeping his Diary long before the early publication of these candid personal records became the fashion. In this he was not unique, and a few of his colleagues generously made all or parts of their own diaries available to me. Comparison with these showed numerous cases of corroboration, many of them quoted in footnotes to Gaitskell's biography, and none of contradiction – though occasionally the two parties to a conversation might have recalled and reported different bits of it. As a historical source the Diary is thus very reliable, subject to one qualification. Except for short periods it was not kept, like Crossman's, at regular weekly intervals, but a good deal less frequently. The record is therefore contemporary but not usually immediate, which naturally limits

its value in, for example, reporting conversations. On the other hand, and again unlike Crossman, Gaitskell was a man who took time to make up his mind and was then reluctant to change it on sudden impulse, and his impressions of events in the recent past are unlikely to have been much distorted in the interval by several successive mental somersaults. There is no sign at all that he ever went back over his Diary 'improving' it for posterity, and only one passage which shows evidence of later inter-polations. That comes at the start of the Suez crisis and is noted there. The dates of many of the mid-1956 recordings are unclear and have had to be deduced from the text: in that single case, most of the entry was clearly dictated before the summer recess but a few phrases must have been added later. His letters from the same period make it clear that no change of view, however slight, was involved.

His irregularity as a diary-keeper is of some psychological interest. He began the moment he became an M.P., recording conscientiously week by week even when there was not a great deal to say. In May 1946 he accepted junior office and was promptly immersed in humdrum detailed work, and for fifteen months he added nothing. He began again only in the summer recess of 1947, and unfortunately failed to complete the subjects he had intended to write about. That autumn he became a full Minister, and kept up the Diary assiduously, once a month or more, throughout and after his first year in that office – during which Herbert Morrison had called him 'the most overworked man in Britain'. In March 1950 he moved to the Treasury, at first as Minister of State, from October as Chancellor of the Exchequer. The intervals became longer, often quarterly rather than monthly, so that only what he saw as really major developments were covered; but the account of these was full and con-tinuous in spite of his repeated lament that the more there was to record, the less time there was to record it in. In November 1951 Labour lost office. After one entry about the changeover, and another four months later about the struggle within the Parliamentary Party, a long period of silence ensued and it was not until November 1954 that he settled down to fill in part of the gap. In early 1955 his battle with Bevan came to a head, and he dealt with that affair in great detail. But as it ended, Labour was plunged into a general election, and over the next nine months Gaitskell fell silent again. Yet those nine months included the climaxes of both his major political struggles of the past four years: the parliamentary assault of October 1955 which drove R.A. Butler from the Chancellorship, and the election for the leadership of the Parliamentary Labour Party in December which saw his victory over Bevan and Morrison. Two weeks after that, at New Year 1956, he resumed: 'It is a long time since I did any diary, but in view of recent events I must start again'. And in those frantic first months, spent simultaneously learning his new duties and carrying them out with his customary conscientiousness, he kept up his Diary weekly or fortnightly for the first time since his back-bench days ten years before.

His own comments about the time available not only fail to explain this pattern, they almost suggest an opposite one. The great gap from early 1952 to early 1956, broken only during one five-month stretch in a period of nearly four years, came at precisely the time when Gaitskell had relatively undemanding daily duties and the greatest opportunities for recording and reflecting. A better clue comes from his hint on 9 November 1954: he had indeed had more time, but the events about which he might have told his story simply seemed much less significant to him than those he had dealt with up to 1951, and so he never drove himself to make the effort. Previously he had been in high office, hoping to make a constructive contribution to policy and taking decisions affecting the fate of the nation. Since 1951 he had been in opposition, waiting in frustration for another chance to act upon his principles and not merely talk about them. But when he became leader, life suddenly regained its interest. Not yet in power, he found himself nevertheless on its threshold, poised indeed for greater power than he had ever wielded in the past, and with the opportunity and responsibility to prepare his Party for success. In short, the Diary is fullest when he felt he was fulfilling himself, and that was when he was actually in government or believed he was approaching it. The pattern is revealing about the outlook of politicians generally, and also about the sort of politician Gaitskell was. Far less obsessed with career and success than some of his fellows, he felt no compulsion to record, even in retrospect, the way in which he had gradually been persuaded to stand for the leadership or the triumph (which had naturally elated him at the time) of winning by much the most convincing margin in Labour's history.

Because the surviving Diary is confined to the first eleven years of his parliamentary life, it gives an impression of Gaitskell's political outlook which is trebly incomplete. First, it begins after his basic views, which he had thought through carefully before the war, were already firmly established. Much is taken for granted. It does not cover his conversion to socialism in the 1920s, or the period of intense intellectual activity in the 1930s when many of the major issues to be confronted by a new Labour government were being thrashed out – often in G.D.H. Cole's socialist think-tank, the New Fabian Research Bureau. Nor does the Diary mention Gaitskell's personal experience of fascism in Vienna in 1934, which greatly influenced his political outlook. He returned to England totally convinced that democracy was an essential precondition of socialist advance, and that it was very foolish and very dangerous for socialist parties to refuse to make a clear choice, explicit and decisive, between the democratic and the revolutionary roads to power. In Vienna, too, he learned the impotence of good intentions and majority votes against superior force. The experience gave him a life-long mistrust both of those who talked glibly of unconstitutional action at home without calculating the consequences, and of those blinded by wishful thinking to the perils abroad if predatory dictatorships were allowed to acquire military predominance.

Secondly, as we have seen, the Diary omits some of his main activities as an Opposition front-bencher in the early 1950s. His principal contribution – the selection, organisation and inspiration of a brilliant Labour finance team – goes almost unmentioned. Altogether absent are the general election of May 1955, and his election to the Party leadership that December. (If he gives disproportionate space instead to battles inside the Labour Party, that reflects his concern, not for his own advancement, but that the Party should continue to be led by those who shared his principles.) Thirdly and finally, only ten quite untypical months of his seven years of leadership are covered.

The power struggle within the Party is a focus of attention in the early 1950s. Yet during the period of the Diary there was less internal disagreement than usual over the main issues of domestic policy. Measures broadly agreed on before the war, and sometimes worked out in detail in the wartime coalition government, were implemented with little or no dissent. In opposition, these conflicts were muted until the 1959 election; and even the subsequent battle over Clause Four arose not over Gaitskell's specific proposals but from unjustified (and soon disproved) suspicions of his long-term aims.

It was on foreign and defence policy that the conflicts developed, though again serious divisions emerged only in and after 1951. Britain's main post-war policies were initiated by *Labour*. They were adopted by a united Labour leadership and a vast majority of the Party: notably the alliance with the United States and acceptance of her economic help in rebuilding Europe, the Atlantic Pact and the military commitments necessary to preserve it. Attlee, Bevin and their colleagues had just survived a major war which might, they believed, have been avoided if the Western democracies had acted in time. The Soviet Union was steadily consolidating its grip on its satellites, blockading Berlin and threatening Yugoslavia, while Communists seized power in Czechoslovakia, suppressed independent political life throughout eastern Europe, and sought to exploit economic grievances to destabilise governments in the West. Bevan, like most of those who later became his leading followers, fully concurred with the rest of the Cabinet; until late in 1950 criticism was largely confined to a few traditional pacifists and a tiny handful of Communist sympathisers.

After 1951 that broad consensus was ripped apart as the implications of resisting Soviet pressure through the American alliance became increasingly distasteful: rapid rearmament with all its repercussions at home, war in the Far East, the restoration of a German army. Gaitskell argued that to demand simultaneously both defence cuts and independence of the United States was to pursue incompatible aims: if Britain refused cooperation in European defence, then at worst American isolationism might revive, while at best we would become even more dependent on her and less able to affect her policies. He warned of the dangers of exploiting the widespread anti-American feelings, while at the same time he suffered from them. Many American attitudes were unpopular, and the reputation of the U.S. was tarnished by the activities of Senator Joe McCarthy. Above all the apparent reversion to the power politics of alliances and military defence, reluctantly and belatedly accepted when Hitler threatened, was always repellent to Labour's instincts and to its traditional outlook in international affairs. Bevanism, though neither fellow-travelling nor pacifist, won the support of both those minority groups and, in addition, revived that tradition, which had deep roots in Labour's history and sentiments.

Those traditions and instincts, however natural in a propagandist movement in permanent opposition, were inappropriate to a party of government. No one knew it better than Bevan, who – like Churchill – was as well aware of the constraints of power when he held it as he could be robust in overlooking them when he was outside and seeking to break in. In office, however, he behaved as a man of government for five years. With his successful ministerial record in introducing the National Health Service, and his seniority in Parliament and in the Party, he was a natural aspirant to major office. Instead, Gaitskell became Chancellor of the Exchequer in October 1950, and Morrison Foreign Secretary in the following March. Resenting his loss of influence and what he saw as the government's drift and loss of purpose, and perhaps fearing to alienate his back-bench and activist followers by his new responsibility as Minister of Labour for the rearmament programme, Bevan became embroiled with Gaitskell over charges on teeth and spectacles at a time when he was already wondering whether his continuation in office would serve either his own interest or his conception of the Party's future. After his resignation he gave expression to anti-American and anti-militarist feeling and, briefly and intermittently, to concern about the H-bomb. But during the period of the Diary he neither pursued a consistent policy nor attempted seriously to build a consensus for an alternative strategy.

Many of his leading followers were also later to show themselves capable ministers and not merely fuglemen of protest. But during much of Gaitskell's lifetime they acted as political opponents, seeking to upset the existing balance of power in the Labour Party in order to win control of it themselves. Other Bevanites, particularly the journalists, used their various platforms to mobilise the critics of Labour's leaders and their policy; *Tribune* and the *New Statesman* concentrated particularly on Gaitskell, pursuing him (and the others) unremittingly, as he said at Stalybridge, with 'grossly misleading propaganda, poisonous innuendoes and malicious attacks . . . [and] vitriolic abuse'. (The sample shown in Document 10 is a singularly mild specimen.) In different degrees with different individuals and at different times, they opposed the leadership because of disagreement about the issues, dissent over the Party's best strategy, or personal jealousies and rivalries.

Here the incompleteness of the Diary can cause some distortion, for Gaitskell's opinions of his colleagues are recorded in the early years – at first a relatively united government, then furious internecine strife in opposition, later the seeds of reconciliation at the start of his leadership – while their subsequent evolution does not appear in these pages. After the busy but harmonious months which fill the last year of the Diary, he was plunged within a few weeks into the great battle over Suez. The early stages of that crisis, recounted here, show both his initial hopes of preserving a bipartisan approach, and also the absurdity of the suggestion that he changed his stand under party pressure. They end before the climax when, convinced that the Prime Minister had personally betrayed him, he spoke for that half of the country which saw Eden's actions as 'criminal folly'.

Many judgments of colleagues were modified over these later years as they themselves developed and his own impressions of them changed. Others had to be revised after those stern tests of character exposed weaknesses, as relationships altered when people came under pressure, or as even Gaitskell's unusual tolerance was strained by the bitterness of these conflicts. His opinions of people as expressed in the Diary thus by no means necessarily reflect his settled or final verdicts. The most obvious case is that of Aneurin Bevan, for whom Gaitskell's view in these pages shows qualified admiration, later deteriorating into bitter hostility, and then beginning to return towards the more balanced and sympathetic appraisal he had arrived at a year later. But he was never obsessive even about those he judged most harshly. When an interviewer in 1961 asked whether he could work again with former colleagues who had tried to overthrow him, he replied affirmatively:

> in politics the situation changes a great deal, and very often you don't understand somebody else's motives, and if you were to sort of be a tremendously unforgiving, ruthless type I don't think again you could do your job properly. I am human and of course

one doesn't like it . . . one must just try and get over it, that's all . . . Politics is a very tense sort of existence . . . part of the price you pay for a very interesting life. [*HG*, p. 751]

Candid and critical judgments, privately felt at the time they were recorded, must therefore be viewed in the light of Gaitskell's conduct at the periods when he had most freedom of action. Long before his election as Party leader he had been seeking to shed his reputation as a factional spokesman, though there was a brief but damaging aberrant period in the spring of 1955, which did not last long. Immediately after his elevation he set out to reunite the Party both by healing bruised personal relations and by working out a new and broadly acceptable policy. At first he was strikingly successful; Bevan, Wilson and Crossman were front-benchers under his leadership, and in 1958 he was described as heading 'a predominantly left-wing team'. The struggles that followed the 1959 defeat, much more memorable but much less typical, have warped recollections ever since; as soon as he had won the battle over defence, he reverted at once to the conciliatory stance that had characterised the early years of his leadership. Within a year he had to face yet another conflict, in which he was opposed by many close friends and supported by many former critics. That ended with his personal authority at its peak – in the Party, in Parliament and in the country. But he never did reap the fruits, for he died three months later.

As editor of Gaitskell's diary I have naturally benefited greatly from the help I received and acknowledged in writing his biography. But I wish to repeat here my gratitude to Baroness Gaitskell and her daughters, Mrs McNeal and Mrs Wasserman, who have agreed to the text being published; to the Warden and Fellows of Nuffield College, Oxford for enabling me to undertake the task, and to its librarians, who made that task manageable. I am grateful also to Nigel Bowles who checked the manuscript; to Nicol Rae and David Bryan, who read the proofs and helped with the index; and especially to Jean Brotherhood, my long-suffering secretary.

ABBREVIATIONS

A.D.A.	Americans for Democratic Action
A.E.U.	Amalgamated Engineering Union (now A.U.E.W.)
A.F. of L.	American Federation of Labor
ASLEF	Associated Society of Locomotive Engineers and Firemen
ASSET	Association of Supervisory Staffs, Executives and Technicians (now ASTMS)
A.T.&T.	American Telephone and Telegraph Co.
B.E.A.	British Electricity Authority
B.o.T.	Board of Trade
C.D.U.	Christian Democratic Union (German party)
C.I.G.S.	Chief of the Imperial General Staff
C.I.O.	Congress of Industrial Organisations (U.S. trade union federation)
C.P.(G.B.)	Communist Party (of Great Britain)
C.P.S.U.	Communist Party of Soviet Union
C.R.O.	Commonwealth Relations Office
E.C.A.	European Cooperation Administration (of the U.S. government)
ECOSOC	Economic and Social Council (of the U.N.)
E.E.C.	European Economic Community (the 'Common Market'; 'the Six')
EFTA	European Free Trade Area ('the Seven')
EOKA	Cypriot terrorist movement fighting for Enosis (union with Greece)
E.P.C.	Economic Policy Committee (of the U.K. Cabinet)
E.P.U.	European Payments Union
E.T.U.	Electrical Trades Union (now E.E.T.P.U.)
F.D.P.	Free Democratic Party (of Germany)
F.O.	Foreign Office

ABBREVIATIONS

H.C. Deb.	House of Commons Debates
H.M.G.	His/Her Majesty's Government (in the U.K.)
I.C.I.	Imperial Chemical Industries
I.C.S.	Indian Civil Service
I.L.P.	Independent Labour Party
I.M.F.	International Monetary Fund
I.P.C.	International Publishing Company
I.T.A.,N.	Independent Television Authority/News
L.C.C.	London County Council[1]
L.P.; L.P.C.R.	Labour Party; – Conference Report
L.P.S.	Lord Privy Seal
L.S.E.	London School of Economics and Political Science
M.E.P.	Member of the European Parliament
M.F.P.	Ministry of Fuel and Power
NATO	North Atlantic Treaty Organisation
N.C.B.	National Coal Board
N.E.C.	National Executive Committee (of the Labour Party)
N.E.D.C.	National Economic Development Council
N.U.G.M.W.	National Union of General and Municipal Workers (now G.M.B.A.T.U.)
N.U.M.	National Union of Mineworkers
NUPE	National Union of Public Employees
N.U.R.	National Union of Railwaymen
O.E.E.C.	Organisation for European Economic Cooperation
P.A.Y.E.	Pay-as-you-earn (income-tax)
P.C.	Parliamentary Committee (of the P.L.P.; the Shadow Cabinet)[2]
P.L.P.	Parliamentary Labour Party
P.M.G.	Postmaster General
P.P.S.	Parliamentary Private Secretary

1 The L.C.C was first elected in 1889, was controlled by Labour from 1934, and was replaced in 1964 by a Greater London Council covering a wider area (except that an Inner London Education Authority survived within the old boundaries).
2 It exists only when Labour is in opposition, and was called the Executive Committee 1923–51. In office, there is a liaison committee instead.

R.A.F.   Royal Air Force

S.D.P.   Social Democratic Party (of the U.K.)
SEATO   South East Asia Treaty Organisation
SHAPE   Supreme Headquarters Allied Powers in Europe
                      (NATO H.Q.)
S.P.D.   German Socialist Party

T.&C. Planning   Town and Country Planning
T.&G.W.U.   Transport & General Workers Union
T.S.S.A.   Transport Salaried Staffs Association
T.U.C.   Trade Union Congress (and its General Council)
T.U. Group   Trade Union Group of the P.L.P.

U.C.L.   University College, London
U.N.O.   United Nations Organisation
USDAW   Union of Shop, Distributive and Allied Workers
                      (based on Manchester)

V.F.S.   Victory for Socialism

XYZ   (a society of Labour financial experts); see p. 447 n.

CHAPTER 1

BACK BENCHER AND UNDER-SECRETARY

Editor's Note
Diary, 6 August 1945 to 12 August 1947
Document No. 1 Hugh Dalton's dinner to new M.P.s, 30 July 1945

[Immense hopes were placed in the Labour Government which came to power in July 1945. The war had just ended in Europe, and was about to end in the Far East. Like most wars it had radicalised popular expectations, and Labour, long committed to greater social justice and stricter government control of the economy, was seen as the appropriate party to handle the post-war difficulties.

Those difficulties were enormous. Industry had been converted far more thoroughly to war production in Britain than in Germany or the United States, and could be reconverted only gradually to peacetime activities. Britain had sold off foreign assets and incurred debts during the war, so that to pay her way abroad she had now to increase exports (by volume) by no less than two-thirds. That ambitious target was achieved in only five years. But for food and raw materials to keep her industries working during this dramatic recovery, Britain depended, until Marshall Aid three years later, on a demanding American Administration, constrained by a mistrustful and hostile Congress.

In those daunting circumstances, keen supporters expected the first majority Labour government to carry out a domestic revolution, while Conservative opponents blamed it for difficulties and austerities they knew to be inevitable. Their recrimination provoked class bitterness among the comfortably-off against both the Government and the unions. But the wartime coalition had given the Labour Party both governmental experience and a new political self-confidence; the Party in those years was relatively free from its inveterate factionalism. Its supporters, too, saw that sacrifices really were being shared, so that in 1950, after five years of stringent austerity, its working-class vote remained almost solid; and the trade unions, enjoying unprecedented bargaining power under full employment, exercised responsible restraint in the interest of their members, of their Government, and of economic recovery.

In 1945 Gaitskell shared the euphoria of Labour's enthusiastic new young M.P.s. He had been a member of the Party for nearly twenty years and a parliamentary candidate for thirteen. Throughout the 1930s he and his close friends had put a vast amount of time and energy into planning the constructive programme which previous Labour governments had never had. At the end of the decade it had seemed that their efforts were all being rendered irrelevant by the advance of Nazi Germany. During the war they had worked in different ways for national survival, and later to ensure that the coming victory was put to better use than in 1918. With the defeat of the Nazis and then the triumphant general election of 1945, they saw opening a great opportunity to shape a new future for the country, and a chance to contribute towards implementing the plans on which they had worked so hard.

Gaitskell spent less than a year on the back benches, becoming Parliamentary Secretary at the Ministry of Fuel and Power in May 1946. It was a crucial Department both economically, since Britain's industrial recovery depended overwhelmingly on the revival of coal production, and politically, because it was responsible for three of the first four industries to be nationalised. That strategic position guaranteed difficulties, and opportunities, to the Ministers responsible for it. He had difficult relations with his chief, Emanuel Shinwell, a veteran who had never trusted anyone, and was not about to start with the new young middle-class Labour M.P.s. Shinwell's suspicions grew after the great fuel crisis of February 1947, in which Gaitskell played a major part not recorded here (see *HG*, pp. 135–8); and after Gaitskell replaced him in the reshuffle of that October, his jealousy and spite lasted for years. The fuel crisis was quickly followed by a summer currency crisis, when the American loan, on which Britain depended for the post-war transition, was dissipated in a few weeks as a result of the U.S. insistence on making sterling convertible long before British industry could supply the goods for which her foreign creditors were clamouring. It was the end of the early Labour euphoria, a blow to party unity, and the start of a long series of financial crises.]

Diary, 6 August 1945

It has been an extraordinary 10 days. Such a lot has happened since Dora and I went up to Leeds on the 25th July. As soon as we got to the Bretts, George said that it was already quite certain we were in.[1] The only question was the size of the majority. He had told our people just to note the proportion of the batches of 50 which were votes for us, and according to him again and again we had cleared about three-quarters of the total.

We got to the Town Hall on the Thursday rather late, but no result had yet been declared. It was soon known, however, that we had won 5 out of the 6 seats. The other, North Leeds, did not seem so hopeful to begin with, but later it became known that on the first count we had lost by only 129 votes and that there was to be a recount.[2]

Meanwhile the results were coming through and the candidates for the various divisions went out on to the balcony, where the Lord Mayor read

1 George Brett was HG's agent.
2 The Conservatives held North Leeds by 128 votes.

out the figures. When my turn came I was rather surprised that he did not even introduce the candidates, but having read out the figures simply pushed the microphone at me. I made the usual sort of speech and Ramsden was very polite.[3] Barford, the Liberal candidate, however, who was cordially disliked by everybody, was foolish enough to end up his much too long speech (he only failed to lose his deposit by 200 votes) by talking about 'national socialism'. Of course he was booed heavily by the crowd.

Later we processed round the middle of Leeds, each of the candidates in a car, followed by a moderate crowd of supporters. One had to stand up with one's head through the sunshine roof and smile and wave. The Yorkshire crowds, however, are not very demonstrative. It would have been more amusing in the South. That evening we started the tour of the division and the women members insisted on hiring a charabanc to follow me round. George and I went in the first car with the loudspeaker and made dozens of speeches. People came out and listened and waved and were generally very friendly, though again not particularly demonstrative. We ended up at the Party rooms where further speeches, and longer ones too, had to be made. I warned them to expect trouble and reminded them what a lot had to be done in the way of party organisations, etc. They took it very well.

Ramsden lunched the next day with Dora and myself. He confessed that his father had been a member of the Fabian Society. He was very sensible about Tory prospects and if he wanted to go on could be of value to them, but I don't think he will.

Dora then caught the train to London and I went back to the Bretts. On arrival there, however, we found that I had to go off to London myself, all Labour M.P.s having been summoned to a meeting on Saturday morning.

Found Jim Milner and Hubert Beaumont on the platform, later Alice Bacon* and Wilfred Paling got in.[4] Though I was tired it was hopeless to try and sleep: they talked all the time.

When we got to King's Cross, I was walking off the station with Alice Bacon and we met the Press Association Lobby Correspondent, who had come to meet her. He said, 'they have just announced the first appointments', and then told them to us. I was naturally delighted: Attlee* has been clever in separating Morrison* from Bevin*. I have always thought HD [Dalton]* would do well at the Treasury and suggested Cripps* in the past for the Board of Trade.

---

3 His Conservative opponent was Brigadier A.M. Ramsden, a Huddersfield solicitor.
* Persons starred when first mentioned are the subject of a Biographical Note.
4 All Yorkshire Labour M.P.s.

Meeting next day in the Beaver Hall – appropriately named, as somebody pointed out.[5] Attlee made an excellent speech. Like his broadcast,[6] it was just the right tone. Bevin also spoke well in praise of CRA [Attlee].

Later Evan [Durbin]* and I lunched with the Chancellor.[7] HD told me I must rest and asked Evan to be P.P.S. E. was somewhat embarrassed, obviously still hoping for a job in the Government. It was finally agreed that he would be P.P.S. if job were not forthcoming.[8] E. and I were both rather shocked by HD's bland assumption that no new M.P.s would or could get jobs.

HD told us the story of how he came to be Chancellor. He had first seen CRA and been offered and accepted the Foreign Office. EB[Bevin] had also been offered and accepted the Treasury. Later CRA said he had changed his mind and they must move round. Probably HM[Morrison] had intervened and pointed out that life would not be easy if he and EB were both on the home front.[9]

HD also spoke critically of HM's frantic and rather absurd efforts to wrest the Party leadership away for himself, right up to the last minute. Ambition driving the most intelligent people mad as usual, I suppose.

Then we talked about the officials in the Treasury and gave warnings against AB, WE and NBG. I spoke up strongly for Dennis [Procter] and proposed that he should try and get John Maud.[10]

I saw Douglas [Jay]* on the Sunday evening. He wants Cripps to bring Franks* into the Board [of Trade]. He also thinks Turner should be put on to Housing.[11]

On Monday evening the Chancellor gave a party in a private room at St Ermin's. I had to make a note of the discussion. I had a curious feeling

5 Perhaps because Labour M.P.s thought they had been helped by Churchill's broadcast suggesting that a Socialist government would have to set up a Gestapo, and Lord Beaverbrook* was believed to have inspired it.

6 In reply to Churchill's.

7 Evan Durbin, another new Labour M.P., was HG's closest friend. They had been Dalton's political protégés for over a decade.

8 Parliamentary Private Secretaries are not, but are often promoted to be, members of the Government.

9 On Attlee's change of mind see Sir J. Wheeler-Bennett, *King George VI* (Macmillan, 1958), pp. 638–9; Williams (1961), pp. 5–6; H. Dalton, *The Fateful Years* (Muller, 1957), pp. 468–75; A. Bullock, *The Life and Times of Ernest Bevin* (Heinemann, 1967), II.393–5; Donoughue & Jones (1973), pp. 344–5. Most of these sources also discuss Morrison's proposed bid for the premiership. (See Bibliography for other publication details.)

10 In arguments about postwar economic policy HG had clashed with the three Second Secretaries, Sir Alan Barlow, Sir Wilfred Eady and Sir N. Bernard Gilbert. Dennis Procter became a Third Secretary in 1948; Sir John Maud (later Lord Redcliffe-Maud) became a Permanent Secretary at Education.

11 Sir George Turner was at the Ministry of Aircraft Production.

most of the evening, having always regarded myself as one of the younger people in the Party, I now suddenly seemed to be one of the older. Sever[al] of those present seemed to be rather inexperienced in politics. The best contributions to the discussion were made by those I already knew, especially Evan, Dick [Crossman]*, Harold Wilson*. I liked Wells, who seemed sensible. Blackburn struck me as a rather less attractive edition of Dick. Ambition very naked, plenty of energy, tendency to speak without thinking. George Brown*, the only non-University man, kept rather quiet. Everyone speaks well of him, though. Perhaps our slightly superior feeling was because we had been in the Civil Service all the war and knew rather more about the real problems of the moment.[12]

On Tuesday I went to the House for the first time. Evan says it is like going back to school, but I pointed out that everybody is much politer, especially the policemen. On Wednesday Dora and I lunched with Henry Drogheda in the House of Lords. Henry produced as the fourth the Clerk of the House, Sir Henry Badeley, who is extremely amusing and very polished. Henry was full of charm, as usual. It occurred to me afterwards that perhaps he might do something for our side, but I doubt it. I promised to tell the film industry that they must ask him out to meals as he says he finds it difficult to get to know them.[13]

Afterwards I went into the House for the first meeting in the Chamber. On the way I ran into Cripps, who asked me searching questions about my health. I said very innocently that, though better, I was by no means fully recovered, and when he said 'is it a matter of a few weeks' rest only?' I said that it would be much longer before I was really 100%. Finally I offered to give him any assistance, whereupon he said rather coldly and mysteriously 'it really depends on your health'.[14]

Only a few minutes afterwards I was sitting squeezed on one of the benches in the House when John Edwards* came up and spoke to me. He said he had been asked to be Stafford [Cripps]'s P.P.S. Looking at me

12 On this dinner, Dalton, pp. 476–8. HG's note appears below, pp. 11–16. William Wells was Bevin's P.P.S. and M.P. for Walsall or Walsall North, 1945–70; Raymond Blackburn for Birmingham Northfield, 1945–51. Unsure of readoption, he became an Independent in August 1950 and called for a coalition government led by Churchill. Later prominent as a campaigner against pornography.
13 The Earl of Drogheda was joint director of the Ministry of Economic Welfare in 1940–42, when Dalton was Minister and HG was his principal assistant. Drogheda was later its director-general, and from 1944 chairman of the Cinematograph Films Council, with whom HG then dealt as a civil servant. Sir Henry Badeley's correct title was Clerk of the Parliaments.
14 HG had had a thrombosis that spring, and had nearly been unable to fight the election. See Williams, *Hugh Gaitskell* (1979; hereafter cited as *HG*), pp. 124–6.

rather hard, he said 'I understand we are going to be more closely associated'. I looked blank, but he could only have meant one of two things: either I was to be the other P.P.S. or Parliamentary Secretary. Later I told Evan about both incidents. He thought it must be P.P.S. But then I had another talk with John Edwards in which Maurice Webb* joined, and it became quite clear that I was being tipped for Parliamentary Secretary. John said quite openly that he understood there were to be two: Ellis Smith* and myself. Maurice confirmed this. I was naturally greatly excited but said I doubted if my health permitted it and that I had already spoken to Stafford about it.

Later that night six of us dined at St Ermin's: Evan, John Wilmot*, Douglas [Jay], H.V. Berry* and Bill Piercy.[15] There was much good conversation and elation that after all the years and year[s] during which we had been advising the Party on financial questions, we were now really in the last stage. After dinner we retired to a private room and got to work on the draft heads of a Bill which Piercy had prepared, and which was to go on to the Chancellor.[16] It was a useful talk.

That evening I discussed with Dora and Evan my own position. Evan said I should try and get them to hold the appointment open until October and try and catch Cripps and talk to him the next morning.

However, the next day I didn't go down to the House until after lunch. Dora and I lunched with Paul[17]. . . .

I caught the Chancellor on his way into the House and agreed to see him immediately after he had been sworn in. We went to his room and I told him of my talks with Cripps and John Edwards and asked him what the truth was. It was clear that the story had been accurate, but equally clear that things had changed, probably that morning. He admitted to having seen Cripps and I think they must have agreed that I was not well enough. Anyway, the Chancellor suggested that as he was going to see Horder at 4.30 I should go with him and we would ask Horder his opinion.[18] He also said, however, that he thought that it was now too late for the B.o.T. [Board of Trade] job. I parted from him in the Lobby,

15 Six members of XYZ, a dining and discussion group of financial specialists who sympathised with Labour. Wilmot (winner of the East Fulham by-election in 1933) and Jay (an M.P. from 1947) were also protégés of Dalton, and Jay was another very close friend of HG. Lord Piercy became a director of the Bank of England and chairman of the Industrial and Commercial Finance Corporation.

16 The Bill to nationalise the Bank of England.

17 Probably Paul Rosenstein-Rodan, HG's closest colleague at the Economics Department of University College London before the war, and later its head until he went to America in 1947.

18 Lord Horder had known HG for 15 years, and advised him during his illness on the amount of political activity he could safely undertake.

agreeing to meet him in New Palace Yard at 4.10; it was then 3.50. I went to the Members' Tearoom and found John Wilmot. He was busily reading the papers, very bad papers like the *Daily Sketch*. I afterwards thought this was a correct sign of great mental excitement. Anyway, I went over and sat beside him and asked him what he had got. He said 'I have promised not to tell a soul, but I am going to tell you because there are special reasons. I am to be Minister of Supply and Aircraft Production'. Then he went on 'Clem asked me who I wanted as Parliamentary Secretary, one of them was to be Leonard who had been Duncan's P.P.S.[19] I said I wanted you (meaning HG). Clem said 'but you know he is ill'. 'Yes', said JW 'but you asked me who I wanted'. 'Who do you want next' said Clem. 'I want Evan' said JW. I then told JW my story and he reminded me that I had said openly on the Monday evening at the party that I would not be well enough to take a job, even if I were offered one. It was all very dramatic. I don't know whether to believe JW but for obvious reasons will not tell Evan.

Then I went to Palace Yard and was told the Chancellor had left a quarter of an hour before, and so I proceeded in my own car to Horder. We had a long talk while waiting for the Chancellor. He said I should not take any job at the moment. I must not have overstrain or too much responsibility until my heart had recovered further. As usual he was charming and answered clearly and on the whole satisfactorily all the various questions I put to him about my physical condition.

Then back to the House to be sworn in, and who should come and sit beside me as we waited, but Ellis Smith. He told me that he had been offered the Parliamentary Secretaryship, but told he was to have a partner and that the partner was to be me. He had since heard that because of my illness this had been changed and that it was to be Marquand*. He was very nice and I told him a good deal about the B.o.T., but I am afraid he will find some of the work rather beyond him.[20]

If Thursday was my day with its inevitably slightly bitter ending, Friday was Evan's day. We went together early to the House and ran into the Chancellor at once. He said he had just seen Horder who had told him about me. I might perhaps be P.P.S., but could be considered later. As to Evan, he said, he was on the list now – 'there may be something for you'.

Later Evan was sent for by CRA and saw him at 10 to four.[21] He came back and described the interview. It was something like this:

19 Sir Andrew Duncan had been Minister of Supply in the Coalition Government. W. Leonard, former President of the Scottish T.U.C., was Labour M.P. for Glasgow St Rollox, 1931–50.
20 He held office for less than six months.
21 Durbin was Attlee's personal assistant during the war.

CRA   'Well, what do you think of the names announced so far?'
E   'I think they are very interesting'.
CRA   'I suppose that means that you don't think it is a good Government'.
E   (mumbling) 'No doubt some of the most surprising appointments will turn out the best'.
CRA   (mollified) 'But I would like to fit you in. What do you want?'
E   'What's going?'
CRA   'Ministry of Supply or Home Office'.

Eventually Evan said Ministry of Supply would be best and Clem said he could not say definitely at the moment, but told Evan to keep in touch with his secretary.

Later, at about 6.30, Evan rang up only to be told by [Whiteley] the Chief Whip* that there was no need for him to hang around, that the P.M. would not want to see him again and that in fact the offers made in the afternoon had been withdrawn. Poor Evan, I had never seen him so agitated or upset. A lot of time that night was spent telephoning to private secretaries and other Ministers to find out what had happened. It was not difficult to guess and in the morning JW had found out and told Evan: they had left someone out – Arthur Woodburn*. However, Clem had said possibly there might be a Parliamentary Secretaryship before long. The next day Evan was completely restored and his usual placid self.

First of all two post-scripts to the events of last week.
1. On the Friday evening when Evan had just heard that he was out, I ran into Creech Jones. He was very angry at being Parliamentary Secretary to George Hall. He said 'I have just been talking to him. He knows nothing whatever about the Colonies'. I said 'Well, he is supposed to be very nice and surely you will be able to get him to do what you want'. He then turned on me in a fury. 'I am sick to death of doing other people's work and letting them get the credit for it. I have done nothing but devil for other people for the last 10 years'. I was pleased to see later that *The Times* particularly singled his appointment out as very unfair, and intimated quite clearly that he ought to have been Secretary of State himself.[22]
2. On Tuesday after the Bank Holiday weekend, the Chancellor rang me up and was extremely cordial. He said that the P.M. was most solicitous

22 Arthur Creech Jones, a T. & G.W.U. official, became the Fabian Society's colonial specialist. M.P. for Shipley (Yorks) 1935–50, Wakefield 1954–64; Bevin's P.P.S. 1940–5; Colonial Secretary 1946–50. George (Viscount) Hall (1881–1965), miners' M.P. 1922–46. Became First Lord of the Admiralty 1946–51. (Titles in brackets were acquired after the date of the reference.)

about my health and anxious that both Evan and I should in due course join the administration. He then went on to re-open the question of P.P.S. He evidently thought that as Horder had said I could do a job of this kind that I might take it badly if he held to his understanding with Evan. I of course reassured him at once. I thought afterwards that the earlier part of the conversation was merely meant to pave the way for the latter, but it is all rather good for one's morale.

Document No. 1

Dalton's dinner to new M.P.s, 30 July 1945

NOTES OF AN INFORMAL DISCUSSION ON
FUTURE POLICY AND PROBLEMS

PRESENT:[23]

The Chancellor	Mr. H. Gaitskell
Mr. J. Wilmot	Major W. Wyatt
Major C. Mayhew	Mr. D. Crossman [*sic*]
Major R. Blackburn	Mr. E. Durbin
Captain G. Chetwynd	Mr. H. Wilson
Major J. Freeman	Major K. Younger
Mr. G. Brown	Major W. Wells

THE CHANCELLOR said he thought it might be a good plan if those present were asked to give their views on the problems now facing the Government and the policies which should be pursued.

MAJOR MAYHEW* said he thought that the Government should announce a production plan for the major industries covering the next three or four years, e.g. that in agriculture the number of beasts should be so much; the output of wheat should be so much, etc. He realised one would have to proceed on certain assumptions regarding the length of the Jap war and, in any case, the figures could only be rough. He felt, however, that the psychological effect of an announcement of this kind would be very great. It would show that the Labour Party were really serious about planning.

MAJOR BLACKBURN said he thought there were two subjects upper-most in the mind of the electorate: Pensions – both Service and Old Age – and Demobilisation. As regards the former he hoped that the Labour Party would be able to make an announcement about the improved rates

23 See p. 7, and Biographical Notes.

fairly soon, and as to the latter he believed that it was, in fact, going to be possible to speed up the pace and, if this was so, the sooner the statement were made about it the better. He also suggested that there should be a visit by Members of Parliament who had been in the Forces to our Troops in the Far East. This would make a very good impression.

CAPTAIN CHETWYND[24] said that while he agreed in general with Mayhew he was worried about the precise manner in which the plans were to be carried out, for example, he would like to know just what was going to be done about coal. He wanted full details published of a plan for coal. In his own constituency he was faced with the question of what was going to be done about I.C.I. and the Chemical Industry. He thought this was by no means an easy problem. On the whole the firm seemed to be relatively efficient. MR. HAROLD WILSON intervened to point out that the Association of Scientific Workers had gone into the question of what was to be done about the Chemical Industry in some detail. A great deal of help had been obtained from Professor Levy.[25]

MAJOR FREEMAN* said he was also very interested in what was to be done in industries other than those which were to be nationalised. He also agreed that Demobilisation was immensely important. Rumours were being spread by Senior officers in the B.L.A. [British Liberation Army] that Demobilisation was to be slowed down, though there was no truth whatever in this. He suggested that it would be a good plan if messages of goodwill could be sent to the Left-Wing Parties in Europe.

MR. BROWN said he thought there would be a good deal of trouble in the work shops during the next twelve months. This could be greatly diminished if leading members of the Government went and spoke directly to the workers and explained the difficulties and their policy for overcoming them.

MR. GAITSKELL said he was rather doubtful about the proposal to announce a definite plan of production. Did not this imply that there was to be control of labour? Yet Mr. Bevin had announced at Blackpool that this was to be abandoned at the end of the Jap war, if not sooner. As regards coal, he thought that it would be wise to subsidize the price quite openly, just as we subsidized food and clothing. It would probably be necessary to pay higher wages still to miners, and there was already some discontent about the high price of fuel. He thought much the most important issue in the next four years would be housing and suggested

24 George Chetwynd was M.P. for Stockton, 1945–62.
25 Hyman Levy (1889–1975) was a well-known Communist who had been a particular *bête noire* of HG's a decade earlier. He was Professor of Mathematics at Imperial College 1923–54, and a former chairman of the Labour Party's Science Advisory Committee. The Association of Scientific Workers later merged into ASTMS.

that the important thing here was to bring more skilled workers out of the Army, even if this involved some departure from the original Demobilisation Scheme. Another difficult problem was that of wages for those workers who had been in munitions and had now to go back to employment which was far less well paid.

Finally, he emphasized the importance of the House of Lords issue. While another General Election should be avoided, if possible, if the House of Lords really proved obstructive then the Party should not hesitate to go to the country, choosing, however, the right issues on which to fight.

MAJOR WYATT* agreed that the building craftsmen should be brought out of the Army in greater numbers. He did not think that this would create any discontent at all. He thought there was a tendency to under-estimate the importance in the public mind of Social Security. He would like to see an increase in Old Age Pensions straight away, even if the full Social Security Act could not be put through this Session.

As regards India and Burma, he thought there should be a General Election soon which would be much less favourable to the Moslem League than many people supposed.[26] He would like to see a considerable speed-up in the programme for self-government of Burma.

MR. CROSSMAN began by referring to two things which 'he did not know about'. Old Age Pensioners were very upset when, as a result of their earnings, many of them found their incomes, including the pension, liable to tax. He thought that pensions granted by the State should be exempt from taxation (this view was, however, hotly contested by a number of other speakers who urged that the right course was to raise the personal and earned income allowances and not to exempt from tax any particular form of income). He thought there was great scope for standardization in cars and certain household articles, such as refrigerators. He would like to see the Labour Party insist on the adoption of methods of production which would reduce costs in this field substantially. As regards the sphere of policy on which he was well informed, broadcasting and foreign affairs, he suggested that we must treat the present situation as though it were another 1940. There should be a series of broadcasts by leaders of the Government to foreign countries. At home the handling of Government publicity was immensely important. At present there were simply a number of competing Public Relations Officers without any appropriate co-ordination. It was desirable that there should be proper planning in this field, not only as regards what was said, but also when it was said. (MR. GAITSKELL suggested that it might be a good plan to ask

26 Wyatt was personal assistant to Sir Stafford Cripps on the Cabinet mission to India in 1946.

one of the Labour Ministers without Portfolio, who would not be very busy, to take in hand the whole question of Government publicity.)

It was, no doubt, desirable to speed-up Demobilisation, but he hoped that we should remember that the Russians could not be properly handled unless we remained strong. They were expecting the Labour Government to be easy to squeeze, and we should have to make it clear that that was not so.[27] In the case of the U.S.A. the position was quite different. To handle them it was necessary to appeal to sentiment. A Labour Ambassador should be appointed in place of Halifax and he should be a non-professional with a background somewhat similar to that of the Master of Balliol.[28] He also thought that it would be a good plan to send a number of Labour speakers to America which was likely to be suspicious and puzzled about the result of the Election.

Finally, it was necessary to make a thorough clean up of our Embassy in Washington. He thought that the whole question of our foreign broadcasts wanted looking into. The idea seemed to be that the Foreign Office should be in control, but this might be dangerous unless Mr Bevin were to clean things up first. He also thought we should be open-minded about the possibility of commercial broadcasts in competition with the B.B.C.

MR. DURBIN said he was somewhat gloomy about the whole position with which we were faced. The major problems – food, homes and fuel – were extraordinarily difficult to handle at any rate in the first two years. It was, therefore, necessary that there should be first-class publicity to make it clear that these difficulties were inevitable and inherited by the Labour Government. He also agreed with Mr. Crossman about the need for co-ordinating publicity and suggested that the Prime Minister should, somehow or other, be given a Public Relations Officer. It was perfectly reasonable, in his view, to provide information for the country at the expense of the Government, while leaving propaganda to the Party. He urged that there should be, among the members of the Government some of the new M.P.'s who were both young and able. He realised that there were dangers and difficulties in this course, but it had been found that during the war new Members of Parliament, who were Ministers, had not necessarily done badly in the House. He would like to see in the King's Speech the nationalization of the Bank of England, the establishment of a National Investment Board, the nationalization of fuel

27 A view associated more with Ernest Bevin than with Crossman who, a year or so later, became his principal critic.

28 Lord Halifax, Foreign Secretary 1938–40, had been Ambassador since 1941. He was replaced in 1946 by Lord Inverchapel (a diplomat, previously Ambassador to Moscow) and in 1948 by Sir Oliver Franks*, former Provost of The Queen's College, Oxford. A. D. Lindsay, Master of Balliol College, Oxford, became a Labour peer as Lord Lindsay of Birker in 1945.

and power. Finally, he agreed about the importance of Social Security. The Legislative programme in the Coalition Government had been held up simply because of the bottleneck in Parliamentary draughtsmen. He thought this was quite unnecessary and the Chancellor should make a special point of overcoming it. MR. WILSON agreed fully about the Parliamentary draughtsmen. He also thought that there should be publicity as soon as possible to show that the major difficulties with which we were faced: coal and houses, in particular, were not due to the Labour Government. If possible this publicity should be combined with the announcement of urgent, even desperate measures, to deal with the situation. It would also be helpful to announce at the same time a speed-up in Demobilisation. As regards the problem of Redundancy, he would like to see the Government, if necessary, placing orders for refrigerators and vacuum cleaners. He also favoured the maintenance of a guaranteed wage.

MR. WILMOT said he had fought the Election largely on the issue of controls. People were primarily concerned with homes and jobs. He would like to see all the vast number of small builders integrated into an effective Housing Drive. He would also line up, at one and the same time, the problem of Redundancy with the production of prefabricated parts for houses. Psychologically the notion of moving from 'war work' to 'house work' was an excellent idea.

MAJOR YOUNGER* agreed on the importance of publicity which he thought was important not only for the reputation of the Labour Government, but also as propaganda for improving production. He was afraid that too many people had voted Labour in the hope that it meant more pay and less work. He had emphasized, in his talks to Trade Union branches, the responsibilities of the Unions for production, but thought that he got very little response.

MAJOR WELLS agreed with the proposal to send a Parliamentary Delegation to the Far East. He thought, however, that it should not go in uniform. One difficult point which caused a lot of trouble was the question of attributability in connection with Service pensions. He thought the industrial workers were quite prepared to accept some cut in wages below the high level they had received while working on munitions, and he was strongly opposed to any further inflationary development. This might suit places like Coventry, but it would be disastrous for the black-coated workers, who had voted in such large numbers for Labour. Finally, he emphasized that one of the great difficulties in speeding up Demobilisation was shipping, and it was not easy to see how this could be overcome.

THE CHANCELLOR expressed his thanks to those present for the very interesting discussion. It was clear that the new Parliamentary Labour Party had plenty of men with courage and intelligence in its ranks. When he had assumed that we should be in opposition he had favoured the idea of creating a number of groups among M.P.'s concentrating on the work of different Departments. The same plan might be appropriate now that we were actually the Government.[29] He hoped that Labour Ministers would keep close contact with M.P.'s and listen to what they had to say. The Session would last some thirteen months and it should be possible to get a lot of legislation through. He agreed that the Parliamentary draughtsmen bottleneck could certainly be overcome. He said it was important for members of the Parliamentary Party to get to know one another and not to allow themselves to drift into disgruntled cliques.

The Tory opposition would probably be sporadic and rather ineffective to begin with, but would become more formidable later on. He thought part of the Social Services programme could be pushed through in the first Session, though some of it might have to be left till later. He did not favour the idea of tackling Old Age Pensions independently.

Monday, 30th July 1945.

Diary, Wednesday, 8 August

Dinner tonight at St Ermin's. There were present Berry, Evan, Douglas, HD[Dalton] and self. Later JW[Wilmot] joined us.

HD was quite amusing at dinner in describing the general satisfaction among all Ministers. They were all very pleased to have jobs and very few were disgruntled because they thought that they ought to be in better ones. He painted an amusing picture of A. Bevan* and others sitting round the Cabinet table, being very thrilled listening to long harangues on the military situation from the three chiefs of staff.

Everything else for the moment is overshadowed by the atomic bomb which we also discussed. Most people are depressed, except of course for the immediate value in the Japanese war. Evan is now saying Europe is finished, possibly parts of North and South America may survive. He also suggests that if only the U.S.A. were more imperialistically minded the thing for them to do would be to govern the whole world.

---

29 They were set up, and a few proved useful – particularly Dalton's finance group.

Thursday

Who should look in to see me this evening but Cyril Joad. I asked him why he had not after all fought the election. He apparently turned down two or three constituencies which were eventually won, because he expected to get Romford, but there was some muddle or else double-crossing. He suggested timidly that he might be a suitable candidate for the House of Lords and pointed out that he was quite a good debater. The idea sounds a bit queer, but there is something in it. He has certainly done the Labour Party a great deal of good indirectly through his B.B.C. influence and, when all is said and done, he has been a member and supporter of the Party for the past 15 years. I shall try it out on Addison* if I see him next week.[30] The trouble, of course, would be that he would be regarded as unreliable, but I think if he were told in advance that he was there not just to air his own opinions but to work for the Party he might behave.

I passed on Evan's idea about the U.S.A. and the atomic bomb. He asked if he could use this at once; he was writing for a Sunday paper. I thought he himself could say anything, but murmured something about bringing the British in.

13 August

Weekend in Leeds. Meetings of Executive and General Committee to discuss familiar subjects of organisation, officers, etc. Highlight of the weekend for me was visit to Beeston Working Men's Club on Saturday evening. In Yorkshire these clubs are quite different from what they are in the South. In particular, women are allowed in. The club was, in fact, a large hall filled with tables with men and women drinking beer. Stage at one end and two or three 'turns' provided. I went with Wilf Webster who introduced me to one or two people.[31] Some others recognised me, but for a good time it was just conversation and drink at our table. Then the chairman was brought up and introduced to me and immediately proceeded to the platform and informed those present of the great honour they had in having their 'worthy' Member of Parliament there. This was greeted with surprising applause and I stood up. Later I was led to

30 Joad, a former civil servant, was a philosopher at Birkbeck College, London and a prolific author and broadcaster; he was one of the original Brains Trust. Addison was Leader in the Lords.
31 Webster, former President of South Leeds Labour Party, was a prominent member of the City Council.

another room, where the same announcement was made and I said a few words to them. Later still the chairman came back and said they were demanding a speech in the main hall, so again I said a few very non-political words. Those present having now drunk a good deal were most enthusiastic, and to my great surprise sang 'For He's A Jolly Good Fellow' and in places the 'Red Flag'. Wilfred complained afterwards that he had to drink a vast amount of beer which had been ordered by various well-wishers for me, as I had to drive the car. If the process of 'digging in' is as easy and pleasant as this I shan't complain. Next time it will be Holbeck Feast and the club I shall visit will probably be far rowdier.

13–24 August 1945

The highlights of these last 10 days have been the opening of Parliament, which coincided with VJ day [Victory over Japan], and the 5 or 6 days of debate following on the King's Speech.

I was lucky to draw a seat in the ballot for viewing the ceremony of the opening of Parliament. We Members of the House of Commons were stuck up in the gallery of the House of Lords, facing the throne, while down below were sitting the Peers and Peeresses. It seems to me all wrong that the seats on the floor of the House should be occupied not merely by the members of the House of Lords but also by their families, while we were tucked up in the background. The ceremony itself was not particularly impressive, but that may be because the full peace-time splendour had not been restored. The King* read the speech in a very flat monotonous tone, but I imagine that this is because it is the only way he can get through without stammering. However, the speech itself has made an excellent impression, containing as it does such a large number of first-class measures – about half the Labour Party election programme.

Later in the day there was a procession to St Margaret's Church for a service of thanksgiving. I walked along with Chris Mayhew. There were large crowds in Parliament Square, but very orderly and only cheering and shouting occasionally when they recognised an M.P. Chris and I felt rather lonely because we represented divisions far from London. However, on the way back somebody started waving to me and I had the pleasure of waving back to a genuine constituent.

The main interest of the debates has, of course, been the large number of maiden speeches. The first day, however, was chiefly taken up by Churchill* and the P.M. The former's speech was a real masterpiece. The greater part of it was, of course, on foreign affairs and spoken almost as though he was still Prime Minister, but the phraseology, the vigour with which it was expressed, and the brilliant repartee to a number of rather clumsy interruptions from our side were all first class. The old boy was really enjoying himself. One somehow felt that he was much relieved to have the election over and those awful broadcasts and now was getting back to his own pastures. The P.M. was not very inspiring but he did quite well within his own limits.

That same evening a rather alarming thing happened to me. I had been dictating and returned to the Central Lobby when Ellis Smith rushed up to me and said the Whips were looking for me and said the Speaker had called my name to make my maiden speech. I was absolutely horrified because, though I had sent my name in, I had had no further warning, was not expecting to get in until later, and had not prepared a speech. However, when I got into the Chamber I found it was something of a false alarm and after talking to the Chief Whip and the Speaker managed to fix up that I would not be called until the following week.

The Labour maiden speeches appeared to have made generally a rather good impression. At any rate that is what everybody says. My own eventually took place on the Finance day and with nearly all the Opposition out of the House. However, it went off well – as indeed it should have done in view of the immense amount of trouble I took in preparing it.

Evan also did very well the next day, speaking with much less preparation than I had on the United Nations Charter. Neither Dick Crossman nor Maurice Webb have so far come in. On the other hand, Raymond Blackburn made a passionate speech at the end of the United Nations debate, which made a considerable impression.

This brings me to the interesting question of malcontents in the Party. Fundamentally this, I suppose, is the greatest danger the Government faces since if it can last the full 4½ years, the underlying forces working in its favour are very strong. Were there to be a split, on the other hand, after say two years, at which point things would be just about at their worst, the consequences would be very serious. Blackburn is obviously a potential focus for dissatisfaction. However, my own view is that he will not cut much ice because he is not clever enough. As for Dick, who certainly has the brains, he is too near ministerial office to risk making a nuisance of himself.[32]

Another interesting move which affects this problem is the proposal to set up groups of M.P.s to specialise in different subjects. This is desirable in itself and it will have the useful by-product of splitting up trouble makers, or to put it another way, canalising their grievances.

I have been put on to the Select Committee on Procedure, a subject of which I know extremely little, but it should be interesting.

32 The first judgment was better than the second. Two years was a good guess.

24 August – 10 September

Took Julia to Cornwall to stay at the Durbins' farmhouse. The holiday rather spoilt by Elizabeth Durbin's bronchitis followed by Marjorie's tonsillitis.[33]

Another weekend in Leeds. Harold and Billy have been elected respectively Secretary and Chairman of the Party. It will not be easy to get them to work together.[34] Indeed, the parochial attitude of the various wards in the division is infuriating. However, one should not be sorry – these things really are trivial and are not likely greatly to affect the future election. On Saturday evening another visit to a Working Men's Club. Reception favourable, though not so overwhelming as at Beeston. Probably because it was earlier and they had not drunk so much.

On the Saturday night after W.M.C. [Working Men's Club] a meeting with the doctors of Leeds and the Health Service. I was rather impressed with them and they, as I subsequently heard, with me. The most remarkable thing was that they all agreed that a doctor should either be 100% in the Service or completely outside it. This is one of the main points on which the Party have insisted. Their chief worry is that of being put under stupid local authority committees or officials and they produced some evidence to show that in the case of voluntary hospitals there was a good deal more self-government. We shall probably meet them again.

Three meetings on the Sunday afternoon and evening at Holbeck Feast. Curiously little interest appears to be taken by the civilian population in demobilisation, though it is the outstanding political question of the moment. Up to now South Leeds electors have been very moderate in corresponding with their Member.

11–30 September

The Select Committee has begun its work. Sir R Young[35] is chairman. He was, extraordinary as it seems, chairman of Ways and Means '29–'31. He is not a very good chairman but on the other hand his questions to witnesses are penetrating and sensible. Our first job is to consider a paper submitted by the Government. Because of this the Tories on the Com-

33 Julia was his own elder daughter, Elizabeth Durbin was Evan's, and Marjorie was Evan's wife.
34 It was not. Harold Watson and Billy Goodwill were his constituency officers.
35 Sir Robert Young (1872–1957); M.P. for Newton (Lancs.) 1918–31, 1935–50; Deputy Speaker 1924, 1929–31.

mittee have tended to treat the examination of witnesses as being an opportunity for scoring points against the Government. Naturally we have reacted the other way, so the whole process tends to be rather like a law court case with counsel on the two sides cross-examining witnesses and trying to get them to say what they want. The proceedings are enlivened from time to time by rows between Lord Winterton, who is always raising points of order, and Mr [Sydney] Silverman, who is calculated to irritate anybody.[36] We shall no doubt let the Government have their scheme in some form, but there is a good deal of disagreement on the Labour side as to when the Standing Committees should do their extra work. I want them to meet on Wednesday mornings and very occasionally in the afternoons. This means, however, limiting the Party meeting to one hour – 10–11 on Wednesdays. Some of the older members are against this, partly I suspect because they like making trouble at the Party meetings (Silverman especially) and partly because they don't want to do the extra work. Consequently they favour adjourning the House one day a week so that the various Standing Committees can get on.

As to the witnesses, Morrison was admirable and dealt suavely but firmly with the Tory efforts to trap him. The Clerk of the House was rather sensational and in my view overcritical of the Government's scheme.[37]

We meet two days a week, morning and afternoon, a very good and cheap lunch being provided in the House of Lords for us. They appear to have a much better manager than the House of Commons to look after their catering arrangements.

The only other development of note is that I have been invited to become Vice-President of B.F.P.A. and accepted the offer on various conditions.[38] I only did this after consulting the Chancellor and the President of the Board of Trade. My independence is very carefully safeguarded and I must say after the talk I had with the film trade press it seems absurd that I should ever have worried about it. They, at any rate, just took it for granted.

Curious meeting at the Treasury took place on the 28th. Willie Hall* had asked me to come and talk about films. When I got there, however, I

---

36 Earl Winterton (1883–1962) was Father of the House; Conservative M.P. for Horsham (Sussex) 1904–51, and in the Cabinet for eight months in 1938–9; his partnership with Shinwell in criticising the Churchill Coalition during the war was called 'Arsenic and Old Lace' after a current comedy. Sydney Silverman, M.P. for Nelson & Colne (Lancs.) 1935–68, was a prominent left-winger, particularly after 1958 in the 'Victory for Socialism' organisation. His main parliamentary cause was the abolition of capital punishment.

37 Sir Gilbert Campion, Clerk of the House of Commons, proposed reforms of his own which did not find favour.

38 British Film Producers' Association. See *HG*, p. 120.

found Waley and Rowe-Dutton both there.[39] It appears that the Chancellor has caused a letter to be sent to the Board of Trade asking them to try and cut down film remittances to the U.S.A. by 50% at once. Naturally the Treasury, with whom I had so often discussed this general subject, had turned to my original scheme for limiting remittances and wanted to discuss it with me, not as having anything to do with the industry but as having originally conceived of it and worked it out when I was at the Board. However, our discussion was rather fruitless because my scheme was not designed for immediate effect. I pointed out that if they were to apply it in that manner the only result would be that the British public would have to live on re-issues and that the proportion of these which would be American and which would therefore cost us dollars would probably be as high as the proportion of new films. I gathered one interesting thing from Waley. They seem to expect the talks in Washington to end in a not unfavourable agreement from our point of view, but that this will be subject to Congress. There will, therefore, be an interval of perhaps several months before we know where we stand and it is during that time that we shall particularly want to cut down dollar remittances.

1946-7: Diary for 1946, written 12 August 1947

Joining the Government happened like this. Early in May [1946] a few rumours started going round the lobbies – particularly that Will Foster, Parliamentary Secretary to Shinwell, had resigned.[40] I did not pay much attention to them at first – rumours of Government changes had been pretty frequent and I was one of the people who was expected to get a job.

However, in the course of an all night sitting on, I think, the Report stage of the Control of Borrowing Bill, the Chancellor led me into the lobby and hinted strongly that I was to get something this time. He urged me not to be fussy and accept what was offered – however unattractive. I reassured him and said that I had long since determined on this course. Then he said the P.M. had asked if I was now fit and he, HD, had said that I was.

A day or two later – by which time Foster's resignation had been announced – I got a phone message to say the Chief Whip wanted to see me. It was Thursday and I was to see him at 2.15 p.m.

That morning I ran into Harold Wilson in the House who said, 'I hear

39 HG had been concerned with films as a Board of Trade civil servant in 1943–5. W.G. Hall was Financial Secretary to the Treasury. Sir David Waley and Ernest Rowe-Dutton were senior Treasury officials.
40 M.P. Wigan, 1942–8.

you're going to a place I'm interested in'. I, thinking he meant Fuel & Power (where he had been Chief Statistician in the war) agreed and suggested a talk. Actually he meant his own job at Works, since that morning Tomlinson*, his Minister, had told him I was to go there and he, Harold, to F. & P. I suspect, however, that Shinwell objected to this and chose me because he did *not* want anyone who was supposed to know about Mining to be his Parliamentary Secretary![41]

My interviews with the Chief Whip and the P.M. were short and utterly undramatic. The P.M. said he understood I was now well; he wished to have me in the Government and wanted me to go to 'Mines' – 'But', he added, 'this doesn't mean going down mines all the time. There's Gas and Electricity, and the Bills coming along.'[42] I was to start on Monday and to get in touch with Shinwell at once.

I remember then going in to Questions – I had one down about Education, and hearing with a tremor the Lord President [Morrison] announce that the business of the first three days of next week was the Report Stage of the Coal Bill! There was some caustic comment from the Opposition about the absence of an Under-Secretary.

Later I rang up Shinwell. This was the conversation.

S 'I understand you're going to be my new Parliamentary Secretary.'
G 'Yes, I understand so.'
S (after a pause) 'Well, that's all right. We've got this Bill on Monday but you won't be able to do much.'
G 'No, I suppose not.'
S 'There's a meeting this evening with the Attorney General and the Financial Secretary – you can come and listen if you like.'
   I said I did like.

The beginning was rather typical of what my experiences at F. & P. were to be for some time. Good publicity opportunity combined with a far from easy Ministerial position.

I decided fairly quickly that I could *not* sit through 3 days and say nothing, and therefore asked Shinwell to let me take some of the amendments. He agreed. I chose a few fairly simple but controversial ones and made, on the first, a successful maiden speech. This was quite easy as I was well briefed and the questions were not technical. But everybody thought it remarkable to be able to do well at such short notice!

There was much jealousy among the Miner M.P.'s about my appointment and I learnt later that a deputation had even gone to the Chief Whip

41 Probably not the case: see *HG*, Ch. 5 n. 65.
42 The old Mines Department of the Board of Trade had become the Ministry of Fuel and Power in 1942.

about it. But it got nowhere, and fortunately I did not know what was happening. They regarded this job, however, as open only to them, and since it was for about all of them the only one they could possibly hope even to be considered for, their dismay and resentment can be understood. However, time was a healer and most of them became in time reconciled and most of them quite friendly – especially those from Yorkshire.

Tuesday, 12 August 1947[43]

A dinner with the Chancellor last night. Arranged at short notice in a private room in the House. Present – Douglas [Jay], Evan [Durbin], Bill Piercy, Nicholas Davenport, Willie Hall, HD and self.[44]

The Chancellor superficially sunburnt and boisterously indiscreet – a contrast with the pale exhaustion of last week – the indiscretions aided by plenty of drink, especially Queensland Rum which tastes more like brandy.

Nicholas amused us by giving his version of the Party meeting held that morning (he was the only one who had *not* been there – but someone had rung him up and given him a second hand story). It was very uneven in its accuracy.

However, it is clear that Nye Bevan had hoped to bring off something and failed. Everybody agreed about that. The Chancellor said that in the last week Bevan's head had swollen enormously. He believed 'his hour had come', had threatened to resign over steel and then organised the 'Keep Left' boys. In the meeting itself he was – so said Bill – signalling to Jennie [Lee*] and (so said Shinwell to me) applauding the critics of the Government.[45]

I think this attempt of Bevan's to stab his colleagues is interesting for two reasons. First its extraordinary naivety – he grossly exaggerates his own popularity and underestimates the notorious loyalty of the Party to its Leaders. Secondly, its failure should weaken his position in the Government because the others – especially the Big 5 – are very angry; his bluff about resignation has been called and these particular bolts having

43 In the original diary this entry follows that for September 1945, preceding that on joining the government.
44 Davenport, a financial journalist, had been a member of XYZ.
45 Jennie Lee was Bevan's wife. On the clash over steel and Bevan's threat to resign, see Foot (1973), pp. 222–7; Dalton (1962), pp. 248–53; Donoughue & Jones (1973), p. 409; G.W. Ross, *The Nationalization of Iron and Steel* (MacGibbon & Kee, 1965), pp. 64–76; Chester (1975), pp. 36–8.

been shot, they can afford to be less frightened of him. This weakening is important because it will strengthen the hands of those who know that we must cut building and probably housing if we are to get our exports up enough.

All the same it would be a great mistake to assume that this is more than a set back for Bevan. He still leads in the race for Labour Prime Minister in 1960! 'Very like LL.G', says Evan. Yes, but I can't help wondering whether LL.G. was really quite so unscrupulous![46]

Strachey* is said to be implicated in the plot. The Chancellor was violent about him. 'I told him', he roared (and we had, despite the great heat, to shut the windows which looked onto the terrace so as not to be overheard!) 'he was the only one of my colleagues whom I so far mistrusted that I had to have a witness to what I said to him.' And again, 'When he came to see me I called in my Secretary to take down what I said – so that he could not double cross me.' And again, 'We can't trust the Minister of Food to carry out the decisions of the Cabinet – but fortunately the careers of his officials depend on the Treasury, and it's been intimated to them that if *they* misbehave they're finished!' And finally and several times, 'Once a communist, always a crook!'

This, I must say, was very much news to me. But though I pressed the Chancellor strongly, he did not go into detail about the nature of the double crossing. It seems that Strachey has been getting away with food purchases which should not have been allowed. But there is probably more to it than that. His vacillations about bread rationing, plus his communist background, plus his obstructive tactics on the crisis cuts all count for something.[47]

There was also talk about the earlier 'plot' to put EB [Bevin] in in place of CRA which never got anywhere and fizzled out completely at the earlier Party meeting. I asked HD how a change of this kind could *technically* be brought about. It seemed really out of the question for the Parliamentary Party to resolve to dismiss its leader in the middle of a Parliament. HD agreed. Then he said that if the other four of the 'Big 5' – Cripps, Bevin, Dalton and Morrison – all agreed that such a change was needed and all told CRA the latter would probably give way. There was, however, no prospect of this, since HM would never agree and EB was not at all keen to leave the F.O. [Foreign Office].[48]

46 David Lloyd George, Prime Minister 1916–22, was the most prominent Liberal of the early twentieth century, mistrusted by the leaders of the other parties and by many of his own. Bevan's ministry was responsible for housing.
47 John Strachey, Minister of Food, had been a prominent Communist sympathiser before the war though never a member of the Party. Dalton (1962), pp. 142–3, 252, 270, 292 hints at his view of Strachey – who had been the earliest advocate first of introducing and then of postponing bread rationing.
48 On this 'plot': *ibid.*, Ch. 29; Donoughue & Jones (1973), Ch. 31.

About HM (whom he at one time strongly supported for the leadership – in 1935?)[49] he said, 'He has a devouring ambition to be P.M. The rest of us, however ambitious, are reasonably satisfied with our "positions". But HM will not die happy unless he has been P.M. He makes this so plain that it is indecent.'

About EB he said, 'Remember he is a Peasant – with all the suspicions of the Peasant – a rural origin. He is afraid people are hoping to get him out of the F.O.'

I must say that HD has made it quite plain to me on earlier occasions that he would really like to go to the F.O. Partly just because a change would be congenial, partly because he thinks he could handle the Russians better than EB.

It is obvious that for some time there has been an alliance between Sir Stafford Cripps and HD. HD spoke warmly of Stafford last night. – 'He really is an intelligent man – he understands.' Whereas in the old days he disliked him for his austerity, serious mindedness, lack of humour and poor judgement.

After this spell of entertaining and illuminating gossip, Evan called us to order and started serious discussion. We all spoke in turn, and there was general agreement – including HD.

(a) that the government policy had deserved a far better reception than it had received.

(b) that this was chiefly due to the fact that the arithmetic of the *whole* thing had not been explained by anyone.

(c) that the Treasury had advised the Chancellor wrongly in not appreciating the rate at which the loan would be drained.[50]

(d) that without waiting until the last moment we really ought to tell Argentine, and Canada, etc. that we could not pay in dollars any more – (we could surely do this at once with Argentine because of their banning the import of so many British goods).

I got up early on the Monday morning and drove from Branc. to London for the Party meeting.[51] I arrived about eleven. The room was hot and crowded. Several angry and excited back benchers made speeches critical of the Government and the P.M. I was depressed because much of what was said was unrealistic. The usual sort of stuff. 'People are ready to follow a lead for austerity, if only you'll give it.' 'People are ready for a more Left Wing policy.' The curious thing is that those who are most

49 It was in 1935 that Dalton was Morrison's strongest backer.
50 On the rapid dissipation of the American loan – within five weeks of sterling becoming convertible – see *HG*, pp. 140–1; Dalton (1962), pp. 255–66; Donoughue & Jones (1973), pp. 404–5, 408–12.
51 HG had often since boyhood spent holidays at Brancaster on the Norfolk coast.

unrealistic about the Left Wing character of the electorate are often the M.P.'s with the most slender majorities (e.g. Ben Parkin).[52] They make the elementary error of identifying their own keen supporters – politically conscious and class conscious Labour men – with the mass of the people, who are very much against austerity, utterly uninterested in nationalisation of steel, heartily sick of excuses and being told to work harder, but probably more tolerant of the Government and appreciative of its difficulties than many suppose.

The P.M. replied rather ineffectively – a very different affair from the last one when he scored a triumph. His speech last week certainly was, as Evan said, catastrophic.

Then we had a brief debate on Steel, when two back benchers (allegedly Bevan stooges) moved a resolution in favour of nationalising steel *next year*. Morrison replied for the Government, said we definitely *were* going to nationalise steel, but that only the Cabinet should decide when. Then there was some confusion. The rebels wanted to go on speaking – Jennie Lee was on her feet, and some others – but the vast majority wanted to vote. Judging by applause it looked to me as though the Government might be defeated.

However, eventually by a narrow majority the previous question was carried. There was a lot of confusion about the significance of the vote – but the Government voted for it and the chief rebels against.[53]

Not a good meeting. People bad tempered, tired and stupid and more unrealistic than I have known them. However, I am sure this is largely due to the fact of having to be here an extra three days owing to this stupid Bill.[54] A first class political blunder that! The Government bringing it in because they wanted to be highly constitutional and really the contrary. All that happens is that they produce a storm of criticism about 'dictators' and give the Opposition another chance of hitting out. It's all very silly and can only be explained by the obvious fact that the Big 5 are all hopelessly overtired.

52 M.P. for Stroud (Glos.) 1945–50, with a majority of 949; and for North Paddington, 1953–69. Stood for Chief Whip as an opponent of HG's leadership in 1961.

53 In the confusion HG was himself denounced by some Government supporters for voting the wrong way. See Dalton (1962), pp. 252–3; and on steel, Chester (1975), pp. 36–7.

54 The Supplies and Services (Extended Powers) Act 1947, prolonging the Government's powers under the Act of 1945 for two years owing to the economic crisis.

SUBJECTS[55]
>SHINWELL
>POSITION OF PARLIAMENTARY SECRETARIES
>THE GREAT FUEL CRISIS
>INDIA
>CROSSMAN AND THE REVOLT

'It is better to be fooled than suspicious' . . . E.M. Forster in *Howards End*. No better example can be found than E. Shinwell whose public life is ravaged by suspicion. Someone described him à la Kipling as 'The Cat that Walked Alone', and that's fair enough. But he walks alone one feels because he has never been able fully to trust anyone. The cause? Basically, no doubt, being Jewish. But there are plenty of Jews who are not suspicious. 'He has always had to fight.' He has always *fought*, but may not that too have been his preference? No, without knowledge of his childhood and boyhood I can offer no further plausible explanation. I have found that if I do not see him frequently his suspicions of me begin to grow. I can only keep them down by seeing him. Otherwise, I suppose, he wonders what I am up to. It has taken me a long time to realise this – chiefly, I suppose, because however much one may say one intends to go all out for a particular object (in this case getting on with him, acquiring influence over him, etc.) there are limits to the extent one can dragoon oneself. As I never really enjoy his company it is an effort to me to see him.

Once not long after the Fuel Crisis,[56] when not having seen him for some time I was becoming highly suspect, I went to see him. The circumstances were these. There was to be a Debate. One of the subjects was likely to be future restrictions on use of gas and electricity. On these as S. knew, I was strongly opposed to the line he at first took – which was to continue the policy of restriction during certain hours of the day. But he pretended to the Cabinet, without saying a word to me, that I was unwilling to speak. This, fortunately, came to my knowledge and naturally I was pretty incensed. I saw him and asked about the Debate. I did not, of course, give away my information or mention the Cabinet, but inquired his intentions. He said he thought I did not wish to speak. I explained this was not so, and that it would look very queer if I did not speak. Even though I disagreed with his policy I was ready to defend it. The tension relaxed and he agreed to my winding up.[57] Then came a release of feeling

55 The last three are not included in the (largely empty) notebook where these entries were originally composed, and probably were never written. For Parliamentary Secretaries see below, pp. 38–9.
56 On the fuel crisis of February 1947 see *HG*, Ch 5–iv (pp. 134–7).
57 See 436 H.C. Deb. 2222–34, 1 May 1947; and *HG*, p. 139.

– in the form of a kind of apology – 'You don't know what it is to have knives thrust into you from all sides – Yes, and stabs in the back, too, from colleagues. Oh, yes, I know all about them, etc.'

His suspicions were not ill founded, because there was indeed strong feeling that he should have been sacked.

Suspicion and aggression went – as usual – together. Thinking he was going to be attacked, he attacked first – his political opponents in public, his party opponents in private. 'Passing the buck' is frequent enough between Ministers. But Shinwell did not just pass it. He picked it up and hurled it. He attacked the Minister of Supply [John Wilmot] about mining machinery and the Minister of Transport [Alfred Barnes][58] over waggons, and in a manner which somehow made them angrier than others would have done. More than one of his colleagues has said to me, 'The Cabinet is really a remarkably harmonious affair, except for S. His presence spoils the atmosphere. He throws apples of discord the whole time'.

And, of course, the whole process was cumulative. Because he was suspicious, he was hostile and aggressive. Because he was hostile and aggressive, he was disliked. There were attacks and much gossip against him. Because of this he was more suspicious, and so it went on.

The position was made no easier because the P.M. during and after the Fuel Crisis (and perhaps before) did not conceal his distaste for ES. At meetings he would be petulant and irritable with ES – rather like a schoolmaster being nasty to the boy he most disliked – criticising and questioning everything he said. And, of course, the very fact that through the Cabinet Fuel Committee, where these scenes used to occur, the Office of Minister of F. & P. was virtually put in commission made ES even more full of hatred and suspicion.

It was a great weakness of CRA's that he was very averse to changing Ministers even when political necessity and merit demanded changes.[59]

Shinwell's chief claims as a Labour leader are oratory, strength of personality and quick wits. He is certainly a good speaker of the platform type – at his best when he prepares nothing – nearly always not so good when he has prepared. I have heard him make some of the best speeches at dinners and similar occasions. He can generally be funny and also even on such occasions serious. It is all a part of this that he does not, as a rule, issue press advances. It inhibits him when he does this. But precisely this has been a main cause of his downfall. Being an emotional speaker he responds to the audience and the audience to him. Some things which sound all right in the heat of the moment read very differently in the cold print next day. And some things do not sound all right, e.g. his reference to the Housewives'

58 1887–1974; M.P. for East Ham South 1922–31, 1935–55; Minister of Transport 1945–51; Chairman of the Cooperative Party for 21 years.
59 The opposite of the conventional view of Attlee.

League[60] ('Lord forgive them for they know not what they do'). (Incidentally, he probably did think of himself as crucified on some occasions.) And more damaging politically, though more excusable – 'Only the organised workers count – as for the rest they do not matter a tinker's cuss'.

As an administrator, however, S. is hardly a starter. He has no conception at all of either organisation or planning or following up. Everything is done by fits and starts, and on impulse. The best you can say is that he contributes at intervals a kind of rugged force and drive which stimulates the officials. He gets worried about something; he calls a meeting; he asks questions and holds forth and perhaps takes some preliminary decision. But there is no follow up and no system.

Because of his strong personality, free language and love of a fight, one expects first of all to find that he will be a 'strong' Minister. This is not so. He will always try and evade an unpopular decision, procrastinate, find a way round, etc. Of course there often is a case on political grounds for this. But S.'s hesitations go beyond natural prudence and amount to sheer weakness and moral cowardice.

I have already referred to his powerful jealousies. I have not spoken of his passion for publicity. It attracted him as a candle does a moth, and in the same way he could not help getting his wings singed by it.

This story illustrates this.

We had planned a series of Conferences on Fuel Economy in the chief provincial cities. Originally S. was to do the first at Nottingham and I was to do various others including a later one at Newcastle.

It was then found that he could not manage Nottingham. He sent a special message while I was on leave asking me to do it in his place. Of course I agreed.

Then it was found that he was also going to be near Newcastle, in his own area, a week before I was due there, and it was proposed that he should do a public meeting and I the Conference. Then I heard that he thought it wrong for us both to be there so soon after one another. He sent for me and explained he didn't want me to go, and consoled me for what he quite wrongly thought was a loss by saying that I would get lots of publicity from the Nottingham meeting. I suddenly saw that to *him* this publicity would have been very important. But the final stage was that without telling me he then told NB to have a press conference in London the very day of my Nottingham speech.[61] This fairly successfully stole all the publicity from my speech!

60 The Housewives' League was a protest movement against post-war austerity. The Conservative press gave it publicity as a weapon against the Labour Government, but afterwards it lapsed into total obscurity.
61 Sir Guy Nott-Bower, Deputy Secretary at Fuel & Power 1942–8, then became the Coal Board's director of public relations.

CHAPTER 2

MINISTER OF FUEL
AND POWER

Editor's Note
Diary, 14 October 1947 to 29 July 1949
Document No. 2 Permanent Secretary to HG, 8 October 1947

[The new Minister's early days were dominated by two urgent problems. One was petrol for private motorists, where the motoring organisations were furiously campaigning to restore the 'basic ration' to which everyone had been entitled until, in August 1947, the Cabinet abolished it to save dollars in the convertibility crisis. The policy was not Gaitskell's, and it was abominated by the middle class; but he defended it loyally, administered it sympathetically and worked hard to end it as soon as possible.

The other was coal production, for which everyone was clamouring: the domestic householder, cut to two-thirds of pre-war needs; manufacturing industry, which got only 85 per cent of its claims, the minimum to avoid economic disaster and unemployment; the booming electricity industry; and the war-damaged Continent with its insatiable demand for exports. To regain any of the lost output quickly, the goodwill of the mineworkers was indispensable. Considering the generations of ill-treatment, their sellers' market and the wails of the middle class at austerity, the miners displayed astounding moderation and responsibility. The Communist Party had always recruited relatively well among them, and its influence worried the Ministry. But it never did attempt massive industrial action for political ends, no doubt fearing to antagonise the other miners' union leaders whose experiences had made them deeply suspicious of Communist motives and tactics. Gaitskell became friendly with these leaders and worked closely with them, particularly those from the northern coalfields.

In the longer run one of his main responsibilities was that of organising three of the nationalised industries, where good managers would not be recruited or retained if they were subject to constant interference by Ministers. Gaitskell told his colleagues in May 1949 that so long as the Boards had statutory responsibility to pay their way and run the detailed administration, they must be left considerable latitude. The Minister must not duplicate their staffs, remove their power of decision, or try to teach them how to do their job. However, Parliament held him broadly accountable for their record, and his own statutory responsibilities entitled him to intervene on matters going beyond the scope of the boards.

Gaitskell's successors did not adhere to the principles he tried to establish. Conservative Ministers set, sometimes for purely electoral reasons, and later Labour ones followed, a bad example of political interference with the nationalised industries, usually unavowed. With responsibility for their management hopelessly blurred, and accountability impossible to enforce, the public corporations have attracted much justified criticism – frequently misdirected against a form of organisation which has never, since those early days, been allowed to work as its originators intended.

Most Ministers of Fuel and Power before and since have been – as one senior civil servant put it – 'blown about by the industries'. Gaitskell, however, saw it as his function to represent the wider public interest as interpreted by government policy, and to ensure that the narrower perspectives of the industries themselves did not prevail over it. That outlook brought him into conflict with some powerful forces, notably the oil companies. Before the war Britain had imported 82 per cent of her oil as finished products, nearly half of it from the Caribbean. Vital dollars could be saved by purchasing Middle East crude from new fields in the sterling area, if only the oil companies would refine in Great Britain instead of on the oil fields themselves. Gaitskell vigorously promoted the policy and by 1951 the new refineries enabled Britain to export more oil than coal. Contrary to official advice, he kept pressing the American firms to supply the oil they sold to Britain from sterling sources under their control. The dollar share of British oil imports fell from 52·6 per cent in 1936 to 32 per cent in 1950 and – largely because of policies he had initiated – to only 19 per cent late in 1953, at an annual saving of £150 million.

Politically it was a period of bitterness, at least on domestic matters. Social tensions were acute, and much of the middle class bitterly resented Labour controls, Labour austerity and the very existence of a Labour government. A generation later a leading political correspondent wrote that he had 'never known the press so consistently and irresponsibly political, slanted and prejudiced'.[†] A fairly flourishing black market enabled many 'spivs' to make a dishonest living by evading the controls: the slender foundation for a shameful whispering campaign against Socialist corruption. It led to the Lynskey Tribunal of Inquiry, which reported at the beginning of 1949. Gaitskell – himself at one point a victim of slander of a different kind – thought that the procedure was most unfair, and the Tribunal quite unjustified in censuring one of the men involved, whose departmental superior he was. His account of this affair, and indeed of several others, show how erroneous is the myth that the period was one of consensus between the parties.]

† James Margach, *The Abuse of Power* (W. H. Allen, 1978), p. 86.

Tuesday, 14 October 1947

The recent changes in the Government took a very long time to mature and for weeks before rumours were flying about. The House of Commons (the Dining rooms are open) had quite an unpleasant atmosphere about it. Everybody was excited and jealous. You could not go in without several people looking at you hard and wondering whether you were involved in some intrigue or other, and also wondering what your position would be in the near future.

However, it is all over now. I have heard a good deal of the inside story from the Chancellor, and guessed a bit more from Cripps and Morrison.

Obviously Cripps has played a major part. Indeed, I have an idea that he wanted to push EB[Bevin] in place of the P.M., but partly as a result of this he was asked himself to do the co-ordinating job on the Home front. That having been settled some other changes followed. HW[Wilson] was obviously Cripps' nominee – a very good one too. I was clearly persona grata with Cripps. Added to which several others, including the Chief Whip [Whiteley], were quite determined to move my predecessor. S[Strauss]* replaced W[Wilmot] evidently also because of the Cripps' insistence. He and W. are, I think, personally antipathetic.

I am sorry for W. I have always liked him and found him sensible and competent, and certainly far abler than far more people left in the Government. At the same time I do not think he was a great success at the Ministry of Supply. He did not seem to me to have the grasp of all that was going on, or to give the administration there the sort of twist that a Minister ought to give it. What is unfair is not so much his being moved from the Ministry of Supply, but his not being given anything else, and that is, I think, due to bad luck in timing. When it was decided to move him there was no other pigeon-hole empty.

The story of S[Shinwell]'s change is fairly clear. The possibility of putting him in Commonwealth Relations was voiced some time ago, but various people, including I suppose the Foreign Secretary, resisted strongly. Further, none of the Big 5 really wanted him in the Cabinet. So everything pointed to a Service Ministry. B[Bellenger]'s stock was not high and so he was replaced by S.[1] S. does not seem to have objected to leaving the Ministry of Fuel. If he had got Commonwealth Relations and had been in the Cabinet there would have been no trouble at all. If he had been War Minister and in the Cabinet there would have been no trouble at all. If he had been War Minister outside the Cabinet with a lot of other

1 Fred Bellenger (1894–1965); M.P. Bassetlaw (Notts.) 1935–68; Fin. Sec. War 1945–6, Sec. for War 1946–7.

Cabinet Ministers, because the size of the Cabinet was reduced, there would have been no trouble at all. What riled him was, undoubtedly, being the only one flung out of the Cabinet. This had the effect of causing the spot-light of publicity to focus on the change here and incidentally gave me much more publicity than I expected.

Inside everybody is happy at the change. The Cabinet Committee meetings which I have attended have been harmonious and friendly. The Big 5 are all without exception very well disposed to me and I think to the other young Ministers. There is no jealousy. They find us easy to handle; they know we know the job and we are not too far away from detailed administration yet (this is one of the great problems).

Cripps wants to run the thing with HW[Wilson], RS[Strauss] and myself as his lieutenants. He made this quite plain to us. We are to have sort of inner discussions on the economic front. He is very friendly and very helpful so far. The only danger is of bees in his bonnet. There have been plenty in the past but certainly fewer and fewer in recent years.

After many vicissitudes the Chancellor and Cripps are staunch allies and on the best of terms. Altogether they have been the architects of the change, and knowing the Chancellor as I do, I do not believe there is any jealousy on his part. He is so tired of stupid, cowardly colleagues and welcomes intelligence and courage. As far as M[Morrison] is concerned he, too, seems more contented. It has been plain to me for months that he could not possibly do both jobs, or rather all four – House of Commons, economic home front, publicity and science. When he was ill I was in favour of his giving up the House, but people said then that he would not do this. Now he has given up the other and the decision is right because Cripps is far, far better equipped and a much abler administrator. Also M. knows that his health is weak and is probably anxious to devote more time to the House. He is still, I guess, ambitious to be P.M. one day, and thinks that the road via the Parliamentary Party is the best one.

Sometimes Cabinet Meetings horrify me because of the amount of rubbish talked by some Ministers who come there after reading briefs which they do not understand. I do not know how this can be avoided, except perhaps by getting more things settled at the official level, and when they cannot be settled there having the issues presented plainly to Ministers.

Also, I believe the Cabinet is too large. A smaller Cabinet, mostly of non-Departmental Ministers, would really be able to listen and understand more easily and hear the others arguing the matter out.

I suppose becoming a full Minister is a great step and a great change. Much more so indeed than I expected earlier. Here is how it happened.

Of course, for ages there had been talk of S[Shinwell] going, but apart from something the Chancellor once said to me in the winter I had never expected to follow him. My line had been, if he goes I shall probably have to stay to see the new Minister in. If he does not go I shall press to be moved, if possible to be under the Chancellor at the Treasury.

When I came back from Leeds I saw Ruth Dalton and she dropped a broad hint of what was to happen. Then I saw Hyndley* who said, 'I shall be disappointed if within a very short time you are not a full Minister'. Then DF*² said to me, 'I am sure that S. is going. He is approving things without looking at them – things which I should not normally have been able to get him to accept. Have you heard anything about your own position?' And finally, the day before, Marquand talking to me outside the Cabinet, said, 'I believe you're going to get your own way in F. & P. in the near future'.

However, the thing had dragged on for so long that I was very sceptical. Then a message came for me to see the P.M. There was nothing startling about the interview. The Chief Whip was there. The P.M. smiled and said in his clipped, muttering way, 'I am reconstructing the Government. I want you to be Fuel and Power.' I said, 'Oh! Well!' He said, 'It is not a bed of roses'. I said, 'I know that already'. Then I asked about the Parliamentary Secretary. They have given me [Alfred] Robens* and I am pleased. I think we shall get on and I think he will be quite capable. Then I was told to keep my mouth shut for three or four days and went off to Leeds. It was funny during the weekend listening to everyone talking about the possible changes without, of course, being able to say anything.

There was a curious coincidence at the end. I had been visiting the Leicestershire and South Derbyshire coalfields, and on the Tuesday evening spoke at a meeting at Swadlincote. Towards the end of the meeting a man with a camera marched down the aisle and started taking photographs of me answering questions. When the meeting was over various journalists came up and offered congratulations and asked questions.

But Swadlincote was a mile or two from a little village where twenty years ago I first lectured to miners. It was my experiences in that coalfield that led me into politics and I had not been back there since. One of the members of my class, now Deputy Labour Director for the Coal Board, was escorting me round the whole day.³ On top of this who should appear at the meeting quite unexpectedly but Tom Baxter, Labour Organiser for the Midland Region, whom I have not seen for years, but who induced me

2 Ruth Dalton was the Chancellor's wife, Lord Hyndley was chairman of the National Coal Board and Sir Donald Fergusson was Permanent Secretary at Fuel & Power.

3 W. H. Sales, later labour director of the National Coal Board 1953–71 and chairman of the Yorkshire Coal Board (1957–67). *HG*, pp. 25–8 on his coalfield classes.

to put my name forward as a candidate for Parliament. He was Evan's agent in East Grinstead in the 1931 Election and it was after that that he suggested to me I might as well stand next time myself, and later arranged for me to be put on the panel from which Chatham selected me.[4]

When I got back from the north I found my family engulfed in publicity, much enjoyed by my daughters who behaved like budding film stars and asked for more and more photographs to be taken, but not so much by my wife. Though, as somebody said, she has handled her publicity admirably.

As I am no longer a Parliamentary Secretary and cannot go back very easily to becoming one – one either goes up along or out, but not down – I must not forget to record some views on the general question of their position.

It is without doubt a very difficult one. I see that even more clearly sitting here as Minister. You are the boss. The Civil Servants look to you. You naturally turn to them and unless you are careful you just forget about the poor P.S. He comes in as a rule without experience, not knowing the game, and in a small Department inevitably tends to get left on the shelf. If his relations are too close with the Minister the Permanent Secretary suspects him. If his relations are too close with the Permanent Secretary the Minister suspects him. So he ends, I think, in many cases by having only tenuous relations with both of them.

Of course, he can be given special jobs, though this is not so easy in a small Department. That is probably the best way out. Then he is a little prince in his own kingdom. But they are generally not very important jobs and so usually he feels himself excluded from the important decisions. If he comes in after the Minister, the Minister cannot be bothered because he assumes the P.S. knows nothing about anything. If he is there when the Minister takes office, then the Minister is probably determined not to let the experience in his colleague put him in the position of running the show.

I believe more could be done to use P.S.'s in Committees. There is a lot to be said for Committees of officials presided over by Ministers. Undoubtedly the Materials and Fuel Allocations Committees which I now give up were successful because of that set up.[5] Indeed, they are among the most businesslike and useful bodies I have ever been connected with. At Ministerial Committees there tends to be too much bickering, talking, woolliness, ignorance and personal feeling. At purely official committees there tends to be too little drive. The combination of a Minister and

4 See *HG*, pp. 49–50. He was prospective candidate for Chatham from 1932 until his defeat there at the 1935 election.
5 See *HG*, pp. 137–8.

officials may give you the drive combined with the expertise, and without the personal feelings and ambitions being too prominent.

Anyway, I shall do my very best to let Robens have a better deal than I had. Though I see I shall have to remind myself of this every week otherwise I shall fall into the old rut.

Wednesday, 22 October 1947

Up to now I have hardly come across the Foreign Secretary [Bevin], and had always rather assumed that he felt shy with and slightly antagonistic to middle class people. However, I have recently had one or two interesting talks with him.

The first of these was actually the day I saw the P.M. EB came and sat down at our table in the House. Somebody else said, 'Well, Ernie and when are we going to get out of this mess?' He looked across the table and rasped out, looking at me, 'When Gaitskell produces the forty million tons extra coal'. (I think he must already have known about the impending change.) After that he held forth a bit about what was to be done. Agreed with me that it was no use talking. Said that if he were Minister of Fuel & Power he would not make a speech for six months. (Of course, they are all inclined to feel like this after ES[Shinwell]). I ended up by asking if I could come and see him about coal. He beamed about this and said, 'Well, certainly, if the old war horse can help some of the younger ones he would be only too glad to'. So last Monday, being now a Minister, I went to the Foreign Office. There he was sitting in rather a small chair at a not very big desk in the enormous, famous room with a picture of, is it George III when young, over the fireplace? And the outlook over St James' Park and the Horse Guards Parade.

I got him talking quite soon. There was nothing very much on what he said on equipment. He thought, as I did, that the Ministry of Labour should take a hand in industrial relations, and suggested I should see [Sir Robert] Goole, Chief Conciliation Officer, of that Ministry. Then we talked about incentives. I said that PAYE and income tax standard rate was really the root cause of a lot of the trouble. It was so close to our noses that we all overlooked it and argued that it did not really count. To my surprise, instead of saying that he disagreed, he said that he had been talking to the Chancellor about this that very morning. Some business man had suggested that any increase in profit tax should be geared inversely to production. He was wondering whether one could not get the same thing for the workers. I was delighted to hear this, and he said, 'Well, you are a younger man than I am; you go away and think it out'.

I asked him about exports, and he was fairly reasonable. I made it clear that if he was to get his exports I must have some means of stopping domestic electricity demand, and gave him a rough idea of the tax proposal. He seemed to swallow it quite well, which was satisfactory as this was one of the main purposes of my visit.

A few days later Cripps, Strachey and I saw him about trade with Denmark and Ireland. After we had discussed all that he suddenly produced a copy of a letter he had written to the Chancellor on income tax and incentives, and read it aloud. It was full of detail, not very logical, but truly remarkable for something thrown off by the Foreign Secretary in his spare time. The Inland Revenue people will probably pull it to pieces, but I remain convinced that something on these lines has got to be done if they are to get the necessary production.[6]

I seem to be doing nothing but seeing Americans these days. I entertained some of the toughest Congressmen to lunch last week, including Mr Taber, an extreme Republican reactionary, who goes round everywhere saying that he has not seen any signs of starvation in Europe. (He repeated it at lunch.) Hyndley and Fergusson were there and we did our best to give them an impression of virility and enterprise. I believe we made some impression on all of them. Anyway, Taber enjoyed his food better than the French cooking, and said he thought we were making a better effort at recovery than other countries. It is pretty intolerable to accept patronising comments from people who are quite so odious, but he is the Chairman of the Congress Appropriations Sub-Committee and will have a big influence on the Marshall Plan question.[7]

A much nicer one came to see me this afternoon – Senator Alexander Smith, who is clearly sympathetic, quick and interested.[8] We also had Walter Lippmann* and wife to lunch on Saturday and showed them round the Mining Exhibition afterwards. I thought Lippmann highly intelligent and sympathetic. It is hard to believe that he is in the late sixties. He said that he thought there was a balance of power at the moment because America could not stop Russia much, but on the other hand the Russians could not stop the Americans smashing Moscow and other cities with long range planes dropping atom bombs. He, therefore, did not expect war.

6 See *HG*, pp. 174–5 on electricity demand, 150 on income tax – where Bevin's ideas were vetoed by Dalton (1962, p. 268).
7 John Taber, Congressman from up-state New York 1923–62, was chairman of the sub-committee dealing with foreign aid in the Republican-controlled House.
8 H. Alexander Smith of New Jersey, a liberal Republican, was senator 1945–58 and a member of the Foreign Relations committee.

I had my first Press Conference last week and put over a long – much too long – statement on the winter fuel position, including allocations for industry. Apart from length it went down quite well. The intelligent papers were glad to have so much information. This is the easy part of my job since I have always been good at arithmetic, and am not easily caught out on figures.

One of the difficulties of my situation is the need for me not to interfere with the Coal Board. Fergusson sent me this note the first day I became Minister, with which broadly I agree.[9]

The trouble is that the N.C.B. [National Coal Board] do not handle their own public relations properly and are, alas, now getting very unpopular with the miners.

Yesterday we had an Adjournment Debate on the National Coal Board and I had the rather ticklish task of once more laying down the firm principle of non-intervention and refusing information. Fortunately the miners played up; although they are very worried about the N.C.B. they had agreed not to make trouble in the House but to confine it to private meetings. I feel my speech, though not exciting, went down fairly well and I hope paved the way for getting these nationalised undertakings out of the cockpit of politics. This is something which has got to be achieved in time.

I have settled the broad lines of the Gas Bill and got them through the appropriate Cabinet Committee. Quite pleased with the rather ingenious idea of giving the Area Boards virtually complete freedom unless and until they get into difficulties. The press say that the gas industry is going to oppose, but I doubt if it will be very serious opposition.

Document No. 2

Permanent Secretary to HG, 8 October 1947

Personal & Private   7 Millbank,
                                                         S.W.1
                                                         8th October, 1947

Dear Hugh,

In considering the policy you are going to pursue as Minister you may care to have my view of the situation, the major tasks that lie ahead over the next two or three years and the best way of tackling them both in the national interest and in your own interest.

9 Printed below by permission of H.M.S.O. (Crown Copyright).

Everything depends on making coal nationalisation a success and getting more coal. In my view there is only one way by which this can be done – simple yet requiring a difficult decision and the greatest courage and resolution in adhering to it. The Coal Board must be given a chance to deliver the goods and it can only have a chance if the statutory position under which the Board not the Minister is responsible for the production of coal is fully and on all occasions recognized and made clear to both the miners and the public. We have carried on since the vesting date as if the Minister was still in the position which he occupied during the war under the control scheme.

In my view this has been a profound mistake – a political mistake as well as a mistake from the point of view of getting the coal, and it has prevented the Coal Board getting on to proper terms with the miners in the pits and with the general public.

The time is opportune for making the necessary change. Everyone realises that the recent intervention of the Cabinet and the Minister was a mistake.[10] And the change is the best way – I am inclined to think the only way – of thwarting the danger of Communist-inspired trouble in the pits and the attempt they will make to set the miners against you and the Government. There are other aspects of the Communist attitude which need to be taken into account and which I think strengthen the need for the change.

This is not to say that we cannot urge on the N.C.B. privately the need for better public relations. But for the rest I suggest it is for them not us to take the steps to get more coal: our task is to back up their requirements. It is hopeless to appoint people to undertake a particular responsibility and then try and do their job for them. They must be trusted and left to get on in their own way or be sacked.

The second point I want to stress is the vital importance of getting the Gas Bill introduced next session.[11] It would immensely strengthen your own personal position in the Party, Parliament and the country. And unless and until gas is nationalised it is not really possible to make much progress with what is now the main responsibility of the Ministry viz: the development of a coordinated fuel and power policy directed to the most efficient utilisation of our fuel and power resources. Moreover the delay makes it almost impossible to promote proper development of the gas industry.

10 Presumably referring to the meeting on August 21 when four senior Ministers saw the N.U.M. Executive and urged them to modify the five-day week agreement in order to increase production. See below, p. 109 and n.
11 There had been a prolonged argument between Ministers over the respective priorities of gas and steel nationalisation: see Chester (1975), pp. 35–8.

Thirdly it is essential to get a proper set up for electricity and I think for the next few months this should have a prior claim on your time to more ephemeral administrative matters. Unless we get the right men for Area Boards and get them set up quickly we shall have a shocking administrative failure in the nationalisation of electricity.

The fourth major problem for the next two years in my opinion is to lay the foundation for a fuel and power policy. Not much can be done till the Electricity Boards are in the saddle and the gas industry is nationalised. But there are preliminary studies to be made in the scientific sphere which will involve a new scientific set-up; and we have got to settle the relations between the Ministry and the Boards in a number of very difficult aspects of fuel and power policy. This will require very careful consideration and very careful handling of the Boards.

As regards our immediate policy problems I think the main issue outstanding is the need to control and restrict domestic consumption of electricity. The other major problem likely to arise is trouble in the pits arising from various causes; but this is a matter where action by the Ministry will in my view only do harm. The only chance is to refuse to be drawn in – this would only play into Horner's* hands.[12]

One last point – the Department itself. I was asked to come here much against my personal wishes to organise and build up what was a new Ministry. When I arrived I found all the troubles that usually occur in a new Department. The old Mines Department (which was not a good Department) felt it was the Ministry. People drawn from other Departments were often the people whom those Departments could best spare or were people who had not wanted to be transferred. There was an enormous proportion of temporary staff; and there had been a great deal of favouritism.

The result was widespread disgruntlement, friction and inefficiency. It takes years of work to remedy such a state of affairs and endless patience. In any case any Permanent Secretary must consider not only immediate needs but how to train and bring on the men who will have to handle the work five or ten years hence.

Therefore I would ask your tolerance of certain present weaknesses and your support in trying to build a really effective team. I know that it is asking a lot of a Minister to put up with things he doesn't like during his term of a particular office for the sake of the future efficiency of a department with which he may not in that future be personally concerned – having passed to other and perhaps higher spheres! But even on the short view the Department has to be looked at as a whole and individual

12 Arthur Horner, a Communist, was general secretary of the National Union of Mineworkers.

cases considered against the background of what will promote general efficiency and not merely efficiency in one particular part or branch.

Yours ever,

Donald Fergusson

Diary: Friday, 14 November 1947

The Baths Episode

How easy it is to say the wrong thing! How easy it is not to recognise one has said the wrong thing!

About three weeks ago I made a speech at a municipal election meeting in Hastings. I had spoken earlier at Eastbourne in the afternoon at a very successful meeting, where there were plenty of good humoured interruptions which enlivened the proceedings. I was tired when I got to Hastings but it was again a good meeting, though rather less lively than at Eastbourne. I tried to keep my speech fairly above Party despite the coming election and inevitably referred to fuel economy in the course of it. Then I let fall two fatal sentences:

'It means getting up and going to bed in cold bedrooms. It may mean fewer baths. Personally, I have never had a great many baths myself and I can assure those who are in the habit of having a great many baths that it does not make a great deal of difference to their health if they have fewer. And as far as appearance – most of that is underneath and nobody sees it.'

Of course the first sentence was said in a joking manner and the second was a pure joke, and the audience laughed and took it as such. It is the kind of thing I have said again and again at open air meetings to liven things up. After the meeting one of the local people who was driving me round referred to this, and said he would not be surprised if it was in headlines next day. Though he, himself, thought it a joke and took it as such. The press did pick it out though not very flamboyantly. However, on Tuesday it so happened that Churchill was making his big speech against the Government on the Address and he made great play of these remarks of mine. I was not present at the time myself but everybody tells me that he was extremely funny at my expense. Since then I have become associated in the public mind with dirt, never having a bath, etc. I am told that at the Command Performance no less than three jokes were made about this by music hall comedians, though they all seem to have been in quite a friendly manner.

First of all, I did not worry at all. It seemed inconceivable to me that anybody could believe it was anything but a joke. However, I now consider I really made a mistake. Psychologically it is probably a bad thing for a Minister to be associated in the public mind with not washing. I had a few anonymous letters and some packets of D.D.T. powder sent to me. And two signed letters which reflect different points of view. The first was from a distant connection of some kind, taking me to task for what I said and asking me when I was speaking in public to be more careful of what I said because the name was such an uncommon one. The second was from my old nurse whom I have not seen or heard from for over thirty years, but who always had a very good sense of humour. I was very touched by this.

Of course it would not matter so much if I had not been preceded by somebody [i.e. Shinwell] who always said the wrong things.

Diary: Friday, 14 November 1947

An incredible thing has happened. The Chancellor has resigned and in the most extraordinary circumstances. These will be public, and indeed history so I need not go into them. But here is what I saw and heard and some of my reflections.

Yesterday morning I was at the Cabinet, the only outsider present for a discussion on wages policy. It dragged on and on very heatedly. Cripps and Morrison being calm and sensible, Ernie [Bevin] flying into a furious rage and accusing Cripps of leading us down the road to fascism. (It was as though Cripps had touched a fuse off.) What EB said was mostly completely irrespective [sic]. In the middle of all this I saw HD [Dalton] sitting rather silent and looking rather tired. I caught his eye and he smiled at me. I did not know then that he must have been in appalling mental agony.

That afternoon I had my questions (I am getting forty to fifty every week) and occupied the stage for the best part of forty minutes. As I finished the last one and sat down I found myself next to the Chancellor. He got up to answer a private notice question and made the announcement, now famous. I whispered to him, 'What's it all about?' and he passed me a copy of the *Star* and said, 'That bloody fool Carvel'. However, Winston [Churchill] got up quickly and appeared to exonerate the Chancellor. I thought it was irritating but all over and left the Chamber.[13]

13 Dalton gave the 'headlines' of his Budget speech to John Carvel, lobby correspondent of *The Star* (a Liberal evening paper) as he entered the Chamber. The paper was on sale before the Stock Exchange closed, and Dalton resigned office. This entry and the last were misdated as Friday 15th.

That night at dinner with Cripps and the others Stafford said that it was all very serious. GS[Strauss] and I temporised and said that we thought it was not to be compared with the Jimmie Thomas scandal.[14] We did not know that Cripps had already become Chancellor himself. The news of HD's resignation was out by 10.30 p.m. that night.

What an incredibly dangerous and uncertain life politicians lead. I cannot understand myself how HD came to mention anything to Carvel on the way in, except that knowing Carvel well (in the war we often used to dine and lunch with him) he must have trusted him completely.[15] It is just possible that Carvel too did not intend the news to be published until later. But it is all a ghastly affair. I have written to HD. It will be very sad not to have him with us in these crucial months ahead. All the same, the general feeling is that he will be back in the Government within a year or less. Moreover, the Party view is that he did the right thing and probably his prestige there is higher than ever.

'No friends at the top.' This is what Asquith[16] is supposed to have said (I must look it up in his Memoirs sometime) and it is certainly true. Cripps showed no remorse and I could not help feeling that he had now satisfied one more ambition by becoming Chancellor. He said to us recently 'I cannot really do this job, you see, unless I am P.M.' Evan, Douglas and I met Ernie the same evening in the corridor at the House. He was very cheerful – he had been drinking – and very friendly too. But he did not seem upset at having lost one of his ablest colleagues. It is a rather horrid prospect. Ambition certainly does seem to kill the pleasanter aspects of human nature. But HD is certainly just the same.

Thursday, 4 December 1947

Postscript on Baths

This subject came up during a Dinner Party last night. Those present included Herbert Morrison, Evan, Douglas, Aidan [Crawley]*, Jack Diamond* and Chris Mayhew. Much to my surprise Chris said that he thought it was a perfectly splendid remark, absolutely right in every way. Jack Diamond and Aidan both thought we had won a lot of votes out of it! Evan, however, made the best remark of the evening about it. He said,

14 J.H. Thomas, Colonial Secretary, revealed details of the 1936 Budget in advance, and dealings took place. He had to resign both his office and his seat.
15 During the war HG had a great many meals with Dalton, as his personal assistant from 1940–42 and also subsequently.
16 H.H. Asquith, Liberal Prime Minister 1908–16. HG often quoted this phrase, attributing it to various sources. I have failed to trace it.

'You all call it a joke, but I can assure you it is a statement of fact. I live with the Minister of Fuel & Power and as far as I know he never has any baths at all!' Herbert said that the Labour Party was rather touchy over baths and had always been regarded as dirtier than the Tories. He went on to say that when a boy he had one bath a week in a tin bath at home. When he grew up this was impracticable and he had to go out to the Lambeth Baths. He found that this took up too much time from his evening studies and so reduced it to one bath in three weeks. I said that I thought that it was quite adequate!

Most of the evening was spent in discussing Kim Mackay's proposals for integrating Western Europe politically and economically.[17] This was, in the main, severely and deservedly criticised on the ground that it was economically irrelevant in the short period and offered no particular advantages in the long period. Politically, however, there was a case. Some, Aidan especially, supported it with great eloquence – 'The only way to prevent the spread of totalitarianism in Europe'; 'England's historic role was to prevent the domination of Europe by a single power'; 'We must lead the world'. On the other hand, Evan no less passionately denounced the idea on the grounds that none of those other countries, except small and uninfluential powers like Belgium, Holland and Scandinavia, were particularly well fitted for the democratic way of life. They were governed by [word omitted] nor had they our traditional tolerance and kindliness. It was all rather amusing.

Much interest being shown in the question of the new Parliamentary Secretary to the Treasury job. Last night Evan seemed to be certain that John Edwards was to get it, and we were all somewhat gloomy; not because we did not like him, but because Evan and Douglas would be technically so much better qualified. However, today Evan tells me that Douglas is to get it which is excellent news.[18] We must now try and bring Evan into the inner Cripps circle. If we can do this I shall really begin to feel quite happy about the Government.

Royal Wedding[19]

I find it difficult to take these things seriously. We had seats in the Abbey and were able to see the Royal personages passing up the aisle fairly well, but I could not get excited. I[t] would, perhaps, have been more fun outside.

17 M.P. for Hull N.W. 1945–50, Reading N. 1950–1. Wartime chairman of Common Wealth Party (see Biog. Note on Acland).
18 Jay became Economic Secretary to the Treasury next day.
19 Princess Elizabeth* married Lieut. Philip Mountbatten (then created Duke of Edinburgh)* on 20 November 1947.

The Weekend in Durham

This is one of the best Divisions in the Coal Board. The Chairman of the Divisional Board is not a coal man but obviously highly intelligent and capable, and interested too in the problems of large scale organisation which they appear to have solved more successfully here than elsewhere.[20] Relations are better here with the miners than in other districts; partly due to the personality of the Chairman, and largely due to the fact that they have Sam Watson* as their leader. I spent a large part of my time with him discussing everything under the sun. He is full of interesting and progressive ideas for improving industrial relations. He wants me to work really hard on the problem of redundancy, or some sort of supplementary pension scheme because he feels that the existence of some such scheme is the key to a successful concentration policy. Otherwise there will be too much resistance from the miners on behalf of the older ones who will probably inevitably be displaced. Concentration is in turn by far the more important method of reducing costs.

I spent some hours with him and his wife before catching the train on Saturday night, and we gossiped away together. She is much younger than him and an unusual type. In fact altogether they are an unusual couple; both coming from mining families in the same village and both having risen so much in the social sphere.

Sam is a prominent member of the Party Executive. He does not much like Cripps (somebody must have put him against him). Very pro HD and did not, apparently know that HD was also my chief friend at the top level.[21] We talked about future leadership. Sam was worried because of the gap between the Big Five and the rest. He does not like Strachey and certainly does not trust Bevan; hinting that I should start collecting supporters like himself and Bowman* and also that I should get together with some younger people.[22] He is a tremendous stand-by and will, I think, be exceptionally helpful in his job.

In the afternoon I addressed a Labour Party Regional Conference. I spoke rather dully and was a bit too high-brow. Mrs Watson said afterwards that I quoted figures like an almanack. However, Sam was pleased because there was no 'trouble'. It seems that even when Attlee or Dalton have been there somebody has been troublesome, and as Sam said – 'And

20 He was an industrialist, H.O. Hindley, who was about to become chairman of the new Raw Cotton Commission.
21 Dalton was M.P. for Bishop Auckland, a Durham mining seat.
22 Sam Watson always refused to leave Durham for a political or industrial post in London. He was the closest of all trade union leaders to HG. Jim Bowman led the Northumberland miners.

I thought in view of who your predecessor was it would be difficult'. But the meeting passed off very peacefully and nothing but goodwill was shown. Sam, incidentally, very, very hostile to Shinwell.[23]

The Gravesend by-election result has cheered everybody up immensely. Those who know, of course, are not enthusiastic about Acland* coming back to the House.[24] What a bore he is! Michael Stewart* and I went to speak for him two days before the poll. He hardly condescended to shake hands and uttered no word of thanks afterwards. In marked contrast, Bishop, candidate for Epsom, wrote me a very nice letter after I had spoken for him three or four days later.

The miners' M.P.s are a problem. Most of them are frustrated men and, alas, abysmally stupid. My relations with them are not so easy to manage. They take offence without much encouragement. We had a meeting this week to which I took Hyndley and Ebby Edwards*,[25] and I got more and more depressed as I listened to the speeches from the various M.P.s. They were so obviously incapable of understanding the most elementary problems facing the National Coal Board. There are exceptions, of course. My P.P.S. – Horace Holmes[26] – is extremely good, most intelligent and honest and shares my gloom about the others.

Our dinners with Cripps continue, and now Strachey has been brought in. This is sensible because it enables us to talk about trade agreements – all the Ministers chiefly concerned being present. Cripps, however, no doubt wants him in the entourage. For my part I reserve judgment about him. He is still, I think, much too inclined to abstract theory. At the moment he is a deflationist and rather anti-control. I think this is rather a rationalisation of the difficulties he has in introducing and maintaining certain controls in his own field. But it is also due to half-baked economics which he learned in the past. At the same time I think he is a very able negotiator, and fairly influential at Cabinet meetings – states his case forcibly, though with exaggeration. Is he to be trusted? Probably not.[27]

An interesting evening on Monday. First of all a party given by Bolton & Paul – John Wilmot's firm. The Ex-Chancellor was present. He talks

23 Shinwell also sat for a Durham mining seat, Seaham.
24 The Labour M.P. for Gravesend had been expelled from the House for selling information about P.L.P. meetings to the press. Sir Richard Acland, who won the by-election, had a reputation for rectitude.
25 Labour director of the National Coal Board.
26 (Sir) Horace Holmes (1888–1971) was M.P. for Hemsworth (Yorks.) 1946–59 and a Whip 1951–9.
27 See below, pp. 164, 184, for a revised and more favourable view of Strachey.

again of launching a great attack on the City. Alternatively of attacking some Minister. All rather crude. He must have an outlet for his aggression. I hope he will do neither. His right course at the moment is to take the loyal, elder statesman line. Later dinner with Hyndley, Street and Fergusson, and an interesting and useful talk about altering the Coal Board. I think we have at last got them down to brass tacks. The idea is broadly that in the spring or summer Reid should go; Gridley should go; Ellis and Lowe should become Chief Executives – leaving only five on the Board, to which we might add Vickers and then three part timers, of whom one might be Reid. This will certainly be a step in the direction of defunctionalisation. We must now leave them to chew it over.[28]

I lunch with Citrine*[29] regularly – more austerely and less privately than with Hyndley. We are, however, always alone which is probably a good thing. He told me this time that he makes a habit of memorising things when he goes for walks in the mornings and evenings. He can now repeat almost all of the Electricity Act. Then in a self-revealing moment he went on to say that he did not feel that the other people on the Board respected him enough, and he felt that if he could quote the Act on any occasion and never be caught out it would impress them.

We talked a little about the international situation, the position in France and the French trade union trouble.[30] Immediately, his eyes lit up and he began to show enormous enthusiasm and interest. I could not help feeling that perhaps it was a mistake to have taken him out of the T.U.C. I think he will do well. The only danger is that he will try and attend to far too many details simply because he will not get used to running such a vast organisation compared with the T.U.C. headquarters at his age.

28 Sir Arthur Street, a former civil servant, was deputy chairman; Sir Charles Ellis, J.C. Gridley, L.H.H. Lowe and Sir Charles Reid were members; Sir Geoffrey Vickers was legal adviser. Ellis was professor of physics at London; Lowe, a chartered accountant, had been director of finance at the Ministry of Fuel and Power; Reid, a mining engineer, had chaired the committee on technical reorganisation of the industry. He and Gridley, who was responsible for marketing, were former directors of colliery companies; both resigned in 1948 (below, pp. 68, 101), and Vickers was then appointed to the Board. On defunctionalisation see Chester (1975), pp. 495, 550–7.

29 For 20 years general secretary of the T.U.C. and now chairman of the British Electricity Authority.

30 Large and sometimes violent strikes, partly provoked by a French Communist offensive against the government, led to a major and lasting split in the recently united French unions.

Tuesday, 6 January 1948

The recent change in the attitude of the Communist Party has caused a good deal of interest – although the mining industry has been given a sort of exemption by Pollitt from the general attack which the C.P. is going to make.[31] Nevertheless within the N.U.M. the new line may lead to complications.

The first of these is likely to arise in connection with the Wigan by-election where the Communists have announced their intention of putting up a candidate. This is, however, a miners' seat and the N.U.M. Executive are putting forward a very nice chap – Ron Williams their legal adviser – as candidate. If, as is likely, he is adopted by the local Labour Party Horner will be in a difficult position. As a Communist representative the Party will expect him to support a Communist candidate, but as Secretary to the N.U.M. he will be expected openly to support the N.U.M. and Labour Party candidate. The view both of the N.C.B. and of Lawther* is that he will have to make up his mind as to which side of the fence he is going to stand. At the moment all the indications are that he will remain with the C.P.[32]

An amusing sidelight on this situation was given by Sir Arthur Street last night at our usual dinner with Hyndley. Shortly before Christmas the N.C.B. gave a dinner to the N.U.M. Executive in the course of which the N.U.M. members mostly got extremely tight. This is no new thing for Horner, or for that matter for Lawther either. Nor is it any new thing for Sir Arthur to drive Horner home after these binges.

On this occasion Sir Arthur got the N.U.M. leaders out of the Dorchester, where the dinner took place, before they passed out, being frightened of a scandal if that were to happen. He pushed them all into the back of the car and then got in front with the chauffeur. Then there arose the most dreadful hullabuloo and argument, and much abuse and filthy language. The first stop was at the Strand Palace where somebody was deposited. Next they dropped Bowman, anti-Communist Vice President, at the Russell Hotel, the row having continued in the meantime. Street said that when Bowman got out he was as white as a sheet, though not so drunk as the others, and he said, 'Well, we have had a real political bust up, and a damn good thing too'. This left Horner and Lawther, and Street overheard Horner then saying to Lawther, 'Well, Bill, you won't desert the workers, will you?' And Lawther, sufficiently sober to be discreet,

31 Harry Pollitt (1890–1960), a boilermaker, was general secretary of the Communist Party of Great Britain 1929–56 (except 1939–41).
32 Williams had nearly 29,000 votes to the Communist's 1,647, and sat until 1958. (Sir) Will Lawther was President of the N.U.M.

replied, 'I have never done that, Arthur' but evading, of course, which side he was going to stand on.

The story ends with Street finally watching Horner trying to get into the wrong house and eventually leading him gently away and getting him into the right house.

I must say that the spectacle envisaged of this extremely distinguished ex-Civil Servant, who at one time was strongly supported for the head of the Civil Service, engaged in shepherding drunken miners round is an extremely funny one, as indeed Street fully realises.

Friday, 30 January 1948

Lots of Trouble

Politics may be pleasant or it may be horrible but it is seldom dull. Just at the moment it is more horrible than anything else. I am faced with a series of insoluble problems, one major administrative nightmare and much public criticism.

The last two are connected with the withdrawal of the basic petrol ration.[33] We decided some weeks ago that we must improve our publicity on this front and finally arranged a Press Conference for the 15th January, the publication of a pamphlet, and a broadcast by myself. The latter was extraordinarily difficult to organise. It was suggested originally by [S.C.] Leslie*, the Chancellor's Chief Information Officer. Then we were told that the prospect of the Prime Minister agreeing to it was very remote. Then I proceeded to draft what I thought was a suitable script. We sent this to the P.M. who passed it to the Lord President [Morrison]. I then received a note from the P.M. saying, 'I doubt whether this broadcast would be well timed even if, as is extremely unlikely, the B.B.C. regard it as non-controversial. I should like to talk to you about it'. I went to see him and to my surprise he did not resist. The Lord President had reluctantly agreed. Then we had to put it through the P.M.G. [Post Master General] to the B.B.C. with the request for them to reserve the time. This fortunately was easier. It was on the whole a success. Though, of course, it provoked a very large number of critical letters.

What was not too good was the film. The next day Movietone News rang up and said they wanted to make a news reel of me at once. I told Murphy* [his private secretary] to ask Leslie what he thought. The latter said, 'Be careful and insist on seeing the film before it is released. It can be

33 See *HG*, pp. 151–2.

a very dangerous medium'. I was very busy but agreed to their coming at six o'clock in the evening. In the intervals between interviews I wrote the words I had to speak, and agreed with my Secretary that they should be written up on a blackboard so that I could read them. A team of men arrived at six o'clock with camera and apparatus of every kind, together with a make-up girl. While I was being made-up I was told I could not have the words on the blackboard because the lights would blind me. Therefore, I would have to learn the piece. I was not very happy when doing it; partly for this reason and partly because the lights were blinding; partly too because nobody really 'produced' me. We went to see the film the following Monday. I did not much like it. I blinked a lot; looked terribly serious and the only good things about it were my voice and the actual words. (I think the script was quite good). However, the experts present, including two from Leslie's office, and Bob Fraser, who came down especially at my request, approved it and on their advice I agreed to its release.[34]

On the following Thursday I went to the First Night of 'Anna Karenina'. I was afraid that the newsreel would come on and sure enough it did. There was a lot of booing and hissing and some laughter. Though also some clapping. I felt horribly embarrassed and really suffered agony for some time, not because of the booing so much as because I felt the film was ridiculous and cursed myself for agreeing to its release.

Later I discussed it with Bob who adhered to his original view and comforted me somewhat. He also promised to find out how it was being generally taken. In a number of cinemas apparently there was no reaction. But it was all intensely depressing, not merely because of what happened, but because it is humiliating to find oneself feeling in that way. Indeed, this is the horrid side of politics – that there is the continual criticism to face and one's own infirmities in being sensitive to it. More than that – the House of Commons is in some ways so like a public school. There is this great community with a keen sense of public opinion, but far more than in most public schools there is the most violent and intense competition and rivalry. HD once said to me, 'Green is the predominant colour in the House. Everybody's eyes are green'. How true that is! One suffers from it oneself and it is humiliating to find that one does suffer. Altogether I very much doubt if I am really suited to this kind of thing.

To turn to more serious topics. The Government is at last going to do something about wages policy. In the absence of the Foreign Secretary – and only because of his absence – the Chancellor and [George Isaacs] the

34 HG's old friend (Sir) Robert Fraser was now director-general of the Central Office of Information (1946–54), and later of the Independent Television Authority (1954–70).

Minister of Labour (the latter having been manoeuvred into it by some official conspiracy) got agreed in the Cabinet a statement which marks an advance on everything else said before.[35] A few weeks ago the same thing was discussed and got nowhere because EB[Bevin] went into a frenzy. Even so, I do not know how much it will achieve. There is very little room between the two horns of the dilemma. To leave things alone so that there is a wage inflation and maldistribution of labour, or on the other hand to regulate wages. Probably this represents the best plan.

The prospect ahead is pretty grim. Indeed, without Marshall Aid it is ghastly, and there is no certainty about that. What will happen if there is a Republican victory and Taft is President in 1949?[36] Yes! the prospect is pretty grim. Even with Marshall Aid there is nothing to be very cheerful about; though somehow or other I must get some sort of basic ration restored in the summer. The plan is to get the Black Market teamed [cleaned?] up and save something that way; to get a new system of rationing which will cut the E and S allowances and simplify administration (Reddaway has come in to help on that) and then to hope that the arithmetic will work out so that we can have a small basic ration back while still saving, say half a million tons a year. Even so, I think I shall have great difficulty in getting the Chancellor to agree. The present thing is administratively a horror.[37]

Looking farther anead for further sources of gloom, one has only to turn to the Middle East. Upon this rather large neck of land between the Black Sea, Mediterranean and the Persian Gulf is centred by far the most important source of oil in the world. Should Russia over-run this area there would not merely be insufficient oil for Britain but for a large part of the rest of the world. And, even without Russia it is difficult enough. The Arab States are making difficulties about the pipe line because of the Palestine question. God knows when we shall really get our expansion programme going there, and how precarious it will all be even when the output is doubled as we plan in the next four to five years.

Coal, however, is a bright spot, not merely because output is getting up but because consumption is extraordinarily low. It is an amazing contrast

35 Isaacs (1883–1979) was Gen.-Sec. of NATSOPA (a printers' union) 1909–49; on the T.U.C. General Council 1932–45; M.P. Gravesend, 1923–4, Southwark 1929–31, 1939–59; Minister of Labour 1945–51, of Pensions 1951.

36 Senator Robert Taft of Ohio was the favourite of the more conservative and isolationist wing of the Republican party, and sought its presidential nomination in 1940, 1948 and 1952. He tried to reduce U.S. aid going to Europe under the Marshall Plan.

37 The economist W.B. Reddaway was the chief statistician at the Board of Trade. When the basic petrol ration was abolished in 1947, E. and S. coupons (Essential and Semi-essential) for supplementary allowances continued to be given quite generously.

with only six months ago. There is talk of people refusing to buy, and even of some merchants having difficulty in disposing of house coal. I must say, I don't believe these stories. But it is not unlikely that the habit of economy which we have [at] last engendered, combined with high prices, will hold back consumption within the expansion of demand. Well, it is all to the good if we can export more. This should be possible. But there are anxieties. What will the Americans do? At present interim aid to France and Italy consists in part of compulsory coal shipments. What if the Marshall Plan itself contains provision for the continuance of large exports of coal to Europe, which in effect will be free. Where then are our markets? This is all fanciful because I cannot believe the Americans would do this.[38] But the position needs clearing up.

As for other headaches, there is a row with the T.U.C. about the Personal Compensation Clause in the Gas Bill; there is a row pending with the Local Authorities about the scandalous way they have dissipated their assets in electricity and gas undertakings; the shortage of fuel oil makes it necessary to halt the coal-oil conversion programme which is embarrassing and there is the perpetual, dreary row about petrol.[39]

Monday, 16 February 1948

Sir Stafford Cripps

Naturally in my present job I see a good deal of Cripps. The more I see the more impressed I am. He has really the most amazingly keen intelligence. This morning at the Cabinet there was a discussion on a Balance of Payments paper – the really vital question of the moment. Part of this paper was concerned with the oil problem which is extremely intricate and involved. The position is that at first sight it looks as though our policy is absolutely crazy, because we are purchasing dollar oil for our own use, the use of the rest of the sterling area, and even possibly some other foreign countries, while at the same time we are exporting oil to quite a number of soft currency areas. When one goes into it one finds all kinds of complications, e.g. some of these soft currency areas have their own tankers and fetch the oil which would otherwise not be sold at all. Some of them are getting the oil in return for some concession in a bilateral

38 They did. See below, pp. 63, 159–60.
39 On the compensation argument with the T.U.C., see Chester (1975), pp. 769–71, 780–2; on the dissipation of local authorities' gas and electricity assets, *ibid.*, 361–2; on coal-oil conversion, below, p. 63; on the row over petrol, *HG*, pp. 151–2.

agreement. To some the oil has to go for political reasons, while in other cases, even if we were to divert it owing to the longer tanker haulage we should not gain very much. These are just a few of the difficulties. But Cripps without the slightest difficulty gave the most lucid and detailed account of the problem, which he began by saying, 'The Minister of Fuel of course knows much more about this than I do'. I sat there just gaping with admiration. I whispered to Strachey what an amazing performance it was, and he said, 'That's what he does when he gets up at four in the morning'.

The second great quality that he has is courage which is closely combined in his case with superb self confidence. As Plowden* [Chief Planning Officer] said to me the other day, 'When he has made up his mind he is absolutely certain he is right and therefore completely indifferent to any criticisms or objections or arguments'. This is where he differs from most politicians. Most of us, I think, are cowards in the sense that we are always counting the political difficulties and probably tending to exaggerate them. You feel with Cripps that almost nothing is politically impossible. He sails on simply concerned with what is the best solution from every other point of view and ignoring all the rocks which lie ahead. As I say, the courage is not obvious as courage; one does not feel there is a tremendous moral struggle because of this great confidence. Perhaps it is something to do with his religion. Perhaps too it is something to do with the martyr complex – at least that is what Evan says.

His third great quality is, I think, patience and, despite what other people say, kindliness. He is a thoroughly nice person to work for. He never loses his temper despite the colossal strain upon him. If you make a mistake he does not shout and rave at you, and probably won't say anything about it. And of course you can always get a decision out of him. No man was ever less frightened of taking responsibility.

His way of life is now becoming quite well known. He gets up at four a.m. and does three hours work before breakfast. He has a walk in the Park; he has a cold bath. He goes to bed, of course, early, if possible by 10.30 p.m. I am told this was not always so; only since the present Government was formed has this very spartan mode been adopted. So also his vegetarianism; this is fairly recent and quite practical because his health was very bad and he had a lot of gastric trouble.

Of course you do feel also that he never really relaxes. One just does not think of Stafford as enjoying a rollicking evening. The most would be a walk in the country; even there one would probably be talking about some deep philosophical problem.

One of the curiosities on the other hand is his poor judgment of people. Some rogues and crooks have fascinated him. Plowden gave Dora several examples the other night. The one we know best is Del Giudice. A man of ebullient personality; considerable gifts of showmanship, no morals whatever and quite unsound from every point of view. The most famous story about Del which I like to tell relates to the second visit that we paid to his house in the country. On the first occasion I had gone alone and he was then living with Greta Gynt, a minor film star, who presided with grace and charm at the dinner table which was loaded of course with most marvellous food despite the war. A year or so later Dora and I went down together and Greta had meanwhile gone off with somebody else. The household was therefore exclusively male. To our surprise, however, we found that Del had given up drinking. This was his story. He had been ill, very ill, and the doctor had said to him, 'You must either give up drinking or women'. 'So', said Del, 'I opt for love.' Can you imagine this with Stafford around?[40]

One or two friends of mine, having observed I was depressed with so much criticism, have been helpful and talked it over with me. Evan says it is entirely due to my public school background. He says that Strachey and I are the worst possible people for the two jobs we hold because of the appalling weight of convention in our youth. We ought really to be minority minded like Evan who, as a Nonconformist, positively revels in unpopularity.

I hear that the late Chancellor is much happier to be relieved of the burden of office. Evan says that he really loathed it at the end, in fact ever since the beginning of the year. All the same I think it is embarrassing and almost humiliating for him to be a back bencher in the House.

The most important recent events have been Cripps' alarming speeches and the statement on what was called 'Personal Incomes and Prices', but really started life as wages policy. Stafford, as I think very belatedly, has issued the grimmest warnings. I have been begging him to do this for some time to ease my position on basic, and he has always agreed but not done it. It was ironical that his weekend statement should follow an unguarded answer I gave to a supplementary Question, saying I would review the position at the end of March. This indeed was my intention, and there must be a review to announce the Government policy for the summer, but it was taken as an encouragement and contrasted with Cripps' speeches.[41] I must say the job of public relations for a politician is appallingly difficult. In a sense it is *the* problem. How not to say the wrong thing and how to get the right thing across.

40 Filippo del Giudice (1892–1961) was managing director of Two Cities, which promoted such famous films as 'Blithe Spirit', 'The Way Ahead', 'In Which We Serve', 'Brief Encounter', 'Way to the Stars'. Cripps may have seen deeper than Gaitskell, for Del Giudice eventually retired to a monastery.
41 HG was criticised for this answer: *The Economist*, 14.2.48. See *HG*, p. 152. On basic petrol, see Editor's Note to this chapter.

Actually, the outlook is probably rather better at the moment than it has been for some time. The prospects of Marshall Aid are nearer and better, and there is a lot of talk about the Bill being through by the end of March. If so, my promise to review, which was so severely criticized, will certainly have been justified.

As to wages policy, the history of this document is as follows. At the very first weekend dinner we had with Stafford this question was discussed. As far as I can remember Marquand and I, and to some extent Strauss, all put forward to Stafford the view that a statement on these lines was about the only thing the Government could do. Stafford accepted the idea and shortly afterwards circulated a paper to the Cabinet. He added, as I think wrongly, the idea of a special tribunal to review all wages claims. There was a most dreadful row. The Foreign Secretary denounced the paper vehemently; [George Isaacs] the Minister of Labour, of course, backed him up, and the outcome was simply an instruction to the Minister of Labour to produce a lot more facts. I thought it was complete defeat and decided we should not get anywhere so long as Ernie [Bevin] was there. I was therefore surprised when a week or two ago the Minister of Labour circulated a paper with a statement of this kind attached. When it was considered by the Government – whether by design or not – the Foreign Secretary was absent, and it went through easily. The Chancellor having produced a better and firmer draft statement than the Minister of Labour. It was considered yet again by the Government and again the Foreign Secretary was absent. I still do not think it would have ever got through if he had been present.

There has been a good deal of grumbling in the Party that it does not do anything about profits and there were threats of a big revolt, but as so often this came to nothing. The Left Wing were appeased by the measures of Price Control announced, and are probably expecting that more will be done in the budget. The real test, however, will not come in Parliament; it turns on whether the Trade Unions will in fact exercise restraint. I think on the whole there is bound to be some restraint, and probably to act as a brake is all that the statement could have done. But, of course, there is a real danger that it will strengthen the Communist power in the Unions. And I rather fancy we shall be in for some trouble in coal on that account.

Another extraordinary development is the difficulty which is looming up of our selling coal in Europe because of the amount sent from America. This does not really matter, except temporarily, so long as dollars have to be paid for it. But if there is free coal under Marshall, not convertible dollars, we are in for real trouble. We have got to make very sure of the position here. But the best advice seems to be that we should get our way with the Americans.[42]

42 But see below, pp. 63, 159–60.

We had the second reading of the Gas Bill last week. It went off very peacefully. I made a conventional and rather dull opening speech, primarily for the record. One never really can make such a good speech when one has very full notes as when one is speaking with almost none. But one must sacrifice Parliamentary effects for security, at least until one has a great deal more experience than I have. We start the Committee stage next week. I fear it will be exceedingly boring since so much of the Bill is like the Electricity Bill. The only hope is that everybody else will be bored and we shall be able to get through it quickly. It will be interesting to see more of Bracken. Whatever anyone may say about him, he certainly is not dull. He made a good speech at the second reading. Good natured, friendly; though, as [was] to be expected from the chief Opposition speech, reasonably buccaneering. The Tories were much better briefed for Gas than they had been for Electricity, which is odd as this time the industry really is co-operating with us. That may be due to Bracken taking Hudson's place.[43]

Friday, 23 April 1948

I am grossly overworked again. Everything is happening at once. The Gas Bill – now three days a week, mornings and afternoons in Committee; the new petrol scheme and all its repercussions; a crisis in the Coal Board; some horrible problems of coal quality and exports, and rather a heavy list of speaking engagements. And then finally the grim world oil situation with all its repercussions on our plans here.

It is a most abominable bore to have to sit for five hours a day opposite Bracken, while the Opposition delay and obstruct the passage of the Gas Bill. Had we known they were going to do this we should have arranged the guillotine. They are quite cunning. They put down an enormous number of amendments. This in itself takes a lot of time unless the Chairman is very ruthless in selecting. If he is ruthless in selecting he has to allow discussion on 'Clause [St]and Part' and this gives more time for talking.[44] I have used the closure three or four times, much to the indignation of the Tories and to the satisfaction of our own side. But it

43 Brendan Bracken, a close friend of Churchill and his Minister of Information 1941–5, replaced R.S. Hudson (Minister of Agriculture 1940–5) as Opposition spokesman.

44 This was the final motion to carry each clause: 'That the Clause stand part of the Bill'.

does not help much; it may save, say, ten minutes on an amendment but the Opposition can then make that up by delays later on.

The real trouble is that we have not got a Chairman with the authority and experience needed to push the Bill through. Jack Diamond is a delightful person, a friend of mine, intelligent and fair-minded, but he does not carry the guns. I made a fatal mistake in asking for him. We should have had a Tory Chairman with experience who would have been able to force the Bill along. There is no doubt that if the Opposition really want to obstruct at Committee Stage they can make the passage of a Bill virtually impossible. Hence the need for the guillotine. We may indeed have to go back to the House for it.

Another difficulty is that Bracken obviously enjoys obstruction. He likes to make irrelevant, colourful and sometimes entertaining speeches; whereas Hudson last year was thoroughly bored with the Electricity Bill and co-operated with us in getting it through. I do not like Bracken; find it hard to hide my distaste and keep my temper. It is difficult to say why I dislike him. He certainly has gifts. He is a good speaker and was, I believe, a good Minister. But he is too emotional and too peculiar for me altogether. Also, he cannot control his own side. It will be interesting to see if he has any position in the Tory Party after Winston goes.

The new petrol scheme has been launched. It received a mixed reception, largely because of the leakage which occurred beforehand and which tended to raise people's hopes. Those with supplementary allowances are grumbling, but I am fairly certain that they will settle down. However, my political instincts in this were quite right; better than those of my Civil Service advisers who wanted me to make a new philosophy out of deducting the standard ration from the supplementary coupons. [45]

The crisis in the Coal Board was precipitated by another of Sir Charles Reid's resignations. [46] He is really using his nuisance value to blackmail all of us. He knows that politically it would be very damaging if he were to resign and make a public attack on the N.C.B. organisation. The awkward thing is that I agree with most of his criticisms of the organisation, so that his resignation in such circumstances would be particularly irritating. Unfortunately I had not so far been able to push Hyndley into making the changes I wanted. I must admit that Reid's threats have achieved this. On Tuesday I took the unusual step of going to see the Board themselves at Hyndley's invitation. I pretended merely to be backing up what their

45 See *HG*, p. 152.
46 Above, p. 50 n. 28.

Chairman wanted and this, I hope, avoided hurting their amour propre. At any rate that plus Hyndley's skill seems to have done the trick. They have agreed to the two essential changes: (1) to set up a Policy or General Purposes Committee, consisting of non-functional members within the Board, leaving the rest to function chiefly as departmental heads, attending the full Board meetings which will now be held less frequently. (2) The Board will invite three outside persons to survey their internal organisation and make recommendations for any improvements which appear necessary.

We were really on a razor edge all the time with the danger of Reid's resignation on the one side and the resignation of the whole of the Board on the other.[47]

I have invited Sir R. Burrows to become a part-time member of the Board. He was Chairman of Manchester Collieries and of the L.M.S.[48] He is an old Tory but I think just the right type that we want, because he knows the industry and is a business man, not a technician; also a man of considerable administrative experience on a large scale. I liked him. He seemed to me to have plenty of common sense and to be pretty shrewd in his judgments. I think Hyndley is a bit doubtful because he fears such a strong character. Anyway I am not sure that Burrows will accept.

We dined last Sunday with the McNeils* and had a good political gossip. Hector says that HD is certain to return quite soon to the Government. He says they would all like him back, though I have my doubts about this. He also says that HD's budget speech was a help because it threatened the Government with some trouble from him. Hector says that HD should make another speech like that, but I am doubtful. Hector is a journalist and I think all this very much the journalist's approach. Hector himself is obviously extremely ambitious. He would have liked to be Secretary of State for Scotland; alleges that he was unofficially approached but Ernie would not agree. He has, perhaps for this reason, no opinion of Arthur Woodburn [Scottish Secretary]. Hector is an attractive person and I like him. For the moment I do not think his ambitions would be such as to make him hopelessly untrustworthy as a friend. He said some extraordinary things about Anthony Eden* which I find very difficult to believe . . .

At our dinner with the Chancellor last night Aneurin Bevan was also present and appears to have joined the group. I must say that Stafford is showing much more political acumen than I expected. He is obviously anxious to have Bevan as an ally. And the group is now fairly powerful

47 See *HG*, p. 155.
48 The London, Midland and Scottish Railway.

consisting as it does, apart from the Chancellor and myself, of the Ministers of Health, Supply, Food, the Economic Secretary, Paymaster-General and President of the Board of Trade.[49] I could not help feeling that Stafford was surveying his future Cabinet. It would be surprising if he did not himself expect to be Prime Minister one day. But these things depend more on accident of age and health than anything else.

We dined with the Prime Minister to meet Princess Elizabeth and the Duke of Edinburgh last week. It was a small, intimate party, the others being the two Attlee girls, the McNeils, Harold Wilson and Christopher Mayhew. Nevertheless there was a good deal of etiquette. We all had to arrive well before the Royal pair and be lined up in the Drawing-room to greet them; the P.M. and Mrs Attlee bringing them upstairs. While waiting we all became very frivolous. We had been talking about capital punishment. Harold reminded us that it was still a capital offence to rape a Royal Princess! Then they came in and we were introduced. Dora, who does not really much approve of royalty, could hardly bring herself to curtsy and made a tiny little bob compared with the others. However, she sat next to the Duke at dinner and very much enjoyed his company. Afterwards, as the ladies left the room, Mrs Attlee suddenly swung round and curtsied low to the Duke and Dora, taken by surprise, did the same thing, contrary to her principles. Afterwards, each of the males was brought up to the Princess and shoved down beside her on a sofa for a quarter of an hour's conversation. She had a very pretty voice and quite an easy manner but is not, I think, very interested in politics or affairs generally. We talked a little about fuel economy and she said that Queen Mary's* house was the coldest she knew; she hardly ever had a fire anywhere.[50] I asked if this was because she was spartan or because of the house, but she said, 'No' – it was because of her national duty.

They stayed quite late and the Attlees were obviously delighted. The P.M. is always in much better form after a few drinks, and I think thoroughly enjoyed himself. Naturally, we were very flattered to be there – presumably as some of the younger Ministers. I am told that great jealousy has been created among the wives of some of my colleagues.

Two major problems are worrying us in the Ministry. We are producing now too much bad coal and too little good coal. This is inevitable as output rises because the shortage of good coal is much greater. The bad

49 Respectively, Cripps, Gaitskell, Bevan, Strauss, Strachey, Jay, Marquand
   and Wilson.
50 Queen Mary was the widow of George V.

coal is open-cast and 'unwashed smalls'. I had hoped that we should be able to sell this in Europe but there are great difficulties because the American coal coming here is screened this side and the residue is much the same as our 'unwashed smalls'. Yet we cannot stop the Americans giving this coal away under E.R.P. because we cannot meet the needs of Europe for the screened varieties.[51] We are taking various steps about this but it is a very difficult one and may lead us into cutting the open-cast programme, now proceeding at record levels, because without a very sharp drop in prices the product just won't be saleable.

The other problem is oil. Already there is a grave world shortage, coupled with a steady expansion of demand. Output can only go up slowly because of the lack of refinery capacity. If American consumption goes on rising, since they already absorb two-thirds of the world's output and have the dollars, I fear they will certainly suck away any extra there might have been for the rest of the world. And if this happens where is the oil to come from to run the new engines, machines, tractors, furnaces, etc., which are being turned out for the use of the rest of the world – a lot of them by our own engineering industry? An American slump would help but there is no prospect of this.

Today after a great battle in the Production Committee I did however manage to get a promise of some more steel for our refineries, but even so the problem is a formidable one.[52] It is thrown up in its most acute form in the coal-oil conversion scheme, started two years ago when there was a coal famine and a surplus of oil; this led to an acute rise in demand for oil which cannot be met. But if we cannot meet it can we avoid compensating the firms which have made the useless conversions, and if we have to do this I don't much relish the Parliamentary row. Though heaven knows it was not my decision or responsibility, and in any case the decision at the time was reasonable enough. Just at the moment we are stalling but we shall have to make a decision on this very soon.

Friday, 7 May 1948

Gas Bill

The situation gets worse and worse. The opposition are delaying everything as much as they can. Next week we have somehow or other got to finish the Bill and if necessary have planned two all-night sittings, in

51 E.R.P.: European Recovery Program [Marshall Aid]. On HG's worry about
    U.S. coal, above, pp. 55, 58.
52 See *HG*, p. 185.

addition to meetings on Monday afternoon and evening. In fact, it is a formidable prospect as I have the Black Market Bill in the House on Monday, though the Attorney General will do most of that;[53] a Supply day on oil and petrol rationing on Tuesday and then Wednesday and Thursday wholly occupied with the Gas Bill. I cannot say whether we shall get it through even then. Jack Diamond is a terrible disappointment as a Chairman and much too weak with the Opposition. The most irritating thing about the Committee is having to sit and listen to a lot of speeches which are often provocative and insulting, but to which one dare not reply because it would only prolong the proceedings still further. Bracken is entertaining enough at times but the chief weakness is that he gives absolutely no leadership. I believe he himself would be prepared to do a deal with me but he says that they agreed they would not and he seems terrified of his own supporters, which is all bound up with his weak position in the Tory Party.

Shinwell Again

That man has entered my life once more to my considerable regret. He has started making speeches about coal and giving advice in public to the Coal Board and incidentally to me. The speeches were calculated to make trouble with the Coal Board. It appears that Hyndley told the N.U.M. leaders of the possibility of the enquiry and I think Horner told Shinwell. Anyway I sent a violent minute to the P.M. asking him to stop this business and this was also backed by the Lord President [Morrison]. The P.M. then saw him at the end of last week and later told me that Shinwell had expressed regret and promised to behave in future. Notwithstanding this however he plunged in far worse over the weekend and made an extraordinary speech more or less admitting the failure of nationalisation. This has caused great indignation in the Party. On Tuesday evening James Callaghan* told me that he had seen the Prime Minister, proposed writing a violent letter to Shinwell and had advised his Local Party on no account to vote for S. for the Executive and was intending to speak about it at the Party meeting next day. I was very touched with this as James' attitude was no doubt partly due to loyalty to me. I did not see the P.M. again, though I sent him a message saying how worried I was about these further speeches. I also saw the L.P.[Lord President] and gave him my views.[54]

53 This was a Bill to break the black market in petrol. See *HG*, p. 152.
54 Shinwell's speech was to a Cooperative meeting in Edinburgh on 2 May. Suspicious as ever, he thought one of his many ministerial enemies had inspired Callaghan; it is quite clear that HG had not.

I was not at the Party meeting being of course in Committee on the Gas Bill, but I hear from K. Younger that S. made a shocking speech about the Nenni business, trying to give the impression that very obviously he had not really agreed with the Executive's decision. This was not at all liked by the Party who are overwhelmingly against the rebels. However, the sensation was James' attack on Shinwell which I gather was pretty fierce – because of his nationalisation speech. S. was not allowed to reply by Frank Bowles the Chairman.[55]

James, however, has just rung me up to say that S. is insisting on raising the matter at the next week's meeting and proposes to justify himself. James thinks this may involve an attack on him as well as on myself, and sought my advice. I told him to see the L.P. and try and get the whole thing stopped. It is an impossible position for Ministers to be slanging each other in front of the Party. Though I ought to be in the Gas Bill Committee, if Shinwell insists on this I shall probably have to go to the meeting and reply if need be. It is all most distasteful and about the last straw coming full on top of everything else. I shall be very glad when we get to Whitsun.

Dinner at the Bank of England on Monday night with the Chancellor and Lord President, Minister of Transport [Barnes] and Chairmen of Nationalised Boards. The Chairmen reacted as I expected to the L.P.'s attempt to tell them what they should do; Citrine particularly violently. It was rather a waste of time but a good thing for the L.P. to see these people himself and appreciate the extraordinary delicacy of relationships between Ministers and these Boards.[56]

Hyndley has now got the Board to accept the Policy Committee idea and has coaxed most of them round to the stock-taking. Burrows is to be Chairman and the idea is to invite a man called [Sir Charles] Renold – Chairman of Coventry Chain – and Sir Mark Hodgson, late T.U.[C]., A.E.U., to participate.[57] The great difficulty is the row between Ebby [Edwards] and Charles Reid. Ebby says no outsiders at any cost. Charles

55 Bowles (vice-chairman of the P.L.P. in 1948) was M.P. for Nuneaton, 1942–64. The 'Nenni business' was a telegram of good wishes sent by 37 M.P.s on the eve of the Italian general election to Pietro Nenni's Socialist party (allied to the Communists) when the Labour Party had just transferred its support to Giuseppe Saragat's Social Democrats. Many of the 37 repudiated their signatures; the others were required to reaffirm their loyalty to Labour policy; and the organiser, John Platts-Mills, M.P. for Finsbury, 1945–50, was expelled as a fellow-traveller.

56 See *HG*, pp. 172–8.

57 Hodgson, the Boilermakers' general secretary and a member of the General Council, 1936–48, had been President of the Confederation of Shipbuilding and Engineering Unions 1943–5.

Reid insists on them. Hyndley however expects both of them to agree now. The position is aggravated by Shinwell's speeches, Reid's leakages to the press and now letters from Tory ex-Coal owner Lancaster to *The Times*, approving belated appointment of Burrows, which all goes to prove how essential it is to get these Boards out of politics.[58] But this is not easy in the case of coal.

Tuesday, 1 June 1948

Gas Bill

Everything went very much as I expected. We had two consecutive all-night sittings on Tuesday and Wednesday and finished the Bill at midday on Thursday. This created something of a sensation, it being the first time that a Standing Committee has ever sat all night, much less two nights in succession. I do not think we should have ever got through the Bill without this. Indeed, it was probably our determination to continue almost without stopping which drove the Tories eventually into submission.

The whole thing created a minor sensation in the Party with the satisfactory result that our Members on the Committee who had been getting very disgruntled ended up much mollified by the limelight, being regarded as heroes and receiving a letter from the Prime Minister, and above all defeating the Opposition.

Highlights of the proceedings were
  (a) The extraordinary capacity of Frank Soskice*, Solicitor-General. He took almost all the amendments on the first night and for another twelve hours the second night, i.e. from 12 a.m. to 12 p.m. He remained patient, lucid and polite to the end and looked as fresh as a baby. He is very popular both with our people and the Tories; much more so than the A.G.[Attorney General, Sir Hartley Shawcross*] who is arrogant though able.
  (b) The fact that we just managed to keep enough for the 'closure' throughout the whole proceedings. This was not easy because several members were away and we had very little margin. Also some of the older ones got very tired indeed; also the two women.

58 Lieut-Colonel Claude Lancaster, a leading critic of the Coal Board, was Conservative M.P. for Fylde or S. Fylde 1938–70, and later prominent on the Select Committee on Nationalised Industries.

Perhaps the crucial moment was on the Wednesday morning at about 6 a.m. when we had one of our rare breaks for refreshments and foregathered in a neighbouring room. It was then decided much to my delight (I had never anticipated they would be prepared for it) not merely to go on the following night but also to go straight through to one o'clock that day with only half an hour for breakfast. Jimmy Murray, ex-miner, aged 60, stupid and tiresome at times but very loyal, was the one who proposed it. Oddly enough the Yorkshire miner in the Committee – George Sylvester – behaved badly and would not sit through either night completely.

(c) Tempers got very frayed by the Thursday morning and I had some difficulty with Frank Collindridge, our Whip, who is rather nervy and uncontrolled. Fortunately we were helped by Julian Snow who was there throughout the night organising much better than Frank.

(d) There was a good deal of humour and wit. First prize goes to Jack Diamond for the following: During one of our innumerable Divisions Julian Snow, 6'6'', was seen escorting Francis Noel-Baker, looking very pale (he was not well) into the room to vote. He brought him in just like a Military Policeman, deposited him in a chair, waited for him to vote and then took him back again. Bracken got up when he saw this and said, entertainingly, that it was a monstrous thing to see Members of the Committee man-handled in this way by large strangers, and ended, 'Mr Diamond, is this a free country?' Jack replied like a flash, 'Yes, this is a free country. Lock the doors.' This wit is only intelligible to M.P.s. 'Lock the doors' is what the Speaker has to say when a Division is about to take place. But Jack's remark brought the house down. Next best was Bracken's music-hall turn of Gas Inspectors; a speech entirely irrelevant and very unwise. I am told that large numbers of protests have been received from Trade Union Branches throughout the country and these are likely to be made public at a later stage.

(e) At the end Bracken and I both made farewell speeches in a general atmosphere of surprising good humour. They are on record and need not be quoted here, except that Bracken's admission about obstruction by the Opposition should be valuable for future evidence.

After having lunch on the Thursday I had to take a Question; immediately after that went home to bed and slept for sixteen hours.

Sir Charles Reid Again

In the middle of all the Gas Bill upset Sir Charles Reid finally resigned. I came back on the Wednesday morning to have lunch in the office and found his letter waiting for me. It was so plainly insulting to the rest of the Coal Board that I clearly had to accept it. Donald Fergusson fortunately handled the next stages for me and arranged for the resignation not to be made public until the Friday and then simultaneously with the announcement of the new Committee. Exactly what led Reid to change his mind at the last moment I do not know, but there is reason to believe that he was advised by an outside person all the time – possibly Lord Leathers.[59] It looked to me as though he wanted to resign all along and realised at the last moment he had been outmanoeuvred, and realised it was his last chance to get out. Although in many ways I regret not having accepted his resignation months ago, on the whole I think we were right to delay it until the other changes had been made. Naturally persons are puzzled as to why Reid resigned at this time. However this did not prevent a considerable uproar in the press and the House. I have stone-walled completely and on the whole successfully up to now, the general line being to play down the resignation as much as possible. I gather that the Coal Board are very glad that Reid has gone, but furious about his behaviour. Reid, on the other hand, is said to be sad but not angry.

Looking back, I do not think he was really at all suitable as a member of the Board, and I doubt very much if he contributed anything useful while he was there. He combined extraordinary missionary fervour (I am told his brother is a Presbyterian Minister) with a lack of balance in judgment and a rather stupid mentality. At the same time, as I think I made clear before, there is a good deal in his criticisms with which I am inclined to agree.

Coal Output

Reid would not matter at all if only output were better, but it has been very disappointing since Easter and I am now alarmed. Today we had a meeting with the N.U.M. and the N.C.B. to see what could be done, but very little came of it. The answer is, nobody knows, or nobody knows of anything which is fairly easy to do and can be done.

59 Minister of War Transport 1941–5; for Coordination of Transport Fuel & Power, 1951–3. On Reid see above, pp. 50 n. 28, 60.

Scarborough Conference

After resting over the Whitsun weekend we went for a few days to Scarborough. The Conference was not very exciting. Some trouble on nationalised industries successfully handled by Jim Griffiths* [Minister of National Insurance], who made an excellent speech. Shinwell in the Chair; admittedly very good, and has rehabilitated himself considerably. Paid our first visit to a Butlin Camp where the N.U.M. were entertaining us on our last night. Very efficient, organised, pleasure holiday making. Everybody agreed they would not go there!

Hugh Dalton Back in the Government

Hugh Dalton back in the Government today very much as Hector [McNeil] forecast. Frank P[Pakenham]* becomes Minister of Civil Aviation which I like because we can discuss common problems. Do not know what HD is to do. Something connected with the Colonies and Empire most likely because the Secretaries of State for Commonwealth and Colonies [Noel-Baker and Creech Jones] will not resist. The Chancellor and the Foreign Secretary would. [60]

Friday, 18 June 1948

Gas Bill

At last we have finished with it in the Commons, though of course it is only too likely that the Lords will make amendments which we shall not accept. No doubt, therefore, in a month's time we shall have yet one more Debate.

The Third Reading ended in uproar, as I had determined to insult Bracken to make up for the offensiveness he had displayed upstairs, also to satisfy the outraged feelings of our own people. He, himself, took it quite well, but his side (the House was packed) got annoyed and decided to shout me down in the last part of my speech. Probably I made a tactical error in not leaving the insults to the end. However, it did not matter very much. The whole thing was not as I wanted it and some people would, I

60 Dalton returned as Chancellor of the Duchy of Lancaster, and led the British delegation to the new Council of Europe.

think, have preferred a more solid reply but I made some good jokes and on balance it should have done no harm.

Socialised Industries

The way things are shaping it seems very probable that nationalisation will become even more of a political issue in the next two years. The Steel Bill is bound to provoke the fiercest opposition. It will no doubt be thrown out by the Lords, and only finally made law, under the new Parliament Bill, just before the General Election. All this is in a way unfortunate because I am sure that the best hope for the nationalised Boards is to keep them out of politics. That will scarcely be possible in the circumstances I have mentioned. We shall have, whether we like it or not and whether we mean it or not, to defend the Boards in public, while the Opposition will continue to attack. It is also of paramount importance that the Boards themselves take a lot of trouble about their public relations.

Hyndley will almost certainly not be staying. His health is not good and he has always said that he did not want to go on too long. The question of his successor is difficult and vital. I should like to get a really national figure who would disarm the Opposition by merely being Chairman. Someone like Mountbatten* or Montgomery*. He would not need to be much more than a figurehead, with a good sense of public relations and a capacity for making people work as a team under him. I had an interesting talk with Herbert Morrison on this and he saw the point. We shall be seeing the P.M. about it before long.[61]

Meanwhile the country continues to be relatively quiet politically. There is a deceptive optimistic air about, but I am afraid that unless the balance of payments looks better we are in for trouble ahead. I told a Press Conference about the coal position ten days ago and they made a sensation out of it. Apart from some lies in the *Daily Express* it was pretty fair, though of course the fact that things were not going so well was used as a weapon against the N.C.B.

The petrol consumption is keeping down and we are holding our breath and keeping our fingers crossed. So far it really does look as though the red petrol business is working.[62] But it is too early – much too early – to be at all certain.

61 Attlee and Morrison scotched those suggestions, but Gaitskell was still tempted by the idea: see *HG*, p. 169.
62 To beat the black market, commercial petrol was dyed red; if found in private cars it was presumed to have been acquired illegally.

I really am blessed with a most admirable Permanent Secretary. The more I see of DF[Fergusson] the more I like him. He is very shrewd and wise and yet not in the least obstructive. He is very hard working and yet has a great sense of humour and a nice healthy enjoyment of good food and drink. What an enormous difference it makes to my life.

One of the things that annoys me these days is that everybody seems to be pitying me. I suppose it is because of the [Gas] Bill and the fact that we in the Ministry are always under fire. Yet on the whole I am pretty well, if at times very depressed.

Leeds

Last time I was in Leeds we had a most extraordinary evening at the Holbeck Working Men's Club. It began with tea with the Chairman and other officials in the Chairman's house. About twelve of us sat round a very small table and consumed an excellent tea with tongue and cakes galore. Then about 7.15 p.m. we went to the Club and upstairs to the Concert room. It was pretty full. Everybody, as usual, with their women, sitting at tables and drinking beer plus some other things too. There were a couple of concert turns and then the Chairman, who was rather nervous, called on me to unveil the war memorial. I made a very short speech and duly pulled the string. The local parson then appeared in full canonicals and proceeded to hold a dedication service, ending traditionally with 'O God our Help in Ages Past' and the 'Last Post' blown by a cornet player. This – all in the middle of the beer drinking and general entertainment. The serious part of the evening being over, we then settled down to an excellent series of turns and lots more drinking! Nobody thought it in the least incongruous, and everybody said how splendidly it had gone off. I somehow do not think that could happen anywhere else except in the north of England.

Reporters came to my meeting in the Park on the Sunday morning for the first time.[63] I spotted them and told the crowd that this would inhibit me and asked them (the reporters) not to take down things that I told them. They agreed to this. Notwithstanding, there was some indignation about their presence and one man wanted to turn them away. This, however, was not possible since it was a public Park. I was very careful. They did not pick up anything and will probably get bored in due course.

I went to lunch with the Indian Finance Minister today. The company was about half Indian and half English, and one could not help being

63 Open-air meetings in Cross Flatts Park on Sunday mornings were an old tradition in the South Leeds Labour Party.

struck by the extraordinarily happy relationships which now exist and which, I am sure, could not have existed so long as we were in control. I sat between the Finance Minister and a man whom I took to be the Governor of their Reserve Bank.[64] He was extremely intelligent, very objective and also very pleasant. They really asked me because they want to get some more oil but in this I am afraid they will be disappointed.

An argument last night with Nye Bevan at our group dinner about nationalisation. Being, of course, a glutton for power he does not like the present policy of setting up the semi-autonomous Boards. He wants to control and answer for them; in fact to have them under him like departments. There is of course a good deal in what he says. Certainly it is no easy job to try and establish just the necessary degree of control without going too far. Also it is irritating not to be able to keep them on the right lines all the time. On the other hand there would, I think, be even greater dangers if, for instance, the Coal industries were run entirely by the Department. In any case we are now committed in the case of my industries to the principle of the semi-independent Board, and that being so one must give this particular form and relationship a fair trial. Stafford [Cripps] did not take sides but kept on saying, 'All I say is we must remember it is an experiment'.

Personality is a funny thing. Bevan, of course, has it very decidedly. He is powerful, though maddening as well. But I feel pretty sure he will be Prime Minister one day and probably at that level will be a good deal better than now. I would not, however, have him as Foreign Secretary, he is much too unscrupulous and would involve us in much too much trouble with other countries.[65]

Tuesday, 29 June 1948

Coal Debate

The Opposition rather tiresomely insisted on one last week before the Coal Board's Annual Report. I had arranged to go to Scotland for four days and was looking forward to some long trips to the Hydro-Electric Stations and sight seeing generally. This had to be cut in half. The Debate, however, went off pretty well. Hudson was not effective (I much prefer him to Bracken as at least he does attempt to argue). The only real

64 On him see below, p. 199.
65 As leader of the Labour Party in 1956, HG made Bevan his Shadow Foreign Secretary.

problem for me was how to put up a good political defence without giving the impression that everything was all right. I do not think there really is an answer to that problem unless the press are exceptionally friendly, which they are not. So it was inevitable that I should appear rather too complacent. Still, on the whole the speech was a success; much more so than my Gas Bill one. I am afraid most people think I am much better at solid arguments and statistics than at political invective and I am afraid they are quite right.

Scotland

The thirty-six hours I spent there was quite pleasant. Loch Lomond and Loch Sloy, in rather cloudy weather, nevertheless looked attractive, and civil engineering is so simple. Driving tunnels to let water go through and then making artificial waterfalls is in the literal sense child's play. Not like the complexities of advanced physics or chemistry. MacColl, full time Vice-Chairman of the S.H.B. entertained us to lunch and showed us round.[66] A funny little, elderly man with an encyclopaedic knowledge of the Highlands and well informed on Scottish history. I am told he believes in ghosts, which is not usual for electrical engineers.

In the evening another Mining Engineers' Dinner and Dance. Lots of drink and friendly people. The next day a visit to a colliery and long discussions with the Scottish Divisional Coal Board . . . Lord Balfour, nephew of A.J.[67] – very aristocratic, perfect manners, serious minded, a little slow, but on the whole I should say a very good Chairman. They somewhat reassured me. No trouble with the men about putting in new machinery and high hopes that they will be able to get through a large plan of concentration involving forty collieries. Housing the real problem here – in Fife and Midlothian, so that miners can be transferred from Lanark.

Exquisite luxury in the North British Hotel where they treated me like royalty. Vast bathroom and sitting room and almost constant attention from the waiter. I do not know whether this is a result of nationalisation.

At the aerodrome on the way back talked with the Captain of the Port. Nice young man, very enthusiastic and polite. The nationalised airways probably have an advantage owing to the discipline and esprit de corps of the R.A.F.

66 Sir Edward MacColl was Deputy Chairman of the Scottish Hydro-Electricity Board, 1943–51.
67 A.J. (later Earl) Balfour was Conservative Prime Minister 1902–5, leader till 1911, and a senior Minister 1915–22, 1925–9. His nephew was the 3rd Earl.

Flew in the pilot's seat on the way back for the first time and was astounded to find they never use the controls at all – everything is done on an automatic pilot. Every now and then they turn a knob slightly just to keep themselves at the right height and on their course, rather like a radio.

Monday, 12 July 1948

Miners' Conference

Dora and I went to the Miners' Conference at Whitley Bay, Northumberland last week. A very dreary, seaside resort, mainly used by day trippers from Newcastle. It was very useful as we spent a lot of time with the miners' leaders, mostly in some form of conviviality. The first night there was a dinner by the Executive, after which we all sat round and sang songs until midnight, some having drunk more than was good for them.

The next day the Foreign Secretary came to speak and partly because he had no notes did extremely well. The only embarrassment was that he suddenly asked for 200,000 tons a week more coal and implied this was necessary to keep up export commitments. The press were mystified and asked if this meant new targets. The next day I had to cover this up by throwing in a lot more statistics which led to the very reasonable complaint that we were confusing the miners. This was the lesser evil.

Lawther, the President, behaved very well and took a fairly firm line with the Communists. He is generally regarded as a weak and inefficient character, though very amusing as an after dinner speaker. Dora spent a lot of time talking to him.

Interesting to see how popular Hyndley and Street are. Both got an excellent reception. Obviously there is real appreciation of their personalities and of the way in which they approach the miners. Street spoke at a dinner on Thursday night given by Northumberland and Durham to the Executive, and made a most moving and impressive speech. He referred to an R.A.F. squadron in the war which had had heavy losses and nevertheless went on and on, and ended by quoting its motto – 'I spread my wings and I keep my promises'. Of course, he applied this to the N.C.B., but coming from a man who lost one, or is it two sons, killed in the R.A.F. in the war, it was particularly impressive. On the same night Hyndley and I were both presented with silver miners' lamps, and Sam Watson spoke so well in handing them over.

There is obviously a C.P. line at the moment on workers' representation. Horner in his speech flew the kite, saying that they might have to consider whether there should be direct representation of the Union on the Divisional and National Boards. He was later challenged on this by Sam Watson and forced to admit that this was, of course, not a Union decision. Meanwhile, however, Moffat and Davies (Scotland and South Wales) had been much more positive in their speeches. I doubt if they are serious on this but probably hope to get support within the Union for themselves by putting it forward.

One of the great difficulties in dealing with the nationalised Boards is to know when to interfere. This has become evident in two matters recently. The N.C.B. and the Unions have been negotiating on a supplementary injuries pension scheme for miners. Before this can be adopted the Minister of National Insurance [James Griffiths] and I have to approve the scheme. The present procedure is that we do not interfere until the negotiation is complete. This has meant that we have had to give private advice to the N.C.B., which the N.C.B. were not always disposed to accept. In any respect they don't want to act as a kind of screen for the Government. In this particular case they behaved well, but nevertheless we had to get a last minute alteration made in the pensions for widows on the instructions of the Cabinet. It would have been much easier had we been openly in touch with them earlier.

Even more difficult is the problem of redundancy. Here again negotiations are continuing, and eventually the scheme will have to be submitted for my approval. But while the negotiations go on the Government has to keep in the background, merely giving the Coal Board advice. This time the Coal Board has really kicked over the traces and offered to [the] miners more than the Government wished. Fortunately, perhaps, the miners have not completely accepted this. So I think the next step is to muscle in on the discussions quite openly; even if we can't persuade the miners and the Board, it makes it easier for us to get the rest of the Government into line.

Kent Coalfield

Another Coalfield visit on Saturday – to Kent where there are only four pits. Chairman of the Divisional Board is a Rear-Admiral called Woodhouse, who seems to have been very successful in getting the confidence of both sides. They also have Chiverton, who used to be here at the Ministry and whom I regard as one of the ablest, younger technical men. Chief difficulty there, as in Yorkshire, is weakness in the Union leadership. If that were remedied I believe the output could go up very fast; though they have not been doing badly this year.

We went to Chislet Colliery and down to the pit bottom where there is fluorescent lighting; a really impressive set of underground offices and even underground lavatories – pretty well unknown anywhere else. In the evening the N.C.B. gave a supper party; good speeches and a happy atmosphere. There is no doubt that there are advantages in having men from the Services in these jobs for the simple reason that doing something for its own sake and because it is their job comes naturally. They have been brought up to believe in service and so, as it were, take to national-isation. The Admiral blurted out in the middle of his speech – 'I have no hesitation in saying nationalisation is already a success'. Then he went on hurriedly to cover himself politically by saying that he did not know anything about other industries.

Peggy Ashcroft came to tea on Sunday, whose brother Edward is an old friend of Dora, and she is one of our leading actresses. This was all for Julia's sake, who has now made up her mind to go on the stage.[68] But Peggy was not very encouraging. Said that she first decided to act when she was twelve as a result of her performances at school. Her husband asked if Julia liked learning things by heart. This was a new one for J. But having heard that it was one of the essentials she finally said to me next morning, 'Can we start next Sunday morning learning things by heart?'

Thursday, 5 August 1948

Northumberland Miners' Gala

Had an interesting and successful two days with the Northumberland miners. Travelled up by night; pit visit in the morning; visit to Rehabilita-tion Centre in the afternoon followed by a meeting in Alf Robens' constituency. Spent the night with Sir Charles Trevelyan, Minister of Education in the 1929–31 Labour Government, who inherited the family estate some years ago.[69] Beautiful 18th century house, or strictly speaking 'and 17th century', full of Macaulay relics. The house is to go to the National Trust on C's death. Though no doubt morally and economically

68 Julia was now aged nine.
69 Sir Charles Trevelyan (1870–1958) was a Liberal M.P. 1899–1918, resigned office in 1914 in opposition to the war, and became a Labour M.P. 1922–31, President of the Board of Education 1924 and 1929–31, and then an ally of Cripps in the Socialist League and later. In 1948 he was probably the only Lord Lieutenant to have his park gates decorated with the hammer and sickle. He lived at Wallington in Northumberland.

sound this gave one the feeling of slight dreariness – that C. and Lady Trevelyan were just living out their time, as though tradition and continuity seemed to be dying. The lovely sitting-room, white panelled with blue paint inlaid and lovely Italian carving seemed exactly like it must have been 150 years ago, and indeed they said that it was pretty much the same. One did not feel, therefore, that it was a museum piece, but just a lovely room full of beautiful things – but lived in.

Next day the Gala at Morpeth. A beautiful setting with the crowd sitting on the hillside in a kind of amphitheatre with the platform down below. I made a good speech and was much congratulated. Jim Bowman, Northumberland Miners' leader, said it was the best speech he had ever heard at one of their Galas. One cannot help being ridiculously pleased with such remarks. As Dora said after EB[Bevin's] speech at Whitley Bay, 'Making a good speech is like champagne; you feel very cheerful after it'.

Other speakers were Jennie Lee, Michael Foot*, as well as, of course, Lawther and Horner. Michael Foot is rather strange. He never seems to talk except when making speeches, and was most silent and reserved all the time. Jennie Lee on the other hand talked. I still think she is a very stupid woman. She and Bevan now positively defend the policy of insulting one's opponents. 'Aggression is what will get us votes' – and such like nonsense. It would be much better if AB simply said that he was Welsh, he spoke as he felt, and sometimes he felt very strongly, instead of trying to make a philosophy out of the use of invective. Perhaps this is really a clash between romanticism and classicism. Jennie Lee said she was worried about the fire going out of the miners because they were getting such a lot. I am afraid I have little sympathy with such attitudes. Final episode was a conversation with Sid Ford on Newcastle platform, waiting to catch the sleeper. Horner as usual completely tight, and brought with the greatest possible difficulty into the train. S.F. is clearly tired of looking after a drunken General Secretary and would like a better job.[70]

We went to our first dinner party at Buckingham Palace the other night, in honour of the Shah of Iran . . . [Dora] arrived nervous and depressed. However much cheered when told she was sitting between Anthony Eden and Montgomery. She liked Eden and obviously liked talking to him. Thought Montgomery a terrible bore with no sense of humour. Monty spoke to me after dinner about the Coal Board. Said he had been to South Wales and talked to Godwin-Austen, Chairman of the

70 (Sir) Sidney Ford was President of the N.U.M. 1960–71. He had been its Administrative Officer and was on its staff from 1925. T.U.C. General Council 1963–71.

Divisional Board who has just resigned (and an ex-General of Monty's). Alleged GA was resigning because he was fed up with National Coal Board and not just because he was bored with the job and wanted a rest. He, Montgomery, said he had urged the General to denounce the Coal Board publicly, but the General had said that was not the thing to do. I was really shocked by this deliberate acknowledgment of disloyalty. How right the P.M. and Lord President were in warning me against my having him on the Board. Montgomery also talked at great length and in a most platitudinous way about leadership. It really is extraordinary that such an unattractive person should have achieved such things. But I fancy these traits – extreme egotism, lack of humour and being a bore – are not uncommon amongst successful leaders.

We ate off the famous gold plate. It was queer having no toasts, not even 'The King' so smoking started at once. Also queer that before we had time to get on with the port or liqueurs we all had to get up and go into another room. Later I was led round the various female royalties and did my five minutes with each. It seems to be a most barbarous custom to condemn the wretched Princesses to nothing but tête-à-tête conversations, so that there is an endless flow of small talk. I do not know why there should not be more than one other person present but it seems to be the rule.

Dora, meanwhile, enjoyed herself a lot, also talking with female royalties. The Queen told her that she thought I was a good Minister because I do not make many speeches; a point on which Dora was entirely in agreement. At the end I spoke to old Queen Mary, who looked pretty good for 81 or whatever it is [it was], in a glittering sort of dress. I said it was the first function of its kind I had been to. She said, with a curious foreign accent, 'Yes, that's the trouble, they won't do enough of this kind of thing now'. Seeming to imply that Their Majesties were much too mean.

A terrible row with the Electricity people, and my first public squabble with Citrine. Some time ago I set up a Committee under Sir A. Clow[71] to consider how far a combination of new technical devices and tariff policy could restrain non-industrial consumption at the peak period. The report is now public, but the only immediate proposal is for a differential seasonal tariff, i.e. higher in winter and lower in summer. This has always seemed to me common sense and I had no difficulty in getting it through the Cabinet. Also easily persuaded Citrine some time ago. But then suddenly, after it had been through the Cabinet, was informed that all his

71 See *HG*, pp. 174–6. Clow, a former Indian Governor, had become chairman of the Scottish Gas Board. His committee was dominated by the economist Professor (Sir) Ronald Edwards, whom HG had known well at L.S.E.

experts were violently opposed to it. Accordingly, we had a meeting with him and them, during which I thought I put it across to them successfully. The next day Citrine seemed to be quite satisfied and told me he thought I would have no difficulty with Area Board Chairmen whom I was to meet afterwards. (Incidentally, one of Citrine's most tiresome weaknesses is that he forgets, or appears to forget, things he has said to you on previous occasions. It is best, therefore, to have things in writing with him, when he is more careful. This is a nuisance.)

The meeting with the Area Board Chairmen was an uproar. After I had spoken they got up and one after another opposed. I did not mind the opposition but the unbelievably stupid and muddled arguments they put forward! I was really horrified that so many men, earning so much money, should be so silly. The trouble, of course, is that they are all madly keen to sell electricity and just cannot get used to the idea that at the moment they should stop people from buying it. When I left there was deadlock but later that day Citrine got them round to accepting the principle of the thing only with a differential which I regarded as far too small.

When, a few days later, we discussed this at a meeting in the Ministry with a few of his advisers, and at the end of a very long three hours discussion on all sorts of other things, there was a real row. Citrine virtually, pretty well, losing his temper and accusing the Ministry of trying to dominate the Board and put things across them and goodness knows what. It was all very painful and unpleasant. The kind of thing which would never happen with Hyndley, who is far too dignified to make trouble in front of a lot of officials. I remained calm and affable but regretted afterwards that I did not change the subject at once. Things have been straightened out somewhat now but we shall have pretty well to accept Citrine's compromise.

In the course of a long, friendly talk with him yesterday he explained that he, himself, was still very much suspected by the Area Board Chairmen and regarded as a politician, and he could not get them to do what he wanted as he used to do with the T.U.C. This would only come in time when they had confidence in him. They would never have this if he did not speak up for them, and he used this reason for his outburst at the Ministry.

He also talked about Bevin. Said he had seen him at the Olympic Games and thought he seemed very, very tired and ill, as though suffering from some kind of stroke. I said I had often seen him very tired and then, a few days later, perfectly all right. Citrine agreed that he had never known anyone with such extraordinary powers of recuperation.

Thursday, 12 August 1948

The Electricity Board

Latest development here is most unsatisfactory. C[Citrine] having promised me to reconsider the size of the differential appears to have done nothing about it, and I have just heard this morning by chance that the B.E.A. [British Electricity Authority] are proposing to announce their decision tomorrow. This they will do without having consulted me or having been in contact with me since the row. Partly, no doubt, this kind of behaviour is due to C's personality. But it also illustrates the extraordinary difficulties of the relationship between the Minister and these Boards.

Yesterday I discussed with DF[Fergusson] the general problem and even he I think is having to come round to the view that the Minister really must have a closer contact and more powers. It is really very unsatisfactory having to deal with the Boards as though they were independent authorities with no special obligations to the Government. Yet if they choose that is the line they can take, and without a major and public row there is very little the Minister can do about it. A possible solution might be to have a Board but make the Minister Chairman of it so that it was quite separate from the ordinary Civil Service department but nevertheless quite publicly and openly under his control. He would then, of course, have to take full responsibility for everything that happened. The closest analogy would be the Board of Admiralty or the Board of Inland Revenue or the Army Council.

Altogether it has been a miserable week with nothing but trouble and no solutions in sight. Coal output is bad. There is this trouble about the electricity tariffs and in addition the critical report from the Estimates Committee about Civil Service petrol. The fact that the report has got it all wrong and that we have really a pretty effective answer is no consolation. The press headlines have done the damage now. It seems to me that my greatest problem as Minister is really to get the truth put out in the press. I never realised how difficult it would be. One might expect the Opposition press to misrepresent, but there ought to be a better method of ensuring that the papers which are fair to the Government put its case across.

A Nostalgic Interlude

Last weekend I went down to Milland to open the new Village Hall.[72]
They were all very polite and kind, though reput[ed]ly extremely Conservative. I visited 'Sweetmans' which I sold three years ago for £2,500
and which was resold a year ago for £6,000, but the present owner is a nice
old lady who loves it. She let us go round the garden and house alone and I
was moved by the experience, for this house and garden has 'atmosphere'
more I think than any other place I have known. You feel your sur-
roundings in a kind of romantic way. I wondered why this was so, and
thought that part of course was from the happiness I have had there, from
the fact that I made the garden and could now see again my trees growing
up. It was because the house stood so much on its own, so I resolved that
we would not again buy a large house which we had to share with others.[73]

Monday, 20 September 1948

Three weeks holiday during which I managed to forget my work worries
for a good part of the time, bathing, eating, sleeping and walking. It is
curious, however, that when you are interrupted on holiday by the office,
you worry quite disproportionately. I was pestered about a particular
Electricity appointment and it really spoilt two or three days for me. Up
in London I would not have thought about it for more than ten minutes.

The Chairman of the Dorset County Council very kindly invited us
over to tea – a lovely eighteenth century house with park, gardens, etc.
Nice friendly people, not very Tory; probably rather Liberal in politics.
The name, 'Pass'; five daughters, all but one married, the other doing
social welfare work in London (somehow or other significant of the
change). They said, rather sadly, that when they died nobody would be
able to keep up the house, but at the same time one felt that they accepted
it as inevitable.

Happiness at the very end of the holiday was shattered by the terrible
news of Evan's death. We had just come back from a long walk to
Abbotsbury – a walk with Ronnie Edwards and his wife, an old colleague
of Evan's, and had just finished dinner when the telephone rang for me. It
was Miss Bolton [a private secretary] who gave me the news. She said that
she thought I would not have wished to hear it on the nine o'clock radio.

72 HG owned a house from 1938 to 1945 in this village on the Hampshire-Sussex
    border. His mother still lived there.
73 As he had before the war, and again in 1944–6.

Later, with the help of the local Police, we got through to Bude and learned from the Police there that Marjorie [Durbin] and the three children were coming up with Nadine Marshall on Sunday. So it was not necessary for me to go down. I met them at Waterloo and was amazed to find Marjorie and, indeed, the children very calm and collected and apparently normal. It was certainly a relief in a way because I had dreaded the meeting.

I do not want to write here and now about Evan. I wrote a small piece for *The Times* which, with the exception of one bit of a sentence, they published. Later, I think it would be nice for his friends to write a good deal more – a sort of memorial volume. But here, I record simply that physically the feeling I most had was one of cold, as though I had had something stripped from me and was exposed much more than before to the elements. It was almost as though one was, although it is over dramatic to speak of it thus, standing in a line and somebody standing beside one was shot and fell. One felt a gap.

I call Evan my best friend, and have done for a long time. Perhaps the words do not have a great deal of meaning because, of course, there are others who are very close. But Frank [Pakenham] said this about him, 'There is nobody I know of whom more people said "he was one of my closest friends"'.

Grief affects people very differently. For me it is sort of chemical in its action. I find it impossible to control my tears. For Marjorie, this is obviously not so. She seems to have been dry eyed throughout; though Dora says this was not so on one occasion. Most painful of all was the Memorial Service; fortunately not entirely appropriate because of its impersonality. I could not have borne anything more personal. Even Tawney's address,[74] admirable in its content, was perhaps fortunately unemotional, and I found it most painful trying to control myself for half an hour and failing, and worrying about the effect on other people; though Dora tells me that others were much the same, including HD[Dalton] and James Callaghan who was sitting in our pew.

Perhaps I should record the story of the accident since some day somebody might want to write a biography. This is what Marjorie told me. It was a bad, blustery day. Nevertheless, Evan wanted to bathe, and particularly to bathe at the Strangles Beach. How well I understand that, as when we were in Cornwall he always wanted to go to some particular cove and almost invariably I used to object because it was not suitable for our children. Anyway, he persuaded them and the whole party went,

---

74 R.H. Tawney (1880–1962) was one of HG's chief political and intellectual mentors. He was Professor of Economic History at London, 1931–49, and President of the Workers' Educational Association, 1928–44. Among his books were *The Acquisitive Society* (1921) and *Equality* (1929).

taking lunch with them and intending to go back to tea. Marjorie came last with Geoffrey whom she had to carry down the cliff path. As she went down Evan, Jossie and a child called Tessa Algar (father is the propaganda man in Transport House), plus Nadine and Tom Marshall were all going in.[75] Marjorie says that she saw that the left hand side of the beach was all right. There were big rollers coming in but they were breaking evenly and smoothly. But the right hand side was horrible, all potholes and whirlpools. She shouted to them to keep to the left and this they did. Nadine and Tom soon came out; they did not like the water and they are not keen bathers, and Nadine said afterwards that she felt the current though none of them were anything like out of their depth. The children then started to come in and moved diagonally (this was the fatal thing) across the beach to where their clothes were; thus passing through the nasty part where they soon got into difficulties; presumably by falling into potholes and being knocked about by even small waves. At any rate, as Marjorie came down, having undressed, she saw the two children in difficulty and Evan going to their help. At this point they were all still well within their depth.

Evan got hold of Jossie . . . and managed to get her into shallower and safer water where Marjorie picked her up and took her back. When she turned round, after depositing Jossie, she saw that the other child had been swept out of her depth and Evan was going after her. She also saw that they were being carried to the right of a line of rocks, going to the sea. So instead of going directly into the sea, she decided to run along the rocks, hoping to intercept them. I gather the whole distance was 100 to 200 yards, though between some of the rocks and the next ones she had to swim or wade. Her feet got badly cut, but as she came in sight of the last rock she saw, to her relief, the child sitting on a rock and Evan in the sea about five yards away. At this point a wave broke over the rock and quickly swept the child off it, and Marjorie decided that she must get the child in at once. This she did, handing her back to Tom Marshall who was following. When she turned round Evan had gone. Nobody had seen him again.

Later, the child said that Evan was completely exhausted; had not been able to put her on the rock; had simply let her go, and told her to try and get to the rock and scramble up, which she did. She was actually swept off once but managed to get back again. She said that Evan had his eyes closed and was very white. Later I heard that Marjorie had only seen the back of his head.

Of course, Marjorie feels she should have left the child and gone to Evan. But Douglas Jay, who knows the beach intimately and says he has

75 Marshall was head of the Social Science Department at L.S.E., and later Professor of Sociology there.

bathed there in all weathers and at all times for years, says that had she done that they all three would have been drowned.

I still cannot get it firmly into my head that he has gone. Every now and then I think about it again. I suppose one's personal loss declines as time passes, at least one will feel it less frequently. But the full loss to his friends and to the country will be there, sure enough. There is nobody else who had his peculiar combination of theoretical and practical knowledge of Labour policy and the intelligence and will-power needed. And, there is nobody else in my life whom I can consult on the most fundamental issues, knowing that I shall get the guidance that I want.

I have been visiting coalfields. First of all Yorkshire and then last weekend Northumberland and Durham. I was depressed in Yorkshire most of the time; and especially by Joe Hall, President of the Yorkshire Miners, and easily the most serious handicap to the success of nationalisation in his area. Holmes, the Divisional Chairman, tells me that JH asked him how much he was going to pay and he had to tell him that things were different now, not as they had been and that he, Holmes, could not behave as the D.A.C. or Sir W. Sullivan.[76] He also told me that Hall boasted of having £45,000 in the Bank. But what is even worse than this alleged corruption is his complete failure to lead the men properly, while at the same time keeping a kind of queer hold upon them.

I spoke to the Miners' delegates at Barnsley, 120 of them, very bluntly. They did not take it well. Yorkshire audiences very seldom do. They were on the defensive and blamed the Coal Board for everything. Ernest Jones*, the Secretary, honest as the day and not on speaking terms with Joe and a staunch supporter of the Government, made an angry speech, abusing the delegates for their utter lack of proportion in raising trivialities after my speech. He was not well received and left shortly afterwards for London. Then Joe waded in with a shocking tirade against the Coal Board – the Divisional Board – I would have walked out had it not been for the fact that I wanted to get a resolution through which Ernest had drafted. We got the resolution. Afterwards Joe was ashamed and insisted on my drinking whisky with him. But he is hopeless and everybody knows it, and what is worse, there is nobody better to take his place.

In Northumberland and Durham the picture is so different. Jim Bowman, courageous, intelligent, confident leader, backing the Board to the full, and the Government too. And Sam Watson in his different way, just as effective and just as reliable. In this coalfield conferences between

76 Major-General Sir Noel Holmes was chairman of the Divisional Coal Board. Doncaster Amalgamated Collieries had been the dominant company in the area before nationalisation.

managers and workers' representatives are held on consultation. I went to two of them, listened in most of the time, spoke freely and frankly. It was heartening to see the excellent relations between the managers and the others. One could hardly distinguish them. There was no trace of bitterness. Perhaps a good deal of anxiety about how to make other people understand the position. I was particularly delighted when one Manager got up and speaking for three others in his group said, 'We think there is nothing in this story about the Manager not having the power. We have all the power we want in our pits'.

Afterwards I had a Press Conference. What an anti-climax. A group of silly and mostly young reporters whose only concern, [it] seemed to me, was to find some story to make bad blood between the Board and the men, or discredit nationalisation. I suppose they were really after news which to them seemed to be the same thing as dirt. They were not really interested in the success of consultation at all. I suppose one really expects too much, but it was depressing.

The King and Queen came to see and shake hands with the Rescue Teams of Yorkshire miners. The ceremony took place at the Earl of Scarbrough's house, Sandbach Park. Afterwards, I talked to Lady Scarbrough, who is a Lady-in-Waiting. Interested to find that they had a flat in London but no servants at all; one daughter being trained in domestic science and doing all the housework and cooking, another daughter being a £5 p.w. clerk in the Foreign Office. Again, however, no apparent resentment. I suppose 40 years ago they would have had an immense house in Belgrave Square with dozens of servants there, as well as a country mansion. Incidentally, the garden pays for itself by sales of the produce. Otherwise they could not keep it up.[77]

Friday, 1 October 1948

The Somerset Coalfield and Cheltenham

I paid a short visit to the South-West this week; one day in Somerset and the other in Cheltenham. In Somerset I went to see the mines. It was curious to find miners speaking with a Somerset accent which is so strongly associated in my mind with farming. The men were friendly and, I thought, easy going, though the local Union Leader is a Welshman.

77 The 11th Earl of Scarbrough was Lord Lieutenant of the West Riding. A Conservative M.P. 1922–9, 1931–7; Governor of Bombay 1937–43.

Impressed by the local Area General Manager who was a Yorkshireman, but had been there for twenty years, knew everybody and was popular and sensible. The Managers a bit shy and probably not getting on quite so well. In fact the position just the reverse apparently from Northumberland and Durham where the A.G.M. seems to be out of the picture and the Managers very much in it.

I thought the Coalfield looked like having no future, but was much reassured by what I learned on the subject. Apparently they expect to increase output very substantially shortly. They are also convinced there is plenty more coal as a result of borings made and hope to get the plans approved for a new sinking. The coal, being near Bristol and Bath, has a ready market and therefore production costs can be above the average because of the low transport charges.

Cheltenham still full of faint, early childhood memories, not particularly pleasant ones. Staying with stuffy relations, and going to Church in a stiff sort of way. All the same it is an attractive town with its many stucco houses, wide roads and masses of gardens and parks. Speech to the Smoke Abatement Society a great success because they felt – quite rightly – that I really was keen on this. A lovely drive to Swindon through the lush upper Thames country, reminiscent of Oxford and 'the Rose Revived'.[78]

Friday, 8 October 1948

Yesterday we had a Conference with the N.C.B. and the N.U.M. Hyndley originally proposed that I should call this and it was sound advice. There was much publicity before it took place and this morning the news about it was headlines.

On the whole I am satisfied with what was achieved. I spoke for an immense time – over an hour – and laid before them the position and prospects. Then went on to action to be taken. A Joint Committee has now been set up to go into the various proposals and I hope something concrete does really emerge. Unquestionably, the main thing to do is to get a concentrated drive against absenteeism. The N.U.M. are, I think, prepared to back this, or rather, the anti-Communist majority are. A year ago this would hardly have been possible, but now I am told the voting in

78 At the age of one HG lived with his parents in Cheltenham for 15 months, but presumably he was mainly recalling later visits. The Rose Revived is a Thames-side pub.

their Executive is on strictly Party lines. Jim Bowman, Sam Watson and Ernest Jones, all of whom knew before pretty well what line I was going to take, are backing us and the politics of the thing from now onwards will be an alliance between myself and them behind the scenes.

It was interesting that at the Conference they proposed that the Ministry should be associated with the Joint Committee. Later the Coal Board strongly supported this, and I have now persuaded DF[Fergusson] to take the chair. He rather disapproves of this 'intervention' but there is no other way.

I particularly picked out one or two lines that I knew the Communists were running, e.g. subsidy of the industry, higher prices, etc., and ruled them out completely. All this is bound to sharpen the conflict within the Union and, of course, we run the risk of local trouble with the C.P. at any time now.

Horner, himself, was very subdued at the Conference and put forward their fairly innocuous statement. Hyndley was not inspiring; this is not really his line of country at all. But Ebby Edwards made a most passionate speech in which he really attacked the Union and the men for not co-operating properly with the Board.

For once in a way the press side of this has been well handled. A week or two ago I invited the M.G. [*Manchester Guardian*] and *The Times* correspondents to lunch in my room and told them pretty well the line I was going to take. The result has been excellent – they gave prior publicity taking just the right sort of line and both are also very helpful this morning. I am going to try some more of these lunches with self-selected journalists. I am sure it makes a great difference.

Another useful press development is the way in which we have managed to spread abroad that the petrol situation is very tricky and that the standard ration may even have to be abandoned. I told our people to get going on this a fortnight ago and they really have been very good. It is a complete contrast to when we brought in the standard ration about six months ago.

To return to coal, the position however up to now is very discouraging, and if we really cannot get a better trend in output, will look very black. Of course, there is no need to have a crisis so long as we keep sufficient for the home market but this means failing on our exports, and that from every point of view would be serious.

Thursday, 28 October 1948

Three weeks ago I met the Coal Board and the miners, and after hearing my statement and making some comments they agreed to set up a Committee on Production. They asked that the Ministry should be associated with it and DF eventually became a sort of independent Chairman. They have just produced a report which I think is a quite valuable document. In particular, the proposals on attendance bring the Union for the first time firmly behind the drive against absenteeism. It will have to be followed up by a lot of propaganda work in the coalfields but the Union seems to be prepared to face this.

Meanwhile there has been an open breach between Lawther and Horner. Horner went to Paris on behalf of the N.U.M. and made statements declaring for the French miners in their strike, which he had no right to do. Lawther openly repudiated him and a slanging match went on for some days. Horner came back, made matters worse by open Communist declarations on arrival at [London Airport] Northolt, and then went to bed. He was said to be ill. Lawther and Co. however suspected he was never ill at all. He was probably drunk in Paris and he may have been got at by the Communist Party there. Today the Union have been meeting to deal with the matter. As I write it looks as though Horner will be very firmly rebuked but not dismissed from his job.[79] Our friends are worried, not about Horner, but about the Communist activities in the Coalfields, in particular in Scotland and South Wales. Most probably, however, the Communists will not come out against the production drive but will content themselves by doing very little about it, and continue to press for higher wages and other improvements which the industry cannot afford.

On a visit to Lancashire last week I spoke with Lawther at a private meeting of the Lancashire miners – about 400 delegates being present. I was extremely blunt and frank especially on absenteeism. Lawther, too, was very outspoken, yet we were well received and the first delegate to get up said, 'It is obvious that attendance and Saturday workings are the important things. I blame the Executive for not bringing these matters up long ago'. But I do not believe that this could have been the reaction a

79 The Communist-led miners' union in France exploited undoubted grievances (below, p. 90) as part of a general Communist offensive against governments which accepted American aid. The British T.U.C. refused to support them and so, on 11 October, did Lawther; two days later in Paris, Horner without authority gave them his backing. On 28 October the N.U.M. executive repudiated his action, and on 16 December it accepted a report condemning his conduct.

year ago. Whether it is the loss the Coal Board made; the growing feeling of responsibility; the growth of anti-Communism, or merely that better pay and conditions have served to weaken the persecution complex, there does seem to be a very different feeling about now.

I also met the Divisional Coal Board and was not impressed. The problem of finding good men to occupy high managerial positions in coal is appalling. The industry just does not breed them. All you have is engineers without any conception of leadership or administration.

A typical incident in the life of a politician happened to me not long ago. Some comedians on the radio – the Western Brothers – told a story in Music Hall about the Coal Board interviewing applicants for a job. It ended with words like this – 'You want to know who got the job? Don't bother to guess. It was Gaitskell's nephew'. I happened to hear this, having supper in the kitchen with Dora. She said, 'That's pretty stiff'. And I said, 'Yes, it seems to go too far'. She said, 'Why don't you ring up the B.B.C.?' So I did. After an interval their Deputy Director General rang back, asking me to do nothing at all until Monday and expressing meanwhile his apologies. Several days then were filled with consultations between lawyers and others. The Lord Chancellor [Jowitt] and Stafford [Cripps] both wanted me to bring a libel action. The Solicitor-General [Soskice] advised that it was unquestionably slanderous, and finally we decided on a pretty stiff apology. There are few things on which opinion differs more. Of course most of our friends wanted firm action; most Tories wanted it treated as a joke. The Tory press of course took the latter line because they would like to go on throwing mud. I hope the incident will stop some of the mud because unquestionably, joke or no joke, this sort of thing sticks.[80]

I managed to persuade the Cabinet to let me give back some of the savings made beyond expectations from suppressing the Black Market. So we are beginning to stop the tiresome business of deducting the standard ration from supplementary allowances. This has got me a tolerably good press. The B.B.C., perhaps to make amends, apparently put on some dramatised version of the whole business, which several people told me was impressive.

The other night I heard something about the Board of Trade enquiry into allegations of corruption. It seems that the centre of this is a man who goes by the name of 'Stanley' and who both HD[Dalton] and I remember

80 See *HG*, p. 181. The slander was the greater because Gaitskell was so scrupulous that he had discouraged his eager stepson Raymond Frost from even applying for a post under the Board.

at a dinner given in honour of George Gibson some months ago, at which the Foreign Secretary and a great many Trade Union Leaders were present as well as ourselves. He seems to have been going round telling everybody that he can bribe various Ministers and officials and getting money by saying so.

The general opinion seems to be that Belcher [Parliamentary Secretary to the Board of Trade] who certainly seems to have known him quite well, is completely innocent of bribes and has got into this position because of what the man Stanley has been saying. However, it will all come out at the tribunal where, it seems opinion is, he will be completely discredited.

HD told me a queer story about how Stanley after the dinner that night tried to inveigle him into having his name connected with a firm . . . which I recall as being highly suspect when I was in the Board of Trade. Needless to say, HD evaded all this.[81]

An interesting lunch with Finletter* who is the man in E.C.A. looking after Great Britain and of whom I see quite a lot. Five British present – the Chancellor, John Strachey, Bevan, Strauss and myself, and five Americans – Hoffman, Harriman*, Finletter, Douglas the Ambassador, and Sigbert, Finletter's number two.[82]

The Americans, rather surprisingly, were almost pro the French miners because they said their conditions were so bad. When I asked if this was relative to other French workers or absolute, they could not answer. But they were absolutely shocked by the complete failure of the French to secure effective rationing and by the consequent gross inequality. It was interesting that Americans should have been driven to this conclusion.

The lunch ended with a wordy argument between Bevan and myself about the use of the word 'democracy', to which everybody else listened

81 George Gibson had been general secretary of the health service employees, was on the T.U.C. General Council from 1928 to 1948, and among many public posts after the war was a director of the Bank of England and chairman of the North Western Electricity Board. John Belcher, M.P. for Sowerby (Yorks.) succeeded Ellis Smith as Parl. Sec. Board of Trade in January 1946. On Stanley and the Lynskey Tribunal see HG, pp. 179–81, and Stanley Baron, The Contact Man (Secker & Warburg, 1966).

82 E.C.A. (the Economic Cooperation Administration) was the American agency administering the Marshall Plan. Paul G. Hoffman was the Administrator, with Thomas K. Finletter in charge of the mission to the U.K. Averell Harriman was the U.S. Special Representative in Europe, and Lewis Douglas, once Roosevelt's budget director, was their Ambassador in London, 1947–50.

in silence. It looked as though it had been staged between the left and right wing of the Government, but it was in fact purely accidental, and provoked by Bevan talking about the Russian peasant's idea of democracy, about which I felt quite certain he knew as little as I did! Strachey and Strauss vaguely supported him, as they would from pre-war days.[83]

I judge from this lunch and from the attitude of the Cabinet that nobody seems to expect war in the near future.

XYZ last night, [H.V.] Berry being over from Hamburg where he is Regional Commissioner. A discussion about policy for Germany on which we were fairly divided. Berry wants us to make an ally of Western Germany, allow them to rearm and build them up. This horrified Chris Mayhew. I do not go as far as Berry but I think the Foreign Office policy of continuing to blow up air-raid shelters in Western Germany while apparently worrying about Russian aggression all the time is really absurd. Incidentally, Frank P [Pakenham] feels very, very strongly about this and was recently on the verge of resigning. I not unsuccessfully persuaded him out of it.

Friday, 3 December 1948

The Stanley case is now the centre of attraction. It is having a very depressing effect on the Party, although most people take it with a grain of humour. The general view is extremely critical of Belcher and Gibson – perhaps a little unfairly so. But I think that is probably because the M.P.s with narrow majorities naturally feel pretty bitter about something which is bound to threaten their positions.

Morgan Phillips* [general secretary of the Labour Party] is very depressed and thinks it will have a very bad effect. My impression is that while the Party members in the country are very depressed and shocked (perhaps rather unduly so because of the apparently glamorous nature of the parties mentioned in the case), the general public does not take quite such a grim view. Anybody who has ever met Mr Stanley is of course nervous in case his name is mentioned. So far, mine has not been although I did meet him on one occasion, i.e. when a dinner was given in honour of George Gibson, the Foreign Secretary proposing his health and I seconding. EB has, of course, been mentioned but nobody else so far.

83 These three had been associated with Cripps' abortive Popular Front campaign in the late 1930s.

On the whole I doubt if it will be very clearly remembered at the Election, but we shall lose some votes. Much will depend on the report of the Tribunal.

This last few weeks I have been visiting the coalfields, addressing Delegate Conferences of the miners and large meetings of the management. I think they have been useful. I have insisted on their being private and so was able to speak very plainly. However, this did not prevent some of the N.U.M. areas turning down the section of the General Production Committee report on absenteeism. The Communists lined up against it, and when really faced with the prospect the men themselves did not much relish the idea of being on Committees with responsibility and power to deal with this problem. However, I am satisfied that we shall get some kind of action against absenteeism as a result. The Areas have all been asked to send in their suggestions and the N.U.M. will then make a fresh approach to the Board.

We have had a worrying time over the Burrows Committee Report. Sir R. Burrows, part-time member of the N.C.B., was asked with Sir Charles Renold, industrialist, and Sir Mark Hodgson, T.U., by the Coal Board to make a stock-taking enquiry into their organisation. The appointment of this Committee was announced when Sir Charles Reid resigned.

The Committee produced the report in August and I told Hyndley that I thought he would have to publish something. However, DF, who read the report (I have carefully avoided reading it until today) took the view very strongly that it would be disastrous to publish it in full, while critical extracts would only be taken from it and used in headlines by the Opposition press. Meanwhile, it would lead inevitably to a rejoinder by the Board and a tremendous public row, as a result of which Burrows would certainly have had to resign.

Discussions between the Committee and the Board took place, the position being further complicated by Sir Charles Renold leaking out part of the contents of the report to the *Manchester Guardian*. At one point Hyndley thought they would have to publish the whole thing. I strongly urged him not to do this, but only the recommendations (in view of DF's advice). Finally, Hyndley got the Board to agree to publishing the recommendations only, with their comments, and they issued a statement on these lines about ten days ago. They hurried this along because we expected a Coal Board Debate, and Rob Hudson told me the Conservatives were publishing their own proposals and expected something from the Coal Board about the Burrows Committee.

What they published, however, had not been approved by the Committee and I was very alarmed at one point lest the Committee should get up and say so. As it happened not only the Conservatives published their proposals, but also Sir Charles Reid published three articles in *The*

Times, all in the same week. This stroke of luck distracted attention from the Burrows recommendations and also from the question of publishing the whole report.

The Debate took place on the second reading of our little Bill, and I was able to deal with the whole thing fairly easily by launching a terrific attack on Reid and the Conservatives' (Colonel Lancaster's) proposals.[84] It was a winding-up speech and seemed to be regarded by many people on our side as one of my best. In fact I have had a lot of flattering remarks about it since.

Today, however, I saw Sir R. Burrows who I knew was threatening to resign. I like him. I think he is a very sensible man and I have a good deal of sympathy with him. We talked most frankly about the Board and personalities as well as organisation. He will not resign yet anyway. But the Committee were only dissuaded from rushing into print with great difficulty and I shall have to see them. I think this particularly awkward corner is nearly negotiated now but it has been very nerve-racking. It is an interesting example of the great difficulty one has with these nationalised Boards when things are not going well. Committees of Enquiry sound all right and look well when they are appointed, but when they report the chickens come home to roost and then the trouble starts.

I am sure it was right to have an Enquiry. Perhaps it should have been a private one (but then it would probably have leaked out anyhow) and once it becomes known it is difficult to resist publication. If, however, there is to be publication, then the thing gets mixed up in politics at once. It is a horribly difficult problem.

Burrows gave me some rather hair-raising accounts of the way the Board does its business. It is astonishing that nine apparently intelligent men should behave in the way that, according to him, they do. At the moment I feel we must make a drastic reorganisation in the spring.

Another nasty headache is the Power Station programme which is hopelessly behind schedule. I saw things going wrong early this year, and although our Ministry has been only partly responsible (the main job being done by Works and Supply) I decided I must take control of things myself. So we have got a Committee going and had a proper investigation for the first time which revealed the true state of affairs. It is obvious that the earlier estimates were hopelessly over-optimistic. It is all very depressing. It will not be easy to make this announcement, which I must do this week, without attracting a good deal of rather unfair criticism.

A man came to see me about a biography of Sir Stafford Cripps. I was astonished to learn from him that Stafford has a letter which I sent to him

84 See *HG*, p. 156. On Col. Lancaster above, p. 66 and n.

when I was still at Winchester. This preceded the first occasion on which we met, when he gave an essay prize and I won it. The circumstances of our subsequent meeting and the line he took are one of my favourite tales to would be biographers of the Chancellor.[85]

Wednesday, 15 December 1948

The Tribunal [under Mr Justice Lynskey] has nearly completed its enquiries. There will be much relief in the Party when it is over. General feeling is a mixture of two elements. (1) That the Ministers and others affected *have* behaved badly. (2) (which very much outweighs the other) that the whole thing has been very much exaggerated and boosted up by the method of the Enquiry and the tremendous amount of publicity it has received. As a result there is a growing feeling against the Attorney-General [Shawcross] who some think has been playing his own hand and getting as much kudos for himself as he possibly can, despite the Party.

There is also much criticism of the original decision to set up the Tribunal, which appears to have been taken by Jowitt, the Lord Chancellor. I spoke to Stafford [Cripps] on these lines and he clearly was partly responsible himself – the P.M. being ill at the time. Stafford, however, took the line that nothing else could have been done. I must say, however, I thought he was not very firm about it. Nye Bevan agreed with me when this was raised at our Group meeting, the general feeling there being that matters of such tremendous political importance should not be decided in this fashion. I believe there is a much wider and growing feeling amongst lawyers and the legal profession that the method of the Tribunal is abominably unfair, and I am sure this point will be argued most strongly when the Debate on this takes place.

We are now faced with the problem of what to do about Gibson. Stafford is anxious to get him off the Bank of England as quickly as possible, and naturally enough. But if he goes from the Bank it is hardly possible to keep him on the Electricity Board. The arguments in the one case apply in the other. I would prefer to wait myself until the Tribunal Report. Stafford is not sure they will deal with Gibson at all. This was all discussed at a meeting with the P.M., Morrison, Cripps and myself. Tewson* [T.U.C. general secretary] has been asked to see Gibson and ask him to resign both jobs. If this fails the P.M. is going to see him. It was

85 Cripps, who had been delayed in court, bestowed the prize (for an essay on international arbitration) on HG in a taxi to Paddington, and told the dissatisfied schoolboy that the world's ills could be remedied only by a union of the Christian churches.

left rather obscure as to whether this would be before or after the Tribunal report.

Nye Bevan suggests also that we should make a terrific counter attack to help overcome some of the damage, and suggest a Bill to compel all political parties to disclose the source of their funds, including individual subscriptions. If this is practical there is certainly something to be said for it.

We have been very successful in raising money for the Durbin family, and it now appears that we shall be able, with the money from the relatives, to provide not far short of £1,000 a year. Some of this, however, will be put aside against heavy contingencies later on. But what a tribute this is to Evan that so many people (not far short of 50) should be prepared to subscribe so generously over a period of years.

In the constituency this weekend on the whole people were not quite so depressed at the Tribunal as I feared. Fortunately, it was being taken with a certain amount of humour. But all the same I think they were glad at the Social that I said a few words about it and urged them not to be too depressed, and pointed out this was only an incident of no significance in comparison with the history of the Movement and the ideals for which we stood.

Monday, 17 January 1949

The Tribunal

Interest subsided remarkably quickly once the Enquiry was finished. The Party seem to be a good deal less worried about it. In my Constituency this weekend they were all very cheerful and optimistic. I think this was partly reaction after the Enquiry which had depressed them.

On the merits opinion is much divided. Some think Shawcross did very well; others that he was very unfair. Some are pro-Belcher and anti-Gibson, and some the other way round. Broadly speaking it depends on connections. Thus, I [am] told that in the North of England feeling is strong for Gibson; whereas in the House it is anti-Gibson because it is felt that he has been responsible for introducing Stanley to other people.

As to Gibson, the following things have happened. Tewson spoke to him and he decided, partly as a result of this, to resign from the Bank. When I heard this had happened I was very worried and spoke to Stafford [Cripps] who still insisted that he had asked Tewson to ask Gibson to resign from both. Subsequently I saw Tewson and Citrine. Tewson made it pretty plain that Stafford had really only talked about the Bank, and certainly he, Tewson, does not seem to have mentioned Electricity to Gibson. Both Tewson and Citrine were inclined to side strongly with Gibson – Tewson saying a lot of people were running away now rather from cowardice who were friends of Gibson's before. They both feel pretty certain that unless the Report is a very black one Gibson will not resign from Electricity, partly because he obviously does not think he has done any wrong and partly because of his financial position.

Since then I have read Gibson's evidence and the evidence about him and I am bound to say that one does not get the impression that he did anything in the least discreditable. Merely that he was a fool to be taken in by Stanley. Reading the evidence made me more and more furious about the unfairness of the Enquiry. People are de facto put in the Dock but not given the right to defend themselves freely by calling any witnesses they like. Also, I thought the Attorney General very unfair to Gibson once or twice, and he even attempted to trap him as though he was a Prosecuting Council. Finally, it is absolutely intolerable that three lawyers, advised by three other lawyers, should be laying down rules as to what is etiquette for Ministers and public men. Their complete ignorance of the machine and other worldly matters comes out very clearly in the questions put.

I saw the P.M. and the Chief Whip about Gibson and we agreed to leave the matter over till the Report of the Enquiry came out. I said that I should then wish to see the P.M. and discuss the findings. They said that feeling against Gibson in the Party was strong because of the damage that had been done to reputable people like Willie Hall. The P.M. agreed that feeling of this kind might change suddenly and develop into sympathy for Gibson if in the findings Gibson was dismissed. Technically I can only dismiss Gibson if in my opinion he becomes unfit to hold office. So it will be pretty tricky to decide.

Russell Vick came in to see me the other day about another matter, but made it clear that he knew that I had been to the dinner in honour of Gibson.[86] I discovered that we had been asked to sign our names on the Menu card and the A.G. [Attorney General] had got hold of one of these cards. He also said that he thought Stanley had written to me on my birthday and I had written back to thank him. I do not recall this, but it is quite possible as one gets a lot of these greetings. Rather indiscreetly I talked about the Tribunal to Russell Vick. I was rather reassured. He seemed to be clearly aware of the pitfalls and difficulties in the way of defining just what should and should not be done in different circum-

86 Russell Vick, K.C., chairman of the Bar Council in 1948, headed the committee on combating the black market in petrol and was a member of the Lynskey Tribunal inquiring into the charges of corruption against Ministers and officials.

stances. I told him how, when I got back from the Gibson dinner, I had said to my wife, 'There was a queer man called Stanley there tonight. I do not know what he was doing in that company'. Russell Vick said, 'There you are! You rumbled to it [*sic*] at once. Poor old Gibson never managed to.' It is not quite fair but there is something in it.

There has been much talk about changes in the Government. I have never taken this seriously. It is clear that the P.M. dislikes making big changes. It took him a long time to face up to the last one. Nor is there any real occasion for changes here, except the filling of Belcher's job. Charlie Key's fate is still unsettled.[87] Personally, I hope he will be allowed to stay.

There will probably be a lot of trouble about Palestine in the Party, and naturally enough Nye Bevan in a private talk with me this morning was strongly anti-Bevin and incidentally anti- the P.M. Part of this, of course, is just ambition and jealousy, but it really is impossible to defend the situation we have got ourselves into in the Middle East now, and if Bevin were not so powerful I would expect changes to be made. In practice I do not think they will be made because the P.M. would never sack him and he certainly will not go of his own accord. Policy may, however, be modified. I think they must realise in the F.O. they have gone a bit too far lately.

Wednesday, 2 February 1949

Palestine

As I expected the whole thing has now subsided, but only after what looked at one moment like a rather critical vote in the House. The Debate took place on the Adjournment and the Tories decided to vote against the Government. About 60 Labour M.P.s abstained. Fortunately the Whips had done their stuff and we had a majority of about 90. I think a good many of those who abstained on our side did not realise they were really risking the fall of the Government. On the other hand I must confess to some sympathy with their point of view, in particular over the shooting

---

87 Minister of Works since 1947, and for a further year; M.P. Bow & Bromley 1940–50, Poplar 1950–64; mentioned but not censured by the Tribunal.

down of the R.A.F. planes, where the British Government action seems to me to have been indefensible.[88]

There was a discussion about this at our Group dinner last week when Nye came out quite openly against Bevin and seemed to be anxious to start an intrigue to get rid of him. While nobody else joined in, I think most of us feel fairly critical of the foreign policy. Nye was particularly indignant because apparently there had been a considerable attack on Bevin in the Cabinet, as a result of which it was agreed that we should recognise Israel. In return for this concession [to] which Bevin unwillingly acceded, he demanded and got a resolution of confidence in his Palestine policy. He then, according to Nye, gradually tried to slip out of the recognition decision on the grounds that other countries must first be consulted. By the time of the Debate it had been agreed that we should not actually go as far as to recognise, but some formula was nevertheless agreed. Nye alleges, however, that this formula was never actually used in the Debate. There is no doubt that if an assurance could have been given on recognition, the trouble in the Party would have subsided completely.

However, we have now recognised Israel and if only the peace negotiations are successful it looks as if that particular trouble will be over. If they are not it may break out again, though this time I cannot help feeling the Government will be a good deal more cautious over, what so many people believe to be, their pro-Arab policy.

The other great event was the Tribunal Report. This is a curious document which primarily sets out very clearly and accurately the facts as they were revealed. But on the most vital issues of all which were not factual but the intentions of Ministers and others the Tribunal are equally clear.

Belcher and Gibson are guilty and everybody else acquitted. They both, say the Tribunal, did things in return for presents or the hope of gain and in fact are corrupt.

The Report came out at six o'clock on Tuesday evening and I found myself in a rather difficult position. I had seen the P.M. and Lord

88 Bevin's policy was widely criticised as pro-Arab by the Israelis, and by the U.S.A., the U.S.S.R. (then pro-Israel) and by British M.P.s of all parties. Five planes were shot down by Israeli fighters on 7 January in disputed circumstances. They had been sent on a dangerous reconnaissance over the frontier three hours before a U.N. ceasefire, a mission denounced as unnecessary, irresponsible and provocative by Churchill and other Conservatives, Liberals and back-bench Labour critics. Although Attlee treated it as a vote of confidence one Labour M.P. voted against the Government and over 50, led by Crossman and Silverman, abstained.

President [Morrison] earlier that day when they had, but I had not, seen the Report. Both said that it was clear that Gibson must go, and I agreed to see him on Wednesday, warning them that he would probably not be willing to resign. When that evening I read the Report and talked with Citrine I felt very uneasy because it did not seem to me a fair judgment on Gibson. Citrine, of course, felt the same. I then had a long talk with Alf Robens whom I like more and more and whose judgment I greatly respect, and finally came to the conclusion that I could not, as Minister, challenge the Tribunal, and one must simply accept their conclusion right or wrong.

It was clear to me that their conclusion made it impossible for Gibson to go on. Nevertheless, I had a further talk with the P.M. late that night to make quite sure that he realised what my own views were and the grounds on which I was going to take this decision. He was very nice though obviously not sharing my views on the Report (but then he knows very much less about it than I do). It was agreed that I should ask Gibson for his resignation, but if he refused go no further for the moment until the Cabinet had had a chance to consider it.

On the Wednesday morning I saw Tewson and told him what I was going to do. He was distressed but agreed that it was the only course to take. This was at 9.15 a.m. At 9.45 a.m. Gibson came in. He looked tired and depressed and said, 'This is a bad business'. I said, 'Have you seen the Report, and have you made up your mind what you are going to do?' And he replied, 'I do not see how I can go on.' I agreed with him. Then he said, 'I want you to know that the Tribunal are wrong about me – all my friends know that.' I said, 'I cannot discuss the findings of the Report. I must not let myself do so, it would be improper. But what has been said there is what makes it impossible for you to go on.' He agreed. Then I arranged for him to dictate and sign a letter of resignation at once. My reply was drafted and in agreement with him we announced the whole thing within one hour.

I was very upset at the interview and he must have seen how terribly sorry I was. I do feel he has had a raw deal. He was a fool and indiscreet but I do not believe he was dishonourable.

Now we have a Debate tomorrow and again I find myself struggling with my conscience. Tom O'Brien[89] has written to me asking me to speak, as he puts it, 'to clear my conscience and vindicate George's honour'. The latter, alas, cannot be done and as to the first my conscience is, I think, clear. All the same I may say something. The difficulty is that it is odd for a Member of the Government to speak, though it may be a 'free' day; that

89 (Sir) Tom O'Brien (1900–70), general secretary of NATKE (Theatrical and Kine Employees) from 1932, was on the T.U.C. General Council 1940–70; M.P. for Nottingham W. or N.W., 1945–59.

I cannot very well denounce the Tribunal without bringing some discredit on the Party because it will be said that one Member of the Government wanted to whitewash the sinners. Moreover, I do feel that Belcher was pretty bad, and of course I cannot be absolutely certain about George. Having said all this, I still believe that the procedure is very unfair. I told the Chief Whip I cannot vote for the Government motion, and he accepted that. He did not want me to speak, but I warned him that I might if Gibson was attacked. It was agreed we should leave it till tomorrow and see how things go.[90]

The Party in all this has been a bit disappointing. Some of the lawyers at the meeting this morning were criticising the procedure but I suppose most of them felt as the P.M. who said, 'Least said, soonest mended'. I am also afraid most of them think pretty ill of George, worse than those who know him. I have written something out which I think I may show to the P.M. if I feel I must speak, but having done so it all looks rather obvious and stale and will no doubt be said by other people.

I wish I was better at making up my mind on these difficult conscience issues. I suppose part of the trouble is that I am too inclined to see every side of the question.

As I thought – no changes in the Government. John Edwards has Belcher's job, which is a good appointment and Blenkinsop has John's which is more doubtful, but will probably do no harm. Another Whip gets Blenkinsop's job. One is impressed by the skill with which the Chief Whip gets his rather dull but safe staff into minor Ministerial posts. Obviously the P.M. is very much influenced by his opinion. Jim Simmons who goes to the Ministry of Pensions is a very nice, very sincere, elderly and loyal Party man, and I suspect that is why the Chief Whip has recommended him.[91]

Thursday, 17 March 1949

A trip to Scotland to continue my series of addresses to Delegate Conferences of the N.U.M. and speaking to the management side. The Communists are very strong in Scotland as was revealed clearly at questions after my speech to the N.U.M. All the same there seem to be fairly

90 He did not speak. (When the day's debate ended in a 'free' vote, no party whips were on.)
91 Arthur Blenkinsop was Parl. Sec. Pensions 1946–9, Health 1949–51; M.P. Newcastle E. 1945–59, S. Shields 1964–79. Jim Simmons was M.P. for Birmingham Erdington 1929–31, W. 1945–50; for Brierley Hill, Staffs. 1950–9.

good relations between the Union and the Board. Up to now the Union has collaborated with the Board in putting across the concentration scheme by which many pits in Lanarkshire are to be closed and the miners moved to Fife and the Lothians. The difficulty is, of course, that the Party line may change at any time (there are even signs of it now) and the Union would then go into opposition to the Board and it would make things decidedly difficult.

A very successful meeting with the Managers of whom about twelve hundred, including deputies, turned up on the Saturday afternoon.

Lunch with *The Observer*; Editor being David Astor*, a friend of Frank Pakenham. Much talk about the Lynskey report [on alleged scandals]. Astor for some reason violently hostile to Dalton. Naturally I defended him. Hugh Massingham, Political Correspondent, with a reputation for getting more political secrets than any other journalist, sat on the other side of me – an intelligent and attractive personality.

We have been looking round for a successor to Hyndley [as chairman of the Coal Board]. It is very difficult. We tried first Sir Geoffrey Heyworth*, Chairman of Unilever. He refused, though quite friendly. Incidentally, having met him at dinner, I was much impressed with his ability. Then we thought of Weeks but he is to become Chairman of Vickers and we knew he would not consider the Coal Board job. Then Gridley, who used to be Marketing Director but resigned a year ago on personal grounds. He, however, is now paid a vast salary by Socony Vacuum and will not leave them for some time. I have now decided to ask Hyndley to try and carry on until the Election.

A lot of trouble about the electricity charges. The Area Boards are trying to get out of the surcharge plus rebate arrangement which I asked them to introduce. They have never liked it and now are terrified of being unpopular. It is, however, clear that they are unpopular where they have had to put up the basic rates a great deal as well. I have decided we must stand firm even if we do lose a few votes.

Also some trouble with the coal merchants who have ganged up with the Coal Board on the subject of fixed margins for wholesalers. I have refused to countenance this. It would mean the N.C.B. boycotting merchants who undercut and that really cannot be stomached.[92]

92 See *HG*, pp. 175–6 on electricity charges; 173, 188 on merchants' margins.

Unfortunately, owing to flu, I missed the Shanklin Conference.[93] By all accounts it was a very harmonious affair. The press were quite extraordinary, the *Daily Mail* even sending their Crime Reporter along to try and track down any kind of information. They even went to the brewery to find out how much beer had been supplied to the hostel [*sic*], and it was as a result of their approach to the local Co-op that they discovered a technical offence about bacon had been committed. Fortunately, I am told that the actual consumption fell within the permitted maximum. How ridiculous it all is.

I sat next to Fred Godber at the Institute of Petroleum dinner.[94] He said he thought we should get the American Oil Companies to play quite well over the question of their share of trade. He thought they would be prepared to buy sterling oil so long as they were allowed to distribute here and commute the dollar profit. But this is a great and important issue which is going to loom larger and larger in the next months and perhaps years. Fundamentally there is a conflict between the American desire to help Europe become independent of dollar aid, which really involves the switching from dollar to non-dollar sources, and the desire of the American exporters, such as the Oil Companies, to continue to supply Europe. As soon as our sterling Companies have a surplus we shall be in a jam for we then either have to continue with restrictions here despite the fact that the oil is available and to spare in our own Companies' refineries, and we have at the same time to import more dollar oil. If we do not do so it will be held to be discrimination and contrary to the Loan Agreement.[95] Alternatively, we should try to get an agreement with the U.S. Government for us to supply more and more of our needs from sterling sources while allowing the U.S. Companies some hold in the market. It will all be difficult.

A trip to Oxford where I addressed a poorish meeting of the Labour Club. It was a rather academic, sober address and fairly right-wing, but seemed to be quite acceptable to them. They have an enormous membership – about 1,500 – and seem remarkably sensible. The papers took up something I said about developing inheritance taxation and when I next saw the Chancellor he greeted me with, 'Well, Hugh, how is your budget

93 Ministers and the National Executive of the Labour Party met on the last weekend of February 1949 to discuss a draft programme for the next general election.
94 Sir Frederick (Lord) Godber was chairman of Shell.
95 In making their loan to Britain in 1945 the Americans had insisted on a clause forbidding discrimination, as well as on currency convertibility within two years.

getting on?' It was, I am afraid, a brick even to mention taxation projects in the most harmless way so near to the Budget. However, really a Socialist Minister must occasionally be allowed to draw attention to the unequal distribution of property.

A weekend in Durham staying with Sam Watson who is the uncrowned king of the area. I travelled up over night and went down a pit on the Friday morning. When we got near the coal face we had to do the last two hundred yards with a roof of about 3'6''. Of all the various forms of exercise one has to take in a pit this is the worst, and I was very exhausted by the time I got to the 18'' face where the men must lie on their sides to throw the coal onto the belts. I referred to this when talking to the press and spontaneously said that I could understand a bit of absenteeism in such conditions. I thought the men were keen and the spirit good. The local Pit Committee had a scheme for demoting absentees from the coal face and were very tough and loyal about everything.

I had a full weekend. A meeting in Durham that night, then a visit to the huge open-cast machine working just the other side of Newcastle, which is designed to cut 15,000 tons of coal a week. Favourably impressed with the care to grade and mark the coal which looked excellent. Then a big L.P. [Labour Party] Conference in the afternoon where I was speaking with Morgan Phillips. Finally, a dinner which the Durham Miners' Executive gave me in the evening. To this they invited some of the Divisional Coal Board as well as Hugh Dalton and Whiteley [the Chief Whip, and a Durham M.P.]. It was a very successful and happy occasion. All the same there is a hell of a problem in West Durham where they are losing a lot of money, and one must not assume that good relations always give a lot of coal. This, alas, is far from being true.

On the Sunday afternoon I went to see the Bishop who once taught me history at Winchester. He lives at Auckland Castle, a vast, cold house. I used to like him but found him rather dull and heavy.[96] Perhaps he was bored with my coming.

Finally, two meetings in the evening at South Shields and Sunderland; well attended and quite enthusiastic.

Everybody is particularly cheerful at the moment because we have won four by-elections in a row and kept up our extraordinary record. General impression is that we shall get back again with a majority of about fifty at the General Election. But, personally, I think it is much too soon to talk. One of the awkward things is that we are having to make a lot of concessions now in the way of removing controls, etc. which it would be

96 A.P. Williams, who became Bishop of Durham, was nicknamed 'Heavy Bill' at Winchester.

better to spread out over the next year.[97] A great deal of the art of politics concerns timing. But this is not always in our hands.

Wednesday, 6 April 1949

There is a strong feeling developing within the Government that we ought not to leave the Election so late. This has been discussed at our Group Meeting on two or three occasions, and the general view is towards an autumn election on the grounds that there is a very real prospect of a trade recession which would lift the unemployment figure to 750,000 by next spring. The chief argument against this is that we should lose the Parliamentary Bill and the Steel [nationalisation] Bill and presumably have to start both again after the Election.[98] There is also the objection that it looks rather like sharp practice, but I have never thought that important because traditionally any Government has the right to choose the timing of a General Election and three out of the last four have been decided quite arbitrarily, and led to the usual criticism from the Opposition which, however, nobody takes seriously.

The Minister of Health [Bevan] is in some ways a very simple person. He has no scruples about denouncing his colleagues. The other evening he launched attacks on the Prime Minister, the Lord President [Morrison] and the Minister of Defence [A.V. Alexander], and of course on previous occasions he has frequently attacked the Foreign Secretary. When this happens everybody becomes embarrassed. Either you remain silent in which case you feel 'pi' which is not a pleasant feeling – you are the good boy, not slandering your colleagues – or you also say what you think, probably in much more moderate terms than the Minister of Health; but this of course makes you feel rather a cad. Stafford [Cripps] usually remains silent when this happens, but the other evening he went so far as to say that he thought the Party could not continue to be run in the new Parliament by the old men at present at the top. I am sure he genuinely believes this, and with some reason for they have not of course anything like his ability. We younger ones sat back rather primly and said nothing. But I personally, assuming we are returned for another period, shall be surprised if there are many changes in the Government for another year

97 Harold Wilson, President of the Board of Trade, had announced a 'bonfire of controls' on 4 November 1948 and another at the time of this entry.
98 The Parliament Act, 1949, reduced the delaying powers of the House of Lords from two years to one.

or two. Stafford also revealed the interesting and curious fact that he had never had a private meal with the Prime Minister since the Government was formed – meaning by that a meal at Number 10 where he and some of the other Party Leaders could meet and talk. Of course the Prime Minister, however, retains his authority partly because he deliberately stands above everything and, as I pointed out, this has great advantages in leaving the rest of us to get on with our jobs without too much interference. However, it would [could?] be much worse in this way. Stafford himself is excellent.

I went back to University College [London] the other day, where I taught for eleven years before the war, to debate against Bracken. I am afraid it left me very unmoved. It is extraordinary that such an important part of my life should have been spent there and left so little impression.[99] They were, of course, all very friendly and rather to my surprise we won the motion. It was the usual one about welcoming the return of a Labour Government, and it was won by quite a handsome majority.

The position in the N.U.M. is constantly a source of anxiety. A Communist General Secretary [Arthur Horner] who is not trusted by the majority of his Executive; a labour member of the N.C.B. [Ebby Edwards] who is friendly with the Communist General Secretary and who was General Secretary himself, and therefore thinks that all business must be conducted with the General Secretary. The result is

(1) Complete absence of leadership inside the Union.
(2) Suspicion growing between the non-Communist members of the Union Executive and the Coal Board because the latter, or rather their Labour Director, deals with Horner and talks to him much too freely.

I came to the conclusion recently that we should never solve this as long as Lawther remains President. We cannot get rid of Horner. Lawther is incapable of directing Horner or doing the work of Horner, but we might by promotion move Lawther on. If this could be done we could get somebody to take his place as President of the N.U.M. That somebody would be Bowman who, I think, would take over from Horner the effective running of the Union. All this is easier said than done, but the present position is worrying. The Board are refusing the Union's demands, quite rightly because they cannot afford them. On the other hand the Union complains that the Board are not taking them sufficiently into

99 On his life at U.C.L. from 1928 to 1939 see *HG*, Ch. 2-i, 3-ii and 3-iv.

confidence on other matters. So we are drifting back to a position much too much like the past.

Soon we shall be making changes in the Coal Board. Hallsworth is likely to become Chairman of the North West Electricity Board in place of George Gibson.[100] I shall not fill his place because I want to reduce the number of full time members. It is just possible that Ebby [Edwards] will apparently also want to come from the National Board and take up a post in the Divisions. But this is only rumour. There is also the problem of the second Vice-Chairman; not easy to find. And, finally, there is the problem of the Chairman [Hyndley] whom I have now asked to stay on because in fact we cannot get either [any] of the three people we thought of as most suitable to replace him. He has not yet made up his mind. If he stays we must somehow relieve him of some of his work. One of the great difficulties is that the standard of the Coal Board officials is far too low, much lower than the Civil Service. The industry has produced so few people who have any administrative ability at all. Yet if we bring people in from outside it causes resentment.

A rather attractive meeting at Cirencester for the Labour Party on a Sunday afternoon. One would suppose it was a hopeless thing, yet members came from all over the place in buses and with the sale of tickets and collection more than twenty pounds was gathered in. There was a good sprinkling of Tories, one of whom persistently interrupted and of course made the meeting more entertaining.

I saw R. Henriques who, as he reminded me, was Secretary of the Labour Club at Oxford in my time.[101] He is no longer a member of the Party for very bad reasons. He is a large farmer and landowner in the district. He came, accompanied by the Secretary of the Local Party who is one of his employees. He sent me an extremely nice letter about my speech.

Crisis on Argentina

We had to agree to offer a lot more coal in the next fiscal year. I told the E.P.C. [Economic Policy Committee of the Cabinet] I did not know where it was coming from but thought we ought to make the offer all the

100 Sir Joseph Hallsworth, former general secretary of the Distributive Workers, had succeeded Citrine on the National Coal Board in 1947, and duly replaced Gibson in 1949.
101 Colonel Robert Henriques, HG's contemporary at New College, was a soldier (wartime commando) and writer.

same. One of the troubles is that the Railways will go on consuming all the coal they want and take no notice of their allocation. They justify this on the grounds that they must put on more and more services to help their financial position. Soon there will be a real showdown on this.[102]

Dora and I went to see Indian dancing for the first time, as guests of the High Commissioner. We were greatly impressed and charmed. At the reception afterwards one could not help being extremely impressed by the enormous change in the relationship between Indians and ourselves as a result of our clearing out. Krishna Menon, an old acquaintance of mine, who for years hung around the L.S.E. scraping a living, is now a very respectable High Commissioner and he received his guests with great dignity.[103] It is all the same an odd turn of fate. One of his people came up and said he had attended my lectures in the past.

A rather nice dinner party with the Pakenhams to meet the Prime Minister and Mrs Attlee; the Jays being the other guests. Elizabeth [Pakenham]* looked marvellous, prettier than twenty years ago and before she had her eight children. Mrs Attlee . . . confessed to Dora that she did not really like Party politics and we have for a long time suspected her as being a bit of a snob, but she does her stuff as the Prime Minister's wife very well and is an extremely pleasant, rather ordinary, middle-class woman.

Monday, 11 April 1949

Last week's sensation was the Budget. It is regarded as very austere although anybody who had looked at the Estimates would have known that tax concessions were most unlikely. The public had been expecting them. This was partly because of a campaign to reduce purchase tax carried on in the press; partly because of all the good news about

102 The British meat ration depended on supplies from Argentina, which was sending reduced deliveries as a bargaining lever in talks for a new 5-year agreement, eventually signed on 27 June. Evidently HG used their pressure in his own bargaining with the (British) Railway Executive.

103 V.K. Krishna Menon (1896–1974), Secretary of the India League 1927–47, first editor of Pelican Books, St Pancras borough councillor 1934–47 and once Labour candidate for Dundee, became Indian High Commissioner in London 1947–52. He sat in the Indian Parliament 1953–67 and 1969–74, and was Minister of Defence 1957–62.

decontrols which has been coming in lately and partly because since it was the Budget and therefore especially secret nobody did any debunking in advance.

However, had the Chancellor simply made no changes whatever there would have been disappointment but no shock. It was the fact that he went further than this in particular directions which gave rise to the trouble. He has at last said that we cannot continue increasing the food subsidies; has cut them to £465 million against the £485 million that they were running at last year and actually announced the increase in the prices of meat, butter, cheese and margarine which will take place. These increases are not much – 3d. or 4d. per head per week, but they have a positively traumatic effect.

There was an interesting Party meeting the morning after the Budget, good speeches being made on both sides. But on the whole, although there was some severe criticism, the Government had very little difficulty in getting the vast majority of Members on their side.

That evening we discussed it at our Group dinner. For once in a way I found myself agreeing with Bevan. Stafford's greatest mistake was to reduce the tax on beer. It would have been better not to have done it, and better still not to have done it and to have kept on the subsidy to that extent. I also urged that he should have increased the petrol tax. With this bringing in say £15 million and no reduction on beer it should have been possible to have kept the increase in food prices to meat only. This would have been linked in people's minds with Peron [President of Argentina] and the Argentine negotiations, and I think fairly easily accepted. As Bevan said, the real mistake made by the Chancellor is that the Budget was 'out of character'. It did not follow the Party line we have been adopting all along, which certainly includes austerity but not reducing taxes on beer and increasing them on food. Of course, it is not really a tax on food, but the way the Chancellor put it has given people this impression. If he had stuck to meat only and simply said that any further increase in costs during the year would have to be reflected in higher prices, that would have been accepted.

Two interesting points emerged from the discussion.

(1) The reduction in the beer tax almost certainly was not Stafford's idea. It is thought to have been very strongly urged by Dalton.
(2) Stafford undoubtedly had been won over by Plowden and Co. into thinking that the food subsidies were really a bad thing. When we suggested the line explained above his only objection was that this would not have shown that we were really opposed to going on with the subsidies. He seemed to make it a point of principle where, as I pointed out, it was really [a] quantitative matter.

This is his first serious political blunder for some time. Probably he was tired and therefore the Budget came out as a kind of unholy compromise between Dalton on the one hand and Plowden on the other.

Bevan after Stafford had gone said he thought the whole thing regrettable, chiefly because it would weaken Stafford's position in the Party. I am not sure whether he really minds about this. It is just possible that he regards Stafford as a very much better future Prime Minister than Morrison, and does not think of himself as competing just yet.

The County Council election results have been, of course, most depressing. It is generally accepted that the Budget influenced them although there were other factors too. There seems to be no doubt that the Tory organisation was exceptionally good and ours rather poor. It is difficult to find any other explanation for the change from the by-election results. On the other hand I have felt for some time that the Party was getting a bit too complacent about the next election.[104]

Thursday, 5 May 1949

The N.U.M. came to see me about going on with the extended working hours.[105] I spoke very frankly to them about the dangers of stopping it. All the same they all seemed to raise difficulties (the whole of the Executive was there). Nevertheless, after I had left them they decided without much delay to go on with the agreement. Jim Bowman and Sam Watson must have done very well to bring them round.

Dora and I spent three or four exquisite days at Abbotsbury. The weather was perfect and of course the setting of the village in the hills and by the sea is something we always go silly about. On Easter Monday we went to Swanage where I opened the Warwickshire Miners' Convalescent Home and acquired my first gold key. They were all very friendly but the speeches after the dinner in the evening lasted for three and a half hours. I spoke for ten minutes. The man who proposed the toast of 'The Ladies' –

104 Labour lost nearly 300 seats, especially around London, and control of five counties; even the London County Council almost fell. This middle-class revolt against austerity foreshadowed the 1950 General Election better than the by-elections, which were not in marginal seats.

105 The five-day week was modified in October 1947 by an agreement between the Board and the Union for longer hours at overtime rates. Each area could choose whether to add half an hour a day (as was done in Northumberland and much of Durham) or to work Saturdays (as elsewhere).

last but one on the list – spoke for 42 minutes. Dora replied in two minutes and was deservedly popular.

Dinner at the Royal Naval College at Greenwich with all the Service big tops. I was invited because of fuel oil and aviation petrol. Oddly enough the Defence Ministers failed to turn up and only Barnes [Minister of Transport], Geoffrey de Freitas [Under-Secretary for Air] and myself represented the Government. I sat next to the Commander-in-Chief in the Mediterranean, Sir John Power, a typical tough Admiral, very popular, with shocking views about almost everything but I believe pretty good at his job.[106] The setting was very beautiful, built I think by Inigo Jones, with the Marine Band playing in Service fashion. No speeches but a lot of gossiping afterwards.

Still more social life. We went to Cambridge for the night. Munia Postan asked me to the Perne Feast at Peterhouse. Cynthia, his wife, gave a party for the women at home. I talked at some length to the Vice-Chancellor, who turned out to be Canon Raven, noted pacifist and supporter of ours.[107] He was extremely friendly. I must say Cambridge was exceedingly beautiful with all the flowering trees in bloom, now quite large and coming to maturity after ten or twenty years.

Went to Edinburgh for the Scottish Miners' Gala. We prepared in advance the press notice of my speech, nailing the colours of the Government pretty firmly to the Coal Board's mast, and supporting them in their development plans. I was, however, worried because:

(a) The Scottish leaders are Communists.
(b) They have been changing sides and withholding support from the Coal Board.
(c) The miners affected at two collieries to be closed were reported in the press to be organising a strike throughout the whole of Scotland.

However, the Miners' leaders, Moffat and Pearson were surprisingly

106 (Sir) Geoffrey de Freitas was Attlee's P.P.S. 1945–6; Under-Sec. Air 1946–50, Home Office 1950–1; High Commissioner Ghana, then Kenya 1961–4; M.P. Nottingham C. 1945–50, Lincoln 1950–61, Kettering 1964–79. Sir Arthur John Power became C.-in-C. Portsmouth 1950–2, and Admiral of the Fleet 1952.

107 M.M. Postan, Professor of Economic History at Cambridge, had been a colleague and friend of HG at University College London before the war. Canon Charles Raven, Regius Professor of Divinity 1932–50, Master of Christ's College 1939–50, was Vice-Chancellor 1947–9. Said to appear as Jago in C.P. Snow's *The Masters*.

friendly.[108] We marched at the head of the procession through Edinburgh with the Pipe Band playing behind us and crowds lining the streets. I got a real kick out of it. At the meeting I did my stuff and they behaved quite well – with no heckling. Moffat also made a much more reasonable speech than had been expected. Lord Balfour, Chairman of the Scottish Board, was I think pretty well satisfied. Later we went back and listened to the Band competitions and at the end they all marched in mass formation playing all together. It was most impressive – a good bit of modern democracy.

Monday, 30 May 1949

At the Group dinner on Thursday the Chancellor was pretty gloomy. What worries him most is the pressure for devaluation which comes to some extent from well meaning Americans and which is in itself making things difficult because people are hesitating to buy British exports in the hope that the pound will fall. He wondered whether he ought to come out with some statement explaining the reasons why we do not intend to devalue. But Douglas [Jay] said that his experience was that any talk about devaluation whatever was said always to increase the pressure on the Exchanges.

I asked whether there had been a real tightening up of controls over capital movements since 1947. The Chancellor seemed to be fairly well satisfied on that point.[109]

There was also general agreement that since the Budget the 'general line' in the country had become rather obscure. I urged the Chancellor to go back to the earlier slogans, and to come out as soon as possible with a strong speech in order to check the pressure for wage increases and the tendency for everybody to think that our worries are really over and that only the tiresome Government prevents them from enjoying a higher standard of living. I got the impression that he agreed with this and had thought of doing it at the Party Conference.

He is obviously also depressed about the great difficulties in Western Union. The Americans, it seems, are always pressing us towards impossible decisions. If it is not devaluation then it is making sterling con-

108 Abe Moffat was president of the Scottish miners, 1942–61, and Communist candidate for President of the N.U.M. 1954 and 1961. Bill Pearson, another Communist, was treasurer and then general secretary also until his death in 1956.
109 The crisis in 1947 resulted from convertibility; that of 1951 was to be worsened by capital movements within the sterling area.

vertible in Europe. Part of this in turn is due to the fact that the administration and Congress are completely at loggerheads now and there is a good deal of anxiety as to whether the necessary E.C.A. [Marshall Aid] appropriation will be made. I was interested that the Chancellor for the first time agreed that Harriman was rather a stupid man and exceedingly vain. I have always rather disliked him and thought him much over-rated. It seems that when Stafford [Cripps] was Ambassador in Moscow there was some function in which he was put on the right hand of the hostess and Harriman on the left. Harriman was so incensed about this that he did not speak to Stafford for three days. Fortunately, we have in Lew Douglas and Tom Finletter two very good characters who could not be nicer, more understanding and more intelligent.[110]

I travelled up to Yorkshire with Sir Arthur Street this weekend (he coming in place of Hyndley), to address Coal Board Conferences of the management at Doncaster and Leeds. We had some very interesting talks. It is quite clear that Street, himself, is really running the whole of the Board. He said that everybody came to him – other members of the Board and the chief officials – for advice and guidance. Hyndley, to whom he is devoted, clearly has for a long time done no more than be there, make comments and create general goodwill. The real work, however, especially the implementation of policy decisions as well as no doubt the reaching of the decision, is really left to Street. In fact, he is a sort of Chief-of-Staff who does all the work rather than a Deputy Chairman. Once again it is clear that the gravest weakness in the Coal Board is the lack of experienced administrators. None of the other members of the Board, except possibly Vickers, are the least good in that way, and apart from one or two exceptions most of the officials do not know how to draft properly and are in general incapable of running a large organisation.

On Vickers, Street was interesting. Hyndley has been criticising him for some time because he will 'think aloud' at Board and Committee meetings and thus wastes an immense amount of time. On the other hand Street says that he is the only other person on the Board with real vision, enthusiasm and intelligence. This is what I should expect. Apparently he has not been able to get as far as he wanted because all the time he comes up against Ebby [Edwards]. Vickers is essentially a progressive in all personnel matters and would dearly like to push on much faster on that side but Ebby is extremely conservative and holds on tightly to his sphere in labour relations.

It had been my idea that Vickers should become Chairman of a Divisional Board, because I had the impression that he was not working very well in the team. On the other hand I knew of his ability and other

110 Above, p. 90 and n. on E.C.A. and the Americans. HG was soon to change his mind about Harriman: below, pp. 190–1, 282, 285.

qualities, including that of leadership, and that he would do well in a Division. Later perhaps he could return to the Board, say, as Vice-Chairman. Street said that he was sure that Vickers would in fact be extremely successful as a Divisional Chairman, but after a lot of thought he finally decided that it would be too much of a loss for Vickers to leave the Board for the moment.

Street made the surprising proposal that [Sir Eric] Young should be the second Deputy Chairman. He no doubt would like this partly because there would be no danger of Young taking away from him any of the administrative work and although he himself would deny this, I have a feeling that subconsciously he fears losing control of the situation which he now has. For my part I have never thought highly of Young. He has no particular attractive characteristics and only moderate ability. Chief argument in favour of making him second Vice-Chairman is that if we did not he might make trouble, and that as the leading Mining Engineer in the country the Management side in the Coal Board would be pleased and have their morale improved. I am, however, exceedingly doubtful and it may be best not to fill the job at all at the moment. What I think I would like to do if I had a completely free hand, is to get rid of Ellis and Lowe who never should have been put on the Board and to bring in some other administrative bloke who with Vickers could assist Street. One might also bring onto the Board McGilvray, who is extremely good on the marketing side and would not, I think, waste the time of the Board in other ways, but I do not see how this can be done because of the contracts which Lowe and Ellis have.[111]

Tuesday, 21 June 1949

I went to the Annual Dinner of the Colliery Managers in Cardiff and was much incensed at their attitude. After I had made the usual sort of speech, moderately serious but not too long and on the whole complimentary to the Managers, their President got up and made a most outrageous speech which culminated in a passionate demand for higher salaries. He spoke a lot about frustration and people leaving the industry – the usual stuff. It was in very bad taste and out of place and I made this pretty plain to him when I said goodbye. Subsequently I have learned that the Production Director in South Wales resigned from the Association

111 Young, a mining engineer and former colliery managing director, served on the Board from 1946 to 1951. William McGilvray (later knighted) became director-general of marketing in 1947. On the others see above, p. 50 and n. 28.

because of this speech, that it was deeply resented by most people there, and that the President's object in doing so was to try and secure the job of President of the Colliery Managements' Association (a different Association concerned with trade union matters).

Matters were not improved next morning because on opening the paper I found, not as I had expected the report of the President's speech, but a report of all sorts of silly and indiscreet things which had been said the previous morning by Sir Eric Young, William Reid and various high officials of the Coal Board.[112] As I rather expected, it seems that the proceedings in the morning were supposed to be confidential but somebody or other let a press man in.

This incident illustrates the difficulties in the industry. There are too many people in managerial positions who are still strongly opposed to nationalisation and quite willing to make trouble with the Coal Board and the N.U.M. The Coal Board has not yet won their loyalty, and it cannot do so easily and at the same time retain the goodwill and support of the Union.

Of course Conferences often bring to the fore the worst types of self-advertisers, particularly in organisations like this. In a trade union there is the great difference that the best people on the whole tend to get office because it is in a way as good, or better, an avenue for promotion than the job they are doing. In the case of professional people this is not so and therefore Association officials are very often irresponsible, poor types.

However, it must not be overlooked that the meeting and the dinner were in Cardiff and there were a large number of Welshmen present. I ascribe to that part of the bad atmosphere in comparison with Harrogate last year.

Another Labour Party Conference, at Blackpool this time. As a Conference, successful in so far as the platform, i.e. Government, dominated the scene and the different Members all spoke with the same voice. Correspondingly dull for journalists because there were little or no debate or scenes, also rather dull for all onlookers like us.

I was also worried because although Morrison and Bevan, who are the two Members of the Executive most powerful in the Government, really ran the Conference and in doing so behaved in everything they said perfectly well, nevertheless the skeleton of the dollar crisis was kept firmly in the cupboard, except during a part of Stafford [Cripps]'s speech and then the door was opened but shut again. I fear that the Party is not

112 Reid was production director for Scotland.

really prepared for the very great economic difficulties now emerging. From this point of view it would have been much better if Stafford were on the Executive.

I was also worried because of the failure of the leaders to defend nationalisation adequately. They are much too apologetic and all tend to assuage criticism by saying, 'Yes, of course, we know things are wrong. Give us time and we will put them right.' This is thoroughly bad politics and quite unjustified. I am going to put a paper to the S.I.M. [Socialised Industries Ministerial] Committee [of the Cabinet] and try and get a change.

Tom Finletter, unfortunately, has left us. His going is a serious loss. He is a curious, shy man but highly intelligent and extraordinarily sympathetic to our point of view. He frankly allowed himself to become our advocate with Washington. Nobody knows who will replace him, but in any case this is bound to add to the difficulties blowing up between us and the U.S.A. When saying goodbye to me Finletter expressed his grave personal anxiety about developments in the next six months. There can be no doubt that the clash between American and British ideas on discrimination and convertibility is certain to become worse. For my part I see no hope of closer links between the dollar and sterling areas. On the contrary the incipient depression in the United States with falling prices and incomes makes our dollar problem worse. Since we will not deflate or devalue – in my view quite rightly – we must restrict dollar imports more and try and develop non-dollar sources of supply. This means bilateral pacts with some form of multilateralism between the non-dollar countries. But it is all anathema to the Americans. The fear is that if we follow this path they may cut Marshall Aid. If so, it will only be cutting off their noses to spite their faces, but unfortunately Congress has often done this before. They seem unable to understand that with the surplus in their balance of payments they must either import more or lend or give us dollars, or their exports must fall. They want to force us to make all the effort to push our exports into the United States, and no doubt if necessary would say that we ought to deflate ourselves to achieve this. Nevertheless, if we were to succeed they would probably be demanding higher tariffs! Between the other two alternatives they decline to choose. They complain that our exports replace theirs in non-dollar areas but will not take the only step to prevent this which is to lend or give away dollars.

The Yorkshire Miners' Gala at Wakefield was a pleasant affair. The Foreign Secretary was going with myself but could not get away from the Council of Foreign Ministers in Luxemburg. So he telephoned his speech to the meeting and this was a great success. It was an excellent speech and came over just as if he had been standing on the platform. Maurice Webb took his place in the 'body' at the meeting and also at the dinner the night before. On both occasions he spoke extraordinarily well. I do not think he is really very intelligent but he has an extraordinarily attractive manner of speech and obvious gifts of leadership. It is a real tragedy for him and probably for the Party that he has had to have his leg amputated and in such a manner as to incapacitate him, I fear, more or less permanently. If this had not happened he would be by now a full Minister.

Tuesday, 28 June 1949

It never rains but it pours! Right in the middle of the dollar crisis comes the news that the railwaymen have decided to adopt Go-slow tactics next Monday. If this threat matures I am afraid we shall have the pits stopping before long, though we are making all possible preparations to postpone this happening. But there can be no doubt that the N.U.R. by their attitude are going to do an immense amount of harm to the Government, and indeed to the whole cause of nationalisation. Maybe it is [the fault of] the Railway Executive as well, though with a heavy deficit on their first year it is not so easy to blame them.[113]

The dollar crisis has become rapidly worse and is now public knowledge. Policy is not yet decided but I feel we are at the parting of the ways. If we continue to aim at convertibility and multilateralism, I do not see how we can avoid deflation and devaluation now that the American slump is deepening. But if we do neither and go in for what is the only problematical alternative, trade discrimination in a big way against dollars and a great effort to replace dollar supplies with supplies from other areas, we risk the cutting off altogether of Marshall Aid.

The Chancellor is obviously torn. Plowden has for long favoured devaluation; other parties in the Treasury favour deflation, but they all seem to want to cling to multilateralism and convertibility as our aim. Douglas [Jay] is opposed to this and has a continual struggle inside the Treasury for Stafford's [Cripps'] soul.

We had an interesting Group dinner last week when Stafford was away and all agreed that the two most important things were:

113 There was trouble on the railways that summer over Sunday shifts and over delays about a wage claim. On 28 June the N.U.R. delegate conference called a national work to rule, suspended three days later when the Minister of Labour intervened. A Conciliation Board was agreed upon on 9 July, and reported in September accepting some minor claims but rejecting the main one owing to the Executive's financial position. (Entry misdated as Wed. 28th.)

(a) to ensure that Exchange Control was operating properly to prevent a flight of capital.

(b) to make the Canadians face up to the possibility that we cannot pay dollars for the balance of our imports.

In other words, we all agreed that we did not want either devaluation or deflation, and we would have to move in the direction of a more closely controlled trade system with discrimination against the dollar, but try to build up multilateralism in non-dollar areas.

The following day there was a very secret meeting of the E.P.C. [Economic Policy Committee of the Cabinet] (in the P.M.'s room in the House of Commons to avoid comment) at which rather surprisingly the general view was very much the same as ours had been the night before. The Chancellor, himself, was obviously fed up with Harriman and what the latter is trying to do on the European Payment Scheme.[114] The Foreign Secretary too showed a surprising disposition against the American attitude. He was at his best, full of imaginative ideas, and quite hopeful that he would persuade the Americans on political grounds that they 'must do the big thing'. There was talk of an Economic Conference, and of the United States supporting sterling, and the hope that they would reflate in their own country, etc. But, as I said to somebody afterwards, it was rather a matter of whistling to keep your chin up. We are to meet again all day on Friday and we shall see whether opinions have changed.

I must say, the technique of modern Government becomes almost intolerably difficult. On the one hand, the key Ministers are hopelessly overworked. Stafford spends his time dashing between Paris, Brussels and London, thinking out and arguing most frightfully complicated questions of international trade and payments, and somehow or other all this has got to be explained to the general public sometime. The P.M. is perhaps so successful because he is content to let others do the work. I noticed that he was at Lords on Saturday morning and Wimbledon on Saturday afternoon, and went down to Chequers for the weekend. Poor Stafford spent most of his weekend in bed writing his latest paper and in a state of complete exhaustion. But I dare say that kind of arrangement is necessary. The responsibilities of the Prime Minister are quite enough without making him work too hard as well.

There have been few occasions since the war when we feel so uncertain as to where we shall be in three months' time. It is pretty awkward with a General Election in the fairly near future – a fact that we cannot ignore when making up our minds on policy, and behind it all, of course, is the great political issue of Russia. I must try to put my thoughts on all this down in a more coherent form.

114 But see below, pp. 178–82, 190–1; and *HG*, pp. 219–25.

Friday, 29 July 1949

The N. U. M. Conference at Porthcawl

I had to cut short my visit to the Conference because of the dollar crisis and meetings connected with it in London. We therefore went down on the Tuesday night; I made my speech on the Wednesday morning and we came back on the Wednesday evening. As soon as I arrived I noticed the difference in the atmosphere from last year. There was a complete cleavage between the Communists and others on the Executive – they hardly spoke to one another and did not mix socially at all.

I made a speech which gained some notoriety for two reasons. Firstly, I laid it on very thick about the crisis and used the phrase, 'a moment of supreme crisis for the Government'. I also referred to the fact that there would probably be an election before the next Annual Conference and, as I think quite naturally, said it might therefore be the last time that I spoke at such a Conference. Secondly, just at the end of my speech, when I had been speaking with some emotion about the crisis and was being extremely frank about absenteeism, etc., I went on to refer to my pride as Minister in the experiences that I had had in the various coalfields. At this point, for the first time in my public life, tears came into my eyes and I had to stop speaking for a few seconds and have a drink of water. From the point of view of the speech it was, I suppose, extremely effective. Emotion is infectious, and as somebody said to me afterwards when I apologised, it was what really made the speech.

However, the combination of these two things produced the most sensational press reports because I was speaking a few hours before the Chancellor was to make his statement on the dollar position. The newspaper comment was to some extent embarrassing (the Tories of course said that I had spoken the truth, as the Chancellor was soft pedalling everything) and to some extent extremely offensive and cutting because of my alleged tears. Some of the comments I must confess turned my stomach and made me hate journalists even more. And I feel that way because as a speech it was a very good one. In fact, Harold Neal, Secretary of the miners' group in the House and no friend of mine, said to many people afterwards that it was the best speech I had ever made or would ever make.[115]

I also believe it may materially have affected the subsequent debates in the Conference about the Coal Board and about wage demands.

115 Neal was M.P. for Clay Cross (Derbyshire) 1944–50 and Bolsover 1950–70; Parl. Sec. Fuel & Power, 1951. With 34 sponsored M.P.s in 1945, the miners were by far the best-represented union in the House.

However, I am afraid it did me no good with the Party because it was of course described as 'defeatist'. I rather expected that the Chancellor or the P.M. might tick me off because I had got out of step. But though I fancy the Chancellor was a bit annoyed nothing was said to me by anyone, and subsequent events have so much proved me right that in the long run it was probably not a bad thing for me to have spoken as I did.

I cannot help smiling occasionally when I think of the chief episodes which the press have headlined about me – my famous baths remark; the story that I refused to allow somebody to sit down in a dining-car with me, and now that I burst into tears at the Miners' Conference.[116]

There has been the usual run of social engagements. Buckingham Palace parties and garden parties, etc. The general feeling seems to be that the shadow of the coming election was visible. The parties seemed to be more Tory and less democratic than before. I do not think this is entirely imagination – all my colleagues seem to have the same opinion.

The Foreign Secretary gave a lunch to the Prince Regent of Iraq and his wife. I noticed that he [Bevin] quite openly took what I think was amyl nitrate for his heart after the meal and this did seem to suggest that he was in a pretty bad way. In the House recently I was walking with him to a Division when he had a slight attack and had to sit down at once. He could not make the Division and later I came back and sat with him again. On the other hand sometimes people can go on for years like that.

A rather nice visit to the new part of my Constituency where I attended the Tenants' Association Fete and later on visited some Clubs.[117] I was impressed with one of them because as well as the usual billiard tables, drinking and smoking downstairs, there was modern dancing upstairs and lots of young people, very well dressed and cheerful, enjoying themselves. How extraordinarily this compares with what it must have been like even fifteen years ago. The Clubs are an interesting form of British culture which are quite important in the North of England and very seldom referred to. They always seem to be completely crowded.

I went and spoke to the National Coal Board Weekend Conference of Managers and was rather favourably impressed by the way they seem to be shaping. One noticed however, that the Chairman of the Divisional Board quite openly spoke of his difficulties with the National Board, in the presence of Sir Arthur Street. It seems that in every walk of life the

116 On the dining-car story see *HG*, p. 181.
117 The recent parliamentary redistribution had added the safely Labour Middleton ward to South Leeds.

unit below always complains of the supervision and direction that it receives from the unit above.

At the special request of Mrs Attlee we went to a 'Save the Children Fund' anniversary dinner having, of course, to subscribe heavily afterwards. I heard at the dinner that some people had offered no less than 500 guineas to be allowed to sit at the top table. How peculiar human nature is! In effect [In fact?], I do not think the guineas were accepted since all at the top table seemed to have official reasons for being there. Princess Marie Louise, who seemed to be about ninety, made a most effective speech.[118]

I had a meeting with the three Chairmen of the Boards and another row with Citrine about the control of investments; the others sat and listened. For Hyndley it was a very familiar experience because he had it so often on the Coal Board. For Sylvester it was more of a novelty.[119] It is all very tiresome. I shall have to try and settle the matter with him alone.

A lovely weekend at Durham for the Miners' Gala. We stayed with Sam Watson and there was also there the McNeils and the Bergers.[120] On the Saturday morning we made our way to the County Hotel in the middle of the city. It took a long time because of the enormous crowds already converging towards the race course. We marched with the procession part of the way and then dodged ahead. Then we stood on the balcony with the P.M., Mrs Attlee and Morrison and waved to the processions as they went by with their bands. There is no traffic allowed within the city on this day, and indeed it could not possibly get through. There is just a solid mass of people in the streets, some standing still watching the processions and the others in the processions themselves.

It was tremendously hot and at the demonstration itself almost unbearably so. I should think it must have been at least 85 in the shade and correspondingly more in the blazing sunshine. Not a very easy atmosphere to get people emotionally roused, but they gave us a grand reception. In the afternoon I sat in the window at the hotel and watched the

118 Grand-daughter of the last King of Hanover, and third cousin of the King; aged 70 in 1949.
119 Sir Edgar Sylvester, former managing director of the Gas Light & Coke Co., was chairman of the Gas Council (composed of all the area board chairmen). Citrine had been on the Coal Board before moving to Electricity.
120 Sam Berger was a first secretary at the U.S. Embassy.

processions coming back; again seemingly endless. I have since heard that they estimated that 300,000 people were there, though I cannot believe that they all came to the demonstration. There were only 200 police controlling this vast mass and so far as I know there were no incidents. I only saw two people drunk and they were harmless enough. Hugh Dalton, Chancellor of the Duchy, being a Durham M.P. was not allowed to speak but of course attended and was with us at the hotel in the morning and on the platform. In the afternoon I suddenly saw him marching with one of the two collieries which are in his constituency. Everybody was glad to see him and clapped as he went by. About an hour later I was again watching and lo and behold – he appeared once again; this time with the other colliery in his constituency. I saw him later on in the evening and told him I had seen him and that he was doing a wonderful circus turn. He replied, 'I did a marvellous piece of election work. I marched with the first lot a mile out of town, where they furled their banners, got into buses and drove away. I came back in a police car and was just in time to pick up the second colliery contingent. It will do me a great deal of good.'

Lunch at the American Embassy to meet the new E.C.A. representative, Mr Kenney, who seemed quite pleasant. The Minister of Health sat on one side and I on the other. Nye [Bevan] typically opened his conversation with the gentleman on whom we depend for dollars by describing his experiences in the great San Francisco Dock Strike of 1933, and made it quite plain, quite pleasantly but unmistakably, that he held the lowest opinion of American Justice. (Mr Kenney is a lawyer.)[121]

121 John Kenney was under-secretary of the U.S. Navy 1947–9, Minister in charge of the E.C.A. mission to the U.K. 1949–50, deputy director of the Mutual Security Agency 1950–2.

CHAPTER 3

DEVALUATION, AND ELECTORAL DEADLOCK

Editor's Note
Diary, 3 August 1949 to 21 March 1950
Documents: No. 3 Draft briefs for Cripps and Bevin in Washington
(officials' draft, September 1949; Douglas Jay's₁ draft)
No. 4 HG to Attlee and others on Economic Policy, 18.8.49
No. 5 HG to Attlee and others on Political Strategy, 18.8.49

[Four years after the end of the war, Labour Britain had made an impressive economic recovery. Exports (by volume) were at a record level, up by half in two years, so that overseas trade was almost in balance. Since 1945 they had risen from 50 per cent below pre-war to nearly 55 per cent above, and paid for 85 per cent of imports instead of a third: the best performance in Europe. Industrial production by volume in the first half of 1949 was 30 per cent above 1938; and output per man-hour had since the war increased faster than in the United States. These achievements depended on strict controls at home, to direct resources into essential activities, and abroad, to check flights of capital and to use scarce gold and dollar reserves only for food and raw materials. Wherever possible non-dollar supplies had to be found, exports channelled to dollar markets, and 'hard currency' conserved for indispensable needs. But that involved discrimination offensive to the Americans' interests and ideology, and to the commitments they had extracted in return for Lend-Lease and the 1945 loan. In 1947 American insistence led to the disastrous experiment in convertibility of sterling, which dissipated most of the loan; and in 1949 a sharp recession in the U.S. curtailed her purchases abroad, reduced the outflow of dollars, and revealed the precariousness of the pound.

The acute crisis which followed led to a sharp struggle over economic policy. Many, though not all, of the government's official and financial advisers disliked the restrictions on trade and capital movements and were, like the Americans, eager to reintegrate Britain into the international economy, for reasons often political as much as economic. But with the gold and dollar reserves dangerously low, dismantling controls would make the stability of the currency dependent on the good will of foreign investors and bankers, and thus would strengthen overwhelmingly those domestic forces which were calling for severe deflation and heavy cuts in public expenditure, especially on social services and food subsidies. Labour Ministers believed those expenditures both desirable in themselves and necessary to retain trade union good will under the full employment which they were determined to preserve.

Nor did they believe with the foreign and domestic bankers that the problem was due to inflation within Britain, curable in orthodox fashion by deflating the domestic economy until the foreign account balanced at a low level of activity. The great export drive could not have succeeded so spectacularly if British costs and prices had been severely out of line; and it was not the U.K. but the rest of the sterling area which suffered the greatest fall in dollar earnings when the U.S. recession reduced her purchases everywhere. The devaluation of the pound in September 1949, in the long run inevitable, was precipitated by the reluctance of foreigners who anticipated it to hold sterling. But in those days of political and economic uncertainty, devaluation was a traumatic as well as a dramatic step. For conservative men it still reeked of immorality; for chauvinists (or politicians who worried about them) it spelt national or party humiliation; for the cautious it was a leap in the dark – though, once decided upon, it had to be on a large enough scale to leave no expectation that another might follow. In all these debates Hugh Gaitskell was a central figure.

Gaitskell agreed with Cripps and Bevan, who pressed the Prime Minister to announce the dissolution of Parliament in his winding-up speech in the devaluation debate on 29 September 1949. But Attlee and the other senior Ministers preferred to wait until 1950, with the result that Gaitskell had feared. Working-class voters stayed loyal to Labour but the middle-class gains of 1945 were lost, and the redistribution of seats damaged the Party severely; it had a comfortable lead in votes but an overall majority of only five seats. In those days a working majority was supposed to be around forty, and a government with a nominal but tiny majority was quite unprecedented.]

Wednesday, 3 August 1949

The Dollar crisis led to four meetings of E.P.C. [the Cabinet's Economic Policy Committee] which took place between the last days of June and July 18th, when the Chancellor left for Switzerland. It cannot really be said that any very satisfactory conclusions emerged. There was, of course, no great difficulty about deciding what short-period measures we should ask the U.S.A. to adopt. But on both the immediate steps which we ourselves might take and also on the long run possible solutions to the problem, the outcome was not really sufficiently clear.[1]

For this the main explanation is undoubtedly to be found in the Chancellor's state of health. It was quite clear from his vacillations that he was not really capable of thinking the problems out for himself; and the papers submitted were a hotch potch of official views – themselves divided on some issues – tempered by what Stafford [Cripps] thought his colleagues would feel.

1 For these discussions, see also Hugh Dalton's unpublished diary at L.S.E., vol. 37, 1.7.49. Some of the official papers are summarised in *The Times*, 3, 4, and 8 January 1980.

It is true that *theoretically* short-period decisions which are supposed to save $400 million on the U.K. account and $700 million in the sterling area have been taken. But on examination these savings prove to be much less certain. In the first place nothing has yet been done about Oil. Where it was expected that we could save $85 million – we cannot without 'discrimination' save more than 30. But all efforts on my part to have this problem discussed and resolved have been blocked by the Foreign Secretary who is terrified of the reactions of the U.S. Oil Companies. I hope to return to the attack before long, but up to now we cannot count on anything here (except possibly the $30 million).

Secondly, the food cuts have not been on the scale originally contemplated and there must be a loss here – though how much it is no one seems as yet to know.

Thirdly, it is still not clear that except as a temporary measure the raw material cuts can be managed without unemployment. I have seen no analysis of this.

And finally, the cuts to be made by the rest of the sterling area are *paper* only and goodness knows how much they will amount to in practice.

In any case it is admitted that the cuts can have no immediate effect – not even the standstill on purchases – and meanwhile the drain continues.

As to the long term proposals, here there is really no clear line at all. There was one rather long, rambling discussion at E.P.C. in which I managed to enlist the support of the Foreign Secretary against a proposal to accept 'convertibility' even in the long term, by referring to this as the 'alternative' solution of the problem. This evidently reminded him of his experience back in 1930 as a member of the Macmillan Commission, for he said, 'Yes, 1844 and all that', meaning of course the Bank Charter Act.[2]

The Chancellor too in answer to some questions of mine seemed to imply that he did not expect convertibility for at least ten years. Nevertheless it is certain that many of his advisers in the Treasury take quite a different view. They use phrases like 'one-world economy and two-world economy' and imply that the choice lies between a kind of 'Schachtian autarchy' on the one hand and beneficent multilateralism on the other.[3] I do not doubt that they would like to see a policy which combined deflation at home with devaluation plus convertibility backed to some extent at least by U.S. dollars.

The Foreign Secretary on the other hand while opposed instinctively to

2 In 1929 the Labour government appointed a committee on finance and industry with a judge, Lord Macmillan, as chairman, J.M. Keynes as a prominent member and Bevin as the only trade unionist.
3 MS version, mistyped as 'Shavian'. Dr Hjalmar Schacht ran the pre-war Nazi economy, as President of the Reichsbank and then Minister for Economics.

any 'cuts' at home – he hates austerity – and opposed also instinctively to 'The Gold Standard' is also determined to rescue the world by successful negotiation in Washington. He would like (he pretty well said as much to me) to have six months more to bring about an economic solution comparable to the political solution which he feels, not inexcusably, he has found in 'The Atlantic Pact'.

Meanwhile the Chancellor – as I have said – was really not capable of thinking out very clearly what exactly he did want to achieve. Undoubtedly the danger is that these two most powerful Members of the Government on their own in Washington and advised by the Treasury, whose views are 'liberal', will agree to long term ties which will be eventually ruinous to us for the sake of some short term gain. They may indeed be driven to this because of the state of the reserves by the autumn.

Meanwhile on one short-period issue there have been important developments. When discussions on the crisis began at the end of June, devaluation was mentioned but not taken seriously as something to be contemplated fairly soon. It was known of course that there had been talk about it for weeks and weeks and indeed this talk was regarded as one of the major reasons for the crisis. Various people were blamed for it – the U.S. Secretary of State of the Treasury [sic], the U.S. Directors of the I.M.F. [International Monetary Fund] – and in this country, the editor of The Economist, Geoffrey Crowther and, in the ranks of Whitehall, Sir E. Plowden. The latter subsequently told me that he had been in favour of it since last February and had striven to convert the Treasury to his view. No doubt the very fact that the crisis was believed to be partly due to devaluation talk itself gave rise to inhibitions on the part of many against devaluation as a policy. Actually at the first of four E.P.C. meetings, the P.M. tentatively, and the L.P. [Lord President, Morrison] more definitely, spoke in favour of it. I think they had both been 'got at' by Plowden – but both also felt that probably it would have to come and that, if so, it was better to do it sooner rather than later.[4]

Harold Wilson now says he also favoured it then, but if so he certainly did not say so. Others were against – Hugh Dalton especially strongly – on the logical grounds that it would widen not narrow the gap. Others were probably opposed because of the problem it created for the cost of living index. There was a proposal at this time put up by the Treasury for cutting food subsidies as well (Plowden says he always thought this silly) and it was thought that, this having been sat upon, devaluation was just another way of reducing the standard of living of the working class. In addition one must remember that there was a good deal of taboo about talking about devaluation – for very sound reasons – and therefore the subject was not really discussed except incidentally.

4 They were opposed by Bevin, Cripps and Dalton: his diary, 1.7.49.

I, myself, was originally opposed on the ground that it seemed unlikely that the elasticity of demand of our exports in dollar areas was high enough to justify it – though I had never been much against it on the ground of internal consequences. I took the view that it was quite probable that we could *only* reach equilibrium in our dollar balance of payments by a policy of deliberate discrimination in imports accompanied by an energetic effort to develop non dollar sources of supply. As for the short period, I hoped that we could prevent any 'capital drain' continuing by more strict application of exchange control – while I also favoured, of course, the cuts in dollar imports proposed by the Chancellor. I also suggested that we should have to make the Canadians face up to the issue of conducting trade on a sterling basis in future or losing the U.K. market. (This last subject was in fact discussed at E.P.C. At first opinion was in favour of taking a strong line with the Canadians. The Foreign Secretary and the Chancellor, however, smothered this – the former[5] because his advisers regarded this as immoral, the latter[5] on obvious political grounds. It broke out again after they had gone away but without producing any effect on policy.)

By the middle of July, however, I had revised my views on devaluation. And I found that at just the same time, Douglas Jay, my closest friend in the Government and Economic Secretary to the Treasury, had changed his too. On 18th July we had lunch with Nicky Kaldor – the economist – working with E.C.E. [the Economic Commission for Europe in Geneva] but due to take up a Fellowship at Cambridge in October.[6] NK had come over to England especially to advise us that we ought to devalue at once because

(a) this would be the only way to stop and reverse the capital drain.

(b) The Americans wanted us to do it.

(c) It would probably help to close the gap.

Douglas and I, of course, just listened and said nothing, but we had in fact both come to much the same conclusion a few days earlier.

That afternoon, the P.M. announced in the House that Stafford [Cripps] was going away, that in his absence he, the P.M., was taking charge of the Treasury, but that the President of the Board of Trade, the Minister of Fuel & Power and the two Secretaries to the Treasury would assist him.[7] I had only heard vague rumours about my position in this, but in view of the fuss about my Porthcawl speech I was rather glad. Just

5 These should perhaps have been transposed.

6 'Nicky' (Lord) Kaldor was at L.S.E. 1932–47; Fellow of King's College Cambridge from 1949, Professor of Economics 1966; Special Adviser to Labour Chancellors of the Exchequer, 1964–8 and 1974–6.

7 Respectively Harold Wilson, H.G., Jay and W.G. Hall – who fell ill himself and played no part.

before he made the statement the P.M. said to me, sitting on the bench beside him, 'Oh, by the way, I am mentioning you in this statement'. And that was the only official intimation I had had. I fancy that I was brought in largely because I happened to be one of the few Ministers in London in the first three weeks of August.

I should also mention that at the end of one of the E.P.C. meetings, the P.M. sent the officials out of the Cabinet room and the Chancellor then said, to my considerable surprise, 'One of my difficulties is that my official advisers are all "liberals" and I cannot really rely on them to carry through a "socialist" (sic) policy in these negotiations'. There was a brief discussion which resulted in the highly satisfactory conclusion that Douglas [Jay] was to be a member of the negotiating team for the talks with Snyder* [Secretary of the U.S. Treasury] and the Commonwealth Finance Ministers.[8] John Strachey also suggested on that occasion that I should be seconded from M.F.P. to assist the Chancellor; but I was not too keen on that and it was not proceeded with.

On Wednesday, 20th July Douglas lunched with me in my room at the office, and we then confessed to each other that we were both now in favour of devaluation –

(a) because exchange control had clearly not been able to prevent the continuation of the capital drain; devaluation on the other hand would not only check it, but bring the money back.

(b) The U.S. Government were clearly not going to be able to do anything in the short term to help us and might insist on very stiff terms for the long term.

(c) The Commonwealth countries were obviously influenced in their import policy by the relative prices of sterling and dollar goods. Thus the control over dollar expenditure was clearly much looser than we had supposed.

(d) The prospect of expanding exports to dollar areas was probably greater than we had at first supposed – because of the great profitability of exporting to these areas as a result of devaluation.

(e) To delay devaluation might be exceedingly dangerous because as the reserve fell we should find it more and more difficult to carry out the operation without the risk of a 'collapse of the currency': in consequence we should be completely dependent on the U.S.A. and be at their mercy.

8 Cripps' comment is also reported by Dalton: diary, vol. 37, 19.7.49 ('10 days ago') and 12.9.49, when 'D.J. repeated several times that it is all due to my suggestion at EPC, when S.C. said he didn't trust the advice of his officials, that D.J. should be in on the brief-making that has saved the situation. If he hadn't been in, nor would H.G. have been, and the officials would have had it all their own way'. (See below, pp. 134–5).

The following night we had a Group dinner with Nye Bevan, John Strachey, George Strauss, Douglas and myself. Harold Wilson did not come.

Douglas and I went over the ground and convinced our colleagues. John S. was already convinced (I remember discussing it with him the previous week). Nye was won over without great difficulty.

The discussion was mixed up with talk of the Election on which the others, except for Douglas, wanted an early one, and we said that in that case it was urgent to devalue as soon as possible.

Earlier that day Douglas and I had seen Harold and explained our views. He had made it plain that he agreed in the main, though he was not so sure on the timing. He favoured devaluation *fairly* soon but not before the Washington talks.[9]

The following Monday (25 July) we had a meeting with the Treasury – apart from Harold, Douglas and myself there were present Bridges*, Wilson-Smith and Robert Hall.[10]

I put some leading questions about devaluation and after some attempt at evading them and further discussion, it became clear that *all* were agreed that it must be done before the end of September, at latest. The Treasury favoured during the Washington talks and Harold supported them. Douglas wanted action at once and I was on the fence between – the great difficulty of early action being Stafford [Cripps]'s absence.

That evening HW, DJ and self saw the P.M. and explained our views. He accepted the fact that we had to devalue but saw great difficulty about doing it during August. The line up was much as in the morning. HW at one extreme, DJ at the other and myself in the middle.

Later that evening DJ and I saw the L.P. [Lord President] very privately and explained the position. He needed no convincing and was in favour of immediate action, supporting Douglas in this. It was agreed that he would ask the P.M. for a meeting with us and Harold before the end of the week.

We also saw HD[Dalton] and persuaded him without difficulty.

That same night (there was an all night sitting on the Steel Bill) John S[Strachey] got hold of me and showed me a letter he was proposing to send to the P.M. It was a strong argument for immediate devaluation. I said the only thing that worried me was the fear that the P.M. would think

9 The regular meeting of the World Bank and International Monetary Fund, due in September in Washington, offered the best (or only) opportunity of keeping secrecy while consulting internationally.

10 Sir Edward Bridges was Permanent Secretary of the Treasury, Sir Henry Wilson-Smith head of its Overseas Finance Division, and Sir Robert Hall director of the Economic Section of the Cabinet Office.

D[Douglas] and I had inspired it! I advised him to *see* the P.M. personally which he subsequently did.

On Wednesday [27 July] Harold complained to me that 'there was too much talking', and hinted that Douglas had been indiscreet. I fancy he was then thinking of our Group discussion which had probably got around to him. But he must also have heard that we had seen the L.P.

On Thursday evening [28 July] we three met the P.M. and L.P. and had a very useful discussion. We really pretty well reached agreement on the basis that it should be done *before* Washington but *after* Stafford was back here. This would (a) enable Stafford to put it across [to] the British people; (b) make plain we were doing it of our own volition and not under dictation.

On this line up I should say that L.P. and Douglas would have preferred it at once; Harold not till Washington and the P.M. and I in between – where we in fact settled.

It was also agreed that HW who was in any case going to Annecy[11] and North Italy should go to Zürich and deliver a letter from the P.M. to Stafford setting out the position and asking for his views.

The next day Douglas drafted the letter (a very good draft too!) and we took it on the Friday evening [29 July] to the P.M. When we got there we saw Bridges and Wilson-Smith waiting – the underground Civil Service had been busy! – and they had to be allowed to see the draft and come in to the P.M. They indicated they wanted to put more forcibly the case for delay till after the Washington talks had begun and as they were the official advisers we could not resist them. Harold would not want the document for a week (it was to be taken to him by his P.S. [Private Secretary]). Therefore they were allowed to take it away and suggest amendments, which were to be discussed at a meeting with D [Douglas] and myself in the following week.[12]

I was much cheered up however by finding out that Plowden [Chief Planning Officer] was going with the Chancellor because he and I were very much in agreement about the whole thing, and he promised to put across my own paper to the Chancellor as best he could. We had lunch

11 MS version, mistyped as Nancy.
12 Dalton reported at this time (diary, vol. 37, end July 1949, pp. 1–2) 'H.G. and D.J. come again to see me after this. H.G. says he'll resign if we commit ourselves again to convertibility. They say there is still very heavy [*sic*] from all official quarters "to do something else" as well as devaluation . . . What they all want is a slash in public expenditure on social services.

'H.G. and D.J. both express distrust of H.W. They don't know what he's up to. They think he's currying favour with Bridges and Treasury officials.'

together that day and I was more than impressed with his sanity and intelligence.

The rest of the story can be told quite shortly. I did not get back to London until September 12th, and following that one or two meetings took place with the Ministers concerned with the preparations for the great event. Finally, on the Chancellor's return from Washington, on the following Saturday a secret Cabinet meeting took place. This was an amusing affair because we all had to go in by the back way, and none of the many reporters who must have been hanging about Downing Street discovered what was taking place. The Chancellor gave a brief report on Washington and we then went through his draft broadcast but no point of policy or substance really emerged.[13]

There was evidently much amusement among the drivers of ministerial cars. Mine told me a story (which I suspect his pal invented) that Shinwell arrived in a false moustache and slouch hat!

Apart from this dramatic and interesting period, it is only necessary to record a very delightful holiday in Jersey, followed by four lovely days at Abbotsbury. And what was much more unusual for us, a visit to the St Leger on the last day of my leave with Dora and Robin and Helen Brook*.[14] I found this very enjoyable because of the completely holiday atmosphere and carefree feeling which we all had. We took our food with us, sat on the highest seats in the grandstand and ate it and drank some red wine which we took with us. We betted small sums on each race and ended about fifteen shillings down on the day.

Wednesday, 21 September 1949

We met accordingly in the middle of the following week, i.e. after the Bank Holiday weekend.[15] Bridges and Wilson-Smith had produced a complete redraft of the letter to the Chancellor. When I read this I exploded and made a scene. I said that they had gone far beyond the Prime Minister's instructions; that I totally disagreed with their approach and we must go back to the original draft by the Economic Secretary [Jay]. They crumpled up after this and we compromised by adding one or two paragraphs to the Economic Secretary's draft, emphasising more

13 On Sunday 18 September the pound was devalued by 30 per cent, to $2.80. After all the discussions about the *date*, the *rate* was settled by Cripps, Bevin and their advisers in Washington. On HG's view see below, p. 148.
14 (Sir) Robin Brook, a banker, had been on Dalton's staff with HG in the Ministry of Economic Warfare.
15 The August bank holiday was then the first Monday in the month.

strongly the need for restricted Government expenditure. (It was interesting that later on I heard that this was the one passage of the letter to which the Chancellor strongly objected. It only shows how hopelessly bad the judgment of the officials was about the way to influence their Minister.)

The next day Douglas [Jay] and I took the letter down to Chequers where we had lunch, and the P.M. afterwards signed it. It was duly sealed and delivered to HW[Wilson]'s Private Secretary who shortly afterwards flew to Switzerland and handed it over to HW. HW then took it on a visit to the Chancellor which appeared to be perfectly natural seeing that he, himself, was in any case in the neighbourhood. No journalists seem to have suspected anything.[16]

In the following week HW returned and we heard the outcome of his visit both to the Chancellor and to the Foreign Secretary (whom he had seen earlier). He reported that the Chancellor was by no means convinced of the need for devaluation, and in any case did not at all like the idea of doing it before the Washington Conference. He could not therefore agree to any of our proposals but wished to discuss the matter on his return to England. The Foreign Secretary's reaction was somewhat similar, although he appeared to be inclined to favour devaluation in due course.

Another week then elapsed before anything more on this vital matter took place. Meanwhile we were engaged with the Treasury officials in preparing the brief for the Washington talks. Although after the earlier explosion our relations had noticeably improved, there was one further major row. They prepared the draft brief, the first part of which might have been written by someone who was completely schooled in the anti-British American press. I got very angry about this – and indeed it would have created a most deplorable impression on Ministers, and Bridges hastily agreed to redraft it. It was clear that he, himself, had not written it but Makins* of the Foreign Office. However, I said that was not enough and I would ask the Economic Secretary to do a redraft. It was agreed that both redrafts should be done and then compared. The fear of the Economic Secretary's draft being the winner had a most useful effect.[17] Bridges, in fact, rewrote the whole thing and an entirely different

16 See D. Jay, *Change and Fortune*, Hutchinson, 1980, pp. 186–91, which prints the text of Attlee's letter.

17 Jay's account of this incident is given by Dalton (diary, 12.9.49, p. 1):
'In the absence of H.M. [Morrison] and me and Strachey – and S.C. in Switzerland – the old fight had gone on. *In spite of all our Cabinet discussions and decisions*, the officials – Bridges, W. Smith, Makins (so the F.O. were in the game too) etc. put up a brief for Ministers, immediately before they were due to leave for W[ashing]ton, with all the old stuff about the "need to restore confidence" and hence to make large reductions, including changes of policy, in public expenditure . . . [*note continues on p. 135*]

impression was created. This time I agreed, after consultation with Douglas [Jay], to insert two or three of his paragraphs in their redraft.[18]

However, apart from this row, there is no doubt[19] that the Treasury had been moving steadily in our direction, and Bridges admitted to me that he was really pretty well indifferent as to whether the date should be the 28th August or the 4th or 18th September. I also found myself on much better personal terms with him. I think this was partly because in the last Cabinet meeting I had spoken out strongly against the doctrine that the level of public expenditure had no relation to our balance of payments problem. Some of my colleagues took a very rosy view of this matter which had to be dispelled.[20]

As regards devaluation however we were still in the position that while the majority view was strongly in favour of very quick and early action nobody knew exactly how the Chancellor felt. The Foreign Secretary had meanwhile returned to London and was reported to be favourably inclined. I had a brief talk with him but could not gather from this whether he belonged to the 'before' or 'after' school.

'H.G. and D.J. fought this out. D.J. praised H.G. *most* highly. He acted as "Vice-Chancellor of the Exchequer" and attacked the officials, both on intellectual grounds and on tacking on decisions already taken . . . under H.G.'s attack, the officials retreated . . . If S.C. had had the wrong paper put up (but it wasn't), he might, having been out of touch and ill, have weakened. If the P.M. had weakened on our general proposition that transfer payments don't directly affect costs (but he didn't, remaining on the contrary, serenely set) all might collapsed [sic] – and the Labour Party be breaking up as in 1931.

'H.G. and D.J. saw eye to eye throughout. H.W. was away at this point, but D.J. doesn't trust him. He trims and wavers, and is thinking more of what senior Ministers – and even senior officials – are thinking of him than of what is right.' [Emphasis in original]

18 Two drafts are printed below as Document 3, by permission of H.M.S.O. (Crown Copyright).

19 Mistyped as 'now doubt'.

20 Dalton reports this Cabinet (diary, end July 1949, pp. 1–2):

'C.R.A. calls on me to open, on a paper of H.M.'s alleging that there is a "close relation" between our high expenditure & our dollar troubles. I say the relation isn't close at all . . . Only backing H.M. gets is from H. McNeil who, primed no doubt by F.O. officials says we ought to "meet half way" those in U.S. and elsewhere who haven't "confidence" in our policy. Deval[n] isn't discussed, but is mentioned, approvingly by H.M., myself, A.B. and J.S. (Only C.A. & A.V.A. were in the Cab in 1931. How differently we Ministers are reacting now! No flicker of surrender) . . .

'Two other points emerged from Cab talks. (1) Canadians must be made to face facts . . . (2) Though we won't retreat on social services, it is agreed that P.M. should ask all Dept[al] Ministers to cut down expenditure by, say, 5% . . . without undue publicity . . .

(Dalton was wrong; only A.V. Alexander as First Lord of the Admiralty was in the 1931 Cabinet, and Attlee as Postmaster-General was not.)

We expected the Chancellor back on 19th August, and our first idea was to have a meeting with him at the Treasury that afternoon, to be followed by a Ministerial meeting with the P.M. or Foreign Secretary either that night or the following morning. We hoped in this way to get the decision taken in favour of 28th August, the idea being that the Chancellor would then put the change across just before leaving for Washington. However, the P.M. decided that the Chancellor's health was not sufficiently good to impose upon him meetings of this kind immediately he came back, and we became reconciled to the second alternative which was meetings in the following week and a decision in favour of 4th September. I had agreed therefore to fly back from Jersey, to which I was going on the 20th, on the following Wednesday and Douglas [Jay] had agreed to come back from Devonshire. We hoped that afternoon to have our meeting with the Chancellor and get the thing settled the following day. On this understanding I agreed with Bridges not to impose myself on the Chancellor immediately on his arrival, and that Bridges alone would meet him at [London Airport] Northolt.

In order, however, to be sure that he would understand our point of view, I wrote a ten page memorandum on the whole thing, which Bridges agreed to give him. I also sent copies to the Foreign Secretary and the P.M. and later to one or two other colleagues. With this I also had drafted a note on the Election date which was sent more or less to the same people.[21]

To my surprise, however, on Thursday night, 18th August, Bridges rang me up at home and said, rather mysteriously, 'You may have to be prepared for a meeting tomorrow, after all. I will explain in the morning.' He came to my office the next morning and said that he had learned that the Foreign Secretary was going to Chequers on Friday and there was to be a meeting between him, the P.M. and Chancellor. Having heard this he had telephoned the P.M. and pointed out that he had promised me there would be no such meeting and if there was to be I and the President of the Board of Trade [Harold Wilson] and he should really be present. The P.M. had agreed to this. Bridges added however that he thought the meeting would be short because he learned that the Foreign Secretary was in favour of immediate action at the earliest date.

I was naturally overjoyed at this because it seemed we had at last won our long battle for early action. And so that afternoon I drove down to Chequers for the meeting which was timed to begin at 5.30 p.m. I got there just before HW, the others had arrived shortly before us and were already in the P.M.'s study. H. and I joined them after having a cup of tea. The Chancellor looked very thin, and it was a thoroughly bad omen

21 Printed below as Documents 4 and 5.

when in my presence he handed to Bridges all the papers Bridges had given him and said, 'I am not going to do any work for a week. I must go home and sleep'.

We then talked for about two and a half hours. It was a depressing occasion. The argument rambled along; sometimes about devaluation itself; sometimes about the date. The P.M. did not intervene at all but sat at his desk doodling and listening to the argument. It was obvious that Stafford [Cripps] was quite out of touch and I felt that I had completely failed to put anything across to him at all. I was, of course, myself arguing both for devaluation and for the earliest date. H. argued strongly against the early date – although on the last occasion when we had met he had appeared to accept it. The Foreign Secretary swayed this way and that, and every now and then we were treated to a long monologue on some event of recent history, such as how he had handled the flour millers in 1924, and what he had said to Ramsay MacDonald in 1931, etc. It was very hot and the room is a very small one. Bridges said little and was quite fair and objective in any explanations he gave. After a bit, however, the Foreign Secretary made it plain that he would support devaluation at some time and, despite some scepticism from the Chancellor, that seemed to be accepted. It became clear that the Chancellor, himself, was absolutely adamant against the early date. So finally the P.M. said, 'The Chancellor does not want to do it before Washington. Therefore we cannot do it before Washington.' And that settled the matter.

We all stayed to dinner but for me it was a gloomy meal because I felt I had failed at the crucial moment and just when I had understood (because of a false impression of the Foreign Secretary's attitude) that we were likely to win. Looking back it is of course obvious that the early date was impossible because the Chancellor's health simply did not permit of his doing the necessary work, such as preparing the broadcast, etc. Moreover, temperamentally he was very anxious indeed to do a lot of consulting with the Americans and others. I suppose really it was something to have got the decision that it would be done on the 18th, unless the Chancellor and Foreign Secretary took a completely different view after going to Washington; and what was even more important that the Americans should be told it was our intention to do it immediately our negotiators arrived in Washington.

We then all dispersed and the next day I went to Jersey. Ten days later, on the 29th, I flew back for the Cabinet meeting which preceded the departure of the Foreign Secretary and Chancellor to Washington. Unfortunately the plane was delayed by bad weather and I did not get to Downing Street until an hour after the meeting had started, and found the devaluation discussion was really over. Apparently there had been some opposition from some less important Ministers, but the Chequers decision was in fact confirmed. [22] The rest of the time was spent discussing the brief, on which there was a lot of anxiety expressed regarding what was to be said about public expenditure here. It was however agreed that strong measures would have to be taken against inflation. I thought the Chancellor seemed calmer and better, though still looking very thin. He said to me then as he had said at Chequers, 'I have not slept'.

Document No. 3

Draft briefs for Bevin and Cripps on leaving Washington talks (probably late redrafts, amended by HG): above, pp. 134–5.

                    Objective of Talks   (Officials' redraft?)

1. The general objective of the Washington talks is:
   (a) To establish a basis of co-operation between the three Governments in such a way as to facilitate equilibrium in the balance of payments between the dollar and sterling areas at a high level of trade. The special objective of the U.K. must be to secure that this is achieved on the basis of a high standard of living for ourselves and without any threat to full employment here.

   Our more immediate objective is:
   (b) To secure action by the U.S. and Canadian Governments which [together with (devaluation and) other steps by ourselves] will enable the U.K. to overcome the immediate dollar crisis. [23]

2. The renewed dollar difficulties of the sterling area during the past few months have been due to four main causes – (1) the U.S. recession, and in particular heavily reduced U.S. buying of rubber, tin, wool, cocoa and diamonds; (2) devaluation talk emanating from Washington in the early months of the year; (3) the removal of wheat and other commodities from E.C.A. financing; and (4) an inadequate effort by the sterling countries to switch their exports to dollar rather than other markets. Up till the spring of this year, when the first two of the above factors were emerging, the U.K.'s effort towards viability was making great progress. Our production and exports were at record levels; our productivity was rising; and our overall transactions with overseas countries was [sic] in balance.

22 Dalton was at the Council of Europe, and has no record of that Cabinet.
23 Punctuation throughout follows the document *before* HG annotated, except in para. 5 (see below) – and including his amendments as the passages in brackets which elsewhere in the Diary denote editorial additions.

3. Despite this, the difficulties of the past few months – though in part inadvertently caused by the North American countries themselves – have been made the text for a campaign of critical propaganda in the American and Canadian Press, founded partly on genuine misconceptions and disappointment at the apparent failure of E.R.P., but partly also on political motives. This campaign, though it should not be exaggerated has evidently produced some effect on Canadian and American public opinion, and even some sections of the administration. It takes three main forms:

(1) A complaint that the U.K. has made insufficient use of E.R.P. aid, which is consequently not achieving its recovery aim.

(2) A suspicion that no progress is being made towards the long-term aims of multilateralism and convertibility enshrined in the I.T.O. and loan agreements.[24]

(3) An allegation that the failure of sterling area exports to rise fast enough is due to the level of U.K. costs, which in turn is blamed on U.K. internal social policy.

4. If these doubts and confusions are allowed to go too far unchecked, they may do real damage to the prospect of the negotiations, and also to the ability of the administration to steer through any resulting proposals. It will therefore be essential, if contentions of this kind are put forward by the U.S. and Canadian negotiators, for the U.K. representatives to counter them vigorously where they are false, and to weed out the elements of truth from the many muddled ideas now prevailing. It would no doubt be a great advantage if discussion of some of these irrelevancies could be avoided; but if they are raised they may have to be answered.

5. We should *of course* admit that there is a clear obligation on us to attain viability and freedom from dollar aid at the earliest possible moment; that our campaign for greater productivity and efficiency must be relentlessly pushed forward; that inflationary pressures still exist in the U.K. and have to be countered; and that we have so far failed in the effort to steer an adequate proportion of our exports to North America. *But* we should repudiate the fallacious idea that the sterling dollar problem is entirely a matter of U.K. effort or U.K. policies. This is patently false, since something like half of the deterioration in sterling area dollar earnings this year relates to goods originating from outside the U.K. *Ministers will also no doubt wish to deal with any arguments put forward on such matters as the confused idea* that British Government social

24 E.R.P. was the European Recovery Program authorising Marshall Aid. On the loan agreement, above p. 125. The Americans had already written these long-term aims into the Lend-Lease terms settled in 1941, and again in the Havana Charter of the abortive International Trade Organisation, signed in March 1948. See Gardner (1956).

expenditure is a major element in U.K. *direct* costs of production; *they will no doubt wish* to point out clearly, if necessary, that money raised in profit taxation and paid out in certain services such as food subsidies and family allowances tends not to raise costs and export prices, but to lower them.[25]

6. On this we shall probably have to make it clear that convertibility and greater multilateral trade, must be the results of equilibrium in the balance of payments, and not steps towards it. If attempts are made to introduce them first, equilibrium will be itself retarded, and the attempted convertibility and multilateralism will collapse, as 1947 plainly showed. We must defend the successful bilateral agreements made since 1947, as vital to the rebuilding of our economy after the misguided attempt at premature convertibility in 1947, and as having certainly increased rather than diminished the total world trade. It should be made clear that these Agreements are flexible and various, and do not by any means always or usually imply an exact two-way balancing of visible trade. Finally, we should perhaps again point out that we maintain in the sterling area the largest multilateral system with widespread convertibility in the world.

7. Nevertheless, there are certain further economic decisions which the U.K. Government ought to take on merits, and quite apart from any North American opinions or pressure. The most important of these are – (1) *devaluation*, which is best calculated to encourage both the purchase of sterling area goods by dollar countries and the impulse of U.K. and sterling area exporters to prefer dollar markets to others. [The full case for devaluation need not be argued here; but all the evidence now suggests that a halt to the dollar drain cannot be achieved otherwise, and that the effect on the U.K. cost of living is not likely to be more than 3 or 4 points spread over a period of months. This should not be so great or rapid as to make it impossible to prevent such a rise in money incomes as would outweigh the advantages of devaluation.] (2) *A check to the rise in Government expenditure*. The need for this arises from the fact that rising Government expenditure is certainly inflationary, and that this is particularly undesirable at a moment when devaluation will give a further impulse to inflationary tendencies. The decision has already been taken to carry out a further intensified drive to eliminate all waste in Government expenditure, to curtail less essential services, and to call a halt to the present steady growth in the total. At the same time redoubled restraint must also be exercised in credit policy to ensure that an expansion of bank deposits does not cancel out the effect of Budgetary disinflation.

8. It is the considered advice of H.M. Ambassador in Washington, and

---

25 Words in italics in para. 5, and the first two words of para. 6, are HG's alterations or insertions.

High Commissioner in Ottawa, as well as the opinion reported by the latter of Mr Norman Robertson* that the U.K. Government would gain rather than lose with North American opinion if it took decisions on these issues on their merits, and clearly in advance of any pressure from the U.S. or Canadian Governments.[26] The case is thus very strong for decisions to be taken, and if possible announced, on both these points in advance of the opening of negotiations. This should both strengthen greatly our hands in the negotiations, and avoid making it appear to the British and European publics that we had only acted under pressure. Clearly there is much to be said for an announcement of both decisions simultaneously, and before the talks begin.

9. In the talks themselves we shall be able to make the most of both these decisive steps. The point can be hammered home that devaluation amounts to a heavy reduction in costs, automatic and immediate, and precisely so designed as to affect selling prices in the dollar market. We should point out that its success, however, depends on two things – (a) our own supplementary drive against inflation; and (b) willingness of the U.S. and Canada not to take retaliatory measures. The first we shall have demonstrated we are doing. On the second, we must ask the U.S. and Canada to play their part.

10. In summary, *our recommendations* are as follows:

    (a) Decisions should be taken about devaluation, reduction of Government expenditure and policy in the monetary field before Ministers leave for Washington.

    (b) The decisions (*about reduction in Government*[27] expenditure with any necessary reference to policy) should also be publicly announced before Ministers leave, as follows:

        (i) In the field of *Government expenditure*, H.M.G. declares, as a positive decision of policy, that the effort to eliminate waste and less essential services is to be intensified forthwith; and a halt called to the automatic growth in the total.

        (ii) In the field of *monetary policy*, it is recognised that the recovery which effective action in the field of Government expenditure should produce in the stock markets would not necessarily restore long-term interest rates to the very low levels of the recent past: but changes in long-term interest rates should not be allowed to affect the short-term rate for

26 Respectively Sir Oliver Franks, Sir Alexander Clutterbuck (below, p. 211) and the former Canadian High Commissioner in London, now Secretary of their Cabinet. (The text has 'overwhelming' as an alternative to 'very strong' in the following sentence.)

27 These words in italics were typed into the original document as an insertion. There was also a question mark in the margin at this point.

Government borrowing. Any rise here would frustrate the effort to reduce Government spending.

(c) Devaluation [Recommendations regarding timing.]

TOP SECRET (Douglas Jay's draft?)

1. 'Our general objective in the Washington talks is to induce the U.S. and Canadian Governments to take such action as will facilitate equilibrium in the balance of payments between dollar and sterling areas on a permanent basis with the highest standard of living for ourselves and without threatening the maintenance of full employment here.

Our immediate objective is to get them to take certain specific steps which, together with the steps taken by the British government, will ensure that the immediate dollar crisis will be overcome.'[28]

2. There can be a section on the U.S. and Canadian point of view – but there must also be a brief on the way to counter this – a vigorous presentation of our own case.

3. In particular we must emphasize the extent of our recovery and remind the Americans of our overall balance position, of the fact that we have a specific dollar problem and nothing else and that we were getting along quite well with this until this Spring. We must point out that since then we have taken no internal measures which are in any way responsible for our difficulties, which are caused wholly by external factors and especially the level of U.S. demand.

4. We must make it plain once more that multilateralism and convertibility in the sense used by the Americans *cannot* be sustained until we reach equilibrium and that bilateralism which has enabled us to make such a substantial recovery is inevitable until dollar-sterling equilibrium is achieved. Convertibility is therefore an outcome, not a remedy, nor even a proximate aim.

5. We should play devaluation as our own major contribution to the situation and point out that this is what they wanted us to do. We have done it and now it is up to them to play their part as well.

6. As regards our own level of costs, we expect devaluation to give us substantial competitive advantages – as much as a 25% deflation would have done – provided (a) the U.S. and Canada do not take any steps to counteract it; (b) we do not allow internal costs to rise too much here.

On the latter, we should say we recognize the danger of inflation and are determined to take all possible steps in the field of budgeting, credit and investment policy to suppress it.

28 HG inserted 'the steps . . . government' instead of 'devaluation'.

Finally, we should divide the action we want them to take into the following groups:

1. Action to raise the level of dollar demand for non-dollar goods;
2. Action to reduce the prices of essential dollar products sold to the Sterling Area.
3. Action to facilitate the substitution of non-dollar for dollar imports into the Sterling area;
4. Investment, Gifts, Loans etc.
5. Miscellaneous.

All the specific proposals in this paper, both short and long term, can be grouped into this heading.

Document No. 4

British Economic Policy[29]

TOP SECRET

1. The essential thing to keep firmly in mind in face of the cataract of advice and propaganda pouring in upon us is *that the only major economic problem is the dollar problem*. Employment is high, production is high, the overall balance of payments is not bad, there is inflationary pressure, but no runaway inflation. If it were not for this dollar gap we should have little to worry about.

2. The gap has become wider instead of smaller. The direct reasons for this are not in dispute. Dollar sales from the rest of the sterling area are heavily down. U.K. exports for dollars have not gone up as fast or as far as they should. Talk and expectation of devaluation have caused all who can to delay converting dollars into sterling while converting sterling into dollars as fast as possible. These are the main causes.

3. But because the gap is wider not smaller, Marshall Aid is not enough to close it. Therefore the reserve falls. It is a very small reserve and we cannot afford to lose much. Hence the need for urgent action.

4. In the circumstances our immediate aim must be to prevent the reserve falling further while maintaining full employment here, with least economic sacrifice to ourselves.

29 'British Economic Policy'. Paper sent by HG on 18 August 1949 to Attlee, Bevan, Cripps, Dalton, Morrison and Strachey; also to Douglas Jay and to Sir Edwin Plowden, Above, p. 136; Plowden wrote expressing complete agreement (cf. pp. 128, 132–3).

5. There are three possible lines of attack –
   (a) reduce dollar expenditure;
   (b) increase dollar earnings;
   (c) persuade U.S. Government to give us or lend us more dollars.

6. The original decisions taken in June and July were to reduce expenditure by cutting imports substantially ((a) above) and to try and persuade the U.S. Government to help. We hoped they would help by facilitating an increase in our dollar earnings, and partly by lending or giving us more dollars. On (b) we decided to do a lot of small things: but we took no major action comparable with the cuts in dollar imports. There is nothing surprising about this. Cutting dollar imports is directly in the control of the British Government. Expanding dollar exports is not.

7. Since these decisions were taken there have been four developments –
   (a) Devaluation of sterling is even more widely expected – and consequently there is even more disinclination to acquire it.
   (b) Little or no help has so far come from the U.S. Government.
   (c) The dollar drain on our reserves continues as before.
   (d) There is a raging press campaign in U.S.A. against the British people in general and the Labour Government in particular. Moreover official opinion seems to have hardened strongly against doing anything to help us, *unless we help ourselves*. Cutting imports, would *not* be regarded as 'helping ourselves': what is meant by this is doing far more to increase our dollar earnings. This is associated with the idea that our costs and prices are too high – and this in turn is ascribed by many to the scale of our public expenditure. We may resent this criticism and we can certainly reply to it at the appropriate moment, but it is to-day a fact which cannot be ignored and of which we must take some account in the decision we reach.

8. The conclusion is surely unmistakable – that we cannot now possibly expect the U.S. Government to stop the gold drain for us or indeed to do anything much to help stop it unless we ourselves act; but that if we do help ourselves, then we can reasonably expect some help from them.

9. It seems to me, in any case, enormously important that we should now take the initiative. Lease Lend, the 1945 loan, Marshall Aid – all of them have meant dollars provided by the Americans. I do not believe we can ever solve the problem on this basis. This time we must take the important step ourselves.

10. But what can we do? To cut dollar imports further, as I have said, would not impress the Americans favourably – though (and this should certainly not be forgotten) it may frighten them. The more serious objection is that we cannot carry it far without producing unemployment and other very awkward consequences here. We may be driven to further

import cuts. But these must surely be our last resource and not our next step.

11. Can we earn more dollars? Something may come of the efforts to improve marketing arrangements. But we cannot rely on these. We are told that our costs are too high. This of course is a very imprecise phrase which is why there is so much confused argument about it. If it means that after allowing for the change in the sterling dollar rate our costs have risen since before the war far more than those of American products, it is probably not true. But if it means that our costs are to-day too high for us to sell all the additional exports that we must sell for dollars in the post war world, it is pretty near the mark. For it is not only sales to dollar areas that count, but also sales in competition with dollar articles. It became clear during the Commonwealth Finance Ministers' Conference that other countries in the sterling area would not substitute U.K. for dollar imports, and so save dollars, beyond a certain point, unless our prices compared more favourably with those of U.S. exports. And the same is broadly true of every country in trading with which we risk dollar expenditure.

12. But reducing the costs of producing our exports is easier said than done. We have firmly rejected a policy of wage cutting which, to be effective, would have to be preceded by deflation and unemployment. And to rely on increased output per man through greater efficiency to get the reasonably quick results we need is clearly absurd. The best we could hope for here would be – say – 5 per cent per annum (compared with 2½ per cent before the war) and we cannot even be sure what competitive advantage this would give us, since U.S. producers will no doubt also be steadily improving their efficiency.

13. *There is no way out of this dilemma except devaluation of sterling.* For devaluation does give the British exporter exactly the same competitive advantage over the U.S. producer which a reduction in his sterling costs would have done. On the assumption that other non-dollar countries devalue too, it does more than this; it gives a special impetus towards exports to dollar as compared with any other destination. For the British exporter finds overnight that at previous dollar prices at which his products were selling he is making a handsome profit (equivalent to the percentage by which the pound is devalued). There is therefore the maximum incentive to him to push sales in dollar areas. And he can, if he wishes, cut prices so as to expand sales because he has a large margin from which to do this.

14. It is, of course, not possible to prove conclusively that dollar revenues will increase. But those who argue that they will not, must also agree that reductions in export prices in dollar areas which result from reduced costs of production at home would also not increase our dollar revenues. And

this they seldom admit. All one can say is that although there cannot be certainty, there is a strong probability that devaluation, taking into account all its ramifications in dollar, sterling and non-dollar areas and its effects on the activities of manufacturers and traders will, in fact, cause our dollar expenditure to decline and our dollar revenues to rise.

15. The changes in trade resulting from devalution are, indeed, not likely to produce short period reactions on our gold reserve. But the effect which devaluation produces on expectations almost certainly will. Provided the change is sharp and decisive, there can be little doubt that it will transform the attitude of those who have been waiting for the pound to depreciate these last few months. Indeed it is clear that the only way to stop this particular drain on our reserves is to convince the commercial and financial world that the pound is not going to fall below the current rate. There is in my view no hope of doing this until devaluation has occurred.

16. Because, then, of the prospect it offers of expanding our dollar revenues, because it is the only way open to us on our own of stopping a further decline in our gold reserves, because it is the one big way in which we can take the initiative, because it goes at one blow to the heart of the problem of dollar exports and sterling costs, devaluation has now become an absolute necessity.

17. Nevertheless we must be quite clear that in taking this step we are not avoiding all difficulties. It must be emphasised that *any* step which we ourselves take to close the dollar gap again is virtually certain to involve some sacrifice. This is clear enough when we do without dollar imports. It should be equally clear when the emphasis is on expanding dollar exports. It is true that some of the expansion which will be produced by devaluation may be at the expense of exports to non-dollar countries or the rest of the sterling area. But the need for some overseas investment, the repayment of sterling balances to India and other countries and the demands of commonwealth countries for U.K. products in place of dollar imports place severe limits on these. Most, if not all of the additional dollar exports will therefore have to come from the home market. We must accordingly expect, as devaluation begins to take effect, that shortages over a fairly wide field will tend to appear or be intensified at home – unless, of course, as a result of longer hours, overtime or greater effort more can be produced to counterbalance the higher exports.

18. How serious these shortages will be it is not possible to say. It depends partly on how much extra work we do and partly on how rapidly we can increase our dollar earnings. This in turn depends on how much we can put up our dollar sales without having to cut prices too far. If the Americans adopt all the measures we propose to maintain and expand demand for sterling exports in the U.S.A., it will greatly help. But we

ought to assume that there will be these shortages and that there will therefore be, on this account, an increase in inflationary pressure.

19. Another inflationary influence which must result from devaluation is the higher sterling cost of dollar imports. The effect on the cost of living index is fortunately not as high as one might expect – four points over a period of six to nine months. But there will also be the higher cost of materials for a number of industries of which cotton and oil, timber and aluminium are the most obvious examples.

20. These inflationary influences must be kept under control. Since we already have a somewhat inflationary situation, this will not be easy. But if we fail, then we are really risking the success of devaluation by allowing our costs to rise to offset the competitive advantage we at first gained.

21. There has recently been much discussion on the level of public expenditure in this country and its relation to our dollar balance problem. It is often said that high public expenditure by keeping industrial costs high makes it impossible for us to sell our goods in dollar areas. There is not much in this argument. The effects of high direct taxation on production costs are to say the least round about and difficult to identify, while some Government expenditure – such as food subsidies – by keeping wages down also keeps export costs low.

22. The real connection between public expenditure and the dollar problem is different. It is an internal inflationary situation – and not high public expenditure as such – which has such adverse effects on the trade balance, partly because it causes costs to rise in the export trade and partly because the strong home demand makes it more profitable for manufacturers to sell in the U.K. instead of exporting. Devaluation introduces two opposing forces into this situation. It provides a special and very powerful stimulus to exports to dollar areas; and at the same time it sets loose additional inflationary influences which if not checked will gradually weaken the impetus to higher exports.

23. The case for curbing public expenditure then is simply part of the general case for curbing inflation. If it seemed possible to increase taxation further without creating undesirable political and economic consequences, an increase in taxation would be just as effective. But though increased taxation may not be altogether impossible in some fields, there are certainly strict limits, political no less than economic, to this. Hence one falls back on the necessity for cutting public expenditure – though this should certainly be combined with stricter control over investment and credit.

24. It may be thought that these difficulties outweigh the advantages of devaluation. I am convinced that this is not so. If we have, in the main, to save ourselves – as now seems clear enough – we cannot avoid a sacrifice in our standard of living. Devaluation enables us to do this in the least

painful manner for the nation as a whole. We preserve full employment; we stand the best chance of getting higher output; and we spread the resulting effects on our standard of living pretty widely over an enormous range of manufactured consumer goods and capital equipment. But we must not let inflation get the better of us!

25. If it be agreed that we must devalue, two questions arise – the extent of the change and the timing of the operation.

26. On the extent, the main consideration is, while not increasing the cost of dollar imports too far, to be sure that we make a job of it. It seems to be agreed by all concerned that the minimum change is 25 per cent, i.e. to £1 = 3 dollars ratio and that it would probably be wiser to go rather further – to – say 2.75 or 2.80 dollars to the pound.

27. There seem to me to be very powerful arguments in favour of *not* going to another fixed rate immediately. We want to create an expectation that the pound *may appreciate*. For this is the certain way to get people to wish to acquire sterling – in order to make a profit. If it is felt that we cannot risk leaving the market free (within the limits set by exchange control), then I should still prefer that we announced that the pound would be held within a band of rates – say 2.60-2.80 dollars to the pound.[30] This would give the authorities the necessary opportunity to let the pound go at first to the lower rate and then have an appreciation. Later if necessary we could of course settle on a fixed rate within the band.

28. On timing my view is emphatically that this ought to take place before the Washington Conference begins. Many of us would have preferred that it should have been done in August. But this may not prove possible. The earliest date which next seems practicable is September 4th. The case for this seems to me overwhelming on three grounds. First that if we wait till September 18th – which is the next practicable date – there will be between now and then a great intensification of the pressure against the pound which may be accompanied by a leakage of our intentions from Washington. If so, we shall lose unnecessarily a lot more gold and dollars. Secondly, it will seem to everyone that we have done it under U.S. pressure and this will create a most unfavourable impression on public opinion here, especially if, as is also necessary, we have to refer in the announcement to our policy on public expenditure. Thirdly, by doing it before the Conference starts we shall be doing the one thing which gives the Conference a real chance of success. We shall have seized the initiative and have cut the ground from under the feet of our critics and enemies in the U.S.A. A great deal of evidence has accumulated during the past few weeks showing that this is the strongly held view of our friends overseas.

30 The speculation in *HG*, p. 203 is thus incorrect.

29. As far as I can see, the arguments for delay really amount to no more than a feeling that it will be cosier and more orderly to devalue when bankers and finance Ministers are congregated together in Washington. But devaluation of sterling is a step which really must be taken suddenly: it cannot possibly be made the subject of negotiations and argument in Washington. There is in any case bound to be 'consultation' in the sense that a lot of Governments including – above all the U.S., Canadian and Commonwealth Governments – have to be informed shortly in advance. Since we know that their reactions are likely to be favourable, I do not see why more than this is needed.

30. It is certainly essential that the Chancellor should broadcast. And it is a pity this could not have been done 'live' in England. But that is now impossible. The difficulty can I suggest be overcome if he broadcasts, from the U.S.A. or the boat or if he records a broadcast in the U.S.A. as soon as he arrives, the record being flown at once back to London for broadcasting on September 4th. Possibly a combination of these two might be arranged.

31. I therefore most strongly urge that devaluation should be announced not later than September 4th together with the statement on public expenditure. Having done this we shall then have created the conditions in which the Washington talks may succeed.

32. For, just as it would be a mistake to think that devaluation was a miraculous and painless cure for all ills, so also it would be quite wrong to imagine that once it has occurred nothing else is necessary. We certainly need, if we can, to get the Americans to take all the other steps which are described in the other papers. We shall need some of them to be quite sure of overcoming even with devaluation, our immediate crisis. We shall need others to assist us, even with the pound devalued, in closing our dollar gap without a too heavy cost to ourselves.

33. But important as it is to persuade the U.S.A. and Canada to assist us in these ways, we must be very cautious about accepting commitments in exchange. In particular we should under no circumstances get committed to convertibility at any particular date – however distant or under any specific conditions. After all, convertibility with the dollar at fixed exchange rates does mean a return to the gold standard, to the 'automatic' system of achieving and maintaining equilibrium in international trade. It is almost certainly *not* compatible with the maintenance of our own full employment policy. It could be used to force deflation upon us and to deprive us of certain instruments of economic planning, which even if they are not always to be used, should surely always be kept handy.

34. We must be wary of definite commitments not only on convertibility with the dollar but also on specific steps towards multilateralism and non-discrimination. Progress here, for which there is no doubt much to be

said, must come gradually as equilibrium is restored. Our proposals to O.E.E.C. [the Organisation for European Economic Co-operation] represent a step forward, but at once we see how our very efforts in this direction are liable to be frustrated because of too rigid commitments on non-discrimination adopted a few years ago.

35. It cannot be too strongly emphasised that anything like a system of complete multilateral trade with free convertibility of currencies is quite out of the question until *after* the fundamental problem of disequilibrium between the dollar and non-dollar world has been solved. It cannot in itself help to remove that disequilibrium. It is an outcome rather than a cause. For if we achieve equilibrium, then the pound will be able 'to look the dollar in the face' and then we can begin to contemplate some gradual dropping of our defences – though even so we should reserve the right to re-erect them if our balance of payments position requires this. We can justly claim that in devaluing the pound, we have taken the biggest step open to us which may make for a solution of the dollar–sterling problem. We can ask the other two Governments now to play their part by adopting those other measures which are plainly necessary.

36. Thus I conclude –

(a) That devaluation is now an absolute necessity.

(b) That it should take place at the earliest possible date and before the Washington Conference.

(c) That we must prepare swiftly for a battle against internal inflation.

(d) That we must ask the U.S. and Canada Governments to play their part in solving the dollar problem by adopting those measures which we propose – warning them that if they do not help us, there may be nothing for it but further cuts in dollar imports.

(e) That we should avoid at all costs any definite commitments on convertibility or on progress towards multilateralism and non-discrimination – making it clear that such progress must depend upon our first solving the dollar problem.

Document No. 5

Political Strategy[31]

Before going on holiday, I should like to put before you some ideas about the date of the General Election.

It seems to me that there are really two alternatives which need serious consideration.

An election in any of the months December to March inclusive would, in my view, be most unwise.

While there should be no danger of a fuel crisis à la 1947 (unless we have a prolonged and widespread strike, which cannot be entirely ruled out), it is certain that if the winter is cold, we shall have electricity cuts in peak hours and much discontent among domestic consumers whose coal supplies will not be by any means sufficient for their needs. In the ordinary way, I should not worry about this. It is the price we pay for exporting to the limit. But if it coincided with an election it would probably lose us a good many votes. Moreover mid-winter is apt to be a depressing season when people feel their other discomforts and shortages more keenly than when the weather is kind.

The winter, however, will scarcely be over before we shall be faced with the formidable problem of the budget. I cannot myself see how this can possibly be popular. At best we shall only be able, by cuts in government expenditure (which means itself, disappointment to some people) to avoid any further increase in taxation. I should have thought there was no chance of tax remission; for we shall almost certainly then be facing strong inflationary pressure.

I conclude that on this account the months of April and May should also be ruled out. This leaves sometime between now and December this year, or, on the other hand, June/July next year as the two possibilities.

But a new register is now being compiled which I understand will be published on October 15th. And though in theory the election could be fought on the old register, it would be very difficult to justify this with a new one so nearly ready. Therefore I conclude that if the election is to take place this year, it must be not earlier than 2 or 3 weeks after the publication of the Register – say the end of the first week in November. This, or possibly a week later, seems to me also the latest sensible date this year if we are to avoid the fog and frosts of winter.

31 'Political Strategy'. Paper sent by HG on 18 August to the same six Ministers. Above, p. 136.

If this reasoning is accepted, the two alternatives are, early November 1949 or – say – late June 1950.

If, as I feel is absolutely essential, we devalue within the next month, then I should expect that by November the following consequences would have emerged:

(1) The drain on our gold reserve would have stopped – because of purchases of sterling by those waiting for devaluation.

(2) The influence of higher import prices for dollar products would not yet have greatly influenced the cost of living.

(3) Additional export orders would have been placed – though for the most part not yet fulfilled. The commercial influence of devaluation (i.e. on the dollar revenue from our exports), whether favourable or unfavourable, would not have become noticeable.

(4) We can be fairly certain that there will be, as now, little or no unemployment.

There is, of course, a possibility that through lack of 'confidence' people will still not buy sterling and that our gold reserves will still be falling. We shall be in a much better position to judge this if devaluation takes place at the end of August instead of later in September – and this is another argument for the earlier devaluation date which is not to be despised. But in my opinion it is far more likely as I have said that by November the immediate dollar crisis will have been overcome though of course the long-term dollar problem will still be with us.

What will the situation be in June 1950? Here, of course, we are very much in the field of conjecture. For this reason alone we necessarily take a bigger risk in waiting. And, to my mind, that means that unless we have good reasons to expect a *definite improvement*, it would be wiser to choose the earlier date.

It is certainly possible that by next June the dollar situation will be a good deal better. Financially there will probably be no great change: any return of 'capital' should long before have taken place. But if devaluation provides a good stimulus to dollar exports and dollar saving in the sterling area, then the dollar trade balance should look much healthier.

But precisely to the extent that this is so, it means that there will be greater shortages in the home market. What we might have consumed at home will be exported instead. This is one reason why the inflationary pressure will be so much greater. The other is of course the higher price for imports. We must assume, I think, that by June the cost of living will have risen by at least the four points expected. And there is the very real possibility that unless the wage stabilisation policy is abandoned we may have some industrial disputes at this time.

If on the other hand the effects of devaluation on our dollar position are less favourable, we may find ourselves by next June in a very difficult position indeed – facing the possibility of further cuts in raw material imports from dollar areas, if indeed we have not already had to make them. It is true that in such circumstances the shortage of some articles at home may even be less acute, because we have not been able to export so much. But against this there is the far more serious threat to employment arising from raw material shortages – a threat which might by then have materialised in contrast with November of this year when we can be virtually certain of full employment.

On this reasoning the case for an earlier election is decidedly the stronger. There remains however one possibility – that the outcome of the Washington talks is so favourable that we can confidently expect that [*sic*] by next June not merely to have gone a long way to solving our dollar problem, but to have done so without the shortages and higher prices at home which seem likely. It is difficult to express this possibility more precisely. But it means that the U.S.A. and Canada would have to take all those steps which we shall be suggesting to them (1) to reduce the prices of the things we must buy from them and (2) to expand the demand in their territories for our products without our prices being materially reduced.

Judging by current reports the prospect of anything of the kind happening is rather remote. But while, for this reason, I am still inclined myself to go for an autumn election, the decision should clearly not be taken until nearly the end of September, by which time the Foreign Secretary and Chancellor will have a clearer idea of the possibilities of U.S. aid. If by any mischance it seems then that devaluation has not had satisfactory short-term results, so that the immediate crisis is *not* overcome, I should in any case be in favour of postponement. For I feel pretty sure that an election in a crisis atmosphere would go heavily against us.

If the prospect of substantial U.S. aid then is really bright – without of course our having to pay a heavy price – then also the case for postponement is strong.

But if devaluation is successful in the short run and the prospect of U.S. aid is not too good – which seems to me far more likely – then I believe we should not risk waiting till next year, but take our chance while we can and plump for November.

Incidentally, if we win, we shall have greatly strengthened our position for negotiating with the Americans. Until we win, I cannot help feeling that the Foreign Secretary and the Chancellor are bound to be greatly handicapped by the political uncertainty at home – a weakness which our opponents both here and abroad are not slow to exploit.

The Foreign Secretary has suggested, I believe, that we ought to go to the country as 'the government which has weathered the storm'. It is an attractive idea. But let us be reasonably sure that if we pin ourselves down to next June, we *shall* have weathered the storm by then and not missed a convenient lull which seems highly probable this November!

(sgd.) H.G.

18th August, 1949.

Diary: Wednesday, 26 October 1949

It is now over a month since devaluation and it is interesting to look back on the political and economic developments since then. Most people would say that things have not gone too well. We have produced our economy cuts and they have had a bad reception. The gold drain has certainly been stopped but the building up of reserves has been very slow. There is to be no Election until next year.

Nevertheless, I do not think there is a great deal wrong with the economic policies and the Economists for the most part are on our side. The real difficulties have been due primarily to the absence of the Chancellor for virtually two months – the middle of July to the middle of September; the absence of the Foreign Secretary for nearly three months – the middle of July to the first half of October; the uncertainty about the General Election date which was only settled about a fortnight ago and the unavoidable difference of opinion among Ministers about the political and economic consequences of the various cuts proposed. By far the most important of these has really been the uncertainty about the Election. Until that was resolved it was impossible for Ministers to consider making cuts at all seriously. There had been little time since then. Because there was little time there had to be a delay in making the announcement. The incidence of delay enabled the press to build up an impression that there were to be tremendously severe cuts. It is quite possible that it was deliberate policy on the part of the Opposition press because this was the way to make the whole plan appear a flop.[32]

The Election decision was taken immediately after the Foreign Secretary's return by the full Cabinet. We happened to be waiting outside for another item on the agenda. They took about an hour, and I was told that

32 Thirty years later the doyen of political correspondents, James Margach, wrote that he had 'never known the Press so consistently and irresponsibly political, slanted and prejudiced' as at this time: *The Abuse of Power* (W.H. Allen, 1978), p. 86.

only three Ministers – Cripps, Bevan and Harold Wilson – spoke in favour of the early Election. The fact remains however that all the Production Ministers were in favour of such an Election and I am more than ever convinced that the P.M. made a great mistake by postponing it.[33] I suspect that many other Members of the Cabinet will come to think this as the weeks and months go on.

We had a very large series of meetings of the Economic Policy Committee to settle the economic cuts. John Strachey and I were present at almost all of these; Plowden having suggested to the Chancellor that my assistance might be useful to him. We began by discussing what the scale of the economies would be. The Chancellor insisted on nearly £300 million and made it pretty clear that it would be a resignation issue for him if it were not accepted.[34] It was accepted though there was a good deal of rather silly sniping from various quarters. The Minister of Health in particular launched forth in a diatribe and [was] backed, as I thought rather dishonestly, by Hugh Dalton.

The next crisis came on the detail of the cuts, the Minister of Health making it quite clear that he would have no interference with the Health Service. Eventually there was a compromise here which meant dropping £20 million but bringing in £10 million. Most of the £20 million was fortunately made up from some extra administrative economies which came in later.[35]

The P.M. has been very nervous throughout the whole of this business, and in a curious way I think this must have got into his statement which was so badly received. Still on the whole, considering all the difficulties of getting people to take action in advance and the inevitable vested interests I do not think the result too bad.

One of the interesting features has been the violently critical reaction of our own middle-class friends. Hyndley and Fergusson both think we have done very badly, but on cross-examination this really boils down to nothing more than a kind of emotional reaction. They did not really have much to recommend and they had to admit that 'bringing the crisis home

33 Attlee dismissed the production Ministers as 'all the intellectuals'. Cripps and Bevan had favoured a 1949 election ever since July, as they repeated, half backed by Wilson, at the Cabinet on 13 October: Dalton diary, 19.7.49, end September, early October, 5 and 13 October 1949; also *HG*, pp. 206–7.
34 See Dalton diary, 11.10.49; Donoughue & Jones (1973), p. 447 (their figure of £700 million proposed cuts is a printer's error).
35 'I take H.G. back with me afterwards. He is now very frightened of "inflationary pressure" . . . If this morning's clash came to a break, he would be with S.C. against A.B. and so he thinks would the country, and most of the Party . . . he finds A.B. very difficult': Dalton diary, 12.10.49, more fully in *HG*, p. 205 – where the striking parallels with the 1951 Budget clash are emphasised.

to the people' did not necessarily have the appropriate effect on production. I do not believe this middle-class reaction at all typical throughout the country, and I doubt if we have lost much ground as a result, despite the terrific onslaught on the part of the press. Even papers like the *Mirror*, friendly to Labour, have been critical because they have failed to get any of the sensations which they love. How I detest them!

I had a rather pleasant two day trip in North Wales. I stayed with Lord Aberconway to visit the hydro-electric schemes. He is President of the Royal Horticultural Society and has one of the most beautiful gardens in Europe. Clough Williams-Ellis, John Strachey's brother-in-law, was also staying there and provided good companionship.[36]

We have at last settled the Coal Board appointments, and what a time it has taken and how much trouble it has caused! Oddly enough it is a comeback to five part timers as I originally intended. In the middle, owing to a row about the Miners' Welfare Commission and the unwillingness of Vickers to take on the Chairmanship, I had tried for another full time Labour member. I offered the job to two of the best N.U.M. officials – Bayliss of Nottingham and Ted Jones from North Wales and both refused largely, I think, on personal grounds.[37] Ted Jones was all set to accept but his wife almost had hysterics at the prospect of leaving North Wales and moving so far up in the economic and social scale that he decided that he could not do it. How few people would expect this sort of thing to happen. I also nearly lost Heyworth and had to bring every conceivable pressure to bear on him to get him to stick to what he had originally promised.[38] However, now it is done and I think the[y] are not a bad lot. It is something to have overcome the objections of the T.U.C. and N.U.M. What a lot of difference is made by taking people into your confidence, as I eventually did with Tewson, Deakin*, Lawson and Bowman.[39]

36 He was a prominent architect, later knighted, who was Vice-President of the Institute of Landscape Architects and of the Council for the Preservation of Rural Wales, the first chairman of a New Town corporation (Stevenage), and designed and built the model resort at Portmeirion. Lord Aberconway, once P.P.S. to Lloyd George, had been a Liberal M.P. 1906–22.

37 Alderman William Bayliss, President of the area N.U.M. and chairman of the county council, joined the National Coal Board in 1952. Ted Jones, the North Wales leader, was Vice-President of the N.U.M. when he retired in 1960.

38 He became one of the five part-time members whose appointments had been announced the day before this entry.

39 Arthur Deakin was general secretary of the Transport Workers; 'Lawson' should probably read 'Lawther'.

Monday, 21 November 1949

So far it has been a fairly quiet month for me. The pressure of work has very greatly diminished during the past two years, partly because the petrol rationing causes so much less trouble owing – as I think I can fairly claim – to sensible administration, combined with judicious but very small improvements which have been made from time to time. For the rest, the main help has been from the weather which has given us adequate stocks of coal and enabled the N.C.B. to export more than seemed possible, with financial benefits to itself and the country.

The Debate on the annual report of the N.C.B. has I suppose been the chief event for me. I made a rather plodding, extensive kind of speech though even so I had to leave out a lot of what I had intended to say. The Tories played their cards very badly and put down an amendment. This made the Debate more of a Party issue and also involved them in continual criticism of the National Coal Board. If they had been wise they would not have put down an amendment but fiercely attacked the Government for failing to produce the men and for carrying out social service schemes which increased absenteeism. Alf Robens, my Parliamentary Secretary, made his best speech in winding up. The combination of the remainder of my notes plus some advice on the substance of the argument, with his own admirable, pugnacious parliamentary style was most effective.

The Debate also brought out I think the fundamental dilemma which necessarily arises about public corporations. [Al]though the Minister is not responsible for details he must carry general responsibility. Therefore he is liable to attack; because he is liable to attack he must defend himself; because he must defend himself the Debate just cannot be carried on in an atmosphere of complete impartiality. The general view was that we had done pretty well. We even got a moderately favourable press from the Liberal papers.

The Production Ministers had a dinner party for a Senator McCarran who is apparently the Chairman of the Congressional Committee on Marshall Aid.[40] He was a typical U.S. politician type; extreme right wing, Republican [sic], Irish and a bit of a rascal. Nye Bevan was an immense

40 Pat McCarran, Democratic Senator from Nevada 1933–54, was chairman of the Judiciary Committee and of the Appropriations sub-committee dealing with foreign aid. He was to become Senator Joe McCarthy's leading Democratic ally in anti-Communist demagogy, and the main author of a restrictive and discriminatory immigration law.

success with him and not because he said nice things. He was extremely rude about Americans but the Senator lapped it up because of the way it was done. There is no doubt that Nye is really a natural witty and amusing conversation[al]ist. If his speeches are brilliant they are not the brilliance of carefully prepared, painstaking research, but something much more spontaneous. The remarks which he is famous for in public are equally made in private, as I have often heard at Cabinet meetings and similar occasions.

I think he is also a more profound thinker than he is sometimes given credit for. The other evening after a Group Dinner we drifted into a discussion about religion and philosophy. In this Nye started attacking religion, not as one might have expected on Marxist grounds, but far more on rationalist grounds – very sympathetic to me. It was a little embarrassing because of the Chancellor's religious views, but did reveal I think that Nye had really read and thought about these matters fairly deeply. I said to him afterwards, 'The other day you called me an "arid intellectual", and I wrote you off as a hopeless nineteenth century mystic but I am glad to welcome you back into the eighteenth century fold after your performance tonight.'

It is refreshing to find that one's colleagues can talk about these subjects in this way. We are all so busy as Ministers we tend to get into a terrible rut and talk shop. John Strachey said he had just finished reading Toynbee's great six volume history.[41] I am really positively ashamed, amongst these friends, not to have read anything worth reading for such a long time.

Friday, 27 January 1950

Electricity Strike

In the middle of last summer Citrine warned me that there might be trouble at some of the Power Stations. Indeed, this was not really his first warning. Over a year ago the possibility had been mentioned by him and we had gone so far as to seek the authority of the Cabinet for telling him that he would have full backing from the Government in resisting un-official strikes. However, in July the thing looked much nearer and we began to expect that we should have to put troops in. The strikers

41 *A Study of History*, by Arnold Toynbee: Royal Inst. of International Affairs, 1935 and 1939.

however thought better of it (no doubt because of the time of year) and the trouble blew over.

However, last December it started up again, and early in the month on a warning from Citrine I asked for a meeting of the Emergency Committee and got authority to put the troops in immediately if necessary. Again the trouble blew over and then ten days later, on a Monday morning – this time without warning – the strike began at four London Power Stations. We put the troops in at once and this made a favourable impression on the public. Unfortunately, however, it proved impossible to get the Stations to anything like full capacity owing to the inexperience of the troops and the shortage of people to train them.

Meanwhile, various negotiations with the Unions took place – the Unions acting as a kind of liaison between the B.E.A. and the strikers, and endeavouring to get them to go back. The position in the industry is complicated by the fact that the E.T.U. – one of the leading Unions – is Communist controlled, and although it denounced the strikers officially, we are perfectly certain the unofficial elements are largely guided and controlled by the Communists as well.[42]

I saw a great deal of Citrine during the strike and was much impressed by his determination and firmness. As things developed it became clear that there was a fundamental difference of view between the B.E.A. and ourselves on the one hand and the Ministry of Labour on the other. The latter were concerned almost wholly with ending the strike; whereas we were concerned with smashing the strikers. I wrote a long minute to the P.M. concerning this issue and other matters, but although some precautionary measures have now been taken, the fundamental issue is still unresolved. It is possible that further trouble will develop within the next week or so. Preparations are again being made to get the troops ready and it is hoped that the handling of the causes of the dispute by the Unions and the B.E.A. will this time prevent the strike from actually breaking out. But it is quite possible that the C.P. would not mind in the least landing this sort of thing on us just before the Election.

When the Election is over the Government ought really to face up to the issue of Power Station strikes, and decide whether they can afford to treat them as ordinary industrial disputes. In my view they cannot.

Rows with the U.S.A.

We are involved in two major rows. The first is over what is called the dual system of the prices of coal, and the second is over oil. The Americans are being extremely tiresome over both; particularly the former. So far,

42 He was probably right, though Citrine was not so sure.

however, we have stood reasonably firm. The dual-price row is an illustration of the way in which muddle-headed theorists in America combine with self-interested Continental consumers to try and impose a condition on us which is directly contrary to our national interest.[43] The latter is a different kettle of fish. This is just the vested interests of the U.S. Oil Companies resisting like hell the policy of H.M.G., which is to save dollars by substituting sterling for dollar oil. You could hardly find a clearer illustration of the dilemma of American policy to grant E.C. Aid [Marshall Aid] in order to help us overcome the dollar crisis; but to resist like anything our efforts to do so if these involve displacing American exporters from overseas markets.

Jim Bowman has become Chairman of the new Northumberland and Cumberland Division of the Coal Board. The incident was a curious one. Apparently Street was speaking to him in the autumn at some function or other about who was to be the Chairman of this new Board. Jim Bowman said, 'Why do you not ask one of our people?' To which Street replied, 'Well, you people never accept these jobs'. Of course, he had in mind the refusals to appointments to the N.C.B. Jim Bowman then said, 'Well, I am not in that position anyhow.' And with that, Street asked if he was serious. Jim Bowman said, 'Certainly, if you will make me an offer I shall be glad to consider it'. Street and Hyndley then asked my advice, and said that they did not think they could very well refrain from offering him the job. From their point of view he would be first-class. Neither of them thought he was serious. Neither did I, and I simply agreed that they should do so. Subsequently, I heard that he had asked for a ten years contract which was more than anybody else had got, and the N.C.B. proposed to turn this down. This seemed to me to confirm the view I held that he had not been serious and was trying to get out of it. However, to my astonishment, just after Christmas I heard that he had accepted a five years appointment. I naturally view this with mixed feelings. It will be a very interesting experience to see how this capable and popular leader manages to retain his hold on the men when he is on the employers' side, and indeed, is the chief employer. I have little doubt that he will make a good job of it.

On the other hand, his departure leaves the position inside the N.U.M. difficult. It seems probable that Ernest Jones of Yorkshire will get the Vice-Presidency. He, although very nice and honest and a strong Labour supporter, has not got the force or intelligence of Jim Bowman. The

43 The government encouraged the Coal Board to keep the price down at home but would not interfere with its pricing policy abroad, where it sought to maximise profits especially by exports to dollar areas.

only hope is for Sam Watson to take a much larger part in the proceedings. Without him I fear Horner will always get the better of Lawther
and Ernest Jones. It is not certain that Ernest Jones will get the Vice-
Presidency. Machen who is a crypto-Communist is putting up against him
in Yorkshire for the Yorkshire nomination. It will be very unfortunate if
Machen gets this. Indeed, it would be disastrous if he got the Vice-
Presidency.[44]

The Election

We are, of course, becoming increasingly absorbed with this. I was in two
minds about the date. On the one hand I wanted an early Election
because of the danger of troubles arising within the next six months. On
the other hand, I did not want a winter Election. On balance I am glad it
has come. It is quite likely, however, that the P.M. only finally decided on
it because the Chancellor just refused to have another Budget before it.
That, anyway, is the gossip.[45] There is a wide difference of opinion about
the outcome. Most of my colleagues seem to be very confident, and
expect us to have a majority of 70 to 100. I am not so sanguine. I fear that
the Tories will get a lot of Liberal votes and that this, together with
redistribution, and some inevitable swing over will make the contest very
even. It is impossible not to be impressed by the results of the Australian
and New Zealand Elections which went against the Government of the
day despite unprecedented prosperity; largely because of a desire for
change and grumbling about controls. Making forecasts is a silly business,
but I shall be glad if we get a majority of over 50 and I think it more likely
that it will be less than that. One other factor cannot be ignored. The
Government interferes so much in people's lives these days that the swing
of the pendulum is likely to be far greater than ever before. This may lead
to a surprise. Only a very small proportion of votes have to change over to
make such a big difference in the numbers of seats.

New Year's Eve Party

We gave a party with the Brooks, mostly to local Hampstead friends,
many of them in the Government. It was an enormous success. I missed
the highlight of the evening when Eva Robens, after drinking in the New

44 Ernest Jones became N.U.M. Vice-President, and President in 1954. Alwyn
   Machen became President of the Yorkshire miners, and in 1960 of the
   N.U.M., but died soon afterwards.
45 Apparently it was correct: Donoughue & Jones (1973), p. 449.

Year and getting more and more restive because of what she regarded as the phlegmatic behaviour of those present, looked hard at Harold Wilson and said, 'You come from North of the Trent, don't you? Surely, you know how to behave!' And then proceeded to fling her arms around him and kiss him passionately, to his very great embarrassment. As he had previously been giving a lecture on why the ladies could not obtain nylons – which was full of statistics but all very sober – this incident gave great pleasure.

Another Party

Another party which was, alas, far from gay was given by the Chancellor and Lady Cripps to the Production Ministers and their wives. There was no drink except sherry and apple juice. The meal was pretty foul and conversation, not surprisingly, drab and common place. I saw John and Celia Strachey the next day and they were both thoroughly depressed by it and both wished it had not taken place. There was no depression in the party politically. It was just the atmosphere of austerity and prudery which affected everybody. Lady Cripps was the originator of most of this, as at our Group dinners with Stafford things are much more lively.

At the Dinner-Party the only lively part was when somebody suggested that we should all make a guess at the result of the Election. So everyone wrote down the figure of the absolute majority or minority which the Labour Party in their view would have in the General Election. We each then put a shilling in the pool. Stafford collected the money and it was agreed that it should be paid to whoever guessed closest. After all this had been done of course we all started going round asking what guesses had been made. So the Chancellor read them out. It soon appeared that nearly everybody had assumed a majority for Labour of 70 or above, the only exceptions being Celia Strachey with 40; myself at 30 and Douglas who reckoned we should lose by 30. When my guess was read out Nye said, 'I would rather not be in power at all'. I said, 'That may well be, but I think you are all too optimistic'.

Wednesday, 1 February 1950

Australian Petrol

Ever since the defeat of the Labour Government in Australia in the Elections last December we have been worried about what the new Government would do about petrol rationing. They are said to have got in to a considerable extent because of their promise to de-ration. To give any rash promise was, of course, the height of irresponsibility, since they must have known that they could only carry it out at the expense of the sterling-dollar [balance?]. Moreover, the Chifley [Labour] Government has been extremely loyal and firm in the face of continual criticism and attacks.

Shortly after the Election result we arranged for a telegram to be sent to Menzies*, the new P.M., drawing his attention to the fact that dollar expenditure was involved and asking him to do nothing without consulting us. There then followed various rumours that they were going to de-ration at once, which however proved not to be the case. Instead, there were exchanges at the Colombo Conference and further telegrams.[16] They have tried to introduce completely specious arguments, while sticking firmly to their view that they must de-ration. Apparently any other course would split the Government [a coalition] wide open. We even offered them a Commonwealth Conference on the whole question of oil consumption. Even this they turned down.

I expect the news to break early next week and we have prepared what I regard as a rather masterly statement which appears to be extremely courteous and polite and high minded, but in fact thoroughly blackens the Australian Government as they deserve to be blackened.

So far, the Tories here have been very cautious about petrol – though we may have some trouble before the Election is over.

On the assumption that we get in, various Ministers are busy with the absorbing sport of Government building. There seems to be a general impression that I shall move from the Ministry of Fuel, and flattering friends have suggested a number of alternatives, in particular, the Board of Trade and the Ministry of Health. Personally I would not be in the least surprised if, with his well known antipathy to making changes, the P.M. were to confine them to the minimum and I were to find myself back here again. It would have the advantage of life being considerably easier than if I had to start and learn a new job. DF[Fergusson] however, thinks this would be very bad for my career and wants to see me moved to another Economic Department. He said to me the other day, not very seriously, that he would like to see Stafford at the Foreign Office and myself at the Treasury. I told him that this was politically quite out of the question.

It is a pity that HW[Wilson], whom I regard as extremely able and for that reason alone most valuable to the Government, should offend so many people by being so swollen headed. It may, of course, be that I am regarded as a rival of his and therefore my friends are always talking to me

46 Foreign Ministers of the Commonwealth met in Colombo in January 1950 to discuss Far Eastern problems.

in deprecating terms about him. But I do not think this is altogether the case. What is depressing really is not so much that he is swollen headed but that he is such a very impersonal person. You don't feel that really you could ever be close friends with him, or in fact that he would ever have any close friends. The dangers of friendship in politics are so great that when one starts with drawbacks of this kind the prospects are not too good. How different he is, for example, from John Strachey with whom one may often disagree, but who is a real person with interests and feelings rising above politics, and with whom one can have that emotional and intellectual intercourse which is really the stuff of friendship though it does not always go with friendship. And, of course, for me there are others of whom that is much truer, such as Douglas [Jay] and Frank Pakenham, and even to some extent Nye Bevan.

HD[Dalton] had a very private conversation with me two days ago, before leaving for his election tour. He told me that he had been talking to the P.M. about the Government after the Election and had said to him that there was nobody among the top Ministers who could possibly be Chancellor except Stafford [Cripps], and therefore it was essential that Stafford should remain Chancellor, especially as he, HD, could not go back there. To this the P.M. apparently agreed. HD then went on to say to him that going below Stafford there was nobody until you came to the younger Ministers, that is really HW, Douglas and myself. Apparently he then suggested to the P.M. that the work done at present by Stafford would have to be divided up because he simply could not continue to cope with it all himself (which is, indeed, the case; his health will not stand it), and there should be carved out of it some part to be handed over to one of the three just mentioned. He appears to have gone on to tell the P.M. that I was the obvious person to do this, though I was a little surprised to find that the conception which they seem to have in mind was not the foreign finance plus O.E.E.C. but the more traditional work of the Treasury. HD wanted to be sure that if the P.M. offered me such a job I would take it. I explained that I would almost certainly take whatever the P.M. offered me unless there were strong reasons against it. I did not commit myself on the details of this thing. I do not want to be a kind of superior Under-Secretary to the Chancellor, and it is essential that I should retain the right to take any dispute between him and me to the Cabinet. I gathered from HD that the chances of being in the Cabinet itself with such a post would be small. That perhaps would be disappointing but would not matter so much in practice, particularly if one were made a full member of E.P.C. [the Cabinet's Economic Policy Committee] which is really the most important body of all now among the things which I am interested in.

One is naturally interested when these sort of things are talked about, but I am resolved to put them out of my mind completely for the time being. I am by no means so sure of the Election result, though lately the Gallup poll has moved in our favour and we are now above the Tories.

The truth is, I suppose, that one is always in a way glad to leave a Ministry because you leave behind unsolved problems and some skeletons in cupboards and shed a load, and you walk into the other job with a free mind without having to accept, at any rate for a few weeks, the responsibilities for what has been done beforehand. I must say that the prospect of being in the centre of the financial and economic policy does appeal to me. I feel there is quite a lot which could be done if one had the opportunity, and if one were helped by the right people.

I went last night to speak for Elizabeth Pakenham. It was strange in a way to be standing in the Oxford Union speaking after her, with Frank there as well. I had been a little doubtful as to whether I should refer to our long friendship, but while waiting to speak found out that Elizabeth had already referred to it. At the end of my speech I told them that I had been responsible for introducing them to each other, without being aware of the consequences which would follow. Later, Frank said a few words and told them we had shared digs at Oxford and that the moment of introduction had been 3 a.m. when he had been asleep at the New College Ball. Later we went on to the Randolph [Hotel] and they had some food and I drank with them and we gossiped away. [47]

Frank is now more friendly with Morrison than any of the others. He does not like Bevan and was rather horrified when I said that I thought Bevan would almost certainly be Leader of the Party and therefore P.M. sometime. Elizabeth admitted that he had great qualities. She said, 'He has every virtue but Virtue'. They were very sweet and flattering about my speech and one could not help feeling what a pleasure it was to have such friends in the middle of all this political struggle. So far at least there does not seem to be any sign of any strain in our relationship. I shall continue to watch this carefully. It would be nice to think that I had disproved the Thomas Morley saying, 'There are no friends at the top.'[48]

47 Frank Pakenham – who lived in lodgings with HG in their last year as undergraduates – was Labour candidate for Oxford in 1945, and his wife Elizabeth in 1950 when he had become a Minister, and a peer.
48 I have failed to trace this quotation, to which HG referred frequently, attributing it to various authors.

Tuesday, 21 March 1950

It seems a very long time since the last bit of my diary. The General Election has been fought and won, if one can use that term, and I have now been three weeks in a new job. Already dirty coal, petrol rationing and the problems of nationalised Boards are beginning to fade from my mind owing of course to the amount of new material which is being fed into it.

As previously, I found the period of the Election going extremely slowly. When one has to make, say 50 speeches in all, it is impossible not to be bored with the sound of one's own voice long before the end. Indeed, if one were not bored it would only show what an intolerable character one was. This time was no exception and already ten days before the Election I was beginning to feel one might as well vote and get it over. Everything went over very smoothly in South Leeds and the result was certainly quite up to my best expectations.[49]

As to the attitude of the electorate, I had no very definite impressions during the campaign. I cannot say, for example, I could detect any great difference in the attitude of the audience from 1945. Perhaps one might say that on the one side they had acquired a sort of additional confidence in the capacity of Labour to govern, and on the other side had accumulated inevitably a collection of grievances against us for the way some aspects of government had affected them.

One result of the Election has certainly been the increase in the stature of the P.M. He certainly displayed his remarkable political instinct and gifts at their very best. He always found the exact words to counter Churchill, and it is generally agreed that his broadcast was outstanding. When one considers that he normally is thought of as a poor broadcaster and a man with no gift for leadership this is rather extraordinary; though of course it is not the first time in British politics that this has happened. One thinks of Baldwin as a most recent example.[50] And in the House now the increased stature has given him increased confidence so that his performances in the Debates have been considerable improvements on the last Parliament. I would also say that in the Cabinet his position is a great deal strengthened.

On the other hand for the time being the position of the Minister of Health [Bevan] is certainly weakened. There was a general feeling that he had been hopelessly wrong about the Election result and that his own

49 His majority of 15,359 was 5,000 more than in 1945, thanks to higher turnout and favourable redistribution.
50 Stanley Baldwin, Conservative Prime Minister 1923–4, 1924–9, 1935–7.

speeches – particularly the 'vermin' speech – had lost us many votes.[51] He got practically no publicity during the Election, so the limelight was not upon him then. And finally, the result of the Election seemed to suggest that the Morrison policy of going slow and retrenchment – a move to the right rather than to the left – would have been appropriate.

In a different way the position of the Foreign Secretary has also weakened. His broadcast was the worst, and he certainly no longer has the reputation in the country of being a really powerful and successful Foreign Secretary. The Chancellor said to somebody that he thought Bevin and Bevan between them had lost the Election, and for him to go as far as that was pretty remarkable. More so as hitherto he has greatly admired the one and been a close, personal friend of the other.

Taking it all in all, I do not feel the result is so surprising. I had guessed a majority of thirty over all at the Group Dinner-Party and therefore won the 14/- in the pool. I shall not cash the cheque but keep it as a memento.[52]

After all there were 42 seats won by a majority of under 1,000, of which the Tories hold 24 and we 17 and the Liberals 1. If we had won the 24 instead of the Tories – which would have meant perhaps 12,000 votes changing over, not more – we should have a majority of between 50 and 60, quite comfortable. I had in any case been impressed by the fact that the Labour Governments in Australia and New Zealand had been defeated in each case by a very narrow turnover of votes. It may, of course, seem disappointing that when we had an extremely good record we could not get back with an adequate majority. But one must remember that redistribution had a big influence,[53] and in post-war years when the Government intervened so much there were bound to be grievances piling up especially among the lower middle class and middle class who had been offended by our words and [felt?] they had at any rate suffered considerable economic disadvantages by our actions.

I do not myself take too gloomy a view of the future. I fancy people vote at an Election just as much 'against' as 'for'. I mean that they are moved perhaps more by opposition than they are by positive enthusiasm. It may well be that we shall lose the next election, though this is by no means certain if we play our cards right, but if we were to I should expect to get

51 On 4 July 1948 Bevan had said of the Tory party, 'So far as I am concerned they are lower than vermin': Foot (1973), p. 238. The phrase became a middle-class rallying cry. Attlee too thought Bevan was Labour's worst vote-loser: Dalton's diary, 27.2.50.
52 It is preserved in the Diary.
53 Estimated to account for between a half and a quarter of Labour's drop of 79 seats between 1945 and 1950: H.G. Nicholas, *The British General Election of 1950* (Macmillan, 1951), p. 4.

back again in the next Parliament with a fairly decent majority. People only compare your record against other people's and I fancy the Tories would have a fairly difficult time if they got back. However, as I have said, it by no means follows that they will win. If we can avoid giving unnecessary offence and quietly improve the economic position there is a prospect at least that the old Liberal fear and hatred of the Tories may swing them more on our side than at the last election, when they see there is a real possibility of a Tory Government if they do not vote for us.

Some people think there will be another stalemate. I doubt that when the turnover of votes is so very small to make so much difference in the number of seats. But nobody can really tell at this stage.

CHAPTER 4

MINISTER OF STATE
FOR ECONOMIC AFFAIRS

Editor's Note
Diary, 21 March 1950 to 3 November 1950
Documents: No. 6 Paris dinner at start of European Payments Union
negotiations, 25 March 1950
No. 7 HG's memorandum on his Washington visit,
8–12 October 1950

[As Cripps' understudy, Gaitskell was concerned with several disparate subjects, of which three were crucial: the argument with Aneurin Bevan over the cost of the new National Health Service; the international talks about forming a European Payments Union; and the negotiations with the United States about financing rearmament.

When the Health Service began in July 1948, no one could predict its cost: a large supplementary estimate was needed to cover unexpected expenditure in February 1949, and a much bigger one a year later. The first was generally thought excusable, the second much less so. The Cabinet had already authorised charging for prescriptions if necessary, and the legislation was piloted through the House by Bevan himself on 9 December 1949. Cripps' budget speech in March 1950 insisted that no more supplementaries could be tolerated; and while charges were not yet to be imposed, a weekly committee under the Prime Minister was set up, with Gaitskell as the Treasury spokesman, to keep a regular watch on health service expenditure and ensure that it did not exceed the (generous) ceiling laid down.

Cripps also gave his Minister of State full responsibility for overseas finance, with the difficult task – among others – of trying to persuade other countries to adopt the same economic priorities as Britain. For with no international commitment to full employment, Gaitskell feared to let the British economy become exposed to strong deflationary pressures from abroad. World trade in 1950 was still largely conducted under bilateral agreements setting quantitative limits on imports from one country to another, which gave both the means and the incentive for manipulation by governments. American foreign economic policy concentrated on removing quantitative restrictions, forbidding discrimination, and working towards convertibility of currencies. Few countries would benefit as much as Britain if total trade could be expanded by a multilateral payments scheme, allowing surpluses with some neighbours to be offset against deficits with others so that only the net balance with the whole group had to be settled.

Britain, however, jealously protected her reserves against any consumption of inessential dollar goods by her own people, and feared to throw them open to finance luxury imports into the rich creditor countries against whose goods she would no longer be allowed to discriminate. Gaitskell thought it essential to protect her reserves of gold and foreign currency, which were dangerously low; for those five disastrous weeks of convertibility in 1947 had shown how quickly they might vanish. On first moving to the Treasury, Gaitskell was therefore extremely suspicious of all these plans for liberalising trade. Yet within two months he was working closely with the Americans, and had become one of the chief architects of the new system. Several factors changed his mind: above all he discovered that the United States Administration was divided against itself, with the New Dealers entirely willing to introduce safeguards to guard against the risks that Britain feared. The talks therefore undermined his deep suspicion of the Americans on economic policy by showing him that some of them could be invaluable allies for a Labour Britain. Undoubtedly this helps to explain his attitude to the rearmament gamble a few months later.

The pressure for rearmament began that summer. Already, Western minds were haunted by the Communists' rapid elimination of all their rivals in Eastern Europe; Socialists above all were sensitive to the Prague putsch, the threats against Yugoslavia and the Berlin blockade. In Washington, a major analysis by the National Security Council had recently anticipated a world-wide Soviet offensive over the next few years. A few weeks later came the Korean war, the first Communist military invasion of a neighbouring country since 1945. Everyone, in power or out, knew what had followed the indifference of governments in the 1930s to acts of aggression in remote places. Within four days President Truman, with almost unanimous approval in Britain, had decided to intervene.

Some people feared a Soviet march to the Channel. Others, who thought that idea alarmist, still took very seriously the risk of another Communist satellite army attacking a neighbour: Yugoslavia, Scandinavia, West Germany or Iran were identified as possible targets (not only by American intelligence sources, but also by Aneurin Bevan, Richard Crossman and the Yugoslav government). So, on 26 July 1950, the Americans offered to contribute to strengthening Western Europe's defences, provided the allies helped themselves also. Britain, apart from her wartime record, had the most stable political system and the most flourishing economy; as the expected leader, she was the key to the others' response.

The promised American assistance did not materialise, and indeed the United States impeded the European rearmament for which it was pressing by competing for supplies with its allies, creating shortages and sending raw material prices soaring. British politicians, serving in a government with a parliamentary majority which could fulfil any commitment it made, never fully understood that no American Administration was in the same position; so that offers of assistance, however genuinely meant, could never be more than pious hopes. Gaitskell, whose previous suspicions of American economic policy had been allayed by the currency negotiations in the spring, discovered these new difficulties in Washington in October 1950. He began a prolonged, and eventually fairly successful, attempt to persuade the Americans of the need to assess how equitably the financial burden was being shared between the allies. Before that occurred, however, rearmament and its consequences had transformed the British economy, British politics, and Gaitskell's own career.]

Diary, 21 March 1950 continued

I have been moved to the Treasury from the Ministry of Fuel & Power. When the P.M. asked me to go and help Stafford [Cripps] he said, 'There is one snag about it. I am afraid you will have to accept a cut in salary. A Minister of State only gets three thousand.' I was a bit taken aback and said, 'Well, I naturally don't welcome that, but it does not worry me much. The only thing is the question of status. Will not that be rather awkward – will not everybody say I have been demoted?' 'Oh!' he said, 'That is certainly not the case and I will make it quite clear in the announcement.' So I went back to the Ministry of Fuel and told Alf Robens and Donald [Fergusson] what was happening, and also that Arthur Woodburn was going to succeed me at Fuel & Power. I then went home to bed with flu. The next morning, to my surprise, I read in the papers that my successor at Fuel & Power was not Arthur Woodburn but Philip Noel-Baker* and that I was after all to receive my full five thousand a year. Later I discovered from the Treasury that it was a pure mistake on the P.M.'s part and that he had got muddled up. They had briefed him correctly and there never had been any question of my salary being cut. I was amused to hear this as I had thought the P.M. had tried it as a deliberate test of my loyalty – rather like the King and the good prince in the fairy stories.

Some of the appointments have given rise to surprise. Patrick Gordon Walker* in the Cabinet as Secretary of State for Commonwealth Relations gets a big jump. But I am told that he has really run that office for some time and Elizabeth Pakenham pointed out to me that he was personally very well in with the P.M., Ernie [Bevin], Morrison and Stafford. They are close friends and warmly welcome his appointment, and I must say on the whole, so do I. I should have been jealous if I had not an extremely interesting job and one with considerable possibilities.[1]

1 Gordon Walker had been Morrison's P.P.S., and from 1947 Noel-Baker's Parliamentary Secretary at Commonwealth Relations.

It is bad luck on John [Strachey] being sent to the War Office. I feel extremely sorry for him because he has been pursued by the most loathsome newspaper campaign.[2] Although he appears to stand it very well I know he really hates it and so does Celia who spoke most passionately on the telephone to me about the whole thing. John is particularly disappointed that he is not in on the economic side, but it is fair to say that he has always been interested in defence and would like to have been Minister of Defence. To console him I pointed out that he could hardly be that without at first being a Service Minister, so perhaps the job was not such a bad one.

The worst appointment of all unquestionably is the sending back of Bevan to the Ministry of Health. He certainly wanted to move and in my view it was imperative from the point of view of finance that he should be moved. Apparently under the influence of Bevin the P.M. decided he must go back to clear up the mess he created.[3] It only means the mess will not be cleared up. Moreover his own position was much weakened immediately after the Election; though as I foreshadowed it has already greatly increased as a result of two speeches in the House. He is so much the best debater; so much the most effective speaker on the Front bench, indeed in the House, that he can always raise his prestige in the House by a performance of this kind. It is a great mistake and one which may cost us very heavily that they sent him back to Health. How much better it would have been if he had gone to the Colonies where he would have been out of the public eye at home and Jim Griffiths had gone to Health.[4]

We have already had a foretaste of the difficulties from the Supplementary Health Estimates. I begged Stafford to insist on two things. First, Treasury control should be established as effectively as it is over other Government expenditure and secondly there should be a definite limit placed on the total National Health Service expenditure. I would have liked this to have been below next year's estimates, so that we should be quietly committed up to the hilt to finding the rest of the money, so far as economies would not cover it, by making charges of some kind.

We had a very energetic 48 hours trying to get the Chancellor, and then one or two Ministers, to back this. As usual, there was a policy compromise because of the threat of Bevan's resignation and the unwilling-

2 As Minister of Food.
3 Dalton (1962), p. 350, attributes this advice to Morrison. (In the original diary there is a blank after the next sentence, apparently leaving space for a following one which had been omitted – perhaps because it was inaudible.)
4 Griffiths had become Colonial Secretary – a post which Bevan himself wanted.

ness of the Cabinet to accept the principle of charging just yet. Of course it was a very difficult problem for the Chancellor not only because of his old friendship with Bevan but also because he had to defend himself for allowing the supplementary estimate this year of £90 millions for Health, and he could only do this by explaining that the money was justified. It was therefore difficult for him, having made this defence, suddenly to switch round and impose cuts.

Personally, I think politically if we could have come out with a sharp statement indicating that there were to be cuts it would have done us a lot of good. However, one cannot altogether complain. He did insist on a limit and on the Treasury control, and although not as clearly worded as I should have liked, most of the papers picked this out pretty well from his speech.[5]

As for my own job, it is of course a big difference to come to the Treasury not as a number one Minister. On the other hand the problems are fascinating and of enormous importance. I had expected that we should at once agree on a certain field for me so that I could take the burden off Stafford. He was opposed to this to start with and said that he wished me to alternate for him and therefore I should be in on everything. This has its points because it gives me an opportunity of exercising influence over a very wide field and also means that I learn a good deal about the Treasury; but it does not ease Stafford's burden and it really will not last for long. The officials are determined, I am glad to say, to get a demarcation and are putting up proposals to the Chancellor. I should take the overseas finance and the planners. That will certainly be quite enough and of absorbing interest.

We are certainly in for some difficult times in the field of overseas finance where the Americans seem to me to be getting on very wrong lines. Personally, I am sure that we shall have to have a complete showdown with them on their whole approach to the world's economic problems. But it is a little awkward at the moment, until I am given special responsibilities in this sphere, for me to press very much my point of view. It is also awkward at the Cabinet or E.P.C. (on which I am a full

5 Cripps had defended this huge supplementary in the House on 14 March, although he had warned a year earlier that the practice must not be repeated, and the circumstances of the repetition indicated serious administrative laxity. Charges had been threatened by Cripps in April 1949, and authorised by Bevan's own Act in December; now they were again postponed. But to impose the expenditure ceiling, the Prime Minister became chairman of a weekly Cabinet committee on health service finance – treating Bevan, in his own department, like Shinwell after the fuel crisis. See below, pp. 192–3 on the committee; and *HG*, pp. 211–13, on the crisis and the background.

member) without a sphere of responsibility because I cannot very well contradict the Chancellor and there is obviously no point in repeating what he says. So I remain too silent for my liking.

I went to see the King just after my appointment. I do not find him very easy to talk to. He does not seem to me very intelligent or very interested in economic problems. He always gives me the impression that he is unquestionably Tory in his politics. He made some rather feeble remarks about the quality of coal and what he thought were the causes of it. I never quite know at these functions whether one is supposed to take the lead in the conversation or not. I have hitherto been rather diffident about this but perhaps it is a mistake. He told me that he liked Patrick [Gordon Walker] who had been to see him just before me. But then he has all sorts of exciting things to talk about, such as Kashmir,[6] Seretse[7] and matters of that kind.

Friday, 26 May 1950

International Conferences

I have had my first experience of representing Britain at International Conferences. I went to Paris instead of the Chancellor for the meeting of the Council of O.E.E.C. [the Organisation for European Economic Cooperation] in March, and to Brussels in April for the meeting of the Western European Union.

The two most striking characteristics of these Conferences at the ministerial level seem to me,

(a) the extraordinary slowness of the procedure, partly on account of the fact that everything has to be translated.

(b) the great care taken to avoid anything in the nature of a row or even an argument developing. As soon as anything contentious appears it is referred to official levels where presumably people can speak more plainly.

6 The frontier province of Kashmir was disputed between the newly independent states of India and Pakistan.
7 (Sir) Seretse Khama, chief of the Bamangwato tribe, married an Englishwoman in 1948; the rights of his wife and children were contested in Bechuanaland, and South African intervention was feared in London. He was excluded from the chieftainship for five years by the Labour government, against Conservative protests, and then permanently by the Conservatives in 1952. He became prime minister of Bechuanaland in 1965, and President of independent Botswana in 1966.

However, in Paris I managed to have an extremely interesting talk with
Harriman and Katz (his chief deputy and the one who really knows all
about it), Stikker, Dutch Foreign Minister and Marjolin, Secretary-
General of O.E.E.C. This was at a dinner party given by Sir Edmund
Hall-Patch who is head of the British Delegation. I have written a long
minute on this.[8]

Very little happened at the meeting of the Council itself. There is a kind
of hierarchy as a result of which either France or Britain seems usually
to speak first, the smaller Powers following on afterwards. My only
important contribution was about the relations of O.E.E.C. to the
Council of Europe in which I explained to them that we in Britain did not
like the idea of Opposition M.P.s cross-examining international officials.
This caused some amusement but went down quite well.

I only had about forty minutes to myself the whole time I was in Paris
and I spent it walking up and down the Rue St Honoré looking at the
shops. There was the usual lovely smell of scent and garlic combined; but
I thought the women less well dressed than one would expect and looking
somehow more English than before the war.

At Brussels things were rather different because the Delegation was
led by Shinwell as Minister of Defence and I was really a kind of Treasury
watch-dog. This proved to be very necessary because his chief officials
made a determined effort to go back on a Defence Committee decision as
soon as we arrived in Brussels, and I had to be very firm indeed. [I] having
won this particular battle, Shinwell was as quiet as a lamb and seemed
quite willing to say at the Conference the various things I wanted him to
say, and which were written down on pieces of paper and passed to him.

At this Conference of course we came right up against the major
problem of how to find the money to finance the defence of Western
Europe, and to this so far there is no proper answer. Part of the trouble is
the deep suspicion naturally existing between the military people and the
finance people. Running across this particular squabble is the issue of
whether or not the United States can be persuaded to pay. The result so
far has been, I am afraid, very limited. There is certainly a good deal of
buck-passing not only between different Governments but also between

8 Printed below. Averell Harriman was the U.S. Special Representative in
  Europe, and Milton Katz (professor of law at Harvard) was his deputy, and
  later successor. They dealt with the Europeans through O.E.E.C. of which the
  French economist Robert Marjolin was secretary-general 1948–55 (and on the
  E.E.C. Commission 1958–67). Hall-Patch, a diplomat and former Treasury
  official, was the British representative 1948–54, also to the I.M.F. and World
  Bank. Dirk Stikker was Dutch Foreign Minister 1948–52, Ambassador to
  London 1952–8, representative to NATO and O.E.E.C. 1958–61; secretary-
  general of NATO 1961–4. On these monetary negotiations leading up to the
  European Payments Union, see *HG*, Ch. 7-iv.

Defence Ministers on the one side and Finance Ministers on the other, with the Foreign Ministers hovering uncertainly in the background.[9]

Document No. 6

Paris dinner on E.P.U., 25.3.50[10]

Harriman, Katz, Stikker and Marjolin came to dinner on Saturday. By arrangement Harriman and Katz came early so that we could talk with them alone first.

After the usual interchange of small talk we got on to the Payments Agreement question – Harriman leaving Katz to put the E.C.A. view. Katz said that he thought the atmosphere of cooperation was much better now than it had been, but made it pretty clear that E.C.A. believed our plan was subtly designed to let us avoid payment! Later on in the evening he said that the experts had worked out what results our plan would have achieved had it been in operation in the last 16 months. They had reached the conclusion that under it we should have been in deficit to Europe to the tune of 120 million (I am not sure if it was dollars or pounds) and nevertheless have been able to draw gold! I said I thought that if they took the latest period of all the opposite might have happened and that it was indeed this possibility which rather worried me about our plan!

However we soon left the details of the problem and came to the principles. I said I thought that there was really no dispute whatever about the desirability of multilateral payments: we were just as keen on that as everyone else. But we were naturally bound to be concerned with even the most remote danger to our gold and dollar reserve. This was still far too low for us to take any risks at all. In these circumstances I questioned the wisdom of bringing into the payments scheme automatic gold points. Was not this really returning to the first year of E.C.A. when off-shore purchases were allowed which they themselves condemned because of the impetus it gave to each country to have a surplus? We were at present in surplus with Europe and under this scheme might well suck up gold and dollars. Was this really desirable? Would it not lead to too much anxiety about their reserves by other countries and therefore act as a brake on liberalisation?

Finally I pointed out that if they took $600 million of the appropriation and put it into the Clearing Union, did they realise that to the extent that countries balanced their payments with each other, this would be sheer

9 He was to revert to the same theme when Chancellor: below, pp. 287, 291.
10 In Diary, dated 27 March 1950; emphasis in original.

waste? That $600 million would not and could not be used to finance any dollar imports for Europe whatever. Had they realised the consequence of this to the balance of payments of the United States with Europe? Katz did not take up this last point, but replied to me in some detail on the question of bringing gold into the scheme. He played down its importance and said that it was in order to bring 'gentle' pressure on debtor countries that eventually, after credits were exhausted, some gold had to be paid. He emphasised that under the scheme creditor countries were also penalised – in that the larger their surplus the less the proportion they could take in gold. (This seems to me by no means clear.)

The discussion also touched on the general question of what debtors should do. I made it plain that we could not accept any obligation to deflate as such.

It was obviously the duty of a debtor to get his balance of payments right, but this could be done in three different ways: devaluation, deflation and restriction of imports. Which of these, or how much of each were used may be left to the debtor – just as at the opposite extreme the choice between the opposite policies should be left to the creditor. Neither Katz nor Harriman seemed to dispute this. Indeed they vigorously disavowed any intention of forcing deflation on anyone. I then asked why it was that they were so keen on the gold movements to which only the vague answer was forthcoming that these were a kind of signal to get the debtor to do something. On the whole I got the distinct impression that they would not object to modification of the scheme which diminished the risk of gold losses. There was, it is true, some talk also about the one-world/two-world business and keeping open competition with dollar goods, but I pointed out that the question of what dollar imports we could [afford] depended on what we could earn and not on what currency system existed, and they dropped the argument.

After dinner the discussion became wider and Stikker, Marjolin and Hall-Patch joined in it. We began on the topic of the relationship of economic integration to the defence of Western Europe against Communism. Harriman and Katz were not quite so much up in the clouds as I had expected. They admitted that there was a good deal of symbolism about this, but based their main argument on the economic advantages. They realised that anything like complete specialisation was out of the question and seemed to have some appreciation of the limits of what could be done. But they undoubtedly held – and Stikker even more so – that liberalisation was right because it made people better off almost automatically.

Marjolin made a very interesting contribution to the discussion. His answer to the question of the connection between economic integration and military defence was on political lines. If there was to be cooperation in the military sphere, there had to be good feeling. This could not exist in the face of acts of economic warfare. What were these acts? His answer was 'discrimination'. There was a general discussion on this to which I shall refer later. But his second point was more original and less controversial. He said he thought it was hopeless to expect a complete Customs Union or any very widespread sacrifice of economic sovereignty on the part of different countries. Nor did he seem to attach much importance to this. More important was common economic and financial policies. If we could have these plus the ending of economic warfare, there was a fair prospect that we would have an economic background adequate to military and political cooperation. His mind therefore was clearly running in the direction of discussions on these subjects in O.E.E.C. To this naturally I gave our blessing. But on 'discrimination' there was something of an argument. I pointed out that we only discriminated to avoid loss of gold and dollars. They all seemed to be a little sceptical about this, partly because they had the impression that even if there was a multilateral payments scheme we should still claim the right to discriminate *unilaterally* against *individual* members. They appeared to raise no objection to our imposing quantitative restrictions unilaterally in face of a serious loss of gold – but they argued with some force that if we desired to stop gold losses, there was no reason for discrimination. I said that it might be a good thing for a creditor to be discriminated against, to which they replied that action of that kind should not be taken without O.E.E.C. having considered the whole problem.

After the others had gone I had some further talk with Marjolin on the discrimination issue. He said that there was very bitter feeling about it, because the countries against whom we discriminated felt isolated and helpless; this would not be so if the restrictions were not discriminating. (Harriman had made a rather similar point earlier when he had complained of the danger to the Italian peasants involved in our threat to stop importing soft fruit.) I pointed out that we discriminated only against gold countries – Belgium, Switzerland and Western Germany – and this was simply because they insisted on putting themselves on a dollar standard. Marjolin admitted the force of this and went so far as to say that we should be justified in telling them that they must come in like the other European countries on a non-dollar basis and therefore discriminate themselves against dollar imports. He seemed to want us to take the initiative on this. But he made the fair point that the less automatic our system, the more we must be prepared for consultation with O.E.E.C.

It was left to Hall-Patch to weigh in with a reminder of the violent issue of dollar viability. There was, he pointed out, little time left either to build up Western Europe, or to solve dollar gap problems. But if we failed to deal with the latter it was difficult to see how we could maintain

European Economic Cooperation. The problem could not be left to us alone to solve. If the Americans had the right to tell us not to discriminate, we must have the right to remind them of their responsibilities in the matter of imports policy. A position in which we were suppliants and they tried to bully, or bribe us into doing things which we did not believe to be sound, or even practicable, was wrong. There must be a much greater chance of equality as between the U.S.A. and Europe.

After a further brief argument about the relative importance of dollar viability and other aims for E.C.A. the Americans then departed. I had a conversation alone with Stikker, which is reported elsewhere. And finally, as I have already mentioned, we talked alone with Marjolin. Apart from the question of discrimination and gold, we also touched on the possibility of U.S. slump. Marjolin said he was sure we must expect a serious U.S. recession within the next 18 months – possibly much sooner. The bankers apparently took the view that the slump had already begun. He was very much afraid that this would lead to the break-up of European cooperation. I said I did not think this was necessarily so. We would certainly wish to maintain a high level of income and employment in the U.K., so that the problem would present itself as another dollar crisis. In these circumstances we should wish to replace dollar supplies wherever we could, and we should be ready to rely more not less on Europe in this respect. But, I said, we cannot do that if Europe is tied to the dollar. He said he was quite clear that when the U.S. recession came Europe would have to abandon the dollar entirely. I said it seemed to me far better to do this in advance.

I would sum up my impressions and tentative conclusions from this interesting talk as follows:

(1) E.C.A. are themselves not so much concerned with getting dollars & gold into the multilateral payments scheme and it should not be difficult to bring home to them the dangers of this. The pressure no doubt comes from the I.M.F. and the U.S. Treasury. But in the battle we shall have to fight with the latter, E.C.A. might become our allies.[11] Nor are the European countries – except Belgium – likely to differ from us greatly on this gold and dollar issue – on principle.

(2) There is however very strong feeling both in E.C.A. and other European countries against discrimination by us though at the same time there is also a clear realisation that we cannot afford to lose much gold.

(3) They seem to suspect – and there is obviously something in it – that our reasons for being pro-discrimination is [sic] not solely our fears of

11 Less than a week earlier he had predicted 'a complete showdown with them [the Americans] on their whole approach to the world's economic problems': above, p. 175.

loss of gold, but also the economic power it gives us vis-à-vis other countries. It is precisely this power to which the others object.

(4) It is worth considering whether we should not be ready to drop the right to discriminate against individual members – if in other respects the payments scheme were changed to suit us. I am inclined to think myself that convertible sterling or extension of Uniscan might be sold to E.C.A. provided we give up discrimination and are less sticky about consultation with O.E.E.C.[12] Of course if *we* want to insert a gold and dollar element that would make it easier still.

(5) The battle with the U.S. Treasury on the part to be played by gold will probably not be settled until we have had 'fundamental' talks – presumably in May.[13] Meanwhile I should personally like to see our working away at a draft Payments Scheme which *would be* [*sic*] (a) acceptable to other European countries – especially France, (b) attractive to E.C.A. because we dropped unilateral discrimination, (c) safer for us because it would reduce the risks of gold payments to negligible proportions. Though much of this is a job for the experts, issues of principle are involved which we must first settle ourselves. I will not explain here why I am against gold payments, but will do so in discussion. But there is no doubt that if we could get agreement on a payments scheme in Europe, it will be very difficult for the U.S. Government to resist in the last resort. They would then be framed as the people who, because of their gold fetish, were actually *wrecking* European Cooperation. If a payments scheme of the kind I have indicated were available, it would help us to win the battle against the U.S. Treasury.

(6) Our present expert discussions on payments must be carried on in the light of these wider considerations and possibilities.

Diary for 26 May 1950 continued

The Budget

This was inevitably not very exciting; granted that we had to have something like an over-all balance we were faced with the alternative of either literally doing nothing at all, or increasing some taxes in order to reduce others. We decided on the latter; put up the petrol tax and reduced income tax. We paid off the private motorists by doubling the standard ration at the same time. This was a move which I had long

12 Uniscan (U.K. and Scandinavia) was a projected monetary union of countries, based on Britain.
13 On 'fundamentals' see below, p. 185.

hoped to make when I was Minister of Fuel. The debate which followed was dull and largely a repetition of the Election speeches; the Opposition sticking fairly firmly to the line that we ought to spend less and therefore criticising our taxation proposals.

I found myself with the rather difficult job of speaking after Churchill and I am afraid disappointed some people by sticking fairly firmly to my speech and not doing much about answering him. One ought always to avoid speaking second in the House if one can because people always like to go out and have tea about then.

The chief criticism of the budget from our own side was that it did nothing for the lower paid wage earner, but the more intelligent ones realised that there was very little we could do without giving away a lot of money to other people. On the whole I think we can say at least this – that while the budget was not vote winning it was not vote losing either. This time too the pre-budget publicity was better organised and false hopes were not raised as they were last year.

Looking ahead, however, the prospect is rather gloomy. We are committed to very heavy expenditure and the yield from some taxes – beer and tobacco – is declining as the pre-war pattern of consumption returns. Concessions have been made on income tax which diminish the yield, while the tendency for wages to increase at the expense of profits, however desirable socially, makes the Chancellor's job more difficult. Unless there is some bigger increase in the rate of saving, which reduces the necessity for such a large surplus, it is difficult to see how taxation can be much, if at all, reduced in the coming years. And on top of all this there is the threat of higher defence expenditure.

We followed up the budget by preparing and circulating a forecast of the national income, investment, saving, taxation, revenue and expenditure for the next two years. I believe this is the first time anything of the kind has happened, and can claim that it was something which I inspired. Its purpose was largely educational and in that it was successful. Nye [Bevan], difficult enough on his own Department, was delighted with it and has really given us quite good support on the general theory of preventing inflation. Without it I do not think we should have got the investment programme through successfully. I hope we shall be able to keep it up-to-date with revised issues perhaps every six months.

Dick Stokes*, the new Minister of Works, who has an amusing and pleasant personality, is unfortunately at the same time pretty much of an inflationist and also a decontroller. I am afraid that his influence in the Ministry of Works will be dangerous, particularly as this is really a key point for the prevention of inflation. We shall probably have little difficulty in squashing him in Committees but I fear his influence on his own officials will do a lot of harm. It is a pity because he is otherwise a definite asset to the Government.

Maurice Webb, the new Minister of Food, who is really not nearly such a nice person is also likely to be very much a decontroller. It was one of John Strachey's qualities that he stood up to his officials and took his own decisions with full understanding. I doubt if the same will be true of Maurice. However, so far he is basking in the sunshine of the improvements which really owe their origin to his predecessor.

The End of Petrol Rationing

Today ends a chapter. We have abolished petrol rationing. It is funny how quickly these changes come. We had, of course, been negotiating for the past four or five months with the American Companies on our twin plans of substituting sterling for dollar oil and at the same time agreeing to take extra oil from them providing it was paid for in sterling. The negotiations have been very sticky and the State Department by no means helpful. Egged on by the American Companies they have thrown in their weight heavily against us. Moreover, when Acheson* [U.S. Secretary of State] came to see Bevin earlier this month one of the things he said must be settled was the oil business as it caused them too much trouble internally.

Just about this time the Standard Oil Company sent one of their leading people, Mr Soubrie, to London. He offered to supply their share of the extra petrol needed if we de-rationed throughout the sterling area. Donald Fergusson, my late Permanent Secretary, rather nicely came over to tell me this as soon as it happened. There was then the usual hectic period of negotiation, and with the help of some extra supplies which the sterling Companies pulled out at the last minute we made the crucial decision. One of our reasons for doing so was that the knowledge of the offer was leaking out. I confirmed that this was so in the following way.

Some people I know slightly – Alexander and Margie Geddes – invited us to dine and dance with them to meet Mr Soubrie about a week ago. We went on, after a crush at the Italian Embassy, to a place called, 'The Twenty-One Club' in Chester Gardens. This was a great excitement for Dora and myself who have not been to a Night Club, even of the most respectable kind, for years and years. I found that the party consisted, apart from the Geddes and Mr Soubrie, for the most part of other persons who had met them on the boat coming back from America. There was also present a Conservative M.P. called Beamish.

We were the last to arrive and as soon as I sat down Beamish and a rather good-looking woman sitting next to him who turned out to be the divorced wife of Sir Bernard Docker, a big and I believe extremely unpleasant industrialist, began to speak about the debate in the House the following day.[14] This was a Private Member's motion on petrol. Mr Soubrie was sitting opposite them, so I guessed that they knew a good deal about the offer. Eventually I managed to dance with Lady Docker and extracted from her the information that Soubrie had talked freely on the boat about the offer to provide oil for sterling if we would de-ration.

In the House today Phil [Noel-]Baker, my successor, was extremely generous and kind about the part I had played when Minister in bringing about these developments. Of course, in reality, there is not much one does oneself, but I can at least claim on this occasion to have been more right in my forecast than anybody else. Very fortunately in my Harrogate speech during the Election I not only said that if the dollar position improved the prospects were not bad but I also specifically referred to the negotiations then going on in Washington to procure more petrol without dollar cost. Nevertheless, the Tories will of course claim that Churchill's speech in the Election really had a lot to do with this, even if it is sheer nonsense.[15]

Inside the Treasury

I am beginning to settle down in the Treasury. There is, of course, a big difference between being in charge of a Department and only being the Number II Minister. The officials inevitably look on you rather differently. But on the whole there has been less trouble than I might have expected. On two major issues I have had rows: the European Payments Union and what we call the 'fundamentals' of our economic policy especially in regard to the United States. My chief opponent on both these has been the Head of the Overseas Finance Division, Sir Harry Wilson-Smith. But I think I can claim to have won both battles. On E.P.U. he has retired from the field and left it all to me; and on the fundamentals also the Chancellor ruled in our favour. As it turned out the decision on fundamentals did not lead anywhere, but E.P.U. is a different story.[16]

14 Colonel (later Sir) Tufton Beamish succeeded his father as Conservative M.P. for Lewes (Sussex) in 1945, and sat until 1974. Sir Bernard Docker was chairman of the Birmingham Small Arms Company.
15 See *HG*, pp. 187 and (on the election speeches) 107–8.
16 The 'fundamentals' essentially concerned the U.S. pressure for free trade and convertibility; see pp. 116–17, 125, 149–50, 171, 204; *HG*, pp. 218–19.

After endless arguments in Paris we finally decided we must talk to the Americans in London and they came to the same conclusion at the same time. We also worked out a new approach to the problem ourselves, and at quite short notice Harriman and his advisers, including Katz, turned up at the Treasury. After about half an hour the Chancellor handed the whole thing over to me and Harriman handed his side over to Katz. We then had some intensive negotiating which ended in effect with our giving way to the Americans on the technical problem of relating sterling to E.P.U. while we made it plain that we would only agree to this if we got satisfaction on the gold and credit arrangements.

In the middle of the negotiations I decided that we must give them some idea of what we meant by the latter, and got up at 6 a.m. one morning to write down what I regarded as the essential conditions. I may say that I only got up at that time because I had dined at the French Embassy the night before and had eaten and drunk too much. However, my mind was quite clear and the proposals we eventually put in were extremely close to what I had scribbled down.

The officials were I think at first all quite horrified and regarded me as much too inflationary, but it was necessary to condition the Americans to our point of view, and although they did not promise us support they did not really make trouble either and, indeed, indicated that broadly speaking they were thinking on the same lines.

I go to Paris next week to try and complete these negotiations, though goodness knows whether we shall bring it off. I noticed, however, that after that weekend the attitude of the officials to me changed decisively and for the better. Up to then they had been reserved, at times resentful – never giving me their reasons for thinking things but just implying that I was wrong. Since then, although they have not just accepted my views, they have been much more open and undoubtedly prepared to follow my lead.

At the end of the final meeting we had before the document went to Paris, Playfair, who is the Under-Secretary and the chief Treasury expert, said, 'Well, it is really rather a good memorandum despite our efforts to sabotage'.[17] I felt this was a great step forward.

As for Harry Wilson-Smith, there is still a long way to go and I am not sure that we shall ever settle down very comfortably together, but on the other main issues that I have had to deal with there has been less reason for disagreement. The truth is that he is not really an expert in this field, does not understand the economics as well as I do, but is extremely good – I suspect – at negotiation.

17 Sir Edward Playfair was later Permanent Secretary at the War Office and Ministry of Defence.

Finally, there are my relations with Stafford [Cripps]. These are, on the whole, extraordinarily good. There is always a danger in such a position either that I should feel resentful because I am kept out of the picture, or that he should feel resentful because I am taking too much upon myself. There have been one or two bad patches where both these things have seemed to happen but they have not lasted long. He seems to have been fully content to leave a good deal to me, particularly where it is technical and complicated; though you never know of course when he will suddenly change round.

One of the illusions about him which I have discovered really is an illusion is that in bargaining either with his colleagues or with outsiders he is particularly tough. This is really not so at all. Indeed, we all of us are nervous when such discussions are going on lest he gives way too much. I find myself in the rather surprising position of having to stiffen him up on almost every occasion. It is perhaps not surprising since that is so that I also find him pretty ready to accept my advice, unless of course it is in conflict with some other close adviser. All this may, of course, be partly due to the fact that he is undoubtedly mentally tired and perhaps physically not well also. But I suspect that his strong point was not so much in deciding for himself and then just being tough with everybody but rather accepting sound advice and then having the courage to put it across to the country – which is really rather a different thing.

As to his health, it is extremely difficult to judge. He certainly regards himself as almost an invalid, and Edwin Plowden mentioned to me the other day that he thought he was rather a hypochondriac. From time to time he still talks of not going on for long, and yet I know that when it looked as though Ernie [Bevin] could not carry on at the Foreign Office Stafford was greatly attracted by the idea of becoming Foreign Secretary. This could hardly have been so if he really felt so very ill.

I am quite hopeful that the present arrangements however may work out quite well. From my point of view so long as he will give me a definite sphere of responsibility in overseas finance and planning, and normally leave me to settle everything there I shall be happy. This will take a great deal of the burden from him and enable him to recover his health.

Perhaps the most awkward feature of the present situation is at Government and Cabinet Committees when I am rather apt to be in the position either of having just to repeat what he says or to contradict him, which is really impossible. But this is really a pretty minor matter so long as the right policy decisions are taken and on that I really have no reason to complain whatever.

Relations with Nye [Bevan] have settled down again after the great row about the Health Services. There also seems to be more harmony in the Party as a whole; although Nye still looks on himself as a sort of leader of the Left wing, his actual attitude on the essential points of policy is not nearly so far removed from Herbert [Morrison]'s as it used to be. Curiously enough too he seems to have accepted his present position in the Party. A few months ago he was always grousing and criticising and complaining either about the Foreign Secretary or the Lord President [Morrison] or the Prime Minister. There is much less of that now. Perhaps somebody really has told him that he nearly lost us the Election.

The thing I like about him is that one can have a terrific row with him in a Cabinet Committee and yet remain on quite cordial terms, with a good deal of friendly back-chat. Another endearing characteristic is that he does not really make much effort to collect around him a lot of supporters in the Cabinet or Government, though his enemies would say that was only because he could not find any. Whether this is so or not, it is one of the unattractive features of the Lord President that he does tend to do this. At some of the earlier Cabinet meetings Shinwell's support for the Lord President was so obvious as to be almost laughable – Herbert having brought him back into things again. Nevertheless, Herbert too is in very good form and mostly on the side of the 'angels', especially where public expenditure is concerned. On the nationalised Boards it is a different story and I have continued my long argument with him, as the attached correspondence shows.[18]

The Foreign Secretary seems to be very much iller than he was six months ago. Indeed, there have been a number of occasions when it seemed impossible for him to carry on. Gossip is that he himself, his wife and his doctors all believe that if he were to give up his job he would die.[19] He still has a remarkable power of recovery. One morning he will be very poorly, hardly capable of coherent speech and the next day he will be shrewd, sensible, imaginative – all his old, best qualities.

Finally, there is the Prime Minister who generally speaking seems to me to have more political sense than almost everybody [sic] else. Undoubtedly, too, his position in the Government is stronger than it has ever been. This is, I think, partly the result of the Election out of which he came triumphantly so far as his personal position was concerned. It is no doubt also partly as a result of the Foreign Secretary's illness and the Chancellor's tiredness. Clem [Attlee] told me himself

18 Omitted. Full summary in Chester (1975), pp. 975–7.
19 He did die five weeks after leaving the Foreign Office.

that he had really positively enjoyed the Election, particularly his tour, and confirmed that he had made no notes whatever for any of his speeches. I think history will record that he was among the more successful British Prime Ministers, as indeed it would have said of Baldwin had he lived in a quieter period. It is one of the interesting features of our history, and perhaps that of other countries as well, that the qualities needed for success in peace-time are by no means the ones usually associated with greatness.

Diary: Friday, 11 August 1950

One of the great difficulties about keeping a diary is that when you are very busy and there is a lot to say you have no time to say it, and when you have plenty of time there is nothing to say. It is now some two months since I last dictated and a great deal has happened during that time.

European Payments Union[20]

We had a whole series of negotiations on this which I found intensely interesting. It was perhaps fortunate for me that I came into the Treasury at a point when such a very abstruse but very important subject had to be dealt with. It was really impossible for the Chancellor to deal with it, and this time at least my previous experience as an economist stood me in good stead. The whole subject of the European Payments Union was therefore almost entirely handed over to me, and the eventual settlement is in fact a result of a series of negotiations which I conducted personally.

On many of these occasions I found myself both United Kingdom delegate and also Chairman of the Executive Committee of O.E.E.C. This gave me especial experience which I found extremely interesting. One discovered, for instance, that nothing is ever settled at the main meetings of even such a small body as the Executive Committee where only seven or eight countries are represented. It makes not the slightest difference whether these meetings are held in private or that no formal record is kept. It is rather that the room they are held in is far too large and the formality of the occasion too great for anybody to commit himself. We found that the only way to make progress was to adjourn the main meeting of the Executive and have a completely informal and

20 See *HG*, Ch. 7-iv.

private meeting in our room upstairs where practically the same people came in but the atmosphere was different. You would get twenty to twenty-five people crowded into a room, around a table which was appropriate for ten. You dispensed for the most part with translation and you allowed everybody to talk. In the case of countries chiefly interested Ministers came; others sent officials. In this way, after a tremendous amount of argument, agreements could be reached. Even this was only possible if this highly informal meeting was supplemented by other more informal meetings by groups on the balcony outside the room.

Another interesting thing is the way opinions change. The people who have made most difficulty about our getting the kind of agreement that both the U.K. and U.S. wanted have been the Belgians and the Swiss. In both cases we had agreed at one point that we would just go on without them if they would not toe the line, but again in both cases second thoughts prevailed and we had to make fresh efforts to consolidate them, which were in fact successful.

Perhaps, too, it is a help to be working to a time-table, and everybody knows that they have just got to come to some decision. Thus, if you keep them late enough at it, they either finally agree to something about midnight or after separating about midnight realise they must agree to something early in the morning.

On the whole the standard of the officials in Paris seemed to me to be extremely high, both our own and those of the other main delegations, and I was interested to see how very well they knew each other. One felt that it was in a way like a number of Solicitors who had business with each other for their respective clients but who were bound together to some extent by a common professional interest.

As far as the Ministers, there is really not a great deal to say. I had several prolonged arguments with Van Zeeland in which I tried to explain the realities of a clearing system to him. Petsche, the French Finance Minister, was pretty difficult on occasions but fortunately was not so much concerned.[21]

The most satisfactory feature was the extraordinarily close collaboration we had with the Americans. It is rather odd that after acquiring a reputation within the U.K. Government for objecting to so much of what the Americans were trying to do in Europe I should yet have been able to get on well with them. I think the explanation is that most of them had fundamentally the same outlook as I had. They were and are economist new-dealer types, and anxious to get the same kind of

21 Paul Van Zeeland (1893–1973) served in eight Belgian governments of the Right, and was Foreign Minister 1949–54. As Prime Minister 1935–7 he broke Belgium's links with France in hopes of propitiating Hitler. Maurice Petsche, another conservative, was French Finance Minister 1949–51.

payment system going as we were ourselves. Harriman wrote me an extremely nice letter after we had got over most of the difficulties, and incidentally wrote a similar one about me to the Chancellor.

In contrast to the Anglo-American economists, with whom we might associate the Scandinavians, we had the Belgian, French and to some extent Swiss banker outlook, who invariably took the side of the creditor and wanted a much tighter system of credit. It is indeed an extraordinary situation that the bankers should have so much power. They virtually control the financial system of Belgium and have a considerable influence on that of France. No doubt this is partly due to the extent of inflation that there has been in these countries vying with a dislike of control. We are much more frightened of deflation and unemployment and are quite prepared to impose controls to prevent inflation. They are much more frightened of inflation than they are of deflation and unemployment and are unwilling or unable to impose controls. Hence their insistence on keeping the volume of credit down.

We had one or two nice occasions of a social character during the Whitsun Recess. I took Dora with me and after working all day went out in the evenings. On one such occasion the E.C.A. were opening an Exhibition in the Bois de Vincennes. We arrived very late but just in time to hear some speeches from Harriman, Stikker and Marjolin. It was literally in the wood in the open, or rather with the Exhibition structure around us. After the speeches were over champagne was handed round to the 200 or so people who were there, and I thought that this could only possibly happen in France. We then went off and had a party in the Bois de Boulogne with the Norwegian Foreign Minister, Lange, the Danish Minister of Commerce and his pretty Swedish wife who is a film actress and writes erotic novels.[22] In addition there were various other people including Katz and his wife.

We have also spent some time in the British Embassy, and both Dora and I were much attracted by Lady Harvey, wife of the Ambassador, who seemed intelligent, artistic and very much a personality.[23]

It is rather fun having participated in something which has really actually happened. I mean a new economic system which is definitely going to make some difference, whatever they may say. It will be very interesting to see how it all works out and I shall watch the figures of our balances with E.P.U. from month to month with great interest.

22 This was a gathering of Socialists. Halvard Lange was Norway's Foreign Minister, except for a month, from 1946–65; Jens Otto Krag, Danish Minister of Commerce, later Foreign Minister (1958–62), Prime Minister (1962–8) and leader of the party, was holding his first office.
23 Sir Oliver (Lord) Harvey had been Eden's principal private secretary 1936–9 and again 1941–3. He was Ambassador in Paris 1948–54.

Stafford's Holiday

About three months ago Stafford [Cripps] took the line both with me and with Edwin Plowden that he was going to resign at the end of the summer Session. He said that he had been wanting to get away and have a complete rest for a long time, but he must now have a rest for at least a year and nothing was going to stop him. I naturally protested about this and reasoned with him but it did not seem to make much impression, and eventually I heard he had written a letter of resignation to the P.M. Edwin and I then really got to work. I saw both Stafford and Isobel Cripps, and Edwin also saw the Lord President. After a tremendous amount of argument we finally succeeded in persuading him. During the course of these arguments I pointed out that:

(a) Stafford was physically much better as a result of not having to work so hard, and having had a Whitsun holiday.

(b) He could not just go away for a year because of the voting position in Parliament. If he were to be away as long as that he would have to give up his seat.[24]

(c) In the new circumstances there was no reason for him to worry about over-working any longer.

(d) It was essential for him to remain Chancellor, but that he could quite well go away for a long holiday in the summer.

We were helped in persuading him of course by the Korean war which made him feel that he could not just fade out at present.[25] However, now he has gone right away as from the beginning of this month and is not intending to come back until towards the end of October. He still reserves the right not to come back at all if he does not think he is well enough. But for my part I am pretty certain he will come back, and may come back earlier, especially if the international position gets worse. Meanwhile I have been left in charge, and in order to impress outsiders and officials, at his suggestion, have moved into his enormous room.

The Health Services Row

One of the more unpleasant jobs I have been made to do is to act on the Committee under the P.M.'s chairmanship which has to keep an eye on the Health Services from an official point of view. This Committee was set up after a series of long arguments in the Government about the Health

24 Labour had an overall majority of three.
25 It began in late June 1950.

estimates. The Government was definitely to limit the expenditure on Health – to put a ceiling upon it – for this year at least. The Committee was set up to see that the ceiling was observed and there were not any supplementary estimates. The Chancellor committed himself, in fact, in the House of Commons very firmly on this point, and his position would certainly be a most difficult one if there had to be a supplementary estimate of anything but a nominal size.

My job at these meetings is, of course, to act as Treasury Prosecutor against the Minister of Health, Nye Bevan, and the Secretary of State for Scotland, Hector McNeil. The meetings are not exactly easy or comfortable, and on one occasion the Minister of Health, provoked by something I had said, slammed his papers down and started to walk out of the room. The P.M., however, summoned him back and smoothed him down.[26] I think we can claim to have made some progress with the help of the Supplies Report produced by Sir Cyril Jones,[27] but it is a very wearing affair – always having to nag one's colleagues, and especially when they are as slippery and difficult as the Minister of Health.

Geneva

I had a rather pleasant interlude about the middle of July when I had to go to Geneva for a meeting of the Economic & Social Council of U.N.O. [the United Nations] to deliver a speech on full employment. This arose on a report by five economists, of whom Nicky Kaldor was one.[28] It was an extremely progressive report and absolutely up our street. (I imagine that Nicky wrote most of it.) We were able to make quite a splash with the speech both with the press here and at Geneva. But the atmosphere there was not very encouraging. One did not really feel, as one does in Paris, that anything much was really being done. Partly I think this was due to the lower level of quality among the delegates; partly perhaps to the fact that until recently ECOSOC, like other arms of U.N.O., had simply been a battleground of propaganda between the Russians and the rest of us. The Russians, etc. were not there this time and that gave opportunities for profitable discussion, but the people concerned were scarcely prepared for it.[29] I was the only Minister present, which was perhaps an

26 Apparently on 28 June 1950. For this row and Bevan's subsequent resentment, see *HG*, pp. 214–15; cf. Foot (1973), pp. 295–7, and above, pp. 174–5, 188.
27 Sir Cyril Jones, a director of biscuit and insurance companies, was vice-president of the Federation of British Industries. His report seems not to have been published.
28 See *HG*, p. 217–18, 228–9; and on Kaldor above, p. 129 and n.
29 The U.S.S.R. was boycotting the U.N. and its organs, in protest against the refusal to transfer China's seat on the Security Council to the new Communist government.

indication of the kind of attitude adopted by most Governments towards ECOSOC.

It was rather surprising to find the Palais [des] Nations, the old League of Nations building, in view of Lake Success [*sic*], absolutely crammed full. It seems that U.N.O. is so much larger than the old League that it needs so much more space. Geneva was of course very beautiful, lying at the end of the lake with the mountains behind, and Mt Blanc coming out in the evening after it had been hidden in a haze during the day. It was very hot and the hotels were fiendishly expensive with rather poor service. But I would gladly have stayed on a bit.

Defence and the U.S.A.

Somewhat out of the blue at the end of July the United States made an especial approach to us and asked what we were going to do about increasing the [defence programme] and how much more we would do if we got assistance from them. We were asked to produce our replies in just about a week. The reply we gave has now been published and need not be discussed. But I think the fact that we were able to produce it at such short notice is a tribute to the efficiency of the planning machine and the Civil Service.

However, what is more interesting is the way in which our proposals were finally settled and the reception they received from the Americans. The figure of £3,400,000,000 over three years was built up from the present Defence expenditure; some additions which we knew we had to incur and about £800,000,000 which was an estimate of the amount of extra equipment which could be produced without putting the U.K. on a war economic basis. The question then arose as to how much we were prepared to provide ourselves and for how much we would ask the Americans.

This was originally settled in the Treasury at a figure of £900 million a year for us, the rest to be provided by the United States. However, the way in which this figure was reached was so doubtful and I felt it was so inadequate that after talking to Bridges and Plowden and others I went back to the Chancellor and pointed out its dangers. He rather surprisingly readily agreed and said he meant £950, and £950 was the figure which went into the Cabinet and was accepted by them, and was then sent on to the Americans.[30]

30 Britain had originally meant to spend £2,300 million on defence over the next three years; in answer to the Americans' request another £1,100 million was added, of which they were asked to provide half. Their £550 million over the three years, added to the £2,850 million promised by Britain, made up the new total of £3,400 million – to which a further £200 million was soon added for Service pay (see next entry).

The Americans had made the mistake of trying to handle this in London through a Working Party on their side at too low a level. They had put in charge a Mr Batch [sic], a near neighbour of ours in Hampstead, and chief commercial man in the Embassy, but with very little experience. On the other hand, we sent our best people – Leslie Rowan*, Makins from the Foreign Office and Plowden.[31] They received our proposals very coldly and seemed to expect that we ought to be doing a lot more. However, they appeared to be more anxious to get some document which could be published, and such a document was prepared. It contained not only the total figures but the amount we expected to get from them. There was then a most extraordinary muddle about publicity. There was a great fear that this document would be published in Washington before it had been given out here, and in order to prevent this a special editorial Conference was called, although the actual timing of the release of the document was not definitely settled. As Stafford [Cripps] had meanwhile gone away I was present at this Conference. It was not a very inspiring affair, and one could not help feeling, seeing the nervous and uncertain way in which Clem [Attlee] handled it, how surprising it was that he had been a successful Prime Minister. I think the answer was that he did not feel very happy in this particular field, and he has not really had much experience at press conferences.

However, the serious feature was that next morning, and before the document had been released, protests started to arrive both from Washington and from the American Embassy here. To make matters worse the protests were of different kinds. In Washington they were objecting to the publishing of the figures of our own commitments and what we expected from the Americans, whereas here they were much more concerned with the demand for free dollars.[32] I attended a rather angry interview with the P.M. with the American Ambassador, as a result of which we had expected to leave our figures in though [if] possible take out the free dollar reference.

Meanwhile Oliver Franks [our Ambassador] in Washington had been seeing [Secretary of State] Acheson and he took the opposite line to the American Ambassador here. He did not mind about the free dollars but he did not want the figures in. Looking back, I am sure that this was right, though at the time I was angry because of the continual chopping and changing. It would have been a bad thing if all the countries had put in

31 The commercial counsellor at the U.S. Embassy was Charles F. Baldwin, a newcomer; there appears to be confusion with William Batt, who succeeded John Kenney as the E.C.A. representative to the U.K. in November 1950 (below, p. 222).
32 'Free dollars' could be spent as the recipient chose, without the detailed U.S. monitoring which Congress demanded.

their claims for dollars and published them. Anyway the document was published without the references to the claims but showing a reference to free dollars, and we managed to get some good publicity including the work done by our own press people and two conferences I took myself, one with the Lobby and one with the American journalists in London.

I am quite sure that at first the American reaction was substantial but it seems to have been much less critical than to begin with. They are curious people to deal with – nice, well intentioned but, I think, often lacking in judgment. And whereas most high officials here are pretty shrewd judges of the political interests, one has the impression that their counterparts in the American Civil Service are often very much at sea.

Soldiers' Pay

In the last few days my biggest headache has been increased pay for the Forces. This has been round the corner for some time and we set aside £30 million a year for it in the calculations of the three-year programme. Increases were foreshadowed in the Defence Debate by Shinwell [Minister of Defence], and the P.M., and the last thing that the Chancellor did [before leaving] was to write Shinwell an angry letter about the failure of the Ministry of Defence to consult the Treasury on proposals which they had just announced were nearly ready. This was just before the Bank Holiday weekend. During that weekend, on the Sunday, the P.M.'s Private Secretary rang me up and said he had been instructed to tell me of a letter the P.M. had sent me, saying we must get on with the question at once and get it settled before the end of the next week.

When I came back to London after the holiday I found that our boys in the Treasury had only just received the details of these proposals and that they amounted to far more than the £30 million contemplated. I then went into work with the Service Ministers and Minister of Defence. After a lot of talk I finally got them to agree to figures which involved £40 million as against £55 million which their own original proposals would have cost.

Meanwhile, however, they had circulated – contrary to an understanding with us – their original proposals to the Cabinet. When I went into the meeting which was called to discuss this I noticed the Chiefs of Staff were present, and I had a strong suspicion that they had been round to the P.M. and got him to surrender to their original proposals. To my disgust the discussion went all against me and in favour of the original proposals. It was a bad Cabinet, many of the more responsibly minded Ministers being away, such as the Lord President [Morrison] and Dalton, Harold Wilson and Patrick Gordon Walker. And, of course, it was flooded out with Service Ministers and Chiefs of Staff, so perhaps it was not surprising that I was routed. But I fear that this will have two bad consequences. (1) It will give the Defence Ministry the idea that they can spend anything they like and get away with it. (2) It will lead to a general feeling that money no longer matters.

I must confess I was horrified by the entirely casual attitude to the £15 million which was involved which was adopted by many of the Cabinet.

I stopped behind and spoke to the P.M. about it, and complained bitterly of the difficult position I was in, not having the authority of the Chancellor and yet having to do his job, and do it without knowing what the P.M. really wanted. I also voiced the fears I have just mentioned. The P.M. smoothed me down; said he agreed with my fears, and it was more or less arrived at that in future in any such situation I would go and see the P.M. beforehand. He said, 'I would like to have backed you up on this first occasion'. Nevertheless, I feel it was his influence more than anything which made the decision go the other way.

No doubt we do need a larger Regular Army, but I am afraid I think it very doubtful whether the substantial increases now being brought in will produce that effect. I am all for spending money if we can get good value for it in the way of strong defences. No doubt we have clearly got to do that, but that is no reason for pouring money down the drain.

Another source of anxiety is the fact that the Chancellor agreed to implementing the Chorley Report on the salaries of higher Civil Servants.[33] Douglas [Jay] feels very bitter about this and accuses the officials of getting at the Chancellor on this point before he, the Financial Secretary, had any chance of stopping it, and I must say there is something in this. The Chancellor was certainly in a very difficult position, and in view of previous undertakings I am afraid this is bound to make the wage situation far more difficult. In fact just at present it is impossible to see how we can avoid some considerable measure of inflation here. Perhaps it is some consolation that the same kind of thing is going to take place in the United States and elsewhere; therefore the repercussions on our balance of payments cannot be so serious.

33 This report, which proposed increases of about 30 per cent for the senior ranks, had been accepted by Cripps on 17 February 1949 but for gradual implementation, in three annual stages beginning on October 1949. The first stage was deferred in the post-devaluation economy drive that autumn, but in August 1950 it was decided to start in the following October. (Lord Chorley, a Labour peer, had been Professor of Law at London 1930–47).

Friday, 3 November 1950

French Leave

Our holiday was rather a miserable one this year. We had originally planned to be away the first fortnight in Cornwall, and took a bungalow there for that period. Unfortunately, Stafford [Cripps]'s illness upset this plan because the Annual Meetings of the International Monetary Fund and the International Bank were fixed for that fortnight, and I therefore had to take his place at them.

As it was, we managed to plan a week at Abbotsbury followed by a week near Exmouth with the children of my sister-in-law's family, after which I was to take them to Cornwall, install them, and then go to Paris. This plan, unsatisfactory as it was, could not be carried out precisely. First of all Cressida [his younger daughter] was ill and we could not leave for two days. Then Dora was ill on the first day at Abbotsbury; then my arm got septic (after vaccination); the weather was foul and even the week at Abbotsbury was broken by a trip to France. This occurred in the following circumstances.

The Foreign Secretary rang me up at Abbotsbury and aksed me to go on the Thursday with Shinwell to argue with the French about conscription. We had already decided to put up our period to two years, but we hoped to persuade the French to do the same before our decision was announced. I had really no option but to agree to go, but made arrangements to be flown as much of the way as possible. Accordingly, at 6 a.m. one morning a car from the Royal Naval Air Station near Yeovil arrived at the Ilchester Arms to pick me up. I managed to wake in time, shave, dress and even have some breakfast, and then saw the car standing in the pouring rain outside, and found to my despair that I could not get out of the hotel. The door seemed to be locked; it was pitch dark inside, and I did not know where the keys were. Everybody else was asleep. Finally in desperation I opened the dining-room window from the top – the bottom would not move – and clambered up and out – all in my best overcoat and black hat. It would have been an amusing sight if anybody but the chauffeur of the car had been there to see it.

It was my first trip in what is called a 'V.I.P.' plane, which was beautifully fitted up with curtains, armchairs, mahogany panelling, etc. They were waiting for me at Yeovil, the guard all lined up on parade, saluting etc. Then we flew off down the coast to Manston. Arriving there I found it was now wholly given over to the Americans, except for the administration. There was a hideous noise of jet Thunderbolts which apparently disturb the citizens of Ramsgate, and no wonder.

The company gradually assembled; the officials flying by plane from [London Airport] Northolt and Shinwell driving over from Broadstairs. Off we went to Paris.

The talks were dull – unsatisfactory on manpower. The French were completely obstructive and produced a lot of very unconvincing arguments. Moch did most of the talking and despite his reputation I was not very impressed.[34] He certainly did not marshal his figures and arguments very well. We all had lunch with Petsche, Finance Minister (you always get an excellent meal; he married a Lazard [a great French banking family] and in any case is very rich himself). And afterwards I had a long talk with him and his officials about the finance of rearmament, which was quite useful.

The flight back was marred by a lot of bumpiness. This time I had to go on from Manston to Northolt where I felt too ill to drink all the wonderful cocktails prepared for me. In the evening we flew back to Yeovil and I arrived at Abbotsbury at about 10 p.m.

I did not much enjoy the I.M.F. and the Bank meetings. By then I knew that I should almost certainly have to speak in the Defence Debate in the specially called meeting of Parliament in the following week. Moreover it was all very rushed and nobody I much liked there. But it enabled me to meet one or two – Deshmukh, Indian Finance Minister whom I was to see a lot in the following three weeks.[35] I was much impressed by him. Quick, highly intelligent, responsible, with considerable charm. He gives one plenty of confidence. I must say that things could be much worse in view of the newness of the Government machinery there. But after all, he spent most of his life in the I.C.S. and married an Englishwoman, and seemed to be entirely free from any prejudices.

I have never had more trouble with any speech before or so far since than the one I had to do for the Defence Debate. When I began work on it nobody had really settled any line of policy at all. Most people had been away on leave and I, myself, felt very disinclined to write. However, with much sweat, if not blood and tears, and a good deal of loss of sleep, we finally produced what turned out to be one of my best performances. Of course, I knew subconsciously that it would be of very great importance to my own personal career. No doubt this worried me, and looking back I

34 Jules Moch, a leading French Socialist, was Minister of the Interior 1947–Feb. 1950, of Defence July 1950–1, and later represented France in disarmament negotiations for many years.
35 Sir Chintaman Deshmukh was Governor of the Reserve Bank 1943–9 (above, p. 72) and Finance Minister 1950–6.

know it was so. I was enormously helped by Clem Leslie and William Armstrong*, the Chancellor's Principal Private Secretary.[36] They thought of words when I could not and worked like blacks to get the thing finished. I was pleased to find that on this first occasion when I had to read a speech that I could do so without anybody seeming to be worried by it. I have seen Ministers go badly wrong in the House when reading. It was rather reassuring to find that there should be no difficulty about that, providing one allowed oneself enough time.

Stafford [Cripps] came back to vote in the Steel Bill Debate in the following week. He came into his own room where I was sitting in the House and I asked him how he was. He looked thin but quite rosy-cheeked. He said that he was getting on well and ought to be ready in about six weeks' time. Later however, I heard, he had some kind of attack and 24 hours later in the Lobby he looked pretty ill. The sequel to this comes later.

There were then three weeks of Conferences – Commonwealth Finance followed by South East Asia. Hard work but I enjoyed it. I like being Chairman. It is a thing I do very easily and without much effort. In fact I have never understood why everybody cannot be good at being Chairman. It was a change for me too to be meeting Ministers from other countries, seeing fresh faces and hearing their points of view. I have already spoked of Deshmukh. [Sir] Ghulam Mohammed, Finance Minister of Pakistan I had met before.[37] He is regarded in the Treasury as a likeable man but rather a rascal, though certainly clever. He, too, has been in Government service most of his life. He is very difficult to understand but I personally found him quite agreeable and he is pretty shrewd. Both he and Deshmukh are really without prejudices and could settle the disputes between their countries easily enough if they were allowed to. One cannot help feeling we did leave the Indians a good legacy in the training we gave them in public administration.[38]

The Finance Minister of Ceylon was much more of a politician and inclined to be difficult at times, though personally rather pleasant and certainly forceful in his manner. I liked Doidge from New Zealand particularly, even though he was once Manager of the *Sunday Express*. He was bluff and hearty, not very clever but friendly and sensible.

At the S. East Asia Conference, the general feeling was that Spender*,

36 HG spoke on 13 September 1950 and was well received: *HG*, pp. 229–30.
37 Finance Minister 1947–51, Governor-General 1951–6 (died).
38 Filial piety? HG's father spent his whole life in the I.C.S. in Burma.

Australian Finance Minister [*sic*], would be as he was at the Sydney Conference.[39] He is like a little terrier, self important, talks a good deal, but on the whole quite sensibly though sometimes before he has really thought things out. He has no inhibitions about raising awkward subjects and is what you would call fairly crude – but then so are most Australians. As it happened he behaved quite well and if he were just a little less self important I would even have liked him.

One night we gave a small Government dinner to the other Ministers, which I thought was very successful. But I could not help feeling how fascinating it was that here were these seven or eight totally different people – a fiery Ceylon Nationalist, a wise and sensible Indian Administrator, a clever but slightly doubtful character from Pakistan, a pushful politician from Australia, a nice elderly man from New Zealand, another rather similar (Mayhew from Canada) and ourselves – all sitting round and talking about affairs of some importance to 600 million people, and doing so in a sensible, friendly way without any signs of racial feelings or prejudices or argument or anger. In a way it was quite moving, as indeed was the whole Conference, because we did certainly feel that what we were after was something worth while.[40]

If my Defence Debate speech was important so also was the speech I had to give at the Mansion House in Stafford's absence to the merchants and bankers in the City.[41] Not so much sweat this time but a good deal of trouble and care, following the advice about not being too long and too stodgy, from Bridges and others. Anyway, it went down quite well.

North American Trip

I think it must be an event in anybody's life when he first crosses the Atlantic. I had been trying to do this for a good many years. Even before the war there was a talk about a Lecture tour. During the war there were one or two occasions when it seemed possible. After the war, before becoming Minister, again I had intended to try and get some lectures, and

39 J.R. Jayewardene was Finance Minister 1947–53, leader of the House 1953–6, of the Opposition 1970–7, Prime Minister 1977–8 and President of Sri Lanka from 1978. (Sir) F.W. Doidge was Minister of External Affairs in the National cabinet 1949–51, then High Commissioner in London until his death in 1954. (Sir) Percy Spender was in fact Australian Minister of External Affairs.

40 On the Colombo Plan for South Asia which emerged from these conferences, see *HG*, p. 225. R.W. Mayhew was Fisheries Minister in Canadian Liberal cabinets, 1948–52.

41 The first such speech for over fifty years not given by a Chancellor of the Exchequer.

even as Minister of Fuel & Power I had always had a vague hope that I might go and act as a negotiator about oil or something or other, but it never came off. I was determined at the Treasury to get there. Fortunately, so long as it was understood that I was not going for any political negotiations the Foreign Secretary as well as the Chancellor was wholly in favour. We flew, of course, there was no time for anything else. I felt quite boyish, the same as we used to when we went to Scotland as children, starting out on this trip. I found it extremely comfortable and not even dull because we flew over-night. The oddest feature of the flight is, of course, the gain in time, so that you find yourself arriving at Gander [Newfoundland] at 9.30 by your own watch but it is only 5.30 by their time. You get out and have breakfast at the airport and then you fly on. At about 12 by our time and 7 by their time you have lunch in the plane. It felt very odd because by then we had put our watches back.

I went and sat with the pilot as we flew in to New York but unfortunately it was cloudy and one could only see the beaches at Long Island, the airport was too far out to see New York itself. On arrival we found that our luggage was not there. We had been treated as so much V.I.P. that they managed to put it on the wrong plane, and that meant waiting. So we decided to go into New York for lunch. I was to go back to the city later and will record my impressions then. But first of all perhaps one notices more than anything else two things. (a) Negroes – quite smartly dressed negresses looking after the lifts, for example. (b) Above all, the cars – endless streams on the roads even on Sunday afternoons. So much so that they partly caused us to miss our plane to Washington, but we got there eventually after a lengthy delay because of weather and a good deal of bumpiness about seven o'clock in the evening. The Ambassador [Sir Oliver Franks] and leading Treasury officials were there to meet me and we rushed straight off to the Embassy to change for a dinner party that night.

How shall I describe my feelings about Washington? It is an attractive place; more especially in its domestic architecture, a pleasing Georgian, Colonial style house built in the wooded country outside; and then the fact that the many, many big white Ministry buildings stand in a kind of Park; and then the trees, mostly fully grown and just with autumn tints on them were, I think, very beautiful. There was nothing much impressive about the shops. It is, as everybody knows, a capital city. Civil servants, politicians, diplomats – the same sort of people whom I tend to meet in London; highly intelligent, cultured, very friendly.

There were dinner parties and lunch parties of one kind or another and in between meetings with X and Y, discussions at the State Department, or with Harriman, or the Treasury or E.C.A. A couple of Press Conferences and highlight of the visit perhaps a trip on a yacht with Snyder,

Harriman (Forbes [*sic*], the head of E.C.A. could not come), Webb, Under-Secretary in the State Department, and a few senior officials of theirs and ours.[42] The yacht was owned by a textile manufacturer whom I had met here, a pleasant, youngish man. Goodness knows how he made his fortune but he started from nothing. The yacht was most luxurious. I sat in the stern with Snyder and drank whisky . . . He talked a lot and he showed me the sights as we went down the Potomac, and we chatted about American politics. He began by saying, 'Of course, I have never been in politics'. It sounded strange but he meant that he had never run for a Governorship or State Legislature. He had simply been a pal of Truman's. As he put it, 'I have always backed Harry Truman.' And presumably he meant that he has subscribed to his campaign funds. Snyder is, I believe, a pretty typical American, quite unimpressive, very friendly. One does not get the impression that he could ever have any idea of his own, but that is perhaps a bit unfair. On the yacht he was most unwilling to talk business, and as I had nothing to raise that suited me fine. We both got a bit tipsy together and very friendly.

Harriman, however, thought that this was not good enough and at lunch – cold but very excellent with every kind of luxury – he tried to turn the conversation on to the British financial position. I said, 'If you want to talk seriously, go ahead. I am perfectly willing'. But Snyder said, 'Oh, no! Let's wait until after lunch.' When we were returning and when there were only about 20 minutes to go Snyder and I, shepherded by Harriman, went up to another part of the yacht alone and began to talk. All it was, was to give me a warning that we were doing too well to get much more aid. Funnily, as we got in I saw that Snyder was really disappointed that we had to stop. He had begun to get interested in the conversation, and I believe was genuinely sorry to break it off.

However, the President was flying to see MacArthur, and we dashed to the airport to try to say goodbye, only to see the plane just moving off as we drove in.[43]

Oliver Franks was as usual extraordinarily shrewd and sympathique. I hardly saw his wife and indeed, I believe they both effaced themselves deliberately from my engagements, presumably to let me get the limelight.

42 See Biographical notes on Snyder, Secretary of the Treasury, and Harriman, Special Representative in Europe. The E.C.A. Administrator 1950–1 was William C. Foster (not Forbes). James E. Webb, Budget Director 1946–9, was Under-Secretary of State 1949–52. On these talks see HG's memorandum below, and *HG*, pp. 231–3.
43 General Douglas MacArthur, the most famous American general of the war, was supreme commander in the S.W. Pacific 1942–5, of the occupation forces in Japan 1945–51 (and its effective ruler), and in 1950 of the U.N. forces in Korea.

We lived like royalty, with a beautiful suite and valeting and so on. I have recorded elsewhere the substance of our conversations with the American Government and therefore will not report it here. [Printed below]

Document No. 7

HG's memorandum on his Washington visit, 8–12 October 1950

Although the main purpose of my visit was simply to make informal contacts with some of the Ministers and officials in Washington, I came prepared to discuss four subjects particularly. These were:
(1) the future of sterling dollar relationships, i.e. the question of progress towards convertibility, non-discrimination, etc.
(2) economic development of South and South-East Asia.
(3) raw material prices and supplies.
(4) the defence finance problem.

I had not intended to raise the first of these questions myself but thought it possible that in pursuance of the correspondence between Snyder and the Chancellor earlier this year the Americans might wish to raise it. In the event they did not do so. Although I spent quite a time with Mr. Snyder he never mentioned the subject, nor did any of the officials or any of the other Ministers in all the talks and informal conversations that we had with them. It is quite clear that they are far too absorbed with other problems to worry very much about this at the moment.

On the other hand there was a very definite reaction to the improvement in the level of our gold reserves which I may as well mention at once. Both Harriman, Snyder and Foster* were at pains to emphasise that the striking improvement in our position was going to make it extremely difficult for them to continue with Marshall Aid as far as we were concerned. Although they did not say so in so many words, I think this was intended as a kind of softening up process in advance of the decision to stop it altogether at the end of the year. Our reaction to this was of course to explain on the one hand the need for higher reserves and on the other the anxieties we felt about the impact upon the U.K. of rearmament plans and the changed terms of trade. I also emphasised to Foster, who was of course the Minister particularly concerned, that we would wish to be fully consulted before they came to any decision on this matter.
2. I described the position we had reached on South and South-East Asia

in some detail to Mr. Webb and the leading officials of the State Department. I also had some private talk with Mr Harriman about it. The State Department, although not of course prepared to commit themselves, were pretty sympathetic. Harriman was much more definitely obviously in favour of the U.S. coming in. I put to them specifically three questions: (a) finance (b) organisation (c) procedure. On (a) I gave them an idea of the extent of the need and of the amount that should be provided by sterling balances, the rest of the Commonwealth and possibly the International Bank, using the rough figures that we had discussed in London. They did not seem to be perturbed by the scale of the figures and indeed one got the impression that if they decided to come in this would not really be a major obstacle. They did however show a good deal of interest in the screening of the programmes and here again, as in the case of defence, the prospect of free dollars seemed to be a pretty remote one. On organisation they took no very definite line. They did not attempt to pursue the idea that it should be a purely Asiatic affair, but indicated that there was a possibility that the U.S. might prefer to have a rather looser association with whatever body was set up, rather than be a full member. On procedure I explained that we were going to publish the report and at a private discussion was advised that it would be best for it not to appear until after the Congressional elections on November 7th. I impressed upon them the need for a fairly speedy decision on whether they were going to participate and was told that they would in fact have to make up their minds by about the middle of November because the Budget plans would be taking shape about then for presentation to Congress. On the question of how exactly the next step should be handled if they decided to come in I put to them the idea that after publication Dean Acheson [Secretary of State] might possibly make a speech welcoming the report and, if they thought fit, inviting the other countries concerned to a conference. They did not commit themselves on this but obviously wanted to think it over. They thought it might possibly be preferable for the U.S. to attend a conference which we would be having in the ordinary way. They showed some interest in the location of the next conference and thought it would help matters for them if it could be held in Asia itself. In particular they suggested that if the Indians could be hosts that would probably be of some value to them. I said that I thought this could probably easily be arranged.

As regards the non-Commonwealth countries, they indicated that they had already, through the usual diplomatic channels, brought some pressure upon them to participate in the scheme.

One could perhaps sum up the outcome of these necessarily highly tentative discussions by saying that if the Congressional elections go reasonably well for the Government there is a pretty good chance that the

U.S. will come in.[44] The leading Ministers concerned seemed to be definitely keen on the idea and quite a large number of the State Department officials as well. They are going to keep in touch with our people in Washington on the procedural issues during the next few weeks.

3. Raw materials. My main purpose here was to emphasise the great importance which the British Government attached to action being taken speedily, both to prevent any further rise in raw material prices and to deal with the problems of shortage which were likely to arise in at least some cases. There was a general acceptance of our point of view including the necessity for some frank talks on stockpiling and a realisation that the discussions which start next week would have to move quickly so as on the one hand to cope with the pressure from O.E.E.C. and on the other to fit in with the work which would be done in N.A.T.O. on the raw material supplies needed for the defence programme. While our main discussion on this subject was with the State Department I also mentioned it to Harriman and Snyder, both of whom were apparently very much in agreement with us.

4. Defence Finance. This was at once the most difficult and the most important subject which came under discussion. We talked about it with Harriman, with the State Department, with Foster and Bissell* and even to some extent with Snyder.[45]

In order to understand what took place it is necessary briefly to mention the previous history of the subject. Following the U.S. approach to us at the end of July about an enlarged defence programme given dollar aid and our reply to that – the £3,600 million dollar programme – talks had been taking place in America about the amount of aid which we might expect to receive. These talks had made no progress at all until the Foreign Secretary arrived in New York. It was evident that the Americans on the one hand regarded our programme as inadequate and on the other were quite unable to agree to the scale of dollar assistance which we had proposed. Quite apart from the merits of the case, Congress had imposed severe limits on the amount of free dollars or rather aid in a non-military form which could be given. We were therefore faced with a rather awkward situation. We had said in public that we would carry out this programme given substantial dollar aid. It was evident that the Americans would not be able to give us that aid. It was, however, equally apparent that some considerable speeding up in defence was necessary. As an interim measure we had decided in London to proceed with two successive expenditures of £100 million each pending the outcome of the discussions with the Americans. The result of the Foreign Secretary's talk with Acheson was in fact to break up the problem into two parts – to

44 They did, despite the Republican gains. See *HG*, p. 225.
45 See *HG*, pp. 230–3, on these talks.

consider what aid might be available in respect of the first £200 million to which we were already committed and, secondly, to consider in tripartite discussions with the French how the long term problem of defence finance might be handled.

As regards the first of these, just before I arrived in Washington the Americans had made us an offer covering the dollar component of the £200 million and estimated at 84 million dollars and had also proposed the sum of 28 million dollars in the form of off-shore purchases of military equipment produced in the U.K. There was however no guarantee that this equipment, which would be purchased, would be handed back to us. The total dollars available in this offer represented of course only about 20% of the programme whereas in our reply of August 4th we had asked for 50%. I did not discuss this matter further in Washington but simply said it was under consideration in London and that it was of course very much less than we had expected but in looking at it we would bear in mind the fact that under the arrangements proposed it was no more than dollars on account which would be mopped up by the final decision on defence finance for the whole programme. As to the latter, tripartite discussions had led to the production of the so-called Nitze memorandum[46] which in effect was a proposal that there should be an examination in N.A.T.O. of the burden which the new defence plans involved and an attempt to decide how that burden could be equally shared among them. This means in fact that instead of the earlier approach of bilateral aid for the U.K. and other countries in accordance with what the U.S.A. thought they might need, we were to have a multilateral examination of the whole problem in the course of which there would be considered not only the immediate repercussions of the defence programme but the whole question of the fairness or otherwise of the share taken in the common defence by all the participants including the U.S. and Canada.

Our discussions were concerned partly with points of principal [sic[47]] arising out of the Nitze memorandum and partly with questions of procedure.

As regards principal, our main concern was to emphasise to the Americans that we interpreted the Nitze proposals as involving complete equality between all the participating countries. It was no longer a question, we said, of how aid from the U.S.A. was to be divided out, but simply how the common burden was to be shared. We envisaged the stages of this task somewhat as follows: that there would first of all be a plan for defence worked out by the military experts of N.A.T.O. This

46 Paul Nitze, a banker, was director of the Policy Planning Staff at the State Department; Sec. of the Navy, 1963–7, Assistant or Deputy Sec. of Defense, 1961–3, 1967–9. U.S. negotiator on nuclear arms control since 1981.
47 And throughout this Document.

would involve the provision by each country of so many divisions at such and such a time and the requirement in total of so many aircraft, tanks, guns, etc. The next stage would be a decision as to where the equipment was to be produced. This would be done by the military production and supply board of N.A.T.O. We should then have a provisional allocation of defence tasks to all the member countries and be in a position therefore to estimate the cost to the various countries of their total defence effort, including of course not only the new programme but what they were planning for all purposes in all parts of the world. It would then be necessary to decide whether the tasks allotted in this way resulted in an equable [sic[47]] distribution of the burden. If, as might be supposed, they did not, then two principals would have to be followed. On the one hand the programmes could be adjusted so that one country carried a heavier burden and others a smaller burden in terms of manpower and equipment. On the other hand compensation could be introduced by the payment of sums of money. A country whose burden was too light in relation to that of others would pay to those others sums of its own currency. We do not insist on these sums being paid into a common pool. We recognise that there would be a bilateral arrangement but we were at pains to emphasise that this was an incident of the procedure and did not entitle the country which supplied the money rather than equipment to any particular control over the way the recipient country, which was carrying the heavier burden relatively in terms of equipment and manpower, spent the money it received.

In almost every case the reaction of the Americans to this proposition was similar. They were disposed to accept it in principal. They certainly recognised that the exercise in N.A.T.O. would have to be done in this sort of way but again and again they were inclined to try and limit the logical conclusion which we drew, namely that any money that was paid over could not properly be regarded as aid and entitle them to any particular control. To some extent this reluctance to accept the logic of the argument was based, we believed, on the feeling that for purposes of Congressional approval, the earlier concept of aid plus control would have to remain. The attempt to escape our logic took various forms however. Sometimes they claimed the right to enquire into the performance of the other countries, not as something which the U.S. alone would have, but as a right which every member had over every other. Sometimes they said it pretty boldly as a right which they would have as being by far the largest contributor to the total defence effort. We all of us felt that while it was absolutely necessary to press our point of view on this as far as we could and that for our own political purposes we must present the Nitze exercise as a new look where we would no longer be in the same relationship as we had been under E.R.P., we would have in practice to be reasonable and not pedantic. When it came to the way in which they presented the programme to Congress and perhaps on the claims that they might wish to make to keep an eye on some of the other N.A.T.O. countries' performances, we felt that in practice the sensible way out of the difficulty was probably to try and get N.A.T.O. missions set up in the different countries in which the U.S.A. aid would play a part but this time instead of acting on their own they would really be acting in and on behalf of N.A.T.O. We decided to put down our ideas on this matter of principal and its implications in the form of a memorandum for possible circulation for the remaining tripartite talks in Washington or alternatively at the seven-power deputies meeting in London.

We did not carry any distance talks on the kind of formula which may have to be adopted to settle the question of equable distribution. The chief attitude of the Americans on this was entirely to fight shy of formulae altogether. They did not, however, attempt to argue when I said that I thought it would be impossible to operate without some kind of principal to guide us. They recognised, I think, that in practice some sort of basic formula modified by various features would probably be found inevitable.

On procedure we made fair progress. The question of N.A.T.O. and O.E.E.C. had already been discussed during my visit to Paris in the previous week and we had found there that there was really no difference of opinion between ourselves and the O.S.R. or, for that matter, the other O.E.E.C. countries, on this subject.[48] It was agreed in effect that the job of working out the division of the burden would have to be done in N.A.T.O. but that we would use for this purpose members of our delegations on O.E.E.C. It was also agreed that it would be foolish to try and settle the precise location of the work. To some extent obviously it would have to be done in London, but there was no reason why, if it was convenient, some of the discussions could not take place in Paris. We did not think that it would be necessary for members of our O.E.E.C. delegations involved to change their residence and there was no question of their being transferred once and for all to N.A.T.O. It was a question really of giving them a second assignment which they would fulfil while at the same time retaining their jobs in Paris. On the question of the secretariat the Swedes and the Swiss had agreed that they would raise no special difficulty about the seconding of some of the O.E.E.C. secretariat

48 The O.S.R. (Office of the Special Representative) handled U.S. aid to Europe, and therefore dealt with both NATO and O.E.E.C. Argument continued for months about which organisation should be used to assess each country's share of the burden, and where the work should be done: see below, pp. 224–5, 265–6, and The Economist, 27 October 1950 and 10 February, 17 March, 5 and 19 May 1951.

to N.A.T.O. providing that they were informed of the moves which were to be made.[49]

In a final meeting with Spofford and the State Department officials, we were able to make even more precise the next stages which lay ahead.[50] The deputies were meeting in London on 18th October. The seven-power group would set up one or two committees on production and finance really to look at organisation and procedure, but this would be followed, it was hoped, almost immediately by the setting up in the deputies, as a result of the seven-power group's recommendations, of the full economic working group which was to do the essential job of settling the division of the burden. Although American opinion was not entirely clear, it seemed that they expected the same persons would be concerned on the finance or economic sub-committee of the seven-power group and on the twelve-power committee.[51] What was perhaps the most important was the news they gave us that Bissell himself was to take charge of the American study circle on the seven-power committee, and so far as we could gather, on the twelve-power committee as well. I emphasised several times our desire that before the twelve-power committee really got down to work we should try to reach some measure of understanding with the Americans both as to the kind of procedure to be adopted and, if possible, the type of formula or principal which would have to be applied. We could not, of course, say whether this could be done in Washington or in London. It would clearly depend on the movements of Bissell and any other persons who were to assist him.

To sum up, the next stage for us is to put down on paper what we regard as the implications of the Nitze memorandum and to try and secure both French and American agreement to them. If this could be done it would enormously facilitate the subsequent work and negotiations. As soon as the deputies have agreed to set up the twelve-power committee and, indeed, in advance of this, if necessary, we should begin to discuss informally with the Americans the technical and detailed question of how this problem of settling the equable shares of the burden can be handled. There was very general agreement between us that we had here a peculiarly difficult set of negotiations because the economic and political features were so closely interwoven. Further we agreed that there would have to be a continual shaping and reshaping of the solution – pulling and

49 Sweden and Switzerland belonged to the Organisation for European Economic Cooperation, but not to NATO.
50 Charles M. Spofford, a lawyer, was the U.S. representative on the North Atlantic Council of Deputies, 1950–2.
51 The Western European Regional Planning Group of NATO comprised only seven of the (then twelve) member countries – the U.S., Canada, U.K., France, Belgium, Holland and Luxemburg, but not Italy, Portugal, Denmark, Norway or Iceland.

hauling as Katz described it to me in Paris. We must anticipate that in all this the Americans probably start with the idea that our economic recovery has now proceeded so far that we ought to be able to carry the kind of burden involved in the £3,600 million programme without much financial assistance. We can, however, reasonably expect that they will be open to argument as a result of considering the whole question of equality – as a result in short of the new look. We may have to be prepared, however, to adjust our ideas as to the form in which the aid should be obtained, in particular as between military, production and dollars. From the point of view of Congress (and incidentally the point of view of economic interest) the former is greatly to be preferred.

Diary: Friday, 3 November 1950 continued

Ottawa

The Canadian Government sent a plane for us. The journey, however, was very bumpy and uncomfortable, and at one point it looked as if we might not land at Ottawa but have to go a hundred miles away to Montreal. But all was well, and in rain and wind we landed. Again a large dinner party but this time less formal. No changing and all men. One noticed the difference at once. As William Armstrong said, 'It is like moving from the south of England to the north'. There was a kind of absence of subtlety, and incertitude about the atmosphere, and – dare one say it? – in some cases a lack of charm, though this was not true of all. Having had a rather crude argument with some of them after dinner, no doubt partly due to the fact that I was tired, I had quite a nostalgia for the more civilised Washington.

But they were all very friendly; especially Douglas Abbott*, Minister of Finance, who was acting as my host, and Howe, the Minister of Commerce.[52] I stayed with the High Commissioner, Sir Alexander Clutterbuck, whom I had met during the devaluation crisis and very much disapproved of. He looked like a rather soppy Guardee Officer and is terribly upper middle class. But oddly enough he is an extremely efficient and effective High Commissioner. He knows everything about Canada and is most popular. He came to me and said we ought to leave him there for a further period, and I must say though I should think he is very conservative in his views he and his wife were extremely kind and friendly.

52 C.D. Howe had been a Minister since 1935; at Commerce 1948–57.

Ottawa of course is like Washington in one way, it is a capital city with a little but not much industry, and the people one met were the top Civil Servants and Ministers, most intelligent and capable and anxious to help. One met the same people at almost every party, and even in my three days there were about five or six. They said that I was unlucky to miss 'the fall' – the leaves were about off the trees.

We went to New York by train on the Sunday night. You stop off in Montreal for three or four hours, and they had asked the Manager of a Bank in Montreal to look after us. He certainly did so! He took us all to supper at the Ritz-Carlton, which I did not much like, and then took us home to his house which turned out surprisingly pleasant. He and his wife, an amusing and jolly person, had a sort of bar downstairs, and after a long talk about financial matters with the Manager we went down and went on drinking whisky and beer and laughing and joking with them until the time for the train came.

And now New York

I liked this best of all, partly I suppose because I had really very little to do except enjoy myself. Two lunches in Wall Street, a press conference, a visit to U.N.O., one meeting of the U.K. U.N.O. delegation. That was about all. It is, as everybody says, a very vital city, but friendly too. You do not have a feeling of fuss and bother. People seem to take things in their stride, and I like the way when you said, 'Thank you!' the 'You're welcome!'

Lake Success [the U.N. headquarters] depressed me. These international bodies which have to meet in public tend to be excruciatingly dull, or else it is just propaganda. O.E.E.C. is so much better in this respect.

I went out one night with Mike Pearson*, Canadian Foreign Minister and Gladwyn Jebb*. They asked me to join them; to have sandwiches first and then go to a broadcast which they were giving in a kind of 'Brains Trust'. Mike Pearson used to be the Permanent Secretary at their Foreign Office. He is a very charming and pleasant person, also very able. Gladwyn I have known for many years – much more able but probably not so pleasant. As an American woman said to me – he looked so like a dissipated Roman patrician. But he is, of course, a great figure there since television has shown him dealing with the Russians more effectively, far more effectively, than anybody else at the Security Council.

On Tuesday evening there was a telephone message in my room, asking me to ring the High Commissioner at Ottawa. I put the call through and rather to my amazement was able to get on at once though it is 600 miles. Clutterbuck began, 'Prepare yourself for a shock' (I thought, 'Oh, God! what awful brick have I dropped in Ottawa – are the Canadians going to claim that we have agreed to import far more?'). Then he went on, 'I have a message for you from the P.M.' I thought that he meant the Canadian Prime Minister, who had been away while I was there. What he said therefore left me still alarmed. Then he read, and I haven't the exact words, that Stafford [Cripps] was not going back for a year and that after consulting with his colleagues, the P.M. wanted me to take his place. Would I agree to having my name submitted to the King? I can never think of the right thing to say without notice on these sort of occasions. So I just said, 'I suppose he wants to know quickly. You had better say "Yes I will do it and I will send him a message myself soon"', which of course I did that night via the U.N.O. delegation.

It was rather a thrill hearing about it that way, in a hotel bedroom in New York and knowing that it would be two or at the most three days before it would be announced. Paul Rodan happened to be with me.[53] We had been shopping together and talking and curiously enough he had been asking whether Stafford was coming back and saying that he hoped that I would succeed him. So when I had finished talking with Clutterbuck I turned round to him – we were drinking whisky in the bedroom – and said, 'Well! I am to be Chancellor'. I told the other officials later in strictest confidence.

My last night in New York while it was still secret was especial fun. I had been determined to go out dancing and had been unable so far to arrange this. New York night life was after all I felt famous, and I must see something of it.

And here is a funny episode. In July of this year I went to speak in Shropshire for a Labour M.P. and on the way to the meeting we had lunch at a pub on the Liverpool Road. The Proprietress knew the M.P. and had been told who I was. She was very polite but after we had started lunch she came over and said, 'We have some very important Americans lunching here. I understand he is President Truman's Assistant.' 'Oh!' I said, 'The Vice President of the United States?' 'I think so', she said, 'he is over here about Korea.' She then pointed out two people – a man and a woman, sitting further down the room. I could not recognise the man and thought the story odd because I would have known had there been an American Envoy here on important business.

The landlady, still very excited, came back later and said that she thought it would be very nice if we talked to him. They had come in a large

53 Paul Rosenstein-Rodan and HG were joint heads of the economic department at University College London before the war.

Rolls and the chauffeur had told her the news. So we went over and talked to them for coffee and found of course it was indeed a tall story. The man was the European Manager of American Airways and the woman, no relative, glittering with jewels, was simply a Mrs Stewart, living in Paris, New York and London – an international American Society woman. We talked international politics for a bit. I told her that I was going to the States in the autumn and she replied, 'Come and look me up at River House in New York. Anybody will tell you where it is.' I thought no more about it.

On arrival in New York there was waiting for me at Essex House a letter from Louise Stewart, saying she was sorry to miss me when in Washington. She had heard all about me from John Snyder who had given her my New York address; and would I please come and be entertained.

I rang her up and then told her on the phone what she did not know before, who the landlady had supposed that she and her friend were. She was very amused but said, 'Oh! we do know the family very well'. She also said that she was a great friend of Petsche, and went on to say that she seemed to collect Finance Ministers.

Anyway, my last evening in New York began with a cocktail party at her extremely luxurious flat, just as one had expected, and the first thing that I saw on entering the room were signed photographs of Truman and Snyder. So I had stumbled unwittingly across the rich hand of the Democratic Party.

Frank Soskice [Solicitor-General] came along as I thought it would be nice to put them in touch with each other, and I left the party with him sitting happily on the sofa beside Mrs Stewart.

Then I went with my friend, Jim Orrick and 'did the town'.[54] The best part being dancing with his sister-in-law in Greenwich Village at a place called 'The Vanguard', with a superb Negro band and most excellent cabaret of informal character. Not more than twenty people there and three or four couples dancing. I loved it. I also got a great kick out of the fact that I was going to be Chancellor the next day. I had told Jim before and told the other[s] too, though I don't think it made much impression upon them!

I have always been most amused by Donald Fergusson's story of Birkenhead, when Lord Chancellor, being seen at Nice with two chorus girls, one on each knee.[55] I would not do that because it would upset my

---

54 J.B. Orrick had been an American graduate student at New College, Oxford, and a close friend in HG's undergraduate days. He became a U.N. official.
55 F.E. Smith, who became Earl of Birkenhead, was Lord Chancellor 1919–22 and Secretary for India 1924–8.

wife, but I did like the idea of dancing in Greenwich Village as well as the reality.

The news broke the next day just before we left New York. I came back from lunch with the International City Bank (very nice and friendly too and I thought more intelligent than our bankers). I am getting quite used to being approached by journalists. It is rather like the novelette business of two detectives waiting for you. They step out and confront you, and of course they showed me what had come over the tape. I gave them a quick message and was photographed – horrible photos – and had to pack.

At the airport we had a press conference and lots more photographs. I had tried to speak to Dora at 4.30 a.m. the previous night when I got back from my gaiety (it was 10.30 p.m. in England) but they could not get through. I wondered how she felt about it all. But everything went all right. We were rather late in arriving. There she was waiting and she came on to the plane so that we could kiss in private, and then we walked down the gangway and faced the cameras and movietone and so on.

I went straight to Downing Street to see Stafford [Cripps] first. He had said to me on his way through Zürich a fortnight before that there was a fifty-fifty chance of his coming back, but I did not take this seriously. I have always felt that there was so much hypochondria about his attitude and he had always rather taken this line. Then I had read that he had left the Clinic quite soon and assumed all would be well. But apparently it was not so. His doctors both in Zürich and in London (though I believe they are all a lot of cranks) had told him that his heart would not stand the strain and he would have a worse attack, in three months' time if he went on, which would more or less cripple him for life. So there was no option.

He was, of course, very charming to me and did everything he could before he left to make my path easier, speaking to other Members of the Government whom he knew best and asking them to support me, and dealing as best he could with the inevitable jealousies.

Then I saw the P.M. As usual one's interviews with him are never very exciting or long. But I made sure that I really was to be Number 4 in the Government as Stafford had been. He warned me about Shinwell and Bevan, but told me that he was going to move Nye from the Ministry of Health to the Ministry of Labour – something I had been hoping for and in my quiet way pushing for a long time. But evidently something has gone wrong since then because no change has been made, and he told me a day or two ago that there had been difficulties. So he was letting it rest for the moment.[56]

56 On HG's selection (for which Cripps was mainly responsible) and on the reaction of his colleagues see *HG*, pp. 236–8. On Bevan's refusal of the Ministry of Labour at this time, and the exasperation caused by it, see Dalton diary, 30.10.50.

Of course it is impossible not to create jealousies, but I am not too worried. I suspect that Nye is not so much jealous but humiliated at my being put over him. But HW[Wilson], and others confirm, is inordinately jealous, though in view of his age there is really no reason for it. But then one does not look for reasons for jealousy. Shinwell, too, is probably put out in the same way as Bevan.

At first it was very strange – one could not get used to the idea of being Chancellor. One did not feel any different, and one could not, so to speak, modify one's idea of the office to fit in with one's idea of oneself. Now I am beginning to get used to it a bit more, and I suppose that in a few months time if I am still here there will be nothing strange about it at all. But we certainly face some very, very difficult problems arising out of inflation and rearmament. More difficult in some ways, though less critical, than the 1947–9 problems. So far everybody is being very nice but that will not last for long.

CHAPTER 5

CHANCELLOR OF THE EXCHEQUER

Editor's Note
Diary, 5 January 1951 to 16 November 1951
Document No. 8 Dollar aid and Defence
(HG to Parliamentary Committee, 23.11.51)

[Because of Cripps' state of health, senior Ministers had known for months that a new Chancellor might be needed. Dalton, who did not want the post himself, had urged Gaitskell's eventual claims on Attlee in January 1950, in the summer, and again in October when he heard that Cripps had finally resigned – only to find that the decision he wanted had already been taken. The decisive influence was Cripps himself, who further insisted that Gaitskell, though young and little known in the Party, must replace him also as the fourth senior Minister, after the Prime Minister, Morrison and Ernest Bevin. Those senior colleagues also approved of Gaitskell and much preferred him to Aneurin Bevan. Morrison did not think himself qualified, turned down various unofficial approaches, and was quite content at the choice of a man too young, as it then seemed, to be a dangerous rival.

On 9 March 1951 Bevin was moved from the Foreign Office and replaced by Morrison. Bevan had thus been passed over for both the senior offices, despite his ability and standing in the Party. As early as Christmas, his unhappiness with the Administration had led him to canvass potential allies in resignation; and the choice of Morrison, further weakening his power in the Cabinet, may have been decisive. For his disappointment had come just as all the tensions and frustrations were mounting to their long-foreseen crunch: the rearmament Budget. It was presented on 10 April 1951, and within a fortnight Bevan, Wilson and Freeman resigned. Yet Gaitskell told Dalton the day after the Budget speech that until noon he had been uncertain whether or not he would be making it.

The Budget was warmly and enthusiastically received in the P.L.P., even by Bevan's sympathisers. In the debate, 20 out of 28 Labour back-benchers applauded it and not one attacked it. Detailed criticism fastened not on health charges, but on the conditions – meant to discourage early retirement – attached to the increased old-age pensions. The charges provoked no spontaneous protest in the Labour Movement, in the P.L.P. or even in a dissident minority. Their impact demonstrated the individual influence, and was due to the individual reaction, of one man alone.

Bevan's objection was not to the specific charges but to renouncing an entirely free health service – though he had agreed to that course earlier, when he had felt that broader political considerations required him to remain in the government. The bitter dispute split the Labour Party for years. But the Chancellor had to take the rearmament programme as given, the basic policy he was expected to finance by colleagues none of whom had as yet challenged its necessity or threatened to resign over its size. Facing that huge extra expenditure, no Chancellor could have failed to seek economies in a departmental budget so large, so long immune and so steadily growing as that of the health service. His proposals would have led to no revolt but for the resignations, and to no bitterness but for the tone adopted by Bevan and his journal (which accused Gaitskell of acting like Snowden in 1931, and of 'dismantling the welfare state').

The Ministers who resigned soon broadened their attack, opposing the rearmament programme initiated by Attlee and Bevin at a time when fears of an imminent third world war were acute: 'possible in 1951, probable in 1952', as the War Office officially told the Cabinet at the New Year. Gaitskell defended it, but he knew the economic risks and worked hard behind the scenes to limit the burden without a breach with Washington: and in the end successfully, though too late to help his own Government. But unplanned international rearmament produced a mad scramble for raw materials and a wild commodity boom on a 1973 scale. First, Britain's precarious wage and price stability was severely threatened; then in the autumn she suffered a balance of payments crisis as sudden as it was massive. Politically the Labour Government thus became vulnerable in the Party to the Bevanite attack on its defence and foreign policy, and in the country to the Conservatives, who narrowly won the November 1951 election with more seats than Labour but fewer votes.]

Friday, 5 January 1951

It is now ten weeks or more since I became Chancellor and a brief review of the situation in various spheres and at various levels is worth putting down.

Inside the Treasury I am fairly well satisfied with the arrangements. I have managed to delegate a very substantial amount of work on to the two Junior Ministers, both of whom are I think much happier than before; though Douglas [Jay] finds all the financial detail wearing and would obviously rather have some other job. But I think he feels now he has more authority and a clearer field of work. John [Edwards] is, if anything, overworked since as Chairman of the Materials Committee he is running into a lot of allocation jobs.[1]

I cannot say that I am entirely happy about the officials. Perhaps it is just that they are not the sort of people one has the same attractive and intimate relationship with as was the case at Fuel & Power. Perhaps it is that they have such a keen sense of their own independent, departmental position as

1 HG had himself chaired the Materials Committee: *HG*, pp. 137-8.

apart from serving me. For example, in the Treasury they are continually using the phrases, 'It is the Treasury view', or at least 'It is the departmental Treasury view', or, 'We think', etc. This is buttressed up by such institutions as the Budget Committee, which is purely official and on its status they lay much emphasis; the Second Secretaries' meetings which [the Permanent Secretary] Bridges runs, and various other similar bodies.

I am perhaps more close to Edwin Plowden than anybody else, but he in particular has a keen sense of his own independence, perhaps because he is not a permanent Civil Servant. Still, these are not serious complaints. On the whole relations are for the most part quite good, though it is always a problem to know how far to go into driving people and interfering with them. The machine can get so easily slack if you leave them alone. But if you harass them then they complain bitterly that you are interfering too much and not delegating, etc.

In the Cabinet too I am reasonably happy with my position. It is, of course, not nearly as strong as Stafford's, but I have not had much trouble with any of my colleagues. Shinwell is the most difficult. Obviously my promotion over his head went very deep. He never loses an opportunity of picking a quarrel with me, sometimes on the most ridiculous grounds. In any case there are often very good grounds for it in view of the terrific defence expenditure.

Outwardly Nye Bevan is quite friendly again, and at least he gives a much more honest view of things than Shinwell does. I do not really feel with him that he is insincere and for long going to take a view simply because of his personal likes or dislikes.

Harold Wilson is probably still exceedingly jealous, but I must say I have had no great difficulty with him. But all this is rather premature because the real struggle will come when we try and settle expenditure policy and get nearer to the Budget.

About the Parliamentary Party there is not much to be said. They seem to have accepted my appointment quite easily. They would, of course, like me to be much ruder to the Opposition than I am, and recently when I was fairly rude to Churchill they cheered like mad, and afterwards a lot of people came up and congratulated me.[2] The Tory press were of course very angry and attacked me bitterly. However, for the most part I have avoided this because of my belief that as Chancellor one must try and avoid too much Party activity. Obviously, however, to the country as a whole I am still, as several of my colleagues and friends remind me, pretty

2 After Churchill's repeated advocacy of scaling down India's sterling balances in London, owed to her on account of wartime supplies, Gaitskell said his attitude to India had always been unrealistic and totally lacking in humanity: 482 H.C. Deb. 542–4 (7 December 1950), and *HG*, pp. 241–2.

unknown. This does not worry me at all. There is plenty of time and one cannot help accumulating a good deal of publicity.

On the other hand, the problems [have] accumulated thick and fast, and it is quite astonishing how different everything is from what it was six or even three months ago. On the one hand we have the spectacular balance of payments where we are at present running a surplus of three to four hundred million a year. On the other hand, the extremely gloomy outlook as regards raw materials, coal and the impact of rearmament.

I suppose the most important event in these last few weeks has been the ending of Marshall Aid as far as I am concerned. The history of this is as follows.

When I was in Washington various people hinted to me that they would not be able to go on helping us much longer because of the improvement in our position. One of these was Foster, head of E.C.A. I said to him that we quite understood their position but that we wished to be consulted first, and I asked him if he wanted consultations to start. He said, 'Not yet'. However, when I got back to London his No. 2, Bissell, was waiting for me, and the rumour was that he was going to tell me that they could not give us any more. We had, in fact, a very strong case for some more Marshall Aid dollars in the light of promises given earlier. This had evidently been made plain to Bissell, before he saw me, by the [U.S.] Embassy here. For when he came he did not say they wanted to cut us off, but merely that they wanted to discuss future arrangements. It was agreed that the discussions should take place with William Batt, the new head of the E.C.A. Mission in London, when he arrived in November.

There was then a period during which it looked as though our ideas of what was reasonable would appeal to them, under which we would have got not only all that was in the pipe-line, but also another $100 million. However, when Batt arrived the position had changed again, and they wanted to cut it off at once. I made something of a fuss about this and argued our case for the extra $100 million. He took it well and indicated that he had not appreciated our arguments before. There was then another long period during which the rumours were that we were to get what we wanted, and I am pretty certain this was recommended to Washington by Batt and also by Katz of the Embassy.[3]

However, just about then the debacle in Korea occurred,[4] and Washington decided that they could not get anything more past Congress. In the circumstances I had no option but to accept. I did however manage

3 Katz was not 'of the Embassy'; he was now U.S. Special Representative in Europe, replacing Harriman.
4 The Chinese not only reconquered North Korea but overran all South Korea apart from one small pocket.

to secure a settlement on the vexed question of counterpart funds as a deliberate bit of bargaining.[5] Of course, the final statements were all agreed and the whole thing went off in the friendliest possible manner and everyone was very pleased about it.

Wednesday, 10 January 1951

Raw Materials

If anybody had said to me six months ago that the major problem which I should be dealing with in the beginning of 1951 would be the shortage of materials for British industry I should certainly not have believed him. Yet I suppose there is nothing upon which I spend more time. Part of our trouble certainly arises from the past. We were obliged to restrict dollar imports after devaluation and one consequence of this, plus a certain amount of credit restriction, was de-stocking here. But the major difficulties have, of course, been due to the enormous United States demand, partly for production and partly for stock-piling. That we should need to convert dollars into raw materials as far as we could was recognised not so long after Korea, and certainly by the beginning of August we had given instructions to the Purchasing Departments to go out and buy whatever they could. All the same, I think they were rather slow off the mark, and one must admit that bulk purchase has a disadvantage in that it takes a long time to induce those concerned to adopt a bold, aggressive and risk taking policy. They are frightened of buying at prices which are too high in case they make a loss and in consequence they sometimes fail to get in in time.

In September we began to talk to the Americans about co-ordinating policy on stock-piling, and by the end of the month we were getting seriously worried by not only the price increases but also the shortages. As my note shows, this was one of the major topics I took up with everyone in Washington.[6]

There then followed a period of very private official talks with the Americans, but this too led nowhere.

Meanwhile, O.E.E.C. had started their survey; all very agitated about it, and a Report was produced for the Council early in December. By now

5 For over a year the nominal sterling 'counterpart' of Marshall Aid supplies had been accumulating in a Treasury account at the Bank of England. The Americans had wanted it used for specific investment projects, but now accepted the British preference for using it to retire government debt.

6 Above, p. 206.

we were getting really disturbed about zinc and sulphur particularly, and to some extent about cotton.

The Prime Minister's visit to Truman[7] provided an opportunity for raising the matter at the highest level with the Americans, and one gathers that there was an immediate response. For the first time all the various Agencies concerned with this problem in Washington – seven of them – were brought together. In one meeting it was agreed there should be International Commodity Groups of the main producers and consumers, and a central group consisting of the Americans, French and ourselves.

Yet a month has gone by since then and nothing however [whatever?] has happened. The reason, fantastic as it seems, is simply the anxiety of the Americans as to whether they can resist the pressure of other countries to come on the central group. Tnere have been various interchanges between the P.M. and Truman, and it is only in the last few days that a formula has been found. It really is depressing to see how terribly slowly the Democracies work and I am bound to say this is mainly due, (a) to the chaotic nature of the administration in Washington, (b) to the extraordinary fear the Americans have of giving any offence to the smallest possible power.

The O.E.E.C. Mission which was sent over shortly after the Attlee visit of course had its nose put out of joint by these developments. This is one of the reasons for the delay in the establishment of the Central Group. Stikker, Dutch Foreign Minister and Chairman of O.E.E.C., has been very upset and we had to have him over this week and discuss things with him. He spoke of a crisis of confidence among the smaller powers. We had to do something to get over this – though he admits the need for the large powers to get together on this. Indeed he agreed with everything we had done. This does not get away from the tiresome prestige question which continually crops up. I expect a very difficult meeting the day after tomorrow in Paris, the more so as one cannot really rely on the French and Americans to take an honest and straightforward line. The French are always anxious to keep in with the smaller powers, and pretend to some kind of leadership among them; while the U.S.A. – Katz – have of course a great softness for O.E.E.C. and would like everything to go through it. This is all part of their internal struggle for power in Washington.[8]

Incidentally, one of the interesting aspects of the P.M.'s visit was the

7 Attlee flew to Washington on 4 December 1950, after President Truman was thought to have hinted that atomic weapons might be used in the Far East.
8 Gaitskell had been pleased a few months earlier when that power struggle had enabled him to use the European sympathies of Katz in Britain's interests: above, p. 181. On Stikker, above, p. 177 n.

reaction of the Foreign Secretary. He did not much like it. He told me that Clem [Attlee] had come to him with a letter from Hugh Dalton urging that he, Clem, should go. EB[Bevin] evidently felt this to be a slight on himself. He said that he would have been much happier if the P.M. had come to him and suggested it himself instead of sheltering behind the Dalton letter. I am bound to think that the trouble we have had since then is partly due to a similar sort of pique on behalf of some of the Departments in Washington.

Reverting back to the O.E.E.C. problem. This had wasted an enormous amount of my time in the past few months. Part of the cause is the sensitivity of those smaller countries, but I am bound to say that part is due to our own vacillations in policy. We always start by taking a tough line by saying everything must be done by NATO, and then giving way, with the result that we get no change and merely become unpopular in O.E.E.C. Again and again I have tried to restrain the Foreign Office and our own people from offending O.E.E.C. unless they are prepared, as they are not, to take a very definite policy decision on the whole matter. However, while we may be to blame in this respect, the real trouble I am sure lies in the personal preferences and anxieties of officials and Ministers, mostly of the smaller Powers, in the Delegations at Paris. They are frightened of losing a very nice job. They don't want to leave Paris. They are to some extent escapists about rearmament, and of course all this attitude is fostered by the Secretariat – interested inevitably in jobs.

What shocks me most about O.E.E.C. is that it is really so full of disaffection for NATO. One hardly dares mention NATO in O.E.E.C. Pella, the Italian Minister of the Treasury, quite openly regards NATO as a sort of gang of militarists whom it is his duty to fight, and some of the other Ministers seem to feel the same way.

We are now going to make an effort to kill by kindness. We have reconciled ourselves to the economic side of NATO being developed in Paris, and hope in that way that both the Delegation and the Secretariat and the Ministers will become a bit more NATO-conscious, but it will be uphill work.

Stikker himself, who is a Brewer by profession, is a pleasant rather sly business man with a good deal of vanity, who generally comes down on the right side eventually, but whom one does not feel able to trust entirely. Perhaps this is not his fault since he has been put in as Chairman to be a kind of conciliator.

I am bound to say that the international outlook gets gloomier and gloomier. If we can stabilise the position in Korea then it is still possible I think that some kind of negotiated settlement may be reached between the Americans and Chinese. But so long as the Chinese are advancing they are not likely to be ready to talk, and if we are actually thrown out of Korea pressure in America for some retaliatory action on China will be very, very strong. They talk of a limited war but we all feel that there is no such thing, and the worst of it is that the Chinese would probably retaliate, if blockade is organised against them or if the Americans bomb them, by occupying Hong Kong and moving south through Indo-China to Malaya. I fear too that a young Nationalist movement with such enormous numbers may be difficult to restrain in any case.

The awful dilemma is that if we cannot restrain the Americans then we have to go in with them in China, which nobody wants, or desert them. If we desert them obviously it may have very serious consequences in their participating in European defence. The immediate issue is whether or not in U.N.O. China shall be declared an aggressor, but even if we get over this hurdle I am afraid there will be others to come later on.

It is not surprising in these circumstances that there is now developing something like a panic about our Defence programme. It is to be accelerated. We do not yet know by how much, nor what this will involve, but inevitably the atmosphere becomes more and more like 1940.

To add to the gloom the coal situation does not improve. This time we have taken, as far as we can see, all possible steps in advance, but are still faced with a real shortage and threat of a crisis. We may be able to keep the Power Stations going and that will be our policy, but whether industry will get enough coal is another matter. We are preparing allocation schemes in case the worst comes to the worst.

There was a meeting at No. 10 with the Miners the other day. I thought to myself, 'This is where I came in'. It followed the usual pattern. Exhortations from the Government; smooth talking from the Union combined with demands for wage and other concessions – some of which will of course have to be met.

I am afraid that Phil Noel-Baker, Minister of Fuel, is having a very rough time. . . . He is a very nice man and deserves better things. But I think he will have to move when the immediate crisis is over. If he is I hope that Alf Robens will get at last the promotion he deserves.

What with raw materials, the Korean and Chinese situation, coal and rearmament, the prospect is really black. I was cheered up today only by one thing. There now at least seems to be some possibility that AB[Bevan] may be moved from the Ministry of Health to the Ministry of Labour.[9] That might make a lot of difference to my financial policy. It is too early to speak but it may be the removal of the obstacle in the way of

9 He became Minister of Labour on 17 January 1951.

general economy on public expenditure not only in the Ministry of Health but in other fields as well, which in turn may make possible various other ideas.

The Governor of the Bank of England has been asking for a rise in bank rate.[10] We had a rather sticky discussion on this. He has tried it on both my predecessors. He admits the case for it is purely psychological, and it would cost the Treasury 16 million a year (even [a]½% increase), but because he resists other direct methods of credit control he presses for what I am personally convinced is a completely antiquated instrument. If we do not use the old signal the question is what other steps do we take to control credit? The answer is that we tell the Joint Stock Banks what to do. If we restrict their cash basis they would merely refuse to take up Treasury Bills and we should be driven to borrow from the Bank of England, and this would frustrate the whole operation. So one would have to say to the Banks that they must take up so many Treasury Bills. Alternatively, one could say that they must restrict their advances or charge a higher rate for them. Or, better still, adopt a selective credit policy. On all of these the Governor is somehow uncooperative.

However, we have turned down his proposal as we were bound to, and urged him to pursue these other ideas. I must say that I have a very poor opinion not only of him – he is simply not a very intelligent man – but of also most of the people in the Bank. Whether they are right or not in matters of judgment, they are singularly bad at putting their case, and judging by experience they are usually wrong in their conclusions. The only thing to be said for Cobbold is that he does not attempt to pursue an independent policy, and seems to expect that on high policy it is for us to decide. This is important.

Dora and I had dinner with Campbell Stuart* to meet the new American Ambassador.[11] It was not a very exciting evening. But among those present was a Mrs Carnegie who at one time had been the wife of Joseph Chamberlain.[12] She is now 86 and a grand old lady. There was a certain thrill about meeting somebody who had such an intimate link with a distant past.

10 The precursor of minimum lending rate. Cameron (Lord) Cobbold was Governor 1949–61.
11 Walter Gifford (1885–1966), Ambassador 1950–53; formerly of A.T. & T. Sir Campbell Stuart had been managing director of *The Times*, and briefly ran British propaganda in both world wars.
12 Chamberlain (1836–1914) led the Radicals until he resigned office in 1886 to oppose Irish home rule. He was Colonial Secretary in Unionist governments from 1895–1903 when he resigned to promote tariffs. He married his third wife Mary Endicott, daughter of an American politician, in 1888. Father of Austen and Neville Chamberlain.

Wednesday, 24 January 1951

The Minister of Labour [George Isaacs] has at last been pushed out and the Minister of Health put in his place. At the same time the Ministry of Health is being split up – housing and local government work going to the Ministry of Town and Country Planning, while the health work stays on its own. Hilary Marquand gets the latter job.

This is the result of a long series of pressures and efforts on behalf of many of us. Shortly before Christmas I spoke to the P.M. about the importance of moving Bevan from the Ministry of Health and putting him in the Ministry of Labour. I urged that this must be done during the Recess while the Conservative pressure about housing was not evident. I had previously discussed it with HD[Dalton, Minister of Town & Country Planning] who had indicated that he was not particularly keen to take housing and would not object if it went to the Ministry of Works. I told the P.M. this and I also put forward the tentative suggestion that it might be a good idea to make Dick Stokes Minister of Supply; George Strauss taking his place at the Ministry of Works with housing thrown in.

The P.M. was rather taken with this idea at that time. I also suggested that since the departure of George Isaacs would mean that another Trade Unionist should be promoted, that [sic] Alf Robens should be made Minister of Health. I knew that Alf would be co-operative on the financial side and would also have the guts to take unpopular steps in the ways of economy vis-à-vis the medical profession.

It did not come off just like this. First because George Isaacs indicated that he wanted to stay somewhere in the Government, and the P.M. proposed Pensions. Secondly because the fuel situation is such that the P.M. did not want to move Alf at the moment. (I must say that I agree with this.) Thirdly because the Treasury advised strongly that housing and Town Planning must go together. Fourthly because I think later the P.M. had some doubts about the change between the Ministry of Supply and the Ministry of Works. I am inclined to think that my suggestion about Dick Stokes was probably not a particularly good one; though I am worried as to whether Strauss has the necessary drive to push through the defence programme.[13]

The change did not get a very good press, mainly because no other changes were made. But, generally speaking, I think people realised that it was a wise move. It will be interesting to see how Nye [Bevan] does at the Ministry of Labour. I suspect that he will become more conservative,

13 Isaacs went to Pensions, Stokes stayed at Works and Strauss at Supply – all outside the Cabinet. Dalton's expanded Ministry was renamed Local Government & Planning, and was in the Cabinet.

thus living up to his reputation of being radical in everybody else's Ministry except his own. He will probably be more cautious about wages policy and the direction of labour than he has ever been in the past. At the same time it is certainly a relief to have him out of the Ministry of Health, and although Marquand was not my first choice I am fairly confident that he will be easy to work with.

Friday, 2 February 1951

The storm is blowing up harder. We have had a bad week: the meat ration cut to eightpence; the announcement of the rearmament programme and the rise in the price of coal. The general feeling is that we should suffer a pretty heavy defeat if there was to be an Election now. Obviously, the Tories are out to try and force one.

All this is bringing stresses and strains within the Party itself and within the Government.

We got the rearmament programme through however rather more easily than might have been expected. It was in fact put through despite the absence of the Foreign Secretary, the Minister of Defence and the C.I.G.S. I found myself acting more or less as the chief spokesman for it, which was rather odd seeing that I have to find the money.

It was expected that Bevan would put up a lot more resistance. I never thought so myself for the simple reason that once the programme had been put forward it was difficult to see what we could do other than accept it. We were committed to some acceleration – we could hardly start arguing with the Chiefs of Staff about what was essential and what was not essential. Both the President of the Board of Trade [Wilson] and Minister of Supply [Strauss] made some effort to resist it, partly I think on political grounds (they are linking up with the Minister of Labour) and partly just as an alibi in case the programme could not be fulfilled or exports dropped catastrophically. [14]

But there has been a far more serious split developing on foreign policy. This came out clearly over the United Nations resolution on China. Until Ernie [Bevin] became ill our line was to try and restrain the Americans in every way; to try and delay the resolution going before U.N.O., but in the last resource [resort?] to accept it. But last Thursday evening, eight days ago, during the final meeting of the Cabinet to approve the defence programme, we were told that we had to decide on our attitude; that it was unlikely that the Americans would agree to any

14 *HG*, pp. 247–8, gives corroborative evidence on the Cabinet discussions.

amendments that would have met us, and that we must assume that the resolution would be put in an unpalatable form. Kenneth Younger was there without any Foreign Office officials, and rather to my surprise without referring to the Foreign Office view, made it plain that he was actually in favour of voting against it. There was a short and rather emotional discussion in the course of which the majority of the Cabinet agreed with him, especially of course the Minister of Labour. Hector McNeil alone had the courage to say that he was in favour of voting 'for'. I then suggested, since it was obvious that we would be defeated on that, that at least we ought to abstain. I think the P.M. agreed with that and so did the Lord President [Morrison] (who had been curiously weak up to then). But the only other Member of the Cabinet to support it was Jowitt, Kenneth [Younger] saying that in his opinion there was no difference between voting against or abstaining.[15]

This all happened very quickly and before getting on to the real job of discussing the defence programme. I felt very unhappy at the time and afterwards had a talk with Hector. We both thought it was a fatal decision, but I then discovered that both he and the Lord President were going to Scotland that night. He did, however, ring up William Strang from my room and asked if the Foreign Secretary was well enough to be told of this decision.[16] Strang said he thought not. Hector confirmed however from Strang that the Foreign Secretary would certainly be deeply shocked by the decision which was contrary to his own policy and so, of course, would the whole official Foreign Office.

Hector urged him nevertheless to try and see the Foreign Secretary in the morning, or at least to see the P.M. and tell him what he thought the Foreign Secretary really wanted.

The more I thought about this the more worried I became, and I had a very restless night. I told Dora everything and she too, though often very anti-American, thought it was very grave.

When I came into the office the next morning I sent for Bridges and Plowden and told them what had happened, partly to test out my own reaction. They were completely horrified. I then told Bridges that he should see Strang at once and try and get him to make contact with the Foreign Secretary, and in any case to see the P.M. I also suggested that they should try and get Franks [Ambassador in Washington] to telegraph

15 McNeil, Secretary for Scotland, had preceded Younger as Minister of State at the Foreign Office. Lord (Earl) Jowitt (1885–1957) was a Liberal M.P. 1922–24, Labour 1929–31, 1939–45; held office in the Labour government 1929–31, National government 1931–2, Churchill coalition 1940–5; Lord Chancellor 1945–51.
16 Sir William (Lord) Strang (1893–1978) was Permanent Under-Secretary, 1949–53.

his views. I also arranged to see Christopher Addison [Leader of the House of Lords] and the P.M.

Finally, I told Edwin [Plowden] – though nobody else – that I proposed to tell the P.M. that unless this decision was altered I would find it difficult to continue in the Government. Later Edwin sent a message through William Armstrong [HG's private secretary] to tell me to make that plain because he was sure it would have very great influence.

Bridges then came back from Strang with the good news that telegrams had come in showing that the Americans were likely to give way to us on one point and on the other the Israelis were putting forward a new amendment which looked all right for us. Strang thought this was good enough to see the P.M. on – a card of re-entry he called it – and I agreed.

Bridges said that Ernie [Bevin] was said by the Doctor to be too incoherent to be told. I then saw Addison and explained my anxieties. I told him that I thought this decision might have the most fatal consequences on Anglo-American relations, and that it would enormously strengthen the anti-European block in the U.S.A. It might lead to their virtually coming [away] from Europe which would, in my opinion, be the end for us. I also urged the danger of voting against all the white Dominions. Finally I suggested that we were being a little unreasonable with the Americans and tried to draw a parallel with the Middle East. If, I said, Russia had attacked in the Middle East and we had to provide the troops to U.N.O. to resist it – we had successfully done so until Russian volunteers intervened and we had been driven back – if then the Americans, who were contributing a very small force, had declined to support a resolution on Russian aggression or had declined to give further help we should feel very sore about the whole matter.

Addison listened in silence but seemed impressed. I also told him about my own position and about the new telegrams. When he heard about these he agreed that there was a complete change and he thought we ought to vote 'for' if we could get amendments on these lines. Finally, he said that he thought I was probably right and we should not have gone further than abstaining. He urged me to see the P.M., and said that he would talk to one or two of the others – Tom Williams[17] and Chuter Ede* [Home Secretary].

I went over to No. 10 and met Strang and Younger with the P.M. They had the telegrams and they rapidly agreed that this was a new situation and the Cabinet would have to be called immediately. I made Strang spell

17 Later Lord Williams of Barnburgh (1888–1967). A miner; M.P. for Don Valley (Yorkshire) 1922–59; Parl. Sec. Agriculture 1940–5, Minister 1945–51; author of the 1947 Agriculture Act.

out in front of Younger what he had said to Bridges about the Foreign Secretary, which was very different from Younger's account of it to the Cabinet. I also got him to confirm that the Foreign Office people believed that there was a very big difference between abstention and voting against. Finally, I asked that he should be present at the Cabinet.

Then I saw the P.M. alone and went over the same ground as I had with Addison. He listened in silence and we had a short discussion. He pointed out the difficulty arising from the fact that so many senior Ministers of the Cabinet held other views, and there was a brief but friendly argument about the Americans. Then I left him.

At the Cabinet meeting the P.M. explained the new situation, but this did not prevent some of them, four in number – Dalton, Bevan, Chuter Ede and Jim Griffiths – from arguing for a time against any change. The P.M. however was now quite firm and very good with them. I only had to weigh in once or twice – especially against Dalton who was the most intransigent and who, I knew, would not wish to row with me in public. Addison too was very good and he won over Tom Williams who recanted and to some extent Chuter Ede as well.

It was left that if the Americans would agree amendments on these lines we could vote 'for'. If they did not the decision would be left to the P.M. I felt pretty certain in my own mind that he would not go further than abstention.

On Monday there had been new developments. The Americans did not agree to the Israeli amendment but had offered a compromise and the P.M. had more or less accepted this. So finally it was decided to vote for the resolution.[18]

It was a dramatic interlude but frightening because of the, as I think, lack of understanding and anti-Americanism displayed in the Cabinet.

A few days later we had another discussion on Foreign affairs over the much wider and more difficult issues of Germany and Russia. But again there is to some extent the same cleavage. The anti-Americans, so it seems to [me], because they are anti-Americans will not admit now the Russian menace. This leads them to oppose a lot of things which the Americans want to do. It leads them for a variety of rather confused motives to a hostility to rearming Germany. It leads to accepting the

18 On this incident see *HG*, pp. 242–4 (based on Dalton's and Younger's accounts as well as HG's). The amendments deferred the preparations for sanctions against China which had mainly provoked the alarm in the British Cabinet.

possibility of an agreement with Russia which some of us think might be extraordinarily dangerous.[19]

The whole situation is extremely difficult with the Foreign Secretary away because Kenneth Younger, whose judgment on this is not I think very good, in any case does not carry much weight; and the P.M. though nominally looking after the Foreign Office is not really continually in touch with the officials, and apt to be swayed very much by the views of the Cabinet Members. Beyond all this lies the division between those who believe it their duty and the right policy to follow opinion in the Party which certainly is pretty anti-American, and still rather pacifist, and those who do not attach a great deal of importance to this, even politically. I belong to the latter. While it is important of course to carry the Party with us, in my view they will follow the right lead and their reaction on issues of this kind is generally not typical of the country as a whole.

One cannot ignore the fact that in all this there are personal ambitions and rivalries at work. HW[Wilson] is clearly ganging up with the Minister of Labour, not that he cuts very much ice because one feels that he has no fundamental views of his own, but it is another voice. The others on Bevan's side are very genuine. Jim Griffiths for pacifism; Chuter Ede because he is anti-American and Dalton because he hates the Germans and cannot bear the idea of their rearmament. On the other side are the Lord President [Morrison], Hector McNeil and I, and of course the Foreign Secretary when he is well. Hartley Shawcross also would be in our camp, and so would Patrick Gordon Walker but he is away.

Friday, 16 February 1951

Meat

We had had a bad time about meat lately and naturally enough for the ration had to be reduced to 8d for carcass meat. Why was this? It is a long and rather interesting story.

Last May we opened negotiations with the Argentine on the price that we should pay for meat for the current year under the five-year agreement. There had been no breach of the agreement. They still refused to

19 See *HG*, pp. 244–6, on this first round in the long Labour Party argument over German rearmament. He told Dalton of his worries about a 'false deal' with Russia over Germany; if it were united but disarmed 'they could just march into it': Dalton diary, 9.2.51.

pay their financial debts. They had accumulated a further £3½ million of trade debts. They would not allow our export of inessentials, reasonable prices in their markets, etc.

We were told by the Ministry of Food that we were in the strongest bargaining position we had ever been in. We had been paying a good deal more for Argentine meat than Australia or New Zealand. So with complete unanimity it was decided to open the bidding at £90 per ton and go up to £97.10s. We had not expected this to be accepted, or that any of our other demands would be either. So after some weeks they suspended shipments. Negotiations were being handled by our Ambassador, who then proceeded to go on leave.

Nothing whatever happened until August when the Argentine Minister here saw Ernie [Bevin] and – as we thought at the time and still think – Ernie started negotiating with him. They paid up the commercial debts and made some vague promises about the financial remittances. On meat we moved to £97.10s. They would not however accept this except on a purely temporary basis. At one point it looked as if the deal would be closed on a three-months basis. We reckoned that they would not suspend shipments again. But at the last moment they withdrew from this and offered a month, which was thought to be farcical.

Meanwhile the Ministry of Food's calculations had gone wrong slightly. There was less meat from Australia and less from home killings. So the ration had to be cut early in December instead of waiting until the New Year. Then at the end of the month they came forward with an offer of £120 a ton, to be met partly by shipping some chilled beef.

For some time I had been growing more and more uneasy about the position, and even in the summer had urged that we must try and come to some settlement. I felt that they would be able to hold out longer than we expected; while the Government would not wish to face a cut in the ration. I managed to influence the offers made a little, but I must confess I did not press very hard, mainly I think because the Foreign Secretary was responsible for the negotiations and the Minister of Food [Maurice Webb] was the person chiefly concerned at home. Also it is not easy for the Treasury to suggest to other Departments that they should spend more money.

By now these anxieties of mine had grown more, and I made it plain that we must try and settle after the Argentine had made their £120 – chilled beef – offer. Unfortunately, this did not prove possible, although the Treasury gave the Ministry of Food quite considerable scope, and I should certainly have been prepared to pay the full price had we been asked by the Ministry of Food. They did not go up to anything like our final offer in the two days of expert discussions which took place. No doubt the Ministry of Food officials expected the negotiations would continue, but unfortunately the Argentine Ambassador went straight to the press and announced they were broken off.

This is a very interesting example of the difficulties of bulk purchase, especially when several Departments are involved. Had only one Department been involved it probably would have been easier to reach agreement. But, undoubtedly, one of the major difficulties has been the great reluctance of the Ministry of Food to pay higher prices when they know I am not going to increase the subsidy. Also, I am afraid they are too much in blinkers so far as the general economic situation of the world is concerned and the rises in money incomes here.[20]

Our position has been seriously weakened by reason of the major row in the country – in press, Parliament, etc. We have asked the editors to be reasonable [and] patriotic about this now, and since then things have been a bit better, but I am afraid the damage has been done, and I am also afraid the Argentine may raise their prices still further.

In the Party there has been, so I am told, strong feeling against Maurice Webb. Not so much about what has happened but as they feel this to be a kind of nemesis for him after what is said to be his stabbing of Strachey in the back when the latter was Minister of Food.

Maurice Webb is a very good public relations man, but I cannot say I think he has much judgment or administrative capacity. A better Minister of Food would have spotted what was going to happen and taken a firm hold on the thing earlier, and insisted on an offer on the higher prices.

I have had one or two talks lately with the P.M. about the future of the Foreign Office. On the first occasion he asked my views very tentatively and I told him that I thought that HM[Morrison] should do the job if Ernie [Bevin] were not going to carry on. The P.M. demurred on this and disagreed with my remarks that I thought H. had good judgment in foreign affairs. He mentioned Jim Griffiths. I said that I liked Jim, but I thought he would be far too weak as F.S. [Foreign Secretary] and referred to his behaviour during the discussions on Lake Success [voting at the U.N.] and Korea. He did not at the time mention anybody else, and our discussion ended with the general idea that it might be better for Ernie to go on for a bit anyhow.

Subsequently I had a talk with Dalton, mainly to try and patch up our disagreements on foreign policy. This was not too difficult. He seemed to agree broadly with my point of view, and it is a mystery to me why he took such [a] strong anti-American line in the Cabinet. Of course, what he is

20 One person who did not fully appreciate the Chancellor's position was his wife, who impressed on him the housewife's irritation by serving him only fish – which he did not like.

really cross about is German rearmament which he detests. He has a violently anti-German approach which incidentally rules him out as a candidate.

However, on this latter point I asked if he had discussed this with the P.M., and he had advised Clem [Attlee] to do the job himself. He was contemptuous of Herbert. Said he did not understand foreign policy at all, or how to handle foreigners – quoted his clumsy behaviour at [the Council of Europe at] Strasbourg. He was against Shawcross because he was a Lawyer and more or less simply ambitious, and said he had told the P.M. whereas he was right to have gone 'down the line' to choose the Chancellor, he must choose a new Foreign Secretary from the older people. He agreed with me strongly about Jim Griffiths, but was very much against Hector [McNeil] whom he described as a Scottish gawk.

Later I had another talk with the P.M. from which I gathered that he had moved a good deal in the direction of making a change. There seemed to have been some discussion with the Chief Whip [Whiteley] and whereas previously it had seemed his idea if he were to go 'down the line' (I ought to have mentioned this earlier) that Patrick [Gordon Walker] was the best candidate, now it appeared to be nearer to Herbert and Shawcross. I again said that I preferred Herbert strongly. Subsequently I saw Herbert himself and urged him to take it if offered. It is quite true that he has very little experience of foreign affairs, but he is essentially a man of good judgment. He sees the main issues clearly enough, and with all the advice and assistance of the F.O. will, I think, do reasonably well, though there is some danger that he will get too much in the hands of the officials. However, he may not take it. He is nervous of giving up the Leadership of the House and the control it gives him over the Party and, as he so much [as] admitted to me, his personal position as obvious successor to the P.M.[21]

A typical but interesting episode has occurred in connection with the prosecution of some Communist strike leaders for conspiracy. The decision to prosecute is, of course, solely that of the Attorney-General. He does however usually consult the Ministers concerned before taking his own decision. I understand that he did this, and the story goes that with some hesitations on the part of Nye [Bevan] there was general agreement that he should act. Subsequently, however, Nye apparently had second thoughts, and I am told stories were going round in the Parliamentary Party – alleged to have been started by Nye – that he had not been consulted or approved Shawcross' action. This had a sequel at

21 On Morrison's hesitation about taking it see Donoughue & Jones (1973), pp. 467–8.

the Party meeting this week, where some of the Members raised the question of the prosecution and started criticising the Attorney-General. Herbert Morrison replied and pointed out that this was a very dangerous subject; reminding them of the Campbell case in 1924 in which the Labour Government was turned out,[22] and at the same time emphasising that sooner or later we had to take a firm line with the Communists in the industrial field. It was suggested that the Attorney-General might speak, but one Member – Arthur Woodburn, ex-Secretary of State for Scotland – got up and said that he very much hoped the Attorney would not speak as it was much too dangerous.

The whole thing might have ended there had not Herbert got up and after a few perfunctory remarks said that the Attorney-General was not going to speak but that he had authorised him to say that he had consulted the Ministers concerned and secured their concurrence.

At this Nye, who was sitting on the other side of the platform near to me, jumped up and began to protest, at least by gesticulation. He muttered that this was monstrous and that it was a bloody disgrace and so on. We managed, with difficulty, to restrain him and said he should raise it in the Cabinet. The Party, of course, saw his behaviour and the whole thing must have created a most painful impression. Whether people thought that Herbert was lying and that Nye was protesting about this, or whether they thought that Nye had been caught out in his stories going round the Party about his non-concurrence and had been shown to be untrue, I do not know.[23]

Last night in the Defence debate, where I had been the first speaker with a long, serious, read speech – suitable for the press and country rather than the House – Nye gave one of the most brilliant performances I have ever heard him give. It was also all in good taste, good humoured, interesting and glittering with striking phraseology.[24]

It is an extraordinary thing – the contrast between this and the previous incident of which I have spoken. What a tragedy that a man with such wonderful talent as an orator and such an interesting mind and fertile

22 Sir Patrick Hastings, Attorney-General in the first minority Labour government, decided to prosecute a Communist editor for incitement to mutiny, then changed his mind after back-bench protests and learning of Campbell's war record. The Prime Minister rather inaccurately denied having been consulted, and the Liberals who had kept him in office then threw him out.
23 Foot (1973), pp. 318–19n, throws little light on this incident.
24 This famous speech by Bevan ended with the most categorical commitment to carry out the rearmament programme in full that any Minister made: 484 H.C. Deb. 739–40.

imagination should be such a difficult team worker, and some would say even worse – a thoroughly unreliable and disloyal colleague. Will he grow out of this? Will he take on the true qualities that are necessary for leadership? Who can say. Time alone will show.

Monday, 30 April 1951

A good deal of this diary inevitably records matters which will probably seem of little or no importance in years to come. But I now come to a series of events which may perhaps not fall into this category and may indeed be regarded as of considerable significance in the history of the Labour Party and even therefore in politics in general in Britain.

However, before I turn to these matters I must mention one other change which has occurred recently. I think I mentioned earlier that Mr Ernest Bevin was becoming increasingly frail and feeble. In January last he got pneumonia and evidently very nearly died. While he was ill it became more and more evident that he could not be allowed to go on any longer at the Foreign Office. Many discussions took place as to who should succeed him, and some of these I have recorded.

It was not however until after Mr Bevin's return to the Foreign Office that the decision was finally taken. The candidates at various times had been Herbert Morrison, Hartley Shawcross, Hector McNeil, Jim Griffiths and Patrick Gordon Walker. The last named fell out quite early. Jim Griffiths was obviously seriously considered by the P.M., largely on the recommendation of Ernest Bevin. However, there was very strong opposition to him from almost everybody, including the Chief Whip [Whiteley], the Minister of Defence [Shinwell] and Lord Addison [Lord Privy Seal and Leader in the Lords] who as always exercised considerable influence over the P.M.

One day Lord Addison asked me to see him and told me that he had been commissioned by the P.M. to enquire from a number of Ministers their views as to the respective merits of Morrison, Shawcross and McNeil. Addison himself made it plain to me as on earlier occasions that he thought Shawcross should have it because of the not very happy relationship existing between Morrison and the P.M. I said that I did not think this was a serious objection and myself favoured Morrison very strongly because he was the only person with the capacity to do it and be acceptable to the Party and the country. I confirmed this again, putting McNeil second (at one time I had favoured Hector McNeil who is a personal friend of mine, but I had told him that in the present circumstances I thought Herbert Morrison should have it). A few days later Bevin did in fact resign and Morrison was appointed to succeed him.

The events which I now record began as far as I am concerned with my earliest examination of how we should meet the budgetary problem this year. It was clear that we were bound to have to impose some additional taxation, and although I was not sure of the extent of this I reckoned that it might be to the order of £200 millions and would not be less than £100 millions. I felt that it was vital from the political angle that we should make a tremendous effort to economise on civil expenditure so that we could say to the country that only part of the burden was being carried by higher taxation. At one time I had even thought of a 50-50 arrangement. Therefore, as early as last November I instructed the Treasury to see what they could do to secure economies of about £100 millions over last year's estimates. Various studies were made and arguments took place with other Departments, but it soon became clear that we might hope for £30–40 millions; anything more than this would involve major issues of policy and that these would occur in the field of Education or Health or both.

At the same time it became obvious to me that we would not be able to avoid some increase in Old Age Pensions. At the beginning of the year however I still hoped that the economies would be sufficient not only to finance this but also to provide some contribution to the increasing cost of defence.

However, as the estimates came in and further arguments took place it became clear that this was too ambitious, and I therefore lowered the target to the more meritorious one of holding the total expenditure on Social Services constant, balancing the increases in pensions with savings elsewhere. I had also come to the conclusion that the only possible place where big enough savings could be made was in the Health Services.

About the beginning of February therefore I had some discussions both with the Minister of National Insurance [Edith Summerskill*] on the pensions issue and also with the two Ministers of Health [Marquand for England and Wales, McNeil for Scotland] on the Health Services. I need not say much about the first. I proposed that we should have some kind of a scheme which while increasing pensions gave incentives to people to stop at work longer, and it was agreed that our officials should work something out. On the second however I found, unfortunately, that the estimates themselves for the Health Services were £30 millions above last year's level. Even so, I began my conversations with the two Ministers with the proposal that they should try and reduce these by £50 millions, thereby contributing £20 millions to the Old Age Pensions increase.

I suggested to them the extremely drastic step of eliminating altogether from the free health service the dental and optical services. We had some discussion on this and they raised a number of very reasonable difficulties, and were able to convince me before very long that the target must be reduced once more. It would not be possible, I found, for them to reduce the estimates by £50 millions without such drastic measures as would not be acceptable to the Government. I therefore compromised and pressed them at least to get the estimate down to last year's level.

Meanwhile I had discovered that there were other increases in the social services of about £20–25 millions and therefore on this account I was bound to exceed last year's level. On the other hand in the remaining civil sector we had managed to secure economies worth about £30 millions.

It was about this stage that we spent a weekend at Roffay Park, the rehabilitation place in the country to which Stafford had taken the Treasury officials before the Budget on previous occasions. Our party consisted of about twelve, including the Economic and Financial Secretaries [Edwards and Jay]. We then planned the Budget as a whole, though necessarily in very rough outline. We found that the measure of the gap was much as I had supposed, though at that stage we thought it would be rather less than it finally turned out to be.

It became clear that in addition to increasing petrol tax, profits tax and purchase tax we should almost certainly have to increase income tax as well.

Up to now although I had on more than one occasion told the Prime Minister what my plans were so far as the Health Service was concerned there had been no formal consultations with any other Ministers, either on this or on the pensions changes. But we now found ourselves confronted with the need to decide on the figure to be put in for the Vote on Account for the Health Services which had to be published in the later half of February. After some argument with the Minister of Health I eventually agreed to a figure which was actually £5 millions more than last year's vote, i.e. £398 millions. He however only consented to this on condition that we took the matter to the Health Services Committee under the Chairmanship of the P.M. so that they would know what was involved.

A meeting of the Committee was then held and a general discussion took place. Much anxiety was expressed about the idea of eliminating the dental and optical services from the Health Services altogether, but it was finally left that the 398 [million] should go in and the Health Service Ministers would try and work out a scheme to be put before the Committee under which they would keep within last year's figure, i.e. 393.

It was shortly after this that I had my first discussion on the Budget with the Prime Minister, Herbert Morrison and Ernest Bevin. I outlined my proposals to them which were greeted with no enthusiasm at all. The P.M. said, 'Well, we shall not get many votes out of this.' And I had to remind him that he could not expect to do anything of the kind in a rearmament year. However they had not much to contribute, except to agree strongly with the need for some concessions on Purchase Tax and to press me for a little on Post-War Credits. I mentioned the Health charges proposals which were still not quite definite at this stage and there was no adverse reaction.

The Health Minister then produced a plan for charges for dental and optical services as well as the shilling charge on prescriptions which had been decided on in the previous year and then abandoned by the then Minister of Health.[25] This scheme was submitted to the Health Services Committee about the middle of March. It was approved by them without amendment.

However, I had already suggested to the P.M. that we ought to have another meeting not of the full Cabinet but of the Health Service Departments (on which the Minister of National Insurance was in any case a Member) and some other Ministers in the Cabinet particularly concerned. I suggested Bevan, who I knew would be opposed to these charges, Jim Griffiths and Hugh Dalton.[26] I did not want the matter to go to the Cabinet too early because I was afraid of the danger of leakage both on the health charges and the pensions proposals.

I had warned the P.M. that I felt extremely strongly about the necessity for imposing some scheme of this kind, and had hinted at my resignation. Herbert Morrison also knew this and I had talked to and secured the support of Addison who felt that we had to hold expenditure in check.

The special meeting accordingly took place. The P.M. was, I thought, extremely weak; although he was the Chairman of the Health Services Committee which had approved the proposals he made no attempt to persuade the meeting to accept them and left it all to me.[27] Most Ministers were on my side, except that there was a good deal of anxiety about the shilling charge, particularly from the Minister of National Insurance and Jim Griffiths. Ernest Bevin however who, as I have said earlier, was failing rapidly and could hardly grasp what was going on, changed over from what I gathered his attitude would be at the Budget meeting and sided with the Minister of Labour [Bevan] who, of course, spoke very strongly against the proposals. He threatened resignation and I hinted, not quite so definitely, at the same step.[28] The meeting therefore,

25 The bill authorising it was piloted through the House by Bevan on 9 December 1949, but it was not implemented.
26 Formerly Minister of Health, Minister of National Insurance, and Chancellor of the Exchequer respectively.
27 HG met McNeil and Gordon Walker in the House on the night of 15 March, and told them 'the P.M. was not steady on this issue and was wobbling': the latter's diary, 16.3.51.
28 At that meeting on 15 March, McNeil said he too would resign if HG did: *ibid*. But they all thought Bevan was bluffing.

although undoubtedly the majority were with me, ended in deadlock. Subsequently I saw the P.M. alone but no progress was made and he simply said, 'Well, the Cabinet will have to decide'.[29] He was himself due to go into hospital within the next day or two [on 21 March].

There then happened to follow a second meeting with the P.M. – it was on his last day out of hospital – Herbert Morrison and Ernest Bevin. This time they were rather more cheerful about my taxation proposals, and having dealt with these I again got the conversation round to the Health charges. After a little Ernest Bevin said, 'Why don't you put a ceiling on the health charges?' I said, 'Well of course that is exactly what I am going to do.' Then he said, 'Would you go as far as £400 millions?' (Up to now the figure was last year's level at 393, despite the fact that we had put 398 into the Vote on Account. In other words I had £5 millions up my sleeve.) I said that I would accept this providing everybody else did; freeing the five millions but adding another two millions. I also thought this would enable the Health Minister to drop the shilling prescription charge to which there had been most objection. Herbert Morrison, now Foreign Secretary of course, accepted this and the P.M. also agreed. I subsequently sent him a letter confirming the proposal in writing and got a reply from him, saying that he agreed in general but that he hoped that it would be put forward on the basis of abuse as well as economy.

I then saw the Health Ministers who had no difficulty in working out a scheme which kept them within the £400 millions and involved charges for teeth and spectacles only. The question then had to come up at a Cabinet meeting held on [22 March] the Thursday before Easter.[30] I saw various Members of the Cabinet myself beforehand and made it plain that I must at least have this, which represented a considerable compromise from where I had originally started. In the main they agreed with me, including Jim Griffiths who had been rather doubtful. I did not, however, see Harold Wilson because I knew quite well that he was almost certain to side with Bevan since he had been ganging up with him for a long time.

The Cabinet meeting took place. There was a discussion for about one and a half hours on this item. Morrison was in the chair but did not throw his weight in very much. Eventually the voices were collected and although the Home Secretary [Chuter Ede] and Jim Griffiths were a little doubtful, all but Bevan and Wilson concurred with my proposals.[31] The

29 It is said that at this meeting Attlee, most unusually, allowed the minutes to record that the Chancellor's proposals were approved with the Minister of Labour dissenting.

30 HG gave the same account as this to Dalton at the time: Dalton diary, 22.3.51.

31 Gordon Walker's diary (12.4.51) confirms that before Easter Bevin proposed a compromise on a £400 million ceiling and no prescription charge; that Attlee supported HG; and that only Bevan and Wilson dissented.

Minister of Health [Marquand] himself spoke up strongly in support of them.

The discussion was not very exciting; the chief row occurring between Shinwell and Bevan when Bevan began to attack the arms programme in the middle of the discussion.[32] The Cabinet of course were not aware at that time of the full Budget proposals. I could only say to them that there were going to be substantial increases in taxation, and I thought that these charges would not in themselves loom very large in the background of the other changes. At the end of the discussion when the voices had been collected Bevan said that it was no use his staying any longer and went a stage further in the threat to resign. (I should, however, make it plain that he had done this on a number of occasions before.) There were some signs of weakening among other Members of the Cabinet at this. However, he was eventually prevailed upon to stay for the rest of the meeting, and the decision was a perfectly clear one – to proceed with the preparation of the Bill on the lines of the Bevin compromise.

That was the last meeting of the Cabinet before Easter. After two days' rest I began to draft the Budget speech, and was occupied the whole of the following week upon this.

No further reference was made to this subject until the day before the Budget, i.e. about just over a fortnight later. But a few days prior to this [on 3 April] Bevan made a speech in Bermondsey in which he said plainly, 'I will not be a Member of a Government which imposes charges on the patient'. There is no doubt at all that this was a blatant threat to the Government.[33] It followed very much the pattern of previous occasions and, of course, was much commented upon in the press at the time. It started up, too, a crop of rumours and gossip in the House.

Meanwhile I had practically completed the Budget speech and the broadcast. On Monday, April 9th, my birthday, I went to the Cabinet where the only item on the agenda was the Budget. Following tradition I then explained it all fully to them. There was little comment on the Budget as a whole, what there was being favourable. Most people thought it was better than it might have been, and indeed apart from some anxieties on one or two points and regret that I had not been able to do anything about Post-War Credits, all the taxation side went through easily. But there was another very long discussion on the Health charges.

32 The first contemporary reference I have seen to Bevan opposing rearmament.
33 HG's immediate reaction was to tell Dalton angrily: 'we could not [*not* 'he would not', as Foot (1973) p. 321] always be blackmailed and give way. If we didn't stand up to him, Nye would do to our Party what L.G. [Lloyd George] had done to the Liberals. It would, he thought, do us good in the country to make a stand on this': Dalton diary, 5.4.51. But Dalton, Callaghan and others counselled prudence, and his private secretary recalls that that belligerent mood was very short-lived. See *HG*, pp. 250–1, 261.

It is hardly necessary to repeat the arguments – they have been given in public both before and since. But it is worth recording that Bevan himself did not raise objections to the other features of the Budget. Nor was there at that time any serious proposition that I ought to increase the food subsidies and raise taxation further.[34] Of course, everybody was aware of his, Bevan's, speech and this caused a certain amount of resentment because it was evident that he had deliberately put himself in a position where he was able to say to the Cabinet that he was forced to resign.

During the discussion that morning I did not say anything about resignation myself, but as soon as Bevan talked about it there was a general tendency from the rest of the Cabinet to appeal to him which, I think, was a mistake because it really flattered his own self importance. One Member after another said that it would be disastrous, catastrophic, etc. and this led him to say, 'If it is going to be all these things why does not the Chancellor give way?' Until one Member of the Cabinet, George Tomlinson [Minister of Education], simply threw up his hands and surrendered. He actually said, 'We cannot have the Minister of Labour resigning. What price must we pay for it?' The Meeting went on until one o'clock, and it was agreed that we should meet again at 6.30 p.m. that evening.[35]

I then went back to the Treasury and, after seeing the Governor of the Bank of England and again in accordance with tradition giving him the Budget details and warning him there was a considerable row going on, managed to write the peroration for the speech which I had still to do.[36] At 5.30 p.m. I went to see the King and gave him the full story. I also told him about the row between Bevan and myself. He said, 'He must be mad to resign over a thing like that. I really don't see why people should have false teeth free any more than they have shoes free', waving his foot at me as he said it. He is, of course, a fairly reactionary person. As to the rest of the Budget the King did not comment on it and never does. So I left him, saying, 'Well, it looks as if one or other of us is not going to be a Member of the Government tomorrow. I am not sure which it will be.'

I then came straight back to the House of Commons for the Cabinet Meeting in the Prime Minister's room. The argument continued for two and a half hours till nine o'clock. This time, though very quietly, I did bring my own position in. I simply said that it would be impossible for me,

34 These were subsequent Bevanite criticisms of the Budget.
35 Between the two meetings, as HG records later (pp. 246–7) Morrison and the Chief Whip went to see Attlee in hospital and returned to report his support for HG. Gordon Walker's diary confirms that that was the reason for the delay, and Dalton's confirms the outcome.
36 His private secretary William Armstrong recalls that he also went home for a family party to celebrate his birthday and his Budget – which he alone knew he might never introduce. He broke down and had to leave.

having had a Cabinet decision in favour of this just before Easter, to have it reversed at the last minute. I said that if I resigned I would make no trouble whatever and would always support the Party.[37] Of course, though nobody said so I imagine they felt it was rather awkward having a Chancellor resign on the eve of the Budget. Nevertheless, a good deal of pressure was put on me as well as on him. The most dangerous proposal from my own point of view came from Tomlinson, who said, 'Could not we have the ceiling of £400 millions without any mention of the health charges?' I objected to that because it was dishonest since the Health Ministers knew they could not keep within the ceiling without the charges; and dangerous because the charges might never come into operation.

The meeting was a very tense one, but the line up was much the same as in the morning. Everybody was on my side except for Bevan and Wilson and George Tomlinson, who threw his vote the other way in the light of Bevan's threat to resign. But it is fair to add that both the Home Secretary [Ede] and the Colonial Secretary [Griffiths] made it pretty plain that they supported me because they felt themselves bound by the previous decision. Dalton, Addison and Shinwell were all very strong on my side. The voices were taken again with the result that I have indicated, and the decision was taken.[38] I was very excited and hungry and rather emotional as well. My Treasury staff, especially the Private Secretaries who had of course watched this drama unfolding for some days, were very sympathetic. I went home and arranged that they should come out in an hour with the speech so that we could go over it for a last time. This they did, and we went through it at home finishing at one a.m.

When I got into the office the next morning William [Armstrong] said to me, 'C.J. Harris, the Chief Whip's Official, says he does not like the look of things'. I recollected that the previous night after the meeting Herbert Morrison had called me back and said that he was a little worried about not persuading me to accept the idea of simply having the ceiling without mentioning the charges. I had objected to this again. He said, 'I think perhaps I ought to tell the P.M. about it'. I must also add that it had been arranged the night before that I should see the P.M. at 11.15 a.m. in hospital. I discovered in the morning that Bevan and Wilson were seeing him at 10.30 a.m.

---

37 Dalton confirms. 'He [HG] promises, if he does so, to go quietly, and not to attack the Government afterwards. This is a high moral attitude compared with Nye': Dalton diary, 9.4.51.

38 Gordon Walker in *The Cabinet* (Cape, 1970) p. 135 confirms that everyone voted to stand by the pre-Easter decision except for Bevan and Wilson, and Tomlinson who wanted delay. In his MS diary he adds: 'Ede somewhat sympathised but could not "act under duress"'.

A few minutes later Patrick Gordon Walker rang up. He said. 'I want you to know that I am backing you 100 per cent. But, don't you think you ought to consider not mentioning the charges – just having the ceiling. It would be such a bad moment for us if we had to have an Election now.' I said 'No' once more, pointing out to him that the essential thing was to have the charges within the framework of the Budget. We should never get them through without.[39]

I then saw the Foreign Secretary, at his request, and once again I said 'No' and told him why. He said, 'Well, you will have to argue it out with the P.M.'

So I went along to the Hospital in Paddington. I had, of course, visited him two or three times before, and he had been kept fully in touch with everything while he was there. As I expected, he tried to get me to accept some form of words on the lines that I have already mentioned. He had something written down that he had done while talking to Bevan and Wilson and which they would accept, to the effect of a ceiling of £400 millions and if charges were necessary then they would have to be passed.[40] But I had made up my mind that I would announce the charges and I refused to give way. I offered my resignation several times, and I thought as I listened to his arguments that he was going to accept it.

We sat there talking quietly for, I suppose, half to three-quarters of an hour, he urging that after all anything might happen within the next few weeks and implying that there would be a lot of opposition to the charges, and I simply saying that my position was impossible unless this went through. I had said earlier on that if there were no resignations we should not have any trouble about these in the Parliamentary Party, and the P.M. questioned this. Finally, he murmured what I took to be 'Very well, you will have to go.' In a split second I realised he had said, 'I am afraid *they* will have to go'.

Just then the Home Secretary and Chief Whip came in. Here again I must break off for a moment to record something else. The Chief Whip had been present at both discussions on the previous day [Monday], though [he] said nothing. But between the two he had been with Morrison to see the P.M., and at the beginning of the evening session Morrison

39 Gordon Walker was acting as Morrison's emissary, and he wrote to HG on 11 April, the day after the Budget, to withdraw his criticism and say HG had been right to have the crisis at once. He decided he too would resign if the Chancellor did so (interview): so the government would have lost three Ministers in any case – McNeil being the other.

40 Bevan had nominally accepted an identical formula from Cripps in March 1950, and the crisis came about because he resisted implementing it. See *HG*, pp. 211–13.

read out a message from the P.M. which in effect gave his vote to me and urged the Cabinet to stand by me.[41]

When I saw these two come in, knowing the Home Secretary was very much a wobbler, I felt very depressed. However, there was no need to be. The first question the P.M. asked was this. He turned to the Chief Whip and said, 'Well, Willy, can we get this through the Party?' 'Not the slightest doubt if there are no resignations – no difficulty at all.' They both expressed the view that they thought Bevan wanted to resign in any case.[42]

I then made my one offer. I said that I was prepared to leave out one sentence that was in the speech, under which the new charges would come into force on April 12th; the legislation to be retrospective. I offered this (having agreed to do so with the Treasury before) because, knowing it would risk losing money because of forestalling, I thought it fair to give a little more time to play with. I said therefore that I would take this risk so that they would not necessarily have to bring in the Bill immediately. However, none of the three thought this very important. It would not stop the resignations, they thought. And finally, the P.M. said, 'Well, there is really nothing much I can do'. And the others said, 'Well, perhaps you had better see Bevan after the Budget speech'. So, I returned to the Treasury about 12.30 p.m., tried to collect my thoughts and look at the speech again.

Dora came in to have lunch with me and shortly afterwards Herbert Morrison rang up again on the same subject. But I told him that it was all settled. I had seen the P.M. and we were going ahead. Then we had lunch in the Treasury and I explained the position to Arthur Allen* my P.P.S. who came over to escort me through Parliament Square.

When I got into my room at the House at 3.25 p.m. Herbert came out of the Chamber and said (I had told him of the offer before), 'I think perhaps you ought to leave out the sentence about the date of coming into force. It might just make the difference.' As I had offered, although it had not been accepted earlier, I agreed and struck out the sentence at 3.28 p.m.[43] Then I went into the Chamber and soon afterwards began to deliver the speech.

41 Dalton confirms: Dalton diary, 9.4.51. Above, p. 244 n.
42 Among others who thought so too were Addison (Dalton diary, 6.4.51) and Strauss (interview). On Attlee's handling of the dispute see *HG*, p. 267.
43 His private secretaries still shudder at the memory. On the speech and its immediate reception see *HG*, pp. 253–5.

Friday, 4 May 1951

Before going any further with the story I must mention first the one other incident. On the morning of the Budget when I had come back from the P.M. Sir Edward Bridges [Permanent Secretary of the Treasury] came in to see me. He said, 'I have really nothing to say and certainly no advice to offer. But I want you to know that not only all those in the Treasury who know about it tremendously admire the stand you have made, but that all the others who do not at present know but will know will feel the same way. It is the best day we have had in the Treasury for ten years.' I was so overcome with emotion when he said this and, as can be imagined, in a fairly wrought up condition that I could not say a word. I just sat at my desk and said nothing, but managed to murmur, 'Thank you'.

I mention this episode not only because it gave me particular pleasure (Bridges is a shy, rather dry, academic person not given to flattery and pretty tough himself – coming from him these remarks were especially moving), but also because throughout the whole long struggle I had been sustained by the determined loyalty of the leading officials here, and particularly my Private Office who, of course, knew exactly what was happening.

In a situation of this kind it is impossible not to feel doubts. Not to feel that perhaps after all you were really being too stubborn, that you had got the thing out of perspective and that you were really risking too much, not for yourself, but for the Government. At such moments it is essential to have people you can talk to and whose advice you can seek. I must say that the advice of Bridges and Plowden and Leslie [head of Information] and William Armstrong, my Private Secretary, never wavered. They did not ask the impossible from me but they always made clear where they thought I should stand and why they thought I should stand. It is interesting that no other Member of the Cabinet, not even my closest friends and associates, were prepared to give such advice. I had it from one other Minister – Alf Robens, my old Parliamentary Secretary in Fuel & Power, in whom I have always had very great confidence and who was privy to the whole thing.

We paid our first visit to Windsor Castle as guests of the King & Queen just after Easter. It happened this way. On Easter Monday I stayed in bed in the morning – beginning work on the Budget speech. Dora came up in the middle of the morning and said that somebody had rung up from Windsor Castle and wanted to speak to me. She asked, 'What on earth could this mean?' I said, 'I expect the King and Queen are asking us down'. This was treated as rather a joke by the whole family and we were in fact laughing about it later on at lunch time in the kitchen when the telephone rang again and sure enough it was Major Adeane, the Assistant Private Secretary,[44] with an invitation for us both to go down to dinner and to stay the night in the following week. I accepted for the Thursday and of course there was then great excitement at home as to what we should wear and how we should behave. This was encouraged by a message later from the Master of the Household, asking what servants we were bringing.

However, as it turned out, it was really a very pleasant trip. We drove down shortly before dinner and were shown to the Ministerial Suite where, presumably, Disraeli slept. It is extremely comfortable and nicely furnished. A sitting-room and two bedrooms; one for the wife and one for the husband, each with its own bathroom. In the man's room there are two portraits of Disraeli and two of Melbourne, indicating Queen Victoria's preferences. I could not see any portraits of Liberal Ministers.[45]

Soon after we arrived Peter Townsend, now Deputy Master of the Household, and a cousin of ours, came in to see if we were all right.[46] We have generally found him rather snooty at Buckingham Palace, but this time he was very friendly. Lady Spencer, the Lady-in-Waiting, also came in and turned out to be extremely nice. After a bit I went up to see the King and had quite a long talk with him. It turned out better than usual. He did most of the talking and we covered a wide field; through the general Budget prospects to foreign affairs, the Gowers Report,[47] some rhododendrons he wanted to buy for Windsor Park, and his attitude to some other Members of the Government. As to the latter, he spoke unusually frankly and said, 'There is really only one of your people that I cannot abide. You can probably guess who that is.' I said, 'Is it Bevan?' He said, 'No, I can manage him. It is your predecessor but one.' So we then talked about Hugh Dalton. I explained that he was a personal friend of mine, and he was really much nicer than people supposed. I gathered that the King's dislike of him (I found this was shared by the Queen as well afterwards) really goes back to the Windsor days when Hugh

44 Sir Michael (Lord) Adeane was Private Secretary to Queen Elizabeth II, 1953–72.
45 While Benjamin Disraeli, Earl of Beaconsfield, Prime Minister 1868 and 1874–80 was of course a Conservative, Viscount Melbourne (1834 and 1835–41) was a Whig.
46 Group Captain Townsend's father served in the Indian Civil Service in Burma; his sister married HG's elder brother Arthur. See also below, p. 542 n.
47 Sir Ernest Gowers was chairman of the Royal Commission on capital punishment. Its report was published on 7 May.

Dalton's father was tutor to King George V, and apparently very like HD in having a loud voice and bullying manner.

Later I went back to change for dinner, and we all assembled rather late as usual with the Royalty, 8.30 p.m. to be precise, in the Drawing Room which was one of the State Apartments, though not one of those with the most famous pictures and furniture in it.

There were about twenty people at dinner altogether. Apart from the King & Queen and Princess Margaret, there were a number of the Court Entourage, and the Birleys – headmaster of Eton and his wife (the latter was at school with me years ago) – were as far as I could see the only other outside visitors.[48] Our morale was very high because we discovered we were the guests of honour and in the past at Buckingham Palace sometimes [we had] felt the whole atmosphere rather cold and snobby, and we noticed the contrast on this occasion.

I sat between the Queen and Princess Margaret at dinner and Dora sat next to the King. I thought the Princess extremely attractive, more so than before, and conversation seemed fairly easy. Oddly enough she had been spending the day at the National Union of Teachers' Conference in North Wales, whose President is my Mr [Granville] Prior in Leeds. She had been with Mr & Mrs Prior most of the time, with whom I stay three or four times a year in a reasonably comfortable but working-class house. I was somehow or other fascinated by the contrast. Princess Margaret at once referred to the Priors, and said that she had told them that she had at least one thing in common with them, that they both knew me. There is a curious feature about talking with royalty. You have a sort of feeling that in the middle they have ceased to listen to what you have to say. Maybe it is a feeling that they must not lose their reserve. They cannot enjoy themselves in a natural way with commoners, or at any rate with politicians.

As I always thought, the King and Queen are extremely conservative in their views. The Queen talked as though everybody was in a very bad way nowadays, not happy, poor, dispirited, etc. She did not say this in anger but implied that it could not be helped and that she hoped it would come to an end some day. I got into an argument with her then and implied that not everybody was quite so miserable and perhaps she did not see the people who were happier. I think she resented this.

Meanwhile, Dora had been getting on quite well with the King, who drank whisky all the evening, and talked a great deal. He said to her at one point, 'I wonder what he has got in his box for us?' (meaning me) 'I hope it will not be too terrible.' Dora replied, 'I don't suppose it will be as

48 [Sir] Robert Birley was headmaster of Eton 1949–63. His wife and HG both went to the Dragon School in Oxford (perhaps the only prep. school to take girls as well as boys at that time).

bad as all that. After all he is rather right wing.' This the King thought a tremendous joke and laughed a great deal at the idea of my being right wing. Incidentally, talking to him earlier about the Budget, the details of which I had not of course disclosed, he said, 'Is it going to be the end?' Meaning was I going to propose the confiscation of all large estates or something of the kind. I assured him that I did not think he would feel it was the end.

After dinner we looked at the miniatures which were very beautiful and I talked to Lady Spencer while Dora talked to the Duke of Wellington most of the time.[49] We had been warned that we might have to play canasta. I was looking forward to this after my training with Cressida [his daughter] but only four sat down to this, Princess Margaret, Peter Townsend and two others. The Royalty retired about 11.30 p.m. and everyone else about half an hour afterwards. Everybody continued to be most polite and friendly to us and seemed to take special care that we should be comfortable and have everything we wanted. There seemed to be a sort of Footman permanently stationed outside the Ministerial Suite to look after us. We had breakfast in our Sitting-room and to Dora's great delight the pats of butter had crowns on them. I suggested putting one in an envelope for the children but we did not do this.

Later, by arrangement, we were shown round the State Apartments by the Librarian, Sir Owen Morshead.[50] I did not realise what a terrific museum it was. Mostly filled by Charles II and George IV, the two most spendthrift of our monarchs. Finally, after saying goodbye to the Queen, we returned to London, having much enjoyed the glamour of the stay.

The Budget speech was very well received and I certainly got a great many compliments on the manner of its delivery and to start with at least on its content. I mention this because looking back I see that if it had not been a great success my position might have been a very difficult one. The P.M. of course was in hospital and not there, but Ernie Bevin sat through it all and when I sat down he said, 'That was a great speech', and he held my hand for quite a long time.[51] The Home Secretary [Ede] said, 'This is just what the Party wanted. It will make all the difference.'

---

49 The 7th Duke: Lord Lieut. of London, 1944–9, of Hampshire 1949. The Countess Spencer had been Lady of the Bedchamber to the Queen since 1937. In 1981 her granddaughter Diana married the Prince of Wales.
50 Librarian at Windsor Castle since 1926.
51 Bevin told Philip Noel-Baker it was 'one of the greatest speeches I ever heard'. But Wilson saw him that evening with Bevan, and thought he sympathised with them.

After listening to Winston [Churchill] who, I think quite spontaneously, went beyond the usual compliments and said that he thought that it was an honest Budget and lacking in malice and hatred, I went to my room and rested for a little. I thanked Winston in the corridor for what he had said about the speech and he more or less repeated it, and then added, 'I am not a very good hater myself. I have to work myself up occasionally into a show of it.' I muttered something about our having rows occasionally but that I had always had a great admiration for him.

Later we had a dinner, following precedent, for the Treasury officials principally concerned, but I had to leave quite soon to go and do the Budget broadcast. We had taken a lot of trouble about this and I had been greatly helped by Clem Leslie and William [Armstrong]. Again, by chance, it was the best I had done. I delivered it more slowly and received a lot of compliments. I could not know this in advance, but it was in the light of what was to happen quite important.

The question however then was, what would Bevan and the others do? There was a Party meeting on the following morning. I found Bevan there and learned that he was to make some kind of statement. But first of all I spoke for about a quarter of an hour. Then Bevan got up and said that they must realise how difficult the position was for him, but that he had decided not to take a certain course. There was a lot of relieved applause at this. He then, however, went on to attack the Health charges and ended a very brief speech by saying, 'There is still time'.

The question of the Health Services Bill was brought up in the Cabinet on the following day. Bevan and Wilson were both there and made an effort to get the whole thing postponed.[52] This, however, was overruled without much difficulty, and it was agreed that the Bill would be introduced on the following Tuesday and the Second Reading would take place a week later.[53]

Two days later Ernest Bevin died. I have already described how frail and ill he was, and I think it came as a surprise to none of us. I cannot say that I ever got to know him well, or that he was the type of man that I would ever have known well. But he was helpful to me sometimes and especially in this last crisis. I learned afterwards from Frank Pakenham that he had said before the Budget to Frank after one of those Cabinet meetings, 'I hope Hugh Gaitskell will remain Chancellor for five years at

52 They claimed Attlee had told them he was proposing a June election (cf. Foot, 1973, p. 323) but Morrison said Attlee had denied that: Dalton diary, 12.4.51.
53 Bevan exploded: '"Why should I have to put up with these bloody absurdities?" glaring at Hugh. But Hugh said nothing and the Cab. dispersed': Dalton diary, 19.4.51. Gordon Walker's diary 12.4.51, confirms the incident and specifies the date.

least. He knows what he wants and will get it'. I was rather surprised at this because so often he had not given the impression that he really understood much the basis for my attitude on economic and financial policy.

The chief consequence of his death is primarily the loss of another of our leaders in the eyes of the public. He was obviously past any effective work, but I suppose the country still felt he was there and that made a difference so long as he was alive. Also the P.M. was always very close to him; much closer than to Herbert [Morrison]. I imagine he must have felt as a result even more lonely.

The Budget Debate went on the rest of the week, and I wound it up on the following Monday with a speech which I myself did not think particularly good, but which curiously enough was very well received by our own people. I have certainly made many better winding up speeches, but there must have been something about my manner or the tone of it which caught on. Again, I was helped by this. But meanwhile the Parliamentary Party was in a considerable state of excitement about the Health charges. It was obvious that Bevan and Wilson were going round trying to win support and to cook up future trouble for the Government if we went on with the Bill. Bevan, who normally never goes into the Tea Room but when he is in the House is in the Smoking Room (where you can get drinks), was seen almost openly lobbying in the Tea Room quite a lot.[54]

How exactly the Party reacted to the Health charges was not known. Some said that there was a majority of two to one for the Bill; others that it was four or five to one. On the following Thursday the question of the Health Bill again came up. It was announced that the Second Reading would be on the Tuesday of the following week, and the later stages of the Bill would be taken a week later. Bevan then said, 'I have already explained that I cannot go into the Lobby in support of this Bill, and I will resign on the Third Reading'.[55] At this point Shinwell, somewhat surprisingly, suggested that perhaps we could [set] some kind of limit to the Bill, or at least explain that it was not permanent. Bevan at once said, 'Ah! that would make a great deal of difference'.[56] I said that I was

54 He had already warned Dalton (quite wrongly), 'The Party will be a rabble, and you won't carry it': Dalton diary, 10 & 11.4.51. See *HG*, pp. 255–7, 260–2, on the P.L.P.'s reaction.
55 Dalton confirms and records 'a general impatience in the Cab. with this continual nerve war – first he threatened to resign before the Budget, then on Budget day, then if the charges were brought in, then he wouldn't vote on a second reading & now this': Dalton diary, 19.4.51.
56 Dalton confirms. Shinwell suggested limiting the charges to a year, and Bevan threw a note across the table to Wilson (seen by his neighbour Chuter Ede): 'We've got them on the run': Dalton diary, 19 & 20.4.51.

prepared to consider giving a further explanation of the phrase I had used in the Budget speech regarding the ceiling i.e. that it was for the time being and need not necessarily be permanent. There was some tendency I think among the others to run away a bit but it was left that the Home Secretary, the Health Ministers, Minister of Labour [Bevan] and I (the Chief Whip was brought in later on) should meet later in the day to try and agree upon a suitable form of words. I met the Health Ministers [Marquand and McNeil] in the afternoon and we drafted something together, and later we saw the Home Secretary [Ede]. He meanwhile had got another form of words from Shinwell which we altered so that it read, 'These charges need not necessarily be permanent' instead of 'Should not be permanent'. This was handed to Bevan when he came in. He read it and tossed it aside contemptuously, calling it 'a bromide'.

He then went on to say that he would not be satisfied with anything except an arrangement which left it open as to whether the charges ever came into force at all. He followed this up with a long and rather excited statement that the arms programme could not be carried out, and that it was all nonsense and that we were really wasting our time over this sort of thing. I gather he had this impression from a meeting of the Defence Production Committee which had taken place that day.[57]

I said that of course if there were to be a complete change in the Defence programme we should need a completely new Budget and many other things would have to be reconsidered, but until a Government announcement on this was made I was not prepared to budge on the Health Bill. Shortly after there was a Division and we did not see Bevan again. He had, however, been asked by the Home Secretary to produce an alternative form of words, and in fact never did so. After the Division, however, I got hold of the Foreign Secretary and the Chief Whip [Whiteley] and we went back to the Home Secretary's room, where we explained to Herbert what had happened. We were all pretty incensed by the complete change of the Minister of Labour's attitude, and the Home Secretary who had become increasingly angry about his behaviour in the Parliamentary Party thought that we could not leave things as they were.[58] We finally decided to go and see the P.M. – the other three

57 Several Ministers had doubts: cf. Wilson's speech in the Budget debate (486 H.C. Deb. 1474–94; 16.4.51); Freeman's resignation letter (published in J. Mitchell, *Crisis in Britain 1951*, Secker & Warburg, 1963, p. 186); Callaghan's comments to Dalton (diary, 2.5.51). But when HG checked with the Service and Supply Ministries just before the Budget, he was told that 'the figures in the Prime Minister's statement . . . were still the best available estimates' and his colleagues never altered them: his article in *Tribune*, 28.12.51, cf. Strauss (Minister of Supply) in 491 H.C. Deb. 60–2 (23.7.51).

58 Ede had just replaced Morrison as Leader of the House of Commons.

certainly and I if I was wanted – on the following day and put the whole facts before him.[59]

That evening there had appeared an issue of *Tribune* which is controlled by Jennie Lee and Michael Foot and which Bevan used to edit and which is generally accepted as reflecting his policy. This contained an attack on the Budget as a whole and a personal onslaught on me. It was with this also in our minds that we went to see the P.M. on the Friday afternoon.

The Home Secretary did most of the talking, supported by the Foreign Secretary. The P.M. who sat there in bed listening, said at the end, 'Well, we cannot go on like this. He must behave properly if he is to remain a Member of the Government. Shall I see him or write to him?' Somebody said that writing would be best. The P.M. then took up a pen and paper and wrote a letter to him which he read out to us, to the effect that he had been told that he was now again threatening resignation; that the doctrine of collective Government responsibility must hold; that he, the P.M., must know where AB stood, and that he hoped to hear from him before the weekend that he would loyally accept and carry out Government decisions. It was decided to mark this 'Private & Personal'.

I saw HD just after this. He had supported me inside but had been rather inclined to urge me not to be too stubborn and had, undoubtedly, had compromise in his mind. But I fancy the *Tribune* altered him for he fully supported the P.M.'s letter and the need for having a showdown.[60] I think the others in the Government must have felt the same for the same reason.

On the Saturday afternoon the P.M. asked me to go round to the Hospital again. He handed me a letter which he had received from Bevan – the resignation letter subsequently published.[61] He proposed that Alf Robens should be Minister of Labour and I agreed very warmly. Subsequently he telephoned in my presence to Herbert [Morrison] who was in the country and this was confirmed.

On the Monday afternoon Bevan made his statement in the House. This is on record and I need not report it or the comments made on it by the press which were quite accurate. It was an extraordinary performance,

59 Ede and Whiteley both gave Dalton their accounts, which do not mention defence but otherwise fully confirm HG's; both now felt Bevan 'must either play with the team or go': Dalton diary, 20.4.51. Jay too confirms HG's account: in W. T. Rodgers, ed., *Hugh Gaitskell 1906–1963* (Thames & Hudson, 1964), p. 100. Shinwell says HG was also intransigent: in *Sunday Telegraph*, 30.7.61.

60 Dalton scrawled on his copy: 'a most wicked publication'. For details on *Tribune* (then kept alive by Lord Beaverbrook's money) see *HG*, pp. 257–8.

61 The correspondence is published by F. Williams (1961), pp. 247–8, and by Foot (1973), pp. 330–3.

totally lacking in any understanding of what people expected, and turned opinion even more sharply against him – on top of the *Tribune* article. The following day a special Party meeting took place. It began with statements by Wilson and John Freeman [Parliamentary Secretary, Ministry of Supply] who had subsequently resigned. Both of these were restrained and in a way more dangerous. I then made a fairly long defence of my position. I had been advised by my friends to ignore the personal attack and to keep the whole thing on a calm and reasonable basis. I accepted this advice with rather remarkable results.

I must say that I received a pretty considerable ovation when I got up to speak. I am sure that the *Tribune* article had a lot to do with this. But when I sat down they went on clapping for a minute or two. Douglas [Jay] said that it was the biggest applause that he had ever heard at a Party meeting. I do not know about that but it was certainly an outstanding success. Bevan made things even worse for himself by following this with a shocking outburst of bad temper which was evidently a revelation to many people in the Party. He almost screamed at the platform. At one point he said, 'I won't have it. I won't have it.' And, this of course was greeted with derision. '*You* won't have it?' called other Members of the Party. Of course in the Cabinet we have had this on [*sic*] a number of times but they had not seen it before.[62]

Some people thought that this was a decisive meeting in the history of the Party, but I am not so sure. Nothing swings more quickly than opinion and even now we are facing a good deal of trouble in the Party on this very issue – far more that we would have had on the day of that meeting itself.

I have tried to tell this story baldly and without comment so that it may be of some value as a historical record. I permit myself now only two comments. First, that although I embarked on this with the knowledge that it would be a hard struggle I did not think it would be quite so tough. I suppose that if I had realised that there were so many things which could have meant defeat, I might never have begun; or at least I would have surrendered early on. If Ernie [Bevin] had not suggested the compromise; if some of the Cabinet had been more frightened; if Bevan had played his cards better; if the Budget speech had not been a success; if the Broadcast had been a flop; if I had not won the battle decisively in the Party meeting. If any of these things had not happened it might have meant failure.

Herbert said to Dora, referring to me, 'He has done very well. He took a tremendous risk, but he brought it off.' Somehow I did not realise the risks were so great. Perhaps that is always the way. You could not do the

---

62 HG's italics. Similar account in Dalton diary, 24.4.51. For Bevan's speeches in the House and at the party meeting, and for their reception, see *HG*, pp. 259–61; Foot (1973), pp. 333–41.

important things which have to be done if you thought in advance of all the difficulties.

The second observation is this. People of course are now beginning to look to the future. They expect that Bevan will try and organise the Constituency parties against us, and there may be a decisive struggle at the Party Conference in October. We certainly cannot say that we have won the campaign. We may make mistakes; we may have bad luck. In either case opinion may very well swing over to him. He can exploit all the Opposition-mindedness which is so inherent in many Labour Party Members who having been agin so many Governments find it pretty hard work supporting even their own, especially when it does something unpopular.

All the same, with all the risks I think I was right. I said in the middle of one discussion to Hugh Dalton, 'It is really a fight for the soul of the Labour Party'. More people understand that this was so now. But who will win it? No one can say as yet. I am afraid that if Bevan does we shall be out of power for years and years.

Much will depend on the attitude of the P.M. Part of the trouble at the moment is that we are not getting enough leadership within the Party. I think if he shows himself strong and firm on all this the Party will rally to him and to us. But if he tries to patch things up; to compromise; to make room for the Bevan faction somehow or other, then I think we shall probably lose. I cannot carry on the fight alone. I have not the standing or the experience. Others who would help me are mostly too young, and apart from the Foreign Secretary, the older ones are disinclined to go in for anything so strenuous. Unfortunately the Foreign Secretary is so absorbed with foreign affairs that I do not know how much time he will have for this.

Friday, 11 May 1951

The final stage of this particular episode can be described fairly briefly.

So far as the attitude of the country is concerned there really seems to be no doubt that people generally did not react unfavourably to the health charges. In some [local] Parties there has been trouble, and the Communists in one or two places have obviously stirred up opposition.

I myself went to speak at a Regional Conference in Glasgow (which tends to be a centre of disaffection because of the I.L.P. tradition) but certainly had very little trouble. I made my main reply to Bevan – broadly speaking the same speech as I made at the Parliamentary Party Meeting, but now in public – and then answered questions for an hour. Although, of course, there were a number of questions from Bevanites the audience seemed to be prepared to accept my explanation.

In Leeds I addressed a meeting of our own Party Members and received the conventional 'unanimous vote of confidence'.

In the House of Commons however the Bill now through was attacked vigorously by the dissidents who challenged a vote at the Committee stage on which thirty or forty people abstained. This worried the Home Secretary, who is apt to get into too much of a panic when there is any rebellion, chiefly because it made our loyal people so unhappy. It was a humiliating spectacle to see the Labour Party quarrelling while the Conservatives looked on and laughed.

We made two small concessions in the course of the passage of the Bill. The first was to make the charges maximum charges. This was, I think, completely harmless and I had no difficulty in agreeing to it, and the other was to limit the Bill to three years unless an affirmative resolution was passed.[63] I mention this only because when the subject came up in the Cabinet there was once again a tendency to run away which rather shocked me. However, despite some pressure from the Chief Whip, the P.M. and the Leader of the House [Ede] we got away with the three year limit instead of a two year limit which had also been proposed.

On pensions there was far more difficulty. I had always expected this and indeed said in the Cabinet and the Party Meeting that if there were any more money available I would not have put it into the Health Services but done better for the pensioners. This time it was not the Bevanites but the Trade Union Group and especially the miners who brought pressure to bear.

I met the Trade Union Group, not on this, but on the Budget as a whole and found that the pensions were the only thing they were worried about. They were quite solidly behind me on the teeth and spectacles. This was followed by a deputation to the P.M., myself, the Leader of the House and the Chief Whip and the Minister of National Insurance [Edith Summerskill], in the course of which they pressed for giving the 4/- p[er] w[eek] to the 65-70s.[64] Both the Minister of National Insurance and I argued vigorously that the higher National Insurance rates would take care of any who really needed the increase in pension. This however did not satisfy them. So we had another meeting of the Ministers alone, in the course of which the Prime Minister and the Home Secretary and the Chief Whip were all obviously worried about the situation. There was a real danger that the Tories would support the rebels up to a point in this stand.

63 Such a resolution could extend the Bill for no more than a year at a time: 487 H.C. Deb. 1619 (7.5.51).
64 To provide an incentive to defer retirement, the Budget had increased pensions for men who stayed at work to 70, and women to 65.

So we had another meeting with the T.U. group to try and test out the strength of their reaction. Before this the Chief Whip who had been absolutely firmly behind me on the health charges told me he thought that the position was very difficult. He had had a meeting of the Whips who had all said that the feeling was very strong in the Party as a whole. The Leader of the House obviously thought the same (though I respect his judgment much less than the Chief Whip as he is always much too inclined to give way). At the meeting I got them to admit that they were really concerned not with the extreme hardship cases but with the others, and after a good deal of argument I finally put forward the one proposal which seemed to me a reasonable compromise. This was to pay the extra to those who were *now* over 65 but not to those who reach the age after the appointed day. This could be defended on the grounds that those who had already retired would have much more difficulty in getting back to work, while those who had not yet retired should with the new increments earn the new higher pension by working only another eighteen months. Moreover, from our point of view the principle of encouraging pensioners to work was preserved and the extra expenditure was fairly small and only temporary.

The Leader of the House weighed in heavily in support of this proposal and after a bit the T.U. Group accepted it with much gratitude. It was announced by the Minister at the Committee Stage which went through quite calmly. We are not quite out of the wood yet. Report and Third Reading come immediately after the Whitsun Recess. But I have made it plain to the T.U. Group and everybody else that I am not budging any further and I am fairly hopeful that the Party as a whole will be prepared to hold this line. If so, we shall not have done too badly. Moreover this is not an issue on which I have ever felt very strongly, and if at an earlier stage in the Cabinet or even before it I had been told that we could not maintain the distinction between those above and those below 70 I would very likely have given way then. Anyhow this was a matter on which I was not prepared even to contemplate resignation, nor was I prepared even to create a really first-class row in the Cabinet or the Party. It really became a matter of judgment as to how strong the feeling was and, as I have said, in this I was much influenced by the views of the Chief Whip.

Persia[65]

A most dangerous situation at the moment is developing in Persia where the Government have passed an Act nationalising the oil wells and refinery and tearing up the concession. There is rather an interesting line-

65 See *HG*, pp. 271–2 on the Iran crisis.

up in the Government on this. Shinwell [Minister of Defence] is all for a 'show of force', reflecting in this way the views of the Services. They consider that if we are ejected from Persia in any forcible manner it will have disastrous repercussions in our position in the Middle East. The Foreign Secretary [Morrison] is also rather a fire eater, though not so much as the Minister of Defence.

The Minister of Fuel [Noel-Baker] and I have been much more cautious. We do not want the oil to stop – that is the important thing – and therefore we argue we must do everything possible to get a negotiated settlement first. In the last resort however even we agree that force might become necessary. The P.M. more or less shares our view. The rest of the Cabinet were a good deal more pacifist, but that I think is because they do not realise how serious the loss of the oil would be, or how hopelessly uncertain the situation in Persia is.

This development throws into strong relief the absurdity of not having a proper Anglo-American policy for the Middle East. I have repeatedly pressed for this in the past but there has been great resistance from the Foreign Office and the Service Departments. The Foreign Office think the Americans are very unpopular and ignorant. (The Americans always tell me we are far more unpopular than they are.) The Service people of course hate the idea of the Americans coming into what is their special territory. At the same time when it comes to any discussion on military action the Services always admit that they cannot do it alone. That is where they are so hopelessly illogical. However the real force of events is driving us towards an Anglo-American policy. The real question is whether we can get that policy and put it into effect in time.

I saw Joe Alsop*, the American columnist, this week. He had just returned from Persia and took an extremely gloomy view of the position. It certainly looks like blowing up in a Communist Nationalist revolution from which the Russians would no doubt eventually gain control of the whole country. In a sense of course a revolutionary coup in that country would give us the justification we need for taking over the Southern oilfields. In this event the Russians would occupy Azerbaijan, and the country would in effect be partitioned. This sounds bad but I think it might be the best ultimate solution.[66]

The Persian Parliament and Government is a corrupt and incompetent affair. There is shocking poverty and gross inequality, and I can see no early way out with all that going on. The Russians have, however, played their cards very cleverly, and if they are wise they will not move at the moment. They will try and get the extreme Nationalist Government to

66 The Americans thought otherwise, fearing that 'we might end up with the British out and the Russians in': D. Acheson, *Present at the Creation* (Macmillan, 1970), p. 507.

seize the oilfields and refinery at Abadan, thereby forcing us either to resist or surrender. If we surrender we not only may lose the use of the oil and the power of controlling its distribution, but we should also incur heavy financial losses; and we should also lose face all over the Middle East. Egypt might then feel disposed to try and turn us out of the Canal Zone. Iraq might tear up the Alliance and try and seize their oil, etc. If on the other hand we do intervene then we should risk having a lot of trouble at U.N.O. and equally strong feeling might be raised against us among the Arabs and other Moslem peoples, e.g. Pakistan. India would almost certainly disapprove.

From all this we conclude that we must get some kind of agreement with the Americans so that between us we can ensure the maintenance of this vital oil supply, and prevent the Communists getting control of Persia. That is where we stand at the moment, but events may move swiftly within the next two or three weeks.

Wednesday, 8 August 1951

The trouble about this diary is that, as I think I have said before, when lots of things are happening which are worth recording there is no time to record them. Contrariwise, when there is plenty of time there is not so much happening. It is three months since the last entry and a great deal has happened in that time. I can only pick out the most important developments and concentrate as far as possible on what has happened behind the scenes, rather than on what has been published in the press and is general information.

Persia

The story of the Persian oil dispute is not yet over, but a good deal has happened since last May. Much of this is public knowledge and I need not bother with it, but I can give some picture of attitudes and policies during this time in Whitehall.

The matter has been dealt with mainly by a small Ministerial Committee consisting of the P.M., Foreign Secretary, the Minister of Defence, the Minister of Fuel & Power and myself, and we have had a very large number of meetings. Of course, the Cabinet has been kept informed and every now and then has taken some decision not wholly in line with the Committee's views, but for the most part the Committee has done the steering.

When I last mentioned the subject I emphasised that we should have to try and secure some kind of agreement with the Americans on a general policy. Approaches were made in Washington and we indicated to them the possibility of military action. As I expected, they shied off this very sharply, though they admitted that if there were to be a Communist coup in Persia they would back us up. If there had been any doubt before, it was now quite clear that we could not easily contemplate military action except to forestall or prevent the Communists getting control of the oil of Persia. It was, of course, also recognised that we might have to use military action to rescue our own nationals if their lives were endangered by rioting or similar disturbances.

In view then of the limits of military action we had to try and seek a solution on the basis of agreement. It was however quite clear that no agreement could be satisfactory to us under which we were simply turned out of Persia (because of the repercussions in the Middle East which would be very serious), or which was quite intolerable from a financial angle. Was there any possibility of an agreement which did not conflict with these two aspects?

From the start it seemed extremely unlikely that the Mossadegh Government would be prepared to make one.[67] But, we felt bound to try. Our first move in this direction was therefore the dispatch of a Company Mission which had power to negotiate a settlement which should be acceptable financially, involving the principle of nationalisation but leaving the Company in control of the distribution and marketing of the oil (to which we attached especial importance) and also its production. The latter could have been carried on on an agency basis from some new Persian Company set up for the purpose.

The Company Mission however did not stay very long since the Persians at once rejected the whole idea of anything which conflicted with the nationalisation law the Majlis [Parliament] had passed on May 1st, and which laid out in some detail the policy of complete nationalisation, and no more than 25% of the profits to be set aside for possible compensation for the Company.

We knew all the time that our strongest cards were really in the fact that the Persians could not manage or sell the oil without us. Moreover, so long as the Company continued to produce and sell, the revenues accrued in London and could not be got at by the Persians. It was not surprising, therefore, that the Persian Nationalisation Board tried before long to put an end to this by insisting first of all on tankers' captains signing receipts

67 Dr Mohammed Mossadegh was Prime Minister of Iran 1951–3, having first held office 30 years before. The Shah went into exile in 1953 and was restored after a coup organised by the C.I.A., which gave rise to lasting resentment against the U.S.

which in effect accepted the fact that the oil was in the ownership of the Persian Government and not the Company, and secondly involving, after an interval, the payment of cash by the tankers before they could take the oil away. This drove us into playing our most valuable card. We refused to do what the Persians wanted. Before long the tankers were withdrawn, and after some weeks the refinery slowly came to a standstill. This was the policy of allowing the Persians to impose economic sanctions on themselves in the hope that they would begin to see reason and that in consequence either Mossadegh would change his mind about the agreement, on the lines we wanted, or that he would be replaced by a more sensible Government.

We had prepared for the situation in advance and the Company reported that it had managed to seal up outlets comparable to 94% of Persian oil. Thus, even if the Persians could have experts to run the refinery, they could not have sold any more than a trickle of oil.

At the same time, realising that the policy of stopping the flow of oil might lead to trouble, we tightened up our military preparations.

This brief summary, of course, glosses over a great deal of differences of opinion and arguments which took place in the Ministerial Committee. The line up there was briefly as follows:- The Minister of Defence [Shinwell] was for the most part an extreme appeaser. He mostly wanted to give way to the Persians. The Foreign Secretary [Morrison] until right up to the end was taking a tough note [sic], and generally complaining that the weakness of our military position did not allow us to be firm.[68] The Minister of Fuel & Power [Noel-Baker] and I took much the same line, which was broadly what was decided, i.e. to allow the Persians to bring sanctions down on themselves, while preparing the ground particularly if a pretext existed for military action. The P.M. tended to sit on the fence generally speaking, and sided with us.

The attitude of the Chiefs-of-Staff was rather peculiar. They started by being extremely warlike and warned us of the dangers of being thrown out of Persia, and they recommended strong action. They were then asked to make various plans. They started and the more they went into this the colder they became. This was particularly true of the First Sea Lord.[69] This was so much the case at one point that they seemed in favour of outright appeasement. Curiously enough, this phase was replaced by another one in which they took a much stronger line, having gone into

---

68 Confirmed by Dalton who with Griffiths opposed Morrison in Cabinet, then complained to Attlee: 'We couldn't have H.M. trying to be Pam [i.e. Palmerston]. He said he agreed': Dalton diary, 2.7.51. Cf. Donoughue & Jones (1973), p. 498.
69 Admiral of the Fleet Lord Fraser of North Cape.

things and found it was rather easier to provide the necessary troops and equipment.

We had a number of discussions with Winston [Churchill], Anthony Eden* and Salisbury*. Their attitude was quite interesting. They were not very far removed from my own, but were clearly anxious that by leaving our people in Abadan we would in effect provoke an excuse for intervention. Their major single point – and it is still so – was that we should not withdraw the British from Abadan in any circumstances. I am sure that they hoped that this would force the Persians to the kind of compromise we wanted or, as I have said, provoke a disturbance which would justify military intervention. They did not think this intervention would enable us to hold Southern Persia, but they thought we should be able to hold the island of Abadan and refine crude oil brought in from Kuwait.

There was a lot of argument from time to time as to whether the Company's employees should be withdrawn from the oilfields into Abadan. Indeed, much of the public discussion was about this. There were those who said that this would bring the Persians to their senses. There were those who thought it would provoke them, and there were others who thought it would look like surrender.

In point of fact just as we were about to withdraw them into Abadan because of the dangers to them and the insults to which they had been subjected, President Truman decided to send Harriman and we had to hold our hand. We were very worried about what this visit would involve, particularly as Harriman might try to appease Mossadegh yet again and split the Anglo-American axis.

It so happened that I had to go to Paris the day before Harriman was due to pass through there. Therefore, with great secrecy, a meeting was arranged between us. I stayed over in Paris for this purpose, carefully arranging a cover – because of the difficulty of seeing Petsche who was trying to form a Government and who had not had time to see me the previous day. I went to Katz's flat to say goodbye to him, and waited there for Harriman who came direct from the airport. We had 40 minutes or so together, and I came away somewhat reassured. He was clearly conscious of the dangers of an Anglo-American split, and of the repercussions on the press and American Companies which a Persian victory might have, but he was also very anxious to avoid a position where the Communists got control even of Northern Persia because of the oil which was believed to be there. He obviously thought that the Company at least had handled its affairs rather badly in the past.[70] After this meeting I was driven to a

---

70 So did Younger, whose scathing memorandum to Morrison is printed in Anthony Sampson, *The Seven Sisters* (Coronet ed., 1976), pp. 134–5.

special airfield and flown in the Military Attaché's plane to Leeds airfield so that I could get there for an engagement.

The outcome of the Harriman mission is well known. He certainly did help to convince the Persians that they could not get along without us; though some would say that this was not so much Harriman as the cold facts of the gradual closure of Abadan. He had mentioned to me in Paris that it might be necessary for a Minister to go out, and it was decided to send out Dick Stokes [Lord Privy Seal]. This was the P.M.'s desire. Herbert [Morrison] wanted me to go, but I was not very keen because I knew it would take a lot of time and I had too much to do here. I was rather nervous about Dick Stokes and so were some others because he was rather an appeaser on the oil issue. However, he seems to be doing quite well. He had Martin Flett from the Treasury with him who is one of our best officials and also Donald Fergusson from the Ministry of Fuel & Power; certainly one of the wisest counsellors one could have on such an occasion.[71]

O.E.E.C.

I have already referred to a visit to Paris. It was the first I had made since January, and its main purpose was to hold informal talks with other Ministers about some new move to improve European morale, and alter its attitude to the Defence programme. Stikker arranged a dinner party at the Crillon. It was attended by Schumacher, Petsche, Pella and Swedes, Norwegians and Belgians, in addition to Marjolin.[72] The latter put forward a project, which he had discussed with us, for making plain to Europe that the burden of rearmament was not nearly so heavy as people thought and it could easily be achieved providing certain production problems were solved.

I took the line that the major problem was dealing with the inflationary position which was brought to us from outside. Katz made a most eloquent speech on the kind of political line to be taken. This was followed up by some individual talks between the various Ministers. All

71 The Americans (who were very critical of the Foreign Office) also wanted HG to go out: Acheson (1970), p. 509. On Stokes and Fergusson see Biographical Notes; (Sir) Martin Flett was an Under-Secretary at the Treasury 1949–56 (in Washington from 1953) and later Permanent Secretary at the Air Ministry.

72 Stikker, the Dutch Foreign Minister, was President and Marjolin Secretary-general of O.E.E.C. (above, p. 177 n.) Petsche was the French and Pella the Italian Finance Minister. 'Schumacher' may be a typist's error for Robert Schuman, Foreign Minister in all ten French governments from 1948 to the end of 1952; Dr Kurt Schumacher, leader of the German Socialist opposition, seems unlikely.

of us broadly agreed that some action was needed. For my part I was concerned to see that it should be economic in character; that it committed America, and that it should be raised in NATO. The old jealousies however came into play and although during this weekend most of the other Ministers appeared to be in agreement with me, subsequently they all urged that the negotiation should come from O.E.E.C. because they said if it came in NATO everybody would say that it was American and this would have a bad effect in Europe. This is interesting as it throws some light on the reactions going on in Europe. They are anxious to have American help, but also anxious to avoid giving anyone the impression that the Americans are running them. They fear this outlook would assist Communist propaganda.[73]

Friday, 10 August 1951

Economic Policy

Since the Budget various things have gone wrong. I think it is clear that we under-estimated the extent of the inflationary pressure at home; this was partly due to dis-saving by the public in anticipation of price increases, partly because the impact of the defence programme, through contracts placed, has been rather greater than we allowed for. At any rate, the level of unemployment has fallen sharply to the 1945 figure.[74] At the same time the balance of payments has gone wrong, chiefly because of a more rapid rise in import prices than we had allowed for,[75] while at the same time the export drive has been very slow in getting under way.

Another thing that has gone wrong has been the Stock Exchange. I had expected that by allowing interest rates to rise and increasing the taxes on distribut[ed] profits I would prevent any move in equities and keep dividends down. Unfortunately, the Budget was followed by a steady rise in equity prices, and this has been accompanied by dividend increases on a scale which I had hoped to prevent.

73 This reluctance impeded any early action on HG's repeated pleas to impress on Washington in good time the disastrous economic consequences of American purchasing policy for raw materials on the economies of her allies. See *HG*, p. 273.
74 This happened precisely at the time when Bevan's resignation speech had predicted mass unemployment in British industry owing to rearmament: 487 H.C. Deb. 37 (23.4.51).
75 As he wrote long afterwards, 'the change in the situation was anticipated, but not the speed with which it took place': HG to Strachey, 15.2.54 (Papers, file P.100).

In addition there has been a growing fuss about the increase in the cost of living. There was nothing unexpected about this. We knew it would go up and decided we could not attempt to offset it by higher subsidies. But politically it has been worrying, accompanied by the resignations in the Party, and a sort of guerrilla warfare going on behind the lines, at the same time as one has been conducting a campaign against the main Opposition.

I had not much time to think about these things while the Finance Bill was still in Committee, but as soon as this was over I began to plan a paper, setting out the position and discussing the steps which could be taken. One thing I wanted to do then was to start a real movement for stabilising world commodity prices. I had it in mind to fly to Washington with Dick Stokes and try and reach some agreement with the Americans. This would have been preceded by talks between officials. The Americans agreed to the official talks which have been very successful, but were horrified at the idea of any publicity. They are terrified [of] being thought to be ganging up with us, either to the exclusion of Europe or producing countries, particularly Latin America. Consequently we lost the political advantage of dramatising this move. On the other hand, their general attitude to the problem is pretty satisfactory. They seem to be as keen as we are to prevent any further breakaway, and a good deal of progress has been made in discussing ways and means of achieving this.

Another step we have since taken is the limitation of dividends. The case for this was, of course, that the tax imposed in the Budget on distribut[ed] profits had not done its job of keeping dividends down. I gave several warnings about this, but originally I had not contemplated taking action in the sense of a definite decision before the summer recess. I had thought of this proposal as something we very well might have to do in the autumn, and for which I could give some warning in advance. I changed my mind on this for several reasons. First, our inability to dramatise the raw materials prices policy left the policy programme rather empty. Secondly, the T.U.C. were showing signs of increasing restlessness – though this was mainly directed against our subsidies policy, and against profits as such. Thirdly, pressure was put on to me from various quarters that some kind of move to the Left was really essential if we were not to lose control of the Party to Bevan. I discussed it in detail with HD[Dalton], who kept me informed of what was going on on the National Executive. He made it plain that he thought the manifesto they were preparing was bound to include a demand for limiting dividends as well as some other things. He also thought that the Party Conference would go very much against us unless we did something of this kind.

I consulted a number of other people on the Right wing of the Party, to see how they felt. Herbert [Morrison] was very strongly in favour, so was

Alf Robens [Minister of Labour], so was Aidan Crawley [Under-Secretary for Air]. The only person who was opposed to it was the P.M., who I suspect may have been briefed in the opposite sense by some officials. However, his opposition only lasted a day. As regards the Treasury themselves, they were pretty fair. They admitted that if we had known what was going to happen to dividends we would have done it earlier. They did not like doing it, but did not resist it.

I explained to Plowden and Bridges the awkward position I should be in if the Executive manifesto included this and I was still standing out against it. I would then have to give way to obvious pressure from outside, or involve myself in a head-on collision with my own colleagues. I made it plain that this was not a matter on which I felt very strongly either way, but if anything I was in favour of doing it on merits. Therefore, there could be no question of my making it a resignation issue like the Health Services charges affair. I should add that Dick Stokes was also in favour of it, rather to my surprise, though Hartley Shawcross [President of the Board of Trade] was nervous about the reaction it might have on his relations with industry.

Anyway, we have now announced that we are going to do it, in a speech I made just before the Recess.[76] It has met with a most furious and violent abuse from the Right wing press and a positive torrent of nonsense, as well as a few good arguments. It has obviously angered the Bevanites who alternate between saying that I have abandoned the Budget completely, and that I have really done nothing at all.[77]

I do not think it will be such an electoral asset as some people think. On the other hand, not to have done it would have been a great liability. I propose to defend the measure at length in the T.U.C. They have invited me there and I have had to alter my plans and give up the sea trip to America and fly later instead.

Relations with the Bevanites continue to be very bad. They are apparently becoming more and more intransigent and extreme. They hope to capture the Party Conference and have, I am told, been forming themselves into a kind of shadow Government. They no doubt have a considerable following in the constituency parties; partly because it is difficult for the Government to put the case against them.

I have addressed a number of Regional Conferences of a private character, which I think have been useful. I had a fairly stormy one at Liverpool where the local M.P.s are terrible, including Bessie Braddock*

76 On 25 July HG announced that during the three years of rearmament, dividends would be limited by law to the average of the last two years; but the government fell before the law was passed. See *HG*, p. 270.
77 Barbara Castle* approved the decision, Harold Wilson was critical.

and Keenan – both very stupid and very left wing.[78] In moving the vote of thanks to me Bessie said, 'We can best defend ourselves against the Russians by having a higher standard of living'. It was greeted with enormous cheers.

There has been a lot of speculation about the Election and opinion is fairly evenly divided. The majority of the Parliamentary Party would like to postpone it, partly because they want to hang on, and partly because they are frightened that the cost of living will lose us any Election in the autumn. Dalton is strongly in favour of an Election; Herbert [Morrison] equally strongly against. Chuter Ede is in favour; William Whiteley [Chief Whip] is against, and so on! There have been some private meetings with the P.M. of a few of us. But I was mainly concerned in giving them some idea of the economic prospect which is far from cheerful, apart from the fact that the cost of living is likely to steady down. My guess is that Clem [Attlee] will go for an early Election, partly because he is tired, partly because the risks of hanging on are so great (that is the real argument in favour) and partly because he wants to get away from the conflict with the Bevanites and hopes that an Election Conference will smooth it all over. Others take a completely different view and think it would be fatal not to have a real showdown with Bevan.

Equal Pay

There has been a great fuss about this. I was in favour of making some small gesture to the Civil Service Unions which would not, I think, have had any repercussions, though equally it would have been pretty negligible in its effect; but the Cabinet, led on by Herbert, turned even this down, and I accepted on condition that I was allowed to make perfectly plain what the reasons were as to why we could not proceed with it. As I expected, the statement I made on these lines led to accusations that we had really departed from the principle. There is a lot of passion on this subject in some quarters, though not in the House of Commons, but I fancy it will die down in a few months' time.[79]

78 Will Keenan, M.P. for Liverpool (Kirkdale) 1945–51, had been the only Labour backbencher to criticise the Budget before Bevan resigned (out of 28 who spoke in the debate). Mrs Braddock soon ceased to be left wing. (On HG's T.U.C. speech see below, pp. 274–5.

79 Governments with ample majorities had been defeated on it twice in recent years (1.4.1936 and 28.3.1944) and had had to oblige the M.P.s to reverse themselves. HG's statement was on 20 June: 489 H.C. Deb. 526–33.

Frank Pakenham [now First Lord] gave a dinner at Admiralty House for the Board of Admiralty and invited the P.M., Lord Chancellor [Jowitt] and myself, plus wives. It was a jolly evening with some good, short and very funny speeches. I sat next to Lady Mountbatten, whom I thought pretty terrible. She is supposed to have led a very loose existence in the past. If so, she is certainly making up for it now by being deadly serious, intolerably heavy and speaking with great earnestness about her work in connection with nursing. She is a near Communist, I believe, although of course also a very wealthy heiress. I would have much preferred her to talk about the Night Clubs of New York. I think he is worth a lot more, but also, I feel, rather emotional and unstable on political issues. They tell me he is best when given a specific job to do, and I have no doubt that is so. But I feel uneasy with Royal Princes who are Admirals, who are also left-wing and what Dalton calls 'viewy' on public affairs.[80] Frank and Elizabeth are evidently enormously enjoying his new job, and all the reports I hear about how he conducts himself are excellent.

I took the children down for the weekend and stayed with the Crawleys at their farm in Buckinghamshire. They are both rather unusual types. She, a successful American journalist [Virginia Cowles] who began writing in magazines immediately on leaving school, and found her way here and all over the world. He, very much out of the top drawer. A fine cricketer and sportsman; Harrow and Oxford; who, nevertheless, turned left-wing in the thirties after a long spell of work on the *Daily Mail*. He gave that up, joined the Labour Party and started making educational films, and incidentally learned to fly. In the war he was shot down in Libya and spent the rest of it in prison camps. He is a great authority on escapes and has written the official history of the R.A.F. camps and of escapes which were attempted. The only time that he got out, he came all the way from Poland to Austria before he was picked up. He is also intelligent and has a good academic record. He and Virginia are both very much on the anti-Bevan side. He is optimistic about an election and still thinks we can win it, and expects to hold his own pretty marginal seat.[81]

My relations with the P.M. have not been, on the surface, quite so cordial lately. Ever since the Bevan resignations he has been pretty cool, I think. It has not affected my work, but there has been nothing which

80 Mountbatten was Fourth Sea Lord and about to become Commander-in-Chief Mediterranean.
81 Aidan Crawley lost Buckingham by 54 votes in 1951.

could be remotely described as intimacy. This may also be due to the fact that Herbert [Morrison] is Foreign Secretary and he feels that I and Herbert get on well, which we do. We both, that is Herbert and I, think that the P.M. has taken a very weak line about Bevan. He is very careful not to come out fully and firmly in the open against him, nor has he really given in our view much lead to the country on rearmament, though it was he and Bevin who initiated the new programme. However, I have no real grounds for complaint. He virtually leaves the economic side to me and has not let me down at all so far. We have only had one row, if one could call it that. The Burmese Government are blackmailing us into lending them five million to buy shares in the Burmah Oil Company. We, in the Treasury, do not like the idea at all. It is totally unnecessary since the Burmese have plenty of sterling and a bad precedent which may be followed up by other producing territories. Nevertheless, when it was discussed there was the usual ganging up between ex-Dominion Secretaries – the P.M., Phil Noel-Baker and Patrick [Gordon Walker] – the first two particularly feeling positively passionate about Burma and insisting on giving them anything they wanted. I have voted against this unsuccessfully.[82] In the course of the argument with the P.M. he accused me in these terms. 'If you go on like this you will lose the whole of the Middle East.' He was very angry and had gone quite red in the face. I replied, 'It is your policy which will lose us the Middle East. By giving way to blackmail here you will have it imposed on you everywhere else.'

Later I got into touch with the Burmah Oil Company and both they and our own official man believe that if we had stood out the Burmese Government would have accepted a different solution which did not involve us in putting up money. But it is no use talking to the P.M. on these subjects with which he was once associated.

My relations with Herbert, as implied above, are very cordial. He is very careful to consult me and seems anxious to have my views on foreign policy issues. Also, he is not extravagant and understands the importance of keeping expenditure under control. I think myself also that in the Cabinet and Cabinet Committees, although a little diffident, he has been quite sensible. He is learning his way, but I do not think he has made any policy errors. He is very anxious for Anglo-American co-operation and understands the necessity for that, but he is also quite good at standing up to them and anxious to keep good relations with Europe too.

I am told that in the House and Party his stock has fallen low. Some say that he has not got the dignity and poise for a Foreign Secretary. Aidan

82 HG's personal links with Burma were far closer than theirs, for his father, mother and sister had all spent most of their lives out there.

[Crawley], who is very much a friend of his, and Tony Crosland*[83] both take this line. But I think they are unfair to him. He has not really had much chance as yet, and as for the Party, if he has less hold on it now it is because he has lost contact. If this were resumed I feel he would get the support he wanted.

Of course there is a little gossip about what would happen if the P.M. went. Aidan was doubtful if Herbert would get the succession. I do not share his doubts myself, and feel pretty certain that there would be no difficulty, except of course to keep down Bevan, which I think we could do.

Going back to the dividend limitation it is difficult not to be upset by the intensity and violence of the criticisms. I suppose that fundamentally when you get criticism of this kind you begin to have doubts about the wisdom of your own policy, and so from that to get a lack of self-confidence. However, I am certainly a good deal tougher than I was, and it is just as well because I am in a very much more exposed position – detested by the Left and now very much out of favour with the Right. The only thing to do is to consolidate middle opinion, and that should not be difficult.

Some of us met together in Aidan's flat – John Edwards, Douglas [Jay], Patrick [Gordon Walker], Frank Pakenham and Woodrow Wyatt – not long ago to discuss countering the Bevan propaganda. We decided to try and organise a few people to write to the press, and we ourselves must do some more speaking in the country. But it is all very difficult because nobody has the time. Ministers cannot write articles and there is nobody to organise. It was left to Virginia, Aidan and Woodrow to do some organisation somehow or other, but so far as I can see nothing has happened.

I have had one tremendous battle with Shawcross about who is to be his Permanent Secretary [at the Board of Trade]. A man, James Helmore, was his candidate – now Deputy Secretary. I detest Helmore – knowing him quite well from being in the Board of Trade [1942–5] and since. Douglas Jay, John Edwards and Hugh Dalton all feel the same about it. We did not trust him. Edwin Plowden cannot stand him. He regards him as one of the major sources of trouble-making between the Board of

83 Anthony Crosland, then M.P. for South Gloucestershire and later author of *The Future of Socialism* (Cape, 1956), became one of HG's closest friends.

Trade and the Treasury. So when Hartley [Shawcross] became President (an appointment of which I was very doubtful) I saw him at once and warned him not to have Helmore. However, his present Permanent Secretary has worked upon him and conducted a great campaign for Helmore. It has been a long battle in which we had to go to the P.M. more than once. But finally I won and Frank Lee from the Ministry of Food has got the job.[84] Hartley has very little political sense in my view. He could, I think, have guessed with so many different Ministers taking this view about Helmore that we were likely to be right. It is funny too how one observes the legal mind at a disadvantage. A 'contract' or 'agreement' means something quite different to Hartley from what it does to most of us. In his letters one notices a kind of solicitor's learning creeping in. He is a fine person and is most intelligent and on many matters of policy I agree with him, but he has, I think, a great disadvantage in knowing no economics and not having any experience in administration. Inevitably, he tends simply to reflect the views of his officials who, at the top, are a rather poor lot. I think it would be better if he were somewhere else. I would have liked Patrick there and Hartley to take Commonwealth Relations.[85]

Staying with the Crawleys the other day we amused ourselves with the usual game of Government making. Aidan is desperately anxious to get rid of Shinwell and Strachey. He would obviously like to be Minister of Defence himself but would have taken Hartley for that job. We agreed that poor Phil [Noel-]Baker really ought to be replaced and the man to replace him would be James Callaghan. We also agreed that my two Ministers must be pushed on. Douglas [Jay] to be Minister of Supply, which he would do extremely well, and John Edwards might be President of the Board of Trade, or possibly Minister of Works; George Brown perhaps going to the War Office. But all this is just pleasant gossip and not to be taken seriously.[86]

84 HG's outspoken dislike – very rare with him – was fairly recent. Sir James Helmore had been his undergraduate contemporary at New College (HG thought him 'dim') and was already in the Board of Trade when Dalton became President in 1942 and HG wrote comments for him on all the senior civil servants; Helmore's was among the more favourable. Having failed to succeed Sir John Woods as its Permanent Secretary in 1951, he held that post at Materials, then Supply, 1952–6 when he retired. Sir Frank Lee, possibly the most influential administrator of his generation, headed the Ministry of Food 1949–51, Board of Trade 1951–9, Treasury 1960–2. HG had worked with him earlier, on allocating materials.

85 Patrick Gordon Walker was Secretary of State for Commonwealth Relations.

86 Shinwell was Minister of Defence, Strachey of War, Noel-Baker of Fuel and Power, Brown of Works. Jay was Financial and Edwards Economic Secretary to the Treasury, Callaghan Parliamentary and Financial Secretary to the Admiralty, Crawley Under-Secretary for Air.

At a dinner for Hyndley the other night – his farewell dinner – I sat next to him.[87] He was very much against Phil [Noel-Baker] and said we should change him. This was most unusual, coming from such a kindly man. But somehow or other they have never got on. I do not think Phil is as bad as Hyndley makes out. He has some tiresome habits and is probably a bad administrator but is quite energetic, and all things considered has not done badly in a very difficult position.

Friday, 9 November 1951

Once again a lot has happened since the last entry in this diary, though that was only two [sic] months ago. On September 3rd I went up to the T.U.C. to address them as the chief guest speaker. I was glad they asked me but rather nervous because the impact of my speech would be important one way or the other, both on the relationship between the T.U.C. and the Government and on the Bevan issue.

We took a great deal of trouble preparing the speech. I gave some of the officials an outline of what I wanted before going off to Jersey for a fortnight's holiday. While I was there various foolish speeches were made by T.U. leaders, very anti-wages policy and rather Bevanite in character. So I decided we should have to reply to this.

I did not like the draft they sent me and spent two days in Jersey rewriting it. It went through still further stages in London after I got back, and I suppose by the time it was finished it had had more time spent on it than any other speech, except the Budget.

I took Clem Leslie with me to Blackpool. On the way up the train stopped at Crewe and a lot of schoolboys on the platform saw my red box open on the seat and after a bit recognised me. There was then a further pause while they summoned up courage to ask for autographs. One of them shouted as we left, 'What are you going to do for the workers?'

We arrived on the Monday evening and I was due to speak on the Tuesday morning. The various leaders greeted me in a very friendly fashion and after dinner with Tewson and Woodcock [general secretary and assistant secretary of the T.U.C.] we went on to a party of the N.U.G.M.W. – Tom Williamson's Union – where almost all the other leaders were. I felt reassured by the friendliness of the reception, and the fact that the leaders did not seem to be too worried about what the Conference was going to do.

I went down and made the speech the next morning. Of course I read it,

87 Lord Hyndley was retiring as chairman of the National Coal Board.

which takes some of the nervousness and excitement away. But there is still the great uncertainty as to whether what you say is going to go down. I could not tell while it was going on because they received it almost in complete silence. But I knew they were listening pretty carefully. At the end they gave me a pretty good reception, and all the people on the platform were overjoyed.

I was more pleased about this speech that almost any other I made because it was very, very frank and confirmed my view that people will take the truth so long as you put it across in the right way. Andrew Naesmith, one of the people who had made a particularly silly speech, walked across and congratulated me in a very obvious manner. We then had to dash off to get into a plane to fly back to London for a Cabinet meeting that afternoon.

Before I go on to this and the American journey, I would say that the speech ought to have done a good deal to cement my relations with the T.U. leadership. Every now and then during the Election (see later) people spoke to me with warm approval about it; even Geddes*, one of the leaders who was hostile to me, said to me a month later, how much he had admired it. He said in fact that it had absolutely stunned him, meaning I think, by the force of the arguments. All this shows, I think, that it is of first class importance for a politician to take trouble about speeches. Some, of course, are purely ephemeral and do not matter, but others can be decisive in influencing a limited body of people. Sometimes it is what appears in the press that matters; sometimes it is how you handle the audience. In the case of the T.U.C. both mattered.[88]

When I returned from Jersey [late in August] I found to my dismay that the economic outlook seemed to have got a good deal worse. In particular, it was now clear that the dollar deficit in the third quarter would be at least $500 million. Moreover, the deficit was likely to continue though possibly at a rather reduced rate, unless energetic steps were taken to deal with it. So, at the last minute, I decided to circulate a paper to the Cabinet, setting out the facts and securing authority to lay all these cards on the table in Washington.

We had a very good trip. Leslie Rowan and Edwin Plowden had gone

88 See Trades Union Congress Report, 1951, pp. 363–71; and *HG*, pp. 270–1. (Sir) Andrew Naesmith (1888–1961) was Gen. Sec. of the Amalgamated Weavers, and on the T.U.C. General Council 1945–53; Charlie Geddes led the postmen.

on ahead the day before. William Armstrong and Clem Leslie came with me, also Eric Roll from our E.C. Delegation.[89]

In New York I had lunch with Gladwyn Jebb [Ambassador to the U.N.], who rents a very beautiful house up the Hudson river about half an hour's drive from the city. We reached Washington in the early evening and went to stay with Dennis and Pauline Rickett. He had been the Prime Minister's Principal Private Secretary and had just succeeded Leslie Rowan in the post of Economic Minister in Washington. They took over the Rowans' house, a most attractive one right on the edge of the town in the woods in Westmoreland Hills. But then most of the houses in this part of the town are very attractive both architecturally and because of the absence of hedges. The lawns run down to the road and you get the impression of everything being in a great park. I do not know why we should not do the same. Hampstead, for instance, would look most attractive if one took away all the hedges and fences.

My first job was, of course, to impress on the Americans the seriousness of the dollar situation which was developing so that they could consider giving us various forms of help. As usual, it was necessary to tell the same story to different Ministers. While my most obvious opposite number was Snyder [Secretary of the Treasury], I had also to see Charles Wilson (broadly the Minister of Production), Bill Foster, the head of E.C.A., Sawyer, Secretary of Commerce, and of course [Secretary] Acheson and [Under-Secretary] Webb at the State Department.[90] We thought the best thing to do was to prepare a document and leave it with each of the Ministers so that the officials could really study it properly.

There were also various subsidiary things to be done. I had to have some discussions with Snyder on whether we should apply for the waiver on interest on the American loan.[91] I also had to find out whether he was going to be troublesome on certain other clauses of the loan agreement about non-discrimination.

89 They flew over on the evening of 4 September, after the Cabinet. Eric (Lord) Roll was on Plowden's planning staff in 1948, and Minister to O.E.E.C. 1949. He became Permanent Secretary at the Dept. of Economic Affairs 1964–6, and a Director of the Bank of England 1968–77.

90 Charles E. Wilson, Director of the Office of Defense Mobilisation, was called 'Electric Charlie' (he had been president of General Electric) to distinguish him from 'Engine Charlie' Wilson of General Motors, who became Eisenhower's Secretary of Defense. Charles Sawyer, a Cincinnati lawyer, who ran for Governor of Ohio 1938, was Secretary of Commerce 1948–53. On the others see p. 203 and n.

91 The loan agreement provided that Britain should repay it, plus 2 per cent interest, from 31 December 1951; but (in a clause with no precedent in U.S. lending) that interest might be waived if Britain felt its pre-war standard of living was threatened. In practice the saving seemed too small to justify irritating U.S. opinion: see Gardner (1956), pp. 211–13.

As for the specific help we wanted, apart from any economic aid which seemed pretty hopeless for the current year since the Americans had thought we should not need any, we wanted steel, a more helpful purchasing policy as regards raw materials by their agencies, and some kind of device whereby though we might not receive direct economic aid we could be helped by other means. I also had to make it plain that we could certainly not, under any circumstances, increase our defence effort, and could not afford to take over from the Germans the cost of the occupation forces in that country.

I began with Snyder. I had, of course, seen him a year before when we had a very cordial discussion in circumstances where it was not necessary for me to raise any awkward questions at all. We had gone down the Potomac in a yacht and drunk a great deal of whisky together. We had exchanged photographs and superficially seemed to get on.

This time he greeted me in a most warm and friendly fashion at the first courtesy call. I gave him the dollar document and warned him a little of what was in it. I asked him about the waiver. He said, 'Well, if you really want it, of course there is no question but that you must have it'. Then he went on, however, to make it plain that from the point of view of U.S. public opinion it would be very much better if we did not have to apply for it. I told him that I did not expect to come to a decision on this until I got back to England and had a chance of consulting the Cabinet. What we really had in mind was that we should use it in a sense as a bargaining counter; that we should deliberately not apply for the waiver, on the understanding that the Americans were going to be helpful in other ways.

Snyder and I also discussed one or two issues arising at the I.M.F. [International Monetary Fund] and International Bank Conferences, which was ostensibly the reason for my visit to Washington. As in a sense these proved to be more important than I expected I had better give a little background. On the International Bank there was really no dispute. We felt that it was now doing a good job under Eugene Black*, and we were anxious to support it. There was no issue of policy which arose except every now and then a hope on the part of the Americans that we should be prepared to lend a little more ourselves.

But in the case of the I.M.F. the story was very different. From the start in 1945 there had been nothing but friction between the Americans and ourselves. Friction based on a wholly different view of the functions of the I.M.F. and what it ought to do in present circumstances. The Americans, in the person of Southard who was their Executive Director, took a very laissez-faire view.[92] They were always pressing for freedom from exchange restrictions and unwilling to allow the fund to be used effectively except in

92 Frank A. Southard, an economics professor from Cornell, held this post from 1949 to 1962 when he became Deputy Managing Director.

order to bully or bribe countries into getting rid of restrictions. In particular, they thought it would be dangerous for the Fund to be used where there was serious disequilibrium.

We, on the other hand, took the view for the most part that the Fund should face up to the realities of the post-war world and try and play a full part in helping countries over exchange difficulties. This difference of doctrine was probably aggravated by the use of the voting system. There was no unanimity rule in the Fund but a system of wedge [weighted?] vote which in effect gave the Americans a majority whenever they wanted it. Undoubtedly they used this majority vote pretty ruthlessly to assert their own viewpoint. In passing I may say that the more I have seen of international organisations, the more I feel myself that contrary to what one might suppose, the unanimity rule has a good deal to be said for it. Certainly in O.E.E.C. far more has been done than in the I.M.F. It is tiresome, of course, to have to beg and press and argue, and finally compromise, as you do when one country can exercise a veto, but providing there is a real desire to reach a settlement I believe it is better to get it this way than by vote, which is apt to lead to a good deal of ill will, particularly where, as in the I.M.F., the cards are all stacked on one side.

Apart from this general difference of dogma and dissatisfaction about the use of the vote, there was another cause for friction this year. Some months before, the Executive Directors of the I.M.F. had voted themselves pensions. I took a very dim view of this, as of course did the Treasury in London. I wrote, protesting, to Gutt[93] who was their Managing Director, and on receiving no satisfaction from him, I asked Douglas Abbott, Canadian Minister of Finance, who was Chairman of the Governors' Conference, to put this question on the agenda.

There was a good deal of anxiety even before I left London lest there should be an open row on this at the Conference. If our financial position had been stronger I might have been prepared for it. But it was obvious by the time I got to Washington that I could not afford to quarrel with the Americans who had really been responsible for this action of the Executive Directors.

Official talks took place in Washington in the first day or two, and as a result Snyder asked me to agree to change the wording on the agenda. This change, in effect, meant that we were not going to discuss the past action of the Executive Board but confine ourselves to putting the matter right in the future. A reasonable compromise resolution was agreed with

93 Camille Gutt, a rigidly orthodox economist, had been Belgian Minister of Finance 1939–45 and successfully stabilised the currency after the war. He was Managing Director of the I.M.F., 1946–51, and had already clashed bitterly with HG over full employment, at Geneva in the previous summer: HG, p. 218.

the Americans which secured that in future this kind of thing could not happen, and that the Governors would be able to control the pay in any form of the Executive Board.

In considering this with Snyder I warned him that I would have to square Douglas Abbott himself, who felt as I did, and – more important – the Australian representative, Percy Spender, who had been their Foreign Secretary and was now Ambassador in Washington. I knew Spender of old as an extremely difficult and aggressive little man. He was, however, at that moment in San Francisco at the Japanese Peace Conference and was not expected back in Washington until the following Tuesday.

Before I continue with the history of this particular episode, I should interpose that in the first two or three days we succeeded in getting the Americans to understand and take seriously our economic plight. Snyder, as I have said, had been quite friendly and seemed disposed to help. Charles Wilson, whom we went to see particularly about steel, was as he had been when I saw him in London, very co-operative and obviously anxious to do his best. Unfortunately, he had said some unwise things to the press just before we met him and they put out a most garbled version of our request for steel. This got Congressmen on their hind legs, and made it all much more difficult.[94] Nevertheless, we all felt that he would do his best to help. Even Sawyer, a rather tiresome, very vain man, seemed to be reasonably friendly, and E.C.A., first of all through Bissell, grasped more quickly than anybody what we were up against.

Acheson being in San Francisco, I saw Webb at the State Department and some of the officials and they all were pretty co-operative. Having made them face up to the problem we then proceeded to draft a document setting out in detail what we wanted them to do. But this took some days and further consultations at official level.

Meanwhile, the harmony of our relationship was somewhat marred by what took place on the I.M.F. pensions issue. As I have said, Spender was supposed to be coming back on the Tuesday from San Francisco. I invited the Commonwealth Delegates to a lunch that day, thinking that I would speak to him about the pensions matter then and persuade him not to be too tiresome. That morning I had not been to the meeting of the I.M.F. because there was a meeting with the State Department on East-West trade and our dollar situation, where I more or less took over from the Foreign Secretary and explained the position to Acheson. I left Leslie Rowan to make a fairly moderate speech on doctrine and the way we saw the international economic situation, which we had agreed beforehand.

I came to lunch and met the Commonwealth Delegates including

94 Congress was prejudiced against a Labour government which had nationalised steel, and was to be a bit less ungenerous to their Conservative successors.

Spender. I spoke to him at once about the pensions and, rather to my surprise, he readily agreed with what I proposed as regards not only the change in the agenda and Resolution, but also as to what he might say. I did not discover until some hours afterwards that unfortunately he had already made that very morning at the opening of the proceedings a most stupid and ill judged speech couched in the most violent terms, not only on the pensions issue but also on the whole behaviour of the U.S. in the I.M.F. To make matters worse he was followed by a South African delegate, a certain Dr Holloway, ex-Governor of their bank, whom I had not reckoned with at all, who said more or less the same thing.[95] This led to the following extraordinary sequel.

About the middle of the week Eugene Black gave his usual dinner to the Finance Ministers and Central Bank Governors. It was an exclusively male affair and we all turned up at his charming, modern house ready for what I thought might have been quite an interesting evening.

There was a slight piece of embarrassment because the Chinese (Chiang Kai Shek) delegate who had not been asked, arrived – coming apparently to the wrong party. However, this was coped with very adequately somehow or other.

Before dinner I was talking to Snyder who . . . proceeded to launch a most violent attack upon me, implying that I had double crossed him on the pensions issue because of what Spender and Holloway had said. I tried to explain that I could not control the other Members of the sterling area. The whole thing was highly embarrassing. He also accused me of attacking him in the British House of Commons, which may have been a reference to some very mild comments of approval on their credit policy where, in fact, the Federal Reserve Board won a small argument with the U.S. Treasury.[96] It was interesting really as showing, alas, what an extraordinarily small minded and rather ridiculous man Snyder really is. For example, on the sterling area he said . . . 'Well, I thought you were a big shot. Don't you control all these people? etc., etc.'

Rather to my dismay I found myself also sitting next to him at dinner, and he then proceeded to embarrass everybody else by shouting to Black at the other end of the table, 'I thought this was supposed to be an International affair. Why do we have to put up the money? Let's go round the table and find out what everybody else is doing'. First of all, nobody took any notice, but he went on repeating this and Black, quite tactfully, proceeded to explain what some of the other countries had done. Snyder

95 Dr J. E. Holloway had in fact been Secretary (permanent head) of the Ministry of Finance 1937–50. Representative at many international conferences, and at the I.M.F. 1948–52; Ambassador to the U.S. 1954–6, High Commissioner in London 1956–8.
96 491 H.C. Deb. 668 (26 July). The comments were very mild indeed.

got bored with it after a bit and said, 'It is all right. I see that it is embarrassing everyone. I will shut up'. He then repeated all over again to me his accusations about the pensions issue, and muttered at intervals that the Americans were always the milch cow; that the American tax payers had to pay for everything and, overhearing something I was saying to the Belgian Minister of Finance[97] about the impossibility of spending any more on defence and misunderstanding it, proceeded to say, 'Well, who is helping who?', and similar expressions.

It was all very embarrassing and unpleasant. No less because, as I have said, it showed what must have been at the back of his mind so often. He revealed himself as a pretty small minded, small town, semi-isolationist.

Two other little stories . . . He gave a very nice party (mixed) on the previous Sunday evening to which the Vice-President of the U.S. came. There were about thirty people there, and after dinner Snyder proposed the health of Douglas Abbott . . . [in a] meaningless sort of speech which, however, just passed without anybody worrying about it much. Douglas Abbott replied in a pleasantly conventional way and Snyder then called on Barkley, the Vice-President, to say a few words.[98] Barkley then got up and . . . did a kind of filibuster which went on for half an hour and said nothing at all. Worse still, Snyder then felt he did not want to be outdone and proceeded to put over a similar sort of affair. Leslie Rowan and I were very astonished by this. Douglas Abbott, however (and this is the second story) told me after the dinner at the Blacks that . . . in Paris the year before the same kind of thing had happened but it was worse because it was the first time the other Ministers had seen this. He also said, however, that he had on many occasions tried to explain to Snyder about the sterling area but had never succeeded.

Later in the week I had another meeting with Snyder alone . . . I once again explained what had happened on the pensions issue and he was quite reasonably cordial. I asked him to do what he could to help us as regards the various proposals which we were then making to the Americans, and he implied that he would. Nevertheless, I had the feeling, and still have it, that this whole episode of what Spender and Holloway said and . . . [that] he had said these very offensive things to me was bound to make our relationship a good deal more difficult. Whether it would have much effect on the attitude of the Administration is less certain. Snyder's only power – and it is an important point – is that he is an old and close personal friend of the President [Truman]. He does not, of course, get on at all well with Acheson, nor I would judge with Harriman.

97 Jean van Houtte, who became Prime Minister in January 1952.
98 Alben Barkley, Congressman from Kentucky 1913–27, Senator 1927–48, became Democratic leader in the Senate and was Truman's Vice-President 1948–52.

It is I am afraid the case that whereas one's conversations with Harriman, Acheson, Foster, Bissell, the Ministry of Defence people, always took place in what one felt was an atmosphere of real friendship in which everybody was trying to help, one cannot honestly say the same about Snyder and the U.S. Treasury.[99]

Apart from the Snyder episode, the ten days of my stay in Washington were crowded with functions and meetings. I established very satisfactory relations with Bill Foster who, however, was made Deputy Minister of Defence during the course of the week, but he struck me as a genuinely nice person, shrewd rather than clever. It should be a help to us that someone with his knowledge of Europe's problems through E.C.A. is now in the Ministry of Defence.

I had a very pleasant hour or so with Tom Finletter [Secretary of the Air Force], who remains as cultured and charming as ever. He too was extraordinarily helpful and obviously anxious to do everything he could to help us. I was interested to have dealings with Acheson for the first time. He is an impressive personality; partly because you feel that he has a sensitive and cultured mind. Oddly enough, I found myself on almost every occasion involved in an argument with him, and I cannot say that I really got to know him at all. Averell Harriman is, of course, an old friend now, and he too can be trusted as somebody who will try and solve the problem for us.

The most important thing that transpired in these talks was the clash between our own economic position (and that of the French which was very similar) on the one side and the attitude of the Americans which to begin with at least was to the effect that the defence effort was not enough.[100] The clash between these two points of view came out very clearly at an early meeting we had with Bissell, who was accompanied by

99 Before H.G. arrived in Washington, Snyder had persuaded the President not to see him: *HG*, p. 275 & n. 40.

100 Acheson claimed that 'we were prepared and sympathetic when Hugh Gaitskell and René Mayer [French Finance Minister] joined us with their tale of woe in mid-September. Even our own Treasury head . . . had softened a bit. Gaitskell reported an estimated deficit . . . of a billion dollars . . . the increased requests of General Eisenhower* were out of the question. Not only was it impossible for them [the British] to do more, but they could not long continue the present rate of rearmament': Acheson (1970), pp. 559–60. On his return HG told Dalton that he had 'said that we could not, as U.S. were pressing us to do, go beyond £4,700 million (rearmament in 3 years) and could only reach it, if certain conditions as to supply of materials, etc., were fulfilled': diary, 24.9.51. He told the Cabinet that the Administration were 'As usual, "taken by surprise" at our account of our troubles, but terrified of Congress, and, in any case, won't settle anything till after an election': *ibid.*, 27.9.51. On the change in their attitude see *HG*, pp. 275–6 (and briefly below, p. 291).

a State Department and Ministry of Defence [i.e. Department of Defense] officials. The danger of all this conflict coming out at Ottawa led to our request for a Tripartite meeting – the U.S., British and French in Washington. Eventually we had that meeting and out of it came the proposal, originally put forward by the French, for a special committee to study the whole situation. I will refer to this later on and how it developed. [101]

I saw a certain amount of the press, though perhaps not so much of the English press as I should have done. Afterwards I found that they were presenting the most garbled accounts of my discussions to London. For the first time I appeared in a television show. This was called, 'Meet the Press' and consisted of being cross-examined by four journalists. It all sounded very alarming, but although to begin with one could not help feeling nervous – there were supposed to be ten million listening – by the end of the half hour one was completely in the centre of it and only wanted more time to explain everything to the questioners.

I had dinner one evening with Joe Alsop, who had also invited a few Congressmen. But this I do not feel was a success. First of all, Joe himself was so anglophile and at the same time so gloomy that it was not very stimulating. The Congressmen also were too friendly. It would have done more good if he had invited some more difficult characters. However, I was very tired that night, so perhaps it was just as well.

I spent one nice afternoon with the Bergers, driving round Washington and seeing something of the town outside the Embassy quarter and the Centre. Staying with the Ricketts was extraordinarily comfortable and they are a very nice pair indeed. I did not see much of the Ambassador [Sir Oliver Franks] who was at San Francisco to start with, and very much occupied with the foreign policy talks when he came back. [102]

One other episode was rather amusing. Before I left London, Wally Phillips who had been President of the American Chamber of Commerce in London for many years, and went back to live in America a year ago, asked me if I would meet a group of American businessmen when I was in New York to discuss dividend limitation as it affected their subsidiary companies. Wally is an old friend and out to be helpful so I readily agreed to this, and left William [Armstrong, private secretary] to make the arrangements. It seemed however doubtful whether I should be more than one night in New York and since Wally wanted a dinner party there was going to be no time for anything else. At one of the functions in Washington however where there were many American officials,

101 See the next Diary entry.
102 Morrison and Shinwell, Foreign Secretary and Minister of Defence, were having discussions in Washington at the same time. Sam Berger had been in the U.S. Embassy in London (above, p. 120).

Winthrop Aldrich, whom I had met over here and who is both an extreme reactionary and also very anglophile complained to me bitterly that I was being entertained by Phillips who was in his view a nobody and in any case not . . . [omission in original] 'It is all wrong', he said, 'that the Chancellor of the Exchequer should come to New York and not be entertained by the Bankers.' He had drunk a good deal and went on and on and on about this. He pressed me to come to New York earlier and offered to send the Chase National Bank aeroplane to fetch me from Ottawa.[103] Eventually, I said that perhaps something could be fixed up that way to the mutual satisfaction of both gentlemen. But I could not help feeling slightly amused by the competition of the bankers and industrialists to overwhelm a Socialist Chancellor with entertainment!

The officials were, as usual, extraordinarily competent and helpful. I was very much impressed by Leslie Rowan's speed and efficiency. Edwin [Plowden], too, was very good and forceful. I was particularly appreciative of something he said to Harriman one night. I had once more explained the gravity of the dollar situation and made it plain, as I had done on several previous occasions, that if they did nothing about it we should not be able to carry through the defence programme – we should have to give priority to exports. I never, of course, said anything of this kind in public.[104] Edwin then joined in and said to Harriman, 'It is easier for me to say this than the Chancellor, but if you let him down now you will be playing straight into Bevan's hands. Moreover don't imagine that if the Labour Party lose the Election it will help at all. If the economic position gets really bad there is a danger that Bevan may capture the whole Labour movement in opposition, and that is the worst thing that can happen to the country.'

Douglas Abbott offered me a lift in his plane to Ottawa which I gladly accepted. He is a very attractive and charming man and very shrewd, though at International Conferences at least he does not somehow strike one as being very forceful. But that may be because Canada plays a subordinate role to the U.S. He was, however, a great success as Chairman of the Conference, and the general expectation in Canada is that he will succeed St Laurent as P.M. in due course.[105]

103 Winthrop Aldrich (1885–1974) had been president or chairman of that bank since 1930. He was US. Ambassador in London 1953–7.
104 See his Note on U.S. Aid (below, pp. 297–8) paras. 7 & 8.
105 He went to the Supreme Court instead.

Friday, 16 November 1951

Ottawa Conference

My main concern in the Conference was to try and get the clash between military requirements and the economic situation in Britain and France properly handled.[106] Indeed, it may be said that this, together with the entry of Greece and Turkey into NATO, were the two big achievements of the Conference.

When we got to Ottawa, however, there was still a good deal of disagreement and confusion between the Americans, French and ourselves about the former question. In Washington we had had a tripartite meeting in the State Department where I had explained very frankly to Acheson, Lovett and Harriman how serious our economic position was.[107] The French had confirmed that theirs was much the same and then they had put forward what became known as the 'Wise Men' proposal.

Their original idea was, I think, that three experts should be appointed to go into the whole matter and report to the Council of NATO. This was, in a way, typically French, who nowadays are so often seeking for supranational solutions because of feeling the instability of their Government. Acheson asked what we thought of this idea, and I said that I approved of a special enquiry but that I thought the issues were far too serious for Governments for them to be entrusted to outside experts. I said, 'It all depends who the "Wise Men" are'. Acheson said that he agreed with that, and on my first point, they were thinking of appointing someone sitting not far from me. I guessed that he meant Averell Harriman who was between us. This, of course, was perfectly satisfactory to us because Harriman was a Minister, and very close to the President as well as Acheson. It was then left that we should meet together in Ottawa and discuss the matter further. As Harriman was not coming to Ottawa the responsibility on the American side fell to Bill Foster.

Accordingly, on the Sunday after we had arrived at Ottawa, and before the Conference had really got very far, Foster, [René] Mayer (French Vice-Premier and Finance Minister) met with our chief officials to try and reach agreement on what should be put up to the Council. It was fairly easy to settle the issue of experts v politicians. The French absolutely wanted Jean Monnet* as their man. He was not in the Government but he was very well known to the Members of the Government. So we had a

106 For the outcome see below, p. 291.
107 On these meetings see above, pp. 282–3 and n. 100. Robert A. Lovett moved up from Deputy Secretary to Secretary of Defense at just the time HG was in Washington, and Foster succeeded him.

formula that the members of the Committee must be persons who had the full confidence of Governments. As it turned out, all the other countries took our point of view very definitely, i.e. that they really ought to be politicians.[108]

We then got on to the question of the size of the Committee. On this there were several possibilities. The original idea of the French had been American, British and French plus one other. But, of course, the difficulty was which other? There were at least three candidates: Italy, Canada and some representative of the smaller countries. So this first proposal developed into one for a committee of five which was backed by the French rather vaguely supported by the Americans. I opposed it, partly because I was sure that we had to have a very small committee if we really wanted to get the job done, and partly because I felt sure that we could not keep it to five, and indeed when one once got to six one might as well have everybody in. I therefore proposed that we should have a Committee of twelve with a smaller body of three to do the work. At first this was turned down by the others, but they came round to it as a possibility. Finally, we agreed to consult the other countries as to which of the three solutions they preferred, i.e. a committee of three only; a committee of five, or a committee of twelve with a smaller executive body of three. I had to see the Portuguese, Canadians and Norwegians and found that they all favoured our proposal.

By now the Americans had swung round in favour of it as well, and it looked as though it was going to go through without further difficulty. Van Zeeland, however – the Chairman of the Conference – a real epitome of insincerity, a 'faux bon homme' as Schuman once described him – was offended because he had not been in on these discussions and made a tremendous fuss. He was also backed up by Stikker for somewhat similar reasons.[109] However, we finally held a special private session of one Minister from each of the twelve countries and after two hours of argument reached agreement. The Italians to the end tried to get a larger committee, but finally gave up when they saw that if the matter came to an election the majority were in favour of three only. To make things easier it was informally understood that the Chairman would be Harriman and the two Vice-Chairmen would be British and French. There was also some face-saving sentence about adding to this small committee of three if necessary.

As to the Conference itself, I feel that it was rather successful, chiefly

108 Harriman, Monnet and Plowden were chosen. The Americans had wanted the three to serve as individuals not as government representatives – so that HG could continue to represent Britain if the Conservatives came in.
109 They were respectively the Foreign Ministers of Belgium, France and the Netherlands.

because you really did get the Finance and Defence Ministers up against each other and against their common problem. On foreign affairs Acheson made much the best speech. It was an impressive, very lucid, survey of the whole world situation. It became clear that they rated the Russian danger in Europe pretty high. Acheson used a rather unfortunate analogy however. He said that the position was comparable to one motor trying to overtake another. The position was dangerous so long as they were parallel, but if we could make a spurt and get ahead we should be all right. Herbert [Morrison] said to him privately, 'That's all very well but it is not a very good thing to try and pass somebody on a bend'.

In the main economic debate I was at first depressed by the feebleness of the Finance Ministers from other countries. It is extraordinary how some of them seem to say nothing whatever, presumably for fear of the Americans. This was true, rather surprisingly, of Douglas Abbott [Canada] and René Mayer [France]. However, the Dutch did much better and Kristensen, the Danish Finance Minister, really made an excellent analysis of the situation, speaking in English and only from a few notes.[110] I then joined in and after describing our situation in broad terms, made it plain that it was absolutely out of the question for us to do any more unless we were to have a war economy both internally and in our relationship between each other. I criticised Acheson for appearing to suggest that we could have guns and butter as well. This was one of the things which continually irritated me – a sort of ganging up between the Americans who always wanted promises of tremendous programmes for Congress and the mendicant Europeans who would promise anything so long as they thought they could get some dollars.[111] However, I think that the stand we took with some of the smaller countries made a considerable impression, as subsequent events showed. Snyder was also there but took very little part in the proceedings. I did not have any further personal conversations with him, my dealings with the Americans at this stage being with Foster and to some extent Acheson.

I was very much concerned to secure while in Washington agreement with the Americans on some kind of statement which could be issued to the press after my departure from the U.S. I wanted, of course, to get them tied up as much as possible in public with helping us out of our difficulties, and I was most anxious to have something official with which to answer questions when I got back to England. Before we got to Ottawa

110 Professor Thorkil Kristensen, an economist and member of the Agrarian Party, was Finance Minister in anti-Socialist governments 1945–7, 1950–3. In 1960 he became Secretary-general of O.E.E.C.
111 HG told Dalton, back in London: 'French and Italians were very weak and mendicant': diary, 24.9.51. See *HG*, pp. 276, 282; *Tribune* headlined its editorial on 21 September 'Has Gaitskell joined the Bevanites?'

I still hoped this was a possibility, but the Americans proved very sticky, partly on the quite reasonable ground that they could hardly have a statement on Britain only when all the other countries were there as well. Eventually, we did get them to put into a communiqué a paragraph which went some way to what I wanted. Looking back, one can see that this was not as important as I thought at the time. All the same I think we could have got a good deal out of them had not the P.M. decided to announce the General Election even before the Conference was over. Since a great many people there assumed we would be defeated, this announcement naturally undermined our position. In the circumstances, it was fortunate that it did not do anything worse, and that most of the important decisions had already been taken.[112]

I spent two very crowded days in New York. On the evening of our arrival we had to change and go almost at once to the Aldrich dinner. This was at a Club called 'The Brook' which was a very passable imitation of a small London Club except that the food was incomparably better. I did not see any other members of the Club; the party being held in a private room. The food, as I said, was extraordinarily good and both William [Armstrong] and Edwin [Plowden], who accompanied me, marked it down as one of the best dinners they had ever had. Aldrich was determined not to be outdone by Phillips. After dinner they asked me to talk, and I told them about the Ottawa Conference. They were very polite but did not ask many questions and the party broke up rather surprisingly early. I should quite have enjoyed some further conversations about things like credit policies and the dollar problem.

On the following evening we went to Wally Phillips' dinner. This was held in an almost similar Club called 'The Links', and again the food, though different, was about as good as you can get. Wally was determined not to be outdone by Aldrich. On this occasion, however, there was very much more discussion. I began by making a long statement about dividend limitation. I explained that something obviously had to be done in the light of the recent profits and I thought the dividend limitation was better than E.P.T. [Excess Profits Tax] which they were going to have in the U.S. This argument appealed to some of them and a certain Mr Breech, quite a young man who apparently runs the Ford Motor Company, was very much on my side.[113] However, there was not a great deal of talk about dividend limitation. I think some of them were a little too shy to talk about their own particular problems in front of the others. Instead, we drifted into the usual argument about production in capitalist America and Socialist Britain. There was one aggressive man from the

112 See *HG*, p. 283, on his dismay at Attlee's decision.
113 Ernest R. Breech, Ford's executive vice-president and later chairman, was born in 1897 – nine years before HG.

Steel industry who put forward the usual Tory extreme arguments about incentives and the level of taxation, etc. When he started implying we just did not work in England he was rather squashed by two of the others. One of the Vice Presidents of General Motors said that at Luton they thought they could produce cars just as efficiently and cheaply as in America if only they had enough sheet steel; and Eugene Holman, President of the Standard Oil Company of New Jersey, said that the Fawley Refinery near Southampton was the best job of its kind they had had done anywhere, including America. Edwin also chipped in very well and defended our position. The others were mostly friendly and it was quite an enjoyable evening. As we left the room Wally said to me, with great pride, that he supposed the guests there represented about two billion dollars.

Meanwhile, that same afternoon at lunch I had addressed the Foreign Policy Association. This was rather a hectic affair, and for once in a way the food was really bad. I had, of course, to read the speech; it had been given to the press beforehand. But they received it extraordinarily well – very politely all standing up when I got up to speak and again when I had finished.

The following day, just before leaving, we had lunch with Mr Luce and his staff of *Life*, *Fortune* and *Time*.[114] They asked me about the election and after lunch one of the others said to William [Armstrong], going down in the lift, that he had got the impression that I thought we were going to lose it. I thought this was rather clever of him as I had been extremely guarded. But apparently they drew this deduction because I was so objective in my comments – something they do not experience in their own country.

The arrival home was very different this time. We got in on the Sunday morning in the rain and to my relief there were only a couple of press men to meet us, though all our families had come.

When I got back to the Treasury I found that the economic situation had deteriorated still further (indeed, they had warned me of this while in Washington and Ottawa, and we had taken some further steps on dollar purchases), but it was clear that the deficit for the third quarter was going to be over $600 million; a good deal worse than we had originally supposed. It was also clear that things were going badly wrong in the sterling area balance of payments with Europe.[115] I found, rather to my

114 Henry Luce, the publisher, was influential in journalism, the Republican party and the 'China Lobby'.
115 The main causes were heavy spending by raw-material-producing countries in the sterling area; capital exports to Australia and South Africa; and unforeseen stockpiling in the U.K. See *HG*, p. 277.

dismay, that they were still some way from being ready with recommendations on dollar cuts, or on measures for dealing with the U.K. balance of payments.

I spent a good deal of the next few days preparing my broadcast for the following Saturday. Somehow or other it caused endless trouble. It was so difficult to get oneself back into the atmosphere of English politics and it is, of course, a very hard job trying to compress into less than 2,000 words a talk on everything and anything.

After the broadcast we went down to the Crawleys and drove with them up to Scarborough to the Labour Party Conference. This was a very depressing affair. I was, of course, extremely worried about the economic situation coming just before the election, and I did not much relish the prospect of the speech I had to make a few days later at the Mansion House. We had done most of the preparation for this before I left London, but I knew it was going to be a pretty cold douche for our supporters. There had been a move while I was in America to try and get me to postpone this. But I made it plain that this was out of the question. It was quite clear to me that while one was entitled to present the position as one thought best, it would be quite fatal to attempt to hide any of the facts. It was very fortunate indeed that I took this line, as after events showed.

Scarborough, however, was also gloomy because of the Bevanite successes in the elections to the Executive. It certainly was pretty grim that the delegates of the constituency Parties should have, not merely put Bevan at the top of the poll, but also given such a person as Tom Driberg* more than Jim Griffiths.[116] Afterwards I learned[117] this was the result of some pretty shameful canvassing and instructions to the Bevanite delegates to plump to vote only for four names and not for any others. This was why Jim Griffiths managed to get so many fewer votes than in the previous year. The Conference was bound to be boring because there was nothing to talk about and everybody was wanting to get away and get on with the Election.

116 Barbara Castle, elected by trade union votes to the women's section of the N.E.C. in 1950, transferred in 1951 to the constituency parties' section and won Shinwell's seat. Driberg, a prominent Bevanite, had recently been censured by the Parliamentary Party for absenting himself on a journalistic trip to Korea for some months, without leave of the Whips, while sick M.P.s had to be hauled along to vote because the government's majority was so precarious.
117 Probably from Dalton (his diary, 4 & 30.10.51) whose evidence was shaky.

The Mansion House speech went off reasonably well, all things considered. The penguins were not so frigid as they might have been (perhaps they were cheered considerably by the prospect of our losing the election); and also the facts I had to relate were gloomy enough for our own people, though there were some better aspects, such as the larger gold reserves, to which I was entitled [to], and did, draw attention.[118]

There is really not much to say about the Election. It was the first one in which I had had to travel around and that made it rather less dull. But it was dull all the same. It is intolerably boring having to say more or less the same thing so many times, even if the meetings are different.

Early on I had to fly from Glasgow to Paris because Harriman had particularly asked that I should go to a meeting of the 'Wise Men' Committee of twelve. So I flew from Glasgow at 10 p.m. getting to Paris about one o'clock in the morning. I was met by Edwin [Plowden] who had been acting for me, and he brought me up to date. They were finding Monnet almost impossible because of his stubbornness and his ideas on what the enquiry should be. We went to breakfast with Harriman the next day and talked about Monnet, and also the American idea to bring over a General to screen the military requirements. I should perhaps have mentioned that even before we left Ottawa the American Ministers – Acheson, Foster and Snyder – had all begun to talk of screening down the military requirements rather than following the only other alternative which was to give us a great many more dollars. And by the time the enquiry began I think this was their accepted idea. After breakfast we went off to SHAPE where we met the other members of the Committee. Oddly enough, many of them had not been at the last meeting in Ottawa where we had settled the terms of reference. That was mostly Foreign Ministers whereas at SHAPE they were mostly Defence Ministers. We then had a talk from General Gruenther*, Eisenhower's Chief of Staff, a rather attractive, highly intelligent youngish man. He gave us a picture of just what forces they believed the Russians had got and what they thought we needed to put against them, and showed us the gaps between what was needed and what was actually available and what had been promised. Some of us began to ask questions but we did not get far before Eisenhower arrived. He gave us a sort of pep talk which seemed to me superfluous, but so typically American. Then we all had a buffet lunch and talked in groups, and finally went out to be photographed. This, the Americans explained, was the best way of dealing with the press because then it was not necessary to give any information.

118 On this speech see *HG*, p. 278.

Afterwards, I went with Harriman to settle some trouble with the Italians who were still pressing to be put on the Committee. They wanted me there because I was, apart from Pella [Italian Finance Minister], the only other person who had been in the original discussions at Ottawa. We managed to settle this without much difficulty, [by] assuring the Italians that the main Committee was going to meet very frequently.

As for the rest of the Election, the meetings varied from extremely rowdy at Lewisham [on Persia] to very stolid and slight [? polite] in Yorkshire. The difference between Yorkshire and the rest of the country is quite extraordinary. It is almost a convention that when one goes to speak in support of another candidate to say something nice about the candidate, and this normally evokes enthusiastic cheers from the audience. In fact it is a good way of getting meetings warmed up. It never failed to work everywhere until I got to Leeds where my first meeting was in West Leeds for Charlie Pannell*. He is a good Member of Parliament and popular in his constituency. But my extremely nice remarks about him were apparently ignored by the audience who did not make a sound. They listened very carefully to everything I said about Persia, which was the first part of my speech, and then when I stepped back for a moment, they burst into applause.

I then resumed my speech about the cost of living and they applauded at the end. On leaving the meeting I was talking to Billy Goodwill [his own constituency chairman] about the rock-like immobility of the audience and he said, 'Yes, you were very clever to step back at that point. They thought you had finished the speech – that's why they clapped!'

On the last Sunday I had a strenuous time, doing four meetings and at a time when my voice was very badly strained. I must mention two of these. At the second, at a place called Todmorden the meeting was at 6.15 p.m. in a cinema. It was completely packed and I was speaking first. I said the usual things about Douglas Houghton*, the candidate, but could not get any response from the audience. They only showed any signs of their presence once when they laughed at a rather unconscious joke I made, but to my astonishment when I had finished speaking they gave me a most tremendous cheer. It was very odd but, of course, also encouraging because one felt they really had listened to the speech.

The last meeting at Leeds Town Hall was a fiasco as far as I was concerned. I was to speak last and the idea had been that there would be some speakers between Shinwell, who was the other main speaker, and myself. However, when I arrived he was still speaking. He was doing a real Music Hall performance. Dora told me she almost vomited, but the audience simply loved it – or most of them. Somebody made a very short speech after him and then I got up to finish up the meeting. My voice, as I have said, was already very strained, and I found it completely impossible to get myself across to the audience. They were so drunk by the emotional nonsense that Shinwell had talked that it was impossible to make them think at all. Rather fortunately for me in a way the mike gave out, and this made it obviously essential that I should wind up the speech quickly. But it was a depressing affair and taught me one lesson that if I were speaking at a meeting with a Shinwell type of speaker I must speak before and not after him.[119]

As to the result, we did rather better than I had expected. Right at the beginning of the election I had told Dora privately that I expected they would get in with a majority of about 75. I became less pessimistic as the campaign went on, but I still expected that they would have a majority of not much under 50.[120]

Document No. 8

STRICTLY PRIVATE & CONFIDENTIAL:
FOR THE PARLIAMENTARY COMMITTEE
PARLIAMENTARY LABOUR PARTY

DOLLAR AID AND DEFENCE

Memorandum by Hugh Gaitskell.

1.   I attach as an appendix some notes on the history of this matter during the past eighteen months, which I hope the Committee will find useful. It is clear that to refuse Aid and cut our defence programme would be quite contrary to the general line followed by the late Government.

2.   The views of Messrs, Foot, Crossman and their friends may be summarised as follows:

> 'We have a dollar crisis which is caused by rearmament. It is now suggested that we should be granted and accept dollar aid so as to enable us to go on with rearmament. This would be wrong because if we accept dollar aid we shall be dependent on the U.S.A. We must therefore refuse the dollars and solve our economic problems by cutting our defence programme'

119 Not until 1956 – after nearly 20 years in Leeds politics – did he make a successful speech in that hall. Below, p. 447.
120 Their vote was 231,000 below Labour's but they had an overall majority of 17 seats.

3.   I shall deal first with the economic implications of this argument. It is not true that the dollar deficit is mainly the result of our own rearmament. It is due to (1) Heavier purchases by the whole sterling area of dollar goods, only partly associated with rearmament, (2) higher prices for such goods, (3) Lower prices for the main Sterling Area materials – wool, rubber, tin – than were being received in the early months of this year, (4) the loss of Persian Oil, (5) Capital Movements.

4.   Although of course a cut in the defence programme would obviously help the civilian economy, it is certainly *not* the case that anything like the whole of such a saving could be converted into dollar exports. Some benefit would accrue to home investment and some to other exports. The dollar gap is now put at about 1½ billion dollars for next year. If the defence production programme were cut by say £200 million a year, which would be pretty crippling in its consequences, I doubt if we could thereby close more than about one quarter of the dollar gap.

5.   We cannot even assume this. For it is not only dollars we need from the U.S.A. We need steel: we may want coal. We want sulphur, various metals which are very scarce and cotton which may become so. We also want them to buy sterling area materials steadily and at reasonable prices. If unilaterally we throw their dollars back at them and just cut defence, there is a real danger that they in turn would cut our supplies of these materials they control. The consequence for output here would be serious.

6.   If the economic gains are inadequate and uncertain, the military and political consequences might be disastrous. Much depends here, however, on the way the proposal is handled. It is one thing to reach agreement in N.A.T.O. on adjustments in the programme: it is another thing to declare openly and without agreement that we will take no dollars and will cut our defence programme.

7.   If we were to follow the latter course we should endanger the Atlantic Alliance. We have promised to provide a certain number of divisions for the defence of Western Europe. Even the £4700 million programme is not enough to equip these as well as the forces we need for other areas. The gap here is very large – some £2,000 million – and at present our only hope of overcoming it is equipment from America in the form of Military Aid. We certainly shall not get this aid if we just back out of our European commitments. Moreover, the repercussions in Europe would be very bad. It is quite possible that General

Eisenhower would quit. For economic easement which would certainly not amount to independence, we should have gravely weakened our military position, seriously damaged Anglo-American relations, and of course left ourselves fundamentally far more dependent on America. Because of our weakness we should be in a very bad position to influence their policy!

8.   If on the other hand the proposal is only that within N.A.T.O. and without any public statements we should present our case for adjustment in our programme as well as or even instead of compensating dollar payments, there is not the same objection. But this really implies no more than that we should seek additional Military Aid rather than Economic Aid, that we should ask not merely for equipment for the divisions whose requirements cannot be met under the £4,700 programme, but also additional equipment to allow us to cut our own programme. It is difficult, however, to see why in this case we should feel any less dependent on America. In some respects we should be much more dependent. The advantage of this course is not that it lessens our dependence on America, but that it enables us to maintain a higher level of exports during the period of rearmament and therefore gives us a better commercial prospect afterwards. The difficulties are chiefly the limits of supply from the U.S.A. in the near future, their other commitments and to some extent technical problems. But the policy of preferring military to economic aid is one which commended itself to the late Government; and there is no reason why we should not follow it, though we should recognise that it is certain that the relief to our own defence programme which might follow will be quite inadequate to close the dollar gap. And if Military Aid is permissible, it is really difficult to see why economic aid which takes its place should be barred.

9.   If the adjustment within N.A.T.O. which is desired is, however, for us to have neither military nor economic aid, it is really impossible to reconcile this with the whole conception of the alliance. We have always seen this alliance as a partnership in which we build up common defence. To stand on our dignity and refuse American tanks and guns and aircraft seems quite absurd. And if we did, and if the alliance did not in consequence wither away, the only effect would be to strengthen the military power of America within N.A.T.O. and to weaken our own. Why on earth by making ourselves more like the Belgians we should be gaining in influence it is difficult to understand!

10.   There is one other argument to which I should refer. It is said that

our dependence on America will be permanent if we have dollar aid because rearmament is permanent. This idea is partly wrong and partly confused. It may be that for some years we shall have to maintain our defences at the higher level to which they are being built up. But the resources we shall need for maintaining our defences will not be so great as during the building up period. Moreover, as the National income rises the burden in any case becomes proportionately less. There is therefore no reason to assume we shall on this account continue to need dollar or military aid – (though whether we shall have solved the long term sterling-dollar problem is another matter). Consequently the distinction drawn between Marshall Aid (which is said to be respectable) and Defence Aid (which is not) is really quite untenable.

11.   To conclude

(1) The economic argument that we can solve our dollar problem solely by moderate cuts in the U.K. defence programme is quite unsound.

(2) There is no reason at all why we should not accept an adjustment of our burden within N.A.T.O. either in the form of more Military Aid – with some reduction in our own programme or in compensating Economic Aid. There are advantages about the former from a long term angle, but from the angle of our dollar position the latter is rather to be preferred. To accept the one and refuse the other seems absurd. We shall probably need and receive both.

(3) To refuse both – and to cut our defence programme – by unilateral decision would endanger N.A.T.O. weaken us militarily and diplomatically without any corresponding benefit on the economic side. It would face us with the alternative of 'neutrality', with all its terrible dangers, or an even greater dependence on America.

(4) We should therefore make it plain that we see no objection to Military or Economic Aid, granted to us within N.A.T.O. provided of course no unreasonable conditions are imposed.

H.G.

APPENDIX

NOTES ON U.S. AID AND THE RE-ARMAMENT PROGRAMME

1. Up to the Korean war the question of any American aid in connection with British re-armament had not arisen. We were, of course, at that time

– May, 1950 – still receiving Marshall Aid and this continued until the end of the year.

2. At the end of July, 1950, the American Government approached us and the other N.A.T.O. countries and asked what we were prepared to do in the way of re-armament. This approach was accompanied by vague promises of substantial aid.[121] We were asked for a very quick reply.

3. Within ten days we had announced the 3,600 million pounds programme, which was really a rough estimate of what could be done without building new production capacity or damaging our balance of payments seriously. We asked the Americans for £550 million as a contribution towards the £3,600 programme, but the former figure was never published.

4. We never got £550 million or anything like it. First of all Congress decided that by far the greater part of the Foreign Aid allocation would be military aid, and not economic aid. Secondly, the U.S. Administration did not think we would need it. They thought we ought to be able to carry a larger programme. At that time our balance of payments position was favourable, both U.K. and dollar,[122] while the Americans took a much gloomier view of the international position than we did.

5. Nevertheless, negotiation took place in August and September in Washington about the question of aid. The final decision was

(a) that we should receive an interim allocation of aid in respect of the first section of our expenditure under the [£m.] 3,600 programme to cover the dollar content involved in 200 million pounds' worth of orders which had already been placed. We have since received this (or are in the process of receiving it). It was of the order of 100 million dollars, mostly to pay for machine tools.

(b) the major problem of aid in connection with rearmament was to be decided through what has become known as the 'burden sharing operation'. This meant that instead of aid being granted on a bilateral basis, a N.A.T.O. enquiry should take place to decide what adjustments would have to be made so that the burden among members could be fairly divided. It was originally contemplated that these adjustments might take

121 An earlier and slightly longer draft of this memorandum in the same file (U.156) of HG's papers adds at this point: 'For example, I remember that the general impression we were given was that the Americans would take care of us if the balance of payments went wrong.' Cf. *HG*, pp. 231–2.

122 This somewhat obscure phrase, repeated intact from the original draft, may refer to the total foreign balance of the U.K. and the dollar balance of the whole sterling area, respectively.

the form either of a country doing less or more (i.e. a change in the programmes); or of a country either paying or receiving money as a balancing item. But while the Americans have accepted this principle, they have always been rather two-faced about it. When talking to Congress they speak in terms of bilateral economic aid; whereas with us they have accepted the idea of partnership implicit in the 'burden sharing exercise'.

6. In the autumn of 1950 the Chinese joined in the Korean war and the Americans decided to press for a greater measure of rearmament among the European powers. This was closely associated with the question of appointing General Eisenhower as Supreme Commander in Western Europe. In December of 1950 the then Foreign Secretary, Ernest Bevin, said in Brussels that we were reviewing our rearmament programme to see whether we could speed things up,[123] and at the end of January, 1951, the £4,700 million programme was announced by Mr. Attlee. He made it plain that our success in achieving it was dependent on getting adequate supplies of materials, machine tools, etc. But nothing was said about dollar aid at that time. There were two reasons for this. First, the whole question had – as already explained – been pushed into the N.A.T.O. 'burden sharing exercise'. Secondly, our dollar position was extremely strong at that time. Nevertheless, when the Americans told us about this time that they were proposing in their submission to Congress not to propose any aid for us at all, we protested very strongly. We had certainly assumed that we should get sufficient to cover at least the dollar content of the Defence Programme. We received an assurance from them that what they put to Congress was illustrative only, and had to be content with that.

7. The burden sharing exercise took a very long time to get going, (partly because the Americans thought the aggregate of the various countries programmes was still quite inadequate), and an interim report only was produced for the Ottawa Conference. Meanwhile, two things happened. The U.S. Congress made a substantial cut in the economic part of the 1951/52 aid programme; and the dollar position of Britain and France turned sharply for the worse.

When I went to Washington in September I at once explained the

123 The original draft has an extra two sentences inserted here. 'I may say that even before this the Minister of Defence [Shinwell] had given his approval to what is known as the "Interim Term Defence Plan" as an ultimate objective, though not an immediately practical project, and this was a plan which involved far more than the aggregate of the defence plans of the individual countries. For us, for example, it would have meant something like six thousand million pounds.' Cf. HG, pp. 245–6 and nn. 60–1.

whole dollar situation to the various American Ministries and made it plain to them privately that unless they helped us, it was doubtful whether in fact we should be able to carry out our rearmament programme as planned. I did not put in any specific request for economic aid because this, we thought, must depend on the N.A.T.O. enquiry. But I asked them to consider from the widest angle how they could help us and I made a number of suggestions. But at the same time the Americans, as a result of continued pressure from General Eisenhower, were still hoping for an increase in the defence effort in Europe.

8. Out of this clash two developments emerged. First, the appointment of the N.A.T.O. 'Wise Men' Committee to try and harmonise military requirements with economic realities. Secondly, discussions continued on a bilateral basis with the Americans regarding the help they might give us. We submitted a draft of proposals to them, e.g. the provision of more steel; steadier purchases of sterling raw materials; off shore purchases of our military equipment which would then be handed back to us etc. Fortunately, General Eisenhower later managed to persuade Congress to replace part of the cut on [sic: ? 'in'] economic aid which they had demanded. Of the total of 6,000 million dollars, 1,000 million is economic aid and 5,000 million military aid, but 500 million can be transferred from military to economic aid.

9. The latest development is that the U.S. authorities have invited the principal countries of N.A.T.O. – in anticipation of the outcome of the burden sharing exercise – to consider proposals for an interim distribution of the provision made by Congress for 1951/52, in order to meet the most urgent needs. The U.K. Government have asked for some share of this interim allocation. It is possible that an announcement will be made about this before Parliament goes into Recess.

10. There will remain for consideration:-

   (a) The question of what final allocation of economic aid is likely to be made out of 1951/52.

   (b) What proposals the U.S. Administration are likely to put forward to Congress for 1952/53.

Both of these will probably be closely linked with the report of the N.A.T.O. 'Wise Men Committee', which was the result of our conversations at Washington and Ottawa. It was the hope of Mr. Harriman, the Chairman of the Committee, that either the military requirements could be scaled down or the proper case could be made to Congress for an adequate amount of economic aid.

23.11.51.

whole while attention to the various American Ministers and made it
plain to them privately that unless this behaviour is modified whether
in fact we should be able to carry out our rearmament programme as
planned. My thoughts on many specific points of the exchange are to some
these, as I thought, must depend on the N.A.T.O. inquiry. But I asked
their rearmament from the French State now they should put us in a much
number of suggestions that at the same price the Americans, as are all
of concerned my part from American ... concerned we will impose by so
impose to the defence effort in Europe.

2. Out of this value to development to congest. First the experiment
of the N.A.T.O. Wise Men Committee to the end harmonise may ...
requirements with economic realities. Secondly, these must continued
on a bilateral basis with the Americans to provide the help they might give
us. We anticipate a rate of progress in home ... in it pressure of may be
more of other problems of settling in a materials, of more that ones, to
our military equipment which would then be handed back to us in performance. ... ince the Chancellor rather intimated in personal Congress to
reduce part of the ... cut on the ... ? in ... economic and what. ... they had
demanded. Of ... tax total of £ 4,500 million dollars, 1,500 million economic
aid and $ 2 billion military and but total million can be transferred from
military measures are the

3. The level development is that the U.S. authorities have called the
... ... of the ... to ... in not attention of the execution of the
burden sharing exercise ... to develop or proposes ... for an interim distribution of the proposed more by Congress for 1954-5. In order to meet the
... at night need ... The U.K. Government in ... may be ... but some ... for
this interim allocation, it is possible that announcement may not be made
about this before Parliament goes into Recess.

4. There will remain for consideration:

(a) The question of what final allocation of contracts are likely to
be made out of 1954-5.

(b) What proposals the U.S. Government are likely to put forward
to Congress for 1955-6.

Both of these will naturally be closely linked with the report of the
N.A.T.O. Wise Men Committee, which was the result of our own
relationship Washington and Ottawa. It was the hope of Mr. Harriman,
the Chairman of the Committee, that either the burden requirements
could be settled or that either case would be unable to Congress in an
adequate amount to economic bit.

A.J.E.M.

CHAPTER 6

OPPOSITION FRONT BENCH

Editor's Note
Diary, 23 November 1951 to 14 December 1954
Editor's Note on 1952
Documents: No. 9 HG's memorandum on Anti-Americanism
in Britain, June 1952
No. 10 HG and Kingsley Martin on the *New Statesman*,
(sample of the Bevanite press), November 1952
No. 11 HG to William Connor ('Cassandra') on party discipline,
26 November 1954

[In origins and organisation the Labour Party is unlike the Conservative in being the political wing of an industrial movement. It was built up from below in protest against a Parliament unresponsive to working-class concerns, as an alliance of the trade unions with the Socialist societies and, after 1918, with the Constituency Labour Parties (C.L.P.s). The unions dominated the annual conference with five-sixths of the votes, which each union cast as a block, and the National Executive Committee (N.E.C.), where two-thirds of the members were chosen solely or mainly by trade union votes. Although ever since 1922 Labour front benchers have formed the actual or the alternative government of the country, the Parliamentary Labour Party could choose only one member of the N.E.C., the party leader, until a second, his deputy, was added in 1953. The N.E.C., representing Conference which settled party policy, and the P.L.P. leadership, representing Labour voters and views in the House and the country, each had a claim to legitimate authority. Conflict between them might embarrass the Party in its battle for public support, and the only real safeguard was a common outlook among members of both bodies. However, up to the 1970s, harmony was usually maintained because the front benchers and the trade union majority agreed.

Structure and traditions allowed rival tendencies to control different segments of the Labour coalition. Critics were strong in the C.L.P.s where many besides the perpetual malcontents instinctively felt that the leaders needed an occasional prod. The front benchers had to accommodate their policies to a political and economic situation which they could not control, and to the need to win over uncommitted voters if they were ever to implement those policies. But the Labour Party was always receptive not only to opponents of specific proposals, but also to rebels against the whole outlook of a leadership which they always accused of lacking determination or vigour or Socialist principles.

Frequently in his first year out of office, Gaitskell warned against demagogy, and of Labour's continuing need to establish its credentials as a serious instrument of government. But many M.P.s wanted more aggressive opposition, and hoped to disengage from some governmental policies which were unpopular among party workers in the constituencies. Bevanism thus revived a tradition which had seemed to be disappearing. To Gaitskell and his associates, it threatened not only their policies and their own positions of leadership, but also Labour's prospects of power. At the 1952 Party Conference at Morecambe, the Bevanites triumphed in the N.E.C. elections, winning all but one of the constituency party seats.

Gaitskell attacked them at Stalybridge the following weekend in a speech which sharpened the Left's hatred for him but led Attlee to intervene at last and quell the feuding for a time. Two years later Gaitskell was elected party treasurer, an office hitherto treated as a sinecure but which he used effectively, in cooperation with the leaders of the moderate Left as well as with those of the big trade unions, to improve the Party's finances and organisation.

As the only office to which election was by Conference as a whole, the treasurership had symbolic value, and Bevan contested it unsuccessfully in both 1954 and 1955. He attributed his defeats to a conspiracy of bureaucratic leaders frustrating the rank and file, and hoped by polarising the Movement to undermine their power within three years. It was an error of judgment in both the short and the long term. On the first occasion his actions weakened his own following in the C.L.P.s instead of Gaitskell's in the industrial wing; then his second attempt forfeited instead of attracting support in the unions.

The clash was not confined to the unions or to Conference. Bevan's first heavy defeat coincided with the parliamentary vote on German rearmament, on which he enjoyed much support and the leadership won by only a tiny margin. To avoid reopening the bitter divisions, the Shadow Cabinet agreed that Labour should abstain on it in the House of Commons, and incurred unpopularity by withdrawing the whip from a few individualists who defied this advice; there were much bigger revolts against the whips in March 1952 and March 1955.

Parliamentary discipline was much stricter in those days than in current practice. Both major British parties, while allowing individual M.P.s to speak as they pleased, required them to vote with their party. Every Labour candidate signed the P.L.P.'s standing orders, which forbade voting against majority decisions of the P.L.P. and allowed abstention only on grounds of conscience; revolts and organised abstentions were very rare. Nor was the Labour Party unusual in this: Socialist parties everywhere had always insisted that their parliamentary representatives must accept majority decisions and act as a single block. Gaitskell, though many of his colleagues felt far more strongly than he, was a believer in this recognised doctrine, hitherto accepted by minorities as well as majorities. It broke down in Britain not long after his death.]

Friday, 23 November 1951

Leaving the Treasury

I discovered even before I left Leeds that R.A. Butler* was going to be Chancellor and that this appointment was going to go through on the Saturday; the seals being returned informally to the Palace on that day. When I got back to London I spoke to WA[Armstrong] on the phone and arranged to go in and say goodbye on the Monday to my old officials. RAB was anxious that I should have as much time as I liked to do this and was not going to move in formally until the Tuesday.

I found a letter waiting for me from Edward Bridges which contained, to my surprise, a very warm message from Churchill. This may of course be interpreted as a kind of first move towards a Coalition; or, on the other hand, it may be simply Winston's impulsiveness. He is certainly a person who can move from violent and almost offensive criticism to apparently spontaneous and warm-hearted tributes in a very short time.

The leave-taking itself was quite short and unsentimental. EB[Bridges] thanked me for being a 'very good Treasury Minister', and there was, as one might expect, a very friendly atmosphere at the main gathering, though rather a sad one in the Private Office itself. Civil Servants in this country, thank goodness, have to be hardened to changing Governments and changing Ministers. It is rather remarkable what close and intimate relations one manages to develop despite this.

Clem Leslie looked in to see me during the weekend, partly I suppose to say goodbye and partly to represent to me the desirability of not taking too strong a Party line. He said that he thought there was no doubt that the new Government would be very anxious for a reasonably friendly Opposition and they were not going to attack me at all or try and pretend that I had misled the country. This was confirmed when I had about ten minutes' conversation with RAB. In Winston [Churchill]'s message he had asked that I should give my successor the benefit of my experience and advice. But I thought it better to confine the latter to organisation points. I therefore said to RAB that I hoped he would see to it that the Chancellor remained the effective co-ordinating Minister, and that the Central Planning machine was kept up. He obviously realised the importance of these things and it was clear that Bridges had also been impressing them on the P.M. But RAB hinted that there might have to be some senior and much older man in the background in charge of economic affairs. 'The P.M. does not want to have anything to do himself with economic matter[s]. But he wants someone of Prime Ministerial status there who would be as it were in the background.' This was broadly what

RAB said. I protested against it and urged that he should not, as Chancellor, accept it. I gather that there was at that time the plan to bring in John Anderson to fill such a position.[1]

RAB's appointment caused surprise in many quarters. Lyttelton had been leading for the Tories on finance ever since Oliver Stanley died, and most people expected him to be Chancellor.[2] I have heard three possible explanations as to why Butler got the job. Here they are in order of plausibility.

1) That RAB insisted on being Chancellor and made it plain this was the only job he would take; that he was backed up in this by Eden and that the P.M. had to give in.

2) That the City objected to Lyttelton because of his past in the City where he was something of a racketeer. Some slight confirmation of this is to be drawn from the fact that at the City functions when I was Chancellor it was Butler rather than Lyttelton who was usually present.

3) That Winston knew the job was going to be an intolerable one; dislikes Butler very much and therefore decided to put him in it.

Of course the structure of the Government and the individual appointments gave rise to a lot of comment. Winston, of course, did exactly what one would expect and appointed his old friends and his family to many of the key jobs. In fact, one could say that the Government is broadly divided between them and the straightforward Tory Party candidates. The most peculiar appointments of all are the co-ordinating 'overlords' on which I spoke in the House.[3]

In my opinion one of two things is likely to happen. If Winston and the old pals try and interfere too much with the younger Departmental Ministers there will be a revolt, which will no doubt lead in due course to Winston's retirement. In fact, if this happens I would not expect him to last much more than a year. Alternatively, he may decide not to try and intervene much either on foreign policy or on the economic side. I think

1 Anderson (1882–1958) was a great civil servant between the wars, Churchill's wartime Chancellor of the Exchequer, and Shadow Chancellor after 1945. He became Viscount Waverley in 1952.

2 Oliver Lyttelton (1893–1972; War Cabinet 1941–5) became Colonial Secretary instead, and was created Lord Chandos when he resigned in 1954. He was chairman of Associated Electrical Industries 1945–51, 1954–63; President of the Institute of Directors 1954–63. Oliver Stanley had been a Conservative Minister from 1934–45; he died in 1950.

3 These were the Prime Minister's wartime friends Lords Woolton (Lord President of the Council), Leathers (Secretary for the Coordination of Transport, Fuel and Power) and Cherwell (Paymaster General). The experiment failed (see HG, p. 313) and they lasted less than two years. He spoke in the House on 21 November (494 H.C. Deb. 431–46) and again on the 28th.

this is the more probable. Eden is certainly very well established at the Foreign Office and need not tolerate any interference from the Old Man. He has a much stronger position in the country and an almost equally strong one in the Party. He is, of course, far stronger in the House of Commons. As for Butler, he has made a good start, and Winston in any case has never understood economic affairs.

As to their policy, so far of course apart from the Bank rate, etc. they have really done exactly what we would have done, and have followed the same lines on controls, economic planning, etc. It is possible that they will change later and go in for relying much more on monetary and budgetary influence. This will mean cutting something, at least food subsidies and perhaps more. But on the whole I think it unlikely. Butler is on the extreme left of the Tory Party and is shrewd enough to understand that what they have got to do while in office is to live down the reputation inherited from their periods of office in the thirties. What the intelligent Tories will, of course, want to do is to be able to say to the electorate when the election comes, 'No war: no unemployment: no cuts in social services. Just good Government.' If I am right about this they will want to stay in power for three or four years, and I do not really see why they should not.

I need not refer to the debate on the Address which is available. On the whole I think that they have behaved reasonably well in not trying to make out that we had hidden the facts from the nation. But for this I can only once more thank my Mansion House speech.[4]

In the first week after the election there was a lunch and dinner party at Dick Stokes', and also on one evening a meeting of the late Cabinet at the same place. The latter was for the purpose of discussing how the Parliamentary Party was to be organised. It did not lead to anything very important. At the other two parties those present were broadly, Hartley Shawcross, Hector McNeil, Patrick Gordon Walker, Herbert Morrison and myself. We discussed who should run for the Parliamentary (or Executive) Committee of the Parliamentary Party which was to be elected. We thought we might cut each other's throats. Eventually, Dick and Hartley said they would not stand (though later Dick not only stood but got on). There was also some general discussion about Bevan, but no very clear line laid down, except of course it was a meeting of those who were most opposed to him.[5]

I also saw and had a long talk with Hugh Dalton who has played a somewhat equivocal part with the Bevanites. Broadly, however, his point

4 The Chancellor's traditional annual address, in which on 3 October 1951 he had given a full account of the state of the economy: *HG*, p. 278.
5 A similar group of ex-Ministers continued to meet in 1952 to discuss organising opposition to Bevan and timing the succession to Attlee: *HG*, pp. 299–301 and n. 36; cf. below, p. 346.

of view is that he does not want Bevan ever to be leader but thinks that if a reconciliation is possible we should have it. He was in favour of AB going onto the Parliamentary Committee. He told me that he is informed exactly as to what goes on among the Bevanites. One of them evidently goes and tells him.

As it turned out the Bevanites decided not to run for the Parliamentary Committee at all; partly because they feared they might be heavily defeated and that even Bevan himself might not get on (I myself think he would have got on, but none of the others) and partly because it leaves them free to say what they want in opposition. From what I hear from other quarters – through Crossman to Crawley and then to me – AB himself is, as I have always thought, not going to be satisfied with anything but leadership and will go on playing for that. Whether he will keep all the others with him in doing that is another matter. I imagine however that their tactics will be to appear as vigorous as possible in opposition and attract support to themselves in this way as well as on any policy issues where they think they can get a considerable following.

The election to the Parliamentary Committee produced the following result.

253 voted	Jim Griffiths	195
	Will Hall	177
	HG	175
	Alf Robens	133
	Chuter Ede	131
	Dick Stokes	117
	James Callaghan	111
	Edith Summerskill	111
	Phil Noel-Baker	111
	Dalton	111
	Shinwell	107
	Tony Greenwood*	99

This seems to me pretty satisfactory and most people seem to be happy about it. Whether the Committee will work will remain to be seen. So far I do not think it is getting enough leadership from Attlee and Morrison (who of course as Leader and Deputy Leader are ex-officio members). Hector and Patrick did badly, getting 50 and 48 respectively.

The general impression in the Party is, I think, that Herbert's stock has fallen tremendously since he took on the job of Foreign Secretary. Whether he can recover his position is not clear. Personally, I think he can. Few things change so rapidly as politicians' reputations in either direction, but to do this he ought to give up foreign affairs. Attlee seems tremendously cheerful and lively, but I do not get the impression that he is going to show any special initiative. It is really a period of transition with Attlee and Morrison in a class by themselves in stature and age groups; the other people in that age group having fallen behind leaving the younger ones moving ahead. At the moment Jim Griffiths is the obvious successor for Attlee and Morrison. His experience and friendliness and charm will probably keep him there but whether he is a strong enough character for the job, especially in view of the threat from Bevan, remains to be seen. Anyway, this is all hopelessly premature.

I am pretty well satisfied with the Party members on the economic side where we have a very strong team, and can, I think, easily cope with any sort of Bevanite attack. But one cannot say the same either about defence or foreign affairs, and it is important that some new and vigorous leadership should be shown in these spheres.

I went to see Stafford [Cripps] the other day. He is now at his house in Gloucestershire. I found him in bed because he had suffered what Isobel [his wife] called a slight set-back in his recovery. They thought that this was the result of just doing too much. Certainly he looked to me much better than the photographs taken when he arrived here from Switzerland six weeks ago. He was fatter, or not so devastatingly thin, and had put on weight. We talked for quite a time, mostly about politics and the economic situation, and he seemed interested and quite lively, though by the end I think he was tired. He has certainly had a most appalling experience. He has suffered from three grave illnesses at the same time: T.B. [tubercular] abscess in the spine; tumours in the stomach and a wasting bone disease. All these are said to have cleared up but left him appallingly weak. The Doctors in Lausanne, Isobel told me, gave him up for lost. But at Zürich they never gave up and somehow or other pulled him through. One gets no clear idea of how this happened, and I rather imagine that they both look on it as a kind of miracle. I asked him if he had made any plans and he said that it was quite impossible. They are to go back to Switzerland in January for a check up at Zürich and then stay out there, or in Italy, until the warm weather comes here when they will return. He reads quite a lot but not very serious stuff. We talked about AB. I told him that I had heard that he was very bitter and I said that I thought that both he and HW[Wilson] had been jealous when I became Chancellor. Stafford said, 'There is no reason why Nye should have been jealous. I made the position clear to him.' I did not tell Stafford what several people have told me, that Nye, however, has frequently asserted that Stafford promised that he would be Chancellor. I thought this might upset him as he had always had a deep sort of affection for Nye and treated him as a charming but tiresome child. I thought it was a little significant that Isobel said that she thought Nye had lost us a great many votes.

As to HW, Stafford said, 'Why on earth did he do this? . . .' Everybody asks me whether Stafford is ever coming back into politics. My guess at present is that he will not. If he is capable of taking up any activity at all, my hunch is that it will be more specialised and more in the religious or educational field.

We were talking about Winston [Churchill], and Stafford said, 'He often sends me flowers and books and has also written quite a lot'. It is interesting how people's reputations change. Few people in the country are more respected than Stafford. I suppose it is partly reaction against all the things which were said against him earlier on. But I noticed at the election that one got far more applause at a reference to Cripps than at a reference to Bevin. Perhaps this is not altogether fair.

Diary, 21 March 1952

The Struggle in the Parliamentary Party

Up to Christmas the Bevanites had been on the whole very quiescent. Bevan himself had hardly made any speeches either in the House or at the Party meetings. There was an attempt to raise the question of defence and dollar aid, the implication being that we should have neither rather than both but the two Party meetings we had on this subject went heavily against the Bevanites.

During the Christmas recess *Tribune* launched an attack on me because Churchill admitted that we should not spend the whole of the money provided for defence;[6] but it was not until Parliament resumed that they really began to attack vigorously.

The Chancellor of the Exchequer had made a statement on economic measures to which I was to reply on the following day. We had a Parliamentary Committee meeting, then a meeting of the Finance & Economic Group and almost immediately afterwards a full meeting of the Parliamentary Party to decide our attitude. There was really not much doubt about what this should be – that we should accept the physical cuts but resist strongly the imposition of Health Services charges. Clem called on me to speak almost at once and I went through Butler's speech rather pedantically explaining what I thought we ought to do, but without any rhetoric or vehemence. This was a mistake because the Party after seven weeks' Recess were in an excitable mood and Bevan immediately made

6 He did his utmost to help the Bevanites make trouble for the Labour Front Bench over it: 494 H.C. Deb. 2601–2, vol. 497 col. 444–7, vol. 504 col. 1495–6 (6.12.51, 5.3.52, 30.7.52). See *HG*, pp. 279–83, 296–7.

an effective speech, which though not exactly demanding a different attitude was by implication critical of myself. He also criticised the motion which the Parliamentary Committee were putting forward (it was only very tentative) as being not strong enough. Although there was no vote or anything of that sort the upshot was a definite step back and an advance for him.[7] It need not have happened if we had had a little more time to think out our tactics.

We did better in the debate. At least my own speech was pretty well received, but even so Bevan made a speech himself on the second day which was full of the most absurd statements and some good phrases and was much applauded.

At the next Party meeting there was a discussion on foreign policy, and again they scored some success; so much so that Woodrow Wyatt and one or two others came to me and urged that we should really try and organise some kind of effective opposition. We had a meeting in Woodrow's flat. Chris Mayhew, Tony Crosland, Roy Jenkins*, Arthur Allen, Alf Robens, Woodrow and myself. We decided that we must get people who could speak well to do so at the Party meetings, especially on defence and foreign affairs. We also tentatively thought of compiling a pamphlet which would contain the answer to Bevan's point of view.

The struggle at the Party meetings has continued, with an interval on account of the King's death, ever since; but on the whole the anti-Bevanites have done a lot better, largely owing to the fact that better speeches have been made as a result of urging the right people to make them. Chris, Woodrow, Tony and Roy have all done well, especially the first, and thus set an example to others.

There have, however, been two reverses. First of all, the speeches made by Morrison and Shinwell in the House of Commons have been very bad, and secondly we certainly scored no more than a partial victory in the matter of the defence debate. This is what happened. In the case of foreign affairs we put down a motion criticising Churchill but specifically not criticising Eden; in my view this was justified by Churchill's behaviour in Washington and the fact that he gave a completely false impression of British policy. The censure motion, for it certainly was that, was moved by Morrison however in a very flat and dull speech and Churchill decided to play a particularly dirty trick in defending himself. He disclosed to the House of Commons the understanding we had with the Americans to bomb the Manchurian airfields if Chinese aircraft took off from them to bomb our troops in Korea. There was nothing in the least wrong about this understanding. The more sensible people realised it was the only

7 Confirmed by the diaries of Kenneth Younger, 8.2.52; Richard Crossman, 29.1.52; and Hugh Dalton who wrote: 'Bevanites pushing. Weak opposition. H.G. not sufficiently combative against the Tories' (29.1.52).

possible one, but the fact that it had not been disclosed – quite properly in my view – made it look as though we had been keeping things back from the Party. The disclosure did of course just what Churchill wanted; it spread suspicion and confusion in our ranks. It is an interesting example of his complete unscrupulousness. I do not think Eden would have done the same thing, for there is a strong tradition that you do not disclose secrets which the previous Government have held up.[8]

The defence debate followed a week later and the Bevanites sent a draft amendment to the Parliamentary Party which, in effect, meant voting against the defence estimates. I took a strong line in the Committee urging first that we should in no circumstances accept the Bevan amendment but have it out with them in the Party meeting, and secondly that we ought not to have any amendment down or vote against the defence white paper. I got my way easily enough on the first, but on the second had to agree to an official amendment which approved the White Paper but criticised the Government's incapacity to carry it out. At the Party meeting we scored a complete victory, Crossman's amendment being defeated by about three to one, and as we reckoned that those who were not there would have voted with us this was highly satisfactory.[9]

On the following day however the Bevanites, despite a three-line whip with careful instructions, abstained on the [official] amendment and voted against the White Paper. 57 also [of all sorts?] went into the lobby.[10]

The question then arose as to what should be done about this. On the following day there was great indignation in the Parliamentary Party. Some, Alf Robens and Jim Callaghan (who were surprisingly strong on this) wanted to withdraw the whip at once from the rebels.[11] After a lot of talk however we decided in favour of a condemnatory resolution, the reimposition of Standing Orders and a written undertaking from the rebels that they would observe Party decisions. The only two who opposed this were Tony Greenwood and Chuter Ede. We could not however have a Party meeting until the following week and had another meeting of the Committee on the Monday. It was decided to alter the proposed resolution somewhat, particularly by making everybody sign the undertaking. This had been urged upon me by a number of persons including Woodrow [Wyatt] in the hope of detaching some of the 57 from

8 496 H.C. Deb. 969–77: 26.2.52. For a Conservative view of that debate see *Harold Nicolson Diaries 1945–62* (Fontana ed. 1971), p. 205.

9 Crossman lost by 115 to 41: Dalton diary, 4.3.52. Younger thought his amendment showed the Bevanites were now deliberately seeking a split: his diary, 9.3.52.

10 They were such a mixed bag that they were called 'the 57 Varieties'.

11 So did the Chief Whip and some powerful trade union leaders outside the House: Hunter (1959), pp. 46–50. Hunter was political correspondent of the Party's official paper the *Daily Herald*, and a confidant of Morrison.

their allegiance to Bevan. Meanwhile however George Strauss had been going round with a more innocuous resolution still, and getting a good deal of support for it. People had been very angry during the previous week, had cooled down during the weekend and began, as so often happens, to be frightened at the prospect of Bevan and some others having to go out of the Party altogether. I was naturally quite prepared for this to happen, and indeed there would have been some advantage for it would have left us much freer to attack him. [12] However, as it turned out, that was not the view of the majority.

At the Party meeting Clem [Attlee] made a fairly strong speech to start with but did not attempt to explain our resolution. It soon became clear, particularly after Strauss had spoken, that most people were in favour of his compromise, and the Bevanites themselves indicated that they would accept it. Bevan himself had made a very bad speech, losing his temper and putting everybody against him. [13] He had also got involved in a row with Attlee but John Freeman was much more effective. I was surprised and shocked to find both Tom O'Brien [14] and Hector [McNeil] speaking in favour of the Strauss resolution which was eventually carried by about two to one. The real blame for this must rest with Attlee who made a very weak speech indeed, and did not in the least give the impression that it was important to him to carry the Committee's resolution. Many people said to me afterwards that either he should have made a strong speech, staking his personal reputation on the Committee's formula, or have accepted the Strauss proposal.

In the following week we presented the draft Standing Orders and Clem began by moving that the resolution suspending the old ones be rescinded. The Bevanites challenged this in a long and confused debate, which showed the Party that they were obviously trying to obstruct. Bevan again made a scene and did himself harm and, despite a much cleverer attempt by Mikardo* to rescue the position for them, we scored a heavy vote in favour of the rescinding of suspension and therefore of the reimposition of the old Standing Orders. The significance of this is that it does not matter if they pursue obstructive tactics, the Standing Orders are in force, and it is they who will want to change them rather than the Committee. [15]

12 Dalton reported HG at this time 'very strung up against Bevanites. Wants a show down!': diary, 3.3.52.
13 Dalton called it 'a violent speech, of nauseating egoism, and sweating with hatred': diary, 11.3.52.
14 A leading trade union M.P.: see above, p. 99 and n.
15 All Labour candidates had to promise obedience to the Standing Orders of the P.L.P., which did not allow M.P.s to vote against its majority decisions and permitted abstention only on conscientious grounds; they had, however, been suspended since 1946.

In the middle of all this the Budget supervened. It is hardly necessary for me to describe its features. It was undoubtedly, from the point of view of the struggle in the Party, very helpful for it

    (a) was much milder than expected

    (b) was based on the view that we did not need to cut consumption at all

    (c) was therefore completely unnecessary so far as rearmament was concerned.

Moreover, we could not have had a better thing to fight than the slash in the food subsidies.[16] I therefore had little difficulty with the Party meeting and Harold Wilson, who could not resist some of his usual jibes, was listened to with some impatience from the members.

Another slightly encouraging sign is that [Herbert] Morrison has, I think, now definitely agreed to drop foreign affairs. I had a long talk with him last week in which I urged him to go back to his old job of Party management. I also suggested Phil Noel-Baker, who has done extremely well and is very sound on foreign policy generally, should step into the lead on foreign policy. One difficulty is that Chuter Ede does a good deal of the job of Party Manager, having been of course Leader of the House in the last Parliament, and it may not be so easy to find room for Morrison as well. However, I think if Clem will agree we could gradually produce the required change. I am going to talk to him next week, with Herbert's concurrence. Herbert in fact said that he hoped Attlee would send for him and ask him to do this job. It is of course a very great handicap in the present situation that these two do not get on at all well.

The Funeral[17]

There is no need for me to describe the funeral ceremonies with which the papers were full. By far the most impressive to my mind was the reception of the coffin in Westminster Hall, and the service which we held there. Perhaps this was because it was a private affair with no press present, or publicity paraphernalia.

The Accession Council Meetings could scarcely be described as impressive – about 200, mostly in morning dress, standing around gossiping and then listening to the Proclamation being read by Woolton, and then signing the Proclamation.[18] Naturally we all wanted to do that – it only

16 Butler's Budget cut them by a third (£160 million).
17 King George VI died on 6 February 1952.
18 Sir Frederick Marquis, Lord (later Earl of) Woolton was a businessman who became wartime Minister of Food 1940–3, and of Reconstruction 1943–5. He was a very successful Chairman of the Conservative Party 1946–55; Lord President 1951–2, Chancellor of the Duchy 1952–5.

happens infrequently. The next time when the Queen came to take the oath there was even more of a squash, and being fairly far back I could hardly catch even a glimpse of her.

As for the funeral at Windsor, this consisted of an enormous amount of waiting about. There were several special trains. I went down with Hector McNeil, Mike Pearson, Canadian Foreign Secretary and Claxton, their Minister of Defence. H. and I then spent an hour wandering round the Park and the Castle grounds. Then there was more gossiping with the other guests. Then an hour's wait in St George's Chapel, sitting in our overcoats, very squashed up, and finally the Service itself. Being in the Nave we could not hear very well and about the only moving part at all was the bagpipes playing 'The Flowers of the Forest' as the procession arrived. I went back with Sid Holland, the P.M. of New Zealand and Walter Nash, Leader of the New Zealand Opposition. They drank a lot of whisky on the way but seemed to be quite friendly.[19]

re 1952

[9th November, 1954][20]

I should record now the account which has reached me of the Government's near miss on convertibility over two years ago. It seems that as early as February 1952, and when the crisis was really at its worst, the Bank of England and the O.F. [Overseas Finance] Division of the Treasury persuaded the Chancellor [Butler] that we ought to go ahead with the convertibility of non-resident sterling. The Cabinet swallowed it with, as far as I hear, no definite opposition at this stage. But Eden was at Lisbon at the NATO meeting, and it was decided that he must be consulted first. Whereupon Sir Edwin Plowden and Eric Berthoud flew off to Lisbon. Both of these two were strongly opposed to convertibility,

19 Presumably this means 'friendly towards each other'. Holland (National) was Prime Minister 1949–57, and Nash (Labour) 1957–60; the former led the Opposition 1940–9, and the latter 1950–7, 1960–3. Brooke Claxton was a Canadian Liberal businessman; Minister of Health 1944–6, of Defence 1946–54.
20 The original diary contains two separate entries dated 9.11.54; this one is printed out of chronological order. For the 'Robot' incident over convertibility from Cherwell's side, see the biography by the Earl of Birkenhead: *The Prof in Two Words* (Collins, 1961), pp. 284–94. For HG's attitude, *HG*, pp. 317–18; for Butler's account, Lord Butler, *The Art of the Possible* (Penguin ed. 1973), pp. 160–2. Sir Eric Berthoud, later Ambassador to Denmark and to Poland, was Assistant Under-Secretary at the Foreign Office at the time of Robot; on (Sir) Donald MacDougall, an economic adviser, see below, p. 646.

Edwin on logical grounds, Berthoud because he mistrusted the people who were in favour of it. Berthoud's account of the matter, when we stayed with him recently in Copenhagen, was perhaps natural – that he was the person who had persuaded the Foreign Secretary [Eden] to reject it. Edwin's account shortly afterwards, when we happened to be dining at his flat, was a little different. He agreed that Berthoud had supported him, but made it plain that he had provided all the arguments. I would guess this was the correct version. Be that as it may, the interesting thing is that Edwin was the man who stopped the Government from doing this, not Cherwell, as I previously heard. It was only later, on another occasion, that Cherwell weighed in, on the advice of MacDougall. I said to Edwin, 'I wish you had not advised him that way. If they had been so foolish as to go for convertibility, we might now be back in power, or at least have a much better prospect of getting there.'

'That', said Edwin, 'is exactly what I told the Foreign Secretary.' 'If you want to stay in power', I said, 'do for heaven's sake reject this proposal.' That is all a long time ago now, and despite a much more favourable financial and commercial outlook, Butler is clearly far more opposed to convertibility now than he was then. He has become much wiser and more cautious.

Document No. 9

ANTI-AMERICANISM IN BRITAIN[21]

Although its extent can easily be exaggerated, hostility to America is fairly widespread in Britain to-day and has certainly increased since the outbreak of the Korean war.

Something of the kind was of course to be expected. So long as America was isolationist we had no really close relationship with her and did not have to face the problems inevitably associated with this relationship. The alliance means we have to try and agree on common policies, that we have in so many ways to try and march together. The process breeds disputes. You have plenty of arguments inside your family, whereas you only nod politely to the people at the other end of the street.

Probably the two major direct causes of anti-Americanism in Britain to-day are (1) Resentment at her wealth and power. (2) Fear that she will involve us in war. It would be surprising if we did not find it difficult to

---

21 This memorandum, undated and unsigned but with a few missing words inserted in HG's handwriting, was in HG's Papers, file P.68, preceded and followed by items dated late June and July 1952.

swallow the great change in the position of America and ourselves. Of course this has been going on for sometime, but again so long as she was isolationist it was much less obvious. Moreover, her relative economic and military power has increased very greatly since 1939 and is in part at least due to the war. This makes it even harder to swallow. Many English people feel America should have been in the war earlier and have shared the economic burden fully.

There is a good deal of poor-relation complex about our attitude – including the keeping up of appearances. For in our military and political association with America we generally try and hold a status which might be comparable with a 2 to 1 power ratio but just does not fit the real ratio of – say – 7 to 1. This tends to impose economic strains upon us and – though not by a long way the most important cause of our difficulties – we find it a heavy burden to carry. America has ceased to be isolationist, but, except in the case of Korea and to a smaller extent her own defence programme, she is still not really accepting a responsibility proportionate to her power.

It must be admitted, however, that even if she did take over, for example, a much bigger share of the defence of Western Europe, it would not necessarily improve relations. For her much greater power would be even more apparent. The truth is that we have a dilemma. We do not like to admit our relative weakness, because we should then look much too like a satellite. But if we try and live up to a military standard we cannot afford, that means economic trouble. A poor relation who is driven to live beyond his means by his rich cousins will not feel well disposed to them. Faced with this dilemma people search for an escape. In England there is not much serious neutralism but there is a good deal of wishful thinking – chiefly about the Commonwealth. It is easy to see how powerful anti-American prejudice can be when to this already difficult relationship is added the genuine fear felt by many people that America will land us all in war. Moreover the war if it comes will engulf and destroy Britain and Europe while very probably leaving the territory of America physically untouched.

Why do people fear that America will start a war? Partly because there is a mistrust of her diplomatic skill and experience. This is, in my view, largely unjustified as regards the U.S. State Department, but it is certainly a widely held view. And experience of the U.S. armed forces lends support to it. There appears to have been a disposition in the last war to settle things by sheer weight and power regardless of cost. The same sort of attitude might lead to rash action in to-day's inflammable atmosphere. Then there is the feeling that when her defence programme is completed she will be so immensely powerful that it will be difficult for her to resist the temptation to use her power to 'end it all'. American

Statesmen in the present administration have shown no signs whatever of this, but again the talk of the Generals is a good deal more trigger-happy. Indeed free talk by military leaders – which is almost unheard of in Britain – has certainly been a cause of much trouble in the last two years. MacArthur, of course, was the extreme example, but not the only one.[22]

The U.S. attitude to China is, of course, the chief source of anxiety. And here even the Statesmen do not seem to show the slightest desire or hope of eventually achieving some settlement with Communist China. It is true that the doctrine of carrying the war to China has been repudiated again and again by Truman and Acheson: and it is also true that the American representatives at the Korean truce talks have shown exemplary patience. But undoubtedly a willingness on the part of U.S. to foresee some coming together with Communist China – and the abandonment of Chiang, neutralisation of Formosa, recognition of Mao's government, or something on these lines would do a vast amount to reassure British public opinion.[23]

If anxiety about American foreign policy is a major cause of Anti-Americanism, for a good many people – especially those better informed – anxiety about her economic stability is scarcely less important. It is understood only too well that the world economic situation depends on what is happening in the U.S.A; and despite the long drawn out boom there is a continual under-current of nervousness that another slump will soon take place. Moreover, even now in conditions of prosperity there is a good deal of conflict between American and British economic policy – the unevenness of stockpiling, the continuous maintainance [sic] of tariffs, the refusal to use the resources of the I.M.F. are only a few examples. Most British people, even when they are genuinely friendly to America, look forward vaguely to a time when we shall not be so dependent on them economically, when we can balance our account without aid or loans. Meanwhile, there is an irritating contrast between the talk of partnership which goes on between the governments and the 'charity dole' atmosphere of Congressional debates on Marshall Aid.

At the moment hostility to America is strongest on the left. There are a number of reasons for this. The left is more open to communist propaganda: it is still somewhat sentimental about the Russian regime: it is even more sentimental about the Chinese Communists: the mere fact that America is large and powerful stimulates some opposition among those who instinctively favour the poor and the weak: being in opposition the

22 General Douglas MacArthur had commanded the U.N. forces in Korea until recalled for insubordination by President Truman in April 1951.
23 The Republicans, after being the most vociferous opponents of this course for twenty more years, adopted it in the early 1970s – though the regime of Chiang Kai-shek survived on Taiwan (known in 1952 as Formosa).

left – or some of them – find it tempting to exploit Anti-American feelings in the electorate and turn them either against the more responsible leaders of the Labour Party or against the Conservative Government: America is a capitalist power and most Americans tend to emphasise this: right wing Americans group socialists and liberals with Communists, hopelessly confusing political freedom with economic laisser faire. The fact that the motive for this is largely internal politics does not help good relations with the left in Britain which seizes on the utterances of reactionary U.S. businessmen as though they and they alone represented America.

To some extent the left in Britain may for these reasons always be more anti-American than the right. But it would be a mistake to think that the right is not also affected.[24] At present the very fact that so many Labour Party members are anti-American makes the Conservatives more pro-American. But this is somewhat superficial. The right no less – perhaps more – than the left feels the hurt to national pride when U.S. admirals are put in command of the Atlantic. There is certainly a good deal of anti-Americanism in the Armed Forces where there is both more contact and more rivalry than elsewhere. If Fascism ever develops in Britain – which is still not very likely – it will probably base its appeal to an extent on Anti-Americanism.

In this brief sketch I must finally mention three features of U.S. behaviour which certainly make things worse.

First of all, the American constitution itself creates trouble. English people are used to government by an executive which in turn controls the legislature. The government speaks for the country and no-one else normally has the right to do so. In America the government is not fully in control of the situation. It is engaged in a more or less continuous war with Congress. Thus what Congressional leaders say is as important as what the government says. Unfortunately, they are much less responsible. It is no exaggeration to say that if Anglo-American relations in these last few years had been left to the two governments alone, things would have gone much more smoothly.[25] Very often it has happened that the government have known what was the right course but been unable to pursue it because of their fear of Congress. And over here Congress comes to be regarded as the body that really counts – and as a body it gives us the impression of being pretty full of anti-British prejudices. Secondly – and closely linked with it – is the preponderance [sic] of silly speeches by

24 This prediction, so apparently implausible when written, was amply fulfilled after the Suez crisis four years later.

25 This comment clearly reflected his own experience in Washington in October 1950 and September 1951, as well as the earlier reports of Congressional debates since the 1945 loan agreement.

various individuals in the U.S.A. which invariably receive more publicity over here than the sensible speeches. I have already mentioned speeches by Generals and Congressmen; one must add speeches by Officials and Ministers have also given rise to trouble. Here again the contrast with British custom is striking. We do not expect Generals or Officials to speak at all and we expect Ministers to speak with the same voice – especially on foreign affairs!

Thirdly, the fact that the new U.S. foreign policy seems to be accompanied by a great deal of hysteria over Communism gives rise to misgiving here. This is one of the reasons for the fear that America will make war – which I have mentioned already. But the anti-Communist hysteria takes another form which is especially repugnant to British liberals – the witchhunt – McCarthyism – the tyranny of the majority. It is indeed probable that if the full truth were known over here about the scale of this movement and the way it seems to permeate the Universities, the Civil Service and business, there would be a really serious revulsion against America. On the rational plane it condemns the main argument of the pro-Americans – that America is, after all, a free democratic country, while Russia is a cruel and ruthless dictatorship.

Editor's Note on 1952

[At the Labour Party's 1952 conference at Morecambe, the Bevanites won six of the seven National Executive Committee seats representing the constituency parties, defeating both Morrison and Dalton after over twenty years' service. HG opened the counter-attack with a speech at Stalybridge on 4 October.[26] Though badly phrased, it gave expression to the resentment at the Bevanites' divisive factionalism which was widespread in the Labour ranks. It led Attlee and many others to demand, and Bevan to agree to the disbanding of their parliamentary 'party within the party', and thus to a comparative truce for about 18 months.

Among HG's targets at Stalybridge was the Bevanite press which he accused of pouring out
'a stream of grossly misleading propaganda with poisonous innuendoes and malicious attacks on Attlee, Morrison and the rest of us.'
Kingsley Martin*, editor of the *New Statesman*, (whom he had known for some twenty years) protested and HG replied that
'the only thing I would withdraw, as far as the Statesman is concerned, is "poisonous innuendoes". But the rest of it certainly stands.'[27]

26 Referred to in his Diary for 6.10.54 (below, pp. 331–2) and in *HG*, Ch. 10-iii.
27 Martin to HG, 9.10.52, and reply 16th.

Martin then threatened to sue him for libel, and HG, after consulting Sir
Hartley Shawcross, sent the moderately worded but appropriately wary
response which the latter had drafted.[28] Martin answered that instead of
legal action he would, in default of a withdrawal, publish the correspondence and leave the Labour Movement to judge – and two more
letters within the week pressed HG for an immediate reply.[29] HG's
answer follows, together with their final exchange of notes.[30] Crossman
called it 'a letter which we couldn't publish without irreparable damage to
the *Statesman*, unless it was followed by an equally long reply . . .
Kingsley had done all this, of course, without consulting . . . the file of the
Statesman'.[31]]

Document No. 10

HG and Kingsley Martin on the New Statesman,
(sample of the Bevanite press),
November 1952

7th November, 1952

My dear Kingsley,

You described my letter of October 16th as strange and indefensible
and my letter of 28th October as an 'unworthy document'. May I
comment on your letters? The first – dated October 9th – seemed to me a
genuine enquiry and its tone was informal and reasonably friendly. I
replied in a similar spirit. But your next letter – that of October 21st —
was bad tempered, hectoring and, if I may say so, a trifle hysterical. It
contained a clear threat of legal action in the face of which it would have
been foolish for me to disclose what might have to become part of a future
defence at law.

I decided, however, to write a conciliatory reply, not because I was the
least alarmed by your threat (my legal advisers were reassuring on this),
but because I felt that it would be more in the interests of the Labour
Party to allow the controversy to die away. I am sorry that you should
have replied to this olive branch with another extremely offensive letter.

28 Martin to HG, 21.10.52; HG to Shawcross, 22nd, reply 24th; HG to Martin,
    28th.
29 Martin to HG, 30.10.52; his secretary to HG, 3.11.52; John Freeman to HG,
    4.11.52.
30 HG to Martin, 7.11.52; Martin's reply, 21st; HG's, 28th. (All from file P.45.)
31 His diary, 10.11.52.

But since you have now withdrawn the threat of legal action, I have decided to make a further effort to explain my position to you. Accordingly, thanks to the courtesy of your staff and with the help of my wife, I have now been through the files of the paper for most of the past two years.

This abundantly confirms the justification of my remarks about the Paper. The impression created by what one absorbs at weekly intervals is powerfully reinforced, when one reads through a long series of issues. You might try it yourself. I believe that you would realise that your claim that the references to myself have been 'personally appreciative of your ability, parliamentary skill and your desire to maintain the Welfare State in peculiarly difficult economic circumstances' applied only to the period before, but not since, April, 1951.

It is a pity that I cannot go through with you, issue by issue, the files of those last two years, showing you in each instance what I object to and why. But since time and space is limited I must content myself with a few of many possible extracts.

The significance of these attacks, in relation to my use of the words 'misleading' and 'malicious', cannot be fully appreciated without some explanation of the real facts. I have therefore given these explanations where it was necessary.

I must mention one significant aspect – though I realise it is a little delicate. Most of the attacks of which I complain were made in unsigned articles. I do not therefore know for certain who wrote them. I do know, however, that two Members of Parliament are on your editorial staff – Mr. R.H.S. Crossman and Mr. John Freeman; the latter of course joining only after his resignation from the Government in April, 1951. Both were prominent members of what was known as the 'Bevanite Group', which has been bitterly hostile to myself and attacked me in various ways during the past 18 months.

As Mr. Crossman and Mr. Freeman are political journalists and are not, as far as I know, engaged on the literary side of the paper or in writing short stories, film reviews, humorous pieces or in setting and judging puzzle competitions, it seems reasonable to conclude that some of the articles of which I complain were written and others inspired or influenced by them.

In passing let me say that the writing of unsigned articles by Members of the Parliamentary Labour Party attacking their fellow Members and colleagues in that Party seems to me a habit the ethics of which might be examined by those who practice it.

And now for the extracts. I have chosen seven – four before the 1951 General Election and three since then.

1. *Leading Article, April 14th, 1951*
'The Chancellor in fact is encouraging the Service Ministers to spend more than they reasonably can, and then cutting the Social Services in order to balance his budget.'

Is not this a good illustration of what I said in my letter of October 16th?[32] The indictment is of course wholly unjustified. There is no truth whatever in the allegation that I encouraged the Service Ministers to spend more. As Chancellor in preparing the budget I had to accept the implications of the defence programme on which the whole Cabinet had agreed, including the figures given me for Service Estimates and probably Supplementary Estimates. As for the Social Services, expenditure was increased by some £60 millions.

2. *Article entitled 'The Devil and the Hindmost' July 7th, 1951.*
'In framing this budget Mr. Gaitskell came to the deliberate conclusion that rising prices would have to be used as one way of paying for rearmament. He reckoned that if a financial ceiling were placed on subsidies and Social Service expenditure, and the Trade Unions persuaded to restrain their wage demands, rising prices would automatically "mop up excessive purchasing power".'

The article ends – 'A Labour Chancellor cannot retreat from socialism and expect the T.U. leaders to protect him from the consequences of that retreat.'

Again this illustrates my letter of 16th. October and again it is a complete travesty. The budget involved an increase of £160 millions in taxation, almost all of it on the rich – profits tax, Income tax, Petrol tax, Purchase tax on cars etc.; increased expenditure on Social Services and the holding of the food subsidies at the ceiling imposed by Stafford Cripps. Total real consumption was planned to fall by £50 million only and this through reduced supplies of cars, television sets etc. which competed with defence. The budget did not leave 'excessive purchasing power' to be mopped up in high prices. The rise in prices both before and after the budget was caused by rising costs – higher import prices and higher wages. To have offset these would have cost some £500 million more in subsidies.

All this was known to you when you wrote that article.

3. *August 4th. 1951. An article entitled, 'Dishing Mr. Bevan.'*
This relates to my proposals to limit dividends – of which I had given

---

32 Where he wrote of 'the policy of the paper for a long time now to paint a picture of me as a warmongering type of person who gave armaments absolute priority, did not care about the conditions of the poor and was in every way far too reactionary'.

warning several times – because the rise in the rate of tax on distributed profits did not sufficiently deter companies from increasing dividends.

I would like you to read the whole article. It is so hostile and so unfair that it certainly justifies strong language from the victim.

I quote two passages.

(a) 'Mr. Gaitskell has repeatedly made it plain that he is opposed to subsidies in principle.'

This is just plainly untrue. I have never said anything of the kind. The allegation can only be intended to create prejudice.

(b) 'In a desperate effort to extricate himself in time from the predicament he has himself created, he is prepared to do anything to dish Mr. Bevan.'

(No malice in this?)

4. *August 25th. 1951. Article entitled, 'Two characters in search of a policy.'*

Again, I should like you to read the whole of this. The two characters are myself and Mr. David Eccles* – one of the leading financial experts of the Tory Party. The only purpose of this article seems to be to prove that there is nothing to choose between us except that Mr. Eccles is more logical. The article is quite remote from the reality of the economic problems facing the country at that time.

Since the Election the policy seems to have been to identify me with Mr. Butler on every possible occasion. Almost no reference is made to the many criticisms I have levelled against him. It is hard to believe that this is not a deliberate attempt to 'smear' me in the eyes of Labour people who read your paper.

5. *November 17th. 1951 'In Westminster'*

(Presumably written by an M.P.)

'Mr. Gaitskell's gentle me-tooing response to the Chancellor's economic speech was not very happily received on his own back benches. At least the Party is sure it wants to fight the Tories. But if the new Government merely carries on the policy of the old, what is there to fight?'

The speech which was based on the principle of responsibility in Opposition and not of 'Opposition for Opposition's sake' was in fact very well received except by the Bevanites.

6. *February 9th. 1952. 'Westminster'*

'Mr. Gaitskell may or may not have advised his party to "go easy" on Butler, but in public he stoically led the attack on policies which look both suspiciously like his own children – or his children's children.'

This is a nice little mixture of innuendo and malice.

7. April 19th. 1952

'Mr. Butler with some important concessions to the middle classes is carrying out Mr. Gaitskell's policy of paying for rearmament by permitting the cost of living to rise.'

As a comparison of the two budgets this is so utterly remote from the truth that one is bound to suspect the motives of those who make such absurd statements.

Perhaps, to avoid any misunderstandings, I should emphasise that I am not questioning your right to publish what you like. It is not I who threatened you with libel action. But then you must not be too sensitive when some of us sometimes say what we think of your paper.

By all means publish our correspondence – provided you publish it all – including this letter – though I cannot agree with the rather extravagant implication of the last sentence in your letter of October 30th that the Labour Movement as a whole is included among your readers.

Yours sincerely,

HUGH GAITSKELL

Kingsley Martin Esq.

KM/IS   21st November, 1952.

My dear Hugh,

I received your long letter on my return this week from East Africa.

Your letter has the result of ruling out the proposal to publish the correspondence, simply on the grounds of space. We should have to reply to your letter, and by then the whole thing would come to two or three pages of the N.S. & N., which would bore everybody.

I do not regret the correspondence. It has probably been good for both of us to consider the controversy in perspective. I have looked through the quotations which Dora has dug out for you, and I must say that I am pleased the result has been so little damaging to us. Considering that the controversy has raged a long time, I am glad to find that you have only been able to quote two passages which I regard as unfair to you. Similarly, I hope that you were pleasantly surprised to find nothing to justify the strong language you used, and so little of which you could legitimately complain. If we have gone rather far sometimes, you appear to me to have fallen into a state of mind which regards differences of opinion as contumacious. You are now so big a man that you should realise that you will be criticised in ways that, if you take them entirely personally, will seem unfair. The Chancellor of the Exchequer gets identified with national policy even when his own responsibility for it is only partial.

Yours sincerely,

[Signed] Kingsley Martin

KINGSLEY MARTIN
Editor†

29th November, 1952

My dear Kingsley,

Thank you for your letter of November 21st. I am sorry you feel unable to publish the correspondence. It would have been interesting to see how you replied to my last letter. Moreover, I fancy that the readers of the New Statesman would have taken rather a different view of the facts and arguments disclosed by the correspondence from the one you seem to have formed.

While I totally disagree with the implications of your last paragraph, I hope at least that the correspondence will make you and your colleagues more careful in future, if you don't want people occasionally to answer back.

Yours sincerely,

HUGH GAITSKELL

1952–54

[This entry, covering three years, is in the original order, but subdivided into five sections with added subheads, dealing respectively with
    (a) Spring *1954*
    (b) 1952–4 generally
    (c) October *1952*

† Letter reproduced by permission of the *New Statesman*.

(d) 1952–4 continued

(e) Summer & autumn *1954*.

During the 18 months between his own Stalybridge speech in October 1952 and Bevan's resignation from the Shadow Cabinet in April 1954, HG was mainly concerned with his duties as Opposition spokesman on finance.[33]]

Diary: 6 October, 1954

It is nearly three years since I dictated my diary. This is partly due to idleness, partly to lack of time, and partly to the fact that in Opposition there is much less to record. I have always tried to keep this diary to what might be called 'inside events', that is to say, what does not appear in the newspapers, but might nevertheless conceivably be of interest to future historians, or even the public generally. It is not a personal diary about my own thoughts and feelings to any great extent, but a political diary, and therefore I quite ruthlessly try and restrict it to what people regard as important events.

During these years in Opposition, the main stream of events of importance has been connected with the struggle inside the Labour Party. I can give no behind-the-scenes accounts of Government upsets, but I can give some behind-the-scenes accounts of the Shadow Cabinet and similar bodies. The only one I propose to give in detail is the account of Bevan's resignation, which occurred last spring.

[A. Spring 1954]

It will be recalled that after the Foreign Secretary had made a statement on Far Eastern policy in connection with the forthcoming Geneva Conference [on Indo-China], CRA[Attlee], as Leader of the Opposition, had got up and put two questions, one relating to the dangers of our siding with colonialism, and the other about the need for cooperation with the Asian countries. He put these questions in a mild tone, so that admittedly some could not hear them very clearly on the back benches. Shortly afterwards AB[Bevan] got up, and in a highly excited voice asked a further question, implying much greater criticism of the Government, and much greater anxiety about the whole of the Eastern policy. It is, of course, a normal rule that different members of the Front Bench do not

33 See *HG*, Ch. 10-v.

cut in on the Leader of the Opposition, except with his permission, or except on some quite minor point. This was a clear attempt to step up in front of CRA, and was so regarded by everybody.[34] The upset in the House was closed by Stanley Evans* asking if the Foreign Secretary [Eden] was aware that it was CRA who spoke for the overwhelming majority of us. I mention this only to show the nature of the immediate reaction. It so happened that that evening we had a meeting of the Parliamentary Committee [the Shadow Cabinet]. Shinwell, to his credit, gave notice that he was proposing to raise this, and he did so in a fairly moderate speech, pointing out that it really was impossible if individual members on the Front Bench behaved as Bevan had done that afternoon, that it was insulting to the Leader of the Party and generally discreditable. He also pointed out that we had in fact not decided our policy, but that was part of our job that evening. Various other people joined in, including, as far as I recall, Frank Soskice, Herbert [Morrison] and myself, all of us putting the case moderately. Bevan tried to make out that there were profound differences of policy, and rather adroitly turned the discussion on to the policy issue. The discussion went on, and I had to leave before it was over. There was a certain amount of agreement on the line to be taken by CRA, and we then agreed to meet at six o'clock the following day, the Party meeting being at 6.30. After this meeting, I myself and one or two of the others were by no means satisfied with the attitude of Clem [Attlee] himself. He had sat there really saying nothing, and I recall saying to Herbert, if only he had simply said he was not going to have this, and it made things impossible for him, AB would have been completely squashed. The following day, however, when we met again, CRA opened by giving a fair statement of what he thought in the light of the discussion he ought to say, which followed broadly the lines that we were in favour of the principle of collective security, but there were particular difficulties in applying it to the S.E. Asian countries; there was the anti-colonialism, and the need for Asians to participate.[35] In other words, very much on the lines of his own questions to the Foreign Secretary. When he had finished, AB spoke in the following terms. 'I think I can shorten proceedings. I have decided that after the Recess (it was just before Easter) I will retire from the Committee and return to the back benches. It is the only way in which I can speak freely. It appears that whenever I open my mouth on the Front Bench, it gives trouble.

34 Cf. Crossman's Diary, 21 April 1954; Kenneth Younger's diary, 27 April 1954. For the incident on 13 April, 526 H.C. Deb. 969–72; for the Bevanite view, Foot (1973), pp. 430–2.
35 The South East Asia Treaty Organisation was set up at Manila on 8 September 1954, with only three Asian members (Pakistan, Philippines and Thailand). Four others, including India, would not join.

Yesterday I was subjected to a most humiliating experience. I do not want to go through that again.' He then put his papers together and got up and walked out. Now this is not the first time that I have seen him behave like this, but usually, when he does it, there is a cry of 'Oh, come on, come back, be sensible'. On this occasion, as far as I remember, although I am not entirely certain, all that happened was that Clem said in his most Haileybury military accent,[36] 'Why can't you be a man and face the music'. One or two other people murmured, 'Let him go'. After he had gone, Shinwell started a long speech about what was going to happen, and what we ought to do. Should we announce that he was going to resign? Others said, No, that was impossible, because he was only going to resign after the Recess. It was not therefore as yet an official resignation. Somebody asked Clem if he thought he really was going. Clem said, 'Yep'. We then went back to considering Clem's statement, and at about 6.25, just as we were breaking up, Clem said, 'I think I will have to say something about that Front Bench business, don't you?' There was a chorus, Yes certainly, and most of us were greatly relieved and pleased, having been afraid that nothing would be said about it, that somebody would raise it at the Party meeting, and that Clem would give a shuffling, evasive answer.

We then went upstairs to the meeting, which was pretty crowded, and Clem made his statement on the lines that we had agreed. This went down well, and seemed to be generally acceptable. He then, to our astonishment, proceeded to speak with the utmost vigour and indignation about AB's behaviour on the Front Bench. We were all of us taken aback, after his silence in the Committee the previous day, and certainly AB was quite taken by surprise. He was sitting there on the platform, and immediately Clem had finished, he got up and said that he would tell them now what he had already said to the Committee, that he was going to resign, and he then left the platform. I have often wondered whether Clem did this deliberately, knowing that it would provoke him into an immediate resignation, for there is one thing you can be sure of with AB, and that is that he reacts violently to any defeat or humiliation. It may have been an accident, but it is possible that Clem decided he would give him a gentle push, knowing he would jump over the cliff as soon as he heard what Clem had said.

There is no doubt that AB did all this without consulting his group. It is thought that he may have intervened originally in the House on the advice of his wife, generally regarded as his evil genius, though I would not say genius was the right word; but he certainly did not consult Wilson or

36 Haileybury was Attlee's old school.

Crossman or the others.[37] His resignation put them in a dilemma, because Wilson was the next man on the list, and there was much uncertainty as to whether he was going to accept the post.[38] There were rumours that he was going to ask for a new vote, but as it turned out, when Easter came and went, at the end of the Recess he decided that he would come in. It is said that B[Bevan] was very angry with him for this, and regarded himself as being betrayed. He was also angry with Crossman, who argued with him, and the following conversation is said to have taken place in the corridor of the House of Commons. C. 'So you regard Harold as expendable, then, do you?' AB 'Yes, and the same goes for you as well.'[39]

Nevertheless, it is a mistake to think that the group will disintegrate. Jumping ahead a bit, the only one who has left them is Donnelly*, who after this upset also had a row with B. and told me that at one point in the summer diplomatic relations between him and AB did not exist. Later he went to Czechoslovakia and Poland and E. Germany, and on returning wrote an article in the *Daily Mail* in favour of German Rearmament. Arriving in Scarborough last week [for the Party Conference], he went up to B. and started talking to him, and offered him a drink, whereupon B. said 'No thanks, not with your thirty pieces of silver', which, as somebody said, not only identified D. as Judas Iscariot, but AB himself as Jesus Christ. This was the background to the scene in the Conference when D. pointed his accusing finger at B. on the platform at the end of the German Rearmament debate.

[B. 1952–4 generally]

For the rest, in these last years there is a kind of wave-like movement. The [Parliamentary] Committee, on the whole sound, takes the bit between its teeth every now and then, and decides to give a lead on some foreign policy issue, and then, if there is a strong minority, or trouble in the Party, they beat a hurried retreat. The best example of this was over German rearmament. Inside the Committee, after a great deal of discussion, we had a majority of about 2 to 1 in favour of accepting the Berlin Conference as justification for German Rearmament.[40] But at the Party

37 Confirmed by Crossman's diary, 21.4.54.
38 As runner-up in the previous Parliamentary Committee election, he was entitled to fill any casual vacancy that arose.
39 This story also appears in Foot (1973), p. 433, and in Hunter (1959), pp. 78–9 (quoting Crossman). On the whole affair see *HG*, pp. 324–7.
40 The four-power conference at Berlin in February 1954 had made no progress towards either German reunification or an Austrian peace settlement.

meeting held unfortunately in the evening, under very emotional conditions, we only carried the day by two votes. The result was interesting. It
did not affect our attitude on German rearmament, but when in the
following week the question of the Defence White Paper came up, there
was a quite extraordinary 'swing to the left' in the Committee, although
there was really no justification for opposing the programme, still less for
asking for a reduction in the period of the National Service – especially in
view of the fact that there was a Committee with the T.U.C. going into all
this – the Committee insisting on drafting an amendment embodying
what was really a demand for a reduction in defence and in National
Service. Only Frank [Soskice] and myself stood against this. I was very
upset at the time, and thought seriously of abstaining on the vote, but my
friends urged me strongly the other way. 'You cannot fight Nye and Clem
in combination. The policy must always be to divide them.' The advice
was sound. It is obviously always wrong for me to go against the collective
decision. The strength of our position must be that we do accept majority
rule.

The other interesting thing about the last three years is the way in which
the prestige and position of various personalities has altered. Immediately
after the Election, Herbert [Morrison]'s prestige was very low. It was felt
he had failed at the F.O., and in one or two debates on foreign affairs he
did not do very well. Eventually I went to him and later got Clem to urge
that he should drop foreign affairs in the main, and get back to the ground
which he knew, acting as deputy Leader of the Opposition, and Home
affairs. Herbert somewhat reluctantly agreed to this, on the understanding that he could sometimes speak on foreign affairs. Clem was only
too delighted. Their relations, of course, have never been good, which
does not exactly help matters. Since then, Herbert's prestige, with some
ups and downs, has largely recovered. He is still extremely good at the
'back-chat' of the House of Commons, the questions after questions, the
winding-up, slightly knock-about speech. He is at his worst when he has
an elaborate brief and something written out in advance. He is perhaps
best of all at the Party Conference, which he knows, and where his
peculiar techniques are seen at their best.

[C. October 1952]

In that connection, I should mention my own Stalybridge speech. After
the Morecambe Conference [in September 1952], when Herbert and
Hugh Dalton were thrown off the Executive, and the whole Conference
was extremely hysterical, I made what was for me an unusually violent

speech, attacking the Bevanites outright. The *Manchester Guardian* described it as a call to battle, and so it was. At the time, most of my friends were horrified. They thought I would lose a great deal of support, and undoubtedly constituency parties did not like it at all. Hundreds of Resolutions were sent in criticising me. Nevertheless, I was returned, as in the previous year, in third place for the Parliamentary Committee, and I think it was this, plus the support from the T.U.'s, that drove Attlee finally to taking a stand.[41]

[D. 1952–4 continued]

The speech did something else. It finally broke down Herbert's suspicions and reserve towards me. It is one of his greatest weaknesses that he is prickly towards middle class people he does not know intimately, with the result that he offends them, and he loses supporters. All the same I still have a great deal of regard for him. He has courage, he is honest, and he really understands the working of democracy. He is the nearest we have to a Scandinavian Socialist leader. As I have said, he does not get on with CRA. He feels all the time that he has had a raw deal, and he should have been Prime Minister (as judged by the 1929–31 period he certainly should),[42] and that he does not really get very much sympathy or help from CRA.

Clem, on the other hand, remains as inscrutable as ever. He has still got extremely good political judgment. His idea of leadership, of course, is more that of an Eisenhower than a Truman. He does a good deal of following as well as some leading. He is always frightened of getting out of touch with the Party. He is very much concerned with Party unity, and this leads him to make concessions to the Left. He is sometimes, I think, not as honest as he should be in Opposition, regarding it as quite reasonable to take a line which he knows he would not take in Government. For this, of course, there are plenty of precedents, and nobody has been worse at it than Churchill. He is still unapproachable, difficult to talk to, and without, so far as one can see, any intimates at all. I record here a story about his relationship with Crossman. He never liked Crossman. I once said to him, after the '51 election, that perhaps it was a mistake not to have given Dick a job. 'Certainly not', he replied, 'I have known him since he was a boy. You can't trust him at all.' The story, however,

41 He polled 179, four more than in 1951. On Attlee's successful stand, see *HG*, pp. 306–7.
42 In 1929–31 Morrison was a successful Cabinet Minister (of Transport) while Attlee was not in the Cabinet.

concerned Crossman's visit to Palestine, when he went out on the Committee appointed by Bevin. Some of us hoped, I remember, I think it was in 1946, that this would be the stepping-stone to office for him. But he quarrelled with the Foreign Office. He did not keep in touch with them. He developed views of his own, and started giving expression to them, without making sure they agreed with him. When he came back, he had some kind of a row with Ernie [Bevin], and demanded to see the P.M. After some difficulty, an interview was arranged. He was given half an hour. So, sitting in the Cabinet Room – Clem always received you there, no doubt in order to overawe his guests – sitting in the Cabinet Room on one side of the long table, with Dick opposite, Dick proceeded to talk. He spoke for some twenty minutes, and then paused, hoping to get some response from the P.M. But the P.M., who sat there doodling, merely looked up and said 'Yep?' So he went on for another eight minutes, and when there were only two minutes to go, he had another shot at getting a response. But once again there was nothing. Finally, when he had half a minute to go, he tried again. But all that Clem said was 'Very interesting. Saw your mother last week'. It is a good story, because one of Clem's peculiarities is that of out-silencing people. It is a useful weapon. Nothing can be more embarrassing if you cannot get a man to talk. I am told that Baldwin had the same capacity, and Bonar Law, and that when they were together they used to sit for hours in silence.[43]

Another character whose position has changed a good deal in the last few years is Jim Griffiths. It is hard to say why, but his prestige has fallen a great deal. He has in each year been elected top for the Parliamentary Committee, but whereas three years ago he was being confidently tipped as Attlee's most successful man, who would unite the Party, a man whom the Bevanites would support against Morrison, etc., nobody speaks in these terms now. He is regarded at any rate for the moment as more or less finished. It is very hard to say why. Somebody told him [*sic*: ? me] it was because he had not stood up to Fenner Brockway,[44] that on the one hand he had not stood up to the Left Wing Colonial people, and on the other hand he had disgusted the Right Wingers. Also, it has been bad luck for him that there have been such a lot of debates, that he has always had to speak in them, and that such a lot of the Party are bored with them. But once again, I am enormously impressed both by the elements of luck and the short-runness of everything. Jim's real weakness is certainly his

43 Andrew Bonar Law led the Conservative Party from 1911, and preceded Baldwin as Prime Minister, 1922–3.
44 Fenner (Lord) Brockway (1888–   ) was M.P. Leyton E. 1929–31, Eton & Slough 1950–64. Chairman, secretary or pol. secretary of I.L.P., editor of its journal and four times Parl. candidate 1931–46, when he rejoined the Labour Party. Pacifist in First World War (Sec. of No Conscription Fellowship in 1917). Chairman or president, Movement for Colonial Freedom from 1954.

softness. He has a not unusual Welsh characteristic, that of disliking an open row. I do not enjoy them myself, but you have to face them or else you lay yourself open to blackmail all the time.

On the other hand, Frank Soskice has advanced a great deal. In 1951 he was known as a highly successful Law Officer, well liked and popular, conscientious but not much more. He has now had two years on the Parliamentary Committee. He is as popular as ever, and manages to combine heavy work at the bar with quite a lot of Parliamentary effort. He has also moved into other spheres. He has spoken in Colonial debates, and takes a keen interest in foreign affairs. He is a possible Foreign Secretary. He is a good linguist, a good mixer, hard-working and conscientious. He can also be tough on occasion. He is perhaps too much inclined to be led on by the constituency parties – his own [Sheffield, Neepsend] is a peculiarly dotty one. But we are friends, and I think trust one another, which is so completely essential in the desperate game of politics. He is probably a little jealous of me, though he hides it as a gentleman.

Alf Robens is an entirely different kettle of fish. We have been staunch friends ever since he became my Parliamentary Secretary at the Ministry of Fuel and although, here again, there must be elements of jealousy and rivalry, he is loyal and honest. He went wrong for a time on German rearmament, but I think that was partly due to his absence in America, and partly to some trouble [at the Council of Europe] in Strasbourg. I rather doubt if foreign affairs is his line. He would probably be better back at the Ministry of Labour. It is a pity he no longer lives near us, and has so many family troubles, which I know worry him and upset him. Another person who will count a lot in future is George Brown, now Chairman of the T.U. group in the House. He carries rather too much of a chip on his shoulder about the middle classes, though I often think he puts it on in order to score some point. But his record in speech and writing is excellent. He has unlimited courage and plenty of sense. In the generation under fifty, I would place these three, Frank, Alf and George, as about the best available, though of course I should add my own close personal friends, like Douglas Jay.

[*E. Summer and autumn 1954*]

[At the Party Conference at Scarborough in October 1954, Gaitskell was elected Treasurer with 4,338,000 votes to 2,032,000 for Bevan. German rearmament, strongly opposed by the Bevanites and many others, was accepted by 3,270,000 to 3,022,000.]

I should say a few words about the Treasurership. When Arthur Greenwood died,[45] it so happened that I had already arranged to have Arthur Deakin to lunch with me. This was purely fortuitous. I tried to keep in touch with T.U. leaders, and I had not seen him for some time. As it turned out, of course, I hoped that the question of my nomination would come up, and it did so. He said quite early on, 'The first thing we must do is to nominate you for the Treasurership', and he proceeded to go ahead and do this.[46] At first I thought I should probably get it unopposed, but then, to my surprise, rumours got about that AB was going to run. People often ask me why he did. I am fairly sure the answer is (1) that he wanted to try and regain some of his lost prestige since his resignation; (2) that if he brought it off, this would be a tremendously successful coup, for he would then have behind him not only the constituency parties, but the Unions, and the impact of this on the Parliamentary Party would be considerable; (3) he really thought he had quite a good chance. He really thought he could get the A.E.U. vote, and he thought as an ex-miner he had a good chance of getting the miners. He knew he would have the majority of the constituency parties. In the event, both the A.E.U. and the miners decided, on the same day, to support me. In the background of the A.E.U. decision was a bit of high T.U. politics. Arthur Deakin told me that he was being pressed by the A.E.U. to vote for their nominee for the National Executive. He said he would make it quite plain to them that he would do that, but only if they nominated me for the Treasurership. This was not the only reason. At least three A.E.U. M.P.s[47] are strong supporters of mine, and worked very hard for me on the members of the A.E.U. Executive. As for the miners, the vote was most satisfactory, being taken by the Conference as a whole, and giving me a two to one majority. This was largely due, I am sure, to Ernest Jones and Sam Watson, and perhaps to the fortunate chance that many of the others knew me as Minister of Fuel. The interesting thing is why AB did not give up after these two Unions had decided, and continue to run, as he could have done, for the ordinary constituency parties. It is clear that he had not made up his mind then, otherwise he would have said so earlier. Or did he make up his mind immediately? I think myself it was largely a matter of pride. As always with him, he cannot ever undertake a voluntary step

45 See *HG*, Ch. 11-ii. Arthur Greenwood (father of Anthony) was deputy leader of the Labour Party 1935–42 and acting leader of the 'Opposition' 1942–5. He was elected Treasurer in 1943, defeating Morrison, and though ailing and overdue for retirement, he clung obstinately on until his death on 9 June 1954.

46 Deakin (T.&G.W.U. general secretary, and violently anti-Bevan) had been planning this for months, as Gaitskell doubtless knew: *HG*, p. 319 and nn. 53–4; Dalton's diary, 23.10.53.

47 Charles Pannell, a neighbour as M.P. for Leeds W., was the most important of these.

down. He has to be pushed off. He cannot retreat of his own volition. So a story is invented to cover up his action, that he intends to go on challenging the power of the block vote, and run against me year by year. Maybe he will. But I am pretty sure this was not his original intention.[48]

[The] Scarborough [Conference] was good from our point of view, not only because of the Treasurership, not only because of the German rearmament decision, desperately narrow, but also because once again AB threw himself over the cliff in his speech at the Tribune meeting.[49] People asked me why on earth does he do this. I replied, 'Any M.P. could have told him that he would do that.' It is quite wrong to think of him as a scheming careful plotter. He schemes only at intervals, and his actions are determined far more by emotional reactions, particularly anger and pride, than anything else. Although softened by British environment, and having a much more attractive side to his character in private, there are distinct similarities to the way he behaved, and the way Hitler behaved during the war. When Hitler lost one campaign after another, having gone against the advice of his generals, he never said, 'I was wrong', and that, I think, is rather the way that AB reacts too. I should add, however, one other piece of information. I saw Malcolm Muggeridge the other night, editor of *Punch*,[50] who is a personal friend of Bevan's, and likes him, though violently disagreeing with his politics. He told me that AB had made it plain that he was completely browned off with his own crowd, i.e. the Bevanites, and I have heard from others that all he wants to do is to go and bury himself in the country.

Yesterday I had lunch with Cecil King*, the Chairman of the *Daily Mirror* and the controller of the whole of that group. It is fantastic how successful he is. The only papers increasing their circulation now are the *Mirror* and the *Telegraph*. They have started a junior edition. They expected half a million, and have had a million sales. His plans for the future, very confidential, include possibly buying up some of Kemsley's provincial papers;[51] and even more confidential, possibly getting hold of

48 HG was wrong. Bevan had told his friends from the start that he was no longer interested in serving on the N.E.C. in a minority, and that while he would not win the Treasurership, he would 'split every union and expose Deakin and Tom Williamson by making them prefer an intellectual like Gaitskell to a miner like me': Crossman diary, 3 May 1954 (and *HG*, pp. 327–9).
49 Where he denounced Ernest Jones, the new N.U.M. president, and attacked the 'desiccated calculating machine' type of Labour leader (it was not clear whether Attlee or HG was meant). See *HG*, pp. 332–3.
50 Editor of *Punch* 1953–7, after work on the *Manchester Guardian* and *Daily Telegraph*. Later a prominent broadcaster. Nephew of Beatrice Webb.
51 Lord Kemsley, whose brother and former partner had bought out his share in the *Daily Telegraph* before the war, sold the *Daily Graphic* in 1952 and the *Sunday Graphic* in 1959 but retained important provincial press interests.

the *Star* and the *News Chronicle*, which are reported to be, particularly the latter one, in a bad way. King told me that if this came off, he proposes to make the *News Chronicle* into a sort of *Daily Telegraph* of the Left, which would be excellent from our point of view, and exactly what is needed – a serious but progressive, moderate Labour paper, sufficiently popular to get a reasonable circulation, but with a good news service, and sensible leaders. It is very foolish of the Cadburys not to have done this with the *News Chronicle*.[52] Frank Waters, the business manager of the *N.C.* told me some time ago that he had urged it upon them; but presumably they were tied by their old Liberal tradition, and there is always a good deal of simple inertia. I pressed King very hard about a weekly, since he had all this money, and since he was broadly in agreement with us. I pointed out how handicapped we were vis-à-vis the Bevanites because of the *New Statesman* and *Tribune*, and incidentally also because of *Reynolds* on Sundays.[53] He said they had run a weekly a short time a few years ago, *Public Opinion*. It had been, however, a complete failure. He admitted this was partly because they had the wrong editor – he thought that was one of the great difficulties. I went on about it, however, and urged him to consider it. It was then that he told me about the *News Chronicle* possibility, and that until that was settled he could not go any further. I suggested that he might consider as a possible editor, Percy Cudlipp, who I heard was not really good at the *Herald*, but might be better for a serious weekly paper.[54] He thought that there might be something in this. He asked if I did not think I should go to Washington and also to other places, and keep in touch with people over there. If so, they would be glad to help. It was not clear exactly what he meant, except, presumably, that I should write them an article or two, and they would take care of my expenses. He said, 'after all, this is a very rich concern, and our heart is in the right place. We would like to help.'

He is a very curious man and difficult to understand. I suppose he must be shrewd in business, and I think that more by accident than anything else he is genuinely in agreement with a moderate Labour policy. But he started a rather silly line about the Civil Service – weren't they getting much too powerful? – and took a highly simplified view about Crichel

52 The *News Chronicle* was an amalgamation in 1930 of two Liberal papers, the *Daily Chronicle* being bought by the Cadbury family who already owned the *Daily News* and the (evening) *Star*. In 1960 they were abruptly sold to Associated Newspapers, owners of the *Daily Mail*: see *HG*, p. 667.

53 The need for a right-wing Labour weekly was a major preoccupation during these years: see *HG*, pp. 319–20, and below, pp. 414, 545. *Reynolds News*, the Cooperative paper, ran a weekly column by Tom Driberg the Bevanite M.P.

54 Percy Cudlipp (brother of Hugh*) was editor of the *Daily Herald*, 1940–53, and subsequently of *New Scientist*.

Down.[55] He seems to have been prejudiced by his experience with people in the Colonial Service. Note: I must bring him together with Arthur.[56] I suppose it is really a combination of being a nephew of Lord Northcliffe, and being educated at Winchester which makes him such an odd and mixed personality. But he is obviously a man of very considerable power and influence, who could be very helpful to us, and I was therefore glad to have had this intimate and fairly exhaustive conversation with him.[57]

14 October 1954

I spent the weekend in the Lake District, in a hotel with the grammar school headmasters of Lancashire and Cheshire. The purpose of this was principally to discuss the Labour Party's proposals for education, and in particular the comprehensive school. The person who I think suggested that I should be asked, and indeed, probably started the whole idea of this Conference, was Eric James, the Headmaster of Manchester Grammar School*.

I had not met him before, but he has made a great name for himself in education. He was a don at Winchester before going to Manchester, and is nevertheless still, I think, only about 45. Alice Bacon and Michael Stewart came with me, and we had a weekend's pretty solid discussion.[58]

The headmasters began in a somewhat truculent mood, and I was rather astonished to hear them say, one after another, that the Labour Party was against the grammar schools, that it had attacked them, that it was trying to destroy them, etc. James himself, in what was obviously a deliberately provocative speech, said that our policy was based on 'ignorance, frivolity and enmity'. He made, however, some telling points, the most important of which, I thought (and it came up several times during the weekend), was the fact that in some areas to start a comprehensive school, instead of the present division between secondary

55 Land at Crichel Down in Dorset had been compulsorily purchased in 1937, and the former owner sought to buy it back. The Minister of Agriculture resigned in 1954 after severe criticism of his department's handling of the case.
56 HG's elder brother Arthur had spent his life in the Sudan Civil Service.
57 King's support cooled somewhat after the 1959 election. He remained an ally until the Common Market issue arose, but HG became much more wary of him: *HG*, pp. 667–70.
58 Alice Bacon became Labour's main education spokesman at the Party Conference, being on the N.E.C.; and Michael Stewart in the House of Commons, being on the Parliamentary Committee. He became Secretary of State for Education and Science in 1964, and she Minister of State there in 1967.

modern and grammar schools, would in fact lead to more not less class division. You would get a residential area on the one side, where there was a comprehensive school and all the people there would be drawn from the middle or lower middle class. On the other hand, you would have a working class area, and equally there all of the children would come from working class parents. This would be in contrast with the present situation, whereby in the grammar school itself, owing to the fact that the places were free and that entry was on merit, there was now a complete mixing up.

The other main argument was, of course, the fear that in the comprehensive school the bright, clever children would be at a disadvantage. They would not get the same specialist teaching, and the stream of boys and girls to do the professional jobs requiring more brains would suffer in quality.

We put up between us quite a good case, I think, for the comprehensive school, and criticised the grammar school on the grounds (a) that half the boys and girls in fact left at about 15 or 16, so that the argument that they were being trained for something higher simply did not apply, (b) that the proportion going to grammar schools differed from 50 per cent in one area to 10 per cent in another, so that the character of the grammar school varied enormously, and they could not be defended on the same arguments. We argued also that provided we were prepared for fairly large schools there was no reason why bright children should suffer, and that there was really no case against fairly large schools, e.g. Manchester Grammar and Eton. We pointed out that in the main the segregation at 11 did lead to a class structure, whereas what we wanted was more social cohesion.

I think that by the end of the weekend we had begun to understand each other's point of view better. My own feeling was that we should not be too precipitate in this matter because of the many local problems that would arise (we had some good contributions on this from Directors of Education), and that if only our programme had been phrased a little more wisely, we should not have had nearly so much hostility from the grammar schools and other people in the teaching profession, as well as some of our own Labour Education Committees.[59]

We went two nights ago to the Hirshfields, where they were entertaining Sam Watson and his wife, Joe Godson* from the American

59 See *HG*, pp. 466–8, for his attitude to educational policy in the 1950s and his problems with the N.E.C. even as leader. M. Parkinson, *The Labour Party and the Organisation of Secondary Education 1918–65* (Routledge & Kegan Paul, 1970) is a succinct account.

Embassy, and Sheila McNeil.[60] I had been speaking at High Wycombe, and only arrived there about 11 o'clock. We had a very interesting three hours' discussion, in which Sam talked very freely, and in a most stimulating way. He was obviously worried that AB next year would make a tremendous effort to win the Engineers' and the Miners' vote. We must do everything to stop this, and if possible to increase our majority. He thought that being Treasurer would be a great help. I should have to go and meet and see the Union people a lot, and there would have to be a series of dinners at which I asked them for money for the Party. It would be a good plan if I soon made a speech appealing for Party Unity for the Election. He talked rather more frivolously about the idea of selling buttons with 'Victory for Labour' on them, and even offered an order for 50,000 of these from the Durham miners. I am not sure how seriously Sam wanted us to take it. He agreed that something would have to be done about the agents, and that the Unions would have to put up some more money in addition to what was needed for an Election. Something between the two extremes of letting the constituency parties appoint the agents themselves, and getting grants from head office as at present, and the opposite extreme of a national agency service would have to be worked out. The main point would have to be to try and improve the morale of the agents, and make them into an efficient and contented body, but under the control of the centre.[61]

He was very amusing about the China trip, and about AB's behaviour, and how in particular he had offended [the Party's general secretary] Morgan Phillips. Apparently there was some discussion as to who should stay with the Governor of Singapore, and AB had said to MP, 'Of course you don't go – you are only a paid servant of the Party'. This had given great offence, and led to a final break between them. Earlier that day I had had lunch with MP and he had told me this story himself, and said that he thought that AB was now finished. The lunch was quite cordial, but we skated around a good deal. He asked if I wanted to be Chairman of the Finance Committee. I said Yes, provided it did not upset Jock Tiffin*. He agreed that it was important not to do this because of his future position in the T.&G.W.[62] On agents, he also agreed that something should be done, though not a National Agency Service. He was not particularly worried about money at the moment. He obviously did not want me sitting in the

---

60 Desmond (Lord) Hirshfield was an accountant of Labour sympathies, called in soon afterwards by HG as Treasurer to advise on the finances and administrative organisation of Transport House; Joe Godson was very friendly with Sam Watson; Sheila McNeil was Hector's wife.

61 HG succeeded in raising more money from the unions, but not nearly enough for an adequately paid national agency service. See *HG*, pp. 349–50.

62 A. E. Tiffin, the current chairman of the N.E.C.'s Finance Committee, was being groomed to succeed Deakin, but died six months after doing so.

office (incidentally, Sam also advised me strongly against doing that). I found that they both knew what Arthur Deakin had told me in Scarborough, and which I thought was quite a secret, namely that the two General Unions were going to increase their affiliated membership, the T.&G.W. by bringing theirs up to one million, and the N.U.G.M.W. bringing theirs up to 600,000. This would give us another 450,000 votes at the next Conference, and was the best way of bringing more money into the Party.

Sam thought that this was not enough, and that the N.U.G.M.W. should go up to the full three-quarters of a million, which was about their limit. I think it would be a good thing if I were to go into this in greater detail, and visit some of the Unions on our side and try and get them to increase affiliation. What we want, if we can get it, is a complete safeguard, certainly against the Engineers going wrong and possibly the Miners, though I am not too worried about this at present. There was much talk at the Hirshfields about personalities. Obviously, Sam has a pretty poor opinion of Attlee because of the kind of leadership, or lack of leadership he gives. He was also very critical of Alf Robens, and we had quite a set-to. Sam kept on saying that he did not like people who said they were against Bevan, but then went on to express Bevanite views. When we said, 'What views?', he said 'On German Rearmament'. We, i.e. Joe Godson and myself, pointed out that other people were opposed to us on German Rearmament, that Alf had considerably altered his views on that, and there were reasons why he had been against us. I mentioned also that I thought at one point that Alf, who had been such a staunch friend of mine before, had begun to cool off because of jealousy, that he had the idea of becoming Leader of the Party and that had introduced an element of rivalry. I was interested that JG confirmed that this was so. Sam thought this a most fantastic idea. Eventually I made a long speech, pointing out how terribly limited we were in personnel, and that the three best people available in the hierarchy and in Parliament were Frank Soskice, George Brown and Alf Robens. They all had disadvantages, but they all had very good qualities, and there was enough confidence between us to make team work possible. The same could not be said of various other characters.

It was altogether a very stimulating evening. I have never seen Sam in such good form. He was very anxious obviously that I should start taking the lead in all sorts of ways, and particularly wished that I really was doing something about the finances of the Party. He wanted me to do this, however, not through messing around with the administration of Transport House and the Regions, but through talks with the Unions and speeches in the country. I think his advice is probably sound, and I shall talk to him further.

What Morgan Phillips really has in mind I do not know. People tell me that he is very very ambitious, and that until recently he has regarded himself as a future leader of the Party, and that at the very least he should become Foreign Secretary. Most people think that if he came into the House of Commons he would sink to a much lower level than all that. He is certainly shrewd. I would expect his political judgments to be good about e.g., elections or conferences, but just how far one can trust him is another matter. He has certainly been playing with both sides for quite a time. Nevertheless, I must avoid any kind of collision with him, and obviously try and work with him. Sam will probably be helpful in this way, as he obviously has a hold over MP. What a pity it is that Sam himself does not go into politics. He really would make, I believe, an outstandingly good leader, and failing that, I believe he would also be a very fine Foreign Secretary. But although he may change, so far he shows no signs of wishing even to leave Durham, much less to move from T.U. into politics.[63]

9 November 1954

I recently attended my first meeting of the National Executive Committee. It is a large and rather ungainly Committee, scattered about the big, bare room in Transport House. The Bevanites sat together – B. Castle being away; Anthony Greenwood sat away from them. We rushed through hundreds of items very quickly, and everything went quite smoothly until we came to a letter from the T.U.C., protesting about the *Tribune* attack on Deakin.[64] The T.U. boys weighed in heavily and without hesitation, especially Sam Watson, Jock Tiffin, Alice Horan, and several others. Jean Mann* was pretty violent, and Herbert [Morrison] came in towards the end.[65] I only made a slight comment on the drafting of the statement of protest, though I notice the papers said the next day that I had given 'quiet but effective support'. The Bevanite defence was mostly Crossman, who argued in his usual rather tortuous fashion. He

63 He never did.
64 Over a dispute in the docks, where Deakin (for once with Communist support) was resisting efforts by the rival Stevedores' Union (see below, p. 344) to poach his members, contrary to a T.U.C. agreement. The T.U.C. General Council protested to the Party about *Tribune*'s violent attack on Deakin, which embarrassed other Bevanites by its wild inaccuracy; this was the context of Wilson's comment that 'Bevanism cannot do without Bevan but it would be far better without *Tribune*': Crossman diary, 27.10.54 and 1.11.54.
65 Alice Horan was an official of the N.U.G.M.W., and sat on the N.E.C. (women's section) 1951–8. Jean Mann sat 1953–8.

talked about the great moral conflict which a journalist had. 'I often find it very difficult to decide what I ought to say in the *New Statesman*.' If I had had the chance, I should have said that we were eagerly looking forward to a startling resolving of this moral conflict – by his resignation either from the *New Statesman* or the Executive. But the opportunity passed.

There is little sign that the Bevanites mean to change. They make the mistake of talking too much, which did not go down particularly well with the rest of the E.C. This is particularly true of Crossman.

The previous evening we had had a private dinner to the Trade Union leaders on finance. Those present, apart from MP[Phillips] and myself, included Deakin, Ernest Jones, Sam Watson, Openshaw, Birch*, Tom Williamson, Stafford (N.U.R.), Poole (Boot & Shoe), and Jock Tiffin.[66]

As to the latter, I discovered that I had made a wrong move. When I got there, before the others arrived, and by arrangement to see Sam and MP, the latter said 'Jock Tiffin is upset because you approached Arthur [Deakin] about the Chairmanship of the Finance Committee, instead of going to him'. Later I had to try and smooth this over, and had a few words with JT at the end of the dinner. I discovered that he was by no means on friendly terms with Deakin, and that he obviously rather resented my wanting to be Chairman of the Finance Committee. I told him that if he wanted to go on, that was perfectly all right by me, and that I would be happy to work with him on that basis. Partly because of this breeze, it was decided to ask Jock to take the chair at the dinner, which he did quite well. He and MP opened the proceedings, after we had eaten, with a statement on the financial situation. He pointed out that it was not so much the General Election that was the trouble, but the need to increase our current income. This was necessary both to meet inevitable increases in costs which would follow upon us [*sic*], e.g. higher rent plus salaries, and even more essential if we were to do anything about an agency service. There was long and fruitful discussion, the general conclusion of which was that it would be necessary not only to increase the number of affiliated members – which was the line taken by Tom Williamson and Arthur Deakin – but that it would also be necessary to increase from 6d to 9d the affiliation fee. There was a surprising amount of support for this. Openshaw, Birch, Ernest Jones and Poole were all

66 Of the first six, all but Sam Watson were on the General Council of the T.U.C.; he and the last three were on the Labour Party National Executive. Deakin was general secretary (and Tiffin assistant general secretary) of the Transport Workers, Williamson of the N.U.G.M.W., Birch of the Distributive Workers (USDAW); Jones (president) and Watson were miners, and Openshaw president of the Engineers (A.E.U.).

prepared to say then and there that their Unions would play. Deakin, who went out early because of the Dock Strike, was much the most difficult. Tom Williamson resisted it, but looked as though he could be won over. The real trouble is quite simply that the big [general] Labour Unions have a very low political levy – in the case of the T.&G.W., a shilling a year; and in that of the N.U.G.M.W., one-and-fourpence a year; and therefore, after deducting what is needed for financing their candidates and other local activities, there is not a great deal in the fund for payment to the Labour Party. Indeed, it seems clear that in order to pay a higher affiliation fee, even to the extent of 3d a year, both Unions would have to increase their political levy.[67] Of course, the other Unions say they ought to do this anyhow. Other Unions also complained that they ought to go even further in the way of increased affiliation, pointing out that their proportion is far lower than the Miners, Engineers, or USDAW. It was finally agreed that after the next meeting of the Finance Committee, we should have another gathering of the same kind, when, however, a more definite scheme for explaining why the money was required would have to be put forward.

One of my difficulties in all this is that the job of Treasurer has simply not been done for ten years.[68] There is therefore no agreement as to exactly what one is supposed to do. This is all the more difficult since I am not Chairman of the Finance Committee. So I never quite know when I should intervene and take the initiative. If I do this too much, it will upset the other members of the Finance Committee. If I do not do it enough, too little will be done. It is bad enough finding the time for all these things, without having these additional complications.

In the staff of Transport House, apart from MP[Morgan Phillips], I find a warm welcome and good cooperation, but I have not yet spent much time there.

Tewson [T.U.C. general secretary] had lunch with me at the Stafford Hotel. He was obviously pleased to be asked, and enjoyed his meal. He talked quite freely. He thought that after Deakin went the T.&G.W. would to some extent crumble, that Tiffin had not got the personality to keep the thing together. He said the Stevedores were a queer Union, not really particularly left-wing, but just a collection of people who for some reason or other are against the T.&G.W. Barrett, the Secretary, was a very poor type intellectually, though he was not particularly

67 Unions could (and can) make political contributions only from a separate fund from which individual members might 'contract out'. The amount and destination of the payments were determined by the union.
68 The period of Arthur Greenwood's tenure.

malevolent.[69] I told Tewson something about our dinner. He thought the best way to get the Unions to pay up was to make it clear to them that the Labour Party would help in their internal troubles with the Communists – in other words, that the Labour Party machine would be put into operation in favour of the Labour Party and against Communist candidates at Union elections. It is said that this is done already, though I have not been able to get any firm evidence. Tewson obviously did not like Morgan Phillips. He made it plain that he did not trust him, and that this was something of a barrier to close cooperation between the T.U.C. and the Party.

We have cleared our first hurdle on Foreign Policy in the Party – the S.E. Asia question. When the Parliamentary Committee first considered our attitude to the Manila Treaty [setting up SEATO], the discussion was chiefly concerned with whether or not we should move an addendum to the Government motion of approval. It was agreed that we could not possibly vote against this motion, because of the Scarborough decision, and nobody tried to argue the contrary.[70]

There was, however, some suggestion that the addendum should range pretty wide, and cover such a point as Chinese membership of the U.N. At the end of the Committee meeting, there was a clear understanding that at the Party meeting which was to follow it, CRA[Attlee] was simply to explain that we could not vote against the treaty, and [we] asked for a free hand in the Committee to decide whether or not to put the addendum down, and if so, in what form.

His opening speech went a good deal farther than this, and leant well over towards the Bevanites. In fact, he made it pretty plain that he did not much care for the treaty. Discussion, however, was on a low tone. There was no excitement, no applause, but just a series of speeches – a very destructive one from Kenneth Younger, who, however, emphasised that we could not possibly vote against the treaty. To our surprise, at the end of it, CRA went much farther than before. He said that none of us really liked the treaty, that it would be much better if we could put our own motion down, and that the Committee would see what could be done in that way. This considerably alarmed Herbert [Morrison], Alf [Robens], myself and others. As we went out of the hall, CRA turned to me and said, 'Was that all right?' I said, 'No, it was not', and took him back into the room to explain why, with Herbert standing there. I said I thought it would be a great mistake to have a motion of our own. There was little we

69 He was a Catholic, and a kind of Trotskyist.
70 On SEATO see above, p. 328 n. and *HG*, pp. 324–6. The Party Conference at Scarborough had rejected a motion opposing it (seconded by Jennie Lee) by 3,669,000 to 2,570,000.

could put down that would make sense, and yet meet with the agreement of the Party. 'I don't agree', said CRA. 'We could say there ought to have been a Commonwealth Conference first.' I said I thought it was absurd to put down a motion on an important debate simply to cover this point, and that anyway he knew perfectly well there had been the fullest consultation within the Commonwealth. We parted somewhat angrily. I heard afterwards that he had approached Frank [Soskice] with the same question, and received much the same answer, except that Frank had no doubt been much calmer than myself, and had simply said that he disagreed with the attitude that Clem was taking. We were rather indignant, because CRA had so clearly departed from the line agreed to by the Committee.

Whether it was the result of various approaches to him during the day, when it came to the Committee meeting that evening, CRA seemed to have changed. The Chief Whip informed us that the Government would have preferred a debate on the adjournment, but were prepared to put down a motion. CRA then said, 'Oh, a motion would suit us much better' (which was, of course, the opposite of what he had said at the end of the morning). We then had a rather long argument about the form of the addendum, but [omission in original] . . . advised some fairly harmless words, going on trying to persuade India, Burma and Ceylon to come in. Against a small minority, Callaghan and Wilson, we managed to insist that it was made quite clear that China was not to be included. We did, however, have a slightly vague tail to the addendum, which enabled those who wanted to talk about the need for a Far Eastern Locarno. We were reasonably satisfied, and felt that we had got the thing back on the right lines after the fiasco of the morning. That same evening, some of us were dining with Dick Stokes, Herbert, George Brown, Hector [McNeil], Alf Robens and myself, and Hartley [Shawcross]. We told them what had happened, and there was general satisfaction. They were, however, much more critical of another decision we had reached, which was to have two party meetings on the Paris Agreements [on German rearmament within NATO], at the first of which the Committee would give no lead to the Party, but simply listen to the debate. George argued with great force that this was not only passing the buck, but also, in so far as it involved two days, making it very difficult for us to mobilise our supporters in the Party. Alf and I argued as best we could the other way, and urged at any rate that the procedure was not so terribly important, and that we would be able to get our people in on the Thursday. Almost the whole evening was spent on this, so that we had far too little time to discuss the wider issues of the Party.

On the following evening, the Party meeting took place, and turned out to be rather remarkable. As soon as CRA had read out our proposed addendum, Bevan got up and made a rather violent speech, saying that this was quite contrary to what had been said in the Party meeting the previous day. He made it quite plain that he wanted an addendum, which in fact implied that we ought to bring China in. He did his usual stuff about 'the encirclement of China'. One or two others followed on somewhat similar lines, and suggested that if we did not name India, Burma and Ceylon, but simply 'Asian countries', that would cover the point. Once again we were taken aback when Clem got up, and instead of pointing out that we did not want China in, and that all that had been decided at Scarborough, proceeded to defend the addendum on the grounds that it did cover the point of China being included. At this point George Brown got up and made a strong, courageous speech, saying he had not been at the previous meeting, but that we could not depart from Scarborough, that talk about encircling China was nonsense. He did, however, make one slip in saying he did not mind if we amended the addendum to read 'Asian countries'. He ended by saying 'Either we should have it on these lines, or have no addendum at all'. Fortunately Woodrow [Wyatt] spotted the weakness of this, and came in in a convincing speech against the addendum, and asked that we should drop it. Both speeches were well received by the Party, and there was a growing murmur of 'No Addendum'. I whispered to Will Hall and Phil [Noel-Baker], who were sitting on the platform, 'Will you accept no addendum?' They agreed, I whispered it to Edith [Summerskill] (who is soft about China because of her visit there). She hesitated a bit, but put up no resistance. So I told Herbert to say that on our side of the platform we were quite prepared to accept no addendum. Clem had simply to put the question, and there was no need to count the votes. There was a substantial majority – 3 or 4 to 1 – against any addendum. But there was even better to come. Harold Davies[71] then said that the Scarborough Resolution really did not dispose of the vote on the main question, and urged that we should in fact oppose the Manila Treaty. There was a bit of an uproar then. Herbert chimed in very heavily against this. Arthur Woodburn then formally proposed we should not vote against the Treaty, in order to get the thing perfectly clear, and this was carried by an even more overwhelming majority, only about fifteen Bevanites voting the other way. Bevan then shouted that he was going to vote against it anyway.

We passed to the next business, and Charlie Hobson[72] asked whether the Committee were going to come forward with recommendations on

71 Teacher, and left-wing M.P. for Leek (Staffs.) 1945–70, when he lost his seat. Parl. Sec. Pensions 1964–6, P.P.S. to Harold Wilson 1966–70.
72 Engineer, M.P. Wembley N. 1945–50, Keighley 1950–9, when he was defeated. Assistant Postmaster General 1947–51.

the Paris Agreements. Clem said, 'No.' It would be free for all on the first day; the Committee would make their recommendation on the second day. Denis Healey* then, to my surprise, made an effective speech, saying that this was not really the best way of doing it. We should get into a muddle if the Committee did not come forward with a definite proposal at the start. This was received with great enthusiasm, and one or two other people spoke, making it plain that what the Party wanted was more leadership. It was then carried by acclamation with no opposition that the Committee should make its position clear at the beginning of the debates in the Party. It was really quite an interesting development, because I do not think this particular point had been organised at all. Both on SEATO and on the procedure over German rearmament, the floor were throwing their weight heavily against Bevan at the start; whether they will keep it up remains to be seen.

In the event, Bevan must have had second thoughts about voting. He did not turn up at the debate on SEATO, and no division was challenged.[73] George Brown, rather unexpectedly, spoke from below the gangway in a much tougher way than Kenneth Younger, who is the official spokesman. George is playing an increasingly important part in all this discussion and argument within the Party. Although he is a difficult person, and at times has an irritating chip on his shoulder, he has great courage, and has persistently taken a sound line in public, however unpopular this has been. I would guess that his authority and influence in the Party had grown a good deal, and he may even get on to the Parliamentary Committee this year, though I should expect him not quite to achieve this.[74]

12 November 1954[75]

The Paris Agreements [on German rearmament] – discussion in the Party

As instructed by the Party meeting last week, the Parliamentary Committee met to decide its attitude, and what it should recommend to the Party. There was an excellent discussion on familiar lines, the line-up

73 His absence, and his failure to lead the Left, caused a 'catastrophic decline in Nye's position' – according to Crossman (diary, 15.11.54). Dalton wrote in his diary at Christmas of Bevan's 'slow suicide'.
74 He was elected in 1955.
75 A separate diary entry, dated 9.11.54 like the previous one, is printed above (pp. 315–16) as it relates to 1952.

being exactly as one expected: Dalton, Callaghan, Harold Wilson and Chuter Ede on the one side, and all the rest of us on the other. I have seldom heard a better debate. For once in a way we each spoke in turn, and as far as our views are concerned they could not have been better expressed. At the first Party meeting there was also a reasonably good debate – Denis Healey was particularly effective. Bevan intervened rather late. He is obviously trying to be as quiet and reasonable as possible. It was therefore a more effective speech than some, although, as so often before, there was an extraordinary lack of logic about his arguments. Perhaps the effect was really to confuse the listeners rather than to win them over. We had hoped to be able to take a vote at the end of Wednesday morning, and there was much criticism of CRA [Attlee] for refusing to do so. Personally, if I had been in his position, I think I should have asked the meeting whether they wanted the vote, and I have little doubt that the vast majority would have agreed. As it was, we had a second day's discussion, in which the only notable speech was by Reggie Paget. He is a curious man, an Old Etonian, an expert bridge player, said to have ridden in the Grand National.[76] His father was a Conservative M.P. He has a lot of charm, but not a very high intelligence. He is courageous and honest, and every now and then he has touches of brilliance. This was one of the occasions. After arguing about the importance of tying up the German forces in the West on technical military grounds, he then launched an attack on the Bevanites. 'The trouble with the Bevanite opposition is that they are so profoundly ignorant of foreign affairs. Only one of them knows anything about it, Dick Crossman, and if the others understood what he wanted, they would violently disagree. What is Crossman's policy? It has been the same ever since the stab in the back debate of 1947.[77] The group received an access of eloquence, if not of judgment, when Nye Bevan resigned from the Government. The policy is that the victory of Communism is unavoidable, that you may as well lie back and enjoy the rape as best you can, hoping that your charms will civilise the victors.' Needless to say, this was received with uproarious laughter and cheers. There was the usual last-minute attempt to confuse the issue by the usual people, i.e. George Strauss and Tony Greenwood, though the person behind them was almost certainly John Strachey. They wanted an amendment, which they later said was an addendum, to be moved, urging immediate talks with Russia. They carefully did not say whether these were to be subject to the

76 M.P. Northampton 1945–74 (Lord Paget); Master of Pytchley Hounds 1958–71; Party spokesman on the Army 1961–4.
77 At the Party Conference of 1947, Bevin complained of being 'stabbed in the back', when negotiating in Washington a year earlier, by a left-wing amendment to the Address which Crossman had moved.

condition that the Russians must accept free elections. Herbert [Morrison] had little difficulty in exposing this point (egged on by myself), and we managed to defeat the amendment by 115 to 82, and then one on the main issue by 124 to 72, a very satisfactory result. One reason for this was that the Parliamentary Committee at its Wednesday evening meeting anticipated the George Strauss move, and had decided clearly what line it should take. How necessary this was was shown by the fact that CRA, when Strauss said that he was quite prepared to have an addendum, not an amendment, was quite inclined to be soft about it. He is an extraordinary man. He is really a very bad Chairman of a big meeting, and nowadays at any rate very seldom says precisely what is intended. For instance, he kept on confusing the recommendation of the Foreign Affairs Group and the recommendation of the Parliamentary Committee. He failed to draw attention to the fact that the Foreign Affairs recommendation on the talks with Russia was subject to the free elections condition – little points like that. They do not really matter much, but they keep one in a constant state of continual nervousness. I sat next to Herbert and made suggestions to him throughout the meeting, which I must say he took extremely well. He was very firm on accepting no amendment.

14 December 1954

Having won by a reasonably adequate majority in the Party meeting, our next hurdle was the vote in the House. It was pretty obvious that there would be some kind of revolt against the Party decision. Some of the pacifists were very likely to challenge a division, and it was possible that the Bevanites would join with them. Our first efforts were directed to trying to prevent this, and various warnings were given both in a special note and also orally to some of those concerned.

We had, however, to face the possibility that these warnings would be ignored, that the vote would be challenged, and we had to consider in that event what advice should be given to the Party. Various people came up to me at this time and begged that we should at any rate give a definite line, because otherwise there would be wild confusion – people not knowing whether to vote with the Government or to abstain.

At first there was some inclination to feel that we should vote with the Government. But there were great difficulties about this. Many would obviously abstain, claiming the conscience clause, and we should have had the party divided three ways. We therefore decided that if a division were challenged we would abstain, and that it would be necessary to tell people this in advance.

(For a full explanation of the whole situation, see the copy [printed below] of my letter to Cassandra of the *Daily Mirror*.)

What happened is well known. Six people voted against the motion,[78] and one insisted on going into the Government lobby.[79] We then had to decide what to do. If we were going to do anything, we would have to do it quickly. Immediately after the vote, Alf Robens ran into me and pointed this out, and urged that we should call a meeting of the Parliamentary Committee on Monday, and a special meeting of the Party on Tuesday – the Executive was in any case meeting on Wednesday. We managed to get hold of Herbert, Clem [Attlee] and the Chief Whip [Whiteley], and I put the point to them. They agreed, and the meetings were summoned.

At the Parliamentary Committee there was very much the same line-up as on German rearmament, except that Dalton was not there and he might perhaps have taken a different line. Callaghan, Harold Wilson and Chuter Ede all put up rather feeble arguments in favour of the rebels, but they made no impression, and the rest of us were agreed that there was nothing to do but withdraw the Whip. I was, however, nervous of whether we should carry this in the Party meeting. Previous experience had told me that the Party was inclined to be terribly sentimental when it came to taking any action. Moreover, it was certain that the Bevanites would organise very heavily in order to get as many votes as possible in favour of the pacifists. The meeting itself took place on Tuesday evening. It was notable for the hysterical speeches made by some of the pacifists, notable too for the fact that they allowed their egotism to come out so clearly. Yates in particular spent a lot of his speech complaining that he had not been allowed to speak enough.[80] If only the Speaker had called him, it would not have been necessary to vote. He said in so many words that 'I have been told that abstention would be enough, but how would people know how I felt if I merely abstained? If the answer is, well, they know how you feel here, that may be true, but how would the country know how I feel?' As if the country was in the least interested in knowing what this very self-opinionated little man really felt about anything!

Another interesting feature was J. Hudson's speech, which I had feared would be damaging to us, he being well liked and respected, and able to turn on an emotional speech at will. But although he formally asked for mercy, he spent most of his speech attacking the six because

78 HG privately called them 'pacifists, egotists and crackpots': to Geoffrey Crowther, 22.11.54 (file P.80). Two were not pacifists: Sydney Silverman and S. O. Davies (Merthyr Tydfil).

79 John McGovern, M.P. for Glasgow (Shettleston), sat as I.L.P. 1930–47, Labour 1947–59. On this occasion he was congratulated in the press for 'having the courage of Mr Attlee's convictions'.

80 Victor Yates, a pacifist, was M.P. for Birmingham (Ladywood) 1945–69.

they had embarrassed him so much. As indeed they had. He pointed out that he was getting letters from all sorts of people, asking why he had not shown more courage.[81]

In the event the vote was not a bad one, better than on the whole I expected. It was a very well-attended meeting, and that may have helped us. We got, however, a very bad Press, partly because the Press always tends to take the side of the martyred minority, and partly because the loyal members of the Party did not go rushing off to the Press to give their view of what had happened. However, I have dealt with all this more fully, both in my letter to Cassandra, and in my 'Birkbeck Oration'.[82]

Document No. 11

HG to William Connor ('Cassandra') on party discipline, 26th November 1954

Personal   26th November, 1954

William Connor, Esq.,
DAILY MIRROR,
Geraldine House,
Rolls Buildings,
Fetter Lane, EC.4.

Dear Bill,

Last Thursday you wrote a piece in the *Mirror* called 'Servile Silence Please'. This is what my letter is about. I only hope it does not annoy you as much as your piece annoyed me. The best thing to be said for what you wrote is that it was short. My letter will be longer, and I apologise for that. But it is addressed to one person instead of five million.

I have little to say about the first two adjectival paragraphs – except just this. If you have to take disciplinary action, it is hard to see any other method more democratic than the one we use in the Parliamentary

---

81 James Hudson, a much better-known pacifist and temperance advocate, was M.P. Huddersfield 1923–31, Ealing W. 1945–50 and N. 1950–5. Members of the loyalist majority very often felt like this towards rebels with whose views they sympathised.

82 'In Defence of Politics' – a case for disciplined parliamentary parties, delivered on 2 December 1954 as the Birkbeck Foundation Oration at Birkbeck College, London.

Labour Party. It may be ponderous and clanking and clumsy, but it is honest. What else would you suggest? That the Leader of the Party should decide on his own? That there should be no procedure at all?

But to come to the main issue. What are you really trying to say? Is it that no member should ever have the Whip withdrawn? Or that this occasion was one which did not justify it?

If the first, consider please the implication. It means really that whatever any Member does, the Party cannot exclude him from its ranks. If you imagine that in these circumstances Labour Members would act together as a coherent body, I am afraid you are wrong.

The temptations to vote as you please are quite considerable, and would be impossible to resist if everybody knew that however they behaved, they could still be treated as perfectly good Members of the Parliamentary Labour Party.

Or perhaps you do not mind whether the Party votes together or not? Perhaps you think that each member should always vote as he pleases? In that case, exactly how are you going to have any kind of stable Government?

In our country we have a two-party system. It is often criticised because, since within each Party there must be many different views, the individual Member often has to suppress his personal outlook in favour of that of the majority of the Party. But it brings with it the inestimable blessing of stable Government – always assuming, of course, that a Government, whether Tory or Labour, knows that it can rely on its majority in the House of Commons. Yes, the Government must be sure of the votes of its supporters, that is the heart of the matter. And it's particularly significant when the two Parties are evenly balanced.

The other system operates in France. You have more parties and less discipline, and the government never knows whether they are going to survive from one day to another. Do we really want that? Do you really think that superior? There is also the American system, with even less party discipline, so that the government never know what they can get through Congress. Is that better?

Possibly you may say that while it is necessary for Members to vote for their own side while they are in Government, this does not matter in Opposition. But what kind of impression will the Opposition make on the country if its Members do not stand together? The electors prefer a Government which has stability. They will not support a Party if that Party cannot rely on the loyalty of its Members in the Division Lobbies. That, however, is exactly what would be said if in Opposition the Party did not vote together. God knows there is trouble enough in the Party already, but in the main, because of the threat of Party discipline, we do manage to vote together in the House.

Or perhaps you do recognise that there must be Party discipline, and that sometimes the Whip has to be withdrawn when the offence is serious, even with all the 'ponderous, clanking authority'; but ask, Why was it done in this case? I will tell you.

The Party came to a decision on the Paris Agreements by a clear majority of 52, not far short of 2 to 1. That settled the Party line. In the debate, people are free to speak as they like. There is really no attempt to control that, at least as far as back benchers are concerned (so long as they do not make personal attacks on their fellow members), because whether a Government survives or not is not a matter of speeches, but of votes.

I do not know whether you read the Hansard. I am tempted to send it you, but I expect the *Mirror* could supply it. You will find the point of view of the official Party put clearly and forcefully enough by the four official spokesmen – Attlee, Morrison, Denis Healey and myself. You will also find it supported by many others. You will find a different point of view expressed by Crossman and Silverman. So far, so good.

But then came the question of how should we vote. The decision of the Party Meeting was that we should accept the Agreements, and therefore it was made quite plain at an early stage that it would be a grave breach of discipline for anybody to 'challenge a Division'. It was known that a few people were likely nevertheless to do this. They were seen. They were asked, for the sake of preserving the unity of the Party, to sink their individual point of view, to be content with abstention. But it was evident that these pleas were not going to succeed with all of them. So we – the elected leadership – had to consider what decision the Party should take if a Division was challenged. We could not have avoided this decision. Members were continually coming up to us and saying, 'What shall we do if, etc.'.

There were only three possible courses. We could have said, 'This is a free vote, vote as you like'. This was never proposed by anyone. It would make nonsense of all the discussion in the Party, which had been about what line the Party should take. It was out of the question for the alternative Government of the country on one of the greatest foreign policy issues of our time. It would have reduced us to a complete rabble.

Secondly, we could have said that we must support the Government. In that case, a number of Members – 50, 60 or 70 – would have abstained, ostentatiously. They would have claimed the right to do this under what we call the 'conscience clause' of the Standing Orders of the Parliamentary Party. The rule is that an M.P. must accept the decisions of the Party, but may *abstain* on important issues of conscience. If we had decided on this course, we should certainly have exposed ourselves as again completely divided. Moreover, it is a course which we are always reluctant to take, because in our two-party system there is strong objection from all sorts of people to going into the same lobby with the Government.

Indeed – perhaps you did not realise – it is very unusual for the Opposition actually to vote with the Government. Abstention, according to Parliamentary convention, more or less implies 'acceptance' of what the Government are doing. To say, as you do in your article, that we 'preserved servile silence on one of the most fateful decisions of this century' is unintelligible to me, in view of the speeches made in the debate.

But voting is always regarded as a rather different matter, because of the need to try and preserve Party unity here. Do you know, for instance, that only 80 Tories voted for NATO when a division was challenged by some of the pacifists on that? Or that on the Bretton Woods Agreement the official order by the Tories was to abstain?[83]

The third alternative was to advise the Party to abstain. We did this reluctantly. Many of us would have much preferred to have voted in the Government Lobby. But we were prepared to sink our individual point of view in order to make it easier for other people to sink theirs. Many of them did so. Such different persons as Jimmy Hudson, the most noted pacifist in the Party (and incidentally the man who was most indignant with the seven people who voted), Hugh Dalton, the biggest German-hater in the Party, and John Hynd*, a persistent advocate for German rearmament, were all prepared to do so. I can see nothing wrong about this. It seems to me a normal act of teamwork. You would admit the need for teamwork in football, in war, in business, in the Press. Why don't you understand that it's also necessary in politics?

But our seven friends disobeyed the rule. Despite all the pleas; despite all the arguments, they insisted on forcing the Division and embarrassing the Party. Their egos had to come first.

Could we have ignored this? Or was there some lesser penalty that could have been imposed? Here I think you should know not only the rules of the Standing Orders of the Parliamentary Party, which lay down quite clearly and definitely that every member has to accept the decision of the Party meeting (apart from the right to *abstain* on conscience grounds), but you should also know that before a man even becomes a candidate for Parliament, he has to sign an undertaking saying that he

83 The Conservatives were divided on the Bretton Woods Bill, which made Britain a member of the I.M.F. and World Bank. On 13 December 1945 the House voted on the American loan, and then on the Bill; the Opposition abstained on both, but 74 Conservatives opposed the first and 47 the second (while 8 and 9 supported them). On the North Atlantic Treaty on 12 May 1949, its 80 non-Labour supporters included Liberals, Independents, and only about one-third of the Conservative M.P.s.

will, if elected, accept these Standing Orders. This is a promise he gives; and for most people it is a matter of honour to observe it.

If we had ignored this deliberate defiance of the Party decision, there is no doubt what the consequences would have been. Here was a most flagrant case where half-a-dozen people, after every effort had been made to stop them, deliberately decided to break their undertakings. The more honest among them admitted this. If we had let it pass, we should never have been able to enforce majority decisions again. Some others in the Party were hoping for this. They themselves were not prepared at this stage to defy the majority decision. They hoped, however, that the pacifists would do so, and would attract sufficient sympathy to make it impossible to withdraw the Whip. That having been done, they would then claim the right to do likewise whenever they thought fit to do so. And it would have been impossible to resist their claims.

Could not a lesser penalty have been imposed? There is really no lesser penalty except just a reprimand. There have been plenty of reprimands in the past. They had been ignored. This was a challenge to majority decision and to the leadership of the Party which could only have been met by withdrawing the Whip. Anything short of that would have meant the end of any serious discipline in the Party.

I apologise again for writing at such length. But it is a subject about which I feel very strongly, and could indeed write much more – about the people involved and their special characteristics, about the attitude of the solid, decent, inarticulate, loyal Members towards them, about the abysmal ignorance of the Press on the whole issue, and why they are ignorant. Oh what a wonderful, debunking, balloon-pricking story there is waiting for a really good political writer.

Why oh Why did our tough, down-to-earth, hit-the-nail-on-the-head, commonsense Cassandra miss this superb opportunity!

[Diary of 14.12.54 continued]

The next day, I lunched with Fred Bellenger and Henry [sic: Herbert] Bowden* (deputy Chief Whip). Fred made no bones about it. He thought it highly probable that I would be leader of the Party before long, and Bowden Chief Whip, and he wanted us to get together.[84] We were both extremely discreet. But Bowden did say, 'There is no doubt at all that what the Bevanites wanted was for these six to challenge the Party, and for the leadership to take no action, in which case we would have been

84 Bowden's promotion came in six months, Gaitskell's in twelve. On Bellenger – an East Midlands M.P. like Bowden – see above, p. 35 n.

open to every kind of challenge to the authority of the Party on any future action. We should then have been unable to enforce the Standing Orders at all'. This, said Bowden, 'is exactly what the b. Bevanites wanted.' He also thought that the withdrawal of the Whip would have a very healthy effect inside the Party.[85]

The Pensions Issue

This seems likely to be the next big fuss in the Party. So far as the Bill is concerned, there has fortunately been no real disagreement, because we all felt that the Government had loaded far too much on the contributors, and too little onto the Exchequer.[86] Mr AB has been making great efforts to lead the miners' group in this matter. He is obviously doing that chiefly in order to try and win their vote for himself for the Treasurership next year, but no doubt also to stage some kind of come-back generally. He is always looking for things to disagree with the leadership about, and he thought he had found one. In this case he was wrong, the wind being taken out of his sails at the Party meeting by Edith Summerskill and Douglas Jay, who were explaining the Executive point of view. He made the usual kind of speech, starting off perfectly all right, repeating what had already been said by the other two. But, obviously feeling that this was not enough, he then charged off on another line, suggesting that we should actually vote against a Second Reading. He had in fact managed to persuade the miners that we should do this, they not understanding that any amendment to a Second Reading Debate could only be put in the form of voting against the Bill. He was quite unconvincing, and before long was causing laughter by saying that he understood what people really felt. Whereupon, when he saw somebody laughing, he got very angry, and the speech tailed off into staple [stale?] repetition of what he had been saying before. He is like a toy engine which starts off all right, but

85 Losing the Whip is not as severe a penalty as it sounds, and the case of Aneurin Bevan (below, p. 383) was soon to show that in itself it did the offending M.P. little harm unless followed by expulsion from the Party. If continued into an election, it would mean an official Labour candidate opposing the M.P. in his constituency, but this has never happened; every M.P. deprived of the Whip since the war has had it returned before the next general election.

86 The National Insurance Bill raised pensions and benefits to match the higher cost of living since 1946, and increased contributions accordingly. Instead of a 'big fuss' it had a quick and easy passage: unopposed Second Reading December 9th, Third Reading 14th, House of Lords 20th, Royal Assent 22nd. Labour had moved amendments to shift some of the burden from contributions to the Exchequer. But, having pressed for the increases in benefits, neither the leadership nor the Bevanites sought to divide on the Bill or delay its progress.

always goes off the rails at a certain point. You can almost predict it, particularly if he encounters opposition.

There was an overwhelming vote against his proposal to vote on the Second Reading, and we did not even have to count. Even the miners were obviously rather shaken from the position in which he had led them.

Nevertheless there is still another danger ahead. The Bevanites are now running the line that we should have a non-contributory scheme. They are doing this quite unscrupulously, without revealing just how much of an increase in income-tax would be involved. Once again, Bevan is trying to bring off the double of standing up as the miners' leader, and at the same time attacking the Executive and the Parliamentary Committee. However, in this case he has to reckon with the T.U.C., who have so far been adamant against the non-contributory principle, and are likely to remain so. Moreover, I think that when the figures are made known and the repercussions on income-tax are realised, there would be rather less enthusiasm among many people for the non-contributory proposals. Nevertheless, all this involved more work and more strain upon those of us who have to think up the arguments, not only for attacking the Tories, but also for defending our flanks and backs against the Bevanites. It is a great bore.

Conversation with Winston [Churchill]

The other night I had to go to a function at County Hall in celebration of the Civil Service Centenary; as Attlee had a bad cold and Morrison was for some reason unwilling to go, I had to take their place and do the honours on behalf of the Opposition. After the speeches were over, we went into a sort of Reception Room – the Privy Councillors being carefully segregated from the Civil Servants (which was silly). Winston was sitting in an armchair with an empty chair beside him. After a bit he beckoned to me, and invited me to sit down, which I did. He then said how sorry he was that I had not been able to accept the two invitations to lunch he had sent me recently. I was surprised that he knew about such things, because they are mostly done by the Government hospitality people, but evidently he did. I in return said I was sorry Morrison was not there that evening, because of his old association with the L.C.C. and his interest in the Civil Service.

The P.M. then said that he thought Morrison had shown great courage over the German question, and added, rather surprisingly, that really one reason why he had said what he did about the famous telegram to Montgomery was to help Morrison. I was mildly astonished with this idea, because quite obviously it would do nothing of the kind, but as the old boy seemed to have it so much on his mind, I said I thought he need not worry very much, that after his apology there would not be much further trouble.[87] We then talked a bit about China and Russia. He said he thought China was greatly over-estimated. Did I know their figures for steel production? I said I thought about three or four million tons. He said, Less than that. I said I thought a lot of English people were really more inclined to like the Chinese than the Russians. Conversation was not very continuous, though quite cordial. He said again to me, as he said in the House, 'The only reason I am here is that I hope somehow or other to persuade Ike to . . . (pause) join with me in a high level meeting'. We spoke about his portrait. He was very frank about it. He liked Graham Sutherland and his wife, but he did not like the portrait at all. He thought it was quite unlike him. I asked what he was going to do with it. He said he thought of giving it to an Exhibition. He said he also thought of having another portrait done.[88]

87 In a constituency speech on 23 November, Churchill had referred to a telegram of May 1945 about stacking captured arms for possible reissue to German troops if it became necessary to oppose the Russian advance. It could not be traced and may never have been sent, as he recognised in his apology in the House: 535 H.C. Deb. 160–78 (1.12.54).
88 Graham Sutherland, O.M. (1903–80) had painted a portrait which Churchill notoriously detested, and which his wife eventually destroyed. He may never have known that the artist's name was proposed by Jennie Lee.

CHAPTER 7

BEVAN EXPELLED?

Editor's Note
Diary, 19 March 1955 to 2 April 1955
Documents: No. 12   P.L.P. meeting, 16 March 1955:
HG's brief for Attlee
No. 13   Crosland, Jenkins and Wyatt to HG,
21 March 1955
Editor's note on 1955

[Ever since the 1930s Bevan had been a prominent antagonist of the principal trade union leaders, and they had reciprocated vigorously. In the 1951–55 Parliament he had led a series of revolts which aroused indignation among Labour MPs. In 1952 he had instigated the first mass abstention in the lobby. At Westminster he had repeatedly offended his colleagues, and in the country he and his friends had kept fanning the flames of Labour's internal feud, and trying to spread them to the industrial wing. In the last twelve months he had challenged Attlee on the floor of the House over South-east Asia, and resigned from the Shadow Cabinet in a fit of petulance; declared war on the union leaders when he failed to win the treasurership; and done his best to reopen the German rearmament wound as soon as it began to heal. Within a week of being warned for that, and without even attending the meeting which decided party policy, he had again challenged the leader in public and staged an open split in the House. His views on the issues changed repeatedly, but in his hostility to the Party leadership he remained consistent. Shadow Cabinet members and back benchers alike, including many who had begun by sympathising with him, were growing increasingly indignant at his persistence in disruptive activities. No one at all defended his conduct, and by early 1955 even his admirers feared he was becoming a perpetual dissident, with nothing to offer a Labour Party preparing for power.

These were the circumstances in which Gaitskell became a belated but committed adherent of a rash attempt to expel Bevan from the Labour Party. Expulsion had never, except for those who seemed indistinguishable from Communists, been a political death sentence for Labour M.P.s: it was a sanction to enforce standards of cooperation with colleagues in the Party, on pain of going into the wilderness in an electoral climate deadly for Independents. A few like Jimmy Maxton, the lovable but futile I.L.P. rebel of the 1930s, had chosen the latter course; most, like Cripps and Bevan himself in 1939, had rejoined – usually quite soon – and later held high office. In 1955 the attempt to expel Bevan failed narrowly, but it brought about the change in his conduct which the threat of it was meant to achieve.

Attlee, who at the end worked successfully to frustrate the move to expel Bevan, could have prevented it altogether if he had made any serious effort to do so in time; as in 1951 over the Budget, and in 1952 before Morecambe, he abdicated the responsibility of leadership by allowing matters to rot before showing his hand. The others involved came out badly too: Bevan by conduct which even his friends did not defend, and his opponents by pressing for harsh measures which reunited the disintegrating Bevanites for a time, and aroused widespread resentment throughout the Party even among the most normally loyal supporters of the leadership. The affair shows how extravagantly politicians in the heat of battle can misinterpret the motives and exaggerate the faults of their temporary adversaries. But Gaitskell learned a lesson from his failure. With the expulsion crisis his Stalybridge period ended, and he resumed his briefly suspended efforts (*HG*, pp. 351-2, 361-3) at reconciliation with the modern Left.]

Saturday, 19 March 1955

The Bevan Crisis, 1955

The latest chapter in this long story opened soon after we resumed in Parliament following the Christmas Recess. It will be recalled that in the closing passage of his speech in the Foreign Affairs debate at the end of November, Attlee, to the astonishment of all of us on the Front Bench, suddenly veered right round and said that he did not see why negotiations with Russia should not be opened pending ratification, provided it was made quite clear that ratification was going to be carried through.[1]

I felt at the time that this was a most dangerous thing to say, and my forebodings were justified by later events. At the end of January Bevan went to see Attlee and suggested that the rift in the Party could now be solved if we were to put down an official motion in the order paper on the lines of the passage in his speech to which I have just referred – in other words we would have an official motion demanding talks with Russia pending ratification. Attlee mentioned this to a meeting of the Parliamentary Committee, which of course strongly objected to the idea, recognising it as an obvious attempt by Bevan to win prestige for himself in appearing to [be] swinging the Party against the earlier decision on the Paris Agreements. Even the opponents of German rearmament, such as Hugh Dalton, were wholly against having any motion on the order paper which would lead to a debate – a debate which could only re-open publicly the differences of opinion in the Party.

It was, on the other hand, recognised that in view of a recent broadcast by [the Soviet Foreign Minister] Molotov*, in which he appeared to go rather further towards considering free elections in Germany, the Government could be pressed to ask the Russians what their intentions

1 HG misremembered. It was in the debate on the Queen's Speech on 6th December: 535 H.C. Deb. 719-22.

were.[2] The matter was discussed by the Foreign Affairs Group, and a formal motion on these lines agreed. It had in fact been drafted by Denis Healey.

There was then a Party meeting [on 9 February], at which Bevan sought to commit the Party to the resolution which he proposed, and which asked for immediate talks with the Russians without waiting for ratification first. He made a moderate speech, but was quite effectively countered by Denis Healey. The issue was rather a confused one, and many people probably did not clearly understand what the precise difference was. It was all the more complicated by the question of whether or not we ought to have a debate. Eventually, however, Bevan's motion was defeated by 93 to 70. Despite this decision, a few days later the Bevanites were cleverly organising signatures for a motion on the order paper, not precisely similar to Bevan's, but with a lot of perfectly harmless stuff in it about disarmament, and bringing in only at the end the reference to immediate talks with the Russians. I was told that the first part of the resolution – the harmless part – was typed in double spacing, and the dangerous part crowded together at the end. I have no doubt a lot of people read it without really understanding it. After they had collected about 100 signatures Bevan and Mikardo informed the Chief Whip – which is required by the Standing Orders – and then proceeded to call a Press Conference and make the thing as public as possible.

This obvious flouting of the decision of the Parliamentary Party caused naturally a good deal of indignation among the majority. Although technically there had been no breach of the standing orders, it was certainly contrary to their spirit – immediately after a Party decision to put a motion on the order paper in the exact opposite sense. The situation was not helped by Bevan getting up after a business question and asking for time for a debate.

The Parliamentary Committee met and decided that we could not ignore this, and that accordingly we would have to have a Party meeting on a motion in general terms protesting against this kind of behaviour. The meeting was fixed for a Thursday evening [24 February]. As it happened we were having a debate on monopolies that day and I was therefore unable to attend, as I had to be on the Bench.

I was also unable to attend a Party meeting in the morning which took place on our attitude to the Defence White Paper. I will return to this later.

2 This incident is more fully described in Hunter (1959), p. 87, who says the Soviet broadcast did not make clear that the elections would be 'free'. Hunter, a confidant of the party leaders, gives in Chapters 9–11 his own very full and generally (though not wholly) accurate account of the whole crisis over Bevan's near-expulsion.

The evening meeting took place, and after about two hours or so resulted in a substantial majority – I think it was about 130 to 70 – in favour of the Parliamentary Committee.[3] Although, as I have said, I was not present at this meeting, the outcome seems to have been quite satisfactory. Attlee made an appeal for unity at the end, and other people, including Frank Tomney,[4] made a kind of appeal to Bevan to sink his personal attitude and join up loyally behind the Committee.

To return to Defence. This presented less difficulty than usual. For some time now we had been criticising the Government in the House for their failure to produce equipment. There were many reports of delays and mistakes, and Woodrow Wyatt had been particularly vigorous in challenging them on all this. Obviously therefore this was going to be one point of attack. But the main piece of information in the White Paper was of course that we were going to produce the Hydrogen bomb. Attlee had already, at a private meeting of the Defence group, said that he thought this was necessary, and had met with surprisingly little resistance. We were able to criticise the White Paper, however, because it did not show very clearly the kind of re-shaping of our Defence arrangements which would become necessary, nor did it give any indication of what the ultimate cost was going to be. We therefore drafted in the Committee a censure motion which was subsequently put on the order paper, and which I therefore need not quote here. It said in so many words that we recognised that pending general disarmament the Hydrogen bomb was a necessary deterrent to aggression, and then went on to deplore the failure of the Government to produce adequate value for the money spent on defence, their inability to produce a new pattern of defence organisation, etc. The motion in fact followed very much the line suggested by the Defence Group and it seemed probable that we would have no great difficulty about it. It was known that Crossman, for instance, and some of the other Bevanites had accepted that we must make the Hydrogen bomb.[5] Indeed, it was fairly obvious; the main argument for this was unwillingness to rely on America in such a matter. Since the Bevanites

3 The motion saying that such conduct 'makes a farce of Party Meetings and brings the Party into disrepute' was carried by 132 votes to 72.

4 The very right-wing Labour M.P. for North Hammersmith, who had won the seat from the crypto-Communist D. N. Pritt in 1950. He was refused re-selection by his local Party in 1979.

5 Their opponents did not realise that Bevan himself supported manufacturing the bomb at first, and that it was he who had convinced Crossman to do so: Crossman diary, 22.2.55 and 3.3.55. Pressed by Crossman and Wigg to support the leadership and by his wife to lead a new split, he told Crossman as they entered the chamber for the defence debate, 'I'm still completely in two minds which I should do': *ibid*. See *HG*, pp. 337–9.

were continually preaching independence of America, it was hardly possible for them logically to argue that we should not make the bomb ourselves.

As I have said, the Party meeting on this took place on the same Thursday [24 February] (but in the morning) as the discussion on the behaviour of Bevan and his friends in putting down the motion on talks with Russia. All went according to plan. Bevan himself did not bother to attend. The Committee's motion was approved with only about 20 opponents, most of them the well-known pacifists. There was also brought up another motion prepared by some loyal characters, F. Peart, Will Blyton, etc.,[6] asking the Government to go ahead with talks with Russia, excluding all reference to Germany. The Committee decided that they would be prepared to make this an official motion with some amendments, and put it down a little later on. This was apparently agreed unanimously by the meeting.

The Defence debate then took place in the following week. There was nothing very sensational on the first day except a long and impressive speech by the Prime Minister, chiefly about the Hydrogen bomb. On the second day, however, Bevan made a curious speech (once again, I was not present, as I had to be at a Savings Rally in Norwich, so my account is secondhand). There is no need for me to report it, because it is in Hansard, but it contained an impudent demand for the presence of Attlee and Morrison, who in fact were at the Parliamentary Committee meeting, and an interrogation as to whether our motion meant that the Hydrogen bomb would be used by us even if it had not first been used against us.[7] This was a fresh attack. It could hardly be described as anything else – and was of course made within a week of a Party decision which in fact ticked off Bevan for his last act of disloyalty.

At the Party meeting on the following day [3 March] in the evening, there was a strong demand for a special meeting on the subject, which was of course at once agreed, though it is important to note that the proposal at this stage came from the members of the Party and not from the

6 Bill (Lord) Blyton, a Durham miner, was M.P. for Houghton le Spring 1945–64. Fred (Lord) Peart, a teacher, was M.P. for Workington 1945–76; Opp. spokesman on education; P.P.S. to Min. of Agriculture 1945–51, Minister 1964–8, 1974–6; Leader of the House of Commons 1968–70, of the Lords 1976–9 (as Lord Privy Seal or Lord President).

7 Bevan, absent from the meeting which approved the motion, had had five full days to raise the question privately with his front bench, but chose instead to interrogate Attlee publicly in the House. The Parliamentary Committee knew of his speech and decided Attlee should not answer: Hunter (1959), p. 91. Sixty M.P.s followed Bevan in abstaining. For the Bevanite version of the incident in the House, see Foot (1973), pp. 461–4,

Committee, which had not in fact had time to consider the question. It was then agreed that the Parliamentary Committee should meet on the following Monday evening to consider what course should be proposed.

During the weekend there was a good deal of discussion about what could be done. Some people of course were for throwing Bevan out – Reggie Paget, for instance, who is by no means a strong anti-Bevanite, said on the Thursday night to me, 'It is no good, we can't go on. We must cut off the head'. Douglas Jay was more doubtful. I myself was doubtful. I thought that if we were to take the extreme step of withdrawing the Whip it might influence the nomination for Treasurership then going on in the Yorkshire coalfield.[8] I was also doubtful whether, since this was not technically a breach of the Standing Orders, we were in a strong enough position. The real right-wingers – Patrick Gordon Walker, Dick Stokes, etc., were of course for stronger action. When I went into the Committee on Monday evening [7 March] I retained an open mind.

I was very surprised when at the beginning of the meeting Chuter Ede, who of course had sided with Bevan on German rearmament, and is generally rather frightened of strong action, proposed at once that we should withdraw the Whip. I was even more surprised when he was strongly supported by James Callaghan, who had also been with Bevan on German rearmament and decidedly equivocal on many occasions. I spoke myself after these two, and said that I had, like them, come to the conclusion that sooner or later he would have to go, but I was not sure whether this was the right moment. I suggested the alternative was a strong censure motion, and I ended by commenting that the attitude of the leader of the Party was extremely important on this, since it was he who had been so grossly insulted. Jim Griffiths followed me with a long alarmed speech, very much opposing the withdrawing of the Whip. This did not surprise me, since Jim is always frightened of any trouble in the Party, and can be relied on to put a timid point of view. I had said, incidentally, in the course of my remarks that we must look ahead and consider what the Executive would do, and what the Conference would do, that I thought this would very much turn on the Miners' vote. Jim Griffiths picked this up and rather implied that we could not be in the least sure either of the Executive or of the Miners. Attlee then spoke and made it plain that he was against withdrawing the Whip, and preferred the censure motion. He did not give any particular reason, and did not speak at any great length.

There then followed a series of very strong speeches in favour of withdrawing the Whip: Morrison, Edith Summerskill, Philip Noel-Baker

8 The N.U.M. took decisions by area block vote, and Yorkshire was thought to be decisive. It voted for Gaitskell against Bevan in both 1954 and 1955.

and above all Shinwell, who made the most impressive speech of all. They took very much the same line, that we really could not go on like this, that the Party was getting demoralised, that people who went canvassing were asked whether they were for Attlee or Bevan, that we should never be right until we had got rid of Bevan, and what he had done now was the culminating point of a long series of acts, etc., etc.

Alf Robens, on the other hand, was rather against action; although sharing the views about Bevan expressed by the others, he favoured the censure motion plus a reference of the matter to the Executive. In this he was supported by Hugh Dalton, who said that on balance he thought that was the right course, though he too made it plain that he was definitely prepared to stand for the more extreme step.

In the middle there was a division. As I walked through the lobby, John Hynd (not a fire-eating anti-Bevanite) said to me, 'I suppose you will dodge it again'. I said something about possibly [?] a strong Censure motion. He was indignant and contemptuous. 'We must go the whole way.' He muttered something about even the Constituency Parties being angry.

I spoke again later and said that in the light of the discussion I had been persuaded that we ought to withdraw the Whip, but I said this must be regarded as the beginning and not the end. If we do start, we must go through with it.

I had forgotten to mention Harold Wilson, who said he regarded Bevan's conduct as indefensible, but as one would expect spoke in favour of the censure motion on the grounds that the extreme course would lead to immense trouble in the country with an election just ahead of us. The counter to this was of course that we were in for trouble anyhow. Attlee then took a vote, and there were 9 people for, i.e. Morrison, Whiteley [Chief Whip], Chuter Ede, Soskice, Edith Summerskill, Shinwell, Philip Noel-Baker, Callaghan and myself. Later Will Hall, who was out of the room at the time, indicated that he would have been with the majority, making it 10. There voted against Jim Griffiths, Harold Wilson, Hugh Dalton and Alfred Robens. When the vote had been taken, both Dalton and Robens said that they were quite prepared to go through with it, and that their difference had been a purely tactical one on which they did not feel strongly. Even Harold Wilson indicated that he would of course stand by the Committee. I do not recall throughout this that Attlee said anything. Certainly there was no statement which could be heard by the Committee generally. We then had a brief discussion about procedure, and resolved that we must keep it completely secret that night (which we did), but that a note should be sent to Bevan informing him of this, and asking if he were well enough to attend a Party meeting on the Wednesday. It was recognised that when he got this he would certainly let it out to the papers, and such proved to be the case. We were told at the time that he would probably be well enough, but that this was not certain.[9]

The thing leaked out in the course of the Tuesday afternoon. It cannot be said that there was any immense surprise in the Parliamentary Party, though of course there were strong differences of opinion. Again, I ought to add here that even at our meeting on Monday there had been talk about our resigning if we did not carry this, and it was certainly the general feeling that we would have to make it an issue of confidence. This had not been contradicted by Attlee or anybody else.[10]

On Wednesday evening [9 March] the Parliamentary Committee met again, and after dealing with the usual business we proceeded to consider the Bevan question once more. Alf Robens raised specifically the question of whether it was to be an issue of confidence, and the most vigorous views were expressed upon this. Attlee, if I recollect rightly, first of all seemed doubtful as to whether we should announce that we should resign if we were not supported, and to everybody's surprise first of all Morrison also seemed doubtful; but everybody else – Jim Griffiths and Harold Wilson were away – said in the strongest terms that it must be made absolutely plain to the Party that if we lost we would all resign. The Chief Whip said in fact that the Whips had said to him that that was what they intended to do. It was clear to all of us that this was necessary in order to win an adequate majority. The overwhelming view of the Committee appeared to be accepted by Attlee. It was also decided that he would have to present this statement, though to start with he said he did not much like the idea of doing this. We told him that of course he would have to do it.[11]

We had been told that Bevan was not well enough to come and we had therefore to fix the meeting for the following week. In fact it took place on Wednesday [16 March], exactly a fortnight after the defence debate in

9 Dalton's account confirms HG's in great detail (including some small points where Hunter (1959), pp. 95–6, had it wrong). He reports HG saying he thought 'that the Party would never do any good till B. was out . . . he lost us votes on balance'. He adds that several members felt that after the seven November rebels had lost the Whip for lesser offences, Bevan should not be treated differently; there would be 'an outbreak of rage from the loyalists': diary, 7.3.55.

10 Hunter (1959), p. 96, confirms that this was mentioned at the end of the meeting. Dalton is silent on that point; he says that earlier on it was suggested that a vote of confidence in Attlee should be moved, a proposal which he and others opposed.

11 Again Dalton (diary, 9.3.55) confirms in detail, including 'Opinion hardened, as we talked in favour of putting it bluntly – Bevan v. present leadership, Attlee down to Hall & Wilson. C.R.A. very unwilling (& H.M. too, perhaps hoping to succeed if C.R.A. alone resigned). Robens, Callaghan, H.G. & I say we're in a fight. Now we must go all out to win.' He also confirms Attlee's reluctance to speak, and (10.3.55) the Whips' intention to resign if defeated.

which Bevan had behaved so badly. The lapse of this week was important, and many people believed that the illness from which Bevan was said to be suffering was diplomatic.[12] We did not, however, get the impression either before or after the following weekend that there was any great weakening among the Party members. On the Friday Bevan put out a statement denying that he had challenged the authority of the leader and this led me into deciding to speak on the subject at Doncaster. I drafted something, read it over to Alf Robens and Douglas Jay (a somewhat earlier version to Hugh Dalton) all of whom agreed that I should say it.[13] It was quite well received by the audience, and indeed there was no pro-Bevan questioning at all at the meeting. There were of course other speeches throughout the weekend, some pro and some against.

The Parliamentary Committee met for the third time on the subject on the Tuesday morning [15 March]. The Chief Whip told us that according to his information if the issue were put as a plain matter of confidence between Attlee and Bevan then we hoped to get 160 people for Attlee and 76 for Bevan and 24 undecided.[14] Some of us said at the time that we thought these figures optimistic, even so it looked as though there would be quite a handsome majority. I had told other people that a majority of 30 or 40 was more likely, though I hoped for 50. It all turned on exactly how the question was put, and we knew of course both from previous experience and from his attitude at the Committee that there was a danger that Attlee would be too weak in his presentation.[15] On the Tuesday evening, many of us attended a silver wedding party of Morgan Phillips, the Secretary of the Party. I took the opportunity to tell both Tom Williamson and Sam Watson that they should speak to Attlee and

12 Including Crossman: diary 8.3.55. The Bevanites naturally used the delay to mobilise protest: Dalton diary, 8 & 12.3.55.
13 Dalton confirms that after Bevan's statement: 'H.G., who is speaking tomorrow at Doncaster & had not intended to refer to this, rings up, & we discuss what he might *now* say. We both think something emphasising B's conduct in the House on March 2nd. (As R. says, most people don't realise this at all)': diary, 12.3.55. [R. was Dalton's wife Ruth.]
14 Dalton confirms. 'W.W.[Whiteley] reports from his whips that 160 votes will be in our support & about 80 against. Total 293, but heavy sick list': diary, 15.3.55.
15 Dalton agreed. 'So it turns primarily on the Little Man tomorrow. If he's firm, he'll win, & by a fair majority . . . George Brown, to whom I speak by phone, . . . was sure we should win tomorrow, but by how much depends on how C.R.A. put it': diary 15.3.55. Dalton had thought from the start that the Parliamentary Party would vote only narrowly (if at all) to withdraw the whip, unless Attlee obliged the members to choose between himself and Bevan. Dalton originally opposed that course, but came round to it when his colleagues overruled his own preference for a censure motion moved so offensively as to provoke Bevan to resign of his own accord: *ibid.*, 7, 8, 9 & 10.3.55.

urge him to be absolutely firm. I know they did this. At the same time, of course, there were movements going on in the Party for compromise motions on the lines of votes of censure, and no doubt many of these people also saw Attlee.

The famous Party meeting on the Wednesday March 16th was described in such detail in the Press that it is hardly necessary to go over it all.[16] Attlee made a fairly strong statement, better than the worst, though not as good as the best that was to be expected, but he carefully avoided any indication that this was an issue of confidence. He did not say anything about resigning. He merely severely criticised Bevan's conduct, giving chapter and verse for this, and indicated that it could not go on and that the Committee had decided that withdrawing the Whip was the only possible course to be followed.

Bevan spoke next, and made a long, aggressive and fairly powerful speech in which he attacked the Committee (and particularly myself for my Doncaster speech). There was no sign of apology or assurance of one. In fact, he did not consider he had done anything wrong whatever. There was a certain amount of rather confused argument about the Hydrogen bomb, but in the main it was an attempt to show that he was really perfectly entitled to do what he had done and that the real villains in the Party were the people surrounding Attlee.

Clem then called Fred Lee and after him Maurice Edelman to move their compromise motion. Here again he did not do what the Committee had decided should be done. We had decided that if anybody moved a motion which included a statement of confidence in Attlee, then Attlee should say that he would not accept such a statement in a motion, because in fact our proposal to withdraw the Whip from Bevan was itself a question of confidence.[17] Attlee carefully refrained from doing this.[18] He refused to accept this phrase of confidence in himself in Fred Lee's motion, on the grounds that it was confusing the issue. So for the second time he was departing from what we in the Committee had expected he would say. There was a third departure when he was asked whether in fact, as had been reported in the paper, we would resign if we were defeated. Instead of saying Yes, he said 'We would have to consider our position'.[19] The debate went on, and need not be described here in detail.

16 Dalton's account confirms HG's fairly precisely: diary, 16.3.55. Michael Foot (1973, pp. 470–1) also writes of Bevan's 'frontal counter-attack . . . a defiant speech'. Crossman (diary, 16.3.55) and Hunter (1959, p. 100) put a much more moderate interpretation on it.

17 Dalton confirms that decision: diary, 15.3.55.

18 Crossman and Dalton diaries both confirm: entries of 16.3.55.

19 Dalton confirms this too (*ibid.*), but says it was Attlee's reply to Elaine Burton at the end of the meeting (see below, p. 373 and n. 22).

Tom Fraser* made a courageous speech on our side, and George Brown
made a courageous and effective speech. There were bad speeches from
Irvine for Bevan and Proctor for us, which lost votes.[20] The final speaker
Clem called was Percy Collick, who made the most effective speech on
Bevan's side, taking the line that Bevan of course had behaved very
badly, but that it was impossible to think of turning him out. It was in fact
a sentimental speech, and it was significant that Attlee afterwards described it as the speech that showed the best spirit. There was a great deal
of rancour in all the speeches, and much talk about disloyalties to Attlee.
Bevan began this, and others of course had to reply.[21] After Collick had
sat down – and he certainly turned some votes – Elaine Burton got up and
asked whether once again this was a vote of confidence, and whether we
would resign if we were defeated.[22] Attlee did not reply to the second,
but he did say 'Yes of course it is a vote of confidence – necessarily so'.
But his voice is weak, and I don't suppose that more than half the meeting
even heard this.[23] The result is well known.[24]

I mention one other passage. During the course of the debate it became
increasingly clear to all of us that Clem was not putting the issue as clearly
as we wanted. Herbert [Morrison] had whispered to him that he should
do so, but as this had no effect I passed round a piece of paper to the other
members of the Committee, and except for Jim Griffiths and Harold
Wilson (who was away) all signed it. It was put in front of Attlee. He read
it, but did not act upon it.[25]

20 Crossman gives much the same impression of the impact of the back-bench
   speakers. Tom Proctor, M.P. for Eccles 1945–64, had been HG's main rival at
   his selection conference for South Leeds in 1937.
21 Dalton is more explicit. Bevan denounced George Brown by name for
   canvassing against Attlee in 1947. Alice Bacon and Percy Daines promptly
   reminded Bevan that he had himself canvassed them in the same cause at the
   same time.
22 Collick was organising or assistant sec. of ASLEF (Locomotive Engineers)
   1934–57; M.P. Birkenhead 1945–64, Parl. Sec. Agriculture 1945–7. Elaine
   (Baroness) Burton was a consumers' champion, M.P. Coventry S. 1950–9.
   She asked her question because her local party threatened not to readopt her
   unless she voted for Bevan: below, p. 400 and n. 64.
23 Crossman says she asked to be told if it was a vote of confidence in Attlee, who
   'characteristically' replied, 'Well, if it's necessary, yes'. Hunter (1959, p. 101)
   says he 'snapped, "Yes, of course"'. For Dalton, who also refers to Attlee's
   'weak voice', see above, p. 372 and n. 19.
24 The votes were 124–138 against Lee's amendment, 141–112 to withdraw the
   Whip.
25 The paper is in the Diary. Dalton writes (16.3.55): 'This is signed by all Parly
   Ctee (except Griffiths to whom I don't show it, & by Wilson who is
   diplomatically absent) and also by W. Whiteley [the Chief Whip]. C.R.A.
   reads it & puts it on his desk. We hope he may be reserving a firm statement for
   the finish.' Crossman confirms that Harold Wilson 'had carefully arranged to

Summing up the result, I should say that the vote corresponded to the kind of speech that Attlee made at the beginning and at the end. He could have made an even weaker speech, in which case we should have been even nearer to defeat. If he had made a really strong speech, convincing the meeting that we were all resigning if we were defeated, I think there is little doubt that the majority would have been 50 or 60 instead of 30 for the withdrawal of the Whip.

It was an unfortunate feature of the whole business that the optimistic forecasts by the Chief Whip had leaked out into the Press. By no means everybody shared this view, and by no means everybody on our side was depressed by the result. They had expected a fairly narrow margin. After all, the Party always hates taking strong action against anybody unless they have committed some terrible moral offence or have in fact left the Party.

Immediately after the meeting I drove to the Russell Hotel, where I saw Sam Watson with Joe Godson, the Labour Attaché at the American Embassy. Sam was rather shocked by the figures. We discussed what should be done in the Executive. I then heard again very much what he had indeed told me the night before, namely that Tiffin (of the T.&G.W.U.) had been talking in terms not so much of straightforward expulsion but of asking for apologies and assurances from Bevan, and only if he refused to give these, expelling him. In view of the vote, Sam was at length inclined to the same point of view, and indeed so was I.[26] It seemed that we might either put the ball into Bevan's court, and if we could draft the apology, etc., in sufficiently strong terms there was a fair chance that he would refuse to sign.[27] This was, however, the first reaction only. I did not see anybody else much that day except Dick Stokes and some of his friends, who of course were all for the strongest action.

I however rang up Alf Robens that night. I should here insert something that really belongs earlier in this narrative. Hugh Dalton, Alf Robens and I had met in the previous week, after the second Parliamentary Committee meeting, and discussed what further should be done

---

be in Paris during today's Party Meeting': diary, 16.3.55. Wilson often managed to be away when awkward decisions were due: cf. above, p. 370.

26 Precisely the result Attlee was working for. Two days before the meeting he had told Leslie Hunter (1959, p. 99) that the Whip would have to be withdrawn from Bevan but he was 'resolutely opposed' to expulsion.

27 Dalton's tactics from the start: diary, 7 and 15.3.55. Presumably it was at this point that Hunter (1959, pp. 104–5) found HG very reluctant to expel: for the Bevanites had the same impression from the same source (Crossman diary, 21.3.55). Syntax as in original text.

to stiffen Attlee. Alf had been very shocked by his apparent weakness about putting the issue of confidence. We decided that I would draft a brief which Alf would then present as coming from him to Attlee, in the hope that he would follow this. This was duly done just two days before the Party meeting, and according to Alf was well received by Clem.[28] We also discussed who should be called on to speak, and having agreed on a short list, this too was given to Attlee by Alf. I mention this to show that he had played a rather prominent part in trying to see the thing through, although he had his doubts in the original meeting. In fact, we took exactly similar views. Doubtful to start with, having made the decision it was necessary to carry it through.

Document No. 12[29]

NOTES FOR CHAIRMAN FOR SPECIAL PARTY MEETING ON
WEDNESDAY, 16TH MARCH, 1955, AT 10.30 A.M. IN
COMMITTEE ROOM 14.

1.   Should Arthur Irvine and Bill Mallalieu persist in moving the Resolution recently submitted to the Parliamentary Committee, namely

> 'That in view of the obvious significance of the occasion to the Labour Movement the individual votes of Members attending the Parliamentary Party Meeting which decides the question of the withdrawal of the Whip from Mr. Aneurin Bevan shall be recorded for publication'

they have already been warned that this will be ruled out of order as being contrary to the established custom and practice of the Parliamentary Party.

2.   In view of the widespread press comment about the Standing Orders, it is just possible that some Member may raise a question with regard to them. It would appear that considerable confusion has been introduced because two quite separate Standing Orders have

28 Dalton records planning this in his flat on the afternoon of 10 March, and receiving HG's note on the 14th; Robens was to give it to Attlee 'who is always most sensitive to working men': diary, 10 and 14.3.55.

29 This brief, with minor amendments in HG's handwriting, is in his Papers, file P.97 (Bevan split). It was addressed to Attlee who, as leader, was also chairman of the P.L.P. (though not of the Labour Party itself).

been coalesced. The Standing Order under which the Parliamentary Committee have proceeded is Standing Order No. 2 which reads as follows:-

'2. The Parliamentary Party have the right to withdraw the Whip on account of things said or done by Members of the Party in the House. The Member or Members concerned shall have the right to be heard at the Party Meeting before the Whip is withdrawn'

and it is quite clear from this that the normal and proper procedure has been followed in the case of Mr. Bevan.

Standing Order No. 4, extracts from which have appeared in the Press deals with other types of disciplinary action other than withdrawal of the Whip [sic], and this reads as follows:-

'4. It is the duty of the Parliamentary Committee to bring before the Party Meeting cases of serious or persistent breaches of Party discipline, and in appropriate cases to recommend to the Party Meeting that the Member or Members concerned shall be reported to the National Executive Committee. The Member or Members concerned shall have the right to be heard by the Parliamentary Committee and the Parliamentary Party'.

It is no doubt the last sentence of this Standing Order (which is not the applicable one in this case) which has been used to introduce a certain element of confusion into the position.

3. The case against Mr. Bevan as elaborated at recent Parliamentary Committees is substantially based on his conduct in the House in respect of three quite separate matters.

4. The first of these arose in connection with the Foreign Secretary's statement on S.E. Asian Defence and Atomic Energy on the 13th April, 1954. The Chairman followed the Foreign Secretary and specified the essential factors in any Agreement on S.E. Asia, but after the Foreign Secretary replied briefly to his observations Mr. Aneurin Bevan interjected as follows:-

'Is the Rt. Hon. Gentleman aware that the Statement which he has made today will be deeply resented by the majority of people in Great Britain? Is he further aware that it will be universally regarded as a surrender to American pressure? Is he further aware that the interpretation that may be placed upon his statement, unless he clarifies it further, is that we shall assist in establishing a N.A.T.O. in South East Asia for the purpose of imposing European Colonial rule upon certain people in that area, and will he realise that if that course is persisted in it will estrange the Commonwealth members in that part of the world?'

It will be remembered that following this incident the question was raised later that day in the Parliamentary Committee as to the rules and obligations of Members of the Front Bench, and there was general agreement that though no Standing Order would be laid down it was desirable that those who sat on the Front Bench should speak with one voice.

5.   During the course of this discussion it was learned that a draft Motion signed by 'Bevanite' supporters, condemning the Foreign Secretary for the Statement he had made had been prepared and the Committee was asked permission for this to go on the Order Paper, but they objected to the tabling of such a Motion until the matter had been ventilated at a Party Meeting.

On the following day, Wednesday, the Parliamentary Committee resumed its consideration of the Eden statement, and the Chairman indicated the line he thought should be taken at the Party Meeting the same evening. After he had spoken Aneurin Bevan said that in view of the unpleasant incidents of the previous afternoon it would be unfair for him to take any further part in the discussions on this matter as after Easter he proposed to go to the back benches and he thereupon left the Parliamentary Committee.

The line suggested by the Chairman was approved by the Committee, and he was authorised to make a further statement to the Party Meeting deprecating the making of contradictory statements from the Front Bench after the Leader had spoken for the Party.

At the Party Meeting that evening the Chairman made a statement defining the attitude of the Parliamentary Committee to the S.E.Asian Proposals, and as arranged said it was 'unfortunate if someone got up from the Front Bench and put a different view from that expressed by the Leader of the Party'. Mr. Aneurin Bevan followed, and referred to what had happened at the meeting of the Parliamentary Committee the previous day and announced his resignation from the Parliamentary Committee. It is perhaps important to note that at no time previous to the statement of the Foreign Secretary had there been any discussion within the Parliamentary Party as to the attitude of the Party towards the SEATO Proposals, and yet despite this Mr. Bevan alleged that there was 'deep resentment in the country to the Minister's statement' and that it was universally regarded as 'a surrender to American pressure'.

6.   The next important difficulty arose over the proposed Motion on the Three Power Talks. The sequence of events in this case is that at a Party Meeting on the 27th January last Aneurin Bevan referred to a suggestion he had made to the Chairman shortly after the House had reassembled after the Christmas Adjournment that the Party should table a Motion asking for an immediate meeting of the big Powers in order to discuss the Soviet Declaration (then recently broadcast in Moscow and Berlin) but added that he did not wish to revive the old question of German Rearmament or Ratification of the Paris Treaties. With other Members he urged that a Special Party Meeting should be held in the early future to discuss his proposition further. It was reported by the Chairman that the Party's Foreign Affairs Group was meeting the following Monday (31st January) for the purpose of discussing the Soviet broadcast and the Parliamentary Committee would wish to have the opportunity of considering any views they might have, and he gave an undertaking that a Party Meeting would be called in due course to deal with the whole question.

The Foreign Affairs Group duly met and John Hynd on their behalf attended the Parliamentary Committee on the 2nd February and reported that the Group had passed a Resolution as follows:-

'That we press the Government to seek clarification from Russia as to their proposals for free elections in Germany under international supervision, but without prejudice to the continuation of the processes for ratification of the Paris Agreements'

After full discussion the Parliamentary Committee resolved

'That the matter should be pressed forward by further questions in the House, but it would be inadvisable to table any motion at the present time and the Party should be advised accordingly'

7.   The Special Party Meeting was held on the 9th February and was opened by Mr. Aneurin Bevan who moved the following motion, of which he had given notice:-

'That this Party Meeting endorses and reaffirms the statement made in the House of Commons on 18th November, 1954, by the Leader of the Party that talks with Russia concerning the future of Germany should be held as soon as possible; and instructs the Parliamentary Executive Committee to place a motion on the Order Paper to the effect that such talks should be initiated forthwith'

The Chairman in reply gave the reasons why the Parliamentary Committee felt that it was undesirable at this time to place any motion on the Order Paper, and explained that he and his colleagues had before them the considered views of the Foreign Affairs Group whose conclusions were expressed in an unanimous resolution. Taking all the circumstances into account, and particularly the changes which had recently taken place in the U.S.S.R. the Parliamentary Committee had come to the conclusion that a debate on the future of Germany would not be helpful at this juncture, but the matter ought to be proceeded with through diplomatic channels with a view to seeking clarification of the Soviet offer of free elections.

At the end of the discussion Mr. Bevan's Motion was put to the meeting and rejected by 93 votes to 70, and the recommendation of the Parliamentary Committee as expressed by the Chairman was carried on a show of hands.

8.   Having, however, failed to carry the Parliamentary Party in his efforts to secure the tabling of an official motion Mr. Bevan tabled a Motion of his own on the 15th February and attracted the signatures of over 100 members of the Party. In this connection the Chief Whip reported to the Parliamentary Committee on the 16th February that Mr. Aneurin Bevan and Mr. Ian Mikardo had seen him about the tabling of this motion and he had pointed out to them that it appeared to conflict with recent Party decisions, and he could not therefore give it his approval: but it was intimated to him that the sponsors having consulted him intended to proceed with the tabling of the motion whether approval was given or not, and the motion did of course subsequently appear on the Order Paper.

The Parliamentary Committee then had to consider the question of what should be done if, on the Business Statement, Mr. Bevan pressed for time to discuss his motion on the Floor of the House, and it was left to the Chairman to deal with it at his discretion. As anticipated, Mr. Bevan did in fact on the 17th February ask the Leader of the House if he was aware

> 'That there appears on the Order Paper a Motion in the names of more than 100 Members? If so, when does he propose to give time for its discussion?'

Having been refused he went on to say –

> 'Is the Rt. Hon. Gentleman aware that hon. Members have their privileges and rights and that if he finds no time for discussion in the ordinary way it might be that we should seek to use the procedure of the House to compel a discussion?'

9.   At the Party Meeting that evening several Members raised the question of the Motion and claimed that it should be made the subject for an early Party Meeting, and an undertaking was given that the matter would be discussed on Thursday of the following week. The Parliamentary Committee, therefore, at its meeting on Wednesday, 23rd February, considered what recommendation should be made to the Party Meeting the following day, and ultimately empowered the Chairman to make a statement which he did the following evening.

10.   At the Party Meeting on Thursday, 24th February, the Chairman expressed the Parliamentary Committee's concern at the position created by the tabling of the Bevan Motion. While not discussing the merits of the Motion he said that its tabling made a farce of Party Meetings, and he moved the following Motion on behalf of the Parliamentary Committee:-

> 'That for Members of the Party to take action in direct contradiction to a decision of the Parliamentary Party taken four sitting days previously makes a farce of Party Meetings, and brings the Party into disrepute.'

Upon this being put to a vote the Parliamentary Committee's Motion was carried by 132 – 72.

The Meeting closed with a strong appeal by the Chairman for Unity in the Party.

11.   The latest cause of complaint against Mr. Bevan which has brought matters to a head arose in connection with [the] last Defence Debate. In his speech in that debate Mr. Bevan saw fit to refer to the absence of the Chairman and Vice-Chairman of the Party from the Bench, though he must have known full well from his own experience that there was the regular meeting of the Parliamentary Committee in progress when he rose at 5.30 p.m. Moreover, in the very last paragraph of his speech he said –

> 'We want from my Rt. Hon. Friends, the leaders of the Opposition, an assurance that the language of their amendment moved on our behalf, does not align the Labour Movement behind that recklessness; because if we cannot have the lead from them, let us give the lead ourselves.' (Col. 2126)

Finally, when the Chairman had wound up the two days debate for the Party, Mr. Bevan rose in his place and pressed the following point upon him –

'There is a matter upon which hon. Members on this side of the House would like to have some clarification. The amendment which has been moved by the Opposition speaks about the deterrent effect upon aggression of the threat of using thermo-nuclear weapons. Paragraph 19 of the White Paper says that we must rely upon this, and that "the knowledge that aggression will be met by overwhelming nuclear retaliation is the surest guarantee that it will not take place". It does not say "nuclear aggression" but merely "aggression" of any sort. In the meantime General Gruenther has said that he has no choice but to use atomic weapons, whether or not the enemy does so. What we want to know is whether the use of the words to which I have referred in our Amendment associates us with the statement that we should use thermo-nuclear weapons in circumstances of hostilities, although they were not used against us.'

The Chairman answered him shortly and to the point, but when the division was called Mr. Bevan and 61 others abstained on the Party's amendment to the Government Motion.

It is important to note that at no time during the meetings called within the Party for the purpose of considering the Defence White Paper did Mr. Bevan seek elucidation of the point raised by him on the Floor of the House; nor did he approach the Officers either in writing or in conversation for any interpretation of the terms of the Party's amendment, and he did not give any notice of his intention to raise this point with the leadership in this debate.

On this matter of Defence special arrangements were made for the White Paper to be fully discussed and the Party line clearly settled. The White Paper was published on the afternoon of the 17th February, and the Defence and Services Group met to consider it on the 22nd February. This was attended by 25 Members, and there emerged from it an expression of opinion which was conveyed to the Parliamentary Committee by John Strachey at its meeting on the 23rd February. After a very full discussion the Parliamentary [Committee] drafted an official Amendment in the following terms:-

'That this House regrets that the Statement on Defence, 1955, while recognising that thermo-nuclear weapons have effected a revolution in the character of warfare, and that until effective world disarmament has been achieved it is necessary as a deterrent to aggression to rely on the threat of using thermo-nuclear weapons, fails to make proposals for the reorganisation of Her Majesty's Forces and of Civil Defence; to indicate what future defence expenditure may be called for; or to explain the grave admitted deficiencies in the weapons with which Her Majesty's Forces are at present furnished, in spite of the expenditure of some £4,000 millions for Defence purposes over the past three years.'

This draft amendment was submitted to a Special Party Meeting on Thursday, 24th February, when a full discussion took place. In the course of that meeting a Motion by Mr. George Pargiter[30] 'That the Party refuses to assent to the Government proposal that Britain should manufacture the Hydrogen Bombs' was discussed, but upon being put to the vote was rejected overwhelmingly on a show of hands. After an alternative Motion proposed by Reg. Paget had been rejected by the Party, the amendment brought forward by the Parliamentary Committee was put from the Chair and approved with one dissention. [sic: dissentient?]

At this most important Party Meeting on this very important subject Mr. Bevan was not present. Had he doubts as to the meaning of the amendment he could have sought enlightenment at that Party Meeting. Moreover the amendment was tabled on the same day as the Party Meeting, i.e. Thursday 24th February, and was on the Order Paper and in the National Press the following day. Mr. Bevan had, therefore, Friday, the subsequent weekend, and Monday and Tuesday the following week during which he could have taken steps to bring his point to the Leader of the Party had he desired to do so. It is difficult to imagine that he did not have his anxiety about the interpretation until the day he rose to speak in the House.

Diary, 19 March 1955 continued

Returning now to the period after the Party meeting, I had a talk with Alf on the Thursday morning [17 March], and we decided that we had better go and see Attlee. We had in mind both expressing our surprise that he had not put the confidence issue more clearly at the meeting, and also testing him out about the Executive. Alf, I think, was more concerned to find out what he was going to do in order that nobody else should get out of step, and I myself wanted to urge that he should take a strong line. It so happened that it was the Silver Jubilee of the *Daily Herald* and a great lunch took place at the Connaught Rooms. I had the opportunity of

30 George (Lord) Pargiter was an A.E.U. M.P., a pacifist, and on the Middlesex County Council 1934–65. M.P. Spelthorne 1945–50, Southall 1950–66.

talking to some of the Trade Union leaders beforehand, and I sat between Tom Williamson and Alfred Roberts.[31] I talked at lunch with Tom who was, as I expected, extremely strong for expulsion. I told him that I thought it would be necessary for him and Deakin to see Attlee.

Later that afternoon Alf Robens and I went to see Attlee. The interview took place in two parts, from about 5.15 to 5.40, and for half an hour or so later after the Party meeting, from 7 to 7.30.

The upshot of it was something like this. Attlee appeared surprised when Alf criticised him for not putting the issue of confidence sufficiently strongly. He thought he had done so, and did not agree that if in fact he had made it perfectly plain that we would resign there would have been a much more favourable vote. On the Executive he refused to commit himself at all, but it was plain that he was rather against expulsion. At the end he said, 'It might be a good idea to keep him on a string for a few weeks and then see'. I expressed my strong dissent from this, and said I thought it would be disastrous to delay things in that way. I told him that Morgan Phillips had said that if in fact he [Bevan] was not expelled it would be a most dangerous position. He would be free to speak anywhere at Party meetings, to stand for any position on the Executive, to have all the advantages and none of the disadvantages. I told him that Alice Bacon said to me that if in fact he was not expelled she would move that the Whip should be returned to him at the next Party meeting. This was in fact much the same point of view as M. Phillips. I warned him that I was at present engaged in delicate negotiations with the Unions with a view to raising the income of the Party by 50 per cent., and that this would be affected by our decision on this matter.[32] But anything we said would not move him at all. I suggested at one point that we might consider suspending him from membership for six months. He said that would be worth looking at. It was an unpleasant interview. He was rather unfriendly, and at one point rapped out, 'You made me the spearhead of a policy in which I did not believe'. Whereupon we both said, 'Why didn't you make that plain at the time and take a strong line?' 'Well', he said, 'we took the vote.' I said, 'You don't take a vote in the Cabinet. Surely if you had really felt that way you should have made it plain that you were not prepared to go through with it'. In fact, what he was really saying was that he felt the Committee had pushed him into an untenable position which he did not want, while of course we – and I suspect other members

31 Sir Alfred Roberts (1897–1963) was Gen. Secretary of the Nat. Ass. of Card, Blowing and Ring Room Operatives 1935–62; on the T.U.C. General Council, 1940–63, chairman of its International Committee from 1958; Director of the Bank of England from 1958.
32 See below, p. 387 n.

of the Committee – feel that he had let us down by not carrying through the policy which he had first of all accepted.[33]

I tried at one point to turn the conversation on to bigger issues. What did he think was going to happen in the future? Did he really want Bevan to be the Leader of the Party? 'Of course not', he said, 'but I don't think he wants to be.' This astonished both Alf and myself. We of course pointed out that if no action were taken against Bevan it would be a victory for him, but none of this seemed to make any impression on Attlee. He said at one point he thought I was 'obsessed' with the fear of Bevan & Bevanism. As we went out, Alf said to me, 'Well, it's quite obvious he is not going to do a thing'. Earlier in the afternoon, George Brown, Patrick Gordon Walker and Dick Stokes had been to see him, and had been received with frigid hostility.

I was naturally very depressed by all this, but later went to see Sam Watson at the Russell Hotel, whom I found with Jim Bowman, now Vice President of the Coal Board, and Joe Godson.[34] We went over the whole ground again. Sam told me that he had come to these conclusions:-

(1) That we must expel Bevan.
(2) That Attlee must at least support this – that we could not move further than Attlee.

He had given up his earlier idea of asking for an apology. After much discussion we decided (a) that Attlee ought to be asked to the dinner on the 21st – the following Monday – which we were having with the Union leaders on Party finance. This would enable the Union people to bring the maximum pressure to bear upon him. (b) that I should try and arrange that Deakin, Tom Williamson and possibly Ernest Jones should see Attlee privately on Monday. (c) that while we should still press for expulsion, if Attlee was adamant on that, then we should try the proposal that had been made to him: namely, suspension for six months. This had the advantage that he would be out of the Party at the moment, and that we could consider in the light of his behaviour in September whether to let him back or not. It was quite likely he would behave badly in the

33 Leslie Hunter records (1959, p. 98): 'he snapped at Gaitskell, "You wanted to expel him, I didn't. I was against it from the first, but you insisted, and now look at the mess we're in". Gaitskell and Robens . . . were amazed at this outburst, particularly as they had both tried to discuss the question with Attlee before the fatal meeting and had been given no guidance at all. Both had been prepared to take a lead from him had it been offered.'

34 Bowman had earlier been Watson's principal ally as leader of the Northumberland miners. Godson, Watson's close friend (see Biographical Note), thanks to his trade-union post was like many labour attachés seen as representing his country's workers rather than its government. But Gaitskell came in time to feel that he was involving himself too deeply in Labour Party affairs.

meanwhile, but if he did not, we would then be letting him back, and we avoided, therefore, the risk of defeat at the Conference. (d) the Tiffin plan would be only a bad third.[35]

Accordingly on the following day I saw Deakin and Williamson, put the position to them, and secured their agreement to see him – Deakin saying that he would try and get hold of Ernest Jones. Deakin himself was very reasonable, and quite realised the dangers of the situation, and was rather inclined to favour my six months' suspension idea. Tom was much more vehement, and it took me some time to persuade him even to consider anything short of flat expulsion. But he was extremely friendly and said finally, 'Well, even though I don't really agree I will do whatever you want'. Although Morgan Phillips was away in Cornwall, we managed to get through to him. He entirely agreed with the idea of asking Attlee and his young personal assistant, Gwilym Williams, telephoned to Attlee about the Monday night. Although we know that he is free, Gwilym told me that he would not commit himself, and was rather 'testy'. I said that this did not surprise me.

Diary, 25th March 1955

(The Bevan Crisis continued)

On the Monday I had lunch with Morgan Phillips. He had been away most of the weekend in Devon and Cornwall, so I brought him up to date with the position. We talked over the possibilities, and he was inclined to accept as the best hope the six months' idea. He had arranged to see Attlee, and I urged him to impress upon him the dangerous consequences of a situation in which the Whip was withdrawn but Bevan remained a member of the Party. He did in fact see Attlee later on in the afternoon, but evidently made no impression upon him, and came away from the interview as gloomy as we had been from ours on the previous Thursday.

When I got into the House, Attlee asked me to come and see him. He was sitting with Jim Griffiths. He wanted to know about the dinner that night. Were there really as many people there as on the list (which he handed to me)? I explained the reasons for the dinner and how far we had proceeded. He then said he thought it was far too dangerous for him to come. He would very likely be seen there, and it would be said either that they were all ganging up, or that the Unions were threatening him that if he did not go for expulsion, they would withdraw the funds. There was force in this argument, and I did not resist it, simply saying that if he felt

35 The Tiffin plan (above, p. 374) was to ask Bevan for an apology and assurances, and expel him only if he refused.

like that he had better not come. We then had a further brief word about the Problem. I once more suggested the six months [suspension of Bevan's membership].

'You mean', he said, 'out of the Party for six months?'

I said, 'Yes, certainly'.

He brushed it aside, muttering something about, 'No, that was no good'.

Later on in the afternoon we had an Election Sub-Committee. Jim Haworth was sitting there alone when I walked in, scribbling in a little notebook.[36] (He is, of course, M.R.A. [Moral Re-Armament].) I asked him what he was doing. He said 'I am drafting a resolution for Wednesday's meeting'. I had of course heard that he wanted the 'apology and assurances' outcome.

After the meeting, and before going to the St Ermin's Hotel for the dinner, I saw Herbert [Morrison] and Edith [Summerskill] and explained just how bad the situation was, viz. that Sam [Watson] was not prepared to go beyond CRA[Attlee], CRA was still hopelessly weak, and that the only hope still existed in persuading him to go further. Herbert, who had also been away for the past few days in Rome, was obviously prepared to go against Attlee. He would prefer straightforward expulsion rather than accept the six months plan. I said that if we could get Attlee on our side this way, it [suspension] would be well worth while. Edith was astonished to hear about Sam's attitude, and very indignant about Clem.

I then went along to the Hotel, where the Union chiefs were already gathering. I found that Arthur Deakin and Tom Williamson had not seen CRA. I said I still thought it important that they should do so. We got hold of Ernest Jones, and it was found that they were all free in the morning. Morgan [Phillips], with some reluctance, agreed to fix up a meeting. He thought CRA would probably not see them. I said that was inconceivable. He could not refuse to see the leaders of the three biggest Unions.

The dinner went very satisfactorily as far as its main purpose was concerned, i.e., future financial problems. We finally got agreement on our plan for raising the affiliation fee to 9d, and agreed that there should be a special meeting of Trade Union Executives before the T.U.C. in September, so that we could try and get agreement from them ahead of the Party Conference.[37] When the dinner broke up officially, there was

36 A trade union member of the N.E.C., 1953–5.

37 The affiliation fee had been only 6d. (2½p.) and was less in relation to wages or to purchasing power than before the war. The increase, though far from adequate, thus raised the Party's trade union income by 50%, and was ratified by 80 union executives at Southport in September 1955: *HG*, pp. 349–50.

then a good deal of to-ing and fro-ing. It is hard to say when the change took place. It may have been before dinner, as a result of Arthur and Tom talking to Sam, but it became clear within the course of half an hour that there was a strong move for carrying the expulsion even against Attlee if this was necessary.[38] Morgan Phillips was active, and so was Bill Webber*. MP came over to me and said 'I think it is going to be all right. Bill is going to have a go at Jim Haworth.[39] Will you tackle Gooch?*' However, we were neither of us successful. Moreover, the idea of actually going against Attlee was such a new one that it was difficult to get it across quickly.

Walking away, however, with Bill Webber and Morgan Phillips, it was clear that they were both anxious to try it, so I drew up a list, and it then transpired that even if we lost Irwin and Stafford (both Unions being Communist-dominated), Haworth and Gooch, the M.R.A. boys, Clem [Attlee] and Jim Griffiths, together with the six Bevanites, we might still carry it against them 16 to 12, counting Edith [Summerskill]'s vote.[40] The crucial question, therefore, was whether we could get assurance from the 16 persons that they would vote even against Clem for expulsion.

I went home a good deal more encouraged and determined to try it out.

I spoke next morning to Hugh Dalton, who has been excellent throughout all this, and sought his advice. Did he think it wise, I asked, to carry the expulsion against CRA even on a narrow majority? He thought on balance yes. He was very discouraged with CRA's behaviour.

I lunched that day with Tom Williamson, and heard from him of the interview they had had with CRA that morning. I gathered that they were very firm and strong, and just put across their point of view without asking

38 Hunter claims (1959, p. 105) that Deakin told him that he and others had warned HG at this meeting that if Bevan were not expelled, 'the unions would . . . certainly not . . . give more money to the party and might decide to withhold some of their current contributions': Hunter attributes HG's decision to this threat. HG never concealed that the Bevan affair and the financial negotiations affected one another; he said so candidly to both Attlee (above, p. 383) and Crossman (below, p. 392 n.). But Hunter's story cannot be accepted. First, HG's candour to others shows that this diary account would have been very different if such a threat had been made or believed in. Secondly, he had found Deakin much less determined on expulsion than Hunter suggests, or than Williamson was (above, p. 385). Thirdly, Deakin had never discussed reducing the contributions either with his own executive or with Williamson whose union was involved along with his own; Williamson denied the whole story with the utmost indignation and others who knew Deakin found it implausible in that form. For a possible explanation, *HG*, p. 343n.

39 Bill Webber was general secretary of Haworth's union, the Transport Salaried Staffs.

40 Gooch (1947–61), Irwin (1947–56) and Stafford (1954–7) were trade union members of the N.E.C., coming respectively from the agricultural workers, the electricians (who were wholly Communist-dominated) and the railwaymen (who were not). Edith Summerskill was chairman in 1955.

him much. They had come away with quite a favourable impression. They thought he ought after all to be all right. I was encouraged by this too, but remained sceptical.[41]

On going to the House I saw Herbert [Morrison], and explained to him what had happened the previous night. We went through the lists, and he undertook to see Peggy Herbison*, Skeffington and Burke.[42] I said I would try and take care of the T.U. members.

It so happened that afternoon that we had a Finance Committee, and it was easy once the proceedings were over for the members to remain behind and discuss tomorrow's meeting. I discovered that Harry Earnshaw (Textiles) was absolutely firm. He said, 'Yes, I have made up my mind, whatever Clem does'. The same applied to Davies (Iron and Steel). I thought it was also true of [George] Brinham, who is a nice chap, and saved the Party on German Rearmament last year.[43] He sat there in a group of us, including Sam Watson, Jock Tiffin, Jack Cooper* and Morgan Phillips, while we were making these plans. But I did not actually put the question to him directly. It was difficult to convince the Union people that Clem really was going to oppose expulsion. They kept on saying, 'The politicians ought to give a lead. Clem ought to do this.' I said firmly to them, 'Forget it – he will not do it. The best we can hope for is that he will follow on behind if we give a lead'.

The question then arose as to who was to propose it. I suggested Jack Cooper, but he was unwilling. Tiffin equally so, because the election in his Union was taking place. It was obviously impossible for Herbert or myself. Then I suddenly thought of Percy Knight.[44] Jack Cooper and I went downstairs where he was waiting. We walked through the lobby and

41 Years later Lord Williamson recalled that Attlee had been altogether unforthcoming, and would discuss nothing but the weather: interview.
42 Representing, respectively, the women's section, the socialist societies (Arthur Skeffington was a co-operator), and the trade unions (Wilfred Burke was from USDAW, the Distributive Workers). He was M.P. for Burnley 1935–59, Assistant P.M.G. 1945–7, and on the N.E.C. 1944–56. Skeffington sat for W. Lewisham 1945–50, Hayes & Harlington 1953–71 (was an under-secretary, 1964–70). He was on the N.E.C. from 1953–8, 1959–71 when he died.
43 The platform won its narrow majority on German rearmament thanks to an unexpected switch by Brinham's union, the Woodworkers. ('They wanted to be the Cabinet-makers', it was said.) Brinham was on the N.E.C. 1952–63, Earnshaw 1942–62, and Dai Davies 1953–67, eventually as Treasurer.
44 Cooper represented the General & Municipal Workers 1953–7, and Knight the Seamen, 1947–55. Tiffin was a candidate for the general secretaryship of the Transport Workers at a ballot due shortly, for Deakin was close to retiring age; Hunter claims that he voted for expulsion only because Deakin threatened otherwise to oppose him at the election (expecting still to be in office at the time): Hunter (1959), pp. 105–6. In fact, Deakin died on 1 May and Tiffin soon afterwards.

Jack said to him jovially, 'Well, Percy, we have decided that you will have to move the expulsion tomorrow'. To my surprise and delight, Percy said, 'Of course I will – I have every intention of doing so. I am not going to miss this chance of getting that so-and-so out'. So Jack then said he would second. I thrust into Percy's hands a long letter I had had from John Murray, of which I had had copies taken, which would serve as a bit of a brief, and we then parted.[45]

I then went back upstairs to the Committee Room, where they were waiting, and told them of Percy's decision.

Greatly encouraged, I came down again and ran into Alice Bacon, who said, 'I have got rather bad news, Jean Mann is wobbling. She wants him expelled, but she seems to want it done indirectly – the apology business, etc. I told her she was being very silly, and I thought I convinced her.[46] I also hear', she said, 'from Skeffington, that Brinham is unsafe.'

I had shortly before run into Wilfred Burke, who said, 'I have to see the President and Secretary of my Union tonight (USDAW is a Bevanite union),[47] but', he said in a low voice, 'it will make no difference. I am quite used to this.' I thought he was splendid and courageous, for all his being so quiet.

The day ended, as far as I was concerned, with my telling Edith the better news, and warning her that Percy Knight must get in straight away. There were two doubtfuls – Brinham and Jean Mann, but I could not believe Jean Mann would not be all right. She has been such a violent enemy of Bevan's, and Brinham too I thought, in the light of his behaviour last year, and his relations with the other Unions seemed sound.

That was how it rested when the meeting began on Wednesday morning.

It all went very much as I expected. I had warned all those I had seen – most of the sixteen – that we would have hurdles to get over. There would be Jim Haworth's amendment – Clem was almost certain to say that we must see him, which I thought would be fatal because of the delay. And then there would be the main issue. My forecast was exactly right, except that there was one new side issue brought in. It became known in the course of the evening that [Clem] Attlee had seen Bevan. I was afraid that

45 This letter is in HG's Papers, file P.97 (Bevan split). John Murray, an industrial consultant active in Lancashire Labour politics, was president of the 1944 Association (of pro-Labour businessmen), and a friend of Gaitskell's.

46 Alice Bacon and Jean Mann were both representatives of the women's section (elected mainly by trade union votes) and strong anti-Bevanites.

47 The President, Walter Padley*, was a Bevanite (and an M.P.); the Secretary, Alan Birch*, was not. USDAW had a left-wing but non-Communist tradition, and among the big unions was the one where the officials had least direct influence.

this meant some new development, that Clem would spring a surprise. But it was not so. After Knight had moved the expulsion without making a speech, Clem at once intervened to say that Bevan had come to see him, but only for four minutes, to say that if he were expelled he would raise the question of Privilege. This was apparently the sole reason for his visit to Attlee. I had heard of this, and taken the precaution of consulting Frank Soskice, who had also been called in by Attlee, and who told me that although there might be a prima facie case, it was almost inconceivable that it could be treated as privilege. There was a brief discussion after Clem had explained the situation (without first of all telling them of Soskice's advice until I mentioned it).[48] But there was a strong reaction from all the non-Bevanites, who were justly indignant with Bevan for trying this bit of blackmail at the last minute. The discussion then proceeded. Jack Cooper made a strong and impressive speech, going to some extent into Bevan's past. Haworth then produced his amendment, which was a fantastic affair, more or less preventing Bevan from ever saying anything at all anywhere. It went in fact much too far, and nobody could have seriously expected him to sign it. He was supported by Gooch. It was, I think, at this point that Attlee intervened, as I had expected he would, saying that we ought to see him, and proposing that we should do so. He did not speak for long, and left it to Jim Griffiths, who followed him to make the usual rather passionate and alarmist speech about the consequences in the country if we expelled him with an election coming up, etc., etc.[49] I think Herbert [Morrison] came next, putting the case for expulsion quite reasonably, though not perhaps replying adequately to Attlee's amendment. He was followed by Sam Watson, who was excellent as usual, forthright and absolutely firm. There were then a series of Bevanite speeches. Tony Greenwood (who made the best for them), Mikardo, Barbara Castle, Driberg and Crossman. There was little discussion of Bevan's behaviour. It was all mostly about what the consequences would be. There was a good deal of talk as well about the attitude of the Parliamentary Party, and claims were made that they were really not in favour of expulsion. I then spoke more or less winding up for our side. It was obvious that the Haworth amendment was going to be rejected, and I did not waste much time on this, except to say that the difficulty in drafting was not an accident, and that I believed it was

48 Attlee told Crossman beforehand 'that it was very serious indeed, since it was a prima facie case': Crossman diary, 24.3.55 (they talked on the 22nd).
49 In Crossman's account: 'Attlee weighed in. He did it with great boldness, saying that the Parliamentary Party had given no mandate for expulsion and that the Conference would not carry it, probably, if the N.E.C. had failed to hear Nye and try conciliation. He was immediately supported by Jim Griffiths on exactly the same line': diary, 24.3.55.

practically impossible to get any form of words which meant anything, and which he could reasonably be expected to sign. I then opposed the Attlee motion on the grounds that delay would be fatal, and that we must face it that if we accepted it, it was almost certain that we would not expel him. Again, the same difficulty arose about assurances that would mean anything. Then I said that on the main issue I believed that on this occasion the assumption in the Parliamentary Party had been that he would be expelled, whereas on the previous occasion when we tackled the seven people who voted wrong on German Rearmament, the assumption was that nothing further would be done. At this point Attlee intervened, saying 'I object to ex-parte statements like that'. I retorted 'If it is an ex-parte statement, it is in reply to other ex-parte statements. I am simply giving my impressions of the Parliamentary Party'.[50] Attlee replied, 'Well, at any rate so far as I am concerned I have never assumed expulsion'. He also said it was a pity perhaps that we could not relate the whole proceedings in the Parliamentary Party. I agreed with this, and said it was a pity we could also not relate the proceedings in the Parliamentary Committee. I then went on with my statement, pointing out that I thought that if we did not expel him the Tories would certainly claim that he was indispensable, and indeed the future leader of the Party & that they would use this against us in the Election. I admitted that we should lose some support in the constituency party membership, but I thought this would be balanced by the gain from marginal voters. Percy Knight then spoke very briefly, and the vote was taken. Fourteen for Attlee's amendment and thirteen against.

The uncertain links had both broken. Jean Mann had indeed spoken early after Attlee supporting the motion, though making it plain that she was in favour of expulsion, but thought that we must go through the motions with Bevan of asking for assurances. Brinham was the other who voted for the Attlee motion.

Edith [Summerskill as chairman] could have given her vote and then given a casting vote against Attlee, but I think wisely she refrained from doing so. I have also forgotten to mention Alice Bacon, who spoke early on, and I think after Jim Haworth and Gooch, and very effectively too. Brinham came up to me afterwards, and half apologetically said he was sorry, but he was under great pressure from his Union. They were worried about their conference this year because of the changeover on German rearmament last year, and I gathered that he could not carry a pro-Bevan-expulsion attitude as well.

50 HG's impression, rather than Attlee's, is supported by Hunter (1959), p. 109, as the view of 'most of the political correspondents who had questioned M.P.s after the vote'; and even by *Tribune*, 25.3.55. But the same M.P.s might well have changed their view subsequently.

There was one curious passage which I should have mentioned earlier. On the Tuesday morning Crossman rang up and asked if I would see him. I thought on the whole it was best that I should. So on the understanding of complete secrecy, I agreed to go and have a drink with him at his house at 7.15. I went there and we talked for about three-quarters of an hour. Naturally his purpose was to urge me not to support the expulsion. He used pretty familiar arguments. The only interesting things about the conversation were that he said at one point that what we really wanted was a left-wing without Nye [Bevan], and a right-wing without Deakin and Tom Williamson. He also said that (presumably if Nye was expelled) Harold Wilson would run for the Treasurership. He (Dick) thought that this was a foolish move, and I agreed. It was quite a friendly talk, though naturally I was very much on my guard. He regarded Nye in a kind of mild pitying slightly contemptuous way. It was clear to me that they were obviously fairly near breaking point, but equally he complained about *Tribune*. In fact, he said we made a great mistake because they were all in bits and pieces, but this move against Bevan had solidified them again. I said we had to think of the morale of the right wing as well, and that they were becoming increasingly exasperated. He thought that we greatly underestimated the power of the constituency parties, and was, I think, genuinely shocked when I said that of course we would have to clean up some of them, including Coventry. He seemed to think that that would be a very difficult thing to do.[51]

A couple of days later I had some confirmation of the tensions in the Bevan movement. Delargy, who is a personal acolyte of Bevan, told

51 Crossman's account of this conversation (printed in part by Foot (1973), pp. 473–4n) covers quite different ground, apart from the points about right-wing morale, and 'cleaning up' Coventry. He reports HG as saying, '"we must consider money, and many of our big backers were asking why we hadn't acted three years ago." I said we knew about his meeting at St Ermin's Hotel and he said, "Oh, that's a pure phoney. We've been having regular meetings on the National Agents Service and last Monday happened to be the last of them. But I don't deny that, in discussing the money, this issue of Bevan has been not unimportant."'

Later, according to Crossman, HG compared Bevan to Hitler as similar demagogues; and Foot's quotation ends there. Crossman goes on that he objected that Bevan cared for parliamentary liberty, and reports HG as replying, 'Oh, there are minor differences [!], but what is striking is the resemblance'; also as admitting that the division would continue until the Party Conference. 'But no one survives in the wilderness and after that it would soon be forgotten.' HG, he said 'criticised Attlee very bitterly . . . he'd merely been a chairman, not a leader', and would not respond to 'prods' about Morrison. Crossman concluded: 'We both promised not to tell our closest friends; and I think I can now occasionally repeat this': diary, 25.3.55.

George Brown what a pity all this was, because Bevan was just on the point of breaking with Crossman and Barbara Castle.[52]

It is not very easy yet to describe the feeling in the Party. The dust has not settled. There is obviously a sense of relief among many people who were frightened of the consequences of straightforward expulsion, even though they knew it was right. The really tough right-wing boys are furious with Attlee. The Bevanites are apparently a bit nervous themselves as to what Bevan will do next week, and one can assume they will be working hard to get him to be reasonable.[53] The papers of course have headlined the incident between Attlee and myself, and I am sure that many of my supporters thought I was very foolish to get involved in it.[54] But the reaction does not seem to be as sharp as when I made the famous Stalybridge speech 2½ years ago.[55]

I saw Deakin yesterday and had a very pleasant conversation with him, but it did not introduce anything new. I said we would naturally try and make the best we could of the situation by putting forward firm assurances which Bevan would either refuse to sign or have to accept as a very considerable restraint in the future. Last night, I saw George Brown and Joe Godson, and we drafted something possible. George took a rather gloomy view of Bevan's position in the Party. He thought he had been growing stronger and that there was still an inclination among so many of them to follow him if only he would behave and get rid of his supporters. I think probably his [Brown's] judgment is at fault here. My impression is that his [Bevan's] position is rather weaker, not stronger than it was a year ago. But George was very firm and good about the things that ought to be done, about the need to resist the Communist infiltration, to do it by building up some organisation between the Labour Party and the T.U.'s, the need to start a weekly paper. We thought that perhaps when all this was over we would get hold of Tom [Williamson] and Arthur [Deakin] and have a talk with them and try and get some action. George is a curious

52 Hugh Delargy, M.P. Manchester (Platting) 1945–50, Thurrock 1950–76, had voted with the Party and not abstained with Bevan (to whom he was devoted) in the division on the Bomb. But his point is obscure since Crossman and Barbara Castle were sharply at odds, both on their advice to Bevan and on the issue itself.

53 Crossman was, as his diary makes clear: *ibid*. But other associates of Bevan influenced him the other way, particularly the *Tribune* editors (his wife, Michael Foot and J. P. W. Mallalieu): Crossman diary, 16.3.55, cf. 31.3.55; also Dalton diary, 14.3.55, quoting Hunter.

54 As shown by the letter of 21.3.55 from Anthony Crosland, Roy Jenkins and Woodrow Wyatt (below, page 394). These three, and Jay, told Dalton of their misgivings soon afterwards: Dalton diary, 7.4.55. Others who thought HG wrong were his closest ally in Transport House – and his wife.

55 In October 1952: above, p. 320.

chap. He can be very difficult with a chip on his shoulder. If he does not see you he thinks you are neglecting him. Recently I had to intervene about the Agricultural Policy pamphlet when he was away.[56] He came up to me and said rather offensively, 'I hear you want to be Minister of Agriculture as well?' On the other hand, he is a courageous and clear-headed person whose public utterances and speeches at public meetings have always been excellent. He and Alf Robens are people with whom you can safely go tiger-hunting. They are not frightened, and once they commit themselves they stick. It is a pity that George by his aggressive manner makes rather too many enemies in the Party. Otherwise his position would be stronger. All the same, he counts for quite a lot, and will count for much more in the future.

Document No. 13

[*Letter from Crosland, Jenkins and Wyatt, in HG Papers, file P.97*]

Personal.   March 21st, 1955.

Dear Hugh,

You must excuse this slightly formal letter, but we want you to consider seriously the views that it expresses. We are aware that it comes at a difficult time, but it is not the result of hurried thinking nor simply a hasty reaction to the flood of constituency resolutions. We held these views before the Parliamentary Party meeting but we deliberately refrained from worrying you and dutifully "voted as we were told."

We think that the Parliamentary Committee was wrong in its decision a fortnight ago, and our views on this have not merely arisen out of the narrow result last Wednesday. We held them and expressed them before-hand. A little less certainly we thought the Parliamentary Committee was wrong in its decision to withdraw the Whip from the seven Members last autumn. We also thought that the tactics and timetable (though not of course the substance) of the German rearmament decision a year last February were faulty. More recently we were unhappy about the handling by the Parliamentary Committee of the Bevan proposal for four power talks. A little more skill by the platform, we thought, could have avoided another narrow vote without giving away anything of importance.

56 A Transport House pamphlet which HG thought too complicated for its propagandist purpose. Brown was the Party's spokesman on agriculture.

On all these occasions, of course, we supported the platform with our votes, although with varying degrees of misgivings. There must, however, be a limit to the number of times on which one can vote the straight "ticket" merely out of loyalty and regardless of our personal views. We therefore feel that we must in future have some freedom of action; and we think you ought to know that this is our present mood. You might argue, of course, that we have the advantages of close consultation with, and perhaps influence upon yourself, and that this is really much more important than the question of a simple vote. We think this was rather more true a year or so ago than it is now when we used to have occasional meetings. Inevitably you are busier than you used to be, but the opportunities for a full political discussion have been very infrequent in recent months.

You know us well enough to realise that this in no way affects our feelings of both personal and political loyalty to you. We are pleased to be called "Gaitskellites"; we want you to be leader of the Party in the future and we shall do everything we can to see that you are.

We have, of course, occasional differences, in particular over Morrison. This is part of a wider view of ours that it is essential that any "Right wing" leader must have the fairly solid support of the centre, which Attlee has, which Morrison does not, and which we want you to have. Our difference of opinion only arises because we believe that you and the "Right wing" must in the future carry many people whose support you did not have last Wednesday morning.

Do not please think you have to write a reply to this – if one comes we shall all be too frightened to open the envelope! Can we not meet soon?

Yours ever,

[signed]   Roy   Woodrow   Tony

Diary, Saturday, 2 April 1955

I went to Oxford and Birmingham for the weekend to do a series of meetings.

Oxford was not too bad. It was pouring with rain. They had taken the Union [Debating Hall] and there were only about 100 there, but it was enough to make it respectable. I suspect the Bevanites boycotted us, because there were very few left-wing questions. There was the usual curious mixture you always get at Oxford: undergraduates, North Oxford ladies, and solid Party workers.

The next day I took a Conference at Birmingham. This was definitely boycotted by the left, with the result that it was quite a good Conference. Again about 100 people, but they were the solid Party workers. We had a good, hard-headed question and discussion time, realistic and definitely directed to vote-winning, instead of airy-fairy ideas.

The following morning I went to a club in Roy Jenkins' constituency, the East Birmingham Labour Club. The Committee received me in a little room, and produced a new bottle of whisky, of which we drank quite a lot, very strong. This was followed by some beer, and about the time I was feeling extremely cheerful they announced they would now start the meeting. I had to speak for ten minutes or so and then answer questions. They warned me that there would be a lot of Bevanites and at least one Communist there. But it all went off very well, no doubt because of the whisky and beer. I was particularly forthright, and spoke out against my critics with great vigour, which delighted the Committee. It was a heartening experience. One felt that here were the good, sensible Trade Union people with their feet on the ground who were not really taken in by all the *Tribune* nonsense.

In the afternoon there was another cheerful experience. *Socialist Commentary* for the first time had a meeting in Birmingham. Selected persons were invited, and came – about 100 of them, including apparently half the Labour Group on the Council. I spoke at length on the development of Socialist thought (too long, as usual, but they liked most of it, and were extremely sensible and objective). I thought Rita Hinden and the other *Socialist Commentary* people were pleased with the meeting.[57] We really seemed to have something there. As Birmingham is one of the worst areas for lunatics there is probably a reaction now in favour of sanity.

The evening was a different story. It had been arranged that I should speak in Wolverhampton, supported by Baird, a completely mad and unpleasant Bevanite, and Stanley Evans, who is on the extreme right of the Party.[58] The attendance was middling. It was a good hall, about half or two-thirds full. Stanley was going to take no chances with Baird, and at once launched a great attack on Mr B[Bevan] and then proceeded to make a very firm right-wing foreign policy speech. He was, of course, heavily heckled, but took no notice. Baird then got up and replied in kind. I think this was slightly comic for a 'Forward to Victory' demon-

57 *Socialist Commentary*, a right-wing Labour monthly, was edited by Dr Rita Hinden.
58 John Baird, a dentist, was M.P. Wolverhampton E. 1945–50, N.E. 1950–64. Evans sat for Wednesbury 1945–56.

stration. He ended with an appeal to me to say that night that I was
against the expulsion of Mr Bevan. I refused, however, to say anything on
this, and after replying to the more extravagant statements which Baird
had made on foreign policy – clear all the Americans out of Europe, etc. –
I proceeded to try and bring the meeting round to its real purpose, and did
my usual Home Front stuff. There were about 20 Communists, and about
half the rest were Bevanites. It all ended reasonably happily, but it was a
reckless idea to put the three of us on the same platform. Fortunately,
though, the newspaper strike is on, and only the local papers reported
what took place.

On the Monday I lunched with Desmond Donnelly, a Bevan renegade
who, however, had voted against withdrawing the Whip. I was hoping to
hear something of the Bevanite views on the situation, but he knew very
little. He said that Mr Bevan had hardly seen any of them for a long time,
and confirmed that they were splitting a good deal before the last episode.

After lunch we had a meeting of the Staff Salaries Committee, and took
the opportunity of considering our tactics (Edith [Summerskill], Percy
Knight and myself and Morgan Phillips) for the meeting the next day. We
explained to Percy that expulsion was now hopeless and that the best we
could do was to get fairly strong assurances. We warned him, however,
that Clem [Attlee] was obviously determined to accept anything.

The meeting on Tuesday was a depressing affair. The eight of us met to
start with on our own,[59] and there was a rather desultory discussion as to
what should be done. It had already leaked out that Clem had seen him
the day before. Clem said that he had come in and told him that he had
drafted a statement which he had read, which contained an apology and
some vague assurances.[60] Some of us tried to insist that we should press
for specific assurances on upholding majority decisions and not attacking
leaders, but we did not agree on any particular form of words, partly
because it was really inevitable that we should first of all hear what he had
to say.

Bevan then came in. He showed no signs of repentance or any change
in his make-up. He behaved exactly as I have heard him behave on many
occasions, giving expression to similar views. There was a general effort
to keep the temperature down. In accordance with this I said very little.[61]

59 A sub-committee of eight to interview Bevan: four who had voted against
   expulsion (Attlee, Castle, Griffiths, Haworth), three in favour (Cooper,
   Gaitskell, Knight), and the chairman (Edith Summerskill). The secretary
   (Morgan Phillips) also came, but had no vote.
60 Crossman privately called it 'a really abject apology to Attlee and unequivocal
   assurances that he [Bevan] would be loyal to his leadership', which had
   horrified all the other Bevanites only the week before: diary, 31.3.55.
61 Contradicting Foot's statement that HG acted as 'chief inquisitor' (1973,
   p. 478) which survivors from that sub-committee deny: HG, p. 344 and n. 124.

Most of the questions came from Jim Haworth and Jack Cooper. The attitude of Clem and Jim Griffiths embarrassed me. They always seemed so frightened of him, and so terrified of any kind of row. So eager to agree. So pleased at any sign of better behaviour. The only time I did intervene nearly led to a row. I said, 'Would you agree that it was a bad thing for the Party if members attack the leaders, and if so, will you agree not to do this in future?'

He said, 'I refuse to answer that question. It is a trap.'

Whereupon there was a sort of uproar and everybody tried to rush in to keep us apart.

Edith [Summerskill] ticked him off gently for being so suspicious. But in general he evaded every question of this kind. After he had gone away we at least prevented the Committee from making any recommendation, but it was clear that Clem was determined to accept the statement and leave it at that. The same was of course true of Jim Griffiths and Barbara Castle, and appeared to be of Jim Haworth. The other four of us plus Morgan Phillips had a brief chat alone and decided that we should have a motion endorsing the action of the Parliamentary Party, taking note of the assurances and giving some warning about the future. It was agreed that MP should draft this and Jack Cooper should move it.

That evening Dora and I went round to Joe Godson to meet Sam Watson, and Sam proceeded to draft a resolution of his own, but in very similar terms to the one we had discussed with Morgan in the morning. He thought the important thing was to try and make it look at least as though we had achieved something. I was a little sceptical about this because the assurances were so obviously useless.

At the Executive on the following morning, the statement from Mr Bevan was read out. There was then a rather long pause. Somebody said they would like to hear the views of the leader of the Party, and then Clem proposed that we should simply accept it. He was supported by Jim Griffiths. Jack Cooper then proceeded to move the resolution which I suppose MP had drafted (probably after discussing it with Sam Watson) and Sam seconded it.[62]

The surprise of the morning then occurred. Jim Haworth announced that after thinking about it all night he had come to the conclusion that there was nothing to be done but to expel Mr. B. and he accordingly moved. This was greeted with a gasp of surprise and some laughter from those of us who had argued for this a week before. Somebody said afterwards they were not sure whether it was God who had changed Jim Haworth's mind or Bill Webber, the General Secretary. Alice Horan

62 The Minutes show that Earnshaw was Cooper's seconder, and Attlee was Griffiths'.

seconded this (she has always been about the toughest person on the Executive). It became clear, however, that virtually everybody else except the Bevanites were in favour of Jack Cooper's resolution. The psychological moment had passed. Also there was the fact that Jock Tiffin was away, so that the switch over of Jim Haworth would only have given us a dead heat. Some people wanted the Cooper resolution strengthened, particularly Alice Bacon and even Brinham. I spoke very late, and simply said that everything had turned out as I expected, that we received no assurances of value, that Haworth's account of the matter (which had been very direct and almost bitter about Mr Bevan's behaviour in the Committee) was perfectly correct, but it was now too late to expel. I suggested one change in Cooper's resolution – to substitute the word 'note' for the word 'welcome'. I said I did not see how we could possibly welcome the assurances, because they meant nothing. Jack accepted this.

Meanwhile Jim Griffiths had been drafting his own resolution, which differed from Cooper's only in the second part, regarding the assurances. It was altogether much more smarmy, and read much more into Bevan's statement in the way of future cooperation.

Then a rather curious incident happened. One of the Bevanites, Mikardo, raised the question of whether the motion could be put in two parts, so that they could vote against the endorsement of the Parliamentary Party's action. Clem, of all people, said he was really not sure whether we ought to have this put in, on the grounds that it was really none of our business. I thought this the most extraordinary statement, seeing that in the [interviewing?] Committee he insisted the only thing we had to consider was Mr Bevan's behaviour in Parliament. Fortunately Herbert [Morrison] and others waded heavily in against him, and even Jim Griffiths refused to cut this out of his resolution.

The vote was then taken, and Cooper's resolution carried by 15 to 10. Haworth, Jean Mann and Brinham all voted with us this time. Jock Tiffin was away. Gooch must have abstained. The Bevanites then moved to delete the endorsement of the Parliamentary Party, and this of course was defeated, only the six of them voting that way. Unfortunately I cannot recall whether Clem abstained on this or actually voted with the majority. Too much importance should not in any case be attached to the vote, because it was clear that the Bevanite amendment was bound to be overwhelmingly defeated. The same applies to the substantive motion on which some papers report that Clem abstained.[63] But again it is not really of any great importance.

63 Foot (1973, pp. 479–80) says Attlee voted against the Bevanite amendment, and abstained on the substantive motion which passed 16 – 7. Dalton says Griffiths abstained with Attlee: diary, 31.3.55.

The rest of the meeting passed off quite amicably, the Bevanites being divided on the H-bomb statement. There had been earlier some discussion on the relationship between M.P.s and constituency parties, particularly the pressure which the latter were putting upon their Members. We had in mind the case of Bessie Braddock, whose reselection had been defeated by 40 votes to 39, and also Elaine Burton, whose position in Coventry was in danger.[64] We are to have a special meeting of the Election sub-Committee on this, and it should be interesting to see how this develops. There is an important constituency issue involved as to just what rights the constituency parties have in relation to Members. Difficulties arise now because of the combination of two things. Redistribution has meant that many Members have to be re-selected in circumstances in which it is fairly easy to organise against them. Where there is no change in the constituency boundaries, the rules of the Party make it very hard for an existing M.P. to be turned out by the local Party, but this is not so where the boundaries have been changed and a new divisional party technically comes into existence. The second factor is of course the Bevanite organisation, of which unfortunately we have very little detailed knowledge, but which most of us are convinced does exist. There is also a widespread feeling that the Communists are taking advantage of all this and trying to exert their influence through certain union delegates against the supporters of the official Party.

This brings to an end a particular chapter in the Bevan story. I have no doubt that the Whip will have to be restored to him before long, and this is bound to be done if there is an election on May 26th.[65] But just where we all stand as a result of it is not so easy to say. One has the feeling that nobody has really come out of it very well, as compared with the position at the start. I certainly would not think Bevan's position strengthened in the Parliamentary Party, though it may be somewhat better than it would have been had we confined ourselves in the first instance to a severe motion of censure. Attlee has maintained his position, which however is really not assailable, but he has certainly lost even more of the sympathy of the so-called right wing. Perhaps this does not matter, because he has

64 The National Executive found irregularities in the behaviour of Mrs Braddock's local party, Liverpool Exchange, which was reconstituted with her as candidate. One of her opponents resigned and stood against her, and she won with 56% of the vote to 35% Conservative and 8½% Independent Labour. Coventry, a left-wing party, had threatened not to readopt Miss Burton if she voted to withdraw the whip in the Parliamentary Party; she did so, and was re-elected much more favourably than the other two Coventry Labour members, Edelman and Crossman, who had supported Bevan. Crossman himself thought her electoral success directly due to her defiance of the local party: diary, 31.5.55.

65 There was, and it was.

always played the game of leadership by not leaning too heavily on one wing or another. This always brings with it the risk of falling between the two, but this is a risk which really is negligible today. As for myself, most of my friends think I was very foolish to allow myself to be carried on by the 'right wing', with the inevitable result that the Bevanites 'framed' me as the 'Chief Prosecutor'. They say that until this upset my own position had been improving sharply and steadily during the past year, but that now there was a considerable set-back, the middle section of the Party viewing me once again with suspicion as a dogmatic, rigid, right-winger. I am sure there is something in this, nevertheless I always find it difficult to behave in these matters in the subtle way which my own friends seem to expect. I don't see how one can have strong loyalties with people like George Brown and Alf Robens, not to speak of the T.U. leaders, and continually refuse to do any of the dirty work for them and with them. But undoubtedly had I foreseen, as I should have done, where Clem's original attitude would lead us, I should have thrown my weight on the first day against withdrawing the Whip and in favour of the censure motion. This would certainly have been a shock to Herbert [Morrison] and other members of the Committee, and also to many people outside, but in the light of what has happened it would have been better.

For the rest, the whole thing may be regarded as a stalemate. The attack was mounted, but no breakthrough was achieved because the Commander in Chief really did not like the plan from the start. The enemy counterattack was only partially successful. We might be said to have gained some ground after heavy casualties. If Bevan misbehaves again in the near future, his position will certainly be more precarious as a result of all this. On the other hand, the right wing is rather dispirited, and looking at it personally, my own position is no doubt weaker. Once again, however, I must say that I do not and cannot regard that as the only thing that matters. One would get no fun out of politics if one spent all one's life thinking in terms of the single object of one's own political success.

Editor's Note on 1955

[In the general election Labour lost ten seats to the Conservatives, who had an overall majority of 58. When the new House met, Dalton publicly urged his colleagues over 65 (except Attlee) to follow his own example and withdraw from the Shadow Cabinet; four of them reluctantly did so. During the summer Gaitskell came under increasing pressure to stand for the leadership when Attlee (now 72) at last retired, and to settle the succession for a generation. In October he made an excellent impression at the Party Conference at Margate, which re-elected him treasurer with a majority over Bevan of nearly five to one instead of two to one. In the House at the end of the month, he violently attacked the autumn Budget in which Butler undid his pre-election generosity, while Morrison performed disastrously. Under growing pressure, Gaitskell now agreed to stand – and abruptly, without warning Morrison, Attlee announced his retirement on December 7. Bitter enemies for the last twenty years, Bevan and Morrison combined in a desperate last-minute joint effort to stop Gaitskell, but they failed and polled only 70 and 40 votes to his 157 – much the most convincing victory in the Party's history.

Gaitskell kept no diary of these events, which are recounted in *HG*, Chapter 12.]

CHAPTER 8

LEADER OF THE OPPOSITION

[Gaitskell, whose diary is silent about his own election to the party leadership, started keeping it again as soon as he began his new duties as Leader of the Opposition. The variety of his engagements and contacts emerges clearly from this chapter, with its succession of diplomatic dinners, talks with officials and experts from turbulent colonies, party activities, dealings with the press and B.B.C., and assessments of parliamentary or trade union colleagues. News of friction and grumbling among the Conservatives comes to him through social and journalistic gossip, for his social activities expanded markedly after 1955. As a guest the Leader of the Opposition is much in demand. This new and unfamiliar side of life gets more attention in the Diary than his ordinary routine social activities ever receive, and consequently gives a rather distorted impression of one aspect of his existence.

Within the Labour Party, Aneurin Bevan still appears as a potential threat, needing to be carefully handled and kept within bounds. It was in these early months of leadership, however, that the first seeds of their reconciliation were being sown.]

[*Dictated on Monday, 9 January 1956*]

It is a long time since I dictated any diary, but in view of recent events I must start again. The first week of the New Year has certainly been active enough. On the morning of January 1st, we woke up in the middle of the so-called 'Tank Scandal'. It had been reported in the Press for some time that disused British tanks had been sold for export and then reconditioned in Belgium and sent on to Egypt. There had been questions in the House, but the Government had been very cagey about the whole thing. Two days before, Alf Robens [Labour's spokesman on foreign affairs] sent a telegram to the P.M., asking him to suspend all further exports of war supplies for the time being. I was mildly annoyed about this, because he did not consult me, so I telephoned him on the 31st, pointing out that he must not do this sort of thing without my consent. He took it very well, and apologised. I asked him to let me know if he heard anything from the P.M. On the Sunday morning [1 January] it was announced that the Government had in fact banned further exports. At the same time there was a story from Liverpool from Bessie Braddock that there were large shipments of arms going to Egypt from that port.[1] She had been trying to get me all day on Saturday – which was quite true. After looking at the papers and answering one or two enquiries from the Press, I decided to call a meeting, and got Alf Robens, Kenneth Younger, and Denis Healey, together with Hugh Pilcher[2] to act as a kind of Press Officer, to come in in the afternoon. We discussed the whole situation, and decided that I should ask for an interview with the P.M., and that we should put out a statement about this. I got through quickly to the Private Secretaries, and without much trouble arranged to call at No. 10 at 6 o'clock on the Monday evening. We drafted out our statement, which was concerned not only with surplus tanks, etc., but with Middle Eastern policy generally.

Of course, this hit the headlines next day, and considerable interest was shown in the fact that we were going to visit No. 10 in the middle of the Recess, and soon after my accession to the leadership. I had lunch [that day] with Cecil King, who seemed quite convinced that Eden was not going to stay very long. He said he had been at 'the House' [Christ Church, Eden's college] with him at Oxford, and that he had never been much impressed. He was, he said, a brilliant negotiator, but that was all. He thought the Government's decline in the last nine months quite spectacular.

Later in the day, Hugh Pilcher called, and we discussed publicity for the evening meeting. It was decided that either we must have a joint statement which was a full one, including the questions we had asked, or else I would put out one on my own. I telephoned No. 10 and spoke to William Clark* [Eden's press officer], and warned him of this. I then made some notes, and Hugh Pilcher suggested bringing in the points about the recall of Parliament. This was all agreed with Alf Robens and Kenneth Younger, who came in to pick me up. We then drove over to No. 10, where we were ambushed by a large crowd of photographers on the doorstep.

The P.M. received us with great cordiality – Christian names and all. He had with him Selwyn Lloyd* [Foreign Secretary] and [Sir] Walter Monckton* [Minister of Defence]. The Cabinet room, I noticed, was brighter and lighter than it used to be when I was last there, over four years ago. I think they must have removed the book-cases, and perhaps redecorated it. We sat on the other side of the long table. The P.M. began by raising the publicity point, and was inclined to urge that we should simply have a statement saying that a meeting had taken place. In defence of this, he circulated the statements made when they had called on us

1 Many of her constituents were Liverpool dock workers. These shipments of arms for Egypt were in accordance with government policy and unrelated to the surplus war material.
2 A prominent journalist on the *Daily Herald*, the official Party paper.

when we were in power. But I said that this was not the same situation. I had not come particularly to hear secrets, though of course we would listen to anything he had to say; but to put some questions and suggestions which had Parliament been sitting would have been put there. I said we could not get away with a short statement – the Press were too interested – and that the best thing was to have a longer statement setting out both what we had asked and what the Government had answered. I then proceeded to put a series of questions about the surplus war material, and after a bit the P.M. answered. He did not really say much, except that he thought the figures were exaggerated, but it was obvious that somebody had tricked them in making out that the tanks were to be used for peaceful purposes.[3] I asked for a White Paper. I also asked for a debate before they left for America,[4] and if necessary, the recall of Parliament. Finally, I put two specific proposals, that the Belgian Government should be asked to suspend exports, and that we should stop not merely export licensing but exports. They had fairly good answers to the last two. They had been in touch with Belgium, but could not get the Government there to agree so far. And on the exports they said they had been going through the licences already issued, and had only found one which they thought necessary to cancel. On the other two questions, they said they would think it over. We then went on to a private discussion of the Middle East, from which I got the following impressions:

(1) They are obviously worried about the Russian arms supplies, which are on a big scale. In fact, the P.M. said 'We could not on our own balance these supplies, even if we wanted to, by giving arms to Israel'.

(2) They argued that up to now Israel had been stronger, and this was their defence for letting Egypt have tanks, etc. But they admitted that the balance would in fact be upset by the Russian supplies.

(3) On being challenged regarding the maintenance of the balance and the Tripartite Agreement, Eden was prepared to repeat what he had said in the House, that he stood by both commitments,[5] and really had no

3 Much surplus war stock had been sold abroad since the war; these were old Valentines, 'demilitarised' (without the breech blocks of the guns) and sent to Antwerp for scrap. Most were duly dismantled but the Egyptian government bought 150 which were re-militarised and re-exported.

4 Eden, with Lloyd and Winthrop Aldrich the U.S. Ambassador, sailed on 25 January 1956. On his visits to Washington and Ottawa see Eden (1960), pp. 332–40.

5 On 25 May 1950 Britain, France and the U.S.A. had declared their intention to promote Middle Eastern peace and stability by taking action to prevent any violation of existing frontiers. Eden had told the House twice (on 2 November 1954 and 4 April 1955) that this bound all three powers to protect Israel against any Arab attacker, or conversely.

reply when I said this was inconsistent with the refusal to let Israel have Centurion tanks, etc.

(4) The only argument the other way which they put forward was that if they supplied Israel, then, said Selwyn Lloyd, you might have Russian Marshals commanding the Arab arms. We said we thought this pretty unlikely. I also pointed out that there was a limit economically to what the Arab States could buy anyhow.

(5) Because of the danger of the situation, they admitted they wanted to get a settlement, and that, rather surprisingly, this was because on the one side the Israelis would realise the danger and make a concession, and on the other the Egyptians would also be frightened in case the Israelis supported a preventive war. The discussion was perfectly friendly, although obviously we did not agree on some points. But it seemed to me that really the Government did not know what to do, and were anxious to put the whole problem onto the lap of the American President.

The following day [Tuesday 3 January] I saw [the Israeli Ambassador] Elath*, at his request, and he told me that according to their information the Egyptians were getting 150 MIGs, and a number of Stalin tanks. He said that these, with the Centurions, were far more powerful than anything the Israelis had, and that their main grievance against the British was their refusal to sell medium tanks. I pointed out the importance of America, and urged that they should do what they could over there. I also urged strongly they must keep the army under control, and not have these large-scale attacks, such as the one on Syria.[6] This made it much harder for us. Finally, I sent a personal message through him to [Prime Minister] Ben-Gurion* on these points, and also urging that they might consider putting out proposals of their own for settlement. I thought this would make a good impression, if they were carefully thought out and reasonably conciliatory.

Developments since then have been all in the Press. The Government first of all issued a rather dusty answer, to which I replied with a fairly sharp statement. But it is now all settled that there is to be a White Paper, that it is to be produced before Parliament re-assembles, and we shall probably have a debate on the first day before the Prime Minister and the Foreign Secretary go to Washington. The Tory Press is now running the line that the White Paper will show that vast amounts of war supplies were sold by the Labour Government, and that the transactions of the last few months are on a comparatively minor scale. This is to be expected.

6 On 10 and 11 December 1955 the Israelis attacked Lake Tiberias, in their fourth attack on Syria in two years and the biggest since the 1948 war. It was condemned by the U.K., U.S., U.S.S.R. and France and there were demands for their expulsion from the U.N.

But I doubt if it makes a great deal of impression. Nobody has objected to the sale of war supplies as such, but to loopholes through administrative weakness which has come at a very awkward moment in view of the situation in the Middle East.

I have been seeing various members of the Parliamentary Committee on their own, in particular Alf Robens, James Callaghan, Tony Greenwood, Dick Stokes and George Brown, and had each talk with me separately. I have urged upon them the absolute necessity of making ourselves into an efficient and loyal team, and dropping all the back-stabbing and intriguing which has been going on in the past few years. I have told them I want to build up a young, energetic team, each member of which has his own job, an important job to do, so that we can prepare ourselves properly for the desperate and dangerous business of Government.[7] There has been much discussion about tactics vis-à-vis AB[Bevan]. Nobody has given me any very precise advice. There has been a dis-position to ask me what I am going to do.

I have been cagey, but I have hinted that I am not particularly per-turbed, as I want to go ahead with the team operation. If he joins in so much the better, if not, well it just can't be helped. I have no intention of taking away foreign affairs from Alf [Robens]; although I have been cautious on this, it is clear that Harold Wilson will have to have the Treasury. If Jim Griffiths becomes Deputy [Leader] the Colonies will be vacant and the question is whether this should be offered to AB. James Callaghan said he would like it if it was free. George Brown also made it plain, as he [sic; ?I] expected, that he wanted something more active. I suggested to him that if he stayed in Supply he might take over Defence, though not at once. Dick Stokes in fact offered to give this up, but I said not at this stage, though I have thought that in time he will wish to get out of it.[8] He told me he was seeing more of AB, and it is clear from other conversations that this has alarmed some of his friends. George Brown assured me in my talk with him [at lunch on Friday 6 January] that he had nothing to do with the famous manoeuvre during the [leadership] election,

7 At the start of the new Parliament Attlee had introduced the practice of assigning front bench spokesmen to shadow specific departments, which has prevailed ever since. It was partly a reaction to the clash with Bevan over SEATO in 1954 (above, pp. 327–8). See *HG*, pp. 407–9; and R.M. Punnett, *Front Bench Opposition* (Heinemann, 1973), pp. 59–73.
8 Attlee had made Robens responsible for shadowing foreign affairs, Wilson for Trade, Griffiths for Colonies, Bevan for Labour, Callaghan for the Admiralty, Brown for Supply and Stokes for Defence. In November 1956, for the first new session with HG as Leader, Bevan took over foreign affairs, Brown Defence, Callaghan Colonies and Robens Labour; Wilson was already shadow Chancellor.

and in fact was not in the House that day. He thought it most foolish.[9] I impressed upon him particularly the need for loyalty to his colleagues. He said he found it very hard to stomach Harold Wilson, and much preferred Nye.[10] He said that Harold Wilson had said far worse things about me than ever Nye had, though I gathered that this was some time ago. I said that nevertheless HW was not only on the Executive, but also Chairman of the Organisation Committee, and high up in the Parliamentary Committee vote. Furthermore, he had in fact worked very well together with me,[11] and although he was a cold fish I thought he knew the need for loyalty. Finally, I pointed out that he was not really dangerous because he would not have much support if he made trouble. George was impressed with this last argument, but had, to start with at any rate, hoped that I was not going to bring HW forward so much. He had said he [Brown] did not want to go on with Agriculture, but showed an interest in the Board of Trade. I did not encourage this, and urged, as I have said, Defence. He responded quite well to this idea.

We had a Parliamentary Committee meeting in the middle of the week [Thursday 5 January] to discuss what I call our Commando Raid on No. 10, Downing Street, and the line we should take after the Government announcement.[12] It went off quite peacefully, although the only persons there were Jim Griffiths, Bevan, Tony Greenwood and George Brown, and two Labour peers. We were informed at the beginning of the meeting that the White Paper would be ready before the debate, and decided to press for Tuesday (which was afterwards conceded by the Government). There was then a long, rather rambling discussion on the Middle East, in which AB took a prominent part, being, however, as usual, rather all over the place. He made no attempt to criticise what I had been doing. He is obviously finding it very difficult to make his mind up whether to run for the Deputy-Leadership or not.

Clem [Attlee] came in to see me during the week, and we had a conversation about this and that. I was anxious to find out how far he had

9 On Thursday 8 December 1955, with nominations due to close next morning, ten fairly senior M.P.s had urged both Bevan and HG to withdraw in Morrison's favour. Bevan, who had dined with his old enemy Morrison the night before, agreed at once; HG declined, and benefited from resentment among supporters of both his rivals at their unholy alliance. See *HG*, pp. 366–7; Donoughue & Jones (1973), pp. 339–40; Hunter (1959), pp. 173–5.

10 This was less surprising than it might appear, for there was much sympathy between the two working-class leaders, who sometimes stood together in dealing with their university-educated colleagues. See *HG*, pp. 476, 493–5.

11 On the National Executive, over reform of party organisation and in attacking Butler's autumn budget in the House: *HG*, pp. 350–2, 361.

12 The visit on the evening of 2 January (above, pp. 406–8).

got with Eden about the House of Lords, pay for its members, and pay for the Members of the House of Commons.[13] Nothing at all has so far been agreed. I gathered that Salisbury has been considering the question of reform, but [sic: ? that] they are very much worried about the decay in the House of Lords, that they would probably be willing to arrange for payment of some allowance for attendance, and that they would also be willing – on the assumption that no reform project is put forward – for the Leader of the Opposition to nominate some additional peers. It is evident that the whole subject bristles with difficulties. Our people in the House are still very angry about the pay situation and the pension situation too, and would not, I think, readily agree to pay for the peers unless something is done for them too. Moreover, there is a great disinclination to think at all about the problem of the Second Chamber.

We have to move carefully in this field, though it will probably be an advantage that Clem is now in the Lords. The Party will listen to his views from his new vantage point with special interest. He made two other quite significant remarks. We were talking about Herbert [Morrison] and discussing what he should do. Clem said, 'Do you think he would like to go to the Lords?' I said, 'No, I can hardly think he would want to go there, especially now that you are there – he would be overshadowed again'. Clem nodded, but said, 'I expect you are right, though of course his wife might have different views'.[14] This amused me, as it probably indicated the influence which Vi [Lady Attlee] has had upon him in this matter. The other bit of evidence here is the invitation to their cocktail party, which has inscribed upon it, 'To meet the Viscount and Viscountess Prestwood, The Countess Attlee At Home'.

The other remark was about Winston [Churchill]. I was saying how extraordinary it was that the Government had gone down so much in the last nine months, and added, 'After all, the only important change is the disappearance of Winston. Who would have supposed that he would make so much difference?' Clem said, 'Yep. It's the heavy roller, you know. Doesn't let the grass grow under it' – which I thought was (a) shrewd, and (b) typical, being a cricketing analogy. It is indeed a possible explanation. Clem also talked about Anthony [Eden]. 'He has never had any experience of running a team.'

Hugh Dalton lunched with me on Saturday, and we talked about a lot of problems. He was strongly in favour of my idea of building up the young team, and strongly supported my line on not giving AB the big jobs. On the Colonies he was doubtful – obviously in the same kind of

13 See below, pp. 415–18.
14 Morrison's first wife died in July 1953 and he married again in January 1955. When he was offered a peerage in 1959, his wife helped overcome his hesitation.

doubt as I was myself. On the House of Lords he was, as always, violently prejudiced. 'Don't do a thing for them unless we get something for the Commons.' And to my plea for some of the poverty-stricken Labour peers – 'Well, they knew, didn't they, when they went there?' He was not quite so down on appointing new peers, except for the general prejudice against doing anything to keep the institution going. He thought we should move first on pensions for the Commons. This would make it easier to get rid of some of the older people, always a passion of his. He was pleased with what I had done on the Tank Scandal, and urged me to attack Eden. 'The boys will like it. Remind him how Chamberlain used to interfere with him when he was Foreign Secretary, and how he disliked it, and warn him against doing the same.'[15] There is some sense in this, but Hugh's great weakness is that he has always paid too much attention to public opinion in the Party and too little attention to public opinion in the nation.[16] It is curious in a way for a person so politically shrewd, and so hard-headed about elections.

Diary, 9–16 January, 1956

I had a useful talk [on Monday 9 January] with Morgan Phillips. Made it plain that I wanted to keep in regular touch with him. I am sure this is necessary in order to prod him into action of various kinds. My theory is if prodded he will do quite well. I suggested we should make some use of Gallup Polls to guide us on policy issues, as well as T.V. and sound broadcasts. He is to follow that up. He is also himself prodding Len Williams about organisation, which seems to be going rather slowly.[17]

Saw Billy Richardson, the Editor of *Reynolds*, [on Tuesday] at his request. Generally regarded (correctly) as a small, insignificant man, far below the level for a paper of this kind; but the usual trouble – the Co-ops pay too little. I believe he gets £2,000 a year. He has been urged by Cyril Hamnett, Chairman of *Reynolds*, to make changes, not trying to compete

15 Eden held the office for just over two years before the war, first under Baldwin who left him alone and then under Neville Chamberlain who did not. He resigned within nine months of the change at No. 10.
16 Not surprisingly, Dalton had privately criticised Gaitskell for precisely the opposite error in the past: his diary, 5.4.51.
17 A.L. (Sir Len) Williams (1904–72) had been Assistant National Agent 1946–51, was National Agent 1951–62 and became General Secretary of the Party 1962–8. Previously he had for ten years been party secretary in Leeds (where HG was first adopted in 1937); and later, from 1968, he was Governor-General of Mauritius.

with the *Sunday Pictorial* pornography, and making the paper more serious, even with a lower circulation.[18] Naturally I welcome this. I agreed to write an occasional article for them, and to keep in constant touch. I also suggested a number of people who could write, e.g. Tony Crosland, Woodrow Wyatt, Denis Healey, etc. I shall try and follow this up. It may be important, because Party members read *Reynolds* more, probably, than any other paper.

Also saw Peter Ericsson, Head of the International Department, at his request, who wanted to consult me about the Middle East and Defence. I shall encourage this contact as well. I shall want to use him for briefing me, and I am anxious to ensure that Transport House keeps in line with the Parliamentary Party.

A rather exhausting T.V. rehearsal [on Wednesday] at a local studio. However, I am now fairly confident of being able to speak to the camera with an audience. The real problem is substance. What to say which will keep the audience for 15 minutes. Today we were not so much concerned with that, because the broadcast on 27th January must depend on the P.M.'s broadcast on the 21st. We definitely rejected the interview idea, after trying it out. The great problem is how to be relaxed. Tony Benn* said at one point, after one rehearsal, 'At least there was one point when you did not look as though you had an ulcer!' I am afraid this is all too true. Perhaps practice is the answer.

Later I lunched with the Polish Ambassador to meet Malik, the Russian Ambassador*. The three of us were alone. We had a terrific meal, starting with smoked salmon and caviare and a good deal of vodka, going on to lobster, then a tournedos, then a chocolate mousse with various kinds of wine. It was very friendly, plenty of banter, but neither of them gave anything away. Malik did most of the talking, and took the usual Soviet line, e.g., on disarmament (it was all the fault of the Americans), Middle East – the Baghdad Pact was the trouble. On that, they tried to make out that there was a sinister Zionist influence here. I pointed out that it was much stronger in the Labour Party, and was not in the least sinister. They had very little answer to what I had to say about anti-Semitism. I asked if Khrushchev* wanted to come [to England]. They assured me that he did.

Later that day I went to the P.M.'s dinner for the President-Elect of

18 (Sir) William Richardson was editor of *Reynolds News*, later called the *Sunday Citizen*, 1942–67, and then Chief Executive Officer of the Cooperative Press 1967–74. Cyril (Lord) Hamnett was a director of the Press 1947–53 and chairman 1953–77; chairman of the paper 1953–67 when it died; on the executive of the Cooperative Union 1953–74, and chairman of its Parliamentary Committee from 1969. Previously, and simultaneously, he was an officer of USDAW.

Brazil.[19] Not a very inspiring affair. I sat between the President-Elect, who had a little English, and another Brazilian, who spoke only Portuguese. This made things difficult. I said a few words in slow, bad French, which he understood, after which he relapsed into rapid Portuguese, which I could not understand. This conversation was observed by Sir Walter Monckton and a Brazilian sitting opposite. Walter said to me afterward, 'The Brazilian asked me, "Does [Mr Gaitskell] speak Portuguese?"' It must have looked quite funny.

After dinner, the P.M., somewhat surprisingly, spoke freely about the Press campaign against him. I said, 'I suppose you are not going to take this too seriously?' And he did not seem to be worried about it.[20] We talked a bit of economics, and I said rather slyly, 'You had better be careful. In six months' time you may be worrying about unemployment.' He said, 'Yes indeed, that is a very great difficulty.' I do not think he really has a clue about how to deal with inflation either, but he has been warned by the more inflationary-minded people of the dangers of deflation. Also spoke with Harry Douglass*, Steel Trade Union, about *Forward*. He was delighted to hear the news, and indicated he thought they could put some money into it.[21]

Finally, a dinner with Harman Grisewood, effective[ly] No. 2 in the B.B.C., anxious to open informal relations between the Director General and himself and me.[22] I was naturally very willing. He sought my advice on one or two things, in particular whom should they recommend as a replacement Governor for Barbara Wootton. I suggested Raybould or Ruth Cohen or Margaret Hall.[23] He told me they were running a series of

19 Juscelino Kubitshek was President of Brazil 1956–61, and built a new capital, Brasilia, in the interior of the country.
20 On 3 January 1956 the *Daily Telegraph* attacked Eden for failing to provide 'the smack of firm government'; the *Daily Mail* joined in; he thought it necessary to issue a public denial of the rumour that he meant to resign; and R.A. Butler promised publicly 'to support the Prime Minister in all his difficulties'.
21 *Forward*, a Glasgow Socialist weekly, passed into the hands of HG's friends in 1956 and so fulfilled his old aim of having a sympathetic weekly journal. Surviving largely through trade union subscriptions, it merged in 1960 with *Socialist Commentary*. See *HG*, p. 320.
22 See below, p. 436–8 and n. 73.
23 Barbara Wootton, Governor 1952–6, had been Professor of Social Studies at London. She sat on many Royal Commissions, and became Baroness Wootton of Abinger in 1958, as one of HG's first nominees for a life peerage. Like her, Professor S.G. Raybould was active in the W.E.A., and Margaret Hall and Ruth Cohen were economists sympathetic towards Labour. The former was a Fellow of Somerville College, Oxford, and her husband was the Government's economic adviser; the latter was a Fellow, then Principal of Newnham College, Cambridge 1939–72, and knew HG in the Board of Trade during the war. Thus all four were among his friends.

talks on Trade Union problems and industrial unrest. I suggested they had better get some allies among the T.U.C., in case there was trouble. He should see Tom Williamson in the first place, and get him later to bring some others in. We also discussed the problem of whether Ministers should be allowed to go on T.V. outside Party political series. So far we have resisted this, since it is bound to build them up. Apparently William Clark had been pressing for Eden to have one of these, but the B.B.C. rightly refused without the agreement of the Opposition. I said I thought we would only agree if we were compensated in some way, e.g. by more Press Conferences.

He also wanted to know about next year's Conference. I suggested he should write to Morgan Phillips informally and propose some talks.

Lunched with Dingle Foot the next day [Friday]. He is a nice man, but thinks himself more important than he is politically. Very much concerned about African problems, where he has a big legal practice. Anxious that I should not be too pro-Israeli. He will join the Party fairly soon, and will write me a letter about it. [24]

Document No. 14a

SECRET
NOTE ON CONVERSATION WITH THE PRIME MINISTER
ON TUESDAY, 17TH JANUARY, 1956 [25]

I saw the Prime Minister this evening following upon certain decisions of the Parliamentary Committee, i.e.,

(1) that I should press that no Debate on Malta should take place here before the Referendum: [26]

(2) that I should take up with him in a preliminary fashion the question of Members' pension and pay.

As I knew this latter point was related to the House of Lords issue on which CRA[Attlee] had had discussions, I decided to bring it in as well.

24 (Sir) Dingle Foot (1905–78, brother of Michael Foot) was M.P. (Liberal) for Dundee 1931–45, and (Labour) for Ipswich 1957–70; Solicitor General 1964–7. Shared a flat with HG in the war, when both were working for Dalton at the Ministry of Economic Warfare (where Foot was Parl. Sec. 1940–5). On 9 July 1956 he wrote publicly to HG together with two other prominent Liberals seeking to join the Labour Party: Wilfred Roberts, former M.P. for N. Cumberland, and Philip Hopkins; Lloyd George's daughter Lady Megan had done so just before the 1955 election.

25 From Papers, file P.118–4.

26 On Malta see below, pp. 429–32.

On Malta there was no difficulty. The Prime Minister said it was their view also that no debate on Malta should take place here before the Referendum. I asked him to make contact with me if for any reason he were to change his mind and before any kind of public statement were made. He agreed to this.

On the Members' Pay/House of Lords issue, I said I understood that CRA had had discussions with him about the position in the House of Lords. We had an elderly and rather ailing band of Labour Peers, some of whom were in financial difficulty or at least found it difficult to incur the expense necessary in regular attendance. Two questions had therefore arisen:

(a) Was anything to be done about an expense allowance for Peers?

(b) Should the number of Labour Peers be increased?

I said I understood that these questions had been linked by the Government with the wider issue of Reform on which Lord Salisbury was making investigations.

I went on to point out that the question of pay for Peers was bound to raise also the questions of pay for members of the House of Commons. I reminded the Prime Minister of the great dissatisfaction among Labour M.P.s at the failure of the previous Government to carry out the proposals of the Select Committee.[27]

I brought in the question of pensions and made it plain that we could not possibly agree to the Members' Fund proposals for a large increase in contributions with no contribution from the Government in order to obtain what was still an inadequate pension.[28] I did, however, add that I thought that, subject to details, we might be prepared for something on the lines of a superannuation scheme in which the Government as well as the Member contributed. I said, however, that even this would be very

27 The Select Committee – of 6 Conservative and 6 Labour M.P.s, with the Liberal leader Clement Davies in the chair – had reported unanimously on 16 February 1954. It found that M.P.s' salaries were worth less in 1953 than when they were introduced in 1911 (though taxation was much heavier and the number of badly-off M.P.s much greater), and recommended an immediate increase from £1,000 to £1,500. On 14 April Churchill's Government refused but offered to consider alternatives. In a free vote on 24 May, the House approved very similar proposals by 280 to 166; but Conservative back-benchers were overwhelmingly opposed, and on 24 June the Government again refused. The Parliamentary Labour Party reacted furiously, withdrawing all pairs, and on 8 July the Government agreed to introduce a new sessional allowance for expenses.

28 The Fund was raised from a levy on M.P.s' salaries, and spent on relieving hardship cases. As these were becoming more frequent and the assistance less adequate, the Select Committee had called urgently for a non-contributory pensions scheme, but this met even stronger opposition than the salary increase, and was not proposed on 24 May.

difficult unless the basic pay were adjusted. I also indicated that we would be quite willing to consider something like the French system under which Members' pay was related to pay in the Civil Service.

The Prime Minister said that, as regards the House of Lords, he himself, as well as Lord Salisbury, was keen on Reform. He believed in a Second Chamber but the present situation was unsatisfactory, not only so far as Labour Peers were concerned but also on the Conservative side. Lord Salisbury was still pursuing his enquiries. What they had in mind was some Peers elected by Hereditary Peers and others – Life Peers – who would be chosen more or less on Party lines. He made it plain that until the question of whether there was to be Reform or not had been settled, it was not possible to make progress either on the question of an expense allowance for Peers or on the question of an increase in the number of Labour Peers, but he hoped that Lord Salisbury would come to a conclusion on this matter in a month or so. He thought that the chances were fifty/fifty – no more than that.

On the question of Members' pay, he said he was aware of the feeling on our side and there was also the difficulty of Junior Ministers both in the Commons and in the Lords.[29] He said he would be prepared for minor adjustments but intimated in rather general terms that anything more substantial could only be done as part of a general package deal. I said that for my part a package deal would not necessarily be rejected by our people. They would be prepared to be much better disposed to changes in the House of Lords – especially expense allowances – if their own conditions were taken care of.

On the Reform of the House of Lords, I said that our people, in general, were not well disposed to this because although the Prime Minister might say – as he had done – that there would be no change in powers for the Second Chamber, there was always the danger that it might be given more powers.

I made it plain that we were likely to oppose the suggestions he had outlined. I thought the only kind of Reform would be one on the lines of the Norwegian system in which the strength of the Second Chamber was determined by the proportional strength of the Parties in the First Chamber, i.e. Peers would be appointed in proportion to the General Election results in the House of Commons. The Prime Minister made it pretty plain that he would have great difficulty in getting a proposal of this kind passed by the Hereditary Peers who were difficult enough about any Reform. He also implied that they might very well drop any attempt at an

29 Junior Ministers usually became worse off by taking office, since they could not draw the sessional allowance or earn money by outside activities. Their grievance attracted much more government sympathy than the others' did.

agreement with us and force through a Reform on the lines he had indicated.

Finally, he suggested that on the question of Members' pay, I should have a talk with [R.A. Butler] the Leader of the House while the Prime Minister was in America.[30]

17th January, 1956.

Document No. 14b

NOTE OF CONVERSATION WITH THE FINANCE MINISTER OF KENYA

18th January 1956

Mr. Vasey, the Minister of Finance in Kenya, came to see me this afternoon. I was much impressed with his remarkably progressive outlook.

He began by referring to the Royal Commission Report and expressed surprise that Arthur – my brother – should have signed a Report which was so antagonistic to the development of Trade Unionism.[31] He and his friends in Kenya regarded Arthur as their trump card and he couldn't help feeling that on this particular point the Commission had made a great mistake. He was perfectly friendly – indeed, more than friendly – about A.G. and I explained how difficult A.G.'s position had been. He had been very near to putting in a Minority Report but, having been a

30 Eden rejected another approach from HG and Clement Davies on 15 June 1956, and his uninformative memoirs (Eden, 1960, p. 327) make his personal hostility fairly clear. On 4 July 1957, six months after becoming Prime Minister, Macmillan introduced legislation which (inter alia) raised M.P.s' salaries to £1,750, gave Junior Ministers an additional £1,000 a year, and brought in attendance allowances for peers. HG attacked these allowances as quite inadequate in the debates next session on the government's Life Peerages Bill, which Labour criticised but did not oppose; the P.L.P. without argument agreed with his view that Labour should put forward names (see *HG*, p. 470). Twelve years later his nominees were still the Party's mainstay in the upper house.

31 The Royal Commission on Land Ownership and Population in East Africa was appointed in January 1953, with Sir Hugh Dow (ex-Indian Civil Service) as chairman and Arthur Gaitskell, who had been manager of a cotton-growing cooperative in the Sudan, as a member. Its report, published on 9 June 1956, favoured minimum wages and wages councils but dismissed attempts to develop trade unions on the British model as a waste of effort for some time to come.

team worker, he decided against it. I promised to pass on these views to A.G.

On the political situation, he made it clear that, in his opinion, it was essential to move towards genuine African self-government. He thought the Coutts Report, so far as it went, was satisfactory, but it left untouched some crucial questions.[32]

For instance, how many representatives were the Africans to have? Under the present arrangements there were six representing six million people – which was absurd. The representation ought to be increased at once to a fifty-fifty basis with the Europeans – say fourteen each – with the Indians having a kind of proportional representation. In due course, when the Africans had had more experience of participation in Government legislation, they would, of course, have to have increased representation. He said the Africans were, in fact, perfectly reasonable. They were not asking for self-government; indeed they had a lot to learn. If we held back too long we were simply asking for trouble.

I asked Mr. Vasey how he managed to get on with the other Europeans as his views were so left-wing. He told me that he had been twice elected as a 'Socialist'. He thought that, even now, if he stood in an election where there were European votes only he would only just manage it.

He said that in the last ten years many Europeans had become far more reasonable and progressive and nearly half of them were broadly of the same opinion as he was, namely, that you have to move on towards self-government. It was only in the interior where the people on the farms were remote from the more educated Africans that the more reactionary views were held.

I was altogether surprised by Mr. Vasey. He was so completely unlike anything I expected. He reminded me of a more left-wing Civil Servant – not particularly pushing or aspiring. A short-sighted little man who spoke with precision and logically – rather donnish in fact. I felt it was all pretty encouraging.[33]

32 The report by W.F. Coutts (who had become Minister of Education Labour and Lands) was published on 10 January 1956, and led to a bill passed in February for the 8 unofficial African members of the Legislative Council to be elected. At the first contest in March 1957, six sitting members (nominated under the old rules) were defeated, and the newcomers – led by Tom Mboya of the Kenya trade unions – pressed for much more rapid political changes. These were conceded in part in November 1957 (when the African seats were increased to 14) and fully in February 1960.

33 (Sir) Ernest Vasey was Finance Minister of Kenya 1952–9, of Tanganyika 1959–62, and later was the World Bank's resident adviser in Pakistan. He had once been a councillor in Shrewsbury, and was Mayor of Nairobi during the war. His liberal views were more widely shared among his compatriots in Kenya than among their counterparts in Rhodesia or Algeria.

He said, incidentally, that he was going to Jamaica and then to America and would be back on February 2nd when he had to lecture to the Empire Society. He proposed on that occasion to take a line similar to that which he had expressed to me.

Diary, 16–21 January, 1956

I lunched [on Monday 16 January] with Sydney Elliott, the Editor of the *Daily Herald*. He is not a friend of mine – in fact, I have often thought his appointment as Editor was disastrous. He comes from an I.L.P. stable, and most of the accounts I hear of him on the *Daily Herald* are not at all favourable.[34] Since his appointment there has been nothing but trouble and friction with the staff, and from time to time the policy of the paper has been in conflict with that of the Party. He has brought lots of people from the *Daily Mirror*, but as far as I can make out, most of them people the *Mirror* was glad to get rid of.

Nevertheless I thought it best to maintain relations with him. We had quite a satisfactory talk. I complained bitterly about an article on the Middle East by Basil Davidson, whom most people believe to be a Communist, and who ought not, in my view, to be employed on the paper. This is not the first time I have complained about him. I have written several letters to Surrey Dane, the Chairman of the Board, about other articles of his.[35]

Elliott made no attempt to defend the article, but blamed Hutchinson, the Deputy Editor, to whom, he said, he had entrusted the responsibility for vetting it.[36] (It was, in fact, an article which managed to say nothing at

---

34 Sydney Elliott edited *Reynolds News*, the Cooperatives' Sunday paper, 1929–41 and strongly supported a Popular Front, which in 1939 the Cooperative Party rejected. He was editor of the *Evening Standard* 1943–4, and of the *Daily Herald* 1953–7. For an example of relations with the *Herald*'s senior staff see Hunter (1959), pp. 162, 168, 170.

35 Basil Davidson, a journalist on the *Herald* 1954–7 (previously on *The Times* and *New Statesman*, later on the *Mirror*) had not yet made his reputation as a historian of Africa. HG's earlier complaints were largely about Davidson opposing German rearmament after the Party decision (see *HG*, Ch. 10 n. 165, Ch. 11 n. 68). This rather unattractive habit of his reflected his feeling that the Left dominated most of the sources read by Labour activists (*Tribune*, *New Statesman*, *Reynolds* and Crossman's column) and that the leadership could not risk losing control of its one official forum. W. Surrey Dane, an Odhams director who had played a big part in building up the *Daily Herald* in the 1930s, was ousted by Cecil King after his takeover in 1961 (on that, *HG*, p. 668).

36 Harold Hutchinson, unlike his editor, was a strong sympathiser with HG.

all about the Arab-Israel dispute, and was a thinly veiled version of the normal Communist line.)

We went to the London Labour Party reunion in the evening (16th). I came away most depressed. It was moderately well attended, but extremely badly supported by M.P.s and Councillors. Also I thought the audience was very cold. The whole thing was badly managed. If only people would spend a little more trouble in thinking out how to organise these things, what a difference it would make. Of course, it was not made any easier for me by the fact that Herbert Morrison deliberately stayed away – London being his own ground.[37] On the other hand, I did not feel there was much emotion about his defeat for the leadership.

On the 18th I spoke to the National Council of Labour. It was well attended by the Trade Union and Co-op people.[38] The interesting feature of it was the complete confusion about their ideas of 'Socialism', and their recognition of the need for a lot more clear thinking.

I lunched [that day] with Harold Wilson, and we had quite a satisfactory talk. But nothing much emerged. He really seems to be getting on with the organisation job. We kept off future [Shadow] responsibilities.

On the 19th I lunched with Derek Marks, the *Daily Express* Parliamentary and Diplomatic Correspondent, together with Hugh Pilcher, who introduced me to him as a friend of his. I do not care much for Marks. He is a typical *Daily Express* product – cynical and rather bumptious – but I must admit his conversation was interesting. It was chiefly about the Tory Party. He confirmed what Virginia Crawley had told me the night before – that the real trouble with Eden is that he has no friends. Marks qualified this by saying that his only friends were people of insignificance. This group was described by the Tory back-benchers as the 'kissing ring' and the 'inner kissing ring'. I gathered it consisted of people like Noble and Nutting.[39] The attack in the *Telegraph* was not, he thought, inspired so much by Pamela Berry* as by the fact that neither Coote, the Editor, nor Donald McLachlan, the Assistant Editor, had any high opinion of

---

37 Morrison had been Secretary of the London Labour Party for 32 years, 1915–47.
38 Meeting monthly, this body comprised representatives of the N.E.C., General Council and Cooperative Movement. It had been important in Labour policy-making in the 1930s.
39 Commander (Sir) Allan Noble, Conservative M.P. for Chelsea, had been Eden's P.P.S. 1947–51. He was Under-Secretary for Commonwealth Relations. (Sir) Anthony Nutting sat for Melton Mowbray (Leics.) 1945–56, and was Under-Secretary at the Foreign Office under Eden, 1951–4, when he moved up to Minister of State. He opposed the Suez invasion and in November 1956 resigned both his office (which Noble took over) and his seat.

Eden and his group of friends.[40] Marks doubted whether Eden would, in fact, stay the course.

On Butler, he said that he had been very much upset by my attack upon him, particularly of my criticism of him for being dishonest. Both Pilcher and I maintained that this was completely justified, and gave a number of instances where we thought in political terms he had been guilty of dishonesty. Marks had no real reply to this, but persisted in the view that he had been upset. He had wanted to leave the Treasury earlier, but agreed with me that he would not be in a powerful position as Lord Privy Seal.[41]

There seems to be no doubt that Macmillan* was not getting on at all well with Eden as Foreign Secretary,[42] and that Tory opinion is rather veering round towards him as the best of the three.

On the subject of Eden we had an interesting talk, comparing him with Attlee. I said that in a sense Attlee too had no friends, but it was in a different sense, in that he had no favourites. He was aloof from the battle. Marks said, 'Well, I will tell you the difference between them. One of Attlee's great strengths is that he did not mind whether people liked him. Eden minds terribly.'

Another person under discussion was Walter Monckton. Marks confirmed, as I had heard from others, that Goddard was absolutely unwilling to give up being Lord Chief Justice in order to let in Walter Monckton, whom he evidently dislikes.[43] This had become known to Walter, who has been waiting for the job. But now, apparently, he has abandoned hope. He is said, according to Marks, to have committed himself to a continued political career. I find this hard to believe. It is much more likely that Monckton is staying in politics because he is still waiting and hoping for the L.C.J. job. He might, of course, have been Lord Chancellor, but according to Marks this had to go to David Maxwell [Fyfe, Viscount

40 (Sir) Colin Coote, a former Liberal M.P. and *Times* leader-writer, was deputy editor 1942–50 and managing editor 1950–64. McLachlan had worked on *The Times* and *The Economist*, and edited the *Sunday Telegraph* 1961–6. As deputy editor of the *Daily Telegraph* (1954–61) he wrote the leader of 3 January 1956 (above, p. 414, n. 20) about the 'smack of firm government'. Michael Berry, Lady Pamela's husband, who was part-proprietor and Editor-in-Chief-for-Life, was abroad at the time.

41 Butler had become Lord Privy Seal on 20 December 1955, seven weeks after HG's denunciation of his autumn budget (545 H.C. Deb. 390–408): 'having bought his votes with a bribe, the Chancellor is forced – as he knew he would be – to dishonour the cheque . . . He has behaved in a manner unworthy of his high office'. Undoubtedly he was upset.

42 Confirmed or hinted at by A. Sampson, *Macmillan* (Penguin, 1967), pp. 105, 111–12; R. Churchill, *The Rise and Fall of Sir Anthony Eden* (McGibbon & Kee, 1959), pp. 206–7; H. Macmillan, *Riding the Storm* (Macmillan, 1971), p. 1.

43 Lord Goddard, a judge since 1932, was Lord Chief Justice 1946–58 when he retired at the age of 81.

Kilmuir*], largely on financial grounds, because the latter had done too little work at the Bar while they were in Opposition, and had no savings; also he had married a young wife and had young children.

There was a curious episode with Lady Pamela Berry this week. We had arranged a small party at home for Wednesday evening, with dancing, and a very select group were being asked to this. In the middle of the day Dora rang me up to say that Aidan Crawley had asked if Lady Pamela could come with Frank Pakenham[44] . . . In the event, she did not turn up.

But the next day we met her at the Fashion Reception which she was giving for Overseas Buyers at Fishmongers Hall, and the following occurred.[45] Dora and I were brought in through the crowd to shake hands with her, as hostess, in the ordinary way. Now normally at these gatherings, having shaken hands, one wanders off, and does one's stuff with the Overseas Buyers, who are supposed to be impressed by the presence of leading politicians. On this occasion, however, partly perhaps because we arrived rather late, nothing of this sort occurred. Lady Pamela was obviously determined to talk to us. She said that she had expected to come to the party, that she had got all ready and 'done her face', because Frank had promised to pick her up, presumably at about 10 o'clock. His story was that he could not get anybody to answer the bell, and she, of course, was bitterly disappointed. There was a lot of badinage about the Edens. Hartley [Shawcross] came up and said, 'Why wasn't Clarissa [Lady Eden] at the reception?' Lady Pamela then turned and talked to me, and said, 'Tell me, Mr Gaitskell, is it possible to get rid of a Prime Minister in peacetime?' I said, 'It is extremely difficult if he doesn't want to go. But you can, of course, make life so intolerable for him that he becomes ill and cannot carry on.' 'You aren't suggesting that I should murder him?' she said.

She continued to talk in this strain, and in reference to the *Telegraph* leading article on the Prime Minister's speech at Bradford, which she said had made it impossible for her husband to bring her to our party the previous night, she was obviously pleased with the title, which indeed she may have suggested herself – 'The Curate's Egg'.[46]

There was a lot of photographing of her with all the Labour people there, but I don't suppose the results will ever be printed. She struck me as being slightly crackers . . . We dined with the Plowdens on the Thursday night, very nice, just ourselves and them. Edwin [Plowden] is extremely funny about Sir Christopher Hinton, who is the genius

44 The omitted passage discussed the invitation, at length.
45 Lady Pamela was President of the Incorporated Society of London Fashion Designers.
46 The speech was Eden's reply to the press attacks on him.

responsible for all the engineering side of Atomic Energy, but is completely and utterly impossible as a man. Edwin always complains about Hinton and the others, and speaks wistfully of the nice people he used to know in the Treasury. He has now apparently ordered Hinton to go away for six months rest, but only after a tremendous scene. Edwin is speaking of giving up after he has completed his five years, but I don't take this seriously.[47] He always talks in that strain. On the following night we dined with the Tyermans*, also alone, and also very nice. Donald did not add very much to the gossip about Eden, but he did say one thing about Macmillan. It appears that Macmillan met the financial journalists and to them proclaimed in the most determined and unqualified way his adherence to the theory of brimful employment, i.e. the maintenance of the Butler standard of Full Employment. Donald admitted he did not know whether this was done deliberately as a kind of cover behind which in fact a deflationary policy would be carried out, or whether it really represented Macmillan's personal views.[48] Eden in his T.V. broadcast appeared to take rather the same line, though less violently.

Diary, 23–30 January, 1956 [dictated Tuesday 31st]

A reasonably quiet week. On the Monday evening [23 January], a largish dinner given by the Indian Journalists in honour of their Republic Day. We talked for some time with Mrs Pandit, who was very affable. I mentioned to her a project which Norman Robertson* had suggested to me: namely, that Nehru should ask the Attlees to tour India.[49] She said that she had heard of this from Norman, and had in fact been thinking nearly the same idea herself. I gather she will propose it to Nehru when she goes there in the near future, but we may hear more of this at the dinner she is giving for the Attlees on February 1st.

National Executive [Wednesday] went very satisfactorily. Mikardo

47 Sir C. (Lord) Hinton, O.M., F.R.S., was Managing Director of the Atomic Energy Authority 1954–7 (and chairman of the Central Electricity Generating Board 1957–64). Plowden did give up as A.E.A. chairman after five years, in 1959.
48 Macmillan had just become Chancellor of the Exchequer, and this sign of early uncertainty about his personal views is noteworthy, since they became so well known later.
49 Mrs V.L. Pandit and Norman Robertson were High Commissioners of India and Canada respectively. She had been Ambassador in Moscow 1947–9, in Washington 1949–51, and was in London 1954–61. She was the sister of Jawaharlal Nehru, Prime Minister 1947–64 (and father of Indira Gandhi).

made a rather mild effort to argue that the Treasurership should go to the runner-up. He was supported by Barbara Castle, and eventually a vote was taken – those two, plus Crossman and Driberg, voting against the rest, who wanted me to stay in the job for the time being.[50]

We got the Middle East statement through quite easily, heavily amended by myself, and even Edith Summerskill swallowed it. It had been, of course, much helped by the debate the day before, and in fact followed the lines of my speech.

The debate itself, incidentally, had been rather inconclusive. We had got into a somewhat dangerous position, partly perhaps owing to my rashness in going to Downing Street, but more because of the Press handling of the whole episode. As in fact we had all expected, the White Paper, while completely endorsing the reports in the Press about surplus arms for the Middle East, and indeed adding to them, showed that they did not amount to a great deal in terms of military power. This looked as though we had been making a fuss about nothing. However, we managed to make our position fairly clear, and then switched the debate onto Middle Eastern policy as a whole.[51]

I was disappointed with Selwyn Lloyd's reply. The most he would say was that they would consider the qualitative balance of arms, and that he liked the idea of some kind of frontier force to help General Burns.[52] My fears in this direction were accentuated when, on the following day, one of the American Broadcasting men came to me with a tape recorder and asked me for a statement. I gave him this, but before I did so he showed me what he was going to say about the British Government attitude. This suggested that they were going to do absolutely nothing at all, that they were much too frightened of offending the Arabs to attempt to maintain the balance, or indeed to take the Tripartite Declaration seriously. However this particular man, Yale Newman, is probably not very reliable.

To return to the N.E.C., the organisation seems to be going along well now. The Sub-Committee [on organisation, under Harold Wilson] have

---

50 HG therefore remained Treasurer as well as Leader until the next Conference, like Arthur Henderson in the 1930s. Bevan, of course, had been runner-up.

51 HG had asked for the White Paper (Cmd. 9676) on his visit to Downing Street, and in his speech (548 H.C. Deb. 54–74; 24.2.56) he criticised the Government for lax administration (over the export licences for the surplus arms) and for tilting the diplomatic and military balance against Israel. Edith Summerskill strongly supported the Arabs (a view then unusual in the Labour Party).

52 Lt-General Burns, a Canadian, was U.N. chief of staff supervising the truce in Palestine; after Suez he commanded the U.N. Emergency Force.

really made progress, and I think we can leave all that to advance to some extent under its own steam.[53]

I lunched with Campbell Stuart* on Thursday. When he invited me he implied he was going to give me all sorts of interesting information. But it did not amount to a great deal. He spoke at length about his own life, and how he had come to live in England. It seems that he had originally intended to go into Canadian politics, but that during the First World War, having raised a Canadian Regiment, he was sent by the Canadian Prime Minister, Sir Robert Borden, to the British Embassy in Washington. His arrival there was not particularly well received by the Ambassador, Spring-Rice, who said to him, 'Your appointment is rather unusual. It is the first time we have ever had a *Colonial* here.' He then said, 'Where were you educated?' Campbell replied that he was educated at some Canadian school which, so he said, was a very good one; and the Ambassador said, 'Oh, all my people here were at Eton'.[54]

Disliking the atmosphere of the Embassy, Campbell noticed one day that Lord Northcliffe had been sent out in charge of the British Purchasing Commission. He had met Northcliffe in London once or twice, and decided to try and see him. So – all this is according to Campbell – he put on his resplendent uniform, dashed to New York, went to Northcliffe's hotel, and asked to see him. The clerks were so impressed by the uniform that they allowed him to go up to Lord Northcliffe's bedroom, although he was in bed. So there he was, standing in the bedroom, and Northcliffe saying 'What the hell are you doing here?' Campbell replied, 'I don't really know. I just wanted to see you. Anyway, what are *you* doing here?'

They got on very well, and within half an hour Northcliffe had said, 'Send a telegram from me to Mr Balfour (then Foreign Secretary) asking that I can have you as my Military Secretary'. Campbell said he went downstairs and sent it off from the hotel, paying for it with his own money. He then returned to Washington. Two days later, the Ambassador sent for him and said, 'I have just had a very queer telegram. Do you know Lord Northcliffe?' He said, 'I have met him two or three times'. 'Well, he seems to think a lot of you. I have a telegram from the Foreign Secretary saying I am to release you to go to him. When could you go?'

53 Wilson had chaired a committee of inquiry into Labour organisation after the 1955 defeat, which was set up partly at HG's instigation and reported on 5 October 1955, condemning the Party's 'penny-farthing machine'. One by-product was this new Organisation Sub-committee of the N.E.C., which he also chaired.

54 Borden (1854–1937) led the Canadian Conservatives from 1901, was Prime Minister 1911–20 and represented Canada at the Peace Conference and at the League of Nations. Sir Cecil Spring-Rice (1859–1918) was Minister to Persia and Sweden before serving in Washington 1912–18.

Campbell said, 'In fifteen minutes, Sir', which surprised the Ambassador, who, however, no doubt quite willingly parted from him.

Campbell was obviously the kind of quick, bold young man whom Northcliffe liked, and they got on extremely well. Northcliffe apparently liked those who push their way through life and show initiative, and that certainly Campbell had done. He continued with Northcliffe in that job, later becoming his deputy, for the next few years. Then, when he was about to return to Canada, still intending to go on to a political career, Northcliffe asked him to stay, and said, 'Are there any terms on which you would stay?' Campbell, again according to himself, said, more as a joke than anything else, 'Well, of course, if you were to make me Managing Director of *The Times* I might consider it'. Whereupon Northcliffe rang for his secretary and said, 'Prepare a contract appointing Sir Campbell Stuart as Managing Director. He can fill in his own salary and the terms of his appointment. I'm going off to Broadstairs.'[55]

Later on, we got on to more up to date things. Campbell thinks that Lady Pamela really does control the *Telegraph*, and that her relationship to Michael Berry is somewhat similar to [what] that of Ann Rothermere (now Fleming)* used to be to Lord R and the *Daily Mail*, only, he said, 'Lady Pamela is a cleverer woman and a stronger personality'. He did not give me any clear picture as to why Lady Pamela disliked Clarissa [Eden].

We talked about Eden, Macmillan and Butler, and found ourselves on the whole in agreement, though Campbell added the interesting bit of information that Lord Birkenhead, Lady Pamela's brother, had in fact been staying with Rab [Butler] at Somerset Maugham's villa in the South of France, so there may possibly be a tie-up there.

Finally, he gave me various bits of advice. He was anxious that I should keep in with the Haleys*. He thought that we ought to ask them out – they would like it very much, and after all, the Editor of *The Times* was important.

On saying goodbye, he said to me, 'Well, I think you have a more interesting life than anybody else I know'.

He is a much disliked man, partly because he is, so everybody says, a pansy; but more because he is not trusted. But he is amusing, and is now, I think, past the stage when he very actively desires to do anybody down. For some reason or other, Dora and he always get on well. She tells this story of how, dining with him one night, he asked her a lot of questions about her past, trying to find out, as she put it, how on earth she came to marry me. Whereupon she said to him, 'It's no use, Campbell, I can

55 Alfred Harmsworth, Lord Northcliffe (1865–1922) was the founder of the *Daily Mail* and of cheap popular journalism, and the first of the press barons; Cecil Harmsworth King was his nephew. He controlled *The Times*, 1908–22.

blackmail you just as easily as you can blackmail me!' Which, of course, amused him.

He talked a little about Beaverbrook*, whom he knows very well, and said that he was convinced that the support of the *Express* group for Eden was deliberate, and done in order to damage Eden.[56] Beaverbrook knew very well that the people he supported suffered harm from it, and he [Stuart] was sure that he had not given up his intense dislike for Eden. Personally, I rather doubt that, and think it more likely that he is merely carrying out Churchill's wishes.

Went [on Thursday] to see Julia act in her school play, 'The Lady's Not for Burning'. It was remarkably good all round. I found it very hard to say whether she can really act, but she certainly has got a very beautiful voice, and said the lines most attractively. I own it is difficult to judge one's own daughter, but I think she should try [to act].

Friday evening was the T.V., for which we had prepared so long. I should say the result was fair. In some ways it was the most relaxed performance I have done, but it was less forceful than perhaps it should have been. It has made a good impression on marginal voters, etc., but very little impact. This may have been to some extent inevitable, but the real problem here is, I think, being sufficiently spontaneous and yet keeping within the time. In order to keep within the time you have to practise, but if you practise too much, and still more if you try to learn by heart, then it loses its natural effect. You have to sacrifice something. If you learn it by heart, you can no doubt get all the best phrases in, but unless you have masses of time and really treat it like an act, it is no good. In a General Election, one would never have time to do this. Therefore I think it is a mistake to start trying. Better rather to practise speaking for exactly the right length on different subjects – possibly a tape recorder or dictaphone will help here. But there will always be an element of chance, just as there is with an ordinary speech. I have made the same speech again and again in the General Election – but it is never quite the same speech – and sometimes it is successful and sometimes not, and I cannot tell in advance just how it is going to go. That is at the moment the uncontrollable element. Perhaps with practice one can bring it more under control. The one clear lesson which comes out of this, I think, is that I must at an earlier stage start getting the timing right – I left it too late to squeeze what I wanted to say into the 15 minutes.

56 When the *Telegraph* and *Mail* began attacking Eden, the *Express* began supporting him.

Went to Buxton for the weekend for *Reynolds News* Co-op Convention – quite a pleasant occasion, and I had some useful talks with the leading Co-op people. They liked my speech in the morning, which indeed some described as a landmark in the relations between the Co-op and the Labour Party. I did not say a great deal, but pointed out the muddle they were all in and the confusion of their ideals of co-operation in relation to socialism.

Dined at the French Embassy last night. On paper, it could not have been a nicer party. It was really in our honour, and those present included Sir Ian Jacob, head of the B.B.C., Oliver Franks, ex-Ambassador in Washington, and head of Lloyds Bank, Edwin Plowden, head of the Atomic Energy Commission, Ifor Evans, Provost of University College and the leading Arts Council figure, Rose Macaulay and Rosamond Lehmann – the men, of course, with their wives.[57] Not only were they quite a glittering list, but many of them are friends of mine. Well, it was really not a successful evening. I had some enjoyable and witty conversation with Oliver during dinner, and the same with Rose Macaulay, whom I met for the second time in my life. She looks about a hundred, but she is extremely lively and engaging. I think the trouble really was that the rooms are too big, and that therefore everybody got scattered and separated. But it is the kind of dinner party that sounds wonderful when you hear the names, and yet somehow it does not work out that way.

[Dictated 1 February, 1956]

A lot of trouble is building up about Malta. Last September, an all-Party Conference went into the question of what was to be done. The alternatives were either some form of self-government on the lines of Dominion status, or what is called integration with the United Kingdom, somewhat similar to the case of Northern Ireland. The Conference plumped firmly for the second alternative, which was that favoured by the Malta Labour Party, and indeed that on which they had won an Election in Malta, though by a fairly narrow majority.

The proposals of the Conference involved a referendum in Malta, and

57 Lt-General Sir Ian Jacob was Director-General (succeeding Haley) 1952–60. Sir Ifor Evans, a professor of English, Vice-Chairman of the Arts Council 1946–51, was head of Queen Mary College 1944–51, and then of University College where HG had taught economics for 11 years before the war. Both ladies were very prominent authoresses.

it was not made clear whether this should take place before or after any decision in the House of Commons.

The Labour Prime Minister of Malta, Mintoff* – a nice little man with an English wife, but with little political experience – favoured having the referendum first. I understood, when I heard about this before Christmas, that that was also everybody else's view. It seemed logical enough that before the British Parliament could pronounce, it must find out what the Maltese themselves wanted. Moreover, Mintoff informed us on the Labour side that he thought it best not to have the question discussed in the House of Commons till after the referendum.

Now, however, trouble has blown up in Malta. And the trouble seems to centre round or emanate from the Catholic Church. They are believed to be opposed to integration, although they have not officially come out against it. But undoubtedly there is great friction between the Church and the Labour Party in Malta. Mintoff has been deluging me with messages asking me to intervene with the Government here on a number of matters, and in particular to bring pressure to bear upon the Vatican, so that the Vatican in their turn may stop the Maltese Church from being so hostile to the referendum. I have left almost the whole of this to Jim Griffiths, who is not only our expert on Colonial affairs, but was also a member of the Conference.[58] What Mintoff wanted was intervention in Rome on the one hand, and also a firm declaration, to answer the subtle propaganda of the Catholic Church, that the British Parliament would not interfere in religious matters in Malta after the integration had gone through.[59]

I could not see any particular reason why the British Government should not do these things. But on Monday, Jim Griffiths and I saw Lennox-Boyd*, the Colonial Secretary, and he rather shocked me by (a) showing great impatience with Mintoff's behaviour, and (b) making it quite plain that the Government were not prepared to announce their attitude to the Conference report until after the debate in the House of Commons. We had some rather sharp words about this, but I was unable to shift him. Lennox-Boyd assured us that he was entirely in favour of integration, and hinted that if it did not go through he would have to consider resignation, as also [Kilmuir] the Lord Chancellor, who was the Chairman of the Conference that recommended it. But he seemed to be rather worried about the Catholics on the Tory side, and also implied, wrongly as far as I can see, that various people on our side were doubtful about integration.

However, Jim Griffiths has put down a question for today, the answer

58 So were Attlee and Bevan.
59 The Church was suggesting it would so interfere; the declaration sought was a denial.

of which we hope will help, even if the Government cannot come out 100% behind the Conference Report, if they make it plain in so many words that that is their intention, and if we then support that, it may help the situation in Malta.

Meanwhile, however, Mintoff says that priests in Malta are saying that those who vote for integration will be refused absolution, and there seems to be a terrific row going on over there.

I also saw the Governor of Malta, Sir Robert Laycock, who was over here last weekend. I have always heard very good accounts of him. He was an outstanding soldier, and was reputed to have a rather progressive outlook. He married the daughter of Mrs Dudley Ward, as she then was, who was Edward VIII's mistress for 18 years, so society gossip alleges.[60] The interview with him confirmed his reputation. But though obviously in favour of integration, he thinks Mintoff has behaved very foolishly. He said it would be far better to have had the debate in Parliament first, and left the referendum till later. Apparently the reason why Mintoff hurried the referendum was because of Lent. During Lent it appears that the hold of the Church on the people of Malta is very much greater. The priests would be able to get to work more effectively during this period, and discourage people from voting for integration. Therefore, thought Mintoff, we must have the referendum before Lent began. This belief, according to Laycock, was a mistake, because it led to every kind of accusation that the thing was being forced before people had an opportunity of making up their minds.[61]

Moreover, when a priest apparently did say in his Church that those who voted for integration would be refused absolution, Mintoff, says Laycock, should have gone to the Archbishop quietly, and said 'Please will you deny this and discipline the priest?' Instead he sent two of his Ministers to the priest's Superior – not the Archbishop – and threatened that if the priest did not stop they would prosecute him. This, of course, upset the Church more than somewhat. There have also been a good many ugly incidents, anti-integration meetings being broken up (the Press is entirely in the hands of the anti's, and to balance this, Mintoff has more or less collared the radio).

My old friend Tommy Balogh* is, oddly enough, in the middle of all

60 Major General Sir Robert Laycock (1907–68) was Chief of Combined Operations 1943–7, Governor of Malta 1954–9, Lord Lieutenant of Notts. 1962–8. On Mrs Dudley Ward and her daughter, see Frances Donaldson, *Edward VIII* (Weidenfeld & Nicolson, 1974; Futura ed. 1976, pp. 57–60, 108–9, 159–60).

61 The opposition Nationalist Party favoured boycotting the referendum, Archbishop Michael Gonzi and the Catholic Church wanted it postponed. See also below, pp. 453–4, 469–70.

this. Some time ago he went out at Mintoff's request to do an Economic Report on Malta, and since then has become Mintoff's chief adviser on everything. The Governor, however, quite approves of him, and even uses him as a person to influence Mintoff in the right direction. Lennox-Boyd, on the other hand, was obviously irritated with Tommy's intervention. He said petulantly, 'Mintoff is such a fool, and he is advised by that Hungarian Jew'. Laycock, however, as I say, thinks Tommy useful, though rather tactless, and when I suggested he should let me know if there was anything the Labour Party here could do, he, Laycock, asked if he could use Tommy as an intermediary with me. I said that would be perfectly all right. Tommy, however, is so like Mintoff in many ways, so apt to get into a panic, so apt to think that unless something urgent is done the battle is being lost, so inclined to suspect persecution, particularly from the Catholic Church, that I am not sure he is quite such a good influence at the moment! Part of the trouble is that Laycock himself has been over here, and Mintoff has been doing all these silly things while he was away. Thank goodness, however, he went back yesterday, and I am hoping he will be able to cope with the situation if there is an open row with the Church in Malta, and the Church comes out openly against integration – if this happens, it could have very serious consequences. But I gather in fact the Government have intervened with the Vatican, and if Mintoff behaves sensibly there is no real danger of that.

Mrs Pandit came to see me yesterday. She is going back to India on a short visit, and said she wished to have a chat with me before she went. I think it was chiefly courtesy, but she made out that she would like to tell her brother [Nehru] what my views were on the existing world situation. She said that the Government in India was in a frightful state at the moment, irritated with everybody, particularly about these Pacts.[62] I said she would know my general attitude to defence pacts, which was favourable. I had been a strong supporter of NATO. On the other hand, whether the Baghdad Pact, which was the one Nehru particularly objected to, was really desirable or not, seemed to me a matter not of principle, but of whether it would work. I do not myself think that it would make much difference either way. There was neither ground for being very enthusiastic, nor for being very hostile. In fact, the Labour Party had been luke-warm to it, but had not opposed it.

We then went on to Pakistan and Kashmir. I made it plain that I thought the Indians were on bad ground here, because of their refusal to accept a plebiscite. Mrs Pandit did not demur from this at all. I also said that if Nehru really wanted to have his foreign policy accepted by

62 The irritation was especially with Pakistan, which had adhered to SEATO in 1954 and to the Baghdad Pact (with Iraq, Turkey and the U.K.) in September 1955, acquiring U.S. aid and allies both to the east and west of India.

Pakistan he should never have quarrelled with them over Kashmir.[63] I was convinced that they had gone in with Turkey partly in order to get military aid from the U.S.A., but partly also just to snub Nehru. In accepting the aid, they were undoubtedly thinking of Kashmir, not in terms of aggression, but in terms of balancing Indian power. If he had had the sense to come to terms with them over Kashmir, it is extremely unlikely that they would have signed the pact with Turkey. She listened to all this, and seemed to accept it. She is a woman of great charm, but how intelligent she really is I do not know. I think she had some difficulty in coping with her brother. She thought the Khrushchev visit had been a great help to Nehru, because it had taken the wind out of the Communist sails in India. This would be useful in the Election next year. But what he said had embarrassed them, and been altogether a bore.[64]

[Dictated on Friday, 3 February, 1956]

The Afghan Minister came to see me yesterday. He is a rather small, pale, pleasant-looking man, who speaks in a very soft voice. It was therefore difficult to follow what he said, but broadly speaking it amounted to this: that there were a fair number of people of Afghan stock in Pakistan, occupying about half the North West Frontier province. They were in a state of more or less continual dispute or revolt against the Pakistan Government, and there was great sympathy for them in Afghanistan. His country did not want to alter the frontiers, which he admitted were those of British India, but they wanted to see some form of semi-independent state created – Pathoonistan. Unfortunately, Pakistan would not even discuss the problem with them. The result was that they might be driven more and more to look to Russia. Khrushchev had been to Kabul, and had made some very friendly speeches, indicating his sympathy for them on this issue, and they had recently had a loan of 100 million dollars without any strings. He said that they knew very well that they could not

63 The dispute went back to the partition of India in 1947. Nehru jeopardised India's reputation for international morality by allowing Kashmir's Hindu ruler to accede to India though the population was Moslem (while applying the reverse principle in the opposite case of Hyderabad). Both countries agreed to settle it by a plebiscite in Kashmir, but then India refused to hold it, imprisoned the Prime Minister who pressed for it, and a little later on withdrew consent to it because of Pakistan's foreign policy moves.
64 Khrushchev, with Marshal Bulganin*, visited India in November 1955. At Bombay on the 24th, and again at Rangoon on 6 December, he blamed the West for starting the Second World War by launching Hitler against the U.S.S.R.

trust the Russians – they were far too near them – but all the same, the pressure to move into their camp would grow stronger unless Pakistan adopted a more reasonable attitude.

I asked him whether there were Communists inside Afghanistan. He said, 'No.'[65] I then pointed out that the position seemed to be not dissimilar to that of the Middle East, where the new Russian tactic was to look around for some existing dispute, and then offer to take sides with the country nearest to them. They had put themselves on the side of the Arabs against Israel, with the result that the Arabs were now more or less blackmailing the West, and threatening to go in with Russia if they did not get what they wanted. It seemed, I said, that Afghanistan was doing more or less the same thing. I put it all very politely and wrapped-up a bit, but he knew perfectly well what I meant. Indeed, he did not really deny it, except he said the position was different because they were actually neighbours of Russia, and the danger of their going into the Russian orbit was much greater.

I of course pointed out that I had no power at all, and that it was extremely difficult anyhow for Britain to influence Pakistan, who no doubt had a good case of their own. I told him of my visit to the Khyber Pass, and how I had been told that the real problem among these tribesmen was economic.[66]

I had a very useful lunch [yesterday] with Hugh Cudlipp* and Sydney Jacobson* of the *Daily Mirror*. First I asked for their help in the matter of the A.E.U. elections. As they knew, there was a real danger of the Communists getting control of this Union. The trouble was that too few people voted. Would it not be possible to give much more publicity to the elections? They seized on this with avidity, thought it an excellent plan, and promised to act accordingly. I suggested that they should get in touch with Charlie Pannell*, who would give them all the necessary information.[67]

I then told them something of our plans for public opinion investigations on matters of policy. They at once offered to help. Their correspondence alone was quite interesting in indicating people's views, though the letters were classified and examined at the moment solely from the point of view of what people liked in the paper. They suggested, however, that they could very easily run a sort of readers' poll on some of these issues, without, of course, saying what it was for. I promised to let them

65 They seized power just over twenty years later.
66 During a three-week visit to the sub-continent in March 1954, when he was a delegate to an unofficial Commonwealth conference in Lahore.
67 A Leeds A.E.U.-sponsored M.P. and ally of HG's. A.E.U. voting took place at branch meetings, where in 1953–4 the average turnout for President, Regional Officers and Executive Council had in each case been 9 or 10%.

have a list of the questions that we had got in mind. It would be a mistake to rely on this only, because large though the circulation of the *Daily Mirror* is, it is after all a particular group of persons who read it.

Finally, we discussed the question of whether and in what form I should write for them. I pointed out that if I had important statements to make, they must be made either in the *Herald* or *Reynolds News*.[68] They accepted that. They thought, however, that I ought nevertheless to be prepared to write for any paper which asked me to. To this I demurred. I did not think it would do for me to write for the *Express* Group, and we had some argument about the matter. They suggested that I could always give the money to the Party, but I pointed out that that would leave me down the drain on taxation! However, as far as the *Mirror* was concerned, we finally settled that from time to time I might do an interview for them. I said I would not mind being paid for this either. They liked that very much. I also told them of my idea of going to S.E. Asia, and possibly Australia, some time in the course of the year,[69] and it was provisionally agreed that I might write, say, six articles for them, to cover my expenses, which were not already covered by other means.

During the course of the talk, Hugh Cudlipp said that whereas at the last election they had really been unable to go out fully behind the Labour Party because of the age of the Leadership, etc., they would be 100% behind us next time. One should not take this too seriously. Things could very easily change. But it is quite helpful.

Finally, Jim Griffiths was elected Deputy Leader last night – 141 against Bevan's 111. The majority was smaller than had been expected. It may be, as [my P.P.S.] Arthur Allen says, that some people voted for Nye, thinking that Jim was going to win anyhow, and as a kind of consolation. I also fancy that his vote may have been put up as a kind of reaction against my own election. Possibly some of the older people, who regard me as having forced out Herbert [Morrison], voted for Nye in order to do me down. But there is no way of knowing this. Anyhow, it does not really matter much.[70]

The Party took it very quietly. There was not much applause, which I

68 Official mouthpieces respectively of the Labour Party and of the Cooperatives.
69 He went to India and on to Burma, Malaya and Ceylon (but not to Australia) in December 1957.
70 Bevan polled 30 more than he had against Morrison in the old House with its larger P.L.P. Yet Griffiths was a strong contender, having few enemies, no ambitions (he was too old to become leader) and an appeal to Bevan's own following among Welsh and mining M.P.s. Wilson, in congratulating HG on becoming leader, had warned of a likely slight reaction (letter of 16.12.55 in Papers, P.101); and there was some attempt to mobilise hostility among Morrison's backers (see *HG*, p. 408). Probably both HG's own high vote and Bevan's showed that many M.P.s wanted to end the feud.

thought was a tribute to them. When you have a contest of this kind, loud applause for the victor is discourteous to the loser. Jim made a nice little speech. I turned to Nye, but he shook his head. He did not take the thing very well. He was muttering away in the course of the discussion on some other subjects that followed, and finally got up and walked out. I don't think, however, there will be any scenes for the time being.[71]

Later, Herbert Bowden [the Chief Whip] and myself discussed, with Jim, the allocation of jobs. But of this more later.

Document No. 14c

NOTE OF CONVERSATION WITH HARMAN GRISEWOOD OF THE B.B.C. ON 8 FEBRUARY 1956[72]

I saw Mr. Harman Grisewood who came at my request. I reminded him that we would shortly be having the Annual Meeting and asked him if there was any particular point which he felt should be made known to me about the B.B.C.'s attitude.[73] He said the only two issues of any importance which he thought would be raised were:-

(1) Ministerial broadcasts – which we had already discussed on another occasion;

(2) The carve up of the Party Political Broadcasts for next year.

This was complicated by the position of the I.T.A. He thought they might probably be prepared to take a full series but it would be necessary to make a clear distinction in future between sound and television – in other words, the option to switch from one to the other would have to be removed.

---

71 A charitable view, as the next entry shows. Dalton's account of the scene in the P.L.P. is characteristically more pungent: 'with a most contorted, angry face . . . [Bevan] made a contemptuous, scowling gesture of refusal, seen by all, and remained seated': diary, 2.2.56.

72 From Papers, file P.118–4, marked Copy to Dep. Leader & Chief Whip.

73 Grisewood, former Director of the Third Programme and of the Spoken Word, was from 1954 to 1963 Chief Assistant to the Director-General (Sir Ian Jacob at this time). He discusses his early dealings with Gaitskell in his *One Thing at a Time* (Hutchinson, 1968), pp. 188–94. The Annual Meeting, which regulated party political broadcasts, comprised the Conservative and Labour Chief Whips and leaders in the Commons, and the Directors-General of the B.B.C. and the Independent Television Authority. It has become more contentious with the rise of other parties.

The Liberal Party had hitherto had a single thirty-minute television broadcast which was also put out on sound. The B.B.C. would propose that in future they would be given a television broadcast of ¼ hour and a sound broadcast for ¼ hour. The distribution would then be

(a) On television – 4 Conservative, 4 Labour, 1 Liberal
(b) On sound – 3 Conservative, 3 Labour, 1 Liberal.

I said I doubted whether twenty minutes was really necessary for sound broadcasts and that it might be possible to reach agreement on cutting it down to ¼ hour.

Later in the conversation Mr. Grisewood raised the question of the Budget Broadcasts. He said that the Government had been thinking this over and he understood that they wanted to have television first and sound second, and intended to bring into their television broadcast various visual aids – charts, etc. The B.B.C. were a bit worried about this because they felt we might not be disposed to accept it and the Government would be abandoning in future the arrangement which had held good for the past four years. I said the best thing would be to ask the Government and draw them out on their plans. Mr. Grisewood also said that they did not think that the combination of television and sound as we had had for the Autumn Budget was really satisfactory. Listeners to sound broadcast had complained.

I discussed with Mr. Harman Grisewood the question of 'jamming'.[74] He said they had made it plain to the Government that it was, of course, the Government who had to decide; all that they, the B.B.C., could do was to put up some considerations which ought to be before the Government in making up their mind:

(1) The general argument, much ventilated in the Press, that we had never before used jamming at any time and that it very much weakened the case in objecting to the Russian jamming if we were to do it ourselves. As far as he knew, none of the free countries resorted to jamming. The only case, apart from the Iron [Curtain?] Countries – and on this he was not quite certain – was the Chinese Nationalists on Formosa. He said Sir Ian Jacob felt that to introduce jamming would create the worst possible atmosphere in Cyprus – quite apart from the more general repercussions of this serious breach with what had been our policy hitherto.

74 The proposal to jam Greek-language broadcasts from Athens inciting the Greek-Cypriot nationalists and terrorists of EOKA: see *HG*, pp. 479–80. It had been briefly discussed in Parliament on 30 January (548 H.C. Deb. 587–92). HG had discouraged official (as distinct from individual) Labour criticism so as not to stiffen governmental intransigence.

(2) There were in fact considerable technical difficulties. He was not sure how these were going to be solved because the B.B.C. were not involved, but he said that there had once been a report that the Russians had needed 300,000 people on the job to deal with jamming. Fantastic as this seemed, there was no doubt that a great deal of expenditure was involved on manpower and other resources to do it effectively.

(3) He thought the reports of the effect of Athens radio on Cyprus were much exaggerated. In fact, it was 400 miles away and reception was not particularly good. Moreover, the distribution of radio sets was by no means universal in Cyprus. He did not believe that it really had much effect on the situation.

I questioned Mr. Grisewood about the alternative policy of replying to the broadcasts. He had little to say on this because Cyprus radio is in the hands of the Government and the B.B.C. had nothing to do with it. He was not sure whether the B.B.C. was broadcasting direct on short wave to Cyprus but they are to Greece. I pointed out that if there was difficulty in receiving broadcasts on medium wave at a distance of 400 miles, it would be extremely unlikely that listeners would be able to receive short wave transmissions from London.

He offered to give me any information I wanted if I would let him know.

H.G.

Diary [Week beginning] Monday, 6 February 1956 [dictated Tuesday 14th]

During the course of the weekend, Mr B[Bevan] made a vitriolic speech attacking me and everybody else, and of course the papers were all speculating as to what we should do about it.[75] I had already come to the conclusion that it was probably best to ignore the whole business, but I had to make up my mind pretty quickly because it so happened that on the Monday morning I was to take a Press Conference at Transport House to

75 At Manchester on 4 February he attacked the Labour Party for not being Socialist, its leadership for playing tiddly-winks instead of rugger, the 'retrograde' idea (HG's) of judging the case for nationalising an industry according to its specific circumstances, and the P.L.P. as an undemocratic conspiracy because it met privately: Foot (1973), pp. 500–1.

launch the Jubilee Celebrations.[76] There was an unusually large attendance of newspaper men, and it was perfectly obvious to me that they were
interested in only one thing – namely, what was I going to say about Mr
B's speech. Well, I said nothing at all, and that was certainly the easiest
way round. Later in the day, I went to the House of Commons, and I was
surprised and delighted to find that virtually everybody who spoke to me
on the subject gave me the same advice – to ignore the whole business.
Charlie Pannell, for instance, one of the toughest of the Trade Union
Members, and a great friend of mine, but who speaks with great frankness always, came in to see me and said, 'What I am saying to everybody is
when you have a delinquent child in the family, you say as little as possible
about him'. And Arthur Allen, my P.P.S., was emphatically of the same
opinion. I am sure that this was good advice, and the Press, I think,
appreciate it now, though they were obviously hoping for some more
news and some more violent language on my side this time.

I dined on Monday night at Wadham College, Oxford, with Maurice
Bowra*. I cannot say it was a very successful evening. I had a beastly cold,
and he gave me much too much to drink. It was their Founders' Day. I
did, however, have some interesting conversation with John Sparrow,
whom I had not seen for years. John Sparrow is the Warden of All Souls.
Coming up in the train, I travelled with Henry Fairlie, and told him what
my view was on the Bevan situation. He is a curious man. He seems to
take everything I say on some occasions, and then on others, well, he will
write something completely different. But this time, when the *Spectator*
came out a few days later, it contained an almost verbatim account of my
views, with strong praise from him.[77]

On Tuesday, I lunched with David Astor [owner-editor of the *Observer*]
to meet Malik, the Soviet Ambassador. Of course, I had met him before,
with the Polish Ambassador. The only other person there was Crankshaw,
the Russian expert on the *Observer*.[78] The lunch followed a pattern that is
now becoming very familiar to me. We started discussing foreign policy,
and argued in particular about disarmament. Malik said, why was it that
we were not prepared to abolish nuclear weapons? Surely that was the
right thing to do. We said, how can you detect the stocks of nuclear
weapons? Wouldn't he agree that in fact, if there were such an agreement, the Russians would not be sure that the Americans were keeping it,

76 Of the Parliamentary Labour Party, which first met to choose its chairman
    (Keir Hardie) and adopt the name Labour Party on 12 February 1906.
77 On 10 February 1956 (*HG*, p. 409); Fairlie was the journal's political
    correspondent. HG had been at Winchester with Sparrow, who was Warden
    1952–77; and as an undergraduate he was a close friend of Bowra (Warden of
    Wadham 1938–70).
78 Edward Crankshaw, author of many books, was the *Observer*'s Soviet
    correspondent 1947–68.

and vice versa? We suggested, therefore, that it was really not much use worrying about the stocks of H-bombs. It would be better to concentrate on getting an agreement on conventional arms. But Malik would have none of this. He evaded every time the question, Could you detect the stocks?, and implied that somehow or other it would be possible to do so. We went round and round in a circle like this most of lunch. It was all quite pleasant, but led absolutely nowhere. One had the very natural feeling that one was arguing with a Communist! Somebody who was simply not prepared to follow the logic of the argument to its proper conclusion.

The only other event of importance during the week, as far as I was concerned, was the Dinner given to the Attlees on Friday evening [10 February]. This had been organised by the [Labour Party] National Executive but the Co-op people and the T.U.C. were taking part, and the whole thing took place at the C.W.S. [Cooperative Wholesale Society] Headquarters, in Leman Street, in the East End. It was a bitterly cold night, and I didn't even dare take the car out. We all assembled, but there was no sign of Clem and Vi. Finally, at about 7.30, just when we were due to go in to dinner, a telephone message came from Clem to say that they'd had an accident, and would be late, and would we start dinner without them. So in we went. We had our dinner, and still there was no sign of them. Half-past eight, nine o'clock went by, still no sign. Morgan Phillips and Jim Griffiths, who was in the Chair, wondered what to do. Some of us would have been content to go on talking, but in fact we had some community singing. This had gone on for about quarter of an hour or so, and then finally Clem and Vi arrived. They had had a bad skid right across the main Oxford road, and another car had run into them. Vi had cut the back of her head – in fact I could see as she was sitting next to me a sort of blood-stained patch on her head – on her hair. I asked if Clem was all right, and she said that she thought he had bruised himself a little, because of the pipe in his pocket. The speeches were then made, and went off quite successfully. I was glad that I had taken such a lot of trouble with mine, because Clem was obviously very pleased with it, and indeed, it was one of my better efforts. The amazing thing was really, however, that Clem and Vi came at all. The next day we heard that in fact he had broken two ribs.

During the weekend I went to Liverpool and Manchester. I was expecting trouble at Liverpool, because it is a troublesome place, and I remember the last Conference that I took there in 1951 was pretty stormy.[79] Of course I was Chancellor at the time, and it was after the Bevan resignation. However, all went off splendidly. I spoke on 'Labour and Public Ownership', and gave them a very frank talk about the situation we were facing. They took it wonderfully, and to my amazement not only was there no personal abuse, which one rather expects in that part of the world, but there were no lunatic questions. There were a lot of questions, but they were all sensible and to the point. Everybody felt that it had been a great success.

Later on, we visited a Labour Club [Walton] on the outskirts of Liverpool, where I opened an extension. All very friendly and jolly, though it is one of the worst constituencies from the point of view of the Trotskyists and the Bevanites.[80] I imagine they kept away.

In the evening, I spoke at the Fabian Society Dinner at Manchester. By now, I was rather tired, but it was not too bad. I was delighted to see Eric James there, though I did not really have time to talk to him.[81]

The following day, I did a day school in Rochdale. I had promised to do this a long time ago, otherwise I would not have taken it on. But all the same it was worth while. It was a small, crowded room, with about 100 people packed in together. It is good, after all, to get close to the rank and file, and on so many occasions one has to be far from them. It too, I think, went off successfully, and I felt that the new ideas I was trying to put across were at any rate making some impression.

Yesterday, that is, Monday the 13th, we had the big Jubilee Celebration at the Seymour Hall. Thank goodness, it really was a success this time. How different from the London Labour Party one about a month ago. The M.P.s turned up in pretty good numbers, and there was a generally happy atmosphere, despite the absence of the Attlees, and incidentally neither Herbert Morrison nor Nye [Bevan] came. What really made the evening from a political angle was the presence of a number of the Labour people from the West Indies who are here for a Conference on West Indian Federation. We got them on the platform, and we made Norman Manley*, the Prime Minister of Jamaica, and Grantley Adams, the Prime Minister of Barbados, speak. They were very good, and it was a huge success. Manley is a remarkably fine-looking man, and an excellent speaker as well. He is a cousin of the famous Bustamante, his political enemy, but he seems to me to have all the virtues of Bustamante, without

79 In 1960 he was to be shouted down by a section of the crowd in both places: see *HG*, pp. 640–1. On 1951 see above, pp. 268–9.
80 Councillor Eric Heffer, who led the shouting down in 1960, became M.P. for Walton in 1964.
81 See above, pp. 338–9.

his demagogic vices. Grantley Adams, whom I had also met before, is equally impressive in a more rugged and less glamorous way. [82]

Today, Tuesday the 14th February, we finally settled the allocation of jobs. We had decided right at the beginning, immediately after Jim Griffiths' election, that we would offer the Colonies to Nye. Then occurred his speech at Manchester over the weekend. Nevertheless we all agreed that it should make no difference to our giving him this opportunity. So we saw him, Jim and I, on the Tuesday. It was rather a funny scene. I sent for him, and Jim and I were sitting there. He came in, evidently expecting that we were going to put him on the mat about his weekend speech – swaggering in in a sort of defensive way. So I said very sweetly, 'Come along, Nye, come and sit down', and went on, 'Allocation of jobs'. He was quite startled, and quite obviously surprised at this development. Then I said, 'We would like you to take the Colonies'. He then proceeded to talk in a more sensible and rational manner than I have heard him do for a long time. He said, 'I would have liked Foreign Affairs'. I ignored that, and then he went on, 'The only difficulty about the Colonies is that I really know so little about them'. This is a very rare admission from Mr B! I said, 'Well, you'll have to learn a lot – it's a job with a lot of work attached to it. But it's something to get your teeth into. You didn't really have much scope when you were doing the Ministry of Labour'. He agreed with all this, and then said he would like to go and visit the Colonies. We said, 'Certainly', and we would help him. Finally, he said, 'All right, I'll take it'. He made another pretty bad speech last Sunday – two days ago. Not quite as bad as the previous one, but it was at Merthyr Tydfil, for the Jubilee Celebration, and Jim Griffiths was the other speaker. I asked Jim about it. He said – and he's a very mild-spoken person – 'It was the worst form of demagoguery, and what was particularly shocking about it was the tremendously egotistical tone'. Jim said this had quite shocked a number of the older people at the meeting. Incidentally, while I was in Manchester, I heard there a story from the wife of the leader of the Labour group in Manchester, Mrs Nally. She works in a remand home, and one of the teachers there has just recently

82 The Federation, planned ever since the war, was inaugurated in 1958 and lasted until 1962 when Jamaica voted in a referendum to secede. It was championed by the Federal Labour Party headed by (Sir) Grantley Adams (1898–1971, Federal Prime Minister 1958–62) and by Manley (father of Michael Manley, later Jamaican Prime Minister). Sir Alexander Bustamante, Chief or Prime Minister 1953–5, 1962–7; led the Opposition in between; his Jamaican Labour Party had favoured federation but in 1962 organised the opposition to it. Gaitskell's view of the two rivals was widely shared.

joined the Party. This teacher, a woman, went off to the Manchester meeting – the Tribune meeting – where Nye was speaking ten days ago. She came back very shocked, and almost inclined to leave the Party. She said to Mrs Nally, 'It was not a Labour Party meeting at all. It was a Bevan Party meeting'. However, we shall have to see. I feel pretty confident that our policy is the right one. We are giving him every possible chance. We are giving him a job which is an interesting one, with plenty of Parliamentary scope, with travelling, with something, as I said, that he can really get his teeth into. If, despite this, he refuses to work in the team, and goes on behaving as he has been doing recently, sooner or later he will simply get himself out of the Party. But whether he will do that, or whether after all he will settle down, we cannot yet say. I am bound to admit that in the light of what has happened so far, I have the feeling that his pride will always make it very difficult indeed for him to work in a team under my leadership, or indeed under anybody else's who is now on the scene.

The other changes in jobs are fairly straightforward. There was an awkward position in the Treasury and the Board of Trade. I felt that Harold Wilson would have to take over the Treasury, but who was to do the Board of Trade? I would have liked Douglas [Jay] to have had it, but that would have been difficult, because of Bottomley's claims.[83] Moreover, I wanted Douglas to continue to help on the Treasury side, and it was equally foolish to cut Harold Wilson completely off from the Board of Trade. So we worked out a special scheme, under which the Treasury and the Board of Trade jobs are combined. Harold Wilson is No. 1 at the Treasury, and Douglas and Arthur Bottomley are jointly No. 1 at the Board of Trade. We also brought Patrick Gordon Walker into this. He has been in a blind alley for a long time at Commonwealth Relations, with no Parliamentary part to play. Now, although it's lower on the scale, he has an opportunity of getting somewhere on the economic side. George Brown takes over the Ministry of Labour, but I am leaving him in the Ministry of Supply as well, since he is giving up Agriculture. Our real difficulty was over Defence, but we have finally got quite a decent team there, with Dick Stokes in charge, and James Callaghan looking after the Admiralty, Strachey the War Office, Geoffrey de Freitas the Air Ministry, and, as I have said, George at the Ministry of Supply.[84]

I had a long talk with Alf Robens this evening. I was glad to find that he

83 Arthur Bottomley had been Secretary for Overseas Trade from 1947 to 1951. M.P. Chatham 1945–59 (& Rochester, 1950); Middlesbrough since 1962 (E., 1962–74). Became Commonwealth Sec. 1964–6, Min. of Overseas Development 1966–7.

84 Each of the three Service Departments was thus shadowed by one of its ex-Ministers. See Biog. Notes; and on De Freitas, above, p. 110 n.

agreed entirely with my estimate of the various people on the Foreign Affairs side. He says that Denis Healey is far and away the best of them. Very sound indeed, very clear, and very firm. On the other hand, Kenneth Younger, said Alf, is really at heart a Bevanite. I said, 'Yes, and he's very indecisive as well'. As for Dick [Crossman], he is of course unreliable as always, full of his grandiose ideas, one moment very good and sensible, at another moment totally lacking in judgment. John Hynd, the other person in the group, is too weak, but can be relied on on the whole to follow a sensible line if somebody else gives a lead.

Document No. 15

HG's engagements, week of 13–19 February 1956

Monday, 13th February[85]

9.45 a.m.	Leave Manchester. 1.5 p.m. Arrive Euston.
1.00 p.m.	Mr. Wedgwood Benn's Broadcasting Luncheon. Room C.
2.30 p.m.	Prime Minister. Room at House.
4.00 p.m.	Home Policy Sub-Committee of N.E.C. House of Commons
7.30 to 11.30 p.m.	[Labour Party] Jubilee Celebration. Reception, Cabaret and Dance. Seymour Hall. Mr. and Mrs. Gaitskell.

Tuesday, 14th February[86]

12 noon	[Cancelled interview]
12.30 p.m.	Car calls at House of Commons. Proceed to Savoy Hotel.
1.00 p.m.	Variety Club Luncheon. Mr. Gaitskell to speak.
4.00 p.m.	International Sub-Committee of N.E.C.
5.00 p.m.	Chief Whip and Deputy Leader.
6.00 p.m.	Mr. Agar and Mr. Eldon Griffiths (News Week)
6.30 p.m.	Miss Hunebelle [the cancelled interview, *Reality*]

Wednesday, 15th February[87]

10.00 a.m.	National Council of Labour. Mr. Robens to speak.

85 Below, p. 446 on the lunch; above, pp. 439 n. 76, 441 on the Jubilee.
86 Herbert Agar was an American journalist and author and a London publisher. Eldon Griffiths was an English writer for American journals, foreign editor of *Newsweek* 1956–63 and later a Conservative speechwriter, M.P. and Minister.
87 The Abbey service was for Viscount Trenchard, creator of the Royal Air Force, who had just died. On the West Indians see above, pp. 441–2; on the 1944 Association cf. p. 389 n. 45.

11.45 a.m.	Church Service. Westminster Abbey. Mr. Gaitskell to read Lesson. Mrs. Gaitskell to attend.
1.00 p.m.	N.E.C. Luncheon to West Indian visitors. House of Commons
2.00 p.m.	Mr. Callaghan.
4.00 p.m.	Organisation Sub-Committee of N.E.C.
5.00 p.m.	Parliamentary Committee [of the P.L.P. – the Shadow Cabinet]
6.45 p.m.	Mr. Diamond.
7.15 for	1944 Association [of Labour businessmen] Dinner.
7.30 p.m.	House of Commons. Mr. Gaitskell to speak on Party's new research programme.

Thursday, 16th February[88]

12 noon	Empire Journalists.
12.45 p.m.	Daily Herald Luncheon. Mr. Deryck Winterton. The Chief Whip will be present. Taxi arranged.
5.30 p.m.	Lobby Correspondents.
6.00 p.m.	Mr. De Freitas Roy Jenkins
6.30 p.m.	Party Meeting.
6–8 p.m.	Reception to Cornelius Dwyer, Mr. & Mrs. Gaitskell.

Friday, 17th February[89]

10.00 a.m. all day	Co-op Commission. 10 Doughty Street.
4.00 p.m.	Mrs. Milchsack, Forum Club.
8.00 p.m.	Dinner: Residence of the Burmese Ambassador, 45 Redington Road, N.W.3. Mr. and Mrs. Gaitskell. Black Tie. (? Cancel "In The News")

Saturday, 18th February[90]

12.5 p.m.	Leave Kings X by Pullman (? 3rd Cl.) 3.21 p.m. Arrive Leeds.

88 Cornelius Dwyer, an American diplomat, had served in the London Embassy in 1948 and 1949.

89 HG was chairman of an independent commission of inquiry into the Cooperative Movement; Anthony Crosland was its secretary and wrote its report. (See *HG*, p. 469.) Frau (Dame) Lilo Milchsack was the founder and hon. secretary (later chairman) of the Anglo-German Association which organised regular conferences of parliamentarians from both countries at Koenigswinter.

90 He was to stay with Granville Prior, President of the N.U.T. (above, p. 250) but had to cancel (p. 447).

4.00 p.m.   [Constituency] interviews. Middleton Arms.
                   Stay night at 26 Sefton Avenue, Leeds 11.
                   Tel. 7-6151

Sunday, 19th February[91]
Evening   Golden Jubilee Celebration of P.L.P.
                   Town Hall, Leeds Rally (J. Anson).
                   Return to London by sleeper.

Diary, 14–23 February 1956

Not much has happened. On Monday the 13th I mentioned something which I should have put into the previous report. I went to join a small lunch which had been organised to discuss the T.V. programme in which our Foreign Affairs experts are to take part. Alf Robens could not be there. When I arrived, I found everybody in a complete state of confusion because of Dick Crossman suddenly taking the line that really there ought not to be any group discussion at all, but that the real purpose was to put forward Alf Robens and Kenneth Younger. He then switched onto a totally different tack, and wanted to urge that we started off with some tremendous, grandiose onslaught on the Government. I mention this only to show what a very difficult person he is. I managed to straighten things out, however, quite easily, and I was told afterwards that the group as a result got round a nasty corner. But it all fits in with what I said about Alf Robens' remarks regarding Dick and the other members of that particular team.

On Friday we had another meeting of the Co-op Commission. I had to leave in the middle of the morning to go and listen to Macmillan's statement in the House.[92] But on coming back, I went off to lunch with Colonel Hardie, and managed to persuade him without very much difficulty to put up two or three thousand pounds – I shall certainly make it three if I can – for *Forward*. He is a curious man. Like so many successful business men, he has flashes of considerable intelligence, and other bits that are completely blind. He still has the most crackpot ideas about prices in nationalised industries, and his comments on Berry, who was one of his co-Directors, or rather, one of his fellow-members on the Board of the Steel Corporation, were most uncomplimentary. As I have a very high opinion of Berry, I cannot accept this. Still, he is doing very well

91 John Anson was Labour's Regional Organiser for Yorkshire.
92 The Chancellor announced a deflationary package including, besides the highest Bank Rate since 1931, restrictions on hire purchase, food subsidies, bank credit, public expenditure and investment allowances.

on the Commission, makes no trouble at all, and is, I think, really going to be useful in his comments on how the various Co-op undertakings are working.[93]

In the evening we went to dinner with the Burmese Ambassador, who lives quite near us in Hampstead. It was not a very successful affair. The Elaths were there, which was nice, and the Indonesian Ambassador and his wife, whom we had not met before, and also a man called Barrington and his wife, who is going back to Rangoon to be head of the Burmese Foreign Office.[94] What was interesting was that Barrington was obviously half-caste, and so was his wife. They were a good-looking pair, and he, I think, had had a University education in England. But it was taken for granted, I suppose, that being half-Burmese he went with the Burmese rather than the English. I should think he would do very well. He seems sensible and intelligent. The Ambassador himself is an extraordinary man who laughs loudly after every sentence, so that during dinner there appeared to be a continual uproar coming from his end of the table.

I had intended to visit Leeds on Saturday to do my interviews, but having some kind of tummy trouble – either a chill, or something that I had eaten at lunch with Colonel Hardie – I decided to stay in bed all day and only go up on Sunday. This seemed to do the trick. Anyhow, I travelled up on Sunday afternoon for the Jubilee Demonstration in the Town Hall. I was rather nervous about this, because I have never made a successful speech there up to now. Indeed, on some occasions they have been really ghastly failures. There was one Election – I think it was 1951 – when I had to speak last, and after Shinwell had spoken. It was my fourth meeting during the day, and I was very tired. Shinwell proceeded to give a complete, knockabout music hall turn. The audience simply loved it. But by the end of it they were punch-drunk, and incapable of thinking at all, and my kind of talk fell as flat as a pancake. To make things even worse, the microphone broke down in the middle.[95]

However, fortunately, on this occasion all really did go well. It was a grand demonstration, very well organised, the Town Hall absolutely packed, and people standing, with coachloads having come in from all the different parts of Yorkshire. They also had community singing, and the

93 Colonel Steven Hardie – with whom HG became less happy as a member of the Co-op Commission – had been chairman of the Iron and Steel Corporation from 1950 to 1952. His colleague there, (Sir) Vaughan Berry, had in 1932 founded XYZ, a clandestine dining club of Labour sympathisers in the City: see *HG*, p. 47.

94 Eliahu Elath was the Israeli Ambassador. James Barrington had been at school at Maymyo, where HG as a boy of five had spent a year, and later at Oxford. He was Burmese Ambassador to the U.S. 1950–6, and he (not his wife) was Permanent Secretary to their Foreign Office in 1956–8.

95 See above, pp. 292–3.

women's choir before we began, so that there was a nice, warm atmosphere when we got onto the platform. I was surprised and naturally pleased when as I did so, and was just sitting down, they began to sing 'For He's a Jolly Good Fellow'. I had taken a good deal of trouble with preparing the speech, and I think I can say that it was quite successful – at any rate, the *Manchester Guardian* gave it a very good report, and I had a charming letter from [my agent] George Murray, who knows my feelings about the Town Hall, saying that it had all gone over extremely well. So I hope that particular bogey is now destroyed.

We had had an economic debate the last two days, and it had gone very well for us. Both Harold [Wilson] and Douglas [Jay] made outstanding speeches.[96] Douglas certainly was in better form than I have ever heard him, and has never received such a fine ovation at the end of his speech. Harold, too, was very good. He managed to combine a good deal of hard argument with considerable wit, and he also adopted a really responsible line. I am delighted that he should do this, because if he is to be Chancellor in the next Government, it is essential that he should build up a store of confidence in the country generally. I think he fully appreciates that. My own speech was a fairly knockabout affair, and I was rather disappointed at the time because I had to leave out two or three things that I particularly wanted to say. However, the Press reports were good, and the Party seemed to like it. The only thing that really went wrong, apart from the omissions, was that I forgot to mention – in praising Harold and Douglas – poor Fred Lee, who is really, of course, far below their standard, but was the fourth Front Bench speaker. People are so touchy on these things. I therefore had to send him a note of apology this evening to cheer him up.

However, the general plan in the House does seem to be going reasonably well. If we can only make the Party understand that they should attack on themes where the Party is most united and the Government most vulnerable, and not attack on the opposite occasions, then I think we shall continue to do fairly well.

Dora and I went to the Guildhall lunch today, given by the Lord Mayor on the return of the Queen and the Duke of Edinburgh from Nigeria. The only interesting event that occurred was the conversation which I had with Lady Waverley. Lady W. is a rather faded, pretty woman who was married originally to a man in the Foreign Office, and was therefore quite well known in London society.[97] After his death she married Lord

96 549 H.C. Deb. 59–80 (Wilson), 205–18 (Jay), 307–20 (HG): 20–21 Feb. 1956.
97 Ralph Wigram, her first husband, was among the first to foresee the threat from Hitler, and to alert his friend Churchill to it.

Waverley, i.e. old John Anderson. The only times that I have seen her so far have been on occasions when she has been rather annoyed with me. She was very angry when I criticised Waverley's appointment as Chairman of the Royal Commission [on Taxation], and indeed through my criticisms forced him to give up the job! It was, in fact, a monstrous appointment, because of his well-known prejudices, strongly expressed, on the subject of taxation. She also objected strongly, on another occasion, to the attack that I made on the Chancellor [R.A. Butler] last year. She regarded this as most unfair, because of the death of Sydney Butler, i.e. the Chancellor's wife, which she felt had really been responsible for his doing so badly.[98] However, today, rather surprisingly, she was quite friendly, and talked across the table. She began by saying that she had heard a number of jokes about me. After a bit, she made it plain she did not mean against me, but jokes in which I had been involved. On enquiring what these were, she said they had to do with Pamela [Berry]. I guessed then that she meant the Fishmongers' Hall episode, and sure enough she did. We talked rather obscurely for a time, in order not to give anything away to the other people who were sitting round us. But later she put the question to me directly. 'Is it true that she asked you whether it was possible to get rid of a Prime Minister in peacetime?' I said, 'Yes, that was true'. She said she had heard that from somebody who had been standing near, and had heard the whole conversation. She assured me that my conduct was irreproachable, according to her friends. But they were very critical of Pamela Berry. She also said that Michael Berry is rather deaf, and therefore Pamela speaks in a very loud voice, which is part of the trouble. She seemed to be rather distressed about the whole episode, but I reassured her, and told her I did not think it was very important. Nevertheless, she said quite definitely that she was sure the attitude of the *Telegraph* had been influenced by Pamela Berry, and then proceeded to relate in some detail the story of her feud with Clarissa Eden.

Apparently this did all start with Duff Cooper writing a letter to Clarissa telling her that Pamela Berry had said something very uncomplimentary about Anthony [Eden] to an American correspondent in his (Duff Cooper's) presence.[99] Apparently after that, according to Lady W., Clarissa made various attempts to heal the breach, but had not been successful in doing it. I was very reticent throughout the whole of this, and explained that I only knew Pamela very slightly. Lady W. said that she thought she had her father's eloquence without his brains,[100] and that

---

98 On these two incidents see *HG*, pp. 313, 360–1. Sir John Anderson, a most
    distinguished civil servant, had been Chancellor of the Exchequer during the
    war and Shadow Chancellor after it. For HG and Butler, above, p. 422 n. 41.
99 Above, pp. 423. The journalist was Joe Alsop.
100 Her father was F.E. Smith, later Earl of Birkenhead.

therefore when she ran out of something to say she often said very foolish things.

Friday, 24 February 1956

We went last night (February 23) to dinner with the Berrys, the famous dinner party which was planned some time ago. In addition to our host and hostess and ourselves, there were present Colin Coote, the Editor of the *Daily Telegraph*, and his wife, Aidan and Virginia Crawley, and Bob Boothby*. It was a most enjoyable evening – plenty of good conversation, and for the most part, quite interesting discussion. Perhaps the most significant points of discussion were about the position of Harold Macmillan. The Berrys and Colin Coote and Bob Boothby are, of course, all of them supporters of Macmillan. In the case of the Berrys, this is, I think, not so much from any positive enthusiasm for him, but because he remains their only hope in the Tory Party. I asked Bob what the opinion of the Tories was about Rab Butler now. He replied, 'Contemptuous disdain'. Since Eden is, of course, an enemy of theirs, there remains only Macmillan. Apparently Macmillan was dining with them the night before, or at any rate quite recently. They described him as extremely gloomy. He kept on saying, 'We've only three months to go'. So it looks as though the Treasury prognostications really are pretty grim. I imagine the real problem is the low level of the gold reserves, and the fear that the confidence factor may set in at any moment, and in consequence the reserves will fall still further. Of course, Bob is influenced in all this by two things: firstly, he has stood out for physical controls – during the debate this week he did get some support from other members of his Party for the first time for two or three years. And in fact it would be a triumph for him if Macmillan were driven to using physical controls, and he will be driven to use those controls if things continue bad. Secondly, I suspect that Bob still has hopes that if Macmillan were to become Prime Minister, he (Bob) might after all be given a job.[101]

There were some amusing stories told of a fairly gossipy character . . .

There was also much discussion about Lord Beaverbrook. Both Colin Coote and Bob Boothby said that they regarded him as the only really evil man they had ever known. Curiously enough, Aidan protested about this, and disagreed quite strongly. But I have heard this story often before – that he has taken a real pleasure in corrupting younger people. Colin Coote said that he certainly regarded him as having ruined Bevan, having

101 Macmillan and Boothby had been two of the most persistently rebellious Conservative M.P.s in the 1930s, and frequent allies.

taken him under his wing when he first became a young Member of Parliament, and drawing him away from what he ought to have been doing – namely, working hard in the House of Commons. Of course, all this was stimulated by Driberg's book on Beaverbrook, which everybody agreed was remarkably well-written and penetrating . . . Afterwards we discussed various other members of the Tory Party. I expressed the view, as I have done on one or two occasions lately, that from our point of view in the Labour Party, the difficult problem was not the top three in the Conservative Party, all of whom seemed to me to be pretty discredited,[102] but the next crust, i.e. Selwyn Lloyd, Macleod*, Reggie Maudling*, and Duncan Sandys*. There was some doubt about Reggie Maudling, but I stuck to my guns. I mentioned Lennox-Boyd, but they all pooh-poohed that, and implied that he was not really a person who counted to any great extent. On Eccles*, they agreed with my assessment that he was a person who had planned his life from the start to include politics, but was not predominantly interested in it.

I sat next to Lady Eccles at the Guildhall earlier this week, and she – who incidentally is a very charming person – had said that David would be quite happy really to give up politics altogether. Pamela Berry remarked how extraordinarily inept he was in the kind of comments that he made. It appears that during their last year in Opposition, he had come to dinner with the Berrys, and in the presence of Randolph Churchill, announced that he had wrested the intellectual leadership of the Party from Rab Butler. Randolph, who is of course mischief-maker No. 1, was delighted with this, and immediately wrote a letter to Rab Butler, telling him exactly what had been said. He did this, not because he liked Butler, but on the contrary, because he disliked him.

We had also some brief discussion about the people in the Labour Party, and I told them some amusing stories about Douglas Jay. Bob expressed doubts about Alf Robens, but thought Harold Wilson was extremely clever. Aidan, on the contrary, denounced Harold in un-measured terms. They asked about Dick Crossman, and I quoted what Denis Healey had said to me earlier the same day. I asked Denis how they were getting on, preparing the T.V. broadcast today (Friday). He said, Well, he thought it would be all right, but Dick was extremely difficult. I said, 'What is the trouble with him?' And Denis replied, 'Well, you see, he's a Bolshie – not that he's a Left-winger, but that he's a Bolshie'. I thought this was quite appropriate, and so did the others when I men-tioned it. The great question about Dick is, in fact, whether he will allow himself to be principally a Bolshie, or whether he will get used in time to adopting a more responsible and co-operative attitude.

102 Not his most perceptive comment.

Going back to Macmillan, it appears that he had great difficulty in persuading the Cabinet even to adopt the measures which he has recently announced.[103] They did not apparently want to do anything at all. In this particular circle that we were in last night, there was some quite free talk about the Tories giving up altogether, and handing over to me. This is not, in my opinion, to be taken at all seriously, but the fact that gossip of this kind goes on is of some significance, and there is really no doubt about the intense feeling against Eden which seems to exist in this circle, and I think it must be in wider circles as well. One can hardly imagine that relations between Eden, Butler and Macmillan could be anything but pretty bad just at present.

The other exciting event of the week is that Dora has changed the colour of her hair! On the advice of Phyllis Digby Morton[104] she had been to some place or other, and had all the other dye she used washed out completely – the very dark kind – and has now got a much nicer, sort of auburn, dye, which is better for the quality of her hair. It is quite extraordinary how it alters her appearance. She is very pleased about it, and so am I. There is something rather entertaining about changing the colour of your hair from time to time, though I hope she will stick to this colour for some time, because it is such a pretty one.

I had lunch yesterday with Maurice Edelman, to meet the French Ambassador [Jean Chauvel] and Jules Moch. Maurice is evidently trying to win himself back into favour after his rather deplorable exhibition over the hydrogen bomb[105] – at any rate, he not only asked me to lunch, but also the Chief Whip [Bowden], and Kenneth Younger and Denis Healey. I must admit I found the French Ambassador a BORE. He talks in a very low voice, so that it is hard to hear what he says, and when you do hear it, it is not really worth hearing! On the other hand, I like Jules Moch. He is a strong and forceful personality, and was a notable [Socialist] Minister of the Interior at a time [1947–50] when Communist strikes were really threatening to break everything up in France. He has for some time been the French Permanent Delegate of the Disarmament Commission, and has become a complete expert in that field. He told me yesterday that he was convinced that the Russians did want a proper system of inter-nationally-controlled disarmament. I asked him point-blank whether

103 On his own views, above p. 424; on the measures, p. 446 n.
104 Digby Morton was Vice-President of the Society of Fashion Designers (above, p. 423 n. 45).
105 Edelman, M.P. for Coventry (W. 1945–50, N. 1950–74, N.W. 1974–5), was chairman of the Franco-British Parliamentary Committee. He had spoken strongly against manufacturing the H-bomb, with early warnings about its genetic effects, in the debate which began the disciplinary row over Bevan: 537 H.C. Deb. 1946–53, 1 March 1955. Jean Chauvel was French Ambassador in London 1955–62.

they would put up with the controls. He said he was quite certain that they would. He thought they had come to the conclusion that they could not stand the strain of all their own internal development needs, the help they had to give China, and a heavy – a very heavy – defence programme as well, and that for that reason they really did want disarmament, or at any rate limitation of armaments. If so, if he is right, of course it is enormously important, and it is something which I think we should certainly pursue further.

[*Dictated Tuesday, 28 February 1956*]

On Friday afternoon [24th] Sir Robert Laycock, the Governor of Malta, came to see me. He is, by all accounts, an extremely fine person. He had a wonderful reputation as a young General in the War, and is supposed to have progressive views. I remember that Herbert Morrison once thought of him as a possible Member of a Nationalised Board. Since he has been Governor of Malta he has shown marked sympathy with the progressive views of the Labour Party, and is clearly a strong supporter of the integration proposal, probably for that reason. The result of the Referendum has, of course, put him in a great difficulty.[106] He tried to persuade Mintoff not to have the Referendum until after the Debate here, but now it has taken place, and there really is a deadlock. He told me that Mintoff was extremely difficult to deal with, and that he was terrified that he would go, which would leave the Church [free?] actually to excommunicate him. He was also afraid that, even if he didn't do this, he might decide to chuck up politics altogether.[107] That, thought the Governor, would be disastrous, because Mintoff was really the only Maltese who was capable of leading the Island. The Archbishop and Mintoff were absolutely at daggers drawn; relations between them had never been worse, and Sir Robert's chief idea seemed to be to allow a cooling-off period. I raised the question of negotiations with the Vatican, in order to bring influence to bear upon the Archbishop. Sir Robert was entirely in favour of this and intended, I gathered, to go back to Malta via Rome. I suggested that we ought really to have Mintoff over here where we might be able to try and get him to behave more reasonably. This also Sir Robert thought was probably right. I gathered that the Government had been against Mintoff

106 The opposition boycotted the referendum, and 40% of the electorate abstained; 45% voted for integration and 13% against. On the Governor, see above, p. 431 n. 60.
107 In both these obscure sentences 'he' appears to mean the Governor at first, but Mintoff later.

coming over here because they had been frightened that the Maltese would regard this, or, rather, the Nationalists of Malta would regard this as another piece of evidence that Britain was trying to force them into integration. I said I couldn't see how that could be so. After all, he was the Prime Minister and it was perfectly natural that he should come over. I heard later on from Jim Griffiths, who saw Laycock on the Monday, that the Government had apparently revised their views on this. The Prime Minister himself murmured to me as we went into the House yesterday, that he thought that we must stand by Mintoff, otherwise the results would be catastrophic.[108]

On Friday evening, Dora and I went to the twenty-first birthday celebration of the Islington Council, or, rather, the Labour-controlled Council; they have been Labour-controlled for twenty-one years, and are now 100% Labour. It was quite a pleasant function. They were all very friendly and pleased, I think, that we had gone. Wilfred Fienburgh was there and mentioned in the course of conversation that Boyle, the Economic Secretary to the Treasury, was definitely in favour of physical controls, and had so spoken to Fienburgh.[109]

On Saturday morning I went with [my younger daughter] Cressida to the H.M.V. place in Oxford Street to buy records, and the following amusing incident occurred:-

It was terribly crowded, and we had great difficulty in getting anybody to attend to us. However eventually I managed to get some records to try – jazz records – and we found a young girl – I think she can't have been more than 17 – to shepherd us to a cubicle where one could play the records. She left me there to play the records, while Cressida went off in search of other ones. As I was listening to the jazz, more or less dancing up and down to the rhythm, the door of the cubicle opened and who should put her head in but Elaine Burton, the Labour Member of Parliament for Coventry. Slightly embarrassed at being caught dancing on my own, I welcomed her. She said 'I must tell you what the girl has just said to us. She said, "Do you know, I believe the Chancellor of the Exchequer is next door".' This is not the first time that, so long after I held the office, people have still regarded me as Chancellor. I suppose it is

108 Below, pp. 469–70 on Malta.
109 Fienburgh was Labour M.P. for North Islington from 1951 to 1958 when he was killed in a car crash. Labour first won Islington and many other London boroughs in 1934, the election that made Morrison leader of the L.C.C. Sir Edward (Lord) Boyle, Conservative M.P. for Birmingham Handsworth 1950–70, was Economic Secretary 1955–6 when he resigned over Suez. Macmillan brought him back to office two months later, and he was Minister of Education 1962–4; Vice-Chancellor of Leeds University 1970; died 1981.

because I have so frequently broadcast and appeared on T.V. on financial questions.

On Monday [27th] I went to lunch at the B.B.C. with the Executives, i.e., Sir Ian Jacob, and the five or six top people there. It was not a particularly interesting or exhilarating affair. Jacob is a very serious, rather conservatively minded, but very successful ex-General. I should imagine he was quite good as an administrator. The conversation was chiefly about the 14-day rule,[110] where, of course, their views are well-known, and also about the difficulty the B.B.C. had in getting across the economic situation. I explained that I thought it was very difficult for them to do this because there were Party issues involved. We didn't have the same atmosphere as we had had, for example, when Cripps was Chancellor. We then got on to the question of taxation, on which most of them took pretty stolidly conservative views and were not, I'm afraid, convinced by my arguments that the effects of taxation on the amount of work done were greatly exaggerated. I think Jacob could be relied upon to carry out any kind of national policy, but his instincts are certainly very pro-professional classes. I learned one interesting fact, and that was that the B.B.C. pay their orchestras much more than the same sort of people are paid in the provincial orchestras; for example, I was told that the B.B.C. Symphony Orchestra rank and file, as they call them, get £17–£20 a week, whereas the Halle Orchestra only pays £11 a week. It seems that the Musicians' Union adopt American techniques by trying to squeeze each of the employers as far as they possibly can.

I was disturbed by what took place in the course of the afternoon following this lunch. It was a Foreign Affairs Debate, and Alf Robens had told me that he would let me have the notes of his speech well in advance of the debate. Indeed he told me that they would be available on the Friday. However nothing turned up, and they cannot have been brought into my room until late on Monday morning. I found, not so much the notes, as the whole speech there when I got to the House about 3 o'c on Monday afternoon. I read it quickly through, and was pretty horrified by what I read. It was neutralist, almost fellow-travelling in places and broadly following the same kind of line as the lunatic fringe such as Zilliacus* and Warbey*, or perhaps I should say the pseudo-Communists. I sent for him at once. He came in with Ericsson[111] and we went over the speech. We only had time to take out the worst passages and then he had to go into the Chamber and deliver it. It is really most mysterious; I

110 This forbade discussion of a topic on the air within 14 days before a parliamentary debate on it. On Jacob, above, p. 429, n. 57.
111 The Transport House official dealing with foreign affairs.

cannot imagine how he comes to produce a speech of this kind. He certainly does not want to be labelled as a fellow-traveller and I had hoped that Denis Healey and Kenneth Younger and, even, Dick Crossman, would have had a better influence upon him. The speech was punctuated by 'Hear Hear's' from the Warbeys, Zilliacus etc., though it was just rescued from being too much that way by certain contradictory statements which he made in another direction. It was altogether a very poor effort, and worrying for me because I could not help feeling that he should have known better.

Immediately after I left the House, Ericsson came in to see me to explain that it was not in any way his fault. He said that Alf had given him, on Friday, an earlier draft, which was far, far worse. He had tried to work over this at the weekend, but, in fact, found it impossible without absolutely re-writing it. Then only after lunch on Monday had Alf produced a completely new draft and they were going through this when I sent for them. He thought that it must have come from somebody else and mentioned that it was, in certain respects, exactly like Zilliacus' memorandum to the Foreign Affairs Group, which had been so completely torn to bits, even by Crossman. Later Denis Healey came in to know if he could, nevertheless, say what he wanted to say, despite Alf's speech. I told him to go ahead and added that it was better not to refer to it at all.

When Alf sat down after his speech, I made it pretty plain to him that I didn't think it was really very good and later in the evening he came in to see me, obviously sensing my embarrassment. We had a long talk, but I still am puzzled by the whole thing. He said that he had worked it out himself, reading the documents (incidentally he got very muddled about quite a crucial point about the second Geneva Conference regarding the security guarantees to be given over German unification), and gave me no indication that he had received help from somebody else. Incidentally Kenneth Younger who is by no means a – what shall I say – staunch NATO man, was horrified as he heard Alf delivering this. Denis thought that it could not possibly have been written by Alf. However, as I say, he gave me no indication as to who had helped him, but implied that he had done it all himself. I explained the dangers to him of taking the line that he was proposing and gave him a short talk on such things as the balance of power. I made it quite plain that we must stick to the Bevin line and that if we were to attack the Government it must be on specific issues. He listened to quite a long harangue from me on these lines,with complete composure and agreement. I told him that I thought we really must get together before any further Foreign Affairs Debates, and urged him to have the regular meeting[s] with those, in fact, who were on the Television team so as to talk about Foreign Affairs all the time . . . However, I am still hoping that after a time he will get to know the whole subject very much better and that this kind of incident will not occur. Dick Crossman spoke to me about it this morning on the telephone, and even he was quite horrified by the line which Alf had originally intended to take and, to some extent, by what he had said. He thought that it must have come from somebody else, and suspected that the Co-op had in some way influenced him.[112] He agreed very much that they must have these meetings, and said that he would arrange regular lunches at his house or at Kenneth Younger's for the five of them to meet. I would come, I said, whenever I could so as to take part in the discussions.

I took Denis Healey out to lunch this morning [28.2.56]. Of course we discussed yesterday's debate. Denis felt sure that Alf must have got his speech from somebody else. He was as surprised as anybody about the whole affair. We discussed how it might be avoided in future. I told Denis I wanted him to do two or three things. First of all to produce, say once a month, a review of the foreign political situation, with notes indicating where we might attack the Government and where we should not. Secondly, I said they must have these regular meetings where they could discuss foreign policy and try and hammer out some common viewpoint. I also asked him to keep in the closest possible touch with Alf and treat himself as his kind of permanent secretary, advising him all the time. Denis agreed to do all these things. Unfortunately he is going to America on Friday and will be away for a month. But it is unlikely that there will be any major foreign affairs debate before he comes back. He drew my attention, incidentally, to a leading article in the *New York Times* which hinted that some elements in the Labour Party were veering again towards a kind of fellow-travelling point of view. It seems that there was an article in *Tribune* urging that the arrival of Khrushchev and Bulganin [in April] should be used by the Labour Party as a way of reaching agreement with them and that certain things said in the television broadcast last Friday illustrated the same attitude. I think this is greatly exaggerated, but it all shows how awkward Alf's speech on Monday was.

When I got to the House, I found that, as I feared, the [Communist] *Daily Worker* had splashed the speech right across its front page, regarding it as quite obviously just the thing for the troops. *The Times* didn't mention it; the *Manchester Guardian* was pretty caustic. I asked [my P.P.S.] Arthur Allen to find out the Party reaction. I doubt if it has been very strong, but Charlie Pannell said to Arthur that, having heard it, he

112 Robens' background was in the Cooperative Movement, which had strong pacifist traditions. Crossman's own diary (2.3.56) records his alarm, and calls the draft 'a rehash of the paper Zilliacus had presented . . . a rather obvious piece of fellow-travelling', and the speech one that 'followed the draft but had been skilfully blurred by Ericsson'.

decided that Bill Warbey evidently would not need to speak! He also said that he had thought of saying to Alf what apparently he said to Herbert Morrison after one of his less effective speeches as Foreign Secretary that he had better go back to Transport or, as it was put more colourfully, 'You had better go back to bus driving'. Part of the criticism actually arose because of Alf having written the speech. Later today I had another word with Alf about it. He professed to be horrified by the *Daily Worker*. I asked him, point blank, whether it was all his own idea or whether he had got any help or assistance from anybody. He said emphatically that it was all his own work; that he had taken all the papers home and worked steadily all Sunday on it and far into the night. I am sure this is true. What seems to have happened is that he read all these documents, including Zilliacus' memorandum, some of the phrases in which must have stuck in his memory. I must add, however, that George Brown said to me today, sitting on the Bench, that this was the sort of line that he took at Strasbourg. George said, 'I have always felt that Alf was a neutralist at heart'. I spoke pretty sharply to him tonight and said that I hoped he realised what kind of an impression the speech had made. He said that he certainly had realised that; people had made it plain to him! I am very fond of Alf, but I felt it necessary to administer a kind of shock to him, as we really cannot go on like this. I gather that Dick Crossman has already fixed up for the first lunch. I am rather sorry that this is taking place in Denis' absence.

This evening I went to a dinner given by a group of Labour M.P.s, whose distinctive characteristic is that they are all under 40. Not all of those under 40 come to the dinner, but there were about a dozen there tonight. The thing was started by Francis Noel-Baker, after consultation with me soon after the last Election. It was quite a useful evening, and I thought for the most part they were quite sensible, though nothing very impressive emerged. I felt Dickson Mabon, the new Member for Greenock, made one of the best contributions;[113] and, of course, Roy [Jenkins], who was there, was, as usual, extremely sensible, though he might have been a little more emphatic.

[Dictated Thursday, 1 March 1956]

I lunched yesterday with Dick Stokes. He told me that he had seen Nye [Bevan] once or twice and had re-established relations with him. (As a matter of fact I knew this already.) He had told him not to say silly things,

113 Mabon (M.P. Greenock since 1955) was Minister of State for Energy 1976–9; F. Noel-Baker (Philip's son) sat for Brentford 1945–50, Swindon 1955–69.

but that didn't prevent him making these speeches in the country. He had asked Nye after the Manchester speech why he had been such a b.f. and Nye had said, 'Oh well, I can't help it'. He wasn't sure whether he would really play in with us or not. I said I thought it was doubtful, and Dick admitted that it must be so. I felt that part of the trouble was the influence of Jennie [Lee] and Michael [Foot] upon him, who dragged him around to these Tribune meetings. He said he thought Michael was a very bad influence. He asked me if I wanted him to go on keeping in touch with Nye, and I said 'Yes, certainly'. Nye fortunately turned up yesterday to do the Colonial Office questions and came along to the Parliamentary Committee. He distinguished himself here by taking a very strong line against the T.U.C. on resale price maintenance. This is a matter on which he knows practically nothing, and, as Harold Wilson remarked to me afterwards, it seemed to be more hatred of the T.U.C. than any hatred of resale price maintenance, which motivated him. But it is a little comic that he should take what is really a very liberal attitude and indeed the kind of thing that the academic people, like myself, have always believed in.[114]

The Defence Debate has gone extremely well. All our Front Bench people, Dick Stokes, John Strachey, George Brown, spoke well. We concentrated our attack on the Government's weak spots, and we really made an impression on the House. George Brown, in particular, was first class yesterday. I only heard the beginning of his speech, but everybody tells me it was excellent. He has come out of this week as well as Alf has come out of it badly. A few days ago I was quite worried about Defence because it has been such a mess in the past. But undoubtedly the last two days has given us the best Defence Debate we have had for years. Great credit is due to the four speakers – incidentally supported by one or two Back Benchers, and also in particular to Dick Stokes, who organised the meetings, invited ex-Generals, Air Marshals, etc., to give their views. He is, I am glad to say, going on with this, at my suggestion, and we ought to have a really strong team before long.

Oliver Franks* came to XYZ last night.[115] Unfortunately I could not stay to the finish of it because I had to go and listen to the wind-up of the debate. But I thought he was most interesting. Clearly he is very worried about the economic situation. He asked me more than once what I thought the chances were of our getting through the rest of the year without a really major crisis. I said I thought 50-50. He thought that a

114 Gaitskell had favoured abolishing the practice at least since his wartime civil service days: see *HG*, pp. 119, 241, 392.
115 XYZ (see above, p. 447 n.) continued as a dining club of Labour politicians interested in finance. Sir Oliver Franks, former Ambassador in Washington, was chairman of Lloyds Bank.

little optimistic. Later, however, he said he thought that if there was a really tough budget, then things might begin to get better about April or May. Robin Brook* said in Zürich it was rather taken for granted that there would be a further devaluation, the only thing discussed was when and by how much. Oliver more or less confirmed the earlier stories that I had heard about Macmillan threatening to resign in order to get through these measures.[116] He thought, however, that Macmillan was, in fact, a strong character and might well have a tough budget. On the more technical side, he was quite interesting about the control of the banking system. He has evidently come down strongly in favour of using the liquidity ratio much more definitely and openly. He thinks the American system is better and does not agree with all the mystique and secrecy which surrounds the Bank of England. Douglas [Jay] asked him what he thought we should do if we came into power at a moment like this. Oliver replied that he thought we should have to do everything, i.e., phsycial controls, severe monetary measures and arrangements with the T.U.C. He thought the latter would be our strong point. He said that of course the confidence factor would weigh heavily against us. It was worth several hundred million dollars in terms of gold reserves to the Treasury. He was interesting in describing in a plain sort of way the feeling in the City; how all the foreigners who still dealt in sterling were watching us like cats to see what was going to happen. They were not interested in the immediate movements of the gold reserves. What they were concerned with was what was going to be the position in about twelve months' time. He was obviously frightened that the French and Dutch would not hesitate to operate against sterling if they thought there was any serious devaluation danger. On the other hand, if they were convinced that we were going to be in the clear by the end of the year, then there was no reason to fear anything from them.

It is a most useful thing to have somebody with his academic background, knowledge of the Civil Service and generally broad outlook in such a key position in the City. Not only can he understand what is happening there better than most people, but he also has the powers of exposition, so that he can tell us, and people like us, about it. He is an obvious possible candidate for the Governorship of the Bank of England, if and when we get back into power.

116 Above, p. 452. Confirmed by Macmillan's memoirs (1971, pp. 13–14).

[Dictated Friday, 9 March 1956]

I had lunch with Tom Williamson [general secretary of the N.U.G.M.W.] or, rather, he had lunch with me on Thursday last [1 March 1956]. The main purpose of this was to discuss the position regarding the Treasurership next year.[117] I told him that really he must get together with Frank Cousins* of the Transport Workers' Union and agree upon a candidate. They ought to do this soon, as otherwise Bevan would continue to get nominations from some Unions, simply because there was no alternative. We went through the names together. He had apparently approached Sam Watson who, however, did not want it. There had also been talk of Herbert Morrison, but I told him that according to Morgan Phillips, Herbert did not want it either. It really then boiled down to either one of the younger Trade Unionists in the House of Commons, or one of those outside. As regards the latter, Jack Cooper's name had been suggested. (He is President of Tom's Union.) But Tom did not think that he was sufficiently well-known, or influential. So ultimately it boiled down to George Brown or Alf Robens. I said I would be perfectly happy with either, and indeed, would be glad if one or other were on the Executive. Tom thought that, on balance, Alf was much more likely to collect the votes because he was better known, and I added that he would presumably get the USDAW nomination which together with the two big Unions would give him about two million votes. He could expect another million from Trade Union sources and stood, therefore, a pretty good chance of winning. On the other hand, I was not sure whether Frank Cousins would be willing to drop George Brown.[118] I pointed out that George Brown had a very good record so far as his public utterances were concerned and drew attention to the excellent speech he had just made in the Defence Debate. Tom said that he fully appreciated all that, but nevertheless thought that Alf was probably the better bet. He promised to act quickly on this, not only consulting Cousins, but also Alan Birch [the general secretary] of USDAW and Ernest Jones, the President of the Miners' Union. We discussed other arrangements for meeting and he promised to arrange a dinner party before very long – in the next few weeks – where he would have about six or seven people from the Trade Union side and there would also be, on my nomination, so to speak, four from the Labour Party. I suggested Jim Griffiths, Alf Robens, George Brown and myself. Later I said we should probably have to bring in Harold Wilson to these talks, but for the moment we could keep it to the

117 HG held the post concurrently with the leadership, but only until the next Party Conference.

118 Robens was sponsored as an M.P. by USDAW, and Brown by the T.&G.W.U.

younger Trade Union people, the Leader and the Deputy Leader of the Party. One of the purposes of the first dinner would be to see what could be done by the Unions to help the new Paper *Forward*.

We had a rather pleasant dinner party on Friday evening. The Plowdens and the Brooks came to dinner. Edwin [Plowden] had his usual argument with Dora saying that as far as he was concerned he did not see why he should work so hard and have so little leisure for so little money. As he was getting £8,000 a year, Dora didn't think much of this! But most of the discussion was taken up with the position of the younger scientists, who, Edwin said, were very disgruntled and dissatisfied with their standard of living. They came in as young men from the Universities, attracted by the glamour of atomic energy. But this glamour soon wore off when they got married and started having children. They were really very poorly paid compared to what they could get in other countries. And, in fact, so he alleged, they were, some of them at least, leaving the country and going to Canada and the United States.

One of the things that has been going rather well lately has been our handling of the Press. I don't think that Clem [Attlee] ever bothered sufficiently about this. I have a Lobby conference every week and I take it quite seriously. Last week, for instance, I took with me Douglas Jay and Lynn Ungoed-Thomas*, our two spokesmen on the Monopolies Bill. I did this because I was anxious to get a good Press for our rather surprising decision to move a reasoned amendment to the Second Reading of the Bill. It was extremely successful. We got an excellent Press and nobody suggested we were behaving out of spite or stupidity or opposition for opposition's sake. The *Observer* came out with a leader, taking very much the same line as we did, and altogether we got our case across in just the right way. And I think, in general, the presentation of the Opposition as a serious, co-ordinated force is enormously helped if you see the Lobby regularly and tell them what you are doing, what your aims are, and correct any mistakes which they may inadvertently have made. We have also had a Press Conference for the foreign press, answering questions for three-quarters of an hour, and that, too, I think, went off extremely well. Fortunately, I find these Press Conferences easy and enjoyable.

Last week has been more or less dominated by the events in Jordan – the dismissal of Glubb and the consequences.[119] On the whole we have managed to extract quite a lot of political kudos. It all happened, or rather the news became known, exactly a week ago, last Friday. Dick

119 Lieut-Gen. (Sir) John Glubb, after serving since 1920 in Iraq, went to Jordan in 1930 and commanded its Army, the Arab Legion, from 1939 until his dismissal by King Hussein on 1 March 1956. For the British Government's reaction see Eden (1960), pp. 347–51; R. Churchill (1959), Ch. 15.

Crossman came in to see me with the evening papers and told me he had put down a Private Notice Question, for Monday. He said he would be willing to withdraw this if we wanted it put from the Front Bench. I told him not to do that just yet. We then discussed the implications of all this in quite a satisfactory way. He was rather inclined at first to attack the whole of the Baghdad Pact but after discussion agreed that we must draw a distinction betwen the Northern tier agreement, the purely defensive agreement between Turkey, Iraq, Pakistan, and Persia, to which we adhered through our Treaty with Iraq in any case, and the attempt of the Government to build a whole Middle East policy and, indeed, an Arab policy out of and upon it.[120] Subsequently, of course, many more discussions took place.

On Monday morning we had to decide whether we would move the Adjournment of the House, and secure an immediate Debate. We had a good deal of discussion about what line should be taken if we did this. I decided that I would not press Dick to withdraw his Question, though I must say that I afterwards discovered that Alf Robens had tried to put one down himself, but found it blocked by Dick's. However, I felt that Dick had a particular interest in Jordan – he has certainly spoken many times on the subject – and that we should not suppress Back Bench enterprise too much. We did, however, agree that if the Adjournment were to be moved, it would have to be done from the Front Bench. Eventually we decided to call a Parliamentary Committee urgently for 2.15. After a lengthy discussion, in the course of which the pro-Arab people, particularly Edith Summerskill and Dick Stokes, proved rather difficult about the whole business and were clearly unwilling to have a Debate, we finally decided that we would press the Government for a full day's Debate later on in the week. We were told informally that they were very much against a Debate on the Monday afternoon and had hinted that it might endanger British lives. This tactic worked and we were informed just before the end of Questions that the Government had in fact agreed to a Debate on Wednesday. Monday, therefore, went off fairly quietly.

We called a further meeting of the Parliamentary Committee for the following evening, Tuesday evening. I must say that it was a rather depressing affair. By then I had thought a good deal about the line that we should take and attempted to explain this to the Committee. While they did not precisely disagree with me, we then, of course, had the different pro-Arab points of view. Edith Summerskill is completely incapable of rational thinking on the subject at all. Mostly, she thinks of herself as a

120 The C.I.G.S. went to Amman in December 1955 to persuade Jordan to join the Baghdad Pact; instead, there was rioting and a new Prime Minister, who refused to accede.

persecuted woman because she stood up for the Arab refugees. And every time the subject comes up, she refers to this. As for Dick Stokes, he merely takes a wildly optimistic view about what the Arabs are likely to do, and insists that there is really no danger that they will do anything to anybody. George Brown, is, I think, much more hard-headed. He simply says that he personally has no interest in Israel whatever and thinks it a mistake that we ever got tied up with the Zionist movement. But he agrees that this is a minority view, and all he asks is that we should not press our official view to such an extent so as to give offence to the Arab States. Nye [Bevan], of course, is, as usual, out of line; though when we last discussed this he was quite sensible. He was strong for the Tripartite Declaration, strong for arms for Israel and generally taking quite a reasonable point of view. But this time he had slumped back into a fellow-travelling attitude. He was all for discussing the whole thing with the Russians and for saying as little as possible apart from that. You cannot, however, really trust him on these occasions since he has so clear an interest in the speech to be made not being successful. Later in the evening Dick Crossman came back to see me with the suggestions of the Foreign Affairs Group. These were much more sensible than the Parliamentary Committee, which is indeed surprising. He told me that 40 of them had agreed unanimously on various points, which he then proceeded to detail to me.

Well, I made the speech the following day preparing it finally on Wednesday morning and being, I may say, extremely nervous about the whole thing. I was not sure how far what I had to say was really sound, and how well it would be received by the Party. But I need have had no anxiety. The day was undoubtedly a triumph for us and for me particularly. At least that is the conclusion to be drawn from the Press. I got a wonderful ovation when I sat down and even when I went into the Tea Room afterwards people started applauding. At the Party Meeting on the following day somebody got up, most unusually, before business and said that they wished to offer congratulations. So everybody was delighted. Indeed I was quite worried by the number of people from extreme left to extreme right who all seemed satisfied. It really is a matter for anxiety when Zilliacus comes up to you and puts his arm in yours and says he is so happy about what you have said. Nevertheless the speech was quite tough and absolutely flat-footed about Russia. And at least three-quarters of it was acceptable even to the die-hard Tories. So it is all rather obscure why they all liked it. I suppose they each found some part which seemed attractive to them. The lesson out of all this is, I think, that if you take people like Dick Crossman into your confidence, discard their foolish ideas, retain their sensible ideas, then, on the whole, you can really make some headway. Undoubtedly the Foreign Affairs Group were particularly pleased because they saw that I had accepted quite a number of their suggestions.

Of course we were greatly helped because of the appalling display by the Government.[121] They had nothing to say at all in the way of policy. Nutting who opened made an emphatic declaration in general terms. But although he spoke perfectly well, there was nothing concrete whatever. Indeed the only new point that he made was a complete blunder. He tried to argue against a treaty with Israel, but his arguments were hopelessly fallacious, and we very soon caught him out on that. As for Eden, his winding up speech was almost pathetic. He made the great mistake of attacking us on very inadequate ground, and then, when our people reacted rather strongly, he did not attack me, but Robens about some rather foolish thing he had said about the Baghdad Pact. When our people reacted to this with interjections and a general uproar, he made the fatal mistake of trying to answer these interjections. This is a bad habit of his which I have often noticed before. When one is Prime Minister or Foreign Secretary, or indeed a Front Bench spokesman of any weight at all, it is very unwise to take any notice of interjections unless you have a really crushing retort which will bring, of course, all your own people out on your side. In the first ten minutes of his speech, Eden was occupied with trying to reply to these interjections, which he did quite inadequately, and it was plain that he was rapidly losing his temper. Of course when our boys saw that, it only encouraged them still further. There was then a sort of period of calm, during which he said little except to criticise Egyptian policy, and then towards the end of his speech he made another mistake in attacking me, saying that what I said seemed to be a faint echo of the Moscow Radio, which absolutely infuriated our people, and received no support from the Tories, who were perfectly aware that I had, in fact, made an unusually good speech, which had commanded the assent of the vast majority of the House.

Eventually Eden sat down and everybody was saying after it that he really could not last much longer. I could not help feeling that if the Tories had been sitting where we had been sitting and seen him that his position would have been still further undermined.[122] He looked thin and tired and ill and one could not help feeling really rather sorry for him, because of all the attacks which he has had to put up with. But what an error of judgment the whole speech showed! If he had just been unable to say anything, one can understand that – though, in that event, he should not have implied on the Monday that two days' wait would be sufficient for at

121 439 H.C. Deb. (7.3.56), cols. 2111–21 (Nutting), 2121–36 (HG), 2223–34 (Eden). For confirmation of the reception see *HG*, p. 410; Churchill (1959), pp. 226–8.
122 His own back benchers, of course, sat behind him.

least something to be said. But even if that was the case, he should have made an entirely different speech. He could, for instance, and it would have been wise, have complimented me upon mine and said that he agreed with a good deal that I had said, but that, of course, it wasn't quite so simple. He could then have explained the difficulties that they faced in the Arab countries, that they had done their best to make it plain that the Baghdad Pact was not aimed against anybody, that they were disappointed with the Egyptian reaction. As for arms for Israel, no doubt there was a case here, they had recognised that, but that there were difficulties, there were risks, they could not move without the Americans, and so on. If he had taken this line and begged the Opposition not to ruin the harmony and spoil the unity of the country, it would have put us in quite an awkward position, whether we should vote or not. By the type of speech he made, he made things easy for me and there was really no doubt in my mind, or in hardly anybody else's that we should have to divide on the Adjournment at the end of the Debate, which is, of course, what we did.

On the Monday [5 March] I had had dinner with a curious man called Bagrit. I was invited to this by an ex-Air Marshal called Sir Victor Goddard, whose wife is a cousin of Hubert Ashton's*.[123] Bagrit is obviously something of a business genius and control[s] a number of firms making automation machines of one kind or another. There were present at the dinner the Third Sea Lord, Admiral Edwards, the Controller of the Navy, as they call him, the man who is responsible for the whole of the supplies of the Navy, also a man called Sir Steuart Mitchell, who I gather was the Director of Guided Missiles at the Ministry of Supply.[124] I liked the Service people. They were friendly and rather sympathetic to Labour. Edwards, in particular, was very anti-Eden. They regarded him as weak. I supposed he [Edwards] would be better described as a kind of Suez-Group man. He, however, did not blame us for Abadan. He blamed the Americans. He knew that we had been prepared to get tough and then had suddenly stopped, and he thought that that must have been due to lack of American support. I told him that, in fact, the Chiefs of Staff themselves in those days, in 1951, had wobbled all over the place in the

123 Butler's P.P.S. and the husband of Gaitskell's sister. Goddard, who was retired, held wartime commands in the South Pacific and S.E. Asia, and was a member of the Air Council 1948–51. (Sir) Leon Bagrit, who founded the first European firm based on automation, was Deputy Chairman and then Chairman of Elliot Automation, 1957–73.
124 Since 1951. He had the same post at the Ministry of Aviation 1959–62, after being Controller of Royal Ordnance Factories 1956–9. Sir Ralph Edwards became C.-in-C. Mediterranean in 1957.

advice they had given us. [125] The conversation was not particularly interesting and I can't say that I learned a great deal. But it is a contact which might be useful later on, and I should certainly like to see something more of Bagrit's enterprises. He is obviously Jewish, and they all of them took the view that we now had to rely much more on Israel, give her arms, etc., etc.

Incidentally, on the Sunday evening, I had a mysterious visit from George Malcolm Thomson, who is the Literary Editor, I think, of the *Evening Standard*. Anyway he writes the book reviews there. However, it appears that he is a kind of general adviser to the *Daily Express* as well. [126] He wanted me to know that I could always use him to get suggestions or ideas or anything else to the *Express*. He thought that I ought to do this. Other people did it (he implied the Bevanites, I imagine) [127] and he would be very happy to serve as a kind of link. We then proceeded to talk about Jordan. He was very anti-Eden, he had tried to swing the *Express* round and get them to take the view that, as he put it, the alliances should now be changed. He thought we ought to force an immediate debate on Monday and that I should speak. I haven't seen him since, but I should imagine that he ought to be well pleased with the effect he had upon me. He is a nice chap, and Dora likes him. His son is a friend of Julia's [and Cressida's] and he lives only about 200 yards away. But whether or not he has much influence with the *Express*, and whether, indeed, it matters in the least what one says to them, is an entirely different matter.

Diary for the week beginning Monday 12 March 1956

We had a photograph taken of the Parliamentary Committee, *i.e.*, the Shadow Cabinet at the request of Transport House because this was the Jubilee year. One member failed to turn up – Mr Aneurin Bevan. One doesn't know whether he just forgot about it, or whether he decided that he could not be seen in this particular company by posterity.

125 See above, pp. 260, 263–4. The Suez Group of Conservatives opposed withdrawal from the Canal Zone in 1954.
126 An author and *Daily Express* journalist, who had been Beaverbrook's ghost-writer before the war and his confidential secretary during it.
127 They had many links with the *Express* group, both through its regular recruitment of journalists from *Tribune*, and through Beaverbrook's close relationships with Bevan and with Michael Foot.

I dined the same evening, on the 12th March, with a body called the British [Socialist] Agricultural Society.[128] They consisted of a mixture of wealthy farmers, who are, of course, members of the Party, and most of whom were Bevanites, and poor, small-holder type of farmers, who seemed to be a good deal further to the Right. It was, nevertheless, quite a pleasant occasion. They were very outspoken and almost all agreed that the present policy was out of date; that the 1947 [Agriculture] Act was really now finished, or at any rate not adequate as a future policy, and that we should have to start afresh. Most of them, I think, did not want to have the present system of subsidies, with threats of eviction against farmers who refused to play, and wanted to have some kind of different system in which efficiency was rewarded more directly and inefficiency penalised by the more obvious consequences, i.e., financial failure.

On the 13th, I went to lunch with Dick Crossman, at the first of the lunches which, at my request, he is organising for the small group on foreign affairs. Kenneth Younger and Alf Robens were there, but Denis Healey had gone to America and John Hynd was away. It was quite a useful and pleasant discussion, though nothing very sensational emerged.

That evening we dined with the Crawleys, the Pakenhams being the other guests, and had a very enjoyable, gossipy time. . .

On the 16th March, I lunched at the Soviet Embassy to meet Malenkov*.[129] It was quite a big squash, the Government being represented by Lord Reading, the Minister of Supply and the Minister of Fuel and Power;[130] on the Opposition side there was Morgan Phillips, Chris Mayhew and myself. I sat between [the Ambassador] Malik and the Deputy Minister of Power in Russia, a pleasant-spoken, pleasant-looking chap who did have a few words of English. Malenkov and I had a bout of back-chat across the table, which, of course, had to be translated, about the role of the Opposition. I explained how important it was in our politics and that even when we had 100 per cent Labour-controlled Councils, opposition naturally developed. I was thinking, of course, that he might be regarded as the opposition inside the Soviet Government. Continuing with the story of the Malenkov visit, the following week, on the Monday, the National Executive Committee gave a dinner for Malenkov. Unfortunately, as I had to address the Political Committee of

128 So named in HG's appointments diary.
129 Soviet Prime Minister till February 1955, then Minister of Power Stations, but still a member of the Praesidium.
130 The 2nd Marquess of Reading was at the Foreign Office 1951–7, as Under-Secretary and (from 1953) as Minister of State. Aubrey Jones, a Conservative M.P. for Birmingham 1950–65, was Minister of Fuel and Power 1955–7, and of Supply (succeeding Maudling) 1957–9.

the Reform Club at a dinner myself that evening, I only arrived at the National Executive affair very late. By then Malenkov had already been answering questions for some considerable time, and when I came in he was still wrestling with the problem of the Communist Party. It was made plain to me afterwards that he had been told clearly that we would have nothing whatever to do with them. When it came to my turn, I asked him some questions about Russian economic development, and, in particular, when they were going to increase the supply of consumer goods, and whether there had been any disagreement in the Russian Government about the plan. He replied rather tartly, but evasively, that consumer goods were increased just as much as capital goods in the plan, and that there was no disagreement whatever but that they were all unanimous. Later on he started to ask us questions and one was addressed to me about disarmament. He followed this up by asking if there was any real difference between us and the Tory Government, and I had to explain that there was, in fact, extremely little, though all would depend on how they handled the present series of negotiations. The rest of the Malenkov visit story is told elsewhere. I have written down my record of the conversations I had with him some time later.[131]

On Friday, 16 March, after the lunch at the Soviet Embassy, I went to 10 Downing St, for a meeting about Malta. On our side there was also Jim Griffiths and Nye Bevan, and on the other side, with the Prime Minister, there was the Colonial Secretary [Lennox-Boyd] and R.A. Butler. We argued very strongly, first, that there ought to be a debate before Easter, and that, if possible, there should be a debate indicating the Government's approval of the White Paper. We also urged that, after this, the Government should bring in a Bill, and that the Bill should go through all its stages in Parliament here, before any further decision was called for from the Maltese people. This was the line which emerged after discussion we had had privately with Mintoff, the Prime Minister of Malta and the leader of the Labour Party there. Government were to some extent forthcoming in that they agreed that there should be a debate before Easter, but they were not prepared to make this a debate on a Motion approving the White Paper. They did, however, say that in their opinion the Colonial Secretary could, and should, say that the Government were in favour of this. There was some opposition from Butler, who was throwing up, rather definitely I thought, the attitude and outlook of the Tory Back Benchers who were against the proposals for integration. We also had some difficulty in persuading either or any of them that the Bill ought to go through all its stages here before any decision was taken in Malta. We saw them again in the following week and our discussion

131 Below, pp. 482–91.

with them was a good deal more satisfactory. Out of this, in effect, emerged the conclusion which we had wanted that there should be a debate before Easter, that the Government should make their position quite clear and that they should announce either at the end of the debate or two or three days later, and in any case before Mintoff went back to Malta that they were going to proceed with legislation. In effect that is what happened and in the light of all their hesitations of which we heard so much from Mintoff, and indeed of their reluctance at the beginning of our first conversation, I think we have achieved a considerable triumph in getting the Malta problem handled just as we wanted. One could not help feeling, watching them, as one took part in the discussions, discussions incidentally in which we did far more talking than they did, one could not help feeling that Eden was really a very indecisive sort of person. He seemed to be very nervous about the Back Benchers and to be by no means sure of his own mind in these matters; to be rather willing to allow himself to be pushed by us. Lennox Boyd, on the other hand, although one gathered that he was in favour of integration, was awfully cautious and, again, was frightened of the Back Benchers. And Butler, as I have said, seemed to be doing all he could to play up his own position in the Government as the man representing the Back Benchers. This is exactly what I should have expected.[132]

Diary for the following week, i.e. beginning Monday, 19 March 1956

I have already referred to the National Executive dinner to Malenkov. On the 20th I had lunch with Charles Forte, who is now *the* great caterer in the country. This was organised by Alf Robens, who is a friend of his. Forte is a supporter of the Labour Party, and the object of the lunch, apart from the interest of his company, was to try and secure some assistance from him for the finances of *Forward*.[133] In this we were

132 Above, pp. 429–32. The White Paper, following the all-party conference, had proposed the integration of Malta into the United Kingdom, but the suspicions of the Catholic Church in Malta were reflected among Catholic Conservative M.P.s at Westminster. Talks followed which were quite successful over constitutional issues, but were disrupted in 1957 by Maltese claims over financial aid and dockyard employment. By 1958 Mintoff was reconciled with the Church at home, but had lost British sympathy in both parties, and support for integration had waned. After riots and a general strike he resigned, and for a year the Governor ruled under emergency powers. In 1964 Malta became an independent republic. (Cf. pp. 593–4.)

133 On *Forward* see above, pp. 337, 414 and n., 446; below, pp. 474, 518, 545 and n. Forte, of Trust Houses Forte, was knighted in 1970.

extremely successful, for after we had talked about the paper and what we hoped it would achieve, he said he was prepared to put in £5,000 now and another £5,000 next year, if this was necessary. I must confess that I think Alf Robens has done very well in getting hold of him in this way. He obviously likes Robens, and it is another illustration of Alf's capacity for getting on with all sorts of people. Even if he isn't very good at foreign policy, he has this other quality very much to his credit.

On the 21st March we lunched with the Swiss Minister and his wife; indeed the lunch seemed to be given in our honour. The only interesting thing that occurred was a brief conversation I had with [Sir] Evelyn Shuckburgh, who is the man in the Foreign Office in charge of the whole of the Middle East. He is also a close friend of Harry Walston*. [134] I gave him a lift back to Whitehall after lunch and talked briefly with him about the position in the Middle East. I told him what I thought in no uncertain terms. All I got out of him was that they did appear to be genuinely frightened about Communism and the danger of the Communists getting control if we gave Israel the arms. But I feel that this is a very biased point of view and probably based on the Embassies in the Arab States who so far as experience goes never seem to know anything about the States in which they are serving. [135]

At the end of the week I went to Scotland to attend the Scottish Labour Party's Conference who were holding a big meeting in Edinburgh. There is nothing special to record. I was very much helped by Arthur Woodburn, Peggy Herbison, Willy Ross in preparing my speech, at least that part of it which dealt with Scottish affairs . . . [136]

Diary for the week beginning Monday, 26 March 1956 [dictated 3 April]

We dined on the 27th with the High Commissioner for Pakistan and his wife. It was a most dreary affair. Again it was really in our honour and some of the other people there were quite nice: Lord Pethick-Lawrence,

134 Walston was a wealthy East Anglian farmer and Labour supporter. Shuckburgh was assistant Under-Sec. at the Foreign Office 1954–6, Deputy Under-Sec. 1960–2, attached to NATO in between and later, Ambassador to Italy 1966–9.

135 The Foreign Office had had no warning of Glubb's dismissal three weeks earlier. Among many other examples, the government in which Gaitskell served had been surprised by the Persian crisis.

136 Ross, a schoolmaster, was M.P. for Kilmarnock 1946–79. Sec. for Scotland 1964–70, 1974–6; P.C. (Parl. Committee) 1971–4; Lord High Commissioner to the Church of Scotland General Assembly 1978.

Lord Listowel, the Robens', but the dinner was very late in starting, because the Attlees were supposed to be coming, but forgot all about it – I ought to add that Lord Tedder was another of the guests – and at the end of it all, Dora first of all had a terrific row with the High Commissioner's wife about politics. [137] I must say I thought she – the Begum – behaved pretty badly. She started denouncing the British working classes to Dora, and said they ought to work much harder. Seeing that Pakistan is a feudal country and that she is their representative here, we thought it was pretty good cheek. Anyway Dora certainly answered back and a fierce argument ensued about the class system and one thing and another. Finally, to cap it all, Dora lost one of her earrings as we were leaving. Fortunately after a bit this was found.

On the following evening, on the other hand, we dined with Anne Fleming*, who is one of the most entertaining and amusing hostesses in London. I must admit that this dinner was not quite up to her usual standard, I mean as far as guests were concerned . . . from the conversational point of view, the evening was not quite so good as sometimes. There was the usual political gossip. Anne Fleming is one of the few Tories who seems to be reasonably loyal to Eden, but there was a great deal of criticism of him. All agreed that William Clark, as the Prime Minister's P.R.O. had been an absolute disaster and, so they said, nobody but a fool would have appointed him to such a position.

Joe Alsop* has been in London. He is more gloomy than usual. He came to see me on the 29th March and he dined with us this evening, April 3rd. I must say he seems to have more reason than usual for his gloom. He regards the position in Washington as completely hopeless. Eisenhower is in cottonwool, [Secretary of State] Dulles* is a disaster and it is impossible for the British Government to get the American Government to do anything. He is naturally rather more kindly about the British Government than I would be and he blames his own Government for most of the British Government's troubles. But he admitted that it is very shaky. Tonight he said, 'You will probably be in power within two years. I do not see this Government lasting as long as that. There is so much

137 Lord Pethick-Lawrence (1871–1961) was a champion of the suffragettes before the First World War, secretary of the Union of Democratic Control during it, a Labour M.P. 1923–31, 1935–45 (P.C. 1935–40) and Secretary for India and Burma 1945–7. The 5th Earl of Listowel succeeded him in 1947–8, held minor offices 1945–51, and was Governor General of Ghana 1957–60. Lord Tedder had been Eisenhower's Deputy Supreme Commander 1943–5, and Chief of the Air Staff 1946–50. Mohammed Ikramullah was High Commissioner 1955–9; a former Foreign Secretary, he attended six Commonwealth Prime Ministers' Conferences.

discontent around'. However, I said that he must not assume that all the discontent necessarily led to action. The Tories very very seldom split, and if they don't split, I don't see them having an Election, unless by any chance they get to the point where they feel they would rather have an Election early than late because they feel they would not do quite so badly. In any event, I see no prospect of one for at any rate two years and perhaps more. Joe is particularly friendly with Antony Head, the Secretary of State for War, of whom he thinks very highly indeed. [138] He told me the Prime Minister was going away for ten days because he was ill. He had seen Butler and Macmillan. He thought Macmillan very difficult to get to know. He agreed that he looked ill and, for the rest, he thought the Colonial Secretary was gloomy about Malaya, but that is exactly what Joe, somehow or other, would expect him to be.

Diary for 5 April 1956

Last night, i.e. April 4th we had a very private dinner with the Trade Union leaders. There were present:- Tom Williamson, Frank Cousins, Jim Campbell, Bill Webber, Charlie Geddes, Harry Douglass and Ernest Jones; [139] almost all the key people in the T.U.C. And on the political side:- Alf Robens, George Brown and myself. Jim Griffiths had been invited, but was unable to be there. I had been pressing for a meeting of this kind for some time, and had suggested to Tom Williamson that the leading Trade Union people should meet the leading Parliamentarians regularly from time to time in order to discuss any matters of common interest. And he had welcomed the idea. Eventually this dinner was arranged. It took place in a private room at the Café Royal. During dinner itself there was some extremely interesting conversation. Firstly, about the line the Communists were going to take, and secondly about the great issues of wage policy. On the Communists, most of the Union leaders took the view that the new Soviet line was certain to be reflected in the demands from the left wing in the Unions for united fronts with the Communists of one kind or another. Most of them seemed to be fairly satisfied that they could deal with moves of this kind, though I thought

138 Brigadier Antony (Viscount) Head was Conservative M.P. for Carshalton (Surrey) 1945–60, Minister for War 1951–6, Defence 1956–7 (including Suez), High Commissioner to Nigeria 1960–3, to Malaysia1963–6. Died 1983.
139 Respectively general secretaries of the General & Municipal Workers, Transport Workers, Railwaymen, Transport Salaried Staffs, Post Office Workers, Steelworkers, and president of the Miners. Geddes was also chairman of the T.U.C. that year.

Ernest Jones of the miners was a little nervous. As to wages policy, the discussion was lively though rather confused. I got the impression that they were continuing an argument which had already taken place up to a certain point in the Economic Committee of the T.U.C. In this argument Frank Cousins, the latest arrival in the T.U.C., but also the General Secretary or General Secretary elect of the most powerful Union, the Transport Workers, was inclined to take the view that they could not make any kind of agreement or have any kind of understanding with the Government, and that there was nothing to be said for restraint of any kind. The others, on the other hand, said that in the interests of a future Labour Government, a policy of no restraint at all was dangerous, even if this was carried out under the Tories.

As I said, the discussion was confused, but I felt that it promised very well for further meetings. It is probably a good thing that all those concerned should let off steam informally in this way and it is certainly highly important that they should give their minds to the problem. After dinner was over, Tom Williamson, who was acting as Chairman, explained why the dinner had been arranged and, after a bit, I also chipped in and together we put our reasons for a gathering of this kind. Tom mentioned the question of the Treasurership of the Labour Party and I did also and I also mentioned the question of *Forward* and the need for getting Trade Union backing for the new paper.[140]

In fact the whole of the rest of the evening virtually was spent on discussing the Treasurership problem. We more or less went round the table and one Trade Union leader after the other made it quite plain that he was not going to support Bevan. Williamson made that absolutely plain from the start and, rather surprisingly, Jim Campbell, of the N.U.R., took just the same line. Geddes was rather anxious to find out my views first, but was stopped by Bill Webber, who said it was quite unfair to ask my views. It was a matter for the Unions to decide for themselves. Ernest Jones of the miners said rather bitterly that this meeting should have taken place three months before in which case they might have prevented the Yorkshire Miners nominating Bevan for 1957. There was then some discussion about alternative candidates. Tom Williamson mentioned Jack Cooper, but it was very clear that he was not very enthusiastic, although Jack Cooper is the President of his own Union. Indeed he said that Jack Cooper, although he wanted it, would, he knew, give way in favour of a better candidate. It was made plain that they had approached Sam Watson and, indeed, pressed him for some weeks to accept nomination, but he had refused. It was also mentioned that Herbert Morrison had been approached, although some thought that

140 On *Forward* see above, p. 470 n. and references there.

he was really a doubtful candidate. The field thus gradually became narrower and narrower, and I was getting a little worried because the two obvious candidates who remained were both in the room, namely Alf Robens and George Brown. I was going to propose, since this was a kind of selection conference, that the two candidates had better withdraw and, indeed, to offer to do so myself. However, as it turned out, this was not necessary.

Frank Cousins, Transport Workers, said quite plainly that he would like to nominate George Brown. He did not press very strongly for this and made it plain that, of course, if there was general agreement in favour of somebody else he would fall into line. But he felt that George was a good candidate, a strong candidate and, of course, he was a member of their Union. Then Alf Robens chipped in. I knew that he had spent the weekend at his Union Annual Conference. I also knew that he was going to discuss with Alan Birch, the General Secretary, the possibility of his being nominated for the Treasurership by his Union [USDAW]. I also knew that Tom Williamson had spoken to him and that Tom had regarded Alf as possibly the strongest candidate. I fully expected that Alan Birch would, in fact, agree that Alf should be nominated by the Union and that he would return from the Conference having arranged this. However, as it turned out, something quite different had happened. Alf explained, quite frankly, to the people at the dinner that he had been at the Conference and that he had discussed both with Alan Birch and with Padley*, the President of the Union, a left-wing member of Parliament who was rather jealous of Alf, the possibility of a nomination. Although they had not ruled this out, neither of them was prepared to say that he could definitely have the nomination and, indeed, Alf felt that they were showing no enthusiasm for this. He said that he thought there was an element of jealousy in it, but that he must accept the position and that it was practically impossible for his name to go forward unless he was assured of the support of his own Union. The implication was, therefore, that he was no longer in the running. That, of course, simplified the whole situation, and it was clear that George Brown was, therefore, going to be the candidate chosen by the Trade Union movement, or most of the Trade Union movement.[141] There was then some further discussion about immediate action. It was generally agreed that George should get himself nominated quickly and finally settled that he should secure nomination in the first instance from his own Divisional Labour Party – he said he could get this arranged on Saturday next – and that about a week

141 Since Aneurin Bevan was standing, the assumption that the candidate of most trade union leaders was the candidate of the movement was rash. HG often over-estimated the leaders' control over their unions.

after that the Transport Workers would come out with their nomination for him as well. So all ended quite satisfactorily.

I had an interesting conversation with Jim Campbell, whom I took home. Jim is, of course, the Secretary of the Railwaymen. He has a rather difficult time with his people, and I have always regarded him as, well not exactly left-wing, but rather timid. But last night he was very firmly anti-Bevan and thought that he could swing the N.U.R. vote in favour of George Brown. He had spoken to me earlier in favour of Brown and said that he had been much impressed by his television appearances and also by his speeches in the House. Later he said to me another interesting thing, that Alf Robens' speech had lost him a lot of support in the Trade Union movement.[142] Those who were anti-Communist were not quite so sure whether they could rely on him. Of course, I was afraid that exactly this would happen. But it is fascinating to see how a few speeches and a few appearances on television can make such a big difference.

Six months ago I do not think that George Brown would have had much chance, but he has suddenly come to the front with his performance in Parliament and with these television appearances as well. I am not surprised about him, because he is a man of great force and vigour and highly intelligent too. His great weakness is that he has a sort of chip on his shoulder, that he is very ambitious and can hardly disguise it and that he goes around, for that reason, making far too many enemies. It is not that one doesn't trust him. In a way his record of public utterances is extremely good. He has always said what he thinks and said it very courageously. But one has, all the same, some feeling that he may be getting agitated and pushing around trying to get himself on rather faster and further. I hope, however, that the success that he has had in the last few weeks will do him good. At any rate he came in to see me this morning to discuss the implications of all this and we went over the arithmetic. It is, I think, clear that, if Bevan gets the Miners' vote, and the A.E.U. vote, and also the N.U.R. and USDAW then he is almost certain to win.[143] But if George can get either the N.U.R. or USDAW then I think he stands a good chance of pulling it off. We were assuming that Bevan would get more of the Constituency Party vote than he did last year. Incidentally, Alf said he thought he could swing the USDAW vote in favour of George, and even Ernest Jones thought there was just a possibility that the Miners might come round. Anyway we shall see what happens. Of course, I have

142 On the speech, above pp. 455–8. Campbell, assistant secretary of the N.U.R. since 1948 and general secretary since 1953, was to lead the opposition to HG's compromise proposals on nationalisation in 1957. He was killed in a car crash in the U.S.S.R. later that year.

143 He did (except for the A.E.U. which voted for one of its own M.P.s, Charles Pannell).

to be very careful about all this, and I only hope that nothing about this meeting leaks out. For the rest, it was an extremely successful evening. We all agreed that we would have regular meetings about once a month and that we might bring one or two other people to them. And we fixed the date of the next meeting. If we can keep this up, it may really make a big difference, not only to the unity of the Party and the Movement in Opposition, but also to our chances of success when we get back into power.[144]

144 Similar meetings were held in later years but were increasingly used to counteract the influence of Frank Cousins.

CHAPTER 9

RUSSIA, AMERICA AND THE COMMONWEALTH

Editor's Note
Document No. 16 HG's two talks with G.M. Malenkov,
29–30 March 1956
Diary, 20 April 1956 to 14 July 1956

[After Stalin died in 1953, Western politicians had a natural curiosity and indeed anxiety about his potential successor. G.M. Malenkov, who had once seemed the likeliest, was approved in the West but repudiated at home for saying that a nuclear war would destroy civilisation. After his demotion, he visited Britain in March 1956, and made an excellent impression. He was soon followed by the two men who had recently taken over his former posts: Nikita Khrushchev the new First Secretary, and Nicolai Bulganin the new Prime Minister. With them, relations were very different. Though later mellowed by experience, Khrushchev at first pursued intransigent policies in the crudest style, revelling in the destructive power of his nuclear weapons, which he insisted would wipe out capitalism while communism would survive.

The Labour Party gave a dinner for the visitors, at which there was a row. Shinwell, who had not been present, tried to use the incident to make trouble for Gaitskell, but found little support even among Bevanites. Relations were formally repaired, and the Russians invited Gaitskell to the Soviet Union; his visit was postponed until 1959 because of their invasion of Hungary and its repercussions, so that he was in Moscow when Macmillan dissolved Parliament.

Gaitskell was an enthusiastic traveller to all parts of the world, and he felt very much at home in the United States. All his life he had a powerful appeal there, mainly though not exclusively to liberal opinion. In 1957, two months after Suez, he was to deliver his main public analysis of international affairs, the Godkin Lectures, to a university audience at Harvard. But on his visit in 1956 he was unusually free of academic as well as official commitments, spent nearly all his time with trade unionists and liberal Democrats, and was impressed to find so many of their attitudes very similar to his own. He was also familiar with many leading Commonwealth figures from his period at the Treasury, met them again as a senior front bencher when they came to London for periodic conferences, and visited the Asian Commonwealth countries twice in the 1950s.]

Document No. 16

TWO TALKS WITH MR. MALENKOV
(from HG Papers, file P.118–4)

On the evening of Thursday, the 29th March, 1956, there was a big reception at the Soviet Embassy in honour of Mr. Malenkov and his Delegation. I myself arrived very late at about 7.20 p.m. when a great many people had already left. Wives had not been invited but, as we were going to Tony Crosland's party afterwards, Mrs. Gaitskell had arranged to pick me up at the Embassy at about 7.45 p.m.

I went in and greeted Mr. Malenkov, was introduced to and talked for a time with Mr. Gromyko* and also had some conversation with one or two other members of the Electrical Delegation whom I had met before.[1] I then went into the entrance hall to see if my wife had arrived. While I was there Mr. Malenkov came out accompanied by a large crowd and I began to talk with him again. There was nothing serious in the conversation; it was mostly banalities and badinage and it was conducted in the hearing of about 30 people – many of them press men – who surrounded us. I did, however, ask him if he would like to come on with us to a private English party – and he replied laughingly that he thought it was his duty to accept all invitations in England! Mrs. Gaitskell then arrived and was duly introduced to Mr. Malenkov and further chit-chat followed.

A little later after I had left Malenkov I was taken on one side by Malik [the Ambassador] who asked if in the course of the next two or three days I would have dinner with Malenkov and himself alone. I said I would be delighted and we agreed on Friday – the following day – at the Embassy. At this point, Mrs. Gaitskell joined us and we asked the Ambassador when [why?] he never produced Mrs. Malik. He said, 'Would you like to meet her?' Naturally, we responded with enthusiasm – whereupon he took us through the crowd to the lift, opened a locked door on the first floor and ushered us in to what was evidently the Maliks' living room. There was a largish table in the middle covered with a lace table-cloth – faintly reminiscent of Chekhov. We three then sat down and the Ambassador turned on a television set. A maid then brought in some drinks. A moment or two later Malenkov came in alone and we began talking (Malik doing the interpreting). Then Mrs. Malik and another woman, Gromyko and his wife, the [Counsellor] Minister at the Embassy

---

1 Andrei Gromyko, Deputy Foreign Minister, became Foreign Minister a year later. Malenkov as Minister of Power Stations led a delegation including electrical specialists.

and finally the official interpreter all joined us. Tea was served (Russian fashion) and cookies and sweets were produced.

We then carried on a long conversation which lasted about two hours and which, together with the one on the following day, is recorded separately. At about 10.20 we got up to go and again asked Malenkov if he would come to the party. There was a short discussion between him and Malik in Russian and after a bit of hesitation he finally said it was too late. But there is little doubt that he very nearly did come.

Malik then said he hoped we would both dine with them the following day and asked me if we would like to bring the children. We turned this down and asked them instead to come and have drinks with us before dinner when I could ask a few friends in as well. This they agreed to do.

We then went on to Tony Crosland's party getting home very late – at about 3 a.m. John Freeman was there and, as one would expect, took great interest in the Malenkov story [as a journalist].

We then had to decide whom to invite to meet Malenkov. We had already asked the Jenkins at the Crosland party and we added the Jays and Frank Soskice. After that I thought it was best simply to ask available members of the Party who had not met Malenkov at the N.E.C. Dinner. Eventually, I got hold of Alfred Robens, Kenneth Younger and George Brown. I could not get James Callaghan. Most of the others concerned were, I knew, away. At 6 p.m. – having earlier in the day sent the chauffeur to find out where we lived – the Russians duly arrived bearing gifts – books for the children and some vodka and brandy for us. Quite a successful party followed in which I left the others who had not met him to talk to Malenkov. The Press, of course, got on to this quickly and within half an hour a *Daily Mirror* photographer was at our door and a reporter from the *Daily Mail*. The Russians came at 6 and left about 7.15. Having got rid of the others we eventually went to the Embassy bearing our few gifts as well – a scarf, some good scent, four Dior earrings and a copy of Evan's book which I duly inscribed![2]

We then had dinner in which I was given lots of caviare (Dora didn't do so well and I noticed the women didn't seem to eat much of it) followed by Schaslik and a fruit sweet. There was lots of vodka and brandy, also some Swedish wine. Once again, the television seemed to be going most of the time until Dora asked for it to be turned off. We couldn't help wondering whether there was some microphone device – or alternatively, whether it was to obscure the noise of the conversation. After dinner we sat on the sofa and easy chairs and another long discussion followed – which is also recorded separately. We left about midnight – all very friendly despite the frankness of the talks.

2 Evan Durbin's *The Politics of Democratic Socialism*, which had recently been reissued with a foreword by HG.

RECORD OF CONVERSATION WITH MR. MALENKOV[3]

I had two long talks with Mr. Malenkov – on the 29th and 30th March, 1956. Both took place in an upstairs room at the Soviet Embassy and on the invitation of Mr. Malik. His approach to me was very informal and, to some extent at least, on the spur of the moment. There were present on both occasions Mr. Malik and Mr. Gromyko and their wives as well as Mrs. Gaitskell.

As the content of the two talks overlapped, there is no point in trying to record them separately. A great deal more time was spent in my answering Mr. Malenkov's questions than in his answering mine or in general argument. I am afraid this makes the record of the talks rather dull. My impression of Mr. Malenkov, however, was that he was genuinely seeking information, that he even seemed to be prepared to believe what I was saying and that, in contrast to Mr. Malik and Mr. Gromyko, he scarcely ever made use of the stock Communist formulae when he spoke. Although he was extremely evasive in replying to some of the awkward questions which I put to him about recent developments in Russia, it is possibly of some interest that he should have thought it worth while spending so much time asking me questions. It may, of course, have been just part of the new Soviet policy of seeking friendship with the Social Democratic Parties. I do not think it was just politeness. I believe that at least to some extent he was really anxious to find out more about Great Britain. Moreover, if Mr. Malenkov expected – as it were – to conduct foreign policy negotiations with the Labour Party in this way he must have been very disappointed. For I made it quite clear very early on that it was not the job of the Opposition here to conduct talks with Russia, or indeed with any other foreign power, and that any serious discussions of that kind must be carried on with the Government.[4] At the same time, I said that I would be glad to try and explain anything to him. The subjects covered during our talks included:-

(1) The Party System here – especially in relation to foreign policy.
(2) The British attitude to Russian foreign policy.
(3) The Middle East.
(4) The position of the Communist Party here.

3 From HG Papers, file P.118–4, marked Strictly Private and Confidential, emphasis his. Copies were sent to the Prime Minister and Foreign Secretary, and to HG's Labour colleagues: only Bowden, Dalton, Griffiths, Wilson and Younger are recorded, but he is unlikely to have omitted Crossman, Healey and Robens.
4 When Khrushchev made such an approach to the Labour Party 18 months later, Gaitskell and Bevan promptly reported it to the Prime Minister: *HG*, p. 460.

(5) The class structure in Britain today.

(6) Recent internal changes in Russia.

(1) *Party System in Britain.*

I explained more than once to Malenkov that there were certain basic differences between the Conservative and Labour Parties – that we represented different interests and different aims especially regarding the distribution of wealth and the role of the State in economic affairs. I told him that the function of the Labour Opposition was really a dual one – first to present and argue for our principles and the policies associated with them against those of the Government; and, secondly, to act as professional critics of the Government's *administration* – exposing its weaknesses, mistakes and incompetence whenever these were discovered.

He asked me more than once about differences between the Parties on foreign policy. I explained that there were some differences here – for example on the Middle East – but that they were far smaller than they had been before the war and that to a large extent the Conservatives had taken over the policies of the post-war Labour Government. I made it plain that the fact that there were relatively small differences over foreign policy was not the result of any conscious effort to minimise them, that we remained completely free to attack and oppose the Government whenever we thought this justified, but that the world situation which confronted us inevitably limited the scope of the foreign policy of any British Government.

(2) *British Attitude to Russian Foreign Policy.*

The most important fact here was our anxiety about Soviet expansionism. Immediately after the war we had hoped – especially in the Labour Party – for genuine co-operation between the U.S.A., Russia and ourselves. For instance, in my election posters in 1945 I had had the flags of the three countries printed together! Unfortunately, Stalin had not wanted to co-operate. He had occupied Eastern Europe and slammed down the Iron Curtain. This, together with other evidence that Stalin's policy was expansionist and even aggressive, drove the Western democracies to band together in self defence. It was no use Malik speaking of 'blocks' – as he did at one point in the conversation – the Soviet had their block very tightly controlled whereas the democracies had a looser alliance with each other. Nor was it any use expecting the West to give up their alliances. They would never do this until they felt absolutely secure. This would be the last stage of a settlement not the first.

Despite our fears of Soviet expansionism, however, I did not expect a major war – because of the 'nuclear deterrent'. The fear of complete destruction by the H. Bomb would stop anyone starting it. The Russian leaders might talk of 'capitalism' being ended by another war, but they must know that it would not only be capitalism but everything which would be ended. At this point Malenkov indicated his complete agreement.

I said I was encouraged by the new Russian proposals for control of 'conventional' arms because they followed a line I had suggested to Malik in a conversation several weeks ago when he had insisted that we must have control over nuclear weapons *including stocks* if we were to have any control at all. Malik smiled at this and said nothing at the time. But later when we came back to the subject of disarmament, Malik rather curiously repeated that there must be control of nuclear weapons. I twitted him with being out of step with the new Soviet line and Gromyko said laughingly, 'He is my opponent!'

I made the point that what we must hope for was a long period of 'quiet' – during which fears could subside and confidence be created. But I said we should never have this if the Russians directly or indirectly stirred up trouble as they had recently done in

(3) *The Middle East.*

This was perhaps the most encouraging part of the whole discussion. In telling them what we felt about the Czech/Egyptian Arms deal, I made the point that the Soviet had not been pro-Arab and anti-Israel before, so there could be no question of principle for them. They accepted this and Gromyko said, 'Yes, I voted at the U.N. for the establishment of Israel'. Malik put up a very feeble defence of the Arms deal and tried to link it with the ban on East/West Trade. But I pointed out (a) that no one was stopping Czechoslovakia from buying cotton anywhere; (b) Malenkov had told me only a few minutes before that Russia had an export surplus in cotton; (c) that the political significance of the deal far outweighed any conceivable economic motive.[5] Neither of the other two made any attempt to support Malik and this line was therefore dropped.

They referred, of course, to the Baghdad Pact – and particularly emphasised their concern about *Iran* – as being their neighbour. I said that Turkey, Iraq, Iran and Pakistan could not be any danger to them and that they must realise that. For the rest I referred them for my own point of view to my speech in the last Middle East Debate and emphasised that we simply could not afford to have them threatening our *oil supplies*.

We agreed that Arab Nationalism was a major cause of trouble and I did not dispute their argument that internal conditions in Egypt were a bigger factor making for disturbance than external communist influences.

5 President Nasser had announced the deal on 27 September 1955; Egypt would pay in cotton for Czech arms.

The most interesting reaction I got, however, was on the question of the guarantee of Israel's frontiers. Malenkov said he was absolutely in favour of this and agreed that we could not let Israel be overwhelmed! I do not think there was any mistake: he said it more than once. Moreover, when I was describing the case of Israel – persecution of the Jews, etc. – he seemed to be wholly sympathetic. I said I thought it would be enormously important (my wife added 'sensational') if the Russians would come out with a statement saying that they favoured a guarantee of the present frontiers of Israel. This would make a profound impression on the West, though I added it would displease the Arab States.

I must admit that while Malenkov showed no sign of withdrawing what he had said on Israel, Gromyko indicated that he was not altogether in agreement with Malenkov.

On the question of Arms, I said that what we objected to was not so much that they supplied arms but that they supplied arms to one side only. They said, 'Would it have been all right if we had supplied arms to both sides?' I said, 'It would have been better, in my opinion, because the balance of power would have been maintained'.

Later, Malik – not altogether seriously I thought – expressed disapproval of 'the balance of power'. So – also not very seriously – I gave him a brief lecture about the advantage of the balance of power in an imperfect world. The others made no attempt to dispute my arguments, and I felt once again the difference between Malik and to some extent Gromyko, who produced stock Soviet propaganda lines, and Malenkov who showed almost no inclination to do this.

(4) *The Communist Party.*

I said there could be no doubt about the harm done by the existence of the Communist Party here to good Anglo-Russian relations. Since it was simply an instrument of Soviet foreign policy, there could be no better reminder of Russian expansionism – or at least her constant interference in other countries. Inevitably it increased suspicions of Russian intentions; it convinced people of her efforts to disrupt; and it made *normal* relations – a situation in which Russia would be treated like any other power – difficult if not impossible. Malenkov said he understood this clearly. The same thing had been said repeatedly at the Labour Party National Executive Dinner. Malik asked how I reconciled this with the Labour Party view that the Communist Party here was unimportant. I said that we did not worry about it politically but it did harm in the Unions. No doubt it succeeded in bringing off some strikes but what real value were these to Russia when set against the disturbance to normal diplomatic relations resulting from the Communist Party? Maybe in France and Italy they would strike the balance differently but not here.

I emphasised that in Britain the Communists and Fellow Travellers had no influence, and I chided Malik with the kind of political contacts he seemed to have. Instead of people who were generally regarded as simply Soviet stooges, he should keep in touch with those who mattered more. This led on to an interesting discussion on the so-called 'Disarmament Conference' to which Ehrenburg and some other Russians had invited a number of individual politicians – most of them well-known fellow travellers.[6] I said this would do no good at all because it was obviously a bit of propaganda. Malenkov made a rather interesting remark at this point. He said he had assumed that no Labour Party member would be allowed to go to a conference of this kind without the approval of the Leader of the Party. He had supposed that Party discipline would ensure this. I explained that this was by no means the case, although a member of our Parliamentary Committee had, it was true, consulted me.

I was then asked what sort of conference would be valuable. I replied first that it should be private, secondly, that the agenda should be drawn up by agreement, thirdly, that it should be arranged through Chris Mayhew's organisation which was known to be untainted with Communism,[7] fourthly, that those who went on the British side should be carefully selected so as to be representative of different interests and points of view here and also people of some importance and that the same should apply to the Russian side. I explained to them how the Koenigswinter Conference was arranged every year by the Anglo-German Society and suggested that something of this sort would be worth trying. But it would be no good if the whole idea was to put across Soviet propaganda rather than to have a genuine exchange of views. Finally, I offered to talk to Malik further about it. Malenkov said he thought this was all very interesting and it was something they ought clearly to consider.

(5) *The Class Structure in Britain.*

Indeed, with one partial exception, to which I will refer in a moment, Malenkov seemed to be ready to accept fairly easily what I said about the Communist Party. When Gromyko rather feebly made the usual comment about Russia having nothing to do with the Communist Party here, he was more or less brushed aside by Malenkov who did not demur when I said, rather sharply, that we were grown up people and need not go in for that kind of pretence. On two occasions, however, he did bring out one Communist Party formula, 'The unity of the working class'. I asked

6 Ilya Ehrenburg (1891–1967) was a prominent Soviet journalist and writer, Vice-President of the 'World Peace Council', and latterly a defender of dissident intellectuals and foreign contacts.
7 See below, p. 503.

exactly what he meant by this today. The class structure had changed a good deal in the last 50 years here as in Russia. How did his phrase apply to America? Did he realise that half the population over here regarded themselves as middle class? Our trouble was that prosperity had made too many workers vote Tory! I quoted the case of a Glasgow Co-operative Factory I had visited where the workers could earn, with overtime, £20 per week. The foreman got £12 a week and even the Works Manager only £14 a week. It was probable that in another twenty years most families would have cars of their own. There were still social evils and inequalities and we in the Labour Party were trying to put them right but the situation could no longer be described in terms of a simple class struggle.

To all this there was no reaction from the three Russians. Malenkov did not in any way dispute what I said. I think he must almost certainly have been impressed with the high standard of living and good factory conditions he found here – though the only remark he made to me with any bearing on this was that he had found England much more beautiful than he had expected. He had thought it was all smoke and dirt – which suggests that he was still under the influence of Dickens before he came here!

(6) *Internal Changes in Russia.*

I spent some time questioning him in a very direct manner about these but got little out of him. I told him that George Kennan[8] had said to me last summer that he was convinced that the Soviet Government today was in a state of revulsion against the Stalin Terror and was determined not to go back to it and asked if he agreed. In reply, he spent much time elaborating the familiar theme of collective leadership compared with the cult of the individual. Important changes had taken place in both home and foreign policy. The latter were not, he emphasised, just changes in tactics, as some had suggested, but real changes.

On home policy he said little, though I pressed him. He first spoke of the collective leadership being 'unanimous' about everything. But later he withdrew this and said that the members of the Government did not change their views but just accepted those of the majority. I gave a brief description of Cabinet Government here including the relationship of the Government to the House of Commons. He said that except for the latter their system worked in the same way. He tried to make out that the Government was controlled by the 'Central Committee'. When I asked how often it met, he said at first every three months but then added that it

8 George F. Kennan, a member or chief of the State Department's Policy Planning Staff 1947–50, was the main architect of America's 'containment' policy towards the U.S.S.R. He was Ambassador in Moscow 1952–3 and in Belgrade 1961–3, and in retirement at Princeton became a prominent author.

was now meeting more frequently. When I implied it was just a rubber stamp he said, on the contrary, there were fierce arguments there (or it may have been in the Plenum).[9] To my question whether it met in public, there was no clear answer. When I asked whether further political changes might be expected in the direction of our democracy, he gave a pretty plain negative.

But my impression throughout the whole of this part of the conversation was that he was being more than usually guarded. Even on Stalin he was much less downright than Khrushchev – 'There were positives and negatives'.[10] (I think he means pro's and con's).

On Beria I put it to him that he had been got rid of because the others feared he was trying to seize power again for himself.[11] Even on this Malenkov was cautious. 'He was doing wrong: he was breaking laws'. 'What laws?' To this there was no clear reply. At only one point was he a little more relaxed. In a last desperate effort to get him to talk about himself, I said, 'Mr. Malenkov, you know why people are so interested in you over here? Many of us feel the really striking thing about the last two years in Russia is your survival! You had to give up being Prime Minister, but they didn't kill you'. At that he smiled and said, 'Yes, at the National Executive Dinner I gave myself as an illustration of the change in Russia!' At the end of all this, I said, 'I hope that collective leadership has come to stay in Russia'. 'There is no doubt about that', was his reply.

There is little that can be deduced from these talks on their own. The most that can be said is that together with other evidence, they may help a little to indicate what Malenkov's outlook really is. As I have said, this may all be just good public relations – but allowing for that I would say that they rather fit in with the view commonly held that Malenkov was for a milder foreign and home policy. His complete acceptance that no one would gain from an H. Bomb war fits in with what he said once before but later had to retract.[12] His attitude on Middle East may be evidence that he did *not* favour the supply of arms to Egypt – the tougher, more aggressive policy. Whether his apparent recognition that better relations with us could not be via the Communist Party – and that was really an obstacle to this end – whether his apparent anxiety to understand my point of view and his freedom from the usual Communist dogmas on policy mean anything, I do not know.

 9 It was to keep Khrushchev in power a year later, when the majority of the Praesidium (including Malenkov) opposed him.
10 Khrushchev had given his 'secret' speech attacking Stalin only a month earlier.
11 Lavrenti P. Beria, the former Minister of the Interior and head of the secret police, had been arrested and executed in 1953, three months after Stalin's death.
12 On 12 March 1954 he had said that *civilisation* would not survive a nuclear war; six weeks later, that *capitalism* would not survive.

I may add that in the exchange of presents we included, together with some Dior earrings, a silk scarf and some decent scent for Mrs. Malenkov; for Mr. Malenkov nothing less than Evan Durbin's book, *The Politics of Democratic Socialism* suitably inscribed! I warned him of its contents – and especially its bitter attack on the 'Stalin Regime'. He did not seem disturbed and said he would get his son who understood English to read it to him. I also said I would send him some other literature which had a bearing on the things we had discussed – including something for which he had particularly asked at the time – any available published statement of our attitude on the major issues of foreign policy.

Finally, one slightly queer incident took place on both occasions. Malik at once switched on the T.V. as soon as we entered the room. This seemed odd when we were there either to talk to each other or, on the second occasion, to eat and then talk. No one made any attempt to look at it. My wife and I could not decide whether this was to switch on some tape recording machine or to allow the noise of the T.V. to drown any recording of the conversations, or was just a bad habit he had picked up in America![13]

H.G.

Diary [Dictated Friday 20 April 1956]

First of all, a few postscripts to the Malenkov visit. The Yugoslav Ambassador, Mr Velebit, came to see me shortly after my talks with Malenkov. The occasion for his coming was to ask whether there was any possibility of our coming to Yugoslavia during the summer. They had asked us last year when, unfortunately, the General Election intervened and we could not go. I said I thought there was a possibility of our coming in the second half of August or early September, since we might be going to Italy for a holiday in any case. We then went on to discuss the Malenkov visit. I asked Velebit whether the Yugoslavs themselves thought that Malenkov was still important. He said that they did regard him as very important. He had, it appeared, a considerable following in the Communist Party and, although he was merely Minister for Power Stations, this, thought Velebit, included the whole of the nuclear energy programme. I subsequently discovered from Khrushchev that this was the case so far as the practical side was concerned. In other words, Malenkov does appear to be responsible for producing the bombs and

13 He had served there in New York, at the U.N., from 1948–52.

everything else. Velebit was quite interesting about the situation in Russia, and particularly the attacks on Stalin. He thought that there was still a kind of pro-Stalin Party and it was partly for that reason that they, the Yugoslavs, had been particularly friendly to Khrushchev and Bulganin when they had visited Yugoslavia. I told him about my talks with Malenkov and also that to me he seemed to have been greatly impressed by what he saw here. I said that he was like a man who had been abroad for the first time and really had his eyes opened. Velebit agreed enthusiastically with this and said that he was perfectly sure that it had been a great surprise to him. Of course, the Yugoslavs naturally wish to take an optimistic view of everything that is happening in Russia because it suits their policy to do so. All the same, this was quite interesting.

Two other Ambassadors also called on me not long afterwards – the Italian (this was really a courtesy visit) and the French – but I suspect that they were both interested, having heard that I had talked with Malenkov, to find out what I thought. The French Ambassador incidentally was most anxious that I should make some contact with Guy Mollet*, the French Prime Minister and leader of the Socialist Party. Indeed he came to call on me to seek my views on the foreign situation before going on to Paris for a day or two. Finally, Elath, the Israeli Ambassador, who is a close friend of ours, came in, and to him I actually gave the record of my conversation with Malenkov. By the time he came to see me, Soviet policy had already appeared to shift in respect of the Middle East. For instance, their statement, which was comparatively mild in tone, that they were interested in preserving peace in that area, their reference to the independence of Israel, the appearance of Molotov and Mikoyan* at the Israeli Embassy in Moscow.[14] All these things suggest that there had been some change of front. Elath had heard from Dick Crossman something of my conversation with Malenkov about the Middle East and he thought that this had really been important. In his opinion, the Russians were anxious to obtain the goodwill of the Labour Party and what I had said to them about Israel had contributed to the decision to make some more friendly gesture to Israel. They must know, said Elath, that there was very strong backing for Israel among the Socialist Parties in Europe. Anyway, it certainly is quite interesting that, after Malenkov's remarkable statement to me that he was in favour of guaranteeing the frontiers of Israel and after we had said that this was enormously important, Soviet policy did appear to have changed.

Another foreign visitor with whom I have recently talked is Skaug, who is now the Norwegian Minister of Commerce, and whom I used to know

14 Mikoyan had lost the Ministry of Trade a year earlier, and Molotov lost the Foreign Ministry a year later. Both were members of the Praesidium.

when I was Chancellor as the chief official in the Ministry of Commerce. He came to dinner [on 17 April] with Eric Roll. Dora and I were there and he told us about his visit to Moscow with the Norwegian Prime Minister. [15] On the following day he came to see me in the House and repeated very much what he had said. He was convinced that Khrushchev was undoubtedly the boss at present in Russia. They had had five days talk in the Kremlin with Khrushchev, Bulganin and Mikoyan and, whereas the others were reasonably deferential to Khrushchev, he had not hesitated to interrupt them whenever he thought they were saying something that was wrong. Skaug also said that they were under very great pressure from the Russians; they were being flooded out with very favourable offers of trade, they were invited to have lots of return visits, and altogether the pressure was being put on pretty firmly. He said that Mikoyan had told him that they, the Russians, intended to go out and collar some of these export markets. As far as the Norwegian Labour Party are concerned, they have firmly turned down all the overtures from the Communists. But the invitations from the Russian Government were more difficult to deal with.

I shall return a little later on to the question of the Russians. Meanwhile here are a few other matters which have cropped up during the last fortnight. I had a private talk with [the Foreign Secretary] Selwyn Lloyd not long ago about the Middle East position. He certainly wished to give me the impression that they had changed their minds a good deal about arms for Israel. Indeed, he said, he recognized that it was essential that she should now have the arms. There were difficulties about our supplying them, partly because we did not seem to have any very good fighters, partly because, if we gave them Centurion tanks, he was very much afraid that this would affect the situation in Jordan which was rather critical. But it was quite clear that they [the Government] have got so fed up with Nasser and Egypt generally, that they are now being driven into accepting our position on arms for Israel. [16] It seems likely that the Israelis will get some from Canada, and I am still hoping that they will get the Centurion tanks before very long. We talked about Malenkov and Selwyn Lloyd agreed with me that he was a very likeable man.

Here is a note on something quite different. We had a rather angry meeting of the Parliamentary Committee; the first difficult one we have had for a long time. It was before the Budget and there was a preliminary discussion about the line to be adopted. It is funny that whenever

15 Arne Skaug held the office 1955–62 and was Ambassador in London 1962–8. Einar Gerhardsen had been secretary of the Labour Party 1935–45 and then its leader for 20 years, and Prime Minister 1945–51 and 1955–65. On Roll see above, p. 276 and n.
16 Said three months before Nasser seized the Suez Canal.

economic matters are raised in the Parliamentary Committee, those who know nothing about it always start talking and always talk nonsense. This happened again. Harold Wilson began with quite a sensible statement of what he thought the Budget was likely to be, which was, in fact, based on discussions that those who were reasonably expert in this field had had over some time. He then went on to suggest speakers, but the way that he put his position, and the reference to the need to have some criticism regarding 'Commonwealth and Sterling Area Policy' obviously nettled Nye Bevan, who proceeded to make the usual kind of rather silly speech, saying that we mustn't have a technical attack, that it must be a very broad one in which we should bring in an attack on the defence policy and goodness knows what else. I, for my part, could not wear this one, and replied rather angrily that we couldn't convert this into a disarmament debate. There was further irritable backchat, both about who should speak and about the line we should take. It was all rather foolish, because obviously we could not decide until we had heard the Budget statement itself. Afterwards, George Brown, who had behaved quite sensibly in all this, but not spoken up as vigorously as I had hoped, pulled my leg about it, and said they were all terrified because for the first time I had appeared really angry. I must say I was annoyed . . . However the whole thing, in a way, is simply a reflection of hostility towards experts, which is always rather marked in the economic field. [17] Shinwell always used to lead the attack in the old Parliamentary Committee and I always took this to mean that he really wanted to speak himself. Yet whenever he did speak in Economic Debates, he always made a complete mess of it, and the plain truth of it is that only those who really do know something about the subject have ever been able to pull off a speech in this field.

There was another incident with Bevan at the Parliamentary Party meeting this week. We were discussing the Budget – I may say in passing that the Budget discussion, after the Budget, in the Parliamentary Committee, was perfectly satisfactory and friendly and gave rise to no difficulties whatever – well, as I was saying, at the Party meeting [on 19 April], when we were discussing the Budget, the main point at issue was the attitude that we should adopt to the premium bond proposals, and, of course, on this there are different opinions. The Committee had, however, after a lot of argument, finally agreed the line proposed by Harold Wilson, namely that we should ask for a free vote on this, but not commit ourselves at this stage to a vote against it, if the free vote were refused. I may say I had some difficulty in getting the Committee to take this line, there being a clear majority for opposing the whole thing, but one or two

17 A view showing how he felt about his experiences as Chancellor and Shadow Chancellor.

of us saw clearly the political dangers of that, and managed to steer the Committee away from it. [18] At the Party meeting, Bevan came in late and was sitting in the body of the hall instead of on the platform where he should have been as a member of the Committee. To my surprise, about half way through the Debate, I saw him signalling to me as though he wanted to speak. I shook my head at him and pointed to the platform, implying that this was where he should be. I took no more notice of him and called a number of other speakers. After a bit, he came up to the platform and, realizing that he might get up and try and speak from there, which would be highly embarrassing, I beckoned him over and asked him what he wanted to do. He said, 'I want to speak'. I said, 'You can't do that; you're a member of the Committee'. He said, 'Why not?' I said, 'Because other members of the Committee will want to speak as well, and we can't have everybody getting up and speaking'. He was most indignant and protested in a suppressed kind of way, but I pointed to Edith Summerskill and Jim Callaghan and I said, 'There you are; they'll want to speak', and he turned to them, but, of course, they said the right thing, i.e., that certainly if they had the opportunity, they would like to speak. He really is pretty impossible. However, he simmered down after a bit and the incident passed over. The truth, of course, is that members of the Committee do not normally speak, though there are exceptions to this. Sometimes there are minor occasions when a member of the Committee can get up and explain a particular point and nobody expects him to ask permission to do that. But this was a major debate, on which the Committee held different views, as I knew, and it would have been quite inappropriate for one member to get up and speak without seeking the Chairman's permission, and it would have been wrong for the Chairman to have granted it. It is only fair on these occasions to allow the member of the Committee in charge, Harold Wilson in this case, to deal with the debate, but it is typical of Bevan that he cannot bear to sit still and not chip in when he wants to speak.

We had a dinner party recently, which was quite interesting. The Tyermans – he is the editor of *The Economist* – and the Chancellors – he is the head of Reuters – came to dinner, and Arthur, my brother, was there as well. Most of the talk was about Africa, from which the Chancellors had just returned. He is an attractive man and surprisedly Left-wing in his

18 HG's attitude shows his populist instincts (see *HG*, pp. 390–2) opposing the puritanical strain so influential in the Labour Party at the time. Premium bonds were the most striking feature of the 1956 Budget, and proved highly popular; so that though Labour did vote against the clause in the end, when Harold Wilson (who had led the attack) became Prime Minister, he increased the maximum prize from £5,000 to £25,000.

views.[19] Indeed he was most vehement against South Africa. He said he thought we ought to withdraw support for them at the United Nations and indeed come out quite openly against them, instead of abstaining as we had done up to now. He was convinced from talking with the South African Government leaders that they were terrified of leaving the Commonwealth. It was the only club to which they could belong. He had pointed out to them that, of course, the Gold Coast [Ghana] and Nigeria were likely to become independent members of the Commonwealth in the near future, and that they would have to make up their minds. He was quite convinced that they would certainly not leave the Commonwealth on that account. He even pictured a more serious development, namely the coloured nations of the Commonwealth ganging up together and saying they would leave it unless South Africa reformed and behaved decently towards the native Bantu population.[20] He was rather horrifying in his account of the South African Ministers. Strydom, the Prime Minister, was fundamentally quite a decent chap, but he was surrounded by an appalling gang of thugs, of whom the worst was Louw. I was able to confirm this, because I remembered negotiating with Louw a few years ago. He compared them to the Nazis, whom he thought they resembled in various ways.[21] I gathered that both he and his wife were very sympathetic to Labour, as, indeed, all his remarks on these colour questions seemed to imply. Arthur, naturally, was in his element and there was a good deal of talk about the problems of partnership with the Africans. Arthur has always taken, I think quite rightly, the extreme view here that you cannot really go on the basis of one representative for a hundred thousand natives and one for each hundred white population. The Tyermans, on the other hand, we are beginning to find rather boring . . . However, he is fundamentally a very nice chap and it's as well to try and keep *The Economist* on the right lines.

Now we come to the beginning of the Bulganin-Khrushchev visit. There was a lunch yesterday at the Soviet Embassy, the first one given since their arrival to which I went. There was a great crowd outside, but they turned out to be a crowd of Russians. Evidently the Embassy had invited the women and children, so to speak, of the Soviet citizens here to come along and give a bit of a demonstration. Anyway, they were all speaking Russian and they seemed to be quite enthusiastic. I had quite

19 Sir Christopher Chancellor was Far Eastern manager of Reuters 1931–9, general manager 1944–59, Chairman of Odhams Press 1960–1 and of the Bowater Paper Corporation, etc., 1962–9.
20 This is roughly what happened five years later.
21 Johannes Strydom (1893–1958), a farmer and lawyer, led the National Party in the Transvaal from 1934 and in the country, as Prime Minister, from 1954. Eric Louw (1890–1968) had been a Nazi sympathiser in the war; he was Minister of Economic Affairs 1948–54, of Finance 1955–6, of Foreign Affairs 1956–63.

a time forcing my way through the crowd in order to get into the Embassy. Malik [the Soviet Ambassador] then took me across and introduced me to B. and K. I said that I had had some interesting conversations with Malenkov, and Khrushchev said, 'Yes. You seem to have made a great impression upon him'. I said, 'Well, he made a great impression on us too'. Whether this was particularly welcome to B. and K. one cannot, of course, say. Later on the rest of the guests arrived; most of the Cabinet were there; I was the only Opposition representative, and we went into lunch, which was done on quite a grand style – caviare, pink champagne, and the rest of it. I sat between Khrushchev's interpreter, Khrushchev being the other side of him, and a man called Kumykin, Deputy Minister of Trade. He looked like an American college professor, with a rather pale face and glasses, and serious-minded. He said he had been in the Ministry for 32 years, and I gather that he is really more of an official than anything else.[22] He spoke French about as badly as I do, so we got on quite nicely! I talked a little to Khrushchev, but it was mostly unimportant stuff during lunch. I formed the impression, however, that he was very much less easy to talk to than Malenkov. He looks like a rather agreeable pig, and, when I mentioned this to Jim Griffiths after the lunch, he made the quick retort 'Yes, Animal Farm again', which I thought was very appropriate. At the end of lunch Bulganin got up and made a few short remarks of welcome, and so on, and Eden replied in the same way, very shortly. Then Khrushchev burst up and made a long speech which, I noticed, was fully reported in the Press today. The interesting thing about it was that he specifically referred to the fact that a number of people here did not want this visit. Whether he had noticed the coolness of the reception or whether he had intended to say this, one doesn't know. He also seemed to take a rather more uncompromising line on politics. We were Capitalists, they were Communists, and one must just accept that. He referred to us as being a bourgeois democracy. After we had listened to all this, I could not resist getting up and saying a few words myself. I said that I wished to make it plain that although Khrushchev had said that the Opposition were also divided about this visit, officially we warmly welcomed it. I also said I thought his frankness was excellent, and that I hoped the –– phone –– [sic in original MS]. I then went on to make a few jokes; in particular I said that while there was this division between Communism on the one side and Capitalism on the other, perhaps they might like to try a compromise – namely, democratic Socialism. This was not very warmly received! However, I said that as I was in a minority of one in this assembly, I would not press the matter. We were, however, the Opposition here, and we should certainly criticise both the British and the Soviet Governments if the talks were not successful.

22 He held the office from 1948 to 1969, after serving in the Ministry since 1924.

Later that day there was a dinner party at No. 10 Downing Street. It was, in a sense, an historic occasion because it was the first time that the Russian leaders, since the Revolution, had appeared at No. 10. Indeed I don't know whether any Russian Prime Minister has ever been there before, and since both Churchill and Attlee, as well as Eden, were present, it was quite an assembly. I found myself sitting between Malik, the Russian Ambassador and one of their academicians, a man with a beard, the atomic physicist, Kurchatov. He was quite agreeable, but conversation was difficult, although we did have an interpreter behind us. But nothing of interest emerged from my talk with him.

On the other hand, I did have quite an interesting conversation with Malik. I asked how the talks were going, and he implied that they were not going very well. It was not clear why, but obviously the atmosphere had not been too good. He then said to me 'I heard you say to Khrushchev this afternoon, when you said "goodbye", that you hoped you would have the opportunity for a more intimate conversation with him. What had you got in mind?' I replied that we were going to lunch at Chequers on Sunday, and then there was the Labour Party dinner on Monday evening and that no doubt this would provide some opportunity. But, I said that if Malik thought it would be a good thing for me to see them alone on another occasion, I would be glad to do so. He then mentioned the reception at Claridges on Tuesday, and wondered whether, perhaps, we could slip away after that, in the same way as we had done after the Malenkov reception. I said that I thought that would be all right (in fact, I happened to have a dinner engagement that night, but that I could get out of it). Then, however, he added, 'I wasn't quite sure whether it would be appropriate, since B. and K. are the guests of the Government, for them to meet the Leader of the Opposition'. I took this hint, and said No, I quite appreciated that and, indeed, as he knew, I had given some warning about it. I said that, in the circumstances, perhaps we had better drop the idea. Now the interesting thing about this is, I think, that the Soviet Ministers have, I think, decided that they are not going to be able to get anywhere, on their own, with the Labour Party. I am delighted that they should feel this way because I have always been a little worried that they would try and burrow in, as it were, and use the Opposition here for their own purposes. It is just as well that they should know exactly where they stand on this.

Later there were the usual formal speeches, but on this occasion Khrushchev did not speak; indeed Bulganin, when he got up, said firmly that he was speaking on behalf of his friend, Khrushchev, as well. After dinner, we went into the Reception Room and people sat round little tables or talked in groups. I had some conversation during the next hour or so about the progress of the talks, which rather confirmed what Malik had said. Selwyn Lloyd told me that he had rather upset them by asking them point blank, 'Was this all a change of tactics or was it a change of aims?' Apparently Khrushchev had seemed very offended by this, and Kirkpatrick, the head of the Foreign Office, took the view that K. was a much more difficult person to deal with than Malenkov. [23] He thought that K. was very definitely anti-British and very strongly pro-Communist. He apparently had said during the course of the discussion to Eden, that, of course, no doubt if we had our way, and could do it, we would liquidate all the Russians just as, if they could do it, they would liquidate all of us. Only, unfortunately, they couldn't do it. If he really said this, it certainly is a bit grim, even in joking. Kirkpatrick said that he thought Khrushchev had accepted co-existence, but only reluctantly because he was forced to. Altogether the prospects for the talks didn't seem to be too good. Winston [Churchill] was standing around and I said that I thought the thing was to have the co-existence but not the competition and Winston quite agreed, and said, 'Of course, if you have the competition it leads ultimately to war'. I thought Winston, incidentally, pretty old, very deaf, he found difficulty in getting up to drink the Royal toasts, and I am not sure that he followed everything that was being said.

I had some further talk myself with Khrushchev, but it wasn't very interesting. I found myself sitting at the same table as him and one had the feeling that it was impossible to raise really fundamental issues. It would have been difficult in any case at a dinner party of this kind. So I asked him questions about their economic progress. He said that they did not intend to export a lot of engineering products, that they were only importing wheat from Canada for their Far East. It was convenient to do that and, at the same time, to export to Norway in the West. I asked him what were the most difficult sectors of the economy and whether agriculture was the worst. He said he thought there were so many economic difficulties. We talked a little about the progress of technical education and, again, he was rather on the modest side. I asked him how long it had taken them to prepare the present technical education programme. He said that they had begun directly after the Revolution.

The only other amusing episode, or interesting episode was one in which Lennox-Boyd took part. After dinner, as we were talking away, he came up and started talking through the interpreter to the atomic scientist . . . He asked why he was wearing a medal and then whether there were different degrees of medals under Communism in a rather abusive and aggressive way and, eventually, I managed to steer him out of the Dining Room and into the Reception Room. Later I was taken by one of the Private Secretaries to the little table he was sitting at, where he was

23 Sir Ivone Kirkpatrick was Permanent Under-Secretary 1953–7, and chairman of the I.T.A. 1957–62. He died in 1964.

talking to the Minister of Culture, a young man called Mikhailov.[24] I soon realised that a very aggressive line was again being taken . . . So I stepped in and more or less took over the conversation. I liked Mikhailov. We had a very frank talk. We were trying to explain to him how their continual intervention in different parts of the world upset any good relations with them. I also made it plain that the exchanges of culture in which he was so interested would only be of value if they were completely outside the propaganda sphere. This Mikhailov seemed to accept quite fully. He had probably realised this by now. He struck me as a young man who was desperately anxious to bring off more cultural interchanges because his job depended upon it. But as soon as we got on to more serious subjects, he really tried to steer the conversation away. However, I said that I would try and see him again because I felt that, at least in his case, even if he had not much power, he had a good deal more understanding. The general view seems to be that Bulganin is very much more amenable, and certainly more polite, than Khrushchev. Whether he counts or not is hard to say. The first impression one has is that he is largely a figure-head, but this may be wrong. One of the Foreign Office people said that during the talks he had tried to stop Khrushchev more than once and, so to speak, pull him down. Anyway one never can be quite sure. They are both of them, of course, quite old. Bulganin, in particular, does not look very strong, and seems to be a definitely elderly man.

Diary for 22 April 1956

We took the Velebits to the theatre last night as a kind of farewell occasion – they are going back to Yugoslavia for good in a few months' time – and after the theatre we went home and had a meal with them. We had some quite interesting further discussion about the Russian position. Velebit, being, of course, a Communist, although a Yugoslav Communist, defended the dictatorship in Russia because, he said, they could never have carried through the industrialisation of the country at such a pace under democratic conditions. He argued that we had achieved the same thing in the 19th century more slowly and with considerable suffering to the working classes. In Russia the suffering had been aggravated by Stalin's sadism. But now, he said, that the standard of living was beginning to rise and that they were getting along so well in the economic field, there

24 Nikolai A. Mikhailov, who was 50, often accompanied Khrushchev on visits abroad. A journalist, he was Minister of Culture 1955–60; previously Ambassador to Poland, and subsequently to Indonesia.

was developing a strong demand for more freedom and easier conditions. I asked him if he had definite concrete evidence of this, and he said yes, that he had. He said the sort of people who were affected were the factory managers. They were tired of being messed around all the time, and suddenly being told that they must leave their work in the Ukraine and go off to the Urals and open a new factory there. They wanted, as I say, more freedom and more opportunity to control their own lives. He thought that all this would develop in the course of the next few years. Apart from that, we also discussed further the possibility of our going to Yugoslavia this summer. He told me that the government there were very enthusiastic about the idea and that they would be very glad to put a villa at our disposal if we went there, or to arrange for our hotel accommodation as their guests. We later on discussed where we might go and they showed us some slides of their own little cottage by the Adriatic. One of the nice things about the Velebits is their complete simplicity. When we were talking about their cottage, he said, rather deprecatingly, that they were very poor. And I said 'Well, so are we'. And I then explained to him about the salary of the Leader of the Opposition! He then told me that all that he would get on his return to Yugoslavia where he was to be, probably, permanent head of the Foreign Office, was £40 a month.[25] For that reason, his wife would have to go out and get a job. In fact she was learning colour printing at the moment. Even here in London he thought he was the worst-paid Ambassador of all. He did not, however, complain at all about this. The country was poor and, well, they believed, as a Socialist country, in not having too great differences.

Today we went to lunch at Chequers to meet B. and K. Jim Griffiths and Alfred Robens came with me. They came up in Alf's car to Hampstead, and I then drove them both down to Chequers. It was a lovely day and we had plenty of time and got there rather early. There was not any great sign of police as we arrived, until right up close to the house, where a Police Inspector, in a car, blocked our way with his car until we explained who we were. Even so, the man in the car, who looked very aggressive, seemed reluctant to move. I fancy that he probably thought that we were the Press trying to get in. I gather that they had a certain amount of trouble with them yesterday. We were received by the Private Secretaries and taken into the large Hall. The talks were still going on, but Eden's son came down with Khrushchev's son immediately behind us. After a bit William Hayter, the Ambassador, came out and we had

25 Dr Vladimir Velebit, a Partisan leader with Marshal Tito, had been Ambassador to Italy and then to Britain. He returned as permanent secretary of the Foreign Office 1956–8, and then became Executive Secretary of E.C.E. (the U.N.'s Economic Commission for Europe) 1960–7.

some drinks. [26] Clarissa Eden then came in, looking very cool and clean, and apologised to me because she had not been able to ask Dora. She said that she was going to be at the lunch because she really refused to be turned out of her own dining-room, but that no other wives could have been accommodated. At lunch I sat between the interpreter, the star interpreter, with Bulganin on his left, and on my right Kirkpatrick, the head of the Foreign Office. Nothing very much happened. I found it rather difficult to talk to Bulganin, through the interpreter, particularly as he spent most of his time talking to Clarissa. I did have some conversation with Kirkpatrick and he mentioned one rather amusing but typical episode about Clem Attlee. We were talking about Yugoslavia and I told him about my invitation to go to Brioni where Tito has a house. He said that he had been there one summer, and there had been some reception, and he had walked in and Clem Attlee had seen him there, and with great delight Clem dashed up to him and said 'Thank goodness you are here. None of these people seem to know anything about the Test Match. Can you tell me what happened?'

After lunch I had some words with the Prime Minister about the way the talks were going. He said there was a slight movement, the ice was cracking a bit, but he did not think they would really get anywhere until the last day of all. That, he said, is what always happens with the Russians. I said that I thought, if possible, we ought to arrange for B. and K. to see something more of how people lived here, because they were obviously quite cut off from the outside world, and had no idea about the standard of living. I felt, and I said the same thing to Kirkpatrick and one or two other people, that the only hope really was that the Russians would settle down eventually and give up their idea of dominating the rest of the world. But they would only do this if they gave up believing seriously in the Marxism-Leninism doctrine. Again, they would only give up these beliefs if they saw clearly that those doctrines were simply nonsense. He said he would bear it in mind. I particularly [stressed] the importance of their going to a new town, where they would see the way people lived, their houses, etc. as compared with the factories, which were really much less important. After lunch we all went out on the terrace and Clarissa took some photographs and there was a certain amount of back-chat, and then the Prime Minister came over and suggested that we should take B. and K. indoors and have a talk with them. So we three all went in to a little room, called the White Parlour, and sat down and began talking to them. We were with them for about 40 minutes or so. It was quite an interesting, though perhaps not very profitable, experience. One really did see the

26 Sir William Hayter, Ambassador to Moscow 1953–7, had been HG's contemporary at school and New College. He was to become its Warden 1958–76 (after being Deputy Under-Secretary at the Foreign Office 1957–8).

kind of man Khrushchev was, but everything that happened confirmed my original view after meeting him the first time that he was going to be much harder to talk to seriously than Malenkov. Indeed, it really confirmed what Kirkpatrick had said to me on the Thursday evening. We had decided, coming down in the car, that, if we had the opportunity of talking to them alone, we would raise two issues. It was obviously impossible for us to talk about the major subjects which they were discussing with the Government, such as the Middle East, disarmament, etc. But we felt that there were two things which we ought to raise with them; one was the position of the Social Democrats in the satellite countries, many of whom were imprisoned, scores of whom, of course, had been executed; the other was the way in which they conducted their relations with us, the same subject which I had touched on during the talks with Malenkov.

I thought it better to begin with the latter, as being the easier of the two subjects. So I explained that we were anxious for good relations with them, but that we felt it was important through what channel these relations were conducted. If exchange visits, [cultural] arrangements, and so on were managed through the Communist organisations here, the Anglo-Soviet Friendship Society or the Society for Cultural Relations with the U.S.S.R., then, in fact, they would get nowhere. Everybody knew they were Communist organisations, they were regarded as suspect, as a method of putting across Soviet propaganda and of building up the Communist Party here. The right way to do it was to work through organisations which were completely free of this taint, and which, in fact, were simply designed for their purpose, namely to make the peoples of the two countries understand each other better. I mentioned, in particular, Chris Mayhew's organisation, or rather, it isn't really his organisation, the Anglo-Soviet Committee of the British Council, of which he is Chairman. I also suggested in the course of my remarks that it might be worth considering forming a new Anglo-Russian Parliamentary Group on the lines that we already had with other countries. There would be representatives from all Parties on such a Group and, of course, it would be quite a different thing from the existing Anglo-Soviet Parliamentary Committee, which again was a tainted affair. This was received, for the most part, in silence by Bulganin and Khrushchev and not with any enthusiasm whatever. They did, it's true, ask a little about Chris Mayhew's organisation and they also showed some guarded approval of the idea of an Anglo-Soviet Parliamentary Committee. However, their reply, first of all, was that they thought they should work through several organisations and they didn't see why an organisation, which had the Dean of Canterbury at the head of it, should be regarded as such a bad affair. Did we really say that people disapproved so much of Dr Hewlett Johnson? I said, 'Yes, indeed we did and, not only that, most people regarded him as a lunatic as well'.[27] This, also, was not terribly well received.

After a bit (it all took rather a long time because of the translation and both Jim and Alf joined in occasionally) Khrushchev then said that he wished to say something to us as well. He then launched into, not exactly a tirade, but a fairly strong attack on the Labour Party. We, he said, were also responsible for the bad relations which existed between the two countries. He made three points in particular. First, that a lot of Labour and Trade Union people had been to Russia and then, when they had returned from Russia, had complained about silly things which were of no importance. They had failed to give a really objective account of what they found. Such things, for instance, as the shortage of toilet paper, as if that really mattered. Then he went on to complain about our foreign policy when we were in power. Had not Churchill said that they, the Tories, were only taking over what the Labour Party had really initiated so far as foreign policy was concerned. And indeed, finally, and thirdly, they really had more polemics with us than they did with the Conservatives. They couldn't understand why this should be so. It was an extremely uncompromising statement and I was getting all prepared to make an equally uncompromising reply when the Private Secretary came in and said that the Prime Minister wanted to see B. and K. before he left for Windsor. I asked for five minutes more, but after a bit Hayter came in and it was evident that we could not go on. We were, therefore, unable to say anything about the plight of the Social Democrats, which would no doubt have been an even stormier subject. I said at the end that I appreciated Khrushchev's frankness; I thought it better that we should understand clearly where we were and that we would have to pursue the subject further on some other occasion. Throughout the whole of this, Bulganin took very little part except, as far as he could, he was trying to keep down the temperature, trying, so to speak, to take a good view from their angle of anything that I said. But everything really confirmed that Khrushchev really seems to be the person that counts.

Going back in the car we discussed it, and all agreed that, undoubtedly, B. and K. have given up any hope at all of making use of the Labour Party, which we all agreed was a good thing and, indeed, they were quite open about regarding us as greater enemies than the Conservatives. And this also we thought was not a bad thing. I asked them if they thought I had gone too far in what I had said about the Dean of Canterbury, but they both agreed that it was right to say what in fact was perfectly true. I think the explanation of the difference between Malenkov and Khrushchev

27 Dr Hewlett Johnson (1874–1966), Dean of Canterbury 1931–63, was a former engineer and a remarkably credulous fellow-traveller of the Communists.

is principally that the latter is the Secretary of the Party, and essentially a Party man, and obviously feel[s] a strong loyalty to the Communist Party, wherever it is. One can understand his point of view; we were asking him to give up associating with the people whom he had been told were his friends. Equally he no doubt had been brought up on the official line which is generally obtained [maintained?] that the Social Democrats were just the lackeys of Capitalism. One gets the impression that he is quite clever, but very limited in his view and that he has a kind of chip on his shoulder, perhaps because he never went to a University. I must say that I would not like to be in the power of a man like this. One really felt, this afternoon, what a ghastly position it must be for those who have to live under the Soviet regime, whether in Russia or any other country.

I must, however, add one more hopeful point: I think it was the Prime Minister, or one of them anyway, who said to me that Hayter in his last dispatch had said that the ordinary people in Russia regarded the changes that had occurred already as the beginning of something and not the end. So to that extent Hayter seemed to agree with Velebit about what was happening. Hayter was very amusing about the Embassy in Moscow. He was referring to the holiday on May 1st, Labour Day, and that he was glad that he would not be back there again. It was so awkward because all the servants went out. I said then do you . . . [omission in original] give up their jobs. One soon got used to the idea that they were being spied upon, and one just took that into account. I asked if there were microphones and so on. He said he was quite certain there were. It was particularly easy to put them in the Embassy because it was hung with a kind of silk panelling all over the place. Every now and then they took down some of the silk and removed some of the microphones, but, he said, since only Russian workmen could put back the silk, of course they could put back the microphones as well. He did say that they had one room which they thought was completely safe and where, if they wanted to conduct private conversations, they went.

[Week beginning 23 April 1956; dictated Saturday 28th]

On the Sunday evening (that is last Sunday) we went to the reception for B. and K. given by the L.C.C. There is not much to record about this. Evidently they had both been told that Dora had been born in Russia, and they stopped to have a few words of conversation with her, saying she should come back and see it – it is completely changed now, said

Khrushchev. The only other conversation of any importance was a brief one I had with William Hayter about B. and K. He said something rather nice about them and compared K. to Ernie Bevin. I demurred to this, saying that that was not at all our experience in the afternoon. We had found him very difficult indeed.

This last week, beginning on Monday [23rd], has certainly been a most extraordinary affair. I had better tell the whole of the B. and K. story first and then fit in, later, any other events of importance. On the Monday evening we were to entertain the Russians to a dinner in the House of Commons. By 'we' I mean the National Executive Committee. We knew that there would be about 60 people there, including, say, 15 Russians. The Parliamentary Committee had also been invited. Before the dinner started, I spoke to Morgan Phillips and Sam Watson, who came over to my room. Morgan said that he had been informed by the Foreign Office that they would not arrive until 8.40 and would have to leave at 10.30. We had already had a discussion, a few days before, in the International [Sub-] Committee about how the dinner should be organised, and it was decided that we would try and put a few questions to them, particularly the question of the imprisoned Social Democrats. Incidentally, we had warned B. and K. at Chequers that we wanted a question [period] and they had accepted this. We had also warned Malik, both Jim Griffiths and I, that we were bound to raise the question of the Social Democrats. To Jim, Malik had said 'Oh, must you bother about a small thing like that?' To which Jim had very properly replied 'It is not a small thing to the people concerned'. Well to return to my brief meeting with Morgan Phillips and Sam Watson: we agreed that the first question might be put by Dick Crossman, and be on internal developments in Russia; the second by Alice Bacon and be about the position of the Jews in Russia, regarding which we had had a number of representations from Jewish organisations. The third, about the Social Democrats, was to be put by Sam Watson, Chairman of the International Sub-Committee. We also had some discussion about what speeches should be made and I urged that we should, if possible, confine them to one from Edwin Gooch [now Labour Party chairman] and one from Bulganin. We all realised that if Khrushchev spoke, he might speak too long and, obviously, there was not going to be very much time.

Then we went downstairs and, after a bit, the Russians arrived, and the dinner began. It seemed to me, that to start with, everything went quite swimmingly. There was a good deal of laughing and talking and joking and friendly conversation. But there is a different view. Some people hold that George Brown during this period gave offence to the Russians. He certainly was talking rather loud and cracking a number of jokes which had a bit of an edge to them. He ragged young Khrushchev a bit and put questions to him like this: 'Do you ever disagree with your father?' 'No', says young Khrushchev. 'How extraordinary', says George, 'I'm always having rows with my daughter', and then George to Khrushchev senior across the table, shouting rather, 'How do you manage that, how do you manage not to have rows with your son?' He also said to Khrushchev senior, raising his glass, 'Here's to the big boss' and Khrushchev is said to have raised his glass and said, 'You look like a little boss yourself'. George says that this was all perfectly friendly, and I must say that this was my impression too, but others take a different view. He also said that Ernie Bevin had once said that the Soviet Union was a break-away from the Transport Workers' Union. Again a joke, but one which could very easily have been misunderstood. However, as I say, I did not think myself that anything had gone badly wrong before the end of the dinner. As far as Alf Robens and myself were concerned we talked to Bulganin. There was a sort of triangle; it was quite a pleasant, interesting conversation, the most remarkable feature of [it being?] Bulganin's apparent continuing belief that there might be a revolution in this country. We tried to disabuse him of that. Then, dinner being finished, Edwin Gooch made a short, appropriate speech, a conventional kind of speech, and Bulganin replied in what was undoubtedly a witty and gracious affair. He said how pleased they were to be there, they were sorry they hadn't seen more of us, they were hemmed in by a protocol and as much exploited by the protocol as any capitalist exploited the workers. Perhaps it was because they had not got Trade Union assistance. And Khrushchev at this stage interjected with a joke. Then Bulganin sat down. Edwin Gooch should then undoubtedly have invited questions, but being a very poor Chairman and rather slow in the uptake, he did nothing for a time and allowed a cry for Khrushchev to speak to develop. This came particularly vigorously from James Callaghan. It was quite natural, but, as it turned out, rather unfortunate. Anyway, the cries went on and so, of course, the Chairman then had to ask Khrushchev to speak, which, rather reluctantly I think, he did.

He got up and began his speech by saying, 'Well, I don't know what I am going to say, but give me a little bit, and I shall get wound up', and he certainly did get wound up. He spoke, including the translation, for an hour, and it was, in places, extremely provocative. The verbatim report, which I have, shows what was said, but it does not show adequately the vehemence, almost brutality, with which it was said. And, undoubtedly, as the speech went on, the temperature dropped and people began to feel gloomier and gloomier. During the course of it he was interrupted. He was interrupted by George Brown on more than one occasion, and particularly when he began to talk about pre-war history. George first of all said, when he was talking about the pact between Hitler and Mussolini,

'What about the Stalin-Ribbentrop pact?'[28] and this certainly annoyed Khrushchev. When he came to the Stalin-Ribbentrop pact and defended it, George said, 'God forgive him'. Khrushchev said, 'What did he say?' and this was translated to him. George, I think, meant Stalin. The Press subsequently gave this out as 'God forgive *you*', but I am sure that it was Stalin and not Khrushchev that George was referring to. Nye Bevan also interrupted, but in a more moderate manner. He said, for instance, 'That was a dangerous argument' when Khrushchev was talking about their need to make a pact with Germany. Two other aspects of the speech were pretty frightening. First, he definitely pooh-poohed the idea of [disarmament] controls and spoke of them as a fantasy, though evidently he must have meant some of the controls which had been suggested, and, secondly, he gave us a very plain threat that if we did not look out they would come to terms with Germany. It wasn't only, as I say, what he said, but the way he said it that upset everybody and the great length which it took.[29] As I have already mentioned, they were supposed to go at 10.30, but Khrushchev did not sit down until 11.15.

Before he sat down, Alice Bacon had sent me a note saying 'I think you will have to reply to this at once', and Edwin Gooch also turned to me and said, 'You will have to speak at once', the idea being, of course, that I would have to make the winding-up speech. Now I was placed in a dilemma. I could of course have made a brief winding-up speech, completely colourless without saying a word about any of our questions. If I had done that, then I think the evening would have come to an end, certainly less eventfully, but also without our doing what we meant to do, namely to raise the question, in particular, of the imprisoned Social Democrats. I felt, therefore, the best thing was to bring this question in myself. But I made, as the record shows, an extremely conciliatory speech, it could hardly have been more tactful or polite and that applies also to the way in which I put the question about the Social Democrats. I particularly said I did not expect any reply tonight. However, immediately I sat down, without being called on by the Chairman, Khrushchev jumped up and made what was an extremely offensive, abrupt and uncompromising statement. Again, this is on the record and the words, this time, do speak for themselves. When he had finished, George Brown again started to say something, but I waved him aside and put the point even more gently, saying that I hoped they would use their influence in these satellite countries (I didn't use the word 'Satellite'). But, again, I

28 The non-aggression pact of 23 August 1939 which immediately preceded the fourth partition of Poland and the Second World War.
29 'I will never forget', wrote Crossman later, his 'couldn't-care-less suggestion that we should join with the Russians because, if not, they would swat us off the face of the earth like a dirty old black beetle': his diary, 6 November 1957.

got an even worse answer, including the famous words 'If you want to help the enemies of the working class, you must find another agent to do it'. Then Sam Watson got up and, following him, Nye Bevan. If I don't record this, it is only because the verbatim report explains exactly what happened.[30] There was some doubt as to whether Khrushchev said the famous thing 'Not with me' right at the end, in response to Gooch or in response to George who, at that time, raised his glass again to Khrushchev, saying 'Well, we've had a row, but I hope we can part friends' or something of that kind. Anyway, Khrushchev certainly did rush out of the room, pretty well without shaking hands with anybody, and said to the Foreign Office man outside, 'That was a complete waste of an evening' and was obviously in a furious temper. The other Russians rather sheepishly filed out, shaking hands, and the whole business came to an end.

Now we had decided beforehand that there would be [a] problem of the Press. I had been approached by the American journalists and asked if I would see them in order to give some account of what took place and prevent garbled, unofficial versions getting out. After discussion with Morgan [Phillips] and Alice Bacon, we decided the only thing to do would be to have a Lobby Conference immediately after the dinner. Of course, we hadn't expected that it would turn out like this. I warned Malik that we were going to do this, and also the Foreign Secretary and the Prime Minister and certainly the two latter quite approved. So I, with my two colleagues, went to see the Lobby and told the story in fairly moderate terms. I did not quote much of what Khrushchev had actually said, but I made it plain that he had turned down in a completely uncompromising manner the request we had made about the Social Democrats. I then saw the American correspondents and gave them a similar version. Then, of course, the next day, it was all in the papers, in the headlines. That was bound to be the case, and immediately a good deal of argument developed. Most of the Press were strongly on our side, all but the [Communist] *Daily Worker* and the *Daily Express* in fact. But there was a good deal of feeling in the Party that it was a bad thing to have done, that the Tories would be able to make a lot out of it, because it could be said that we had quarrelled with the Russians, whereas they had managed to get on with them.

On the following day [Tuesday 24 April], there was a Speaker's lunch to B. and K. I sat next-but-one to Bulganin again, but did not have much conversation with him. He did, however, say at one point, in quite a friendly way, 'Was I satisfied with what happened last night?' and I said I

---

30 It is in the Papers, file P.105a. For other accounts see *HG*, pp. 413–14 and note 47.

was not entirely satisfied and asked if he was, and he said 'No'. After lunch, George, who was there, spoke to Khrushchev and Khrushchev did refuse to shake hands with him. He also said to George, with Nye Bevan standing by, 'I haven't met people like you for 30 years'. I went up to say Goodbye to him, as I thought, saying that we would probably not see him at the reception because of the crowd. He shook hands with me. I also said that I was sorry that yesterday evening had turned out as it did, but that we would hope for a better understanding in future. As I say, he shook hands with me, but then immediately launched into another terrific statement which was to the effect that we must not interfere with each other, that they were Communists, we were Capitalists and that they must do what they liked in their own part of the world, etc., etc. Bevan, who was standing near, was getting more and more irritated with this and said, as Khrushchev was being taken away to go to the Gallery, 'He's impossible. It's time he grew up', in a loud voice, which was not, however, I think, translated to Khrushchev. They went to the Gallery and reports of what they looked like there appeared in the Press.

In the evening we went to the reception at Claridges, but it was an enormous squash and we did not see the Russians – I mean B. and K. We talked to various other people, some of the fellow-travellers came up and complained to me about the previous evening, but there wasn't really very much to say about it.

On the following morning [Wednesday 25th], we had a meeting of the National Executive Committee, and, of course, the whole question came up, and there was a long discussion. Barbara Castle made an attack on us for the Press Conference. But she had really no support on this, the overwhelming feeling, including other Bevanites or ex-Bevanites, was that we were perfectly right to do this, and that if we hadn't had the Press Conference, the thing would have been much worse. Nor was there any disposition to criticise the fact that we raised the issue of the Social Democrats. This, after all, had been brought up at the International Sub-Committee and, in any case, this was very much a matter which the Executive was bound to handle. The chief criticism was directed against George Brown and it came from all quarters. It came even from Peggy Herbison, Edith Summerskill, Jack Cooper, Harold Wilson – all said that they thought he had behaved shockingly and that even before Khrushchev's speech he had been making a lot of unfortunate remarks and they blamed a good deal of the whole thing on him. Though I think that some of them anyway, certainly Peggy Herbison, took the view that Khrushchev would have behaved just as badly.[31] All she regretted was that George had put us in a bad light. Eventually, it was decided that we

31 In this clumsy sentence the word 'anyway' should have come at the end.

should go and say 'Goodbye' to them. There was a disposition from Edith Summerskill, I don't think anybody else, to say that we ought to apologise. This was most emphatically turned down. There was also a discussion about whether we should publish the verbatim report of the proceedings. Jim Griffiths proposed that this should be done, but it was decided that this really would create too much of an international incident and instead it was settled that we would warn the Russians that we had the verbatim account and tell them that if they put out misleading reports, we should have to correct them in this way, by publishing the verbatim. Mikardo [?][32] said that he had heard that they were about to publish something, and this was later affirmed by Barbara Castle as well. Morgan Phillips was told to try and fix up then a meeting with the Russians, where we could say 'Goodbye', and it was agreed that the Chairman and Deputy Chairman, the Leader and Deputy Leader should go to do this job.

In the afternoon there was a meeting of the Parliamentary Committee, and, of course, the same subject came up. This time George Brown, of course, was there and Alf Robens made a direct and detailed criticism of his behaviour. I encouraged this, because I thought it better to have the whole thing out in the open, and I knew that Alf had been going round denouncing George. George made what was quite a reasonable and dignified reply, saying that he realised that some of the things he said had seemed rather foolish, but they had been meant as jokes, up to, at any rate, Khrushchev's speech. There was further criticism from Harold Wilson about George Brown's behaviour and from one or two other members of the Committee, including Edith. Bevan, on the other hand, took the view that this was all being tremendously exaggerated and that it had done Khrushchev far more harm that it did us and that he would probably get into trouble when he got back to Russia, and, of course, I took very much the same view. It was agreed that I should speak to the [P.L.P.] about it at tomorrow's Party meeting. I had already, I may say, got the permission of the Executive to do this, because, of course, the dinner was, strictly speaking, a National Executive affair. Later in the evening, I was told about a round-robin which was being circulated for signatures by Julius Silverman[33] and the fellow-travelling group, in effect apologising for what had taken place. It was proposed that this should be sent with the signatures to the Russians direct. Naturally, I did not like this at all, nor indeed did most of the Party. When I heard later from Morgan Phillips that we had arranged to see the Russians at 11 o'c the following morning, I thought it best to immediately inform the Lobby,

32 The MS has 'McAdden'. No N.E.C. member had a name sounding like that.
33 M.P. for Birmingham (Aston) 1955–74; (Erdington) 1945–55 and since 1974. A housing specialist and extreme left-winger.

and make it plain that this had been decided at the Executive and without any pressure being put upon us. I also made it plain that we were not going to apologise, but only to say 'Goodbye'. Though, I admitted that, of course, there might be some further talk developing from it. This was extremely helpful as it turned out because the Press had exactly the right account of the thing the following morning. The Lobby were obviously grateful to me for keeping them so well informed, and repaid this by reporting pretty well what I wanted reported.

Well, then, the next morning [Thursday 26th] we went off to Claridges. Of course, there was a crowd of photographers and pressmen there, and photographs were taken, and then we went upstairs. We were shown into the Sitting Room, and there were B. and K. We shook hands with them rather frigidly, no smiles, and they motioned to us to sit down on sofas, armchairs, and so on. And it was clear that they wanted to talk, and talk they did. I began with a short statement, saying that we had come to wish them 'goodbye', that we hoped the talks had been a success, that we also hoped they had had some pleasure from the visit, I referred to the Covent Garden opera the previous night, that as far as their dinner with us was concerned, we regretted the way it had turned out, which was contrary to our hopes and intentions. We hoped, nevertheless, that there would be better relations in the future. Khrushchev then said what did I mean by 'better relations', between whom? I said 'between the Soviet Government and the Labour Party'. I was very careful, of course, not to mention the Communist Party. He then made a long speech, not as violent as he had made on Monday, but pretty grumbly. He attacked us for the way George, in particular, had behaved the previous night and implied that this was not what he had expected from us, and things of that kind. He didn't really say anything new, but he implied that we had sabotaged the whole thing, and, indeed, seemed to think that we had organised it all quite deliberately. Bulganin then was very careful to come in at once and said that he agreed entirely with everything that K. had said, and that the Press reports of him not agreeing with K. the other night were quite without foundation. I judged that there had been some kind of a row about this and B. was jolly careful to line himself up with K. He was less friendly, accordingly, than he had been on previous occasions. Jim Griffiths then came in and proceeded to explain, very well, why we had to raise the Social Democrat issue and what we felt about these people, and I then followed it up still further.

During the course of his remarks, Khrushchev said that they would, of course, have to publish something on the whole matter when they got back to Russia. So I took the opportunity of saying what, indeed, we had agreed should be said, namely that we had not put out anything ourselves, that I had warned Malik that there would, of course, be reports in the

Press, but we had a verbatim report, and that if they put out in Russia, and it was re-published here, things that we thought were untrue, we should have to correct them and publish the verbatim. I think, looking back on it, that this did have an effect on the Russians. Later, Khrushchev said, about his own speech, that he had said nothing new. So I then turned to him and said 'You believe in being blunt. Do you agree that other people, therefore, have the right to be blunt in reply?' and I waited for an answer. Of course, he could only say 'Yes' to this, and I said, 'Well, Mr. K. believe me, everybody there on our side thought you said several things that were very new indeed', implying that it was a pretty shocking statement. I think this took him aback rather, although he began to argue a bit about the pre-war position, contradicting himself incidentally about Chamberlainism and the attitude of the Labour Party and so on. Well, not very much more, I think, was said. Earlier than this I had looked at my watch, and said, 'Well, I don't know how [much] time you have', and they, after a consultation in Russian, said 'ten minutes', and then a moment or two later said, 'No, there's no hurry, it's all right, you can go on'. Quite evidently they had expected and wanted to have this talk with us. However, finally, after nearly an hour, I got up and said, 'Well, we must be going now'.

Up to then the whole atmosphere had been pretty grim, not as bad as Monday, but certainly unfriendly. Then, however, Khrushchev suddenly changed and said, 'Well, it's no use going over it; let's forget all about it; let's put all personal recriminations on one side; and let us look forward to friendship in the future'. Then he added as we were shaking hands – he held my hand incidentally a long time, 'Well, perhaps sometimes after a quarrel, relations are better', and I said 'I was just going to say that'. And Jim and I both said, 'Well what we say is "it clears the air"'. Then there was some talk about George Brown, and we said that when K. knew him better, he would probably get on very well with him, and I said, 'I'll tell you a secret – as a matter of fact you are rather alike'. And K., I must admit, did burst out laughing. And I said, 'You both are very outspoken, you are both fairly abrupt, you are both very strong, and so on'. Then they said, 'Well, now, what about coming to Moscow?' and K. said, slightly maliciously, I thought, 'Well, of course, you are the Opposition, and we are the Government, and we can't ask you. Mr Gaitskell can't come with Sir Anthony Eden. We could invite you through the Communist Party or through the Trade Unions'. I was amused at this bit of knowledge about democratic procedure. However, I said, 'Well, there are various ways which could be discussed with the Ambassador. We do get invited as an Opposition by foreign governments sometimes, and individuals can be invited and we can arrange, through the Ambassador, which individuals or, possibly, we could go through the Unions'. They said that they thought it would be an excellent thing to talk it over with the Ambassador. And so everything finished in a friendly, smiley way, with continual handshakes and general cordiality.[34]

As I was going out, I spoke to young Khrushchev and said that I was sure that George Brown would wish me to say that if anything he had said the previous night had given offence, he was very sorry for it. He had only been joking, that was the way we did things here, but, possibly, with translation, and so on, it had been misunderstood. But young K. said, through the interpreter 'I took it as political joking', something I was later able to report to the Party meeting. We then went outside, met the Press, took them in for a moment to an inner room, and told them that, while each of us had stuck to our principles – a point I was at pains to emphasise in the final cordial hand-shaking with B. and K. – nevertheless misunderstandings had been cleared up and everything had ended on a very friendly note. All of which was true. Incidentally, they did appear to suppose that we had organised the whole dinner in this way. I think we managed to point out to them that this was not so. We told them, of course, how the thing had gone off with Malenkov and said that we [had] hoped it would have gone off in the same way with them.

The same evening there was the Party meeting. Of course, by the time that took place the news of our morning visit to Claridges had got out, and the round-robin was pretty well dead. But Shinwell, who was behind most of the trouble here, was thoroughly disgruntled, and nothing more than a mischief-maker, then had drafted another letter, saying, in effect, exactly what we had already said to the Russians, which he proposed, and he was going round getting support for it, should be sent to them on behalf of the Party. This was an improvement on the round-robin, because it wasn't any kind of break-away. But still, it was not very satisfactory. Well, there was an enormous attendance at the Party meeting and, after getting over some preliminary business, in a friendly kind of fashion, I proceeded to take the bull by the horns and made a long statement. There is no need to repeat all that here, because I was really telling them what had happened. I referred to our happy relations with Malenkov and how we had hoped that we would have the same kind of arrangement with B. & K. that we had had with him. I told them that we were bound to raise the question of the Social Democrats, that this was the only official meeting with the National Executive and that we had decided beforehand to put a question

34 HG assumed he would soon be having serious talks in Moscow. But he was not invited until 1958, in circumstances which precluded immediate acceptance. He went in 1959, but plans for a second visit were hampered by Khrushchev's continuing resentment over the 1956 dinner; it was finally arranged for New Year 1963, but prevented by Gaitskell's fatal illness. See *HG*, pp. 414 and notes 51, 52; 529; 761.

to them on this. And, indeed, it was to have been put by Sam Watson. I told them how the dinner had started, I referred to George Brown, and said that he had made facetious remarks, which may very well have been misunderstood. But that I did not think that this made as much difference as some people had supposed. I told them about K's speech and, without going into detail, said it had deeply shocked everybody present. I then told them about my own and told them how conciliatory that had been and went on to tell them about his reply, and I did quote the famous phrase about the enemies of the working class. I then of course told them about the meeting in the morning, and sat down.

I think this pretty well cleared the air. But, nevertheless, Shinwell got up and made a grumbly sort of speech, making really the two points – we shouldn't have raised the question there of the Social Democrats, and George Brown obviously had behaved very badly indeed. He wanted his letter to go. He did not get much support. Unfortunately, Alice Bacon, whom I called next, made a rather silly speech, got into a muddle, although it was fairly obvious that she was trying to make the point that the real trouble began with K's speech the night before. She also spoke of Nye replying equally belligerently to K. and, of course, Nye resented this. He found himself in a rather awkward position. On the one hand, he behaved admirably at the dinner, lining up with us; on the other hand, many of his friends feel that he missed an opportunity to attack us. And he did not want, therefore, to get associated with George Brown on whom they were, most of them (the Bevanites), in fact all of them except Bevan himself, putting all the blame. So he got up and protested about this and I had some difficulty in calming the whole thing down. There was a division in the middle of this. Then we all came back. Shinwell went on with his speech, there was, as I say, this incident with Alice Bacon and Nye, and various other people spoke, but, at the end of it all, after perhaps half-an-hour or so I got up – obviously they wanted to bring the thing to an end – made a final speech, showed them what had actually been reported in the Press about our meeting with the Russians, defended the raising of the question at the dinner and also told them one other fact, namely that already at Chequers Khrushchev had said that they found it much easier to get on with the Tories. This really finished the matter. I asked Shinwell if he wanted to withdraw. He said 'No'. I put the question to the vote, whether Shinwell's letter should be sent and less than a dozen people voted for it. So that was that.

There really is very little else to report. There are, of course, repercussions in the Press going on and I did a T.V. interview last night (on Friday, that is). It was rather difficult to know how far to go. I wanted to defend our action in holding the dinner, on the other hand, I did not want to kick up any further dust. But I did say that I thought Khrushchev was very much inclined to speak, that he flew off the handle rather easily and that he was a fanatical Communist. I contrasted him with Malenkov. There will probably be, even on this, some further complaint that I shouldn't have gone on T.V. at all.[35] But, on the whole, I am inclined to think it was worth doing. Incidentally, one rather satisfactory feature about the Party meeting was that, when I said that, contrary to what some had argued, we really had got a lot of good out of this for ourselves because we had been standing up for our principles, there was a tremendous volume of applause. Most of the Party really did, I think, genuinely believe that. The only argument the other way is, of course, that people may say that we couldn't manage to get on with the Russians and, in particular, that we misbehaved, and so on. The trouble, of course, is that George did rather misbehave, though I don't think it was very serious. But he has so many enemies, both personal and, so to speak, professional, who are only too quick to take advantage of any mistake he makes and, therefore, played this up like anything. No doubt, also, some of them wanted to push all the blame on to him in order to escape any odium for themselves. And that certainly – the fact that all the Brown business has been played up so much – will not do us any good.

However, I don't myself feel that we could have behaved any differently without really feeling pretty ashamed of ourselves. I could, I suppose, have simply dropped the Social Democrats and made the little speech, but, well, personally, I would have felt very unhappy about it, and I think I should be prepared to take the risk. If it were very near a General Election, there might be some danger, but, as things are, I don't think we have to worry a great deal about public opinion. And certainly as far as public opinion in other countries is concerned, I should guess that it has done us a lot of good. That is most certainly the case in the United States and, I think also in the other Western European countries. And if, at the same time, we have spiked the Communist guns on the united front, well, that will have done a lot of good as well. But, of course, at home within the Party we must continue to expect repercussions and it may be that in reply to complaints which I suppose may be made at the Party Conference later in the year, we shall have to do the only thing which I think will finally kill this business and that is to publish the whole of the proceedings. If that were done, I don't think the Communists and fellow-travellers would really have very much more to say.

The only other things which have happened in the past week and which are worth recording are (1) a lunch I had with Retinger.[36] He was quite

35 There was.
36 Dr Joseph Retinger, a Polish historian and former diplomat, was private secretary to General Sikorski (the Prime Minister in exile 1940–3) and parachuted into Poland at 57 as an envoy to the Resistance. He became a founder

interesting about what he thought was happening behind the Iron Curtain. Undoubtedly, there was a lot of loosening up in Poland, and, he thought, in Hungary as well.

(2) A meeting, or rather two meetings with a man called Suhrawardy, whom Patrick Gordon Walker and I had met two years before in Karachi, and who is now technically leader of the Opposition in Pakistan.[37] A little man who strutted up and down, talking rather endlessly. The interesting thing about him was that he has obviously decided to support a pro-Western foreign policy, contrary to the views of most of his Party. He said that he had deliberately gone alone to their Parliament to support the decision to stay in the Commonwealth on the part of the Government there, although all his Party, I gathered, stayed away and more or less boycotted it. But I gather that he pretty well controls the Party all the same. I think the reason why he has taken this line is to strengthen his position on the Kashmir issue; that dominates everything in Pakistan and he is intelligent enough, indeed he is extremely clever, to realise that if Pakistan is to deal firmly with India on Kashmir, she must have Western support. She will not have Western support unless she remains within the Commonwealth. So he was at pains to emphasise all this and to show how anti-Communist he was.

He also spoke about the way in which he had become leader of the Opposition. He had been a Minister of Justice in a kind of Coalition Government and had evidently expected to be Prime Minister. The principle there is that the Governor General comes from one part of Pakistan and the Prime Minister from another. Suhrawardy comes from East Pakistan. When the present Governor General – Iskander Mirza – became Governor General, Suhrawardy thought that he would become Prime Minister, because really Mirza is from West Pakistan.[38] However, Mirza's ancestors apparently came from East Pakistan, and it was so decided; so they more or less squeezed him out. However, I should have thought that if fair elections are held in, I think it is 18 months' time, this chap had a pretty good chance of coming back into power. He certainly

---

of the European Movement and of the Bilderberg Group (below, p. 542, n. 78) and was chief organiser of the Hague Congress in May 1948 from which the Council of Europe developed directly and other institutions indirectly. He married the daughter of E.D. Morel, the Labour critic of British foreign policy before, during and after the First World War, after an adventurous career in revolutionary Mexico.

37 Leader of the Awami League and Prime Minister from September 1956 to October 1957. He died in 1963.

38 Major-General Iskander Mirza was Governor of East Pakistan – now Bangladesh – in 1954, Governor-General 1955, President 1956–8, then exiled by a military coup and lived in London until his death in 1969.

would have a big majority in East Pakistan. As far as I remember from our previous meeting and from what I have heard about him, he is rather a rogue, but Patrick Gordon Walker said, when I told him about S's views on foreign policy, 'Indians who drink are always sound on foreign policy'.

(3) I had lunch with Sydney Jacobson and Hugh Cudlipp, of the *Mirror*. Of course, most of the time we talked about the B. & K. business. They thought there was some danger of me [being] regarded as a chap who did not get on with K. and that this would do harm, though they entirely agreed that on the general issue of whether we should or should not have raised the question of the Social Democrats public opinion was heavily on our side. I am a little worried, however, because since then the *Mirror* seems to have turned round pretty completely and suddenly become much more pro-Russian. I must try and find out why this has happened.

(4) I had lunch with Alan Sainsbury. He is an extremely intelligent and nice man. I wanted to get some money out of him for *Forward*.[39] He has been a member and supporter of the Party for years and, of course, he is a very rich man. I could not tie him down to any particular figure, but he did show a great deal of interest, including an interest in taking part on the business side. So I hope something more will come of this.

[Dictated about Monday 4 June 1956]

On the 1st May we went to a Reception at the High Commissioner for Canada's to meet Mike Pearson, the Canadian Foreign Secretary. He is undoubtedly one of the ablest and most sensible international statesmen. I have for long admired him and often found myself thinking on much the same lines. I had a few words of conversation with him, and said I would like to talk further, and he seemed to welcome the idea, and said he would be coming back to London in June. I also saw at the Reception Gromyko. Malik was in the distance, and I didn't have a chance of speaking to him, but I did speak to Gromyko, who was perfectly friendly, despite the dinner, and, indeed, laughed about it. I said that he hadn't been there, and he said that if he had known what was going to happen, he certainly would have made an effort to get there.

Later, we had our second Trade Union Dinner. The striking thing about this was the way in which none of those present were in any way weakened because of the events of the dinner in their support of George Brown. But it must be added that neither Frank Cousins nor Alfred

39 Alan (Lord) Sainsbury took over the family business and was chairman 1956–67, then president. He stood three times as a Liberal before the war, and joined the Labour Party in 1945. On *Forward* see above, p. 470 n.

Robens were present. The others, Tom Williamson, Jim Campbell, Bill Webber and Harry Douglass, were all absolutely firm. Rather to my surprise, Jim Campbell said that he thought, indeed he said that he felt quite confident, that the N.U.R. would *not* support Nye Bevan, even *after* the dinner. Subsequent events, however, proved that he was wrong because in fact, dictating now over a month later, I must record that by a narrow majority – 13 to 12 – the [N.U.R.] Executive decided to back Bevan.

On the following day [Wednesday 2 May] I went to the Royal Academy Banquet – always a tiresome occasion, when you have to dress up and hang around and wait through a lot of dreary speeches. The only interesting event which happened to me was a conversation with Sir Gerald Templer, the C.I.G.S;[40] just as we were going away, he came up to me and said that he wanted to tell me about his experience with Khrushchev. He said that he had had to look after Khrushchev at the Greenwich Dinner, when the Russians had been entertained in the famous painted hall built in the time of William and Mary. Khrushchev had said to him 'I understand that you are the head of the British Army'. Templer replied 'Well so I am; anyway, I try to be'. 'Well then,' said Khrushchev, 'What do you think of the prospects of thermo-nuclear warheads on guided missiles?' Templer professed himself to be deeply shocked by this, and said that he said 'We really did not come down here, to this beautiful place, to talk about that kind of thing'. He afterwards said that he found Khrushchev quite unbearable and even added 'I have never wanted to kill a man with my own hands so much'. Templer, of course, is a very tough guy and may be exaggerating. I had also heard that Bulganin had, in fact apologised to the Admiral in charge of the proceedings at Greenwich because of Khrushchev's speech down there.

During the following weekend, I had to do some meetings in the South West of England. We began with a Conference in Taunton. I was delighted to find quite an intelligent audience. I dealt straight away with the B. and K. dinner, not telling them a great deal, but giving them a broad outline (it was a crowded Conference). I then went on to speak about other things. I then answered questions for an hour. I only had one question about B. and K. That was an anti-George Brown question, clearly coming from an elderly Left-Winger. He seemed to get no support from anybody else.

That evening I attended the Taunton Labour Party dance, which was enormously enthusiastic. They seemed delighted that I had turned up and taken part in the proceedings. Nobody talked at all about the dinner.

On the following day [Sunday 6 May], we went to Plymouth. It was a

40 C.I.G.S. 1955–8; previously High Commissioner in Malaya where he defeated
    the Chinese Communist guerrillas (cf. above, p. 473).

beautiful day and really delightful to come down to the famous Plymouth Hoe, and look at the Bay sparkling in the sunlight below us. In the course of the afternoon I was driven round by three of the leading Councillors, who showed me what a tremendous building job had been done in Plymouth and the way in which the City was now being planned and the plan was being carried out. In the evening, I spoke in Devonport with Michael Foot, of all people, at the May Day Demonstration. The meeting was packed and it all went off perfectly well. Michael behaved himself, and there were no incidents, heckling or disturbances of any kind whatever. So I returned to London somewhat relieved.

In the following week, we had dinner at the Swedish Embassy, and there was a good deal of conversation about the frog-man.[41] I am afraid I was rather indiscreet. I made it fairly plain that I intended to attack Eden about this, because of the way he had behaved over the B. and K. dinner. In fact, the Conservative Party propaganda had been disgraceful. They have tried, and are still trying, to make as much Party capital as they can out of this, and are trying to build up the idea of Eden as a kind of peace-maker. In view of the circumstances in which the whole visit took place, and the reasons for our row with the Russians, I took the view that this was pretty bad behaviour. However, as I say, I was unwise in talking so freely, because rumours got round that we were going to make a tremendous attack on the frog-man issue and, to anticipate here, when it came to the Debate in the following week and we made a reasoned criticism, this was heralded as running away.

I also had lunch at the American Embassy. I must say that I have never been so enthusiastically received there before. Ambassador Aldrich was all over me, and so were the other members of the Staff. The other leading people in the Party were there, and it was a very happy and cheerful occasion. It was a lunch for me, preceding my visit to the U.S.A.

On the 10th May, Dick Stokes, George Brown and myself went over to Paris. The occasion was a visit to SHAPE [Supreme Headquarters Allied Powers in Europe] and NATO, but we went early in order to see Guy Mollet [the Prime Minister] and Pineau*, the French Foreign Minister. I had arranged this with Gladwyn Jebb, our Ambassador in Paris, who invited Mollet to come in in the morning to meet us and Pineau to come to lunch. The talks were quite interesting, and have been recorded elsewhere.[42] Mollet seemed to be extraordinarily confident about the position in Algeria. Obviously he thought that militarily the French were now on

41 A naval frogman, Commander Crabb, had disappeared in Portsmouth harbour trying to inspect the hull of the cruiser which had brought the Soviet leaders to Britain. The espionage was unauthorised, as Eden publicly stated, and the Labour attack was cautious and not very effective: *HG*, pp. 414–15.

42 Not included here.

top, and he seemed to expect that it would be possible to negotiate an armistice in the near future, and that thereafter there would be elections, and negotiations would then take place with the people elected. Pineau was not quite so optimistic, but took a rather similar line. I can't say that, apart from their comments on Algeria, the two French politicians contributed a great deal. Mollet certainly strikes me always as being very sensible and reliable. He has a great deal to his credit in having swung the French Socialist party in favour of accepting German re-armament – no easy task – and nobody could doubt his sincerity in resisting the Communists.[43]

In the afternoon we went out to see General Gruenther, [the NATO Commander] at his house, and had a private talk. There were present, apart from the three of us and Jebb, Gruenther, Norstad*, his successor, Montgomery, Schuyler, the Second in Command, and Steel, the U.K. Representative on the NATO Council.[44] It was an extremely interesting discussion. The main parts of it were as follows: (1) They were all of them worried about the possible ending of conscription in the U.K. Gruenther did not mind quite so much as the others, and thought that so long as we were able to keep up our four Divisions in Germany, it, perhaps, would not matter. Montgomery, on the other hand, thought that it was extremely unlikely that we would be able to maintain these Divisions there, because, he said, we had often tried before to increase the number of regular troops by raising the pay and never succeeded. Even, however, supposing we did do this, it would still have a very bad psychological effect on the rest of Europe. This was also the view of Norstad. (2) There was much discussion about the exact plan in the Central Front – which I take to be Europe. Here they told us that they aim to have 30 Divisions of which 12 would be German. It was quite plain that at the moment they hadn't even got the 18 non-German Divisions. We discussed why it was necessary to have ground troops at all. Their argument was (i) that even if you relied wholly on the H Bomb as a deterrent, if there were no ground troops at all, the Russians could advance and over-run the air defences, which were protecting some at least of the air bases from which the V Bombers would fly; (ii) that if there were no troops there, the effect on the morale of Germany and France and the other NATO countries would be disastrous. It is true, however, to say that there was no specific defence of the precise number of Divisions which they claimed to be necessary; (iii)

43 Mollet and Pineau were both Socialists. The Prime Minister's optimism, typical of French governments throughout the Algerian war, soon proved unjustified; his reputation, still high in June 1956, never recovered from his record in office during the next 12 months.
44 General Cortlandt Schuyler was Chief of Staff at SHAPE, 1953–9. Sir Christopher Steel was at NATO 1953–7, then Ambassador to Bonn 1957–63.

Montgomery was very interesting about the defence arrangements in the U.K. He said that the key really was to subordinate the Secretaries of State for War and Air and the First Lord of the Admiralty wholly to the Minister of Defence. They would have to become Under-Secretaries and accept orders from him. That was the only way in which the Ministry of Defence could exert its authority. He did not believe that it was practicable to merge the three Forces.

On the following day [Friday 11 May], we went to NATO and I had a talk with Ismay.[45] The two interesting things which came out of this were (1) that Gruenther's retirement was simply due to financial reasons. If he stayed on in NATO and retired from the American Army in the ordinary way, he would simply get his pension as a four-star General. If he went now, there were apparently very lucrative business offers open to him and he would be able to make much better arrangements for his wife, or widow. I could not help feeling how very unfortunate it was that this man, who is regarded by everybody as quite outstanding, particularly in that job, possessing as he does not only the military skill and experience, but also quite remarkable diplomatic ability, should be leaving Europe at a crucial moment simply because they have made no proper arrangements to pay him as he should be paid. The other point in my conversation with Ismay was about Churchill. He said that he had seen Churchill lately, who had become very quiet and demure. He had said to Ismay 'I hope it will not be long before they send for me'. I thought, at first, that Ismay meant back into the Government, but, of course, he didn't, he meant he hoped it would not be long before the end of his life had come. Apparently, he also said 'I can no longer clothe my thoughts in the appropriate words'.

In the following week, on Tuesday 15th, we left for the United States. I have written about this visit elsewhere[46] and I do not think it is worthwhile recording every detail of it. But some of it is, perhaps, worth mentioning. We had an excellent flight over in a tourist plane, which was less than half full. I was very tired when we began, and, consequently, slept quite reasonably well – perhaps 7 hours in all, in the 20 hour flight. On arrival, as I expected, there was the usual collection of Press, film cameras for television purposes and Pressmen waiting to ask me questions. I got through all this reasonably well having anticipated more or less what would be asked and finding that they seemed more interested in the frog-man episode than in anything else. But I was rather taken aback when, just as we were going away, the T.V. part was all finished, somebody said to me 'Why did you travel tourist?' It appeared that, before we

45 General Lord Ismay (1887–1965) was NATO Secretary-general 1952–7. He had been Chief of Staff in the Ministry of Defence 1940–5, and was Secretary of State for Commonwealth Relations 1951–2.
46 In *Reynolds News* on 3 June.

arrived, this had caused a lot of comment, but fortunately, Joy Wright [of the British Information Service in New York], who is a tower of strength on these occasions, had given a very tactful reply which was later put into my mouth. As we walked away, the two Trade Union people, who had come to meet us from the Garment Workers [his hosts], said 'We hope you didn't really come tourist in order to save us money'. It appears that the Union itself is enormously rich, and was quite horrified that their guests should not travel in the maximum of luxury and comfort. I had to spend the rest of that day preparing my speech for the Garment Workers' Convention. I had made the notes only in the plane coming over, but of course it was one of those occasions when one has to put out an advance to the Press. Therefore I went to the British Information Services Office and dictated it in the afternoon to relays of typists. The whole office, I am afraid, was completely upside down as a result of this. However, they did a fine job and got it finished, and it was handed out to the Press that night.

On the following day, very early, we left by car for Atlantic City, where the Convention was taking place. We drove down through rather pleasant wooded country, without a great deal of traffic and arrived in good time at Atlantic City, which is a sort of Margate in relation to New York. It was breezy and clean. The Convention building itself was enormous, apparently large enough to house two Conventions at the same time. We were taken into a kind of back-room and I had hurriedly to finish the notes of my speech, because, of course, the part you put out to the Press isn't the whole of it. And then, at last, at the appropriate moment, we were led in. We received a most staggering demonstration; everybody stood up as we came in and clapped, and clapped, and clapped. They went on doing so for about 5 minutes, even after we had got on to the platform. We were greeted there by Dubinsky, a most lively, small, vital, jolly character, quite elderly, but in complete command of everything, and a real showman.[47] He then made an introductory speech which built me up in a tremendous way, and then I delivered my speech. We had been a little worried about it; Dora, particularly, thought it was too academic and difficult for them, but, all the same, they stood it, and, in fact, they applauded continuously throughout. It was a success. Everybody seemed to be delighted. A large part of it was being tape-recorded for broadcasting later that evening over one of the big networks. After the speech

47 David Dubinsky was born in Poland in 1892 and went to the U.S. in 1911. From 1922 he was a leader of the International Ladies Garment Workers Union, and from 1932 its president, and among the leaders of the A.F. of L. (except 1936–40 when he was in the C.I.O.: below, p. 528 n. 57). An old Socialist, in New York State he helped found the American Labor Party in 1940, and (when it fell under Communist influence) the Liberal Party in 1944; and nationally, in 1947, A.D.A. (below, p. 529 n. 60).

was over, the Convention adjourned and we went and had lunch with what I took to be the Executive Committee in a private room in the hotel. It was all very jolly and friendly. The only other guest I could see was the Governor of Puerto Rico;[48] there are quite a number of Puerto Ricans now in the Union who, of course, are recent immigrants into New York. After lunch, at the request of Dubinsky, I gave them some account of the B. and K. dinner, which, of course, fascinated them, but it was made very plain that this was all completely off the record and not for quotation anywhere at any time.

We then returned to New York and all went well until we got to the outskirts of the City. We then ran into the biggest traffic-jam that I can remember, far worse than London, and it took us about an hour to get from the other side of the Hudson River back to River House, Louisa's flat, where we were staying.[49] On arrival, I had to rush out again almost immediately to go and do a radio interview with one of the well-known radio commentators. I rather resented this, but still I went along to do it. He turned out to be extremely nice and I think it was valuable. Later that evening we went out and dined with a friend of Joy Wright who is editor of the *New York Daily News*, a rather anti-British paper, and following dinner we went on to the St Regis Hotel and danced.[50] Apart from the fact that I was now extremely tired, it was a very pleasant evening.

The following morning I had to be up early and along to the B.I.S. [British Information Service] to do another radio interview for more or less permanent use by them and also have a film made, also for permanent use. This took the greater part of the morning. Lunch was in Wall Street. It had been arranged by S.G. Warburg, the rather Left-Wing financial man whom I know quite well in England, and who happened to be in New York at the time.[51] I can't say it was particularly exciting; there was quite a good collection there, and I talked to them a little about the economic situation. They then asked me a few questions and that was that.

On the following day [Saturday 19 May], we went to lunch with the Harrimans and had a very pleasant time indeed. I must say that Averell [Governor of New York State since 1954] and Marie, his wife, both seem to thrive on politics. He was looking fatter, much more confident, and she was looking as though she really enjoyed it all immensely. There were photographers waiting, and we were photographed with them both outside the house. There was quite a nice collection of people at lunch, including

48 Luiz Muñoz Marin, the first elected Governor, served four terms from 1949 to 1965.
49 On Mrs Louisa Stewart see above pp. 213–14.
50 Richard W. Clarke, the editor since 1946, married Joy Wright in 1959.
51 A German by origin, he was director of S.G. Warburg 1946–69 and president 1970–8. He was knighted in 1966.

Chester Bowles*, former Ambassador to India, with whom I talked at some length. I had read a certain amount of his writings and found myself very much in agreement with them. He is perhaps a slightly puritanical type of man, faintly reminiscent of Moral Rearmament, but nevertheless full of sound ideals and one can understand this slightly priggish outlook because he is undoubtedly rare among Americans and far in advance, so far as his views are concerned, about the handling of India and other neutral countries. He had sent me his book *The New Dimensions of Peace* before I left for America, but I had not had time to read it. Dubinsky was there and also a number of other Union people, including a Mr Alex Rose of the Hatters' Union, and also Carmine de Sapio, the boss of New York, or, if you prefer to put it that way, the Harrimans' political manager.[52] We had a very enjoyable lunch, lots of good conversation, and, again, at the end of it, I was asked to tell the story of the dinner, which I did, to their evident satisfaction and interest. I talked to Averell privately for half-an-hour or so afterwards. He is evidently very keen to get the [Presidential] nomination, though few people seem to think that he has much chance of doing so. He criticised Stevenson* because he did not feel he was fighting Eisenhower hard enough. I complained that in England the Tories were now pursuing a sort of soft, appeasement policy towards the Communists, and that I feared they were going all out for home popularity without regard to the real interests of the country. Harriman said that exactly the same thing was happening in the United States. The truth was [in] fact the Democrats would be far better at dealing with the Communists than the Republicans. As to Eisenhower, Harriman thought that the only thing to do was to go all out and attack him. He complained that Stevenson was much too gentle and moderate in his views. He, Harriman, thought you had to fight in order to have any chance of winning at all.

Later we went on to a Reception which Dubinsky had organised for us, where we met most of the Labour Movement of New York. A good many of the Union people were there, as well as the Liberal Party, including a friend of Aidan [Crawley]'s called Stuart Schaeftel and his wife, an actress called Geraldine Fitzgerald – very charming. We were photographed continuously; indeed, it was rather like being in a studio, the number of photographs that were taken, from all angles, at all times, and with all sorts of people. We then had a very queer dinner with some of the high-brow anti-Communists. This was organised by a man called Beichmann, who I gather was associated with the A.F. of L., the rather

52 Dubinsky and Rose ran the New York Liberal Party which tried to push de Sapio's Democratic machine in a reforming direction. De Sapio was leader of Tammany Hall 1949–61, and New York Secretary of State 1955–9.

right-wing Trade Unions;[53] but, in fact, the people we met were supposed to be the Committee of the Congress for Cultural Freedom, and, in particular, Mr and Mrs Trilling. Now Lionel Trilling is a well-known novelist and critic, who wrote a rather remarkable book called *The Middle of the Journey*, which was supposed to be all about Whittaker Chambers and the [Hiss] case.[54] There were some other people there, but they were not of very great importance. I sat next to Mrs Trilling and found her neurotic and rather boring. She insisted on asserting throughout dinner that there was a great gap between the British and American intellectuals, and this was, in her opinion, illustrated by Graham Greene's last novel *The Quiet American*, which was heralded in Britain as a very fine novel, but which they regarded as just more or less anti-American pro-Communist propaganda; 'an anti-American political tract', Trilling called it. In fact, of course, the Trillings turned out to be ex-Communists who have gone to the opposite extreme, and Mrs Trilling was almost [McCarthyite?] in her outlook. It was very nice of them to give us dinner, but I was relieved to find from talking to other people afterwards that they by no means typified the intellectuals of New York.

I also should add that in the course of the morning I was interviewed by a man from the *New Yorker*. As we had both been to bed at 4 a.m. the night before, we were not feeling too bright, but he was very pleasant, and I enjoyed it. I was also interviewed by a very right-wing columnist called Sokolsky, who, nevertheless, was quite interesting on Russia – he was, of course, Russian by origin – and what was happening there now. I find myself broadly in agreement with him. He took, oddly enough, although being extremely right-wing, much the same view of Eisenhower as Harriman had done, that he was much too weak, that he was really incapable of doing anything and that nothing would be done for the next four years, because in fact Eisenhower was certain to be re-elected as President.[55] After the dinner with the Trillings, we went to see the latest

53 They had just healed the breach with the rival trade union federation, the C.I.O.

54 Congressman Richard M. Nixon made his reputation by the prosecution of Alger Hiss, a high State Department official, who was convicted of perjury in January 1950 for denying Communist Party membership in the 1930s. Whittaker Chambers was the chief witness against Hiss and said to be the model for Maxim, the central character in Trilling's novel. Trilling was a professor at Columbia University.

55 George Sokolsky was American-born but had been an editor in Russia and China between 1917 and 1930. He was director and then president of the Jewish League against Communism from 1948, and a prominent columnist and commentator for the American Broadcasting Co. As he had supported Senator Taft for the Republican nomination, his criticism of Eisenhower was not really odd.

rage of New York, 'My Fair Lady'. Following that, I addressed a Jewish Demonstration called the 'Workers Circle' for about five minutes. I was so tired and so were the audience that it was really a failure, and, finally, on top of all that, the Schaeftels took us to a rather amusing party full of film and stage people, including in particular Groucho Marx, whom we thought rather disagreeable. I would have liked to have stayed there longer – the food and drink was excellent and the company by no means bad – but we were frightfully tired and we had to get up fairly early the next morning, so at about 2 a.m. we left.

We flew down to Washington in the morning [Sunday 20 May] and were met at the Airport by the B.I.S. people, and also the Ambassador's Private Secretary. We had lunch with the Edmondsons – very pleasant indeed;[56] lovely day and we ate out in their garden. There was a pleasant collection there; in particular I had some conversation with Dean Acheson's daughter and quite a long talk with Walter Lippmann, whom I had seen quite recently in London. I always find him just a little too much of a fellow-traveller, perhaps that's an unfair word, but just a little too soft in his attitude and I had quite an argument with him, but he is awfully nice and quite reasonable. His wife struck me as being rather less reasonable and rather more to the left than Lippmann himself. There were various other people – some Congressmen and some newspaper people, and it was altogether extremely pleasant. My only anxiety was that I had the Meet the Press T.V. programme in the evening and I was very tired. However, this eventually went off quite successfully. Questions were by no means difficult; my only worry really was that I would commit some indiscretion, but I managed to avoid this and everybody seemed to be satisfied. Anyway, immediately after it Schaeftel and Dubinsky both telephoned their congratulations. It's amazing what an enormous number of people watch this programme, not only just millions of people – I believe it's 12 or 14 million – all over the U.S.A., but the people one meets in politics all seem to look in on it. For instance Mr Dulles [the Secretary of State] had watched it and almost everybody else that I met in Washington and New York. It's comparable, I suppose, to a kind of big House of Commons occasion for us over here, except that it's on T.V. and a vast number of people see it.

In the evening there was a very pleasant supper party, where I talked to some of the Pressmen, especially on the subject of the disintegration of NATO.

On the Monday morning [21st] I went off to see George Meany the

56 George D'Arcy Edmondson worked for British Information Services in the U.S. from 1942, as Director-General 1953–9.

President of the Merger between the A.F. of L. and the C.I.O.[57] Meany is rather like Arthur Deakin to look at – a rugged, strong, tough kind of man, though quite quiet in his conversation. I found him easy to get on with. We talked for about three-quarters of an hour. He was very calm and collected about everything. He made a remark about Khrushchev which I thought particular[ly] significant. He said, 'He does not really behave as if he were a strong man'. I thought there was a good deal in this, but it was the first time I had heard anybody suggest it. On automation, he was not particularly perturbed and seemed content to point out that they were studying it. He also said that it would be very expensive to introduce and that therefore it would be slow in coming in because of the capital involved, and that as far as individual firms were concerned they would not be able to introduce it unless they expected a big increase in volume of production. This would be necessary to cover the very heavy capital charges involved. Then I went on to see the Eugene Mayers, the pro-prietors of the *Washington Post*. They were both very old. He is over 80 and she is certainly in the middle 70s, but both quite lively.[58] They called in two of their editorial people and asked me questions for some time. I noticed that Mrs Mayer, although very much of the same mind as myself on international politics, was critical about [the] British Economy, and seemed to hold the usual view that the Welfare State, nationalisation, and one thing and another had undermined our moral fibre. I pointed out to her as I did on many other occasions in the course of the trip that our increase in productivity since the war was actually greater than that of the U.S.A. This was obviously complete news to her. She was very interesting about Eisenhower. She said that she had voted for him in the last Election, but that she was now going to vote for Stevenson who she thought would be certain to get the Democratic nomination. Eisenhower, she said to me, 'is a nitwit, that's the conclusion I have reached. Don't for Heaven's sake ever tell anybody that I have said this! But I have a certain amount to do with him on social work.' In fact, she held the same view as Harriman and Sokolsky, that he was really content to do nothing at all most of the time, and merely to come in and make the decision when something was thrust in front of him.

57 The Congress of Industrial Organisations, comprising unions in the mass-production industries, split from the old American Federation of Labor in 1936 and reunited with it 20 years later. George Meany (1894–1980) was leader of the Plumbers' Union, secretary-treasurer of the A.F. of L. 1940–52, president of the A.F. of L. and then of the A.F.L.-C.I.O. 1952–79, and the dominant figure of American trade unionism.

58 Eugene Mayer (1875–1959) held various financial posts 1917–33, and was the first president of the World Bank in 1946. He was publisher and later also editor of the *Washington Post* 1933–46, and chairman from 1947.

Then I went to lunch with Mr Dulles. I had met him before, when I was Chancellor, and, I think, on an earlier occasion and I had not much cared for him. We had had a long argument about Japanese gold and I thought he was extremely obstinate and rather dry and unfriendly, but I must say that on this occasion he was certainly very forthcoming and I could not help, at the end of it all, feeling rather sorry for him. I sat next to him at lunch and I had intended to explain to him how desperately important it was for the Western Powers to work more closely together. In fact, I found the words taken out of my mouth. He spent the whole of the lunch telling me precisely that. Indeed, he went so far as to say that if we did not get closer together we should continue to drift further apart. After lunch he took Makins [our Ambassador] and myself back to the State Department and we had a further half-hour conversation in his room on the same theme. He talked rather vaguely about the possibility of America joining the Council of Europe. I pointed out the difficulties of NATO being used as an institution to handle questions, many of which were outside the geographical area of NATO, but he rather brushed this aside, saying that he didn't really see why they shouldn't talk about matters outside their own area. Roger Makins told me afterwards that the reason for this was that the U.S. actually belonged to NATO and it would be extremely difficult to get them to join any new organisation. Therefore, anything that was to be done in the way of greater co-operation would be done much more easily through NATO which at least was in existence. After this talk, I went along and answered questions at a meeting of the State Department officials. There were about 50 of them there and the questions covered an enormously wide field. Murphy* took the Chair, who I imagine is now one of the Assistant Secretaries. He used to be regarded as very anti-British, but he seemed friendly enough. Then we went on to tea with Eugene Black and his charming wife, and had a very pleasant hour with them. Raymond came too and we forgot about politics and even economics for the time being.[59] Then on to a special cocktail party organised for us, where we had to meet other people whom we hadn't met before, especially some from the A.D.A.,[60] and from the Labour Movement and some more Press people as well. The evening ended with dinner at the Embassy in our honour; rather boring; Senators and Congressmen were the chief guests; also Under-Secretary of State Hoover,[61] but I did not have any very satisfactory talk with him. He was against my U.N.O.

59 Black was president of the World Bank where Gaitskell's stepson Raymond Frost was an official.
60 Americans for Democratic Action was founded in January 1947 to organise liberals within the Democratic Party.
61 Herbert Hoover junior, son of the ex-President, was an engineer and businessman. He held the post 1954–7.

proposal, but mainly because they were already, he said, doing a great deal for U.N.O.

On the following morning [Tuesday 22 May] I went with the Ambassador to see the President. We wandered through a kind of ante-room where a lot of people were sitting. I asked what they were doing there, and apparently they were just hanging around, not exactly hoping to see the President, but hoping to see somebody. It all reminded me rather of a sort of Eastern Potentate's Court with a lot of people waiting to have their case heard. After a bit the Appointments Secretary came out and apologised that the President was still with the Congressional Leaders, but eventually we were taken in and we had twenty minutes conversation with him. He did almost all the talking. He looked quite well, and, on the whole, he talked quite sensibly. Part of it was just purely small talk. He did not like Mr Spivak, the man who runs 'Meet the Press'.[62] He said 'I don't like a man who has made a fortune out of other people's mistakes.' Apparently Spivak built this programme up out of the number of bricks dropped by people and then sold the rights in it at an enormous profit, while still agreeing, of course, to continue to manage the programme himself. I then turned the conversation on to NATO and SHAPE and told him that I had recently seen Gruenther; told him also of their views on conscription. He said that he would agree with that, but that he also thought that there was a lot to be said for having new people in SHAPE because the nuclear changes made such a difference. It was good, he thought to have a fresh mind on the whole subject. He was more forthcoming on China trade than anybody else. He said that he thought it was hopeless to try and stop the Japanese trading with China (Makins told me that he was well in advance of anybody else on this subject), and then finally the photographers all came in with a sort of rush and took photographs of us, so we all began to smile at each other, and I asked the President if he was coming to England, and he said, 'Well, the difficulty is, if I come to London, I shall have to go to Rome and Paris and Berlin, etc.' and I said, 'Well, why not do all that?' He said, 'Over here the Latin American Presidents are all meeting me in Panama'. So I suggested that perhaps the same kind of thing might be arranged by us in Europe. All this helped to give us good photographs, and it was particularly appropriate because, of course, the newspapermen were listening in. When I went out I found I had to do another T.V. thing or, rather, films for T.V. on the interview, and what I said to the President about his coming to Europe provided a very convenient excuse for avoiding any of the other things we had talked about.

62 Lawrence E. Spivak was manager, editor or publisher of the *American Mercury* 1934–50, and became a radio and television producer.

I then went on to see Burns, the chief Economist in the Government.[63] He is an academic sort of figure, whom I knew slightly. He is rather difficult to talk to ordinarily, but for some reason or other, on this occasion and on the previous one he had talked to me very freely. He was quite frank about the American position and thought the Federal Reserve Board had made a great mistake in putting up interest rates at a time when the economy was already more or less stable and stopped expansion. He thought the effect of the credit squeeze being tightened would be bad. I said to him, 'Do you expect serious trouble?' He said, 'Yes, I do.' I said, 'When?' He said, 'Well it's already beginning', and he instanced the position in the automobile industry, private house building, and he thought that small businesses generally would be badly affected by it. I had, of course, heard before about the row between the Federal Reserve Board and the Treasury, but it was interesting to hear Burns taking such a very definite view. He did not, however, I must add, think that investment would go back; that was booming. I then went to see the Secretary of the Treasury, [George] Humphrey, who impressed me a good deal. He is a businessman, obviously intelligent, genial and strong. He did not take such a gloomy view as Burns, but perhaps, in any case, he would not have said so to me, though he made it plain that he had not agreed with the Federal Reserve Board. He was worried, so he said, about the danger of both Britain and America being priced out of the markets by Germany and Japan because of our wage situation. He had David McDonald, the Steel Trade Union Leader coming to lunch with him and asked me if I could stay.[64] I knew McDonald; I had met him in London. Unfortunately, I couldn't stay, but I was interested that he was seeing him, because the steel workers have a big wage demand at the moment and many people think that what happens will be rather crucial to the economy.

Then on to the Overseas Writers, which is a collection of American newspapermen who cover foreign affairs. We had lunch, and I gave an off-the-record talk, very much the same as one I had given, but I have not referred to in this piece of dictation, in New York to the Council on Foreign Relations: broadly that I was profoundly worried about the way the Western Powers seemed to have lost the habit of consultation and illustrating my point from the military, economic and propaganda and

63 Arthur F. Burns (born in Austria in 1904) was professor of economics at Columbia 1944–69. He was chairman of the Council of Economic Advisers 1953–6, Counsellor to the President 1969–70, chairman of the governors of the Federal Reserve 1970–8, Ambassador to Bonn from 1981.
64 George M. Humphrey was president of the M.A. Hanna Co. (steel manufacturers) 1929–52, later chairman; Secretary of the Treasury 1953–7. Dave McDonald was secretary-treasurer of the Steel Workers Organising Committee and then of the United Steel Workers of America, 1936–53, and later its president.

diplomatic fields. After this I still had to go and make another speech, addressing the Amalgamated Clothing Workers Union. This was not very enthusiastically received; quite different from the Garment Workers of Atlantic City; although what I said was, I think, sensible enough. Then, after doing a one-minute bit of a film in the form of a message for the automobile workers, we were allowed to go back to the Embassy, collect our bags and go off to the plane to New York. No sooner had we got there, than I had to change and go off to see Norman Thomas, the Socialist leader. He had with him two younger men, one of them, I think, the Secretary of the Socialist Party, and the other the leader, I gathered, of the Social Democratic Federation. They wanted to know if I would help them merge, I asked if there were any doctrinal differences. They said 'No. Not really'. Apparently some of the S.D.F. people didn't want to merge with the Socialists, partly because they were frightened of the name. But they thought it would be a great help if I would write them a line, saying that I thought it was a good thing. I said I would be glad to do this, but suggested that they should write to me in London first.[65]

Then we went off to dine with Sir Pierson Dixon, the British Ambassador to the U.N. This was rather a nice party. Quite a different lot of people from Washington, most of them were working at the U.N. either as Ambassadors there or employed there. I was particularly impressed with [Ralph] Bunche, the rather paleish negro, who has made such a reputation for himself.[66] He seemed to have a completely white wife, who was sitting next to me and came from Alabama. After dinner I again told the story of the B. and K. dinner at the request of Dixon and it received the usual interest. Unfortunately we had to rush off rather early in order that I could do a radio interview – this time with what is called the Tex and Jinx Programme. It is remarkable how the Americans do these things. This programme is conducted from part of a big hotel and behind a kind of glass screen. People are sitting around tables having drinks, and then in the middle there is another table with a microphone on it, and the two people Tex and Jinx do the interviewing. She was a tennis star and is

65 The Socialist Party split in May 1936 when the old leaders, following their trade union allies like Dubinsky (above, p. 523) in supporting Roosevelt, formed the Social Democratic Federation; they reunited in 1957. Norman Thomas (1884–1968) was Socialist candidate for President six times from 1928 to 1948.
66 Sir Pierson Dixon was Deputy Under-Secretary at the Foreign Office 1950–4, Ambassador to the U.N. 1954–60, to France 1960–4. Ralph Bunche, a professor at Howard University 1937–50 and at Harvard 1950–2, was a U.S. delegate at many international conferences and a U.N. representative in many trouble-spots. He was director of the U.N.'s trusteeship division 1946–54, under-secretary for political affairs 1955–67, and then Under-Secretary-General. He won the Nobel Peace Prize in 1950.

rather an attractive woman. He is a very good-looking man. And you just go and sit at a table to start with, and then when it's your turn you wander up to the table in the middle and then they just ask the questions. It's all done in a wonderfully informal and friendly kind of way and I should think it is very effective. Much the same, incidentally, is true of T.V.

The following morning [Wednesday 23 May] I had to do a T.V. programme at an unearthly hour. I had to be there at about 7.45 and again it was the same sort of business, very informal; you go and sit down with some well-known personality. In this case it was a man called Will Rogers, Junior, and he asks you questions and you reply, and then there's a commercial, then they put you on again and ask you a few more questions and so on. Well that's about all I think I need to say about the U.S. trip. I don't think there's very much doubt from the public relations angle it was abundantly worthwhile. I got a good Press here, and fortunately the big T.V. programme 'Meet the Press' which was the sort of highlight of the whole visit went off well. Most people whom I met seemed to think that it had done the Labour Party in America a lot of good, though of course, it was an easy wicket because after the B. and K. dinner American opinion generally was extremely well disposed to me and to the Labour Party.

There are only two episodes which I think I need mention which have happened since our return from America. The Catlins[67] gave a lunch for the Mountbattens the other day [Tuesday 29 May]. This had been arranged a long time ahead; and we went along, finding there some other Labour people, including the Summerskills in particular. I sat opposite Mountbatten, and I must say I was not particularly impressed by him. The truth is I never have been greatly impressed by him, and I often wonder whether he isn't an overrated man. He came out with a great plan, which he said had been in his mind for some time, so far as defence went. But all that it really amounted to was the best argument he could think of for maintaining the Navy. He said in effect that we had to make up our minds to choose between being a World Power, in which case we had to have a Navy and Air Force, of course, and being a Land Power. We couldn't do both. And he was, in fact, really suggesting that we should give up bothering to have land forces in Europe and should rely instead on the Navy and the Air Force. I was not particularly impressed by this. Most people I know think it far more sensible to give up the Navy altogether. He argued that, on the contrary, the Navy was by far the best base from which to fly atom-bombers. He did say one interesting thing. He thought that Gruenther was by far the best and ablest soldier that he knew,

---

67 Professor (Sir) George Catlin was the husband of Vera Brittain the writer, and the father of Mrs Shirley Williams the politician. An Englishman, he taught at Cornell and McGill Universities, and knew a number of Labour Party leaders.

despite the fact that he had really had no experience, or practically no experience, of active service. I told him what Gruenther had said about conscription, which I think he was rather surprised to hear. But, on the whole, the lunch, was, I thought, rather a ghastly failure. Dora at her end of the table complained even more than I did, and as for Edith [Summerskill] and Mrs Catlin they apparently also complained. Mrs Catlin is a pacifist and therefore not particularly interested in hearing Mountbatten put forward his views on defence and Edith, I think, was just annoyed because Mountbatten did all the talking and she hardly got a word in.

The other episode was a lunch on Saturday last [2 June], where I met Malik for the first time since the famous dinner. This was arranged by Arthur Henderson,[68] who had himself had lunch with Malik a few days ago. It appeared that at this lunch Malik had asked Henderson whether he thought the attacks on me, presumably including the attacks in *Pravda*, were doing me any harm, and Henderson, according to his own story, had said that Malik had better make up his mind that I was going to remain Leader of the Labour Party for probably the next 15 or 20 years and that it was very likely indeed that I should be Prime Minister within the next three and that, therefore, they would do as well to have good relations with me. Henderson had understood that Malik was going to Moscow on Sunday, and thought that it would be a good plan if I were to see him before he went. He therefore arranged this lunch, which was given by Lord Inman, a wealthy Labour peer, in a flat in St James's Court.[69] In fact, when Malik arrived, he explained that he was not, after all, going back to Moscow. He said that the change of plan had nothing to do with Molotov's dismissal as Foreign Minister [on 1 June], though I strongly suspect, all the same, that it had. Anyway, the lunch was a very good one and the conversation started. For a great part of the time it was about disarmament and it went round and round and round as it always does with Malik. I had the same experience with him at David Astor's and also at the Polish Ambassador's some months ago.[70] The only difference is that the Russian line has slightly changed as so indeed has the line of the West.

However, after a bit, the famous dinner was brought up. It was really

68 Son of Labour's Foreign Secretary, 1929–31, and himself Secretary for Air 1947–51. He was an M.P. 1923–4, 1929–31, 1935–66, and held minor offices 1942–7.
69 Inman (1892–1979) was President of the Charing Cross Hospital. Attlee made him Lord Privy Seal in 1947, and it was said that M.P.s asked for new Cabinet Ministers to meet the P.L.P. so that they could be recognised. Inman held office for less than six months.
70 See above, pp. 413, 439–40.

introduced by Will Henderson, Lord Henderson, Arthur's brother,[71] who was there as well and who did it quite deliberately (I think), hoping that perhaps it would clear the air. I can't say that it was a very satisfactory conversation. The only interesting thing was that Malik said that B. and K. after our meeting at Claridges had been very pleased and that everything had been perfect. I then said, why had they on returning to Moscow made these attacks? And continued the attacks in the Press? Malik said something about the[ir] having read in the British Press that we were going to publish an account of the dinner. Now this was plainly untrue. What happened, as I told him, was that we had warned them at Claridges that we would do this if they published anything. It is true that at a later stage there were references in the Press to the fact that we had a verbatim account of the whole business, but as far as I recollect, these did not appear until after B. and K. had made their attack on us on returning to Moscow. So it still remains something of a mystery as to why they changed round. Maybe they just thought it over, maybe they were upset by the weekend Press, but if they had been upset by what I said on the I.T.V. News on that Friday evening, Malik surely would have said so because it was an obvious point for him to make. It is very queer that he should have referred to these wholly imaginary references to our verbatim account of the proceedings. He also seemed to have the idea I had attacked them a great deal in America, which was indeed quite untrue. I was most restrained in my comments there. And I replied to all this. I also told him pretty frankly what we thought of Mr K's two speeches at the dinner. I said I thought he ought to know that, because not all the feeling was on one side in this matter. However, I continually reiterated that we wanted good relations and that we drew a sharp distinction between relations with the Communist Party on the one side and the Soviet Government on the other. On this Malik was entirely in agreement. Indeed, he said that they did not wish to bring in ideological considerations into their negotiations and discussions with other Governments. However, he kept coming back to the point, why had we not discussed the things that really mattered, why had we concentrated on this one item. I pointed out that, of course, we had no chance to discuss anything else because of K's very lengthy speech. I rather liked the man they [he?] had with him, who was their disarmament expert and who seemed to me to be a good deal more reasonable than Malik. Incidentally, I kept on reminding him of the very successful talks we had had with Malenkov, so that he could not possibly say that I was anti-Soviet in any way. I understand that as he went downstairs, he complained to Arthur Henderson that it was a pity the

71 A journalist, and M.P. 1923–4, 1929–31. He was Foreign Under-Secretary 1948–51, and on the Parliamentary Committee as a peer, 1952–5.

conversation had got on to these controversial matters, and he objected to Willy Henderson having brought them up. It is very difficult to know what to make of all this. On the whole, however, I think it was just as well that he should hear from me exactly what I thought about the whole thing, though I doubt very much if anything will come of it.

[Dictated Saturday, 14 July 1956]

It is about six weeks since I did any diary, and consequently it is much more difficult to remember what actually happened. During this period, there has been the [visit of former President] Truman, the Commonwealth Prime Ministers Conference, some developments within the Party and one rather interesting conversation with Prince Bernhard of the Netherlands.

President Truman came fully up to expectations. He looked extra-ordinarily well for 72 and struck me as being a much firmer, stronger man than his pictures implied, though, indeed, his career showed this clearly enough. He was extremely pleasant to me personally, and, though I did not have much time to talk to him at the bigger receptions, when we met at the American Embassy [on 19 June] for instance, nevertheless he went out of his way to arrange a more intimate gathering. I was just wondering whether we ought to ask him to dinner in the House of Commons when Joe Godson, of the American Embassy, came along with a message from Truman saying that he would like to entertain me and one or two other leading Labour people to lunch [on Monday 25 June]. Joe and I discussed possible names and decided on about three or four people from the Party: Jim Griffiths, Alf Robens, myself, and Tom Williamson, Tewson and Harry Douglass from the Trade Union side. It was a very pleasant lunch and gave me a chance of saying to Truman the kind of thing which I had been talking about in America, namely the danger of the break-up of NATO and the enormous importance of the West working more closely together. We talked a little about the American Election and he more or less whispered to me that he hoped Harriman would get the Democratic nomination, though, of course, he pledged me to secrecy on this. He was very much against Kefauver and regarded him as bogus.[72] He was quite friendly to Stevenson though, as I have said, he obviously preferred Harriman. He appeared to have every intention of taking an active part in the campaign himself and gave the impression of being extremely optimistic.

72 Senator Estes Kefauver of Tennessee had won early primaries against Truman himself in 1952. He tried again for the Democratic presidential nomination in 1956, and was eventually nominated for Vice-President (narrowly defeating Senator John F. Kennedy).

The Commonwealth Prime Ministers Conference also brought with it a tremendous number of social functions, dinner at the Palace one evening, followed by dinner at 10 Downing Street the next. The contrast between them was really most remarkable. At the Palace [on 27 June] the whole thing was so formal and, as far as I was concerned, it was impossible to enjoy it. There was no reception before dinner; you just stood around until the Royal Family were ready to receive you, and then you all troop in and shake hands, after which, with about five minutes for a glass of sherry, you go into the Dining Room (the Dining Hall, rather), you have your dinner and, of course, whether you enjoyed it or not depends principally on whom you sat next to. I haven't had very good luck in that way recently. After dinner, the best part of it begins which is when the men are left alone and you do get a chance of wandering around and talking to other people, but then when you go in to join the ladies with varied Royalty scattered around everything again seems to become rather formal and frankly, on this occasion, I thought it was exceptionally boring. On the other hand at No. 10 the absence of Royalty also involved an absence of restraint and I had a very friendly and interesting conversation with Menzies [Prime Minister of Australia] who asked if I and some of my Labour friends would go and see him some time or have a meal with him. In fact it never came off, but I think he meant it quite genuinely. I have always liked him, although he is a Tory, but he has a pleasant, slightly cynical, but extremely shrewd attitude to politics.

Another episode in the Conference, or rather in the social functions accompanying it, has been Mr Nehru's behaviour. He and Mr Holland, the Prime Minister of New Zealand, received the Freedom of the City [on Tuesday 3 July]. There was the usual ceremony before lunch, which went off quite smoothly, except that Dora and I and the Attlees, to whom we had given a lift, arrived late and had to sort of steal in by the back door, instead of being introduced properly. We then all went along to the Mansion House for lunch. Fortunately for myself, I slipped away before the after-lunch speeches with R.A. Butler, on the excuse that we had to be in the House of Commons. It was just as well for me because Nehru then proceeded to speak for about 50 minutes. Dora was extremely bored by it all and, I gathered, [so] were most other people; they didn't get away from the Mansion House until nearly 4 o'c.

We had a similar experience on the following day, when I had to go to an India League Reception for Nehru and say a few words as Leader of the Opposition. Clem Davies, the Leader of the Liberal Party was there, and so was Selwyn Lloyd, the Foreign Secretary. We each said our little piece to an audience consisting mostly of Indians who were sitting on the floor in the St Pancras Town Hall, there being a buffet ready with, presumably, drinks or tea or sandwiches or something on one side of the

Hall. We all, of course, said much the same thing in praise of Nehru. He then got up and spoke for one hour and ten minutes. Remember this was a Reception, and presumably the idea was that there should be a general mixing-up together, but it wasn't his idea. Admittedly, they were mostly Indians, and he wanted to talk to them. What he said was not particularly interesting, certainly nothing sensational, nor was it particularly well said. There was one odd interchange between Nehru and myself. I had said, in the course of my little speech, which was extremely friendly, that although the Congress Party was not a Socialist Party, nevertheless the Government of India was clearing [carrying?] out definitely Socialist policy. Nehru seemed to be rather annoyed by this because in the course of his opening remarks he said, rather petulantly, that although they didn't call themselves Socialists, they accepted the ideas of Socialism and, he said, carried them out further than the British Socialist Party. He is a very arrogant man; I think that is one reason why he makes such long speeches. He really thinks everyone wants to listen to them. He is a complete aristocrat and although of course he accepts, no doubt genuinely, democratic constitutions, nevertheless he certainly does not behave in what you would call a democratic way when it comes to mixing with other people. He is most aloof and almost unfriendly. Some two or three years ago Dora sat next to him at a lunch at No. 10 and had the greatest difficulty in getting him to talk at all. Incidentally during the course of his speech at the Mansion House apparently he hardly made any reference to Clem Attlee; there was a great deal about the Mountbattens, and even a reference to Winston [Churchill], as the Leader of the Opposition at the time when India got her independence – a friendly reference too. Seeing that Winston opposed independence with considerable vigour and violence, while Attlee carried it through, this seemed to be extraordinarily impolite, to say the least of it.

Another Prime Minister, who made a good impression, was Mohammed Ali of Pakistan. He used to be Finance Minister, and I knew him slightly then. He asked me to lunch with him alone, which I did [on Thursday 28 June] and we had quite a long, interesting talk about the situation in Pakistan. He asked me at the end if I could give him some information about Party organisation here. He struck me as an ex-Civil Servant who was rather enjoying going into politics; a gentle, highly intelligent and sensitive man. I am told that he made a very deep impression at the Conference itself.[73]

73 Chaudry Mohammed Ali resigned in disgust, and for good, two months later. He had been the first secretary-general of the Pakistan government. He was Finance Minister 1951–5 and Prime Minister 1955–6, utterly confusing infidel chroniclers by succeeding (respectively) Sir Ghulam Mohammed and Mr Mohammed Ali.

I also had a talk with Mike Pearson (Lester Pearson, as his real name is), the Canadian Foreign Secretary. I urged him strongly to sell to Israel the fighter aircraft for which they were asking. I rather got the impression that he was willing to do this, but that the Prime Minister, St Laurent, was doubtful about it.[74] Pearson said, not unreasonably, that he rather objected to the Americans telling everybody else to supply arms to Israel, but not doing so themselves.

The situation in the Party seems to be going reasonably well. We had a Party meeting on foreign policy [on Wednesday 4 July], which was regarded by almost everyone as the most successful for a long time. It was opened by Alf Robens with quite a fair statement of our attitude, but he went a good deal further on Germany than we wanted. Our attitude, I should say, was broadly that we stand by NATO and the Atlantic Alliance, we think that NATO should review the defence situation, we think that the Middle East should be handled on a U.N. basis, we think that the Government should be criticised about not doing more about disarmament, I mean international disarmament, for the line they have taken on manpower and also on insisting on political solutions coming first,[75] and on Germany. Alf wanted to go as far as saying that Germany really now ought to be neutralised. He denies this word, but he means it all the same if, by such neutralisation, i.e. abandoning NATO, re-unification can be achieved. He gets this idea, I am sure, from the German Socialists. However, in the main, the Party responded very well. We managed to draw the line clearly between those who wanted to break up NATO and those who wanted to stand by it. The former were in a tiny minority. An interesting feature of the Debate was that Crossman came out quite clearly and openly against the break-up of NATO in favour of maintaining the Alliance and I called on him deliberately to speak after Jennie Lee, which he did with great effect. Strachey also made a very good speech and the only ones on the other side were people like Zilliacus, in addition to Jennie Lee, and other more or less fellow-travelling types of the same kind. Another feature of the discussion was that it was extraordinarily harmonious and friendly and rational and there was no attempt even to challenge our recommendations at the end of it all.

74 Louis St Laurent, a lawyer, was Liberal Prime Minister of Canada 1948–57.
75 In 1953 the Western Powers had proposed fixed manpower ceilings for the armed forces of the leading countries once disarmament negotiations were complete; the Russians scored a propaganda success by putting forward the same ceilings for unconditional implementation. Since they would have meant American withdrawal from Europe, the Western countries insisted that political differences must be settled first; HG thought they should do more to explore whether disarmament agreements could assist political settlements. See H.C. Deb., vol. 551 cols. 682–90 (16.4.56) and vol. 552 cols. 833–8, 1628–30 (7 and 14.5.56).

The meeting on defence which followed a week later [on 11 July] did not go quite so well, partly because Dick Stokes, who opened it, did not put the case too well and partly because we didn't have as many good people talking sense as we did in foreign affairs. Nevertheless it went reasonably well, and I am fairly confident that we shall get the Committee's views accepted when the discussion is finished in the coming week.

One of the curious features of the situation at the moment is the behaviour of Nye Bevan. He has absented himself from most Party meetings altogether, and he very often keeps away from the Parliamentary Committee. He did not, for instance, turn up when the Committee was to talk about defence. I expected there would be a tremendous row and, well, nothing happened. Much the same was true of foreign affairs; he came in at one stage of the discussion but didn't come to the continuation. George Brown thinks, because of this, that he is not really trying to fight at the moment at all. It is possible that he is waiting until the question of the Treasurership is settled and wants to keep very low until then. It certainly makes things very much easier when he stays away. If he were to come back, still in the Committee, it would perhaps not matter a great deal, but it would certainly prolong the proceedings and it might be awkward for me. One of the difficulties is that a number of the members of the Committee, though well-intentioned, are very weak and timid people with some Left-Wing background and might be willing to follow him; people like Tony Greenwood and Tom Fraser, for instance. There were signs of this during the discussion on defence, although the majority took the more sensible line.

Another member of the Committee who causes me a bit of concern is James Callaghan. He is a most talented Parliamentarian and a man of very considerable charm, but he seems to me to have absolutely no philosophical basis. You never know what he is going to say. He is far too inclined to take a dem[agogic] line, though admittedly every now and then he will swing to the opposite. He is not really particularly intelligent; not nearly as intelligent as George Brown, and sometimes I think he takes a negative line just for the sheer cussedness. On the whole, of the five or six leading people, he is the least satisfactory at the moment, though, of course, he may improve.[76] Harold Wilson has behaved, as far as I can see, very well. He has handled the Finance Bill successfully; though there are complaints that he talks in the House far too much. But in the Committee he has been quite satisfactory and quite loyal to me.

Jim Griffiths is extraordinarily good and helpful and can be relied upon almost always to back me up. George Brown has been remarkably good.

76 HG's view of Callaghan did become much more favourable later, as his correspondence shows.

It is a pity that he still makes enemies so easily; but he has some very fine qualities. He is, first of all, extremely quick and intelligent – one notices that in conversation all the time. And, secondly, he certainly would not allow his views on a political issue to be diverted, as it were, for personal reasons. He will stand up in public and say what he thinks without regard to the consequences. In other words, he has a lot of courage and he has integrity. It is possible that he will turn out to be an intriguer if things go wrong, but at present I feel that he has more than anybody else in the Committee the qualities needed in the Government. Dick Stokes is very well-intentioned, but, again, is not really a clever man and is peculiarly bad at expressing himself. I do not think we can leave him in charge of defence. There is another difficulty. Although he is absolutely sound on policy, he can very easily be out-manoeuvred and, to some extent, I think, bullied by Crossman and Bevan.

Another man who is causing a good deal of worry at the moment is Frank Cousins, the newly-elected Secretary of the Transport and General Workers Union. He likes to think of himself as being Left-Wing and different from Deakin, and in the T.U.C. itself, I am told, he is continually criticising what you might call the more solid points of view. There again, I don't think he is really very clever. Indeed, I don't think he has really thought out the basic issues of policy at all, but it is much too early to write him off, and most people think that with a little more experience of office he will behave and talk more sensibly. Bill Webber, for instance, the Secretary of the Railway Clerks Union [the Transport Salaried Staffs], is quite satisfied with the way he is going, and thinks that before long he will be, so to speak, one of their group.

We have got through now our first three policy statements: housing, personal freedom and equality.[77] It is remarkable how peacefully and easily this has been accomplished. There was more trouble about the housing document than anything else, because the members of the Group were far too non-political and, therefore, put into the original draft a lot of things which would have been highly dangerous from an electoral point of view. However, we managed to get most of the proper changes made without great difficulty when the document came to the Policy Committee of the National Executive. The other two went through very easily, especially the one on equality, which I have been mostly responsible for. But it has not received a very good Press. It is a very funny thing how all the Tory papers, and even the Liberal papers, cannot bear to talk about the subject, and accuse anybody who does as being filled with envy. Nothing could be more absurd, because, in fact, the people who care most about equality in the Labour Party are the middle-class people, who

77 See *HG*, pp. 468–9 on the housing statement; and briefly, pp. 387 (personal freedom), 415–16 (equality), 471 (the policy statements generally).

are themselves quite well off. I am well aware, of course, that it has no great popular appeal, not as much of an appeal as security and jobs and better education, higher pensions, and so on. But I am convinced that, fundamentally, this is the thing that matters to Socialists more than anything else. If you don't feel strongly about equality, then I think it is very hard to be a genuine Socialist, and if we were to abandon this, then I think there would be very little left to distinguish us from the Tories.

I had an interesting talk with Prince Bernhard the other day. He came over here for one of the meetings of the Steering Committee of the Bilderberg Group.[78] I couldn't go to the meeting itself, but I went to lunch [on 12 June] and sat next to him. He talked with remarkable zeal about his own life and the life of the Royal Family in Britain. He thought that here they were much too constrained and not allowed to mix as much as they should. He had been astonished to find that when President Auriol of France[79] had asked him to shoot and asked Prince Philip also, he had gone without even bothering to consult anybody, but Winston [Churchill] had objected to Philip going. I gathered that in both cases they were supposed to take their wives, i.e. Queen Juliana and Queen Elizabeth.[80] Bernhard was astonished that this should be the case, though, of course, it is obvious that the movements of the Queen of England are more important than the movements of the Queen of Holland, a point which I did not think it was quite appropriate to make to him at lunch. He said he thought it was a great pity that [Princess] Margaret was not allowed to marry Peter Townsend.[81] He knew Peter Townsend and liked him very much. He said

78 The Bilderberg Group took its name from its first meeting in Holland in 1954. It was formed to allow periodical confidential discussions of long-term political, economic and strategic problems between the most prominent leaders – in politics, business, labour, the armed forces and the intellectual professions – from all the NATO countries and some others. Prince Bernhard of the Netherlands was chairman and Dr J.H. Retinger (above, p. 517) its first hon. secretary. HG belonged from the start; the British M.P.s on its steering committee were Denis Healey and Reginald Maudling.

79 Vincent Auriol, a French Socialist leader, was President from 1947 to 1953.

80 Prince Bernhard, born in Germany in 1911, married Princess Juliana in 1937 and commanded the Dutch forces in the liberation of Holland. She succeeded to the throne when her mother abdicated on her 50th anniversary as Queen in 1948, and herself abdicated in 1980.

81 Group Captain Townsend was born in Rangoon in 1914; his family knew HG's as their fathers were both in the I.C.S. (see above, p. 249 n. 46). After a distinguished war record he became Equerry to the King, 1944–52, and then to the Queen Mother and to Princess Margaret, whom he had accompanied to Queen Juliana's coronation in 1948. There was some disapproval of their marrying because he had divorced his first wife. In 1953 he was sent to Brussels as Air Attaché; in October 1955, Princess Margaret announced that she had resolved against the marriage; the Church of England and *The Times* commended a decision which much of the Press regretted.

it was so rare for people in that position to be so much in love. I said that I understood that Philip and the Duke of Windsor [the former King Edward VIII] had both been against it. But he, Bernhard, said that as far as he was concerned he had heard nothing of the kind. He also spoke of his eldest daughter, and said that if she carries on for 10 years, I suppose he meant without having to become Queen or getting married, she would be able to go all over the place, and would eventually be the best Queen Holland has ever had. He reminded me that all the girls had been educated at ordinary State schools. He thought that was absolutely right. I must say I found him a most sensible and intelligent man. He said that he had often spoken to the Queen and to Philip about the need for mixing far more with ordinary people.

Some time ago, the Colonial Secretary [Lennox-Boyd] announced at the end of a Cyprus debate that we in the Labour Government had also refused self-determination to the people of Cyprus.[82] In doing so, he referred to our telegrams or despatches which were secret. There was quite a hullabaloo at the time, and demands for their publication, etc., were made, particularly by Bevan. Now this is not the first time this Government have played a rather scurvy, shabby trick of this sort. Winston Churchill, when he was Prime Minister, in the course of a foreign affairs debate disclosed some telegram or other which had been sent by Bevin or Morrison in connection with the Korean war.[83] It is a very dangerous practice because, of course, it could involve diplomatic complications. The whole situation is, in fact, rather curious. When a new Government comes into power in Britain all the files in the Department are put away so that the new Ministers may not see the minutes of the old Ministers. Nor do they have any access to Cabinet conclusions, or records of Cabinet discussions or anything of this sort. They are, however, allowed to see the telegrams and despatches which have been sent between our Government and other foreign governments. But, up to now, however, they have treated such telegrams as completely confidential.

Now for the second time since 1951 disclosures have been made. What do we do about it? We started by pressing for publication in the House, then, rather more cautiously, when the Government offered to publish if we wanted publication, Jim Griffiths wisely asked if the Government would publish all the documents connected with the Cyprus problem, not only under the Labour Government, but also under the Conservative Government as well. Lennox-Boyd, the Colonial Secretary (or it may

82 Labour were criticising the Conservatives for doing so, and indeed for saying it would 'never' be conceded.
83 See above, pp. 311–12.

have been Selwyn Lloyd, the Foreign Secretary) refused to agree to this. Subsequently Selwyn Lloyd, however, wrote me a letter more or less saying again that they would be prepared to publish if we were. I thought it best to call a meeting of Clem [Attlee] and Herbert [Morrison], who had been Prime Minister and Foreign Secretary at the time, Jim Griffiths and myself. Herbert Morrison had also had a similar letter from Selwyn Lloyd and had obtained from the Foreign Office the actual documents. In fact what was involved was the record of a meeting between Herbert (just after he became Foreign Secretary) and the Greek Ambassador. The latter had come to see him and asked for a plebiscite in Cyprus on the issue of self-determination. Herbert who was no doubt briefed on the same lines as Bevin was briefed and the brief, incidentally, may have come from the Colonial Office, replied that we could not entertain any such suggestion and he went further than that. He went on to say that he did not see any prospect of a change in our attitude in the foreseeable future.

This was rather a difficult one for us, and we decided, without much difficulty, that we certainly would not agree to the publication of the telegram. I, therefore, drafted a reply, which will be sent off tomorrow, explaining that, while there may be something to be said for publishing a whole series of telegrams and other documents about the whole of the Cyprus problem, there is a good deal more to be said for not publishing any at all. There is nothing at all to be said for singling out one or two documents and publishing them out of their context. I have gone on, however, in this letter to point out that we are seriously concerned about this practice which has sprung up of referring to documents and giving away the contents of documents which are supposed to be secret. I have warned them that we shall certainly claim the right to do the same, as things are, when we get back into power. But I have offered to discuss the matter with the Foreign Secretary and the Prime Minister, since we don't really think this is a desirable practice, and it might be a good idea to have some kind of understanding between the Parties about it. It will be interesting to see how they react to this. But it is a serious thing and has some constitutional importance as well.

The Government does not seem to be doing much better. It gives a curious impression of disunity or lack of co-ordination, and I can only suppose that this is due to the Prime Minister's personality. He is a queer person; every now and then he treats me as though I were a member of the Government. For instance, he greeted me in the House the other day: 'Have you heard the good news? There's to be an enquiry into the steel strike.' Actually the news had been in the paper this morning, and no doubt it was good from the point of view of the nation, but he spoke urgently, as though I were one of his closest colleagues. Very odd altogether. On the other hand, he is in the House of Commons very often petulant and undoubtedly resentful of criticism[84] . . .

Going back for a moment to the Commonwealth Conference, I am told that Menzies and Nehru don't get on at all well. At the Australia Club dinner, where Menzies was the chief guest, he made an obvious and somewhat slighting reference to Nehru on more than one occasion. Quite early in his speech he said, 'I shan't be speaking for more than about 50 minutes, which seems to be nowadays the custom' – clearly Nehru was what he was thinking of then, and he then went on to make a strong speech about the Commonwealth, arguing that we really must have something in common, otherwise the thing made no sense at all. This was obviously in answer to Nehru's Commonwealth speech, which was, as one would suppose, much vaguer because India's links with the Commonwealth are so much slighter and because she does not agree with the British and, incidentally, the Australian foreign policy. I must say that Menzies is a very good speaker. He was most witty, as well as quite impressive in the kind of appeal that he made. I found myself at that dinner sitting next to a young parson who has just become the Vicar of St Martins-in-the-Field.[85] He had one of those deep Welsh voices which must be such a help in the church. He was obviously sympathetic to Labour and asked me a lot of questions about Parliament and how we managed. No doubt we shall meet again.

We had a small Trade Union dinner party for *Forward* last night. Frank Cousins, Bill Webber, Tom Williamson and Charlie Geddes, as well as Jack Diamond, myself and Francis Williams, who is going to edit it, were present.[86] It was quite successful. The four Trade Union leaders all agreed to place orders for the paper of what one hopes will be quite a substantial character and generally to support it. At one point I had to come in rather vehemently to make it plain that we could not just stand aside and try to be above the battle all the time, and that if we really

84 He was quite unused to it. Before becoming Prime Minister he had made his whole career as a specialist in foreign affairs where his approach, both before and after the war, had gained him a good deal of Labour sympathy.
85 The Revd. Austen Williams is still at St Martin's in 1983.
86 Francis Williams, who had known HG from the early days of XYZ (above, p. 447 n.) edited Labour's official paper the *Daily Herald* from 1936–40, and was Attlee's public relations adviser 1945–7. He edited *Forward* 1956–60 when it merged with *Socialist Commentary*, and wrote about it in his autobiography *Nothing So Strange* (Cassell, 1970), pp. 309–13. HG persuaded him to take a life peerage in 1962.

wanted to counter *Tribune* and the Communists generally, we must throw our weight behind the paper. I also urged that there should be a more direct Trade Union association in the shape of one Trade Union, one member of the General Council of the T.U.C. on the . . . [next page missing]

CHAPTER 10

SUEZ

[By the summer of 1956 the West was taking alarm at the ambitions of Egypt's President Nasser: his sponsorship of Arab nationalists from the Atlantic to the Persian Gulf, his subversion of traditionalist Arab regimes, and his hostility to Israel whose shipping, in defiance of the 1888 convention and a U.N. resolution, he barred from the Suez Canal. For Eden, the last straw was General Glubb's dismissal by the King of Jordan; for Dulles, it was Nasser's big purchases of Czech arms. On 19 July the United States abruptly withdrew her promised support for building the Aswan High Dam to promote Egyptian economic development. A week later, without notice or negotiation, Nasser seized the Canal installations by night; in manner even more than substance, it was a blatant challenge to the Western powers. Bevan later remarked: 'if the sending of one's police and soldiers into the darkness of the night to seize somebody else's property is nationalisation, Ali Baba used the wrong terminology.'

Gaitskell's views did not shift. Britain had a major legitimate interest in the Canal, for most of her oil came through it and nearly half the ships using it were British. While nationalisation alone gave no justification for imposing an international solution by force, the manner in which Nasser had acted showed he had an ulterior aim: to score a prestige triumph over the West and so promote the expansion of Arab nationalism – or the aggrandisement of Egypt. Gaitskell disapproved of ambitious military dictators, and sympathised with the Israelis, like most Labour people since the 1930s. But any action to block Nasser's expansionism needed American backing. So did the economic pressure which he hoped would bring Nasser to the negotiating table. That policy might have worked in 1956, when Britain and France enjoyed the good will of most other countries and particularly the United States. Developments after the period of the Diary, outlined briefly in this introduction, isolated them totally and deprived that policy of any chance of success.

Gaitskell thought an attack on Egypt, in defiance of the Commonwealth and the United States, would be inconceivably reckless – especially after the assurances he believed he had from a Prime Minister who had always seemed the incarnation of modern liberal Conservatism, devoted to an internationalist foreign policy backed by domestic bipartisanship. All his speeches during the crisis therefore put precisely the same point of view, but with an emphasis that changed with the situation. On 2 August he sought to prevent his own party becoming Nasser's apologists, and so stimulating both antagonism at home and intransigence in Egypt. On 12 September he feared an immediate naval confrontation in the Canal, and concentrated on demanding a reference to the U.N. instead. On 4 November, after the British and French Governments had sent Egypt an ultimatum and vetoed an American resolution in the U.N., he denounced their 'criminal folly' which could lead only to catastrophe.

Both the Conservative press and Gaitskell's Labour enemies propagated the myth that he had supported Eden's policy of using force, but changed his mind because of a Labour revolt. It was quite false. His views, right or wrong, reflected his own judgment. He never hinted either that Labour might support seizing the Canal by force, or that he personally favoured doing so. Instead he said exactly the opposite in the House itself, and then, before any breath of Labour criticism had reached him, gave Eden three separate private warnings.

The crucial issue was whether or not to impose international control of the Canal on Egypt by force. A control scheme was agreed in August 1956 by the conference of eighteen user nations, mostly small and some from the Third World. When Nasser rejected it, the U.N. became a field for tactical manoeuvre. The British and French Governments proposed to go to the Security Council, expecting a Soviet veto and intending then to attack Egypt. Dulles suggested instead a new Suez Canal Users Association which, hoping to commit the United States to oppose Egypt, Eden accepted – though he alarmed Parliament by an apparent threat to provoke a clash, which he then appeared to withdraw.

The danger of war was not over. Gaitskell, though apprehensive, was distracted from public affairs by his mother's death on 14 October; and he could not believe that any British Administration would embark on so crazy an adventure in 1956. He never conceived of a sick but stubborn Prime Minister rigorously excluding all unwelcome news or views. Eden's colleagues, senior officials and British Ambassadors were kept in the dark; communications with Washingon were cut; the angry Commonwealth countries were told nothing. Eden and Macmillan relied on intuition to predict the response abroad, and then, after the invasion, expressed pained surprise at the furious reactions they had inexcusably misjudged.

When the invasion finally came, Gaitskell believed that Eden had deliberately misled him, and his indignant condemnation of the policy was sharpened by an angry sense of personal betrayal. Aware of the divisions in the Cabinet, in his broadcast denunciation he appealed to dissident Conservatives to overthrow the Prime Minister. Probably he hoped that a senior Minister would resign to lead the revolt; when none did so, the appeal proved counter-productive and rallied waverers to Eden. Yet, if he had omitted it, the outcome would no doubt have been the same.

Like all political leaders who condemn the catastrophic military adventures of their governments, he met the most virulent hostility – especially

when Eden's policy visibly collapsed and frustrated Conservatives eagerly
hunted for scapegoats. 'The Americans come first with the Labour Party
a close second,' wrote Gaitskell; and a strange by-product of Suez was an
extraordinary press campaign, begun in the Beaverbrook press, praising
Bevan at Gaitskell's expense. Yet far from reviving the conflict between
the former rivals, the crisis consolidated their rapprochement, for they
agreed from the very start. In both big foreign affairs rows – first the
Russian visit, then Suez – Bevan had supported rather than embarrassed
Gaitskell; 1956 ended with Bevan as Labour's foreign affairs spokesman.

Harold Macmillan took over the leadership of an unhappy party at an
unpopular moment, with the Conservatives in a violently anti-American
and resentful mood, British foreign policy in ruins, and the economy hard
hit. In restoring Conservative unity and morale he displayed brilliant
political leadership. Yet in May 1957, when the Government advised
British shipping to return to the Canal on Nasser's terms, the full folly of
the fire-eaters was exposed. The show of military force had demonstrated
Britain's political impotence, and in doing so had destroyed a negotiating
position which had once been quite strong. Suez was soon seen as Britain's
last imperial fling, both displaying and accelerating her decline. In default
of the military power she could no longer wield, Britain might still have
exercised considerable political influence; Suez undermined it both in the
Middle East and generally. The Government's policy thus led swiftly to
the total disaster Gaitskell had foreseen. But the Conservatives saved
themselves by sacrificing their Prime Minister, and it was the Labour
leaders who suffered politically from it; after May 1957 Macmillan's
government was secure for the rest of that Parliament.]

Diary [Dictated on Thursday 26 July 1956]

During the past fortnight or so the King of Iraq has been here and there
have been various functions: one at Buckingham Palace, another at the
Iraq Embassy and a third this evening at No. 10 Downing Street. The
King, who is a boy of 21, brought with him the Crown Prince, his uncle,
and also Nuri es-Said, the old Statesman, now aged 67, who has been
Prime Minister of Iraq on and off for the last 30 years.[1] Dora and I went to
the first two functions. The third was a men only affair, and I was there

1 Crown Prince Abdul Illah had been Regent 1939–53 during the minority of his
nephew King Faisal II. General Nuri es-Said headed 7 Iraqi governments
between 1930 and March 1958 when he became Prime Minister of the new
Federation of Iraq and Jordan. All three were to be murdered in the military
coup in Baghdad on 14 July 1958.

tonight. The dinner at the Palace [on Monday 16 July] was rather more pleasant than the Commonwealth Prime Ministers' dinner. It was not smaller – it was a State Banquet – but somehow or other it was a little less formal, and we both enjoyed ourselves a certain amount. The Iraqis certainly seemed to put themselves out to make themselves pleasant to us – I mean to Dora and myself. At the first party, at the Palace, Nuri es-Said asked me to come to Iraq, bring as many people as I liked, and they would pay for everything. They wanted me to see the country, etc., etc. On the second occasion, the Chargé d'Affaires at the Embassy, a rather nice man called Askari, not apparently knowing that I had talked to Nuri the night before, said he had a special message from the Prime Minister: they wanted Dora and myself to come as their guests, bringing with me at least other selected friends. And, subsequently, the King and the Crown Prince also said that they hoped that we were coming to Iraq, so we shall probably go next Spring. I had some talk with the Crown Prince at the Embassy Party about the political situation. I found him quite reasonable. I asked him for his views on Nasser, but on this he was rather cautious. As to Jordan, he said the situation was dangerous. 'They may go and do something silly with Israel and attack them, and then we shall get drawn in, which is rather worrying'.

But the most dramatic moment was tonight at the dinner at No. 10. At about 10.45 I was sitting next to the King talking to him in one of the apartments, with the Lord Chancellor [Kilmuir] sitting near. We had been talking away for some time about this and that, when Eden came up and said, 'I want you to know – and I think the Opposition should know as well – what Nasser has done tonight. He has made a speech announcing that he is going ahead with the Aswan Dam, that they cannot get any foreign money, but that, nevertheless, they are going ahead, and, in order to finance it, they are taking over the Suez Canal Company, and will collect the dues which the Company receives from ships using the Canal'. I asked if he had taken action in support of this. Eden said that he understood that the Egyptian police had taken over the offices and the buildings of the Company already. A little later, Eden corrected what he had said and added that Nasser had apparently also indicated that he was going to increase the dues very substantially in order to raise the money for the Dam. Naturally, this was a somewhat dramatic thing to say just at this moment. I asked him what he was going to do. He said he was getting hold of the American Ambassador immediately. He thought perhaps they ought to take it to the Security Council, and we then had a few moments conversation about the consequences, Selwyn Lloyd the Foreign Secretary standing near.

I said, 'Supposing Nasser doesn't take any notice?' Whereupon Selwyn said, 'Well, I suppose in that case the old-fashioned ultimatum will be necessary'. I said that I thought they ought to act quickly, whatever they did, and that as far as Great Britain was concerned, public opinion would almost certainly be behind them. But I also added that they must get America into line. This should not be difficult, since, after all, the Americans had themselves precipitated this by their decision to withdraw all financial assistance for the Aswan Dam.[2] There was some discussion about what the Russians might do. Evidently, said Eden, they had not provided the money, but, he said, they may, of course, back them [the Egyptians] up on this. I said that I was not so sure, especially if they have to pay the higher dues themselves on their own ships. Moreover, they wanted to be with the big boys now, and it might not suit their policy to support Egypt. In a half-joking way, I said, since the King and Crown Prince were both standing there, 'What do you think about it?' The Crown Prince rather wittily replied, after a bit, 'We had better send for our Prime Minister too – that's the constitutional position'. Whereupon there was general laughter.

Earlier in the evening, I had had a long talk with Nuri es-Said about Israel and one or two other things. I was sitting next to him at dinner, and he started the conversation himself. He was fairly reasonable. He said that it was essential that Israel should make some kind of gesture so that talks could begin. He wanted talks, if only they would indicate by some gesture or other that they really wanted to live in peace with the Arab States that would make a big difference. I asked him what kind of gesture. He said that if only they would accept the 1947 United Nations' Resolutions *in principle*, although they could add that these were not practicable now, that would make a big difference.[3] I said that I thought that was very difficult for them, since, after all, the U.N. Resolutions were hopelessly out of date. The Arab States had rejected them in 1947 and, moreover, the Arab States had lost the war. In fact they had only been rescued by the intervention of the Great Powers from what would have been a much bigger Israeli victory. Moreover, since 1948, the population of Israel had increased by at least ¾ million Jews, who had come in from North Africa, Iraq, and other places. Nuri admitted all this, but still said that there must be some kind of gesture. He said that as far as he was concerned, he would certainly want good relations with Israel.

2 Aid in building the Dam, which it was hoped would transform the Egyptian economy, had been offered by the USA (and Britain) in December 1955. The U.S abruptly withdrew the offer on 19 July, alleging doubts about Egypt's economic prospects, particularly after her cotton crop had been pledged to Communist countries in return for arms (above, p. 486 and n.).
3 In December 1947 the U.N., against furious Arab opposition, had proposed partitioning Palestine into separate Arab and Jewish states, the latter much smaller than Israel became.

I asked him if he had ever met Ben-Gurion. He said 'Yes. Many years ago', but, he said, 'he explodes all the time'. Sharett, he said, is much better. I said that I agreed with that, and that I hoped Sharett would, in fact, come back before long. But, at the same time, I said that Ben-Gurion was a real man, a real personality. Nuri also complained about the map which he said existed in the Knesset, showing the spread of the Jewish State right up to the Euphrates. I said that I had been to the Knesset, but never seen this map there.[4] This is a familiar complaint of the Arabs, and I very much doubt if it has any foundation at all. I did, however, feel that as far as Nuri was concerned, he would genuinely like a settlement with Israel, and would be prepared to try and get it with a little help from the Israelis. He was also quite realistic about the 1948/9 war. Naturally we did not agree on Israel, but the conversation was very amicable.

He then said he wanted to speak about another subject with me, namely the Baghdad Pact. After he had explained how it had come to be formed, that the Iraqis themselves had wanted protection against Russia and had therefore approached the Turks and then the Persians and the Pakistanis had come in, I interrupted and explained to him that we did not oppose the Baghdad Pact, but that we did oppose the way in which the Government – the U.K. Government – had declared that the Baghdad Pact was the basis of the whole Middle East policy. I drew a distinction between the so-called Northern Tier Agreement, which was a defensive alliance against Russia, and the attempt to impose British influence through the Baghdad Pact on the Middle East as a whole, and I pointed to the difficulties which this had created with Jordan and with Egypt. But I said that as far as defence against Russia is concerned, you can rely completely on us – meaning the Labour Party. He was very grateful for this, and I rubbed it in by saying that, after all, he must have known that on Tuesday of this week I was attacking the Government because of their failure to maintain the strength of NATO and because they were allowing it to disintegrate. In fact, I said that as far as taking a strong line with the Russians is concerned you would find that we are really much better than the Government. After all, think of the B. & K. visit, who was it who really gave them a tough time? It was the Labour Party. Nuri was quite emotional when I said all this and clasped my hand warmly and said 'You have made me so happy. I am so pleased'. He really seemed to think that we were not sufficiently staunch anti-Communists and that this was in some way mixed up with our lack of enthusiasm for the Baghdad Pact.

The only other episode at the dinner worth mentioning was a brief

---

4 The Knesset is the Israeli Parliament. Moshe Sharett, Foreign Minister 1948–56, had briefly been Prime Minister during Ben-Gurion's voluntary retirement for two years, 1954–5.

conversation I had with Eden about the changes at the top of the Civil Service. I said that I was a little surprised that [Sir] Roger Makins had been transferred to the Treasury. 'Well', said Eden, 'I will let you into a secret. It was Harold who wanted it.' Meaning, of course, Harold Macmillan. I am not altogether surprised at this. I had an idea that it must have been his initiative because of his contact with him [Makins] while he was Foreign Secretary and, no doubt, in the old days, during the war.[5]

There have been one or two other interesting developments in the last two or three weeks. We have had a tremendous discussion in the Party on defence and, in particular, manpower. The method of conducting this discussion could hardly have been more incoherent and unsatisfactory. For a variety of reasons, it was done to start with through a thing called the Tripartite Committee, on which the National Executive, the T.U.C. and the Parliamentary Labour Party were represented. But what made it even worse was that, owing to an accident, all sorts of people represented the Parliamentary Party who really shouldn't have done so. What happened was that two successive years' appointees were apparently allowed to remain on, or something of the kind. The initiative in this was probably taken by Dick Crossman rather rashly, and on one or two points I had to throw my weight about to prevent them adopting something really silly. In particular, when Bevan joined the Committee, again by accident, he shouldn't have been on it at all, he managed to bull-doze them into some very silly proposals for precise cuts in defence and for verbal amendments which played down the importance of NATO. However, eventually, chiefly owing to the hard work put in by George Brown and his influence with the T.U.C. representatives, the document that emerged was not too bad. We improved it further only after great arguments in the Parliamentary Committee, and at the Party meeting all went extremely well. In fact, at the moment, the truth is that the Party is much easier to deal with than the Parliamentary Committee, which is a reversal of the position two or three years ago.

The eventual outcome was a decision to call on the Government to make a plan for abolishing National Service, starting in 1958, to submit this plan to NATO for discussion and thereafter to make up their mind and decide one way or the other. On the whole Dick Crossman has really behaved very well throughout most of this; so long as he is kept on the right lines by somebody or other he plays up perfectly adequately. Bevan, of course, has been difficult, but we managed to overrule him in the Committee. Though there again, some members of the Committee are

5 Makins, on returning from the Washington Embassy, became Permanent Secretary of the Treasury. He had been on Macmillan's staff when the latter was Resident Minister in the Mediterranean, 1943–4.

particularly weak. The worst case is James Callaghan who, having criticised the document as not going far enough and having persistently argued for abolishing conscription without qualification, at the last meeting of all when we were settling the terms of the Motion to be debated and the names to be put on it, suddenly indicated that he had changed his view and that he thought that he was much more inclined to support George Wigg*, who had been, in the Party, the most persistent Right-Wing critic of the proposal. Incidentally, Wigg himself . . . only took the line against abolition of conscription quite late in the day.

Another person who has done well has been John Strachey [Shadow Secretary for War] who has been sensible, level-headed and very helpful indeed. Best of all has been the reaction of the Party. At the final meeting I had expected that we would certainly have amendments moved to insert a figure for the cut in defence. That is what the Left Wing have been demanding, particularly in view of the fact that Clem Davies, the Leader of the Liberal Party, has himself asked for a cut of £500 million. I had argued against this very strongly myself, and nobody even moved an amendment. The only amendments moved were one by George Wigg that we should make no change at all in our policy and simply stick to what we had said in February, which was no more than to complain that the Government had not put forward any plan for the abolition of National Service. This received only two votes – George Wigg and Herbert Morrison. The other amendment was one by Warbey – one of the Left Wingers – who did not want consultation with NATO, but simply wanted them informed. This, too, only had negligible support – perhaps half-a-dozen people voting for it. After all the troubles and tribulations of the last few years, this is by no means unsatisfactory. Of course the case is an uncertain one, but we can fairly argue that the present situation is an intolerable one and that the Government themselves have given repeated hints that they intend to bring conscription to an end. In fact, I fancy that they have got into great difficulties over this and that they are now backsliding fast.[6]

Bevan has rather come to the surface again recently. He has been attending the Committee meetings and the Party meetings and, as I have said, one can usually be sure that in the Committee meetings he will be somewhat obstreperous, always arguing, always talking too much and generally, though not always, arguing the wrong way. However, as I say, we managed to avoid any disaster this way, though I wish we had a rather

6 This forecast proved wrong. Duncan Sandys became Minister of Defence in 1957 and produced a drastic new policy, relying on the deterrent threat of massive nuclear retaliation, which included abolishing conscription. Labour deeply disliked it, but was embarrassed in its opposition by the unpopularity of conscription both electorally and within the Party and the unions.

stronger Committee. It will be an excellent thing when Frank Soskice gets back on it, as I think he is bound to next Autumn.[7]

The Foreign Affairs Debate [on 23 and 24 July] went off reasonably well. Eden made a curious speech in opening it; a very short, clever, quite sensible, but fairly easy analysis of the present situation, followed by two proposals: one relating to Germany, more or less on the lines that we wanted, i.e., to have another look at the problem of unification, linking it up with disarmament and a security pact for Europe and the acceptance of what we had been pressing for on the H-bomb tests, namely that the negotiations on this should take place separately. It was very well received and he got a good Press. But on the following day, when people began to realise how many questions he had left unanswered, the enthusiasm cooled perceptibly. Alf Robens spoke after Eden and did reasonably well. I must say that we had worked very hard to make sure that he didn't make the kind of speech he made at the Foreign Affairs Debate last February.[8] I was very nervous that he was going to say something on Germany that would commit the Party to the idea of a neutralised Germany and I went so far as to draft part of the statement myself to make sure that this would not happen. The worry about Alf is really that one needs to take all this trouble. He depends very heavily on people like Dick Crossman and Denis Healey for advice from them, and one is never quite sure what line he is going to take.

He also has a curious habit of raising awkward questions almost deliberately. We have been in a jam on the H-bomb tests. We have supported producing the bomb and, obviously, if you want to produce it, you must be able to test it. At the same time, we demanded the abolition of all tests. This was the position at the last Election and still is supposed to be the Party line. But I have managed to get the Front Bench away from that by getting them to ask for control rather than abolition of tests. I knew that sooner or later somebody was going to get worked up about this and ask why we were not demanding abolition, and, sure enough, this happened at one of the evening Party meetings a little while ago. We then had a discussion in the Parliamentary Committee of a rather acrimonious kind, at which I had the utmost difficulty in making them see how inconsistent the position of the Party was. It was clearly a subject which we might have to face up to, but which the leadership ought to avoid raising in Parliament because of our vulnerable position. Despite this, Alf Robens twice went out of his way to raise the matter in Supplementary

7 After his constituency was abolished in the 1955 redistribution, Soskice returned to the House at a by-election in July 1956, and to the Committee in November.

8 Above, pp. 455–8. For the July debate: 557 H.C. Deb. 37–47 (Eden), 47–62 (Robens).

Questions, although one would have supposed he would realise how awkward it was.[9]

I don't think there was anything malicious in this. I think he just simply did not understand the delicacy of the situation. It is really just the same with Germany. I had to point out to him several times that whatever he might think, it was dangerous to say certain things at the present time. However, he certainly did do better, and the Party, I think, was reasonably pleased with his speech. I spoke on the second day. It was not one of my best efforts; I spoke too long – 54 mins., and I was probably rather tired, though I said what I wanted to say, i.e., criticism of the Government for allowing the disintegration of NATO, criticism of their disarmament policy, backing up what Alf had said on Germany, and then lines of policy toward the uncommitted areas on more or less the same theme as at the speech I had made in America at the Garment Workers' Convention.[10]

[Dictated on Monday 30 July 1956]

The Suez situation again. On Friday morning last, that is, following the dinner at 10 Downing St, the Prime Minister made a statement in the House. I asked Jim Griffiths and Herbert Bowden [the Chief Whip] and Alf Robens to meet me beforehand. Actually Alf did not get there in time, but Dick Crossman and John Strachey walked in. We had a brief discussion. It was agreed that I should complain about Nasser's highhandedness and also suggest blocking the sterling balances. This is pretty well what happened in the House itself.[11] Eden made a reasonable statement, fairly cautious. I said rather firmly that we deeply deplored the high-handed and totally unjustified step taken by Nasser. Whereupon, of course, the Tories all cheered and our people, on the whole, seemed to be reasonably content. At any rate, there was no sign of any demonstration from the Left Wing or the Pacifists against me. The rest of the questions were rather taken up by the Suez Group on the Tory side and Reg Paget, who thinks very much the same as they do upon [this?]. Then we went off for the weekend.

On Monday [30 July] I summoned a meeting of the Parliamentary

9 HG's concern was proved well founded in the following May. New British tests made a parliamentary discussion unavoidable, and though his compromise on this most contentious subject satisfied the P.L.P., it left him dangerously open to criticism by Macmillan: see *HG*, pp. 453–4.

10 Above, p. 523; 557 H.C. Deb., cols. 223–42.

11 557 H.C. Deb, 777–80: 27.7.56.

Committee after lunch, to which I will refer in a moment. But I must mention the fact that I had lunch with Don Cook, the *New York Tribune* correspondent here.[12] He told me that the idea of the talks at the moment between the three Powers was to produce some kind of international system of control over the use of the Suez Canal under the United Nations. I said I thought this was a good idea. He was rather gloomy about what the Americans were likely to do. He gathered that [Under-Secretary] Murphy, who is representing them, is continually sending back for fresh instructions. He entirely agreed with me when I complained of the fact that the Americans had precipitated all this by withdrawing their offer on the Aswan Dam, and yet now seemed to have cold feet pretty badly. He thought it was all the electioneer fears. When I said I didn't see how a firm line by the United States could possibly do the Republicans any harm at the moment, he said 'Well, they don't think of it that way. All they know is that they have promised peace and prosperity, and that everything would be spoilt if there is no peace'.

The Parliamentary Committee was over quite quickly. We agreed without much difficulty that we should have to have a debate before Parliament rises, but that it would have to be a short one and would need very careful handling. On the point of substance, there was some anxiety about our going too far in a bellicose direction and it was felt important that we should stress exactly what our attitude was to nationalisation, as contrasted with the breaking of international agreements or concessions. Nothing much happened at Question Time. I thought it wise not to press Eden in view of the fact that talks were still going on, and he had undertaken to keep us informed. But Bessie Braddock asked very pointedly about the sale of arms to Egypt and Eden announced that all that had been stopped. He also said that the two destroyers that we had just sold them were being, or would be, detained.

In the course of the [Monday] afternoon Elath, the Israeli Ambassador, came to see me and we had a long and most interesting talk. He said that the immediate effect of Nasser's move was far more likely to be upon the Arab States than upon Israel. If he got away with it, so far as the Arab States were concerned his stock would rise enormously and the situation would become extremely dangerous for people like Nuri es-Said in Iraq. (Later on Gladwyn Jebb said much the same thing – that if Nasser got away with this, it would be the end of Nuri.) So far as Israel is concerned, there was no immediate danger, because it was unlikely, thought Elath, that Nasser would risk involving himself in war with Israel until he had straightened things out as far as the Suez Canal is concerned. But, in the long run, the situation would be highly dangerous for Israel,

12 He was head of the *Herald Tribune*'s London bureau, and had been one of its European correspondents since 1945.

because as soon as he felt himself strong enough, he would be certain to go in for what was his ultimate aim, which was the elimination of Israel. Elath said that the Commando raids from Jordan were, in fact, being organised by Egyptian officers, and he reminded me that in his [Nasser's] speech on Thursday he said openly for the first time 'our object is to destroy Israel'.

All this was likely to happen if he won the gamble on which he had embarked. On the other hand, if he lost, there was some risk that, in desperation, he might turn to aggression as well. Thus, whichever way one looked at it, Israel was now entering on her most critical period. There had been further talk about the possibility of a preventive war. This had been urged apparently in the Cabinet, but Elath assured me that the idea was once again rejected. He rather resented the fact that the Foreign Office had approached him urgently during the last 48 hours and begged him not to make any fuss either to thank them for what they were doing or to intervene in any way at all. He felt this was rather tactless of them, and assured them that he knew perfectly well that it would be a mistake to do anything of this kind and that all that he was anxious for was that they (the British Government) should win this battle.

He had heard rather gloomy news about Murphy, who apparently was putting forward the idea that both America and Russia should keep out of all this, and leave it to Britain and France alone. The position of Egypt financially was, he thought, pretty desperate. It was all nonsense for Nasser to talk about using the Suez Canal money to pay for the Aswan Dam. He would, in fact, need it merely to keep Egypt going on current account, so to speak. All the cotton had been sold to pay for the arms, and there was just nothing coming in at the moment. I then asked Elath what he thought we ought to do in present circumstances. He said it was essential that we should make Nasser see that this kind of thing did not pay, even if it involved some sacrifice to ourselves. He thought, therefore, we should adopt every kind of economic measure that was open to us. He mentioned the possibility of building a pipe line from Elath on the Gulf of Aqaba to Haifa, and in reply to a question from me, said that it would only take about 3 months to lay. Tankers could, therefore, come round from Basra and Abadan and Kuwait to Elath, the oil could go into the pipe line there, out at Haifa, where it could be taken up by other tankers. This seemed to me a rather good idea and one well worth pursuing.[13]

Apart, he said, from economic measures of this kind (and incidentally the fact that the Egyptians had so quickly withdrawn their first prohibition on exports to the sterling area showed their underlying weakness), it was, he thought, essential on the political side to show a firm front. This could

13 HG's speech in the debate of 2 August (cols. 1609–17) shows many traces of the influence of this conversation.

be done best by helping our friends, not only Israel but also, for instance, Iraq. Arms should be provided both for Israel and for the Baghdad Pact as well. Finally, as far as propaganda was concerned, this could be very greatly improved. It would be an excellent thing, if for instance, the station in Cyprus, instead of attacking Israel and France as they had done, were now to attack Nasser. Naval vessels might be sent to Haifa, on the one side, and to Basra on the other. A demonstration of this kind always helped. Finally, as to the danger of Russian intervention, he did not believe that this was really very great. He thought Russia really had been frightened by our insistence that we must have control of the oil in the Middle East, and that if necessary we would go to war to keep it. He did not think that they wanted to have a war in the Middle East. They were on the side line and would cheer the Egyptians along, but would take care not to get heavily involved themselves.

Shortly after this, Jim Griffiths and I went to see Eden at my request, because I thought we ought to make plain to him how we felt about the whole situation. I was a little concerned lest he might suppose that we would back force as a Party in the same way as the Suez rebels would back it, or were, indeed, demanding it. I said that this was not the case; that while, of course, there were certain circumstances in which force would be appropriate, it had to be in self-defence or, at any rate, in circumstances which could be properly justified before the United Nations. We could not follow the advice of people like Hugh Fraser who had been writing in the Sunday papers.[14] Eden said, rather contemptuously, 'Well, you surely don't believe that we are going to pursue Hugh Fraser's policy'. He thanked me for making the position clear and then told us something of the consultations up-to-date. The French were extremely good and very keen for firm action; the Americans were much less satisfactory. As far as the French were concerned, they wanted to be in with us in any display of force which there might be and indeed had managed to offer to produce not merely naval vessels and, presumably, aircraft, but also a parachute brigade and an armoured division. Eden said laughingly that he didn't know where they came from because he thought all the French troops were now in North Africa. On the question of arms for Israel, I gathered that the French were going to be encouraged to sell them some more Mystère fighters. At any rate, to my suggestion that we ought really to see that Israel got some more arms, but privately, Eden appeared to agree.

I gathered that there were going to be some troop movements in the near future of a precautionary kind because, said Eden, it was possible

14 (Sir) Hugh Fraser, a member of the militant Tory Right, was Conservative M.P. for Stone 1945–50, Stafford & Stone from 1950. He held junior office 1958–62, and was Secretary for Air 1962–4. He married Lady Antonia Pakenham, daughter of HG's old friends, in 1956.

that Nasser might do some foolish thing, and we had to be ready. He confirmed what Don Cook had told me, namely that their idea was – that is, [for?] the consultations – to put forward a proposal for international control of the Canal under the United Nations, I think, with the hope that Nasser will accept this. I said 'What happens if he doesn't? Do you then use force?' Eden said 'Well, I don't want to take that hurdle yet'. I had already made it plain, I may say, that I doubted whether we could support force merely on those grounds. Eden also said that he was seriously worried about the position of the British employees on the Canal, as Nasser had said in effect that if they left their jobs, they would be put in gaol. I gathered that this was one of the reasons for the movements of troops, and so on, which were taking place. We had very little difficulty in getting him to agree to a debate on Wednesday. We pointed out that, in fact, if we didn't organise a debate, it would take place on the adjournment and the Front Benches would be seriously embarrassed. It was far better, therefore, to take the debate officially and get on with it from the Front Bench and control it in this way. He agreed with this and the announcement will be made tomorrow. He promised to keep us in touch with any developments.

Later in the [same Monday] evening I took Sir Gladwyn Jebb out to dinner. He did not add very much to what I knew already. He told me that Pineau [the French Foreign Minister] had gone back to Paris that night, and confirmed more or less what I had already heard about the attitude of the French and the Americans. In fact, he was curiously unconstructive about the whole affair. Nevertheless, we spent quite a pleasant evening talking about this and that – in particular Roger Makins' (who, of course, has always been Gladwyn's great rival) appointment to the Treasury, which Gladwyn obviously very much approved of.

One other rather curious remark was made during the day. Don Cook told me that Byroade, who had been American Ambassador in Cairo, was not moved because of any change of policy in the United States . . . We should not, therefore, take the movements of these two very seriously. When I say 'these two', I mean Byroade and Allen, who has been in the State Department, and who were supposed to be pro-Nasser and anti-British.[15] Gladwyn Jebb, on the other hand, said to me later in the evening that he could not believe there had been no change in American policy. He had never heard the story about Byroade and, after all, what

15 Henry A. Byroade had just become U.S. Ambassador to South Africa. He had been on secondment from the Army to the State Department until 1952, and was then Assistant Secretary for State for Near Eastern, South African and African Affairs until appointed to Cairo in 1955. George V. Allen, his successor in the Departmental post 1955–6, had previously been Ambassador to Iran, Yugoslavia and India, and had just been sent to Greece.

with the cancellation of the loan for the Dam, the change of the two officials and the rumours about Saudi Arabia, there seemed to be pretty good evidence. Of course, the trouble about American foreign policy is that it is so difficult to be sure what line they are really taking when it comes to the Middle East.

[Dictated on Thursday and Friday, 2 and 3 August 1956]

The last dictating was on Monday night. On Tuesday morning we had a meeting with the Labour Peers. I had arranged this after myself having had a discussion with them about a fortnight ago [on 17 July]. At the meeting I had with them, I was deeply impressed first by their feelings, their very strong feelings of frustration and discontent about their present situation, and, secondly, by the serious way in which they took the project of the House of Lords reform. I thought in the circumstances, the best plan was to have a joint meeting between the Labour peers and the Parliamentary Committee, and this is the one which took place on Tuesday morning [31 July]. Unfortunately, there was a very bad turn up from the Parliamentary Committee side. To begin with, there was only Jim Griffiths, myself, [Herbert Bowden] the Chief Whip and Kenneth Younger. After a bit, Edith Summerskill came in, and she was followed later by Tom Fraser, Alf Robens and Harold Wilson – half the elected members were actually missing. The meeting itself followed much the same pattern as the discussion that I had had with them a fortnight before. They made their case extremely well. They pointed out that most of them had been in the Party for many years and had only gone into the House of Lords because they had been asked to by the Prime Minister – Attlee – that they worked very hard there for nothing at all, and that on top of that, they were treated with contempt, if not abuse, by other members of the Party, especially in the House of Commons. This was simply not good enough. In the short run, two things were needed: first, they must be paid some expenses and, secondly, they must have some fresh blood, so that the burden could be more widely spread.

They were all pretty convinced that the Government intend, in the next Session of Parliament, to introduce a reform measure. Equally they were all convinced that it was no use the Labour Party going on taking its head in the sand attitude about reform. It was simply impossible to leave things as they were, because the Government were not going to do that. The Labour Party really must face up to the question of policy as regards a second Chamber. If the Party was against a second Chamber, well and good. Then, of course, all reforms would be pointless and abolition was the only solution. But most of the members of the House of Lords, including Attlee in particular, were strongly of the opinion that a second Chamber would be necessary. That happens also to be my view. If this was the case, then we could no longer expect that we could continue with the House of Lords as it is now, and we had to make up our minds what sort of a second Chamber we wanted. Only when we had done this, would we be in a position to decide what line to take when the Government brought in their new measure. All this was explained by many of the Labour peers present. I thought Listowel was exceptionally clear and cogent about it and Pethick-Lawrence, although he is 84 was, as usual, very impressive. Jack Lawson, now Lord Lawson, gave us a really moving picture of his own financial position. He said that had it not been for the fact that he was Chairman of the Parks Commission and, therefore, got an income from that, it would have been impossible for him ever to come to London at all – he could not have afforded it. He would have had to stay in Durham all the time, and could not have taken part in any of the proceedings of the House of Lords.[16]

The only other episode worth mentioning at this meeting was a rather extraordinary scene between Edith Summerskill and Alf Robens. Edith spoke rather later in the morning, and made a rather querulous speech in which, in a sense, she chose to attack the peers, while, at the same time, agreeing that reform was essential. The more I see of her, the less my opinion of her. She is extremely emotional, she does not listen very carefully, she is not really intelligent, she is governed almost wholly by some association in her mind. I think what set her off on this occasion was that, apart from Pethick-Lawrence nobody had made any suggestion that there should be women peers. Alf Robens, however, took this as a very offensive speech and rushed to the rescue of the peers in an almost equally silly speech, saying that reform was not our business. We were not there to consider that. I had to intervene and try and smooth things over. But neither of them came out of it very well.

The same evening [31 July] we discussed in the Parliamentary Committee the proposal which I had thrown out in the morning, namely, that there should be some kind of a joint committee between the Parliamentary Committee and the Labour peers to work both on the question

16 Jack (Lord) Lawson (1881–1965) who worked as a miner from the age of 12, was M.P. for Chester-le-Street (Durham) 1919–49, held minor office in 1924 and 1929–31 (P.C. 1939–40), and was Secretary for War 1945–6. He was Vice-Chairman of the National Parks Commission 1949–57, and Lord Lieutenant of Durham 1949–58. On Lords Listowel and Pethick-Lawrence see above, p. 472 n. M.P.s were reluctant to agree to expenses for the peers when their own pay was so inadequate.

of their present situation and also on the question of reform. I was not surprised to find that those who had not been present in the morning were resistant to this idea. In particular, Bevan opposed it on the ground that it would leak out and it would be misunderstood. There was no need for us to think at all about the problem of the House of Lords until the Government introduced their measure. When they did, then we should be able to make up our minds at the time. He was backed up by Callaghan, who had not been there in the morning, who has a kind of artificial prejudice – I describe it as that because I do not feel it is in the least genuine – against the House of Lords. He was rather offensive to the peers who were present and I had to speak rather sharply to him. There was a long, long wrangle about this. Most of those who were there in the morning, with the exception of Kenneth Younger, were convinced that we ought to have the committee and must begin to think about reform. Dick Mitchison, who had not been there in the morning, also took the same view.[17] Eventually, I achieved a compromise; we agreed to a joint committee to look into the present and future position of the Labour peers. I proposed Jim Griffiths, Bevan and Mitchison should be our representatives. I was anxious to get Bevan heavily involved in this, because if we were going to have reform, it is important that he should not be given an opportunity of making trouble in the Party, which is apt to be highly emotional about the whole business. The real truth is that most of them haven't really thought out what they want at all or attempted to reconcile this with the practical possibilities.

The long discussion on the House of Lords question was, in a sense, a blessing in disguise, because it cut short very sharply the discussion on the Suez problem which followed. On this there was no great difficulty. I told them roughly what I proposed to say in the debate which, by then, we knew was not going to take place until Thursday, and there was no great disposition to argue with me. Bevan made a rather lengthy speech saying that all waterways like the Suez Canal should come under international control, and not only the Canal itself.

Meanwhile the Defence Debate had been taking place in the House of Commons. George Brown made an admirable speech. He spoke for rather too long – about an hour – but, personally, I listened to all of it with enjoyment. He gave a really masterful exposition of our case. He pulled no punches. He made it absolutely plain that we would stand by all our commitments. And he made a very good impression on the House, including some of our people who had been worried about our proposal to ask for a plan to abolish conscription, and might have abstained had it

17 G.R. (Lord) Mitchison (1890–1970) was M.P. for Kettering 1945–64 and an assiduous front-bench spokesman (P.C. 1956–64); he held junior office in the Lords 1964–6. In the 1930s HG was very friendly with him and his wife Naomi, the author.

not been for George's speech. Strachey, later in the Debate, also did well. In fact, I felt really pleased with the way the thing had gone; although the Suez crisis made it all look rather ridiculous, nevertheless our people – those two in particular – managed to handle it in such a way that we have come out of it with a much less mad [sic: bad] Press than at one time seemed likely.

One of the most absurd speeches was made by Shinwell. At the Party meeting, when we discussed this matter, he had come down in favour of the abolition of conscription, for which, indeed, he had been pressing for a very long time, over a period of two or three years. His main criticism at the Party meeting of the Committee's proposals was that we had not put in any figure for the cut in defence. He thought we ought to put in a large figure of something like £500 million. But, lo and behold, when it came to the speech in the House, he announced that he did not believe that we could abolish conscription in the time that we envisaged, and he did not see how we were going to make any economies in defence at all. I found it quite extraordinary that people can so blithely and cheerfully completely contradict themselves. George Wigg made an attack on the policy, and later abstained from the vote. But he at least had been criticising it for some time, though not originally when the Committee first met.[18]

That same evening I had a long talk with Frank Soskice about the Suez position. He was most helpful, and put me right on all the legal points, and agreed very much with the line which I proposed to take.

On the following day [Wednesday 1 August] I saw Denis Healey. To begin with I thought there was a bit of difference between us, and perhaps there is still in emphasis. He was inclined to be anti-Government and also less inclined to be worried about Nasser; more pacifist, more neutralist, shall I say, than I had expected. However, after a talk it soon transpired that there was no great difference between us. He readily admitted the great dangers if we did nothing to resist Nasser; he fully agreed that the prestige factor was very important and that the effect in the Middle East would be very serious. He also warmly supported my proposal for a pipe line across Israel, and he took the view that if we were to use force in an unjustifiable way, we would have the whole of the Middle East against us, and much of the rest of the world also. This would be extraordinarily serious and we really could not contemplate it. After a bit I made a rather good joke to epitomise the situation. I said 'The trouble with the Arabs is that if we fight them, they hate us, and if we don't fight them, they despise us.' I added 'This just about signifies the difference between the two Parties – the Tories dislike being despised most and we dislike being hated most.'

18 557 H.C. Deb. 1167–89 (Brown), 1205–16 (Shinwell), 1250–63 (Wigg), 1267–
68 (Strachey): 31.7.56.

I also had a talk [that day], accompanied by Jim Griffiths and the Chief Whip, with the so-called Foreign Affairs Steering Committee. They had asked, or rather some of them had asked, for a Party meeting. The Committee had turned it down on the ground that it was impracticable and, in any case, we didn't know what the Government were going to do. I decided, however, to ask this Committee to come along, partly in order to smooth them down and make them feel that they had been consulted. John Hynd, Warbey, Tony Benn*, as well as Denis [Healey], Kenneth [Younger] and Alf [Robens] turned up. I was not much impressed with what the three first had to say. It is extraordinary how they rush to the defence of any eastern country and how completely they ignore the fact that Nasser is a dictator. John Hynd, having been to the Arab States, instinctively seemed to side with Egypt, until I told him what Nuri es-Said had said the night the news came round, and how anxious he was that we would take a firm line with Nasser. This seemed to come as a complete shock to Hynd, which only goes to show that he is really rather a stupid man. As for Warbey, he is still fundamentally a softy, still fundamentally against using force in any circumstances, though there is some improvement there. Tony Benn, similarly, although talented in many ways, a good speaker and a man of ideas, had extraordinarily poor judgment. He is the last person in the world I would go to for advice on policy. They all of them tried to wriggle on the Israel/Arab question. Altogether it was not an impressive performance. I was able to reassure them on a number of points, e.g., that we distinguish sharply between the act of nationalisation and the question of controlling the Canal, that although I thought that action was necessary against Nasser, force could not be used and should not be used unless there was real justification for it. And, finally, as regards the plan of control, I agreed that this ought to come under the United Nations, and that Russia should be asked to the [proposed] Conference [of Canal users].[19] I think this did something to satisfy them.

The debate was finally fixed for Thursday [2 August] – the last day before the Recess – to begin at 12 and go on until about five. It was hoped that by then the Conference between Britain, America and France would have ended and some conclusions reached on the lines of calling a conference of the Canal users.

The discussion in the Parliamentary Committee which took place on Monday and Tuesday had been quite satisfactory. There was a feeling that the debate would be awkward for us because of differences of opinion in the Party, but it was agreed that we had to have such a debate. As to the line to be taken, nobody seemed to object to my condemnation of Nasser on the first Parliamentary occasion on the previous Friday, nor

19 Russia was asked, as the Americans (though not the British Government) wished: Eden (1960), pp. 433, 438.

to the economic measures to be taken against him. The Committee was most concerned that we should make plain that we did not oppose nationalisation in itself, and that the United Nations should come into the picture. For the rest they were disposed to leave it to me, George Brown saying, 'It will be an awkward speech to make, but somehow or other you will have to find your way through'.

On the morning of the debate Eden asked me to see him about 11.30, but it was really only to tell me that the [three-Power] Conference had not yet ended and therefore he would be able to say very little. We were alone together but I pressed him once more about the use of force. There was not disagreement on the military precautions but I said, 'What is your attitude to be if Nasser refuses to accept the conclusions of the further Conference?' As I recollect and so implied in what I subsequently wrote to him, he said, 'I only want to keep open the possibility of force in case Nasser does something else'. I must add, in fairness, that he claimed later that he had said that he only wanted to keep open the possibility of force *or* if Nasser did something else [*sic*]. But at any rate I certainly thought he said the first, because I went into the House of Commons and told John Strachey who was sitting beside me just before the debate began – having an interest in the War Office – that Eden had said force was to be used only if Nasser did something else, and we agreed that that was satisfactory.

While I was preparing the speech which was really on the previous day [Wednesday], Kenneth Younger came and offered me some valuable help as to what exactly I should say on the United Nations, and as it turned out these paragraphs suggested to me by him were immensely important. I say this because there have been moments when I have been critical of Kenneth, but I must say that he has been very helpful recently.

I had made it plain to the Committee and to other people with whom I talked, such as Denis Healey, that I did not think it was wise to attack the Government on this occasion despite our criticism of Middle East policy, and this was generally accepted. I think most people felt as I did, that had we attacked the Government at this moment we could very easily have been framed as unpatriotic and behaving in an irresponsible manner. I was also advised to make a short speech – no doubt my advisers had in mind my rather dangerous tendency to speak at length, and this meant that I could not spread myself at all.

Eden's speech was very short and told us little. It contained a criticism in fairly severe terms of Nasser but rather on the illegality of the action than on the Middle East generally. I tried in my speech to preserve a balance, not mincing my words about Nasser and deliberately bringing in a passage on the Middle East in which I maintained the importance of prestige and the danger of Nasser's ambitions. This part was not popular with the Left-Wingers, but apart from this the speech was reasonably well received. The only direct criticism made to me was from Edith Summer- skill, who is pro-Nasser because she once met him or once went to Egypt, and who is a woman whose political views are almost entirely dependent on personal contacts. She is also a fairly notorious pro-Arab and has had many rows with the Executive over this. Edith said, 'The first third and the last third were excellent; middle was bloody'. What she objected to, of course, were my remarks about Nasser and his ambitions and his speeches being like Hitler. I heard later that Arthur Henderson had expressed doubts to Hugh Dalton about the passage on prestige, and HD rounded on him and said, 'You should not talk like that. Your father was never afraid to tell the truth.'[20]

The later stages of the debate became rather ragged and, presumably by chance, almost all of those called on our side belonged to the extreme right wing, and most of them went rather further than I had, indicating they were prepared to back the use of force now – in particular Herbert Morrison, Reggie Paget, Frank Tomney and Jack Jones.[21] Denis Healey and [Desmond] Donnelly both made sensible speeches, fairly near my line; but only Warbey from the Left was able to speak. As it turned out this was important because they had a grievance owing to their enforced silence on this occasion.

I was a little embarrassed by far too much praise from the Tories, including Waterhouse and other members of the Suez Group.[22] Pre- sumably they did not listen to the last part of my speech in which I made it very plain that force should not be used, [except?] in accordance with the Charter. Looking back on it now the criticisms of the speech made in the Party owed more to my decision not to attack the Government than to anything I actually said, though the pro-Arab element did not like my attack on Nasser.

Now we go away I hope for a fortnight to Pembrokeshire leaving the Government to cope with the situation. Eden told me that he hoped to get the Conference [of Canal users] meeting within a fortnight, and later Butler told me that the fifteenth of August was the date they had in mind. Eden also told me that they very much wanted to have it in London and later on I heard that in fact the Americans and French had agreed to this. I had told him before that he should not stick out for London if that was a

20 Arthur Henderson senior, as Foreign Secretary 1929–31, had Dalton as his under-secretary.
21 Jack Jones, a junior minister 1947–50, was M.P. for Bolton 1945–50, for Rotherham 1950–62. On Paget and Tomney see above, pp. 349, 366 n.
22 Captain Charles Waterhouse, M.P. for Leicester S. 1924–45, S.E. 1950–7, was the recognised leader of those Conservatives who had opposed evacuating the Suez base in 1954. HG knew him well, for he had been Dalton's Parliamentary Secretary at the Board of Trade 1941–5.

real difficulty and suggested that if he didn't want Geneva they might go to Amsterdam which was also, after all, a big shipping centre.[23]

Document No. 17

HG's correspondence with the Prime Minister, etc.

3 to 12 August 1956.[24]

1. HG to Eden, 3 August 1956.
2. Eden to HG, 6th.
3. HG to his secretary Mrs. Skelly, 8th (manuscript).
4. Eden to HG, 9th.
5. HG to Eden, 10th.
6. Griffiths' report to HG of interview with Eden, 10th.
7. Eden to HG, 12th.

COPY   HOUSE OF COMMONS
                                                    London, S.W.1.
                                                    August 3rd.

My dear Prime Minister,
    Before leaving for Wales I feel I must write to you on one matter – a very important matter – in connection with the Suez crisis.
    You will recall that when Jim Griffiths and I saw you last Monday and again when I saw you yesterday just before the debate the question of

---

23 There are several late interpolations in this entry: two phrases beginning 'later' in the last paragraph, the final sentences of both the two preceding paragraphs, and also earlier on – the 'he claimed later' in the paragraph beginning 'On the morning of the debate', and the 'as it turned out' phrase in the one that follows. There are no signs of amendment to the typescript, and other words show that the main text was originally dictated at the dates given: e.g. the 'Now' at the beginning of the last paragraph, the first sentences of the entry of 2–3 August, the start of the entry of 30 July, and the 'tomorrow' at the end of the last paragraph but two of that entry. For once, therefore, HG must have reviewed his account at a later date, and the start of the entry of 22 August appears to confirm that. But the letters to Eden, which follow, show that the diary record gives an accurate impression of his attitude as he had formulated it before any Labour criticism had arisen.
24 From Papers, file P.106–1.

whether you proposed to use force if Egypt refused to accept the proposed international control of the Suez Canal was raised. On both occasions I expressed anxiety about this and indicated that it was extremely doubtful whether in the absence of any other aggressive action by Colonel Nasser the Labour Party would feel that this was justified. At our first meeting you said, if I recollect rightly, that you would 'prefer to take that hurdle when you came to it', and yesterday I understood you to say that you only wanted to be free to use force if the conference did not succeed in its object and if Colonel Nasser 'did something else'.

In the course of my speech I uttered some warning words about the circumstances in which force was and was not justified. But I deliberately refrained from putting the hypothetical question in public 'Was it proposed to use force to compel Nasser to accept the International Control Scheme?'. For I felt that it might embarrass you to do so. Had I said in reply to my own question that we could not support such action, it might, I felt, have gravely weakened your chances of achieving a settlement. Even to have said publicly that we were uncommitted on the issue would have done harm.

But in view of the reports in the Press this morning, which I gather came from the Foreign Office, that Britain and France intend if necessary and without active American participation to use force – even if there is no further aggressive action by Nasser – I feel I must repeat to you privately the warnings I have already uttered privately. While one or two members of our Party indicated in the debate that they would support force now, this is, I am pretty sure, not the general view.

Naturally our attitude in the event of this situation arising would depend on the exact circumstances. If Nasser were to do something which led to his condemnation by the United Nations as an aggressor, then there is no doubt, I am sure, that we would be entirely in favour of forceful resistance. But I must repeat, what I said in my speech yesterday, that up to the present I cannot see that he has done anything which would justify this.

I am sorry to trouble you again. But in view of the importance of the issue I thought I should give you this further word of friendly warning so as to avoid any possible misunderstanding in future.

I am showing this to Jim Griffiths, who, I know, would be happy to discuss it with you in my absence.

Yours sincerely,

HUGH GAITSKELL.

COPY   10 Downing Street,
                                                    Whitehall.

                                               August 6, 1956.

Dear Hugh,

Thank you for your letter of August 3.

Of course I could take no objection to your stating in the debate on August 2 your position on the use of force if necessary in connection with the Suez Canal. I understand your reasons for speaking as you did and that your attitude about the use of force must depend on the exact circumstances.

As regards my own position on this question, that must rest on what I said publicly in the House last Thursday. I think that what I said privately to you was that I only wanted to be free to use force if the Conference did not succeed in its object or if Colonel Nasser 'did something else'. Certainly the Government's attitude to the use of force would also have to depend on the circumstances at the time.

I am very glad that the debate last Thursday showed such a wide measure of agreement.

I hope you will have a few days peace in Wales.

                                    (SGD.) ANTHONY EDEN

The Rt. Hon. H.T.N. Gaitskell, C.B.E., M.P.

COPY [House of Commons notepaper]

                                               Wednesday Aug. 8th

Dear Mrs. Skelly,

I enclose the reply to my letter from the P.M. It is guarded and not very satisfactory. Please show it to Mr. Griffiths. I am a little worried about the continued preparations for fighting. Sometimes they seem to go beyond mere 'precautions'. The P.M. should know both from what I said in the House and my last letter of our anxieties about 'Force'. But I think if I were in London I would go and have a further and longer talk with him. Perhaps Mr. Griffiths, to whom you should show this letter, may think it worth seeing the P.M. – though if he does it might be a good plan to take someone with him (as a witness!). Tell him too that if he thinks it advisable I will gladly come up for a day or two. It will be easier to decide this when we hear Nasser's reply. Hope all goes well. We have had miraculously a fine week end!

H.G.

COPY   10 Downing Street,
                                                       S.W.1.
                                              August 9, 1956.

Dear Hugh,

You may like a few impressions of how things are moving, but I am bound to admit that they are tentative and may easily be proved wrong.

The acceptances to the Conference are coming in well. The response has been steadier and better than I expected. In particular, only Greece so far has asked for a different place or date. You will know how often this problem of bright ideas by others makes preparations for a conference difficult. At least we have been spared that.

We have also had some solid support both for the Conference and for its purpose from which [sic] countries as Italy, Holland and Sweden. The Press in the last-named has been firmer that I would have expected. Spain is proving difficult, but I do not think anybody will be upset if she does not come.

Soviet Russia. From Shepilov's remarks to Hayter and other Ambassadors it looks as though they will accept. Their grumbles so far have been mainly about membership, e.g., Poland and China should be admitted and the successor States to Austria and Hungary. They have also complained of place. But on the whole they could have been much more difficult – so far.

You will have seen Nehru's comments. He ignored of course the fact that seizing an international company in this way was in itself an act of violence. But he was speaking to Congress and he was telling them that he was going to the Conference. Macdonald has the impression that he is moving towards the acceptance of some form at least of internationalisation. We shall see.[25]

Other Commonwealth countries are in close touch and helpful, except South Africa.

The Administration apart, the Americans are taking more interest publicly in the situation. That is all to the good. I am sure that they are doing all they can to get people to the conference table.

Unless something very unforeseen occurs, I now think we can regard the arrangements as set for the opening of the Conference next Thursday.

Yours sincerely,

Anthony Eden.

The Right Hon. H. T. N. Gaitskell, C.B.E., M.P.

COPY   As from Whitegates,
                                                 Little Haven,
                                               Pembrokeshire.

                                                    10.8.56

Dear Anthony,

Thank you for your further letter of August 9th containing your impressions of how things are going. I have spoken to Jim Griffiths on the telephone this morning and he is going to try and see you. But there are a few things which I feel I should put on paper. I am very worried lest we should get ourselves into the very position described in my speech – being denounced as aggressors in the Security Council and having the majority of the Assembly against us. You speak of 'seizing an international company' as being 'in itself an act of violence'. Whether that be so or not I certainly do *not* regard this as justification for a declaration of war by us. And I fancy my view would be shared by world opinion generally.

You will no doubt have seen the letter in the Times signed by Healey

25 Malcolm MacDonald, son of a Prime Minister and himself a former Colonial Secretary, was High Commissioner in India. All invited countries eventually attended the conference, except Greece and Egypt; but four, including Russia and India, opposed the plan agreed upon by the other 18. See below, p. 589.

and Jay.[26] There is great force in what they say – which, broadly speaking, coincides with my own view. If I have been less precise in my public statements this is partly because we, as a Party, have as yet come to no collective decision and partly because I did not want to say anything which might encourage Nasser's intransigence. I thought it wise for these reasons to confine myself to the more general statement at the end of my speech and to express to you privately for the moment, as I have done now on four occasions – twice orally and twice in writing – my misgivings and anxieties.

Lest there should still be any doubt in your mind about my personal attitude, let me say that I could not regard an armed attack on Egypt by ourselves and the French as justified by anything which Nasser has done so far or as consistent with the Charter of the United Nations. Nor, in my opinion, would such an attack be justified in order to impose a system of international control over the Canal – desirable though this is. If, of course, the whole matter were to be taken to the United Nations and if Egypt were to be condemned by them as aggressors, then, of course, the position would be different. And if further action which amounted to obvious aggression by Egypt were taken by Nasser, then again it would be different. So far what Nasser has done amounts to a threat, a grave threat to us and to others, which certainly cannot be ignored; but it is only a threat, not in my opinion justifying retaliation by war.

Finally, as you will possibly have heard from Jim Griffiths, I propose to break my holiday on Sunday, travel up that night to London and spend Monday there returning Monday night to Pembrokeshire. This should enable me to see and talk with you and with my colleagues after Nasser's statement on Sunday. I hope you will be free sometime in the later morning or early afternoon of Monday.

Yours sincerely,

Hugh Gaitskell.

Confidential

Report on Interview which Mr. Griffiths and Mr. Robens had with the Prime Minister who was accompanied by the Lord President of the

26 Dated August 5; reproduced in D. Jay, *Change and Fortune* (Hutchinson, 1980) pp. 254–5.

Council, Lord Salisbury, at No. 10 Downing Street, on Friday, 10th August 1956, at 3 o'clock.†

I. We told the Prime Minister that we were deeply concerned at this stage with the following matters:-

First. At the scale of the military preparations, which seemed to be going beyond precaution and were therefore creating a bad impression outside in the world, leading people to think that they were preparations for a war rather than precautions against an emergency.

Second. We were anxious to know, if that were possible, what would be the procedure to be followed at the Conference and in particular, whether H.M.G. were proposing to put any specific plan or proposals to the Conference and if so, how did they propose to handle it at the Conference.

Third. We wanted once more to underline what Mr. Gaitskell has said in his speech in the House and what he said in his letter about the view that he and the party hold about the use of force.

The Prime Minister's reply

The Prime Minister said that he had been in some difficulty with the French and to some extent with the Suez Company and had in fact been accused by the French of dragging his feet. He told us that he had been very anxious indeed that the preparations should take place in such a way as not to create public alarm. He remarked that we would know from our own experience in Government that it took six weeks to position troops in places where they could be available if necessary.

He had been very anxious that the canal should continue running during this period and had impressed upon the company the necessity of allowing the pilots to continue at work so as to keep it going. The company had been very loth in this but had agreed. However he said that one of the flash points would be if some of the pilots wished to resign and Nasser prevented them from so doing or took some other action against the pilots. Another flash point would be if he did something to prevent the ships using the canal, and yet another if he interfered with the base which he had not as yet done, (although he had prevented the movement of some materials out of the base). At this stage, there was no intention to take anything out of the base (*the Chiefs of Staff are advising on this*).[27]

There is no intention at this moment to use Libya.

---

† Printed below by permission of H.M.S.O. (Crown Copyright).
27 The italics here indicate a handwritten addition by HG.

On the question of force:

Both Mr. Griffiths and Mr. Robens again emphasised to the Prime Minister what Mr. Gaitskell has said both in his speech and in the letter about the use of force and asked him to bear that in mind.

The P.M. replied that he could assure them that unless we were provoked by some act of aggression on Nasser's part he was resolved not to use force until the Conference.

Conference:

He outlined to us the proposed scheme that H.M.G. were to put to the Conference, and indicated that this had the approval of the French and the United States.

Although he anticipated that both the French and the Americans might submit some alternatives in the course of the Conference, we also got the impression that he was hoping that the Americans would sponsor the final plan. We asked him – let us assume that the Conference agrees to some plan for international operation of the canal – what would follow then? He said that it would be for the decision of the Conference to be conveyed to Nasser and everything thus would depend upon his reactions. Here again it seemed to be his hope that this would be done by the Americans. We again mentioned to him the view put forward for us by Mr. Gaitskell that any such plan should be under the aegis of the United Nations and therefore, we again expressed strongly the view that when the Conference has arrived at a decision that the matter should be taken to the United Nations, preferably to the Assembly. He did not rule this out entirely and indeed favoured some association with the U.N. but would not be specific about what form. It might be just restrictions, it might go further, but he would prefer not to commit himself on that. We pointed out that from what he had told us it seemed to us that the crucial time would be when the Conference had arrived at a decision, and Nasser's reactions, acceptance or rejection, were known. We again emphasised our major point that the use of force must be in conjunction with our obligations under the Charter, and this is an added reason why the United Nations must be brought into it. He told us that Hammarskjöld was being kept in touch with what was taking place – this indicating that he and the Government were of course, not adverse to the United Nations being brought in in some way.[28]

28 Dag Hammarskjöld, a Swedish diplomat, was Secretary-General of the U.N. 1953–61. The pencilled emphasis in this document was evidently added by HG.

He told us that he is having a Cabinet at 5 o'clock on Monday 13th August, and would be very glad to see us after the Cabinet meeting if we so desired. If it was felt that we would like to meet him before our meeting at 3.p.m. on Monday, he would do his best to meet our wishes.

. . . .

10 Downing Street
Whitehall

August 12, 1956.

Dear Hugh,[29]

Thank you for your letter of August 10 and for letting me know your views. Salisbury and I had a full talk with Jim Griffiths and Alfred Robens on Friday afternoon. I was very glad to see them. I made it clear to them that the use of force could not arise so far as we were concerned at the present time, nor while the Conference which we had called was working for a solution, unless of course Colonel Nasser took some further action.

It is, I feel, only in the light of what happens at the Conference that we can decide our future course.

In the meantime, I would repeat what I said in my broadcast that we do not seek a solution by force but by the broadest possible international agreement. We have, however, thought it necessary to take certain precautionary measures.

As regards your meeting with your colleagues on Monday, when I saw Griffiths and Robens I understood that they did not think you would feel it necessary to see me before this. I myself had made arrangements to stay at Chequers on Monday, to have a few hours' break from the continuous series of meetings which the Suez Canal problem has naturally made it necessary for me to hold, including some this weekend.

I therefore trust that you will understand if I do not see you on Monday, though I should be very ready to do so on Tuesday or any later day.

Yours sincerely[29]
[Signed] Anthony Eden

The Rt. Hon. Hugh Gaitskell, C.B.E., M.P.

29 This was handwritten, along with the signature.

Diary, [Dictated on Wednesday 22 August 1956]

I dictated most of the last part on Thursday, August 3rd,[30] today is August 22nd. The very same evening of August 3rd Douglas Jay rang me up and said that [W.N.] Ewer, the diplomatic correspondent of the *Daily Herald* had told him that the Foreign Office were putting out a story that the Government, with the French, had every intention of [imposing?] a solution by force upon Egypt. The idea was that they would have the Conference; that they would push through the plan they wanted, and that once that had gone through they would simply send an ultimatum to Nasser. If he refused to accept it – well, then, it was just too bad, and the troops would go in. I said to Douglas that I could hardly believe this because it did not fit in with what Eden had said to me. But the next morning, it was obvious that Douglas was right. The papers carried the story; there were no quotations from Ministers, but the press said in terms, both *The Times* and the *Herald* and I think the *Telegraph* and the other papers, that this was the intention. This so much alarmed me, that although we were supposed to be leaving early in the morning [of Saturday 4 August] by car for Pembrokeshire, I sat down and wrote to Eden a letter in my own hand, telephoning Mrs Skelly, my Secretary, to come and fetch it and see that it was safely delivered at Number 10. In this letter, I warned him that he could not assume that the Labour Party would support the policy of force despite what had been said by some speakers on our side in the Debate, notably Herbert Morrison. In a sense I was simply repeating what I had said to him in the two discussions, one with Jim Griffiths and one on my own, earlier in the week.[31] I said it much more emphatically in the letter. We then went off to Wales.

I received from Eden what was no more than an acknowledgement, really, of the letter, shortly after the weekend. His reply was evasive in the sense that he did not take me up at all; he simply said that he quite understood why I had spoken as I did upon force during the debate, but he gave no assurance in this letter that they were not going to use force. As the week went on I became increasingly worried because of the tone of the Tory press which continued to put forward the story apparently sent out by the Foreign Office that force was to be used. Other developments also took place. Douglas [Jay] had said that in view of the situation he was proposing to write a letter to *The Times* attacking them for their leader which they had already come out with, of course. I gave him my blessing

---

30 3 August 1956 was a Friday.
31 In fact he saw Eden together with Griffiths on Monday afternoon, 30 July; and alone on Thursday morning, 2 August.

on this, and suggested he should talk to Denis Healey. He did and Denis eventually signed the letter.[32] Then, it was also obvious that the Tory press in particular were associating me with the Government's policy of imposing force. At least they were implying that I was in favour of this, despite the fact that in my speech I had made it abundantly plain that this was not the case. Finally, there was some trouble from our left wing who were drafting and collecting signatures for a letter which was plainly anti-Government. I could not find anything very wrong with the letter, it did not go much beyond what I had said in my speech, but it was also partly aimed against me, at least so I supposed. Eventually Douglas himself rang me up, in the middle of the following week, and we had a brief conversation in which he expressed some alarm about these tendencies, though he mentioned that they had been corrected as far as I was concerned, and to some extent by the *Manchester Guardian* who came out incidentally staunchly in my favour, quoting what I had actually said in the Debate.

Later, I spoke to Jim Griffiths and we decided that the best thing to do was for me to come back to London on the following Monday [13 August], that is to say ten days after going down there, since Jim himself was going off on leave on the Tuesday. Moreover, by then, the Conference arrangements would have been completed and we would know what Nasser had said as he was to make a statement on the Sunday. We decided that in all the circumstances the best thing was to call the Parliamentary Committee together. Accordingly, I returned to London on the Sunday night, and after having various consultations in the morning [of Monday], we had the Parliamentary Committee in the afternoon. I had a long talk with Jim Griffiths and Alf Robens, and I must say found them both extremely helpful and sympathetic. At my suggestion they had been to see Eden a day or two before, on I think the Friday, to give him yet another warning. I also should add, something I had forgotten, that during the course of the preceding week I had received another letter from Eden which was principally about the way in which the answers from various countries invited to the conference were coming in. But one phrase in this, about the attitude of India, alarmed me and I wrote him another letter myself, this time in even stronger terms – about the issue of force. This letter did not reach him until after Alf Robens and Jim Griffiths had been to see him and they had been making the same sort of points to him already.

32 Above, p. 575. Healey did not know that HG had approved the letter and inspired Jay's approach, for he saw it partly as a means of influencing his leader. The words 'of course' (here punctuated as in the original) should probably begin the sentence ending 'Healey'.

In our conversation before the Parliamentary Committee they were both extremely helpful and anxious to ensure that the Committee should endorse my speech in view of the misrepresentation which had been taking place. And Jim, in fact, agreed to propose this. As it turned out, this was not necessary.

The Committee met, and I am bound to say that the discussion was most satisfactory. There was virtually unanimous agreement on quite a number of points. First, that my speech should be endorsed; there was really no criticism of it at all, at any rate openly expressed. And it was not Jim Griffiths but Jim Callaghan who said he thought it most important that the Committee should endorse it; that he had read it, he had not been at the debate – he had read the speech and agreed with all of it. And even Tony Greenwood who is disposed to be rather pacifist, though of course he is pro-Israel, made the same point. So that was agreed. It was also agreed that we should reiterate particularly the warnings that had been given about force; that the system of control to be set up should be under the United Nations, and that the whole matter should be referred to the U.N. to a special meeting of the Assembly after the Conference was over.

To my particular astonishment Nye Bevan himself was very much in agreement with me; he did not of course say he agreed with me but he made a speech at the Committee which was very much on the lines that I had made in the House. He was in no doubt about Nasser being a thug, and he was in no doubt about the need for international control, he even set out the reasons for it and we put them into the statement. In fact I had already covered most of the points in my speech the week before in the debate. There was one point which [had] rather worried me. There has been a good deal of talk in the party about the need for having international control of all waterways of the kind of the Suez Canal. Of course, there is a great deal to be said for this in principle, but I knew very well that if we insisted on raising this now it might be embarrassing to the Americans, because of the Panama Canal. And I thought it would be hard to handle this in the Committee when to my surprise Nye Bevan himself opposed the proposal to put in a reference to the desirability of general internationalisation of waterways. He said, 'You will be surprised to hear this from me but I think it would be a great mistake to say anything at the moment which would embarrass the Americans'.[33] So really, I was very pleased with the meeting which could not have been more harmonious or friendly or turned out better from our point of view. They left the drafting of the statement to Jim and myself and I asked Alf Robens

33 A notable change since the previous week: above, p. 565 and *HG*, p. 426. For the U.S. concern over Panama see Eden (1960), p. 435; S. Lloyd, *Suez 1956* (Cape, 1978), p. 100.

and Kenneth Younger to stay behind and help.[34] We drafted it quite quickly, but I think quite satisfactorily. I then went off to a lobby conference which presented no special difficulties. I was particularly anxious to emphasise what my own point of view had been in the debate. And I think the journalists on the whole took it quite well. I also after the lobby, had an interview with [Deryck] Winterton of the *Daily Herald*; in fact it wasn't an interview, I simply dictated the statement which was in answer to questions, and that was published as well on the following day.

Jim and I had also hoped to see Eden that same night. The Committee had been in some doubt as to whether we should see them – Bevan taking the view that it was a mistake to go and see the Prime Minister because it created a kind of coalition atmosphere. And undoubtedly there is something in what he says. On the other hand there was the danger that if I simply came up to the Committee meeting and then dashed back to Pembrokeshire it would create rather a bad impression. In the event, Eden said he could not see us that day, he was down at Chequers and very tired, and asked if we would wait until the following morning. So the following day [Tuesday 14 August] at quarter to eleven Jim Griffiths and Alf Robens and I went to Number 10 and saw Eden, Salisbury [Lord President] and Selwyn Lloyd. We had a good forty minutes' discussion with them, urging our points in the statement, and in particular the desirability of their making a statement that the precautionary military measures were purely for self defence. We did not get very far with them, they were very cautious in their replies and rather evasive. But I felt myself that we had made some impression, and Selwyn Lloyd's broadcast the following night did, I think, show some traces of this. At any rate they certainly were left in no doubt about our views on the whole situation.

The same evening I had dinner with André, of the French Embassy, whom I do not know well but who is an intelligent young man and had taken some part in the previous discussions. He said one or two interesting things. First, that Selwyn Lloyd had in fact himself been rather concerned about the danger that Britain and France might be denounced as aggressors; that he had also wanted to refer the whole question to the United Nations but that Dulles had opposed this, presumably because of the American elections. André, himself, was disposed to agree very much with our line and thought that force could not be used, but he was also emphatically of the opinion that somehow or other we could not let Nasser get away with it. He said rather dramatically, 'If he does we shall

34 With no reference to any of the meetings mentioned or correspondence published above, Eden pretended in his memoirs that with this Opposition statement 'the retreat then began' from the position he had deluded himself into thinking they had taken up: Eden (1960), p. 445.

lose the whole of North Africa, France will go communist and the Atlantic Alliance will be wrecked'.

I am afraid this previous section has got a little muddled because I spoke about the meeting I had with Eden before the dinner I had with André on the previous [Monday] night. After the meeting at Number 10 I went off to make a short film for I.T.V. and had a few words with Geoffrey Cox who used to be the Lobby Correspondent of the *News Chronicle* and whom I know very well.[35] He was very glad that he [we?] had issued the statement and that I had come back to London because, as he put it, [of] the story given out by the Government – [and] he absolutely confirmed my suspicions that the Foreign Office News Department was responsible – together with the left-wing letters and the Tory press which had given the impression that my speech was entirely in support of the Government. All this was creating for me an awkward position, but he thought that the statement had cleared things up. And he also said, though he later retracted this, that the Government were playing up all the publicity about troop movements and so on. At any rate, he was pretty critical of them and, as I said, confirmed my suspicions. So did Sydney Jacobson with whom I lunched immediately afterwards, and who said that at a news conference with editors which Eden gave he had himself given the very definite impression that they were going, as Eden put it, to railroad through the proposals – the Americans, Eden said, were very good at that sort of thing – and then it was simply going to be imposed upon Nasser. Of course, by now, that is by the Tuesday morning of which I am speaking, the Government had certainly got much colder feet and the press had been beginning to pipe down a great deal.

I went back to Pembrokeshire on the afternoon of the 14th and we returned here two days later. Apart from a [weekend] visit to Scotland I have been in London since then, and in the course of the last few days seen a good many people who are connected with or here for the Conference on Suez. I have had a number of quite interesting conversations as follows.

1) With Chipman of the American Embassy. He said the Americans were amazed when they came over first of all at Eden's emotionalism, as he put it, about Suez. They very much agreed with the Labour Party line and we had a good deal of laughing about Dulles and the Labour Party for the first time being in agreement.

---

35 A New Zealander, (Sir) Geoffrey Cox had just left the *News Chronicle* to become Editor and Chief Executive of Independent Television News 1956–58; later he was deputy chairman of Yorkshire T.V. and then chairman of Tyne-Tees T.V.

2) Don Bliss,[36] an old friend, who thought the only economic measures that were really worth while were the building of new pipe-lines, not through Israel but across the Arab States. He pooh-poohed the idea of large tankers. He said they [the U.S. Administration] had worked out plans by which the Western hemisphere could be supplied with all the oil we wanted if necessary.

3) Hansen, the Danish Prime Minister, who confirmed what I had heard about Eden's emotionalism and who also was very much of our view on the matter of force. As was also Lange, the Norwegian Foreign Minister, who if anything was rather more pacifist than I was, and I think a little less appreciative of the danger of Nasser getting away with it. Though in practice so far as policy is concerned there was no difference between us.[37]

I also saw Peter Thorneycroft at the Downing Street dinner [on Monday 20 August] and had an argument with him about force.[38] Curiously enough he still insisted that they must still reserve the right to use it, perhaps not now but perhaps later on, [as] if there must be a kind of official Government line. He talked in exactly the same way as Eden, although really the logic of it is difficult to understand. All one can say is I suppose that they want to go on with the bluff. Pineau the French Foreign Minister I also saw and he took very much the same line. 'I don't want to use force,' he said, 'but I want Nasser to think we may use it.' And I am sure that really is the basis of the Government's policy. Perhaps at the start they really did contemplate using it. But it was more a question of appeasing the Suez Group on the one hand, taking perfectly legitimate precautions on the other, in case Nasser did something silly, and finally the bluff, as well of course, as I have mentioned already, the desire to use force or to be free to use force.

36 Don C. Bliss had been commercial attaché at the U.S. Embassy in London during and after the war, and Counsellor 1948–50.
37 H.C. Hansen, leader of the Social Democrats, was Minister of Finance 1945, 1947–50; of Foreign Affairs 1953–8; Prime Minister 1955–60 when like his predecessor he died suddenly at 53. On Lange see above, p. 191 and n.
38 Peter (Lord) Thorneycroft was Conservative M.P. for Stafford 1938–45, Monmouth 1945–66; at the Board of Trade 1951–7, Chancellor of the Exchequer 1957–8 when he resigned in protest at government spending – which the Prime Minister, Macmillan, dismissed as 'a little local difficulty'. He returned as Minister of Aviation in 1960–2, of Defence 1962–4, and served as Chairman of the Conservative Party 1975–81.

[*Dictated about Sunday 26 August 1956*]

Continuing now with the various people I met during the Suez Conference, I must mention a conversation with [Brentano]* the German
Foreign Minister, not about Suez, but about Europe. I said that we were
rather [concerned?] about the state of German public opinion. There
seemed to be a danger that the strength of feeling about reunification
might become so great that a German Government – not this one
perhaps, but another one, would decide to negotiate direct with the
Russians, and come to terms with the Russians which would be very
unsatisfactory for the West; and perhaps ultimately for Germany as well.
For these reasons I thought really we ought to see whether there was any
step we could take (we being the three other powers – Britain, France and
America) which would reassure German opinion in [*sic*] that we really
cared about reunification. Brentano was obviously rather pleased with
this approach; he admitted that there was a danger of the kind that I had
suggested and although he had no positive proposal to make he readily
fell in with the idea that there ought to be some kind of informal discussion.
What he said actually was that he would like to see leaders of both Parties,
both Government and Opposition in the three or four countries, if
America would come as well, discussing the problem together. I suggested that if he was thinking in those terms there might be something to
be said for getting the Bilderberg Group to organise a Conference. He
had heard of Bilderberg, he knew that Professor Hallstein, the head of the
German Foreign Office had been to one of the Bilderberg Conferences
and other people he knew in Germany.[39] He also said that he realised that
the Chancellor, Adenauer*, was very difficult with the Socialists. He was
tactful about this; obviously he did not wish to criticise the late
[? great] Chief who he said was extremely well at the moment, but he
was clearly aware, Brentano, that there had to be better relations with the
Social Democrats. He spoke most warmly in favour of Fritz Erler, whom
I told him I had seen; and he thought that Ollenhauer's speech at the
Party Conference was really first class.[40]

I also spoke to Sir William Haley, the Editor of *The Times*. It was
rather interesting that he was actually at the Downing Street dinner which

39 Konrad Adenauer, Chancellor 1949–63, was an implacable opponent of detente
with Communists abroad or Socialists at home. Heinrich von Brentano was his
Foreign Minister 1955–61. Walter Hallstein, a professor of law, headed the
foreign office 1951–8 and was then President of the E.E.C. Commission
1958–67, and of the European Movement from 1968. On the Bilderberg
Group see above, p. 542 n. 78.
40 Erich Ollenhauer led the German Social Democrats 1952–63, and Fritz Erler
was their spokesman on defence and deputy leader in Parliament.

was principally confined to the heads of delegations, plus a few other people like myself. I told him I could not agree with the line taken by *The Times* at the beginning of the crisis when they had gone right over in favour of force. I had assumed, incidentally, that Haley himself must have given directions to that effect; though as subsequently turned out, I was wrong. However, at Downing Street Haley didn't argue with me about what might have been done, he simply said he agreed that force was now out of the question. 'It's like a child', he said. 'If you smack it, you must smack it at once, but not after a time.' I also had some conversation with Casey, the Australian Foreign Minister. I did not much care for him. He was curiously English and un-Australian. He was very critical of the Labour Party in Australia and kept on urging me to go out there – perhaps I would be able to show them how to behave as an Opposition. He thought Evatt, the Leader of the Opposition, was a very wicked man. No, I did not much care for Casey.[41]

There were one or two other meetings which were worth recording. I saw eventually [on Friday 24 August], Dulles himself, after the Conference was over, at the American Embassy, or rather at the Residence. The Ambassador was there and also Norris Chipman. I congratulated him on the success of the Conference which owed so much to him. I was really concerned to make three points. First, to let him know that as far as the Labour Party was concerned we could not possibly support the use of force merely to impose a solution on Nasser if, for instance, he refused to meet the negotiating Committee. I said I felt it was my duty to tell him that because we, after all, represented about half the population. He made no comment on this, except a rather confused statement about the difficulties of opposition. But Norris Chipman told me afterwards that he, Dulles, was in fact rather worried about Eden's attitude; and that it was a very good thing that I had spoken to him as I did.[42] The second thing I wanted to mention to Dulles was how I felt the talks with Nasser should be handled; very much on the basis of consumers or users of the Canal talking to Egypt, not threatening force; pointing out to Nasser the great advantages of a settlement and one which would really develop the Canal, bring him in plenty of money and generally create a good impression, keep the pilots happy and so on. If he refused, on the other hand, to play, why, then, as I say, there was no question of using force but the

41 Richard (Lord) Casey had been a Minister since 1935, and was Governor-General 1965–9. Dr H.V. Evatt (1894–1965) led the Labour Party 1951–60 when he became a judge. He was Minister of External Affairs 1941–9, as was Casey 1951–60.

42 Eden rebuffed Dulles' attempt to warn him of the danger of dividing the nation: Eden (1960), p. 492. Norris Chipman was First Secretary at the Embassy.

users of the Canal would simply give up any hope that it was going to be properly developed and they would have to look for other means of transport, including pipe-lines; and, said Dulles at this point, 'large tankers too'. I was slightly amused at this because Don Bliss, one of his delegation, had been very sceptical about the tankers. Dulles' general comment on this point of mine was that he thought they were thinking, the Committee that is, on precisely those lines. Then, thirdly, I asked him why they, the Americans, had withdrawn the offer on the Aswan Dam. He gave a rather confused reply. He said that there were a number of reasons. What it really boiled down to was this:

1) That they had come to the conclusion that Egypt, herself, would not be able to do her fair share. It would impose too much sacrifice on the Egyptian people if they had to provide, say, two-thirds of the colossal investment required. He therefore thought in practice there would be continual friction. America would always be being pressed to provide more because of the difficulty of keeping down living standards in Egypt where they were already so low.

2) There was also the question of the purchases of arms. Dulles would give no figure for these, though Don Bliss had told me the rather startling story that they had discovered that the Egyptians were committed to purchasing no less than 300 million pounds' worth of arms from Czechoslovakia. Dulles referred to it in general terms, without as I say giving a particular figure. He mentioned also the difficulties in Congress coming partly from the Southern States, with a fear that there would be an increased supply of cotton which would keep prices down.[43] Dulles himself obviously laughed at this, but it must presumably have been one of the elements. On the question of why it was done so brusquely, Dulles simply said that they had felt they should turn the thing down before Congress turned it down, which was not of course a very adequate excuse. I then said I thought it would be a very valuable thing if some fuller explanation to the world could be given about the negotiations on the Dam and why the thing was turned down. And Dulles seemed to be impressed with this and said to the Ambassador and to Chipman that they ought to get something done about that.

Desmond Donnelly rang me up towards the end of the Conference week and sought my advice about an article he was to write in the *Spectator*. In the course of our conversation I asked him if he knew what the attitude of the Suez Group was. I said I was not sure that Eden would come out of this quite so badly. He might be able to turn round on the Suez boys and say, 'Well there you are, I tried to do what you always want, but you see what kind of a mess we got into'. Desmond was a bit

43 Southern Senators and Congressmen, representing states which depended heavily on cotton, were disproportionately powerful in Congress.

sceptical about this, and I suggested that he should ask Julian Amery who was a friend of his, what his attitude was. An hour later he rang back and said that Julian was as tough as ever and that the slogan was, either Nasser or Eden must go before October.[44] However, I still feel sceptical myself about the influence and power of the Suez Group. It is very rare in English politics for a minority to be able to dispose of a Party leader unless he is very weak indeed.

Document No. 18

HG's talk with the Secretary of State, 24 August 1956.[45]

CONFIDENTIAL

USDel/MC/86

UNITED STATES DELEGATION
TO THE
SUEZ CANAL CONFERENCE
London, August 1956

Date: August 24, 1956
Time: 3:00 P.M.
Place: Ambassador's Residence

MEMORANDUM OF CONVERSATION

Participants:
The United States
The Secretary of State
Mr. Norris B. Chipman

UNITED KINGDOM
Rt. Hon. Hugh Gaitskell,
Labor Party Leader

Subject: Suez Canal Crisis

Distribution: Dept. of State, Amembassy London
G, C, S/P, EUR, BNA, NEA, NE, P, and L

The Secretary received Mr. Gaitskell, and the usual amenities were exchanged. Mr. Gaitskell congratulated the Secretary on his 'great achievement' in handling the Conference so as to avoid a sharp break

44 Julian Amery, Macmillan's son-in-law and a leader of the Suez Group, was Conservative M.P. for Preston N. 1950–66, Brighton Pavilion 1969– , and held office 1957–64, 1970–4. As Minister of Aviation he launched the Concorde project and ensured that no successor could cancel it.
45 Sent to HG by a friend at the U.S. Embassy. From Gaitskell Papers, file P.118–4.

between the East and West. The Secretary remarked that given the original position of France and Great Britain, 'we got as strong a demonstration as possible in favor of a position that was acceptable to certain "Asian" as well as other countries'. The three countries that did not go along, Indonesia, Ceylon and India, were against the so-called Dulles' proposal not because they were against its intrinsic value, but because they thought that Nasser would not accept it. They would have been only too glad to accept it themselves, if they had thought that Nasser would accept it. They would want Nasser to accept it, whereas the USSR feared that Egypt might accept it. By its action at the Conference, the USSR has made it more difficult for Nasser to accept negotiation.

Mr. Gaitskell asked, 'What will Nasser do? Will he turn down the 5-Nation Plan?' The Secretary replied, 'No, in my opinion it would be difficult for him to refuse to meet'. One good thing accomplished in this Conference, continued the Secretary, had been the avoidance of a split between East and West. Great efforts were made and skill exercised by Turkey, which was the key figure in bringing about the 4-Nation Amendment to the U.S. proposal.[46] The U.S. had exerted influence on Ethiopia, which is having trouble with HMG.

Mr. Gaitskell remarked that the real worry was what would happen if Nasser turned down the proposal to talk. In his opinion HMG 'could not successfully go it alone in the use of force', and the Labor Party would be strongly opposed to any armed action which could not be brought within the UN. Mr. Gaitskell thought that not only would the Labor Party be strongly opposed, but at least half the nation. The Secretary then remarked that in times of crises like the present one it was absolutely essential for a nation to give the appearance of unity; that any appearance of weakness or division was always taken advantage of by the enemy. The United States had been fortunate in recent years in that Congress had given full support to the Formosan Resolution.[47] At the beginning of the Suez crisis he (the Secretary) and President Eisenhower were worried over the possibility of an East-West split and possibly war with all the attendant risks. Mr. Gaitskell interjected that he thought the best way of handling the matter at the present time was to have someone like Mr. Menzies quietly inform Nasser that the 18-Nation Proposal was a practical, feasible plan and advantageous to him; that Egypt would do

46 The Baghdad Pact countries, particularly Turkey, wished to ensure that Egyptian sovereignty was not eroded by international control of passage through the Canal. (Turkey has a narrow waterway of her own.)

47 It warned the Chinese Communists that the U.S.A. would fight if necessary to protect the island (now Taiwan). This advance commitment passed the House by 410 to 3 and the Senate by 85 to 3, and was signed by the President on 29.1.55.

well to accept it; and that he (Nasser) would be a great statesman if he recognized the advantages of cooperation with the most important users of the Canal. Gaitskell continued to the effect that it would, of course, be important to continue to put financial and economic pressure on Nasser until he had become more reasonable. Alternatives to the Canal should be found. The Secretary replied that 'this is very much in our minds'. The Secretary, however, pointed out that the process of easing away from the Canal would entail economic and financial burdens and that this should be recognized. The West, however, should take measures so that they would be less dependent upon the Canal and in this connection a Turkish pipeline and bigger tankers might be required. Egyptian control of the Canal and the possibility that Syria might cut its pipeline could endanger the oil situation and bring about stringencies, he said, but the United States could greatly increase its oil production.

Mr. Gaitskell then requested the Secretary to clear up what he called 'the mystery' of the Aswan Dam. He pointed out that many people did not understand the abrupt manner in which it was turned down, and he asked for information. The Secretary then explained that it became clear that the cost of the Canal would have placed too great a burden upon Egyptian finances and that in the long run the sufferings of the Egyptian people would have been blamed upon the United States, the International Bank, etc. When the United States turned down the Aswan Dam he had thought the USSR would move in quickly and that it would have to take the punishment in the long run, although gaining an immediate victory. Congress, he further explained, had become anxious over the possibility of an even closer rapprochement between Egypt and the USSR and that the USSR would furnish at great cost to Egypt further arms that would result in an arms race between Israel and Egypt. Moreover Congress entertained fears that economic aid to Egypt might result in increased cotton production that would compete with American cotton. When the Aswan Dam was turned down Congress was on the point of passing a limiting amendment to the Mutual Security Act, which probably would have affected more than the Aswan Dam and might have cut off all economic aid for Egypt. The timing of the announcement was necessitated by the desire to avoid such a complete cutoff. Mr. Gaitskell said that this story should be told to the British public, since it was not understood, and he thought that someone like Jimmy Reston of the *New York Times* could be usefully used for this purpose.[48] The Secretary thanked Mr. Gaitskell for this suggestion and said he thought something could be done along this line.

48 James (Scotty) Reston began as a sports writer and became a leading columnist. He was head of the paper's Washington bureau.

Diary, Dictated on Monday, 3 September 1956

Last Wednesday [29 August], Jim Griffiths, Bevan and myself went to see Lennox-Boyd, the Colonial Secretary. This was at his request. It was a curious interview, and even now I don't know why he invited us. He had nothing new to tell us; he gave away no secrets, and in fact the proceedings took the form of an argument between us and him about Government policy. He had told me a few days earlier when we met at dinner that they had found this diary of Grivas, the terrorist leader [in Cyprus], and that it showed that the terrorists were very much at rock-bottom, and apparently now relying only on those who had come over from Greece.[49] About the only new point which Lennox-Boyd made in the interview was that the diaries also showed that the truce proposal made by the rebels was simply for the purpose of regrouping. We had no difficulty in showing him that whether that was so or not it was extremely foolish to have assumed the responsibility for provoking the terrorists again by the surrender offer made by [the Governor] Harding. In fact, Bevan put the case extremely well. He was very cogent and Lennox-Boyd had very little to say in reply. The same thing applied in the case of [Archbishop] Makarios whom Lennox-Boyd had denounced in a Press Conference held on the previous Sunday.[50] In fact in the Press Conference where he disclosed details from the diaries which implicated Makarios, there was really no new fact which had any particular significance at all. Lennox-Boyd was very amiable, he gave us a lot of sherry and certainly was very quiet and patient in the face of some fairly strong attacks from Bevan. But why he invited us round is hard to say. He can hardly have assumed that our attitude was likely to have changed; nor that anything that he could say to us would make very much difference.

---

49 Lt-General George Grivas (1898–1974) was a soldier and conspirator seeking Enosis, the union with Greece of his Cyprus birthplace. He led several terrorist organisations: 'X' in Athens in 1944, against the Communists on the side of the British; EOKA in Cyprus 1955–8, against the British in favour of Enosis, a cause promoted by Archbishop Makarios and the Orthodox Church; again in Cyprus 1971–3, against the independent government headed by the Archbishop. Commanding the Greek National Guard on the island 1964–7, he conspired against the mainland government. Greek Cypriots owe a lot to him, mostly misery.

50 Field Marshal Sir John (Lord) Harding was C.I.G.S. 1952–5, and Governor and C.-in-C. Cyprus 1955–7. Makarios III (1913–77) had been Archbishop of Cyprus since 1950, and was exiled to the Seychelles from March 1956 to March 1957. In 1960 he became President of the Republic of Cyprus, and he was re-elected in 1968.

Perhaps, I said, it was really a guilty conscience and feeling that they really had made a mistake, but even that seems unlikely.

There was a curious incident before we went along there which I mention only because it throws a little light on Bevan's personality and his relationship with me. In the ordinary way and with other people I would not dream of mentioning it. But this is what happened. I had arranged for us to see Lennox-Boyd at 11.30 and I had told my Secretary to invite Bevan to come round a little before so that, together with Jim Griffiths, we could discuss the line we were going to take. I got into the House myself about five or ten past eleven, and a little later – five or ten minutes later – I was joined in my room by Jim Griffiths. There was no sign of Bevan. We waited until nearly half past and then I told my Secretary to find out where he was. She came back after a bit with the news that he was in the Colonial Office, he had gone there on his own. I asked her whether she was sure he had got the message about coming to the House first. 'Yes', she said – she had sent him a letter, although I gathered she had put no particular time on it. When we got round there he was waiting for us, in fact he was already in the Colonial Secretary's room, and he said that he had come to the House at eleven o'clock to my room but finding nobody there had assumed there was some mistake. Now most people in those circumstances coming at eleven o'clock to my room would, pre-sumably, [have] waited to see whether I was going to turn up, seeing that the interview with the Colonial Secretary was not till 11.30. But I don't think that Bevan would wish to do that; wish, so to speak, [to] hang around waiting for me. That is the psychological explanation of why he, just finding nobody there, wandered off, instead of waiting for us.

There is not much more to report on Suez except that towards the end of last week there was another flare up through the left-wing press this time about the Government's intention to impose a solution by force, in fact to go to war. This was run by the *Manchester Guardian*, the *News Chronicle* and the *Herald*, and prompted me, partly because of what I was told by the *News Chronicle* lobby correspondent, to demand the recall of Parliament once again. I also had a conversation with the London Editor of the *Manchester Guardian* on the telephone and told him that I still could not believe that it was the Government's intention. He said that most of their information came from Service sources and I pointed out that no doubt all the military plans were made but that did not mean that the button would be pressed. This I believe to be the case, but undoubtedly they seem to have given the impression to all the military people – that it is intended to go to war. The same day [31 August] an interview with the *Guardian* that I had done at their request appeared which was very much on the same lines as an article I wrote on the previous Sunday [26 August] for *Reynolds* and did I think do something to check an impetus the

Government may have had. At any rate, Wadsworth, the Editor of the *Guardian*, seemed to be very pleased that I had done it.[51] It is extraordinary how difficult one finds it to get across to the public exactly what one thinks. If you make a speech, then only part of it is reproduced in the press and you can never be sure that they will not reproduce just one part rather than another, thus giving a totally false impression. If on the other hand you write an article where you can set out the whole of your position, of course it is only published in one newspaper and no other newspaper ever dreams of referring to it. It was perhaps just as well that I wrote both in *Reynolds* and they printed the interview in the *Guardian* because between them they certainly cover quite a wide section of the interested public.

This afternoon I saw Mintoff, the Prime Minister of Malta. He is involved in one of his usual rows with the Government. More and more people are saying that he is completely impossible. But they admit that so are all the other Maltese. We had a rather long discussion in the presence of Tommy Balogh and John Hatch.[52] The interesting thing about this is that relations between Tommy and Mintoff have obviously deteriorated. He used to be very close to him, his most intimate adviser, but now even Tommy is obviously getting fed up with him. It is not necessary to record the details of our conversation. But one thing Mintoff said rather worried me. He said that the people of Malta were sympathetic to Nasser as were all the Mediterranean people, because he represented a small country acting against a Colonial power, and that was very different from Mussolini who being a large power was attacking a smaller one. Hence if there were to be war with Egypt over Suez the Maltese people would be much less enthusiastic than they had been during the last war. Tommy and I argued a good deal about Nasser's position and in particular his threat to Israel (I always assume that Mintoff has Jewish blood in him somewhere). But Mintoff said well, even Israel was regarded as fairly well off with a lot of wealthy people and Western backing behind it, whereas the Arab countries were poor under-dogs, therefore sympathy in Malta lay with them. However, I think this is all largely a build-up in order to extract concessions from the British Government. And our dispute with him was really about how far he should go. I tried to warn him politely and in as friendly a way as I could that people were getting rather fed up with his antics and that if he went too far with the

51 A.P. Wadsworth, a journalist on the paper since 1917 and its editor since 1944, died two months later. Gerald Fay was its London editor, and it opposed Eden's Suez policy early, persistently and vigorously.
52 John (Lord) Hatch was secretary of the Labour Party's Commonwealth Department 1954–61. He had been national organiser of the I.L.P. 1944–8, and has written 11 books on Africa.

Government they were quite likely to call the whole of the integration thing off and simply resume Colonial Office rule.

Mintoff is an interesting character. I was told the other day that one of the reasons why he is so difficult is a sense of grievance because he married an English woman, a Cavendish-Bentinck as a matter of fact, therefore from an aristocratic family and he feels that she is not given the proper prestige and treatment which is due to her. But I doubt if there is much in this; it is more a question of his general Mediterranean outlook. He has a good deal of charm, but he certainly is extremely tiresome in argument and I imagine very slippery indeed. However, he relies to some extent on us. He knows that we have helped a great deal over integration and over subsequent difficulties he has had with the Government. And I fancy though he didn't much like it, he will take some notice of both what Tommy and I had to say to him.[53]

Wednesday, 5 September 1956

I had an interesting day yesterday. I lunched at the French Embassy. There was present only the Ambassador, Chauvel, and André who, I suppose, is the First Secretary.[54] André did not talk very much. I had already discussed the whole Suez situation with him on more than one occasion. But this was the first time that I had had a chance of talking with the Ambassador. We had the usual kind of argument about the use of force in which I put the case against using force on the basis of what Nasser had done so far, and Chauvel put the other side. Eventually, he more or less gave up, and said, 'Well, what you really mean is that it is a question of public relations'. I said, yes, that was what I meant; that we had to so conduct ourselves to get world opinion on our side. I had criticised the Government to Chauvel because they seemed to be so oblivious to the need for making a better showing and looking a bit more pacific and reasonable in the eyes of the world. He then said that he was going to Paris that afternoon and would be seeing Pineau [his Foreign Minister]. So I asked him to tell Pineau that in my opinion that if the talks with Nasser were not successful then France and Britain together should immediately refer the matter to the United Nations. I said I thought there were several good reasons for this. First, if we did not do it somebody else would, India, America or Russia. Secondly, it provided a new forum for further negotiations with Nasser. Thirdly, obviously Nasser himself did not want this; he clearly would be embarrassed at the U.N. partly because

53 He did not, and the integration plans were abandoned: see above, p. 470 n.
54 Gérard André was Second Counsellor.

of the failure of Egypt to carry out the Security [Council] resolution on the Israeli ships.[55] And finally I said that whatever we may have to do eventually it can only be an advantage to have been to the United Nations, whatever the exact outcome of that would be. Chauvel seemed to be impressed with these arguments and promised to pass it all on to Pineau when he saw him.

We had, as one always does at the French Embassy, an extraordinarily good lunch – trout in aspic, partridge although it is the very beginning of September, and a wonderful sort of chocolate confection. And in addition the usual excellent wine with the flunkey whispering to you the name of the wine and the vintage – you can never hear it, but it sounds terribly good. The only other interesting things that came out of this conversation were firstly, that Chauvel was quite certain that the press leakage, or unofficial press stories, about the intention to use force had come not from the Foreign Office but from 10 Downing Street, i.e. from William Clark*.[56] This is in accordance with some of the things I have heard from other quarters. But Chauvel himself was quite emphatic on the point. Secondly, he said that the whole idea of the Conference had come from Dulles who had thought of it in terms of the San Francisco Conference over the Japanese Treaty,[57] although he, Chauvel, could not help noticing all the differences. I drew him out a bit on his views on Eden and Selwyn Lloyd. He said that they thought Eden was very nervous; on the other hand they had a considerable opinion of Selwyn Lloyd, or rather Chauvel had. He saw him a lot, he thought he was clear-headed, knew his own mind and was very balanced. He takes everything into account, he said, including the internal position here. From this I deduced that Selwyn must have told Chauvel that the Government would be in some difficulty in going to war because of the position of the Labour Party and a lot of the country in addition.

The second interesting thing that happened was a visit from Sir Francis de Guingand. He was [General] Montgomery's Chief of Staff during the war, beginning with the 8th Army and if I remember rightly going on right through in the European campaign. He wrote a book called, I believe, *Operation Victory*. When I became Leader of the Party he wrote me a letter congratulating me, although I had never met him or had any contact with him, and saying that in his opinion, the Tories ought either to get a

---

55 Approved on 1 September 1951, it called upon Egypt to allow Israeli ships to pass through the Canal. Egypt had been defying it for five years.

56 Clark was Eden's press officer until he resigned in protest at the Suez invasion.

57 The San Francisco conference of 52 nations met from 4 to 8 September 1951, and ratified the treaty which Dulles had previously negotiated for the U.S. No amendments were allowed, so the U.S.S.R., Poland and Czechoslovakia would not sign; no Chinese were invited.

new leader or give way to a new Government altogether. He mentioned in this rather extraordinary letter that he had known Eden during the war, that was the reason why he said this. He had telephoned a few weeks ago, but we had been unable to fix up a meeting time. But he arrived yesterday afternoon. He was a man of about only 55, I suppose, quite bright and chirpy.

He launched at once into an attack upon Eden. He said that he had in his book written a great deal about him, but the lawyers had insisted on cutting it out, because of libel. But it appears that he had been connected with him over the Greece campaign. Apparently he, de Guingand, who was then Chief of Staff to Wavell,[58] had been sent over to Greece with Eden to examine the possibilities of our fighting there if, as was expected, the Germans attacked. All the military evidence according to de Guingand was absolutely against the campaign. It was clearly going to be a disaster from the start. But Eden had obviously made up his mind that we had got to do it, and according to de Guingand he was quite unscrupulous and tried to make him fudge the figures, counting rifles as guns, and things like that. He said that in fact the campaign had not been more of a disaster only because of very good luck and some extremely good generalship. He also objected to the fact that Eden had claimed that the Germans had delayed their attack on Russia because of our rearguard action in Greece. De Guingand thought there was nothing in this at all, and in fact he quoted other authorities, German ones, to the effect that the attack on Russia had been delayed entirely on account of the weather. He went on to talk about Suez, and said that the general view in Africa was very much the same as the Labour Party. They thought the whole thing had been gravely mismanaged; they didn't like Nasser; on the other hand they didn't see seriously how we could go to war. He, de Guingand, is now working for Tube Investments, I suppose as their General Manager in South Africa, and knows Stedeford who is one of these rather enlightened businessmen who was a friend of Stafford Cripps.[59] Altogether quite an interesting interlude.

Then, finally, Hugh Cudlipp rang me up, and said he had some important things to communicate to me which he couldn't do on the phone and could we meet. I said I would go over to the *Daily Mirror* and see him that evening about six, which I did. He told me that in the past two days Cecil King and he had seen two leading members of the Govern-

58 General Sir Archibald (Field Marshal Earl) Wavell was C.-in-C. Middle East 1939–41, India 1941–3, and Viceroy of India 1943–7.
59 Sir Ivan Stedeford was Chairman and managing director of Tube Investments 1944–63; de Guingand was born in 1900, and published *Operation Victory* in 1947.

ment, it turned out to be Macmillan and Monckton, and a third person I knew, which was Donald Tyerman, the Editor of *The Economist*, had seen Butler. From these conversations emerged the following picture. The Tories are not 'bluffing'. Macmillan is determined to have a show-down with Nasser. Just as, if not more, determined than Eden. He and Eden will, if necessary, resign on this issue. Everything is ready and they are quite convinced that they are going to win, and win quickly. On the other hand Monckton is very much more cautious and apparently said to Hugh [Cudlipp] that he thought the line I had taken was perfectly right from the start. Butler is also said to be cautious. He is in favour of force but only as a last resort. I asked HC exactly what was meant by this. Did it mean that if the Menzies-Nasser talks broke down he would then put the troops in straight away?[60] Cudlipp thought not. The implication seemed to be that there would be some provocation by Nasser and they would then take action. They all seemed to be expecting this. Incidentally this fitted in to some extent with what the French Ambassador said also. I said, 'But supposing Nasser does not give any provocation'. Then Cudlipp admitted that it did not seem that Macmillan and Co. could do anything. Nevertheless they were all very worked up. Macmillan had talked to Cecil King and spoken in terms, as I say, of resigning if necessary. 'If the country hadn't got the guts to stand up to this tinpot dictator it's no use'.

The exact implication of this was not clear. King had thought that he meant that there might be a dissolution. Macmillan it appears intended to convey that he was staunchly with Eden and there was no question of his replacing Eden. They would, so to speak, go out together. King had thought this so important that he had asked Cudlipp to see me – he himself was just going off to Africa – because he thought there might be a change of Government. This fitted in with a rumour I had heard about a dissolution during the course of the previous day or two. We then had some discussion about this, and I pointed out how unrealistic the whole thing was. If they went to war with Egypt they could hardly have a General Election while that was going on. If, on the other hand, they did not go to war, they would not have a General Election on the issue of whether they should go to war; that would be completely crazy. Would they be forced to have a dissolution? Well, that would depend on exactly what hap-pened. If Eden did not get the backing of the Conservative Party and resigned, and they were split, of course conceivably they would have to give way to us as a Government and we would no doubt have our Dissolution and a General Election. But all this seemed to me to be far, far too good to be conceivable. They would hardly destroy their own

60 Menzies led the five negotiators who put to Nasser the 18-power proposals approved in London on 23 August. Their talks, in Cairo, lasted from 3 to 9 September.

Party quite so obviously.[61] Hugh agreed that the whole thing sounded rather improbable, but nevertheless wanted to emphasise that Macmillan did seem to be extremely worked up about the whole business still. At any rather [rate?] Hugh was obviously fascinated by the idea that I might become Prime Minister within the next few weeks. Wanted to say to me that I should be thinking about who was to be Foreign Secretary. He did not think it should be Alf Robens, in fact it clearly should not be. Had I thought of bringing back Shawcross for this purpose? I said that while I was most anxious to have Shawcross back I did not think of him entirely as Foreign Secretary. As a matter of fact I have not, of course, made up my mind on this, but I mentioned the possibility of Jim Griffiths doing it – this had many advantages. He would not be there permanently, people would accept it; he would work well with me; he is experienced, nobody's nose would be particularly out of joint and so on. Hugh thought there was a good deal of force in this argument.

Later that same evening [Tuesday 4 September] we dined with Woodrow Wyatt. He had said he had spoken to Julian Amery who of course is Macmillan's son-in-law and Amery's line was that the Government were determined to have war; that the Whips were going to find out if there was enough backing from the Tories to justify this. If there was then they would recall Parliament and announce it. If there was not they would go ahead without recalling Parliament before they actually went to war. Then, of course, having gone to war they would expect the Tory Party to back them. This seemed to me also to be pretty lunatic. But it is interesting as it fitted in pretty well with Cudlipp's story to me.

One other small incident which may be of interest. Herbert Morrison came to see me yesterday afternoon, ostensibly the reason for the visit was that he had received an invitation from the Prime Minister to be a member of a small Committee on the question of higher civil service salaries. I was a little surprised that he should ask my views before agreeing to accept this. We then had a conversation about Suez; he of course takes a much more pro-Government line. But he did not argue with me very much on the issue of force. He did however let slip one thing, he said that as an ex-Foreign Secretary, the only one at present in

61 However implausible, these speculations do not depend only on the melodramatic imagination of Cecil King. At the same time the permanent head of the Foreign Office was telling the Canadian High Commissioner that 'a very senior Minister' was urging that if the country would not support the use of force, Eden should resign and let the Opposition take responsibility for appeasement – and for a stoppage of oil supplies, and 5 million unemployed: T. Robertson, *Crisis* (Hutchinson, 1964), p. 90.

the House, he said, meaning presumably on our side, he had seen the Prime Minister, I rather gathered on more than one occasion. 'I am going to see him again this afternoon', he said. This struck me as slightly unusual, not that Herbert should have seen the Prime Minister but that the Prime Minister should have sent for him. Could it conceivably be that Eden has some vague idea of getting some support on the Labour side, and is using Herbert Morrison for this purpose? It would be, I think, a bad miscalculation on his part, but it could not be ruled out altogether.[62]

Friday, 14 September 1956

This has been a most fascinating week. A week during which Parliament in its emergency Session has debated the Suez crisis. I will come to all that later. But first a record of some events during the week.

On Tuesday [11th] I saw Guy Mollet, the French Prime Minister, at his request. At any rate the interview was arranged on the suggestion of the French Embassy. I went to the Residence early in the morning, about nine o'clock and spent the better part of an hour there. Mollet I thought was rather defeatist and highly emotional about Suez; this of course was the main subject of our discussion. He put forward the familiar view for which of course there is a great deal to be said, that it was essential that Nasser should not be allowed to get away with this. If he did get away with it, then it would be the pre-war story all over again. This was the same episode all over again in 1956 as the reoccupation of the Rhineland. If we had stood up to Hitler then there would have been no war. If we stand up to Nasser now there will be no war. As far as exactly what would happen is concerned, well first of all if he got away with it he would form an Arab Federation. Then he would make war on Israel. There would be anyhow a North African Arab State formed and this of course would be fatal for France.[63] These were the lines on which Mollet argued, as I say, rather passionately, vehemently and in a sense despairingly also.

I naturally put the other point of view. Not that Nasser should be allowed to get away with it, but that we could not go to war – quite apart from tearing up the United Nations Charter, the physical consequences would be disastrous, and no solution. On the other hand, if we played the

62 Morrison went to the United States later in September and was abroad during the Suez invasion – to Eden's lasting regret: Donoughue & Jones (1973), p. 546. Eden also approached the T.U.C.: *HG*, p. 248.
63 The French blamed Nasser for the continuation of the Algerian war, and feared that newly independent Morocco and Tunisia would also turn hostile.

hand slowly and applied economic pressure we could reduce Nasser's prestige. This did not, however, impress Mollet at all. He appeared to think the United Nations was more or less a sham, it would lead to delays, and meanwhile Nasser would get away with it. About the only new point which came into the discussion at all was about the exact proposal to use force. Mollet said of course they had no intention of just putting in the troops, when negotiations with Nasser broke down. There would have to be an excuse for it. What they had in mind was some kind of action they would take which Nasser would either have to give way to or resist, and if he resisted then there would be an excuse for force.

He was rather vague about this, but it filled me with some misgiving. As far as I remember I said that they would have to be very careful not to do something which appeared to be direct provocation.

We also had some discussion on our own and later when Morgan Phillips arrived about a visit to Paris. There had been a plan for a meeting between Mollet, Ollenhauer the German Socialist leader and myself;[64] each of us accompanied by a few other people to discuss the problems of European security. And this had been arranged for September 13th to the 15th. The Germans, however, made difficulties about this at the last minute, and for us it became impossible because of the recall of Parliament for the debate on Suez. But Mollet was very anxious however that we should go over on Saturday, not to discuss Europe but to discuss Suez. He was obviously much concerned with the criticism in France of the attitude of the British Labour Party. He had been asked questions about why we took this view, and pointed out that he was always very careful not to blame us. He had before the meeting written to me about a speech of John Strachey's in which Strachey had attacked France.[65] I gathered he wanted the meeting to make a kind of show of solidarity.

We said we would consider it. At first we were inclined to think it would be possible but we did not commit ourselves. Later that day I told the Parliamentary Committee about this proposal and they urged me very strongly not to go. They argued with force – Bevan and Edith Summerskill in particular – that it would be most embarrassing. There would have to be a press statement; what were we to say; it we said we agreed, that would be highly embarrassing to me and perhaps to Mollet as well; whereas if we said we disagreed it would advertise the difference between the Parties. Moreover, Eden might make out that I was trying to go behind his back and influence Mollet. I thought these arguments so good that I immediately telephoned to Morgan Phillips telling him to wash the whole thing out. Despite this, two days later Mollet rang up, through a secretary, and

64 The typescript reads 'Mollet, Adenauer, . . .' but this is clearly a typing error.
65 Strachey had attacked Mollet's Algerian policy, not for the last time. In December, HG was himself to clash violently with the French Socialists.

asked again if I would not go to Paris. But I told him no, and promised to write him a letter, explaining the reasons, which I have now done. On the same day, Tuesday, a very odd thing happened.

Alf Robens said, 'There's an Egyptian who wants to see you. He says he has a message from Nasser for you.' I gathered that Alf had had lunch with him. So, after the Parliamentary Committee, this Egyptian came in. I cannot recollect his name. He produced a bit of paper, then proceeded to give me the message. It was roughly as follows. Nasser wanted me to know as far as the spy trials were concerned that the English people had confessed, not because they had had any ill treatment or anything of that kind but because they had been confronted with documents which proved their guilt. The trials would take place and they would be convicted. Nevertheless, he wanted to assure me that he had no intention of punishing them. He would, in fact, send them back, all of them, to this country.[66] He was anxious to make it plain that he wanted to co-operate on the Canal, but there would have to be some kind of a new start; though he did not specify exactly what that should be. He knew my views on Israel and wanted to assure me that here too he wanted peace, but it could only come slowly. It was not possible to move fast. I thanked the Egyptian for telling me all this and said in a pretty reserved sort of way that I would of course treat what he had said to me in a completely confidential way, especially about the spy trials, though I was glad to hear of Nasser's intentions, that our judicial system was, of course, quite different, and that once people were in the hands of the Courts the Government could not intervene. On the other hand, equally, they could not cross examine them. As for co-operation, if this was really the case it was important that when the next round of negotiations took place Nasser should be willing to meet the users of the Canal half way. Perhaps this could be within the United Nations. And finally, as far as Israel went Nasser himself could do something very valuable here. He could make a really important gesture which would be to let the Israeli ships through the Canal. The Egyptian, incidentally, had already said that he couldn't do that because he was entitled under the 1888 Convention to stop them since Egypt was still at war with Israel. I pointed out that that wasn't in

66 Thirty people had been arrested a fortnight earlier, four of them British nationals. Twenty (including eight British) were tried in May 1957 and seven (five British) acquitted. One Englishman had been convicted in absence, one served 3 years of a 5-year sentence, and a Maltese served 4 years of 10, being released as soon as diplomatic relations were restored in 1961. Both were sentenced to hard labour but did only six weeks of it, and said after their return that they had been well treated. For the behaviour of British Intelligence, showing the charges to have been well founded, see their favourite press spokesman: Pincher (1979), pp. 93–4. He blames George Blake for betraying the agents.

fact the grounds for stopping them. It was supposed to be for Egypt's self-defence, but that this was a transparent excuse. The Egyptian then said that he couldn't really do this because of the effect in the other Arab States. It was altogether an odd episode. I suppose Nasser wanted to influence my attitude during the debate. I ought to have added that he prefaced the message by thanking me for what I had done in trying to restrain the Government from making war.

The Parliamentary Committee went off quite satisfactorily; we did not have much discussion on policy since we had done that pretty thoroughly in the previous week. And anyhow there was really no serious disagreement. It was settled that I should speak first after Eden; that we would not put down a Motion until we heard his speech. The Government were in fact doing exactly the same thing, i.e. waiting before putting down a motion. We agreed that Kenneth Younger should wind up the first day and Alf Robens open the second day. That opened the question of who should wind up the meeting [sic]; many of the Committee saying that they thought I should speak again. I said that I was not anxious to do this, but I thought possibly Jim Griffiths should do it. I may say a little later on, during the course of the debate when we were settling who was to wind up, Jim pressed me again to do so. By now I knew the Prime Minister was going to wind up and so I agreed. But he said the reason he wanted me to wind up was to strengthen my position in the Party. Both he and the Chief Whip then said in a kind of guilty way, which was rather charming, that they thought I ought to know now that there had in fact been a good deal of trouble about my speech on August 2nd in the Constituencies. Some organisation had undoubtedly been at work, spreading it round that I was really playing in with the Government, and in favour of war, etc., etc. The decision which he and Morgan Phillips had made to circulate my speech to the Constituency parties had undoubtedly done much to stop that,[67] and what had happened in the meanwhile, including of course my speech of the day before, had really brought it to an end. But all the same it would be best if I were to wind up the debate. I really do consider myself extraordinarily lucky in having such a wonderfully loyal and thoroughly decent person as the Deputy Leader. Jim said at one point, 'I am 66. I have no interest in that [sic] – I merely want to help'. And that is exactly what he does.

During the opening stage of the second day's debate, when Selwyn Lloyd was attacking me, and giving various openings, I couldn't help turning to Jim; 'I am glad I am speaking in the debate'. And he said 'I told

67 Made on 9 August and at once notified to Gaitskell (Griffiths to HG, 9.8.56, file P.106–2). They underlined the U.N. passages in the speech.

you so!' And he said the same thing again after what turned out to be quite a successful second speech.

There had been some talk about trouble at the Party meeting over the second speech, but in fact there was none at all. I explained what had happened exactly while the House had not been sitting; what we had done in the Committee and what sort of line we should follow during the debate. The discussion was not very good and rather patchy; and few people made good speeches. There was rather too much inclination to ignore the danger of Nasser. But there were one or two encouraging signs. Particularly Sydney Silverman of all people said he thought we must make it quite plain that there was danger, not so much for the Canal users but for the rest of the Middle East. I had already made this plain, but he thought I should make it even plainer in my speech. Perhaps this greater unity in the Party is having another good effect, namely that the extremists seem to become a little more sensible. Even Zilliacus made quite a reasonable speech during the debate. And finally perhaps most extraordinary of all Warbey who is one of the most tiresome and persistent people on the Left came over and had supper with me on the Wednesday evening after my first speech and more or less apologised for attacking the August 2nd speech. He even gave me a joke for my winding up speech – the Cape Users' Association.[68]

Still leaving the general discussion of the week on one side, I have to record two or three other small incidents. Hegloff, the Swedish Ambassador, came to see me on Thursday morning [13 September]. He had been a delegate at the London Conference and had also been to Cairo with Unden, the Swedish Foreign Minister. He had suggested, he told me, to Unden, that he should come and see me, and tell me what had happened at Cairo, and Unden had thought it a very good idea. Hegloff is a charming man with a very nice wife too, a gay, socialite figure to whom I have referred in this diary before. He said that Nasser had not been during the talks quite as adamant as appeared from the written record. He had been perfectly courteous and friendly, but he hadn't really given way much. They had, however, derived the impression, not so much from their talks with him but in their talks with the Persians and the Ethiopians, and presumably other people as well, that he really was a most dangerous man.[69] Hegloff said that the Middle Eastern countries generally were

68 Left-wing Jewish M.P.s were (as in 1967) ambivalent about the Egypt-Israeli conflict: see L.D. Epstein, *British Politics in the Suez Crisis* (Pall Mall Press, 1964), Ch. 8. (Silverman was Jewish, Warbey and Zilliacus not.)

69 The Ethiopian, Iranian and Swedish Foreign Ministers, with a U.S. diplomat, constituted Menzies' mission to put the 18-nation proposals to Nasser (above, p. 597 n.). Bö Unden had held his office in 1924–6 as well as 1945–62.

terrified of his building his Arab empire; particularly the Ethiopians and the Persians were frightened. Maybe the people in those countries did not mind but the Governments certainly did. On the other hand, they did not think, said Hegloff, that Nasser was fanatical about the Suez problem. They had argued with him on the lines indicated in Menzies' letter, that he would be much better advised to accept the 18-Power proposals as a basis for negotiation, and that if he didn't, then he would have to face rather undesirable economic consequences. Hegloff said he thought that Nasser didn't understand at all about economic consequences. He was really just an Army Officer and all that kind of thing was above him. He thought purely in political terms.

As to what should be done Unden and the other Scandinavian Ministers all took the view that the use of force was pointless. It was certainly true that Nasser must not be allowed to get away with it, but other ways must be found. They thought by far the best way was economic pressure, and they believed that this could be quite effective. It was not only or so much a matter of going round the Cape, although there was much to be said for that, because really the Canal itself was not terribly important to Egypt. Other things were much more important. If only, said Hegloff, the United States would take the same financial measures as we had done – that would be important.[70] And perhaps even more vital, if only they would make use of their power in cotton they could create a very serious situation in Egypt indeed. In short, it appeared from what he said, that the Scandinavians were really very much of the same opinion as we in the Labour Party. The only difference was that they appeared to be doubtful about taking it to U.N.O., on account of the long delays. I pointed out that this did not really matter, as long as Nasser was under pressure, and it was a mistake to suppose that time was on his side. Hegloff said that he entirely agreed with that, the opposite was the truth, and time if we played our cards rightly was on our side.

Then, finally, this evening Gerald Fay, the London editor of the *Manchester Guardian* rang me up and asked me to see him because he had some material from Washington about Dulles' view on the Canal plan. I went down and met him at the Garrick Club and he gave me the stuff to read through. The chief point which emerged from this, which was evidently a kind of background talk to a few newspapermen, was that Dulles himself claimed to have brought forward the Users' plan in order to stop Britain and France making war. Dulles told the press people that there appeared to be no alternative, Britain and France could think of nothing else except force, and so this plan was produced. There were a number of other things that he said, but this was the key point that

70 Eden (1960, p. 455) complained of American reluctance to use economic pressure on Egypt.

emerged. Dulles appeared to try to treat the British and French point of view very fairly, and indeed rather to lean over backwards in criticising Nasser and admitting that there was a good deal to be said for the British and French point of view. One couldn't assume that small nations were necessarily always right when they did this sort of thing. But he equally made it perfectly plain that the U.S. would not use force themselves and that if Britain and France used force they would not have the moral backing of the U.S.

And so, now, a few general observations on this extraordinary week. So far as we in the Labour Party are concerned there is not much to record. It was quite obvious that the Party was substantially united, and what I am really pleased about is that I think they have completely swallowed all the condemnation of Nasser that was in my original speech. The only thing they always want made clear is that we are not against nationalisation as such. We got the condemnation of Nasser into our amendment, and I was able to say, with no opposition at all from the Party, that I stuck by everything I had said on August 2nd. But the really interesting thing is what has been happening on the other side of the House. It seems to me that three things have really happened simultaneously to produce yesterday evening's result. First, of course, the pressure of public opinion has begun to worry the Tories, and the non-Suez Group have certainly begun to wake up to the danger of the situation. How far this has been egged on by the more cautious members of the Cabinet, I don't know. Monckton said to me during the course of the week, 'I am very, very unhappy, I don't think I shall be there much longer'. I said, 'Well, you ought to stay as long as you can, and as long as you have any influence'. He said, 'Yes, that's what I am doing. I am doing all I can.' But he is, of course, a person who is rather inclined to talk about resigning frequently. Nevertheless, I think he would have done so if we had gone to war.[71] This growth of a peace movement, as it were, in the Conservative Party seems to have culminated in the speech of Heald, the former Attorney-General, which certainly created a deep impression on the Government Benches.[72] He was really saying in so many words exactly what we were saying. Very different from the howling mob which barracked us on the previous day. Then, secondly, there is of course

71 Ten days later he told Eden he could not continue, but was persuaded to become Paymaster-General. Antony Head took over as Minister of Defence on 18 October. ('Yesterday's result' earlier in the paragraph, refers to Eden's supposed assurances at the end of the debate.)
72 Sir Lionel Heald, M.P. for Chertsey 1950–70, Attorney-General 1951–4, spoke at 558 H.C. Deb. 182–7.

public opinion which indeed has produced this result on the Tory side. The Tory Central Office must have been getting worried about warmongering, and they must have been worried about the Gallup poll, and the strong demand that the dispute should go to the United Nations and so on. And finally, of course, there was Mr Dulles himself. Eden played his cards, I think, very badly here, because he described the Users' Association in the most provocative way, and almost forced Dulles therefore to use the famous phrase, that the U.S. would not shoot their way through the Canal. This in turn gave me my opportunity, and enabled me to force the admission from Eden that Britain would not do so either. But that admission itself was in contradiction to what had been said the day before, and gave the impression at any rate that Eden had really abandoned force. I may be too optimistic but my feeling is that we are probably over the hump now. Certainly the danger of immediate war provoked by trying to break through the Canal seems to have been averted.

What I guess happened is this. If there was, as I suppose, a division in the Cabinet, it would have come to a crisis point after the failure of the Menzies mission. Salisbury, Macmillan and perhaps Eden and some of the others would have been saying, 'Well now at it boys, we must go ahead'. The others, Monckton and Co. would have been saying, 'No, we really can't do this, it must go to the U.N.' The Americans on the other hand seem to have objected to going to the U.N. At this point along comes the Canal Users' plan, and the Cabinet jump at it because it is a way out. Chipman of the American Embassy, to whom I spoke about this, said they knew very little about it, except that it was very much wanted by the British Government. And of course they wanted it because on the one hand the Moncktonites could treat it as Dulles did, as a bit of negotiátion, while the others could still regard it as provocation. But this duality was brought to an end pretty clearly last night. The Left wing seemed to accept the speech and indeed I received many compliments.

Sunday, 23 September 1956

Following on the account of the debate, on the next day, that was last Friday [14th], the papers carried a pretty confused picture of what Eden had agreed to. And *The Times* had a leader in which while they seemed to be quite certain that Eden had indicated that we would take the dispute to the U.N. Security Council if Nasser refused to co-operate with the Canal Users' Association, [they] made the mistake which has been made by so many other people in this last few weeks, including Eden in the debate;

confusing what it was we were really after. In their leader they referred to Eden's answer to my demand that the problem would go to the Security Council before force were used. I decided in view of the confusion to take the rather unusual step of writing to *The Times* myself, and did so. Some people have been surprised that I should have done so because in my letter I questioned whether Eden really had given definite assurances, and therefore in a sense played down my own achievement of getting the assurances out of him. But I thought first of all, that I must clear up the confusion about reference to the Security Council, which was what I was supposed to have asked for, and undertaking not to use force outside the Charter, which is in fact what I did ask for. And in the course of preparing the letter, I thought I might just as well look and see what Eden had actually said about the Canal Users' Association, and what he would do if Nasser refused co-operation. In Hansard there is no full stop at the end of this famous sentence but – 'interruption' – I could not resist therefore in the letter drawing attention to this and the contradiction, or the difference at any rate, between the statement made by Eden at the last minute of the debate and the two previous statements he had made on the same subject. The letter will be available in my papers. [73]

On the whole I think the Party thought it was a good plan to have written, even although it has provoked as one would expect, angry retorts from Tories.

Document No. 19

HG to *The Times*[74]

The Editor   14th September, 1956.
The Times.

Sir,

The answers given by the Prime Minister in the Debate yesterday have still left behind confusion about the intentions of Her Majesty's Government regarding the use of force in the Suez dispute. According to your leading article today, he has made it plain (in reply to my question, quoting Mr. Dulles, whether he would say on behalf of Her Majesty's Government that they too would not 'shoot their way through the Canal')

---

73 It follows. Eden spoke at cols. 2–15, 297–308, and HG at cols. 15–32, 287–297. The 'difference' involved cols. 11–12, 304–5, 307–8.
74 From his Papers, file P. 110. His emphasis.

that if Egypt refused to co-operate with the Canal Users' Association 'we should take them to the Security Council'. I hope this is correct. But there are some grounds for uncertainty.

First, Hansard records at the end of the sentence which you quote not a full stop but '– interruption –', implying the possibility of further words which were not recorded.

Secondly, it must be remembered that, only a few minutes before, the Prime Minister gave a different answer to the same question when he spoke of a case being brought against Egypt 'at the Security Council or *by a similar method*'.

Thirdly, on the previous day he used different phraseology altogether when he referred to taking further steps in the same situation 'either through the United Nations or *by other means*'. Many at the time presumed that by other means he meant the use of force.

In all the circumstances, it is highly desirable to remove any remaining doubts, that the Prime Minister should now confirm that your interpretation of his definitive statement is the correct one.

But there is another of his answers which is even less satisfactory. Your leader states 'and as for Mr. Gaitskell's demand that he give a *pledge not to use force except after reference to the Security Council*, he said "neither I nor any British Minister standing at this Box could give it as an absolute pledge or guarantee".' Fair enough. But, though the Prime Minister attributed it to me, I made no such demand. What I asked and what our amendment proposed was a declaration that force would not be used '*except in conformity with our obligations under the Charter of the United Nations*.' We put the question in this form because the Charter recognises very properly, under Article 51, the right of 'individual or collective self-defence if an armed attack occurs against a Member of the United Nations, until the Security Council has taken the measures necessary to maintain international peace and security'.

The real issue is whether even apart from Article 51 and the rest of the Charter the Government contemplate the use of force. To that crucial question we have, unfortunately, still no reply. Since Parliament is now in recess we cannot put it in the House of Commons. I hope, nevertheless, that the Prime Minister will take an early opportunity of making his position clear.

Diary for 23 September 1956 continued

Last week I went to Germany for a couple of days and had quite an interesting time. I arrived on Wednesday morning [19th] and was driven to Bonn where I had lunch with the British Chargé d'Affaires, a man called Roger Allen, very conventional type, a Tory, not very exciting, very cautious.[75] He had asked Brentano to lunch and a number of other people, most of them officials, I gathered, in the German Foreign Office. After lunch I had a talk with Brentano alone for about 20 minutes. It was entirely about Suez. He was just about to leave for England for the latest Conference. As I expected, he took a pretty poor view of the Users' Association. He seemed to be rather indignant that this had been launched without any consultation with the eighteen powers who had backed the Menzies mission. I told him roughly what had happened in the debate and urged strongly that he should try and get the new Conference on the line of reference to the Security Council and then negotiating in a half way position with Nasser. As far as I could make out, he was very much in agreement with the line we had taken, though one never can be quite sure. My view is that Germany is being very cautious about moving away from Britain and France. They are not really taking an independent line at all on this. And they also want to keep in with the United States.

Later in the afternoon I saw Adenauer, the Chancellor, at his request. I had not really talked with him before; only just met him at functions. In fact we had an interesting talk, which he obviously took seriously. We sat down in his room on sofa and armchair with an interpreter, but I found it very easy to follow what he said as he spoke slowly and distinctly. Although he is now 81 he is a good deal more vigorous physically I would say than Churchill, and there was nothing wrong with his mental powers. We talked for a time about Suez, there was nothing really very novel to say there, except that he was very critical of the United States for the way they had handled the Aswan Dam business. For the rest, I think he took pretty much our view as to how the dispute should be handled.

We then got on however, to what he really wanted to talk to me about, which was Europe. He was extremely gloomy about the situation; thought that America was going to go isolationist, perhaps not this year or next year but it would come in time. The democracies were getting more and more divided and the Russians were simply laughing at us. He begged me to give my support to Confederation in Europe in some form or other, he used the word Staatsbund and I gathered that he meant by

75 (Sir) Roger Allen, Minister in Bonn 1955–6, later Ambassador to Greece, Iraq and Turkey.

this the kind of political council on which although there would be no veto, there would have to be a certain-sized majority before any action could be taken. I told him I thought he was much too gloomy about America. I did not really think they were going isolationist, and quoted the interest they were showing in NATO. I also said I didn't think that a change of machinery in Europe would really matter. What was important was that Foreign Ministers should make an effort to get together and settle their disputes and differences before coming out into public. Adenauer was apparently particularly incensed over an interview he had had with the United States Secretary of Air,[76] who had talked about the United States not using the hydrogen bomb until the Russians did; but arguing that the Russians probably would not use it because of the fear of deterrence [sic]. I said to Allen afterwards, that I couldn't quite see the point of this, and he said that what Adenauer had really got in mind was the intolerable feeling of being left in the middle between these two powers with neither of them caring about you, and also the implication that there was no need for conventional arms.

I also said to Adenauer as my parting shot, although indeed the discussion was extremely friendly, that one thing I thought was essential, was that people should conduct their foreign policy on the basis of what was good for the Western Alliance, and not on the basis of what was helpful for internal politics. I think he guessed that I was getting at him because of his stern refusal to have anything to do with the Social Democratic Party. He said this with a smile: 'Well, in that way, you seem to have made more progress than we have'.

I must say that everywhere one went in Germany one got the impression that Adenauer was becoming increasingly unpopular. Everyone assumed that his Party were going to lose the next election, in [the] sense that they would no longer have an absolute majority at the end of it, and there seemed to be no doubt that the result of the election would be for the Socialists to be the largest party with about 40% of the votes, and Adenauer's C.D.U. about the same, might be less, with the rest of the votes going to the F.D.P. which would really hold the balance.[77] I will turn to this subject in a moment. The point of mentioning it here was that Adenauer's extreme gloom [is] no doubt rather mixed up with the fact that no doubt he feels that he has been rather let down by Britain and

76 Donald Quarles (of the Bell Telephone Co.) had been Assistant Secretary of Defense, responsible for guided missiles and other research work, until becoming Secretary of the Air Force 1955–7.
77 His informants were quite wrong. In 1957 the C.D.U. won (uniquely) an absolute majority of both votes and seats and their longest-ever lead over the S.P.D., who did not approach 40% until 1965, or exceed the C.D.U. vote until 1972.

America; he has put himself out on a limb in Germany by sticking out for conscription and the 500,000-strong German Army, and also against any further kind of negotiations with Russia. At the same time while he has been doing this, of course America and Britain and France have all been cooling off quite considerably as far as defence is concerned, and there has been a great deal of talk about abolishing conscription.

After the talk with Adenauer I met some members of the Socialist Party – the SPD – and answered questions. Nothing very much came out of that. They seemed more or less to take our view; indeed one of them asked how on earth could I explain how people in the twentieth century at this date could think in terms like the Suez Group of the Tory Party.

Later that evening I gave my lecture. The hall was completely packed and indeed people could not get in and were standing. This, I think, was largely due to the Suez crisis and the fact that I had been so prominent in it. I felt a bit sorry for them because I [had] decided not to talk about Suez, nor to any extent about German rearmament. So they had to stand there and listen to a pretty academic lecture on foreign affairs generally. About the only interesting point that emerged was, in fact, connected with German rearmament. In the course of my talk I said that I did not believe that disarmament should be made dependent upon a political settlement. This obviously created some disturbance or, at any rate, opposition. It was put to me best perhaps on the following day by a rather remarkable woman called the Countess Dönhoff, who I think came from Eastern Germany and escaped to Hamburg where she lived and was now editing *Die Zeit*, one of the German periodicals.[78] She came to see me on the following day in Düsseldorf, and incidentally came to my talk there as well the following night, and she argued very much against me on this. She said they were really all frightened that if there were a reduction of tension then everybody would forget about German unity, and the status quo would gradually become accepted. I gave the obvious arguments against this view and indicated that unless you really were prepared for war it was impossible to put forward the need for German reunification as a kind of obstacle for [? to] reducing tension. I also argued that in fact it would be more likely that the Russians might agree to reunification if there was disarmament and less tension than the other way round. But psychologically it is clear that quite a number of the Germans feel that way. My Chairman at the second lecture at Düsseldorf [who] was a very respectable member of Adenauer's Party and had been in their Parliament, whispered to me when that part of my speech was being translated, 'We don't all agree with you on this'.

I spent the second day at Düsseldorf, and in the course of it met at lunch the young men of the F.D.P. These people have been described as

78 And one of Europe's best weeklies. She still runs it (1983).

neo-Nazis, yet the curious thing is that the Socialists in North Rhine-Westphalia, of which Düsseldorf is the capital, have a coalition with them at the moment in the Government, and it appears to work extremely well. However Frau Milchsack, my hostess, thought it was a good plan for me to see these people. She also invited to lunch Rosenberg, who is one of the best people in the German T.U.C.[79] He is in fact the chief economic man. The three young men she asked were a man called Döring, Scheel and Weyer; the latter in fact did very little talking – he is the Finance Minister in the local Government, and a sort of Deputy Prime Minister. Döring turned out to be quite a charming, vigorous, youngish man with considerable personality, but I thought not a great deal of vanity. The interesting thing was that both he and Scheel let Rosenberg do almost all the talking even for them. When I asked, for instance, for their views on economic policy, Rosenberg gave a very fluent explanation which they seemed quite content to let him do. He put what they thought, and then what the Socialists thought as well.

Before the lunch the British Consul in Düsseldorf, a man called Haley, had come over to see me at his own request to give me the sort of background of these people.[80] He compared them as the flotsam and jetsam of 1945. He said they had really no obvious place in Germany; that they were completely opportunist, wanted power for its own sake; that they were nationalist, but otherwise had no particular views. Altogether he painted a pretty gloomy picture and rather implied that they were Nazis, though he admitted that he was on quite good terms with them, and incidentally that Döring was a very able man. It seemed to be generally agreed that Döring would take charge of the F.D.P. Party before long and get rid of Dehler who is at present the leader. I can't say that I felt that they really were particularly Nazi. They struck me as being very Americanised, they had both been to America quite a lot, and their ideas on economic policy were frankly American. Their cynicism was also largely American in character, though they were, particularly Döring, good humoured and obviously rather full of vitality and laughing quite a lot.[81] They seemed very pleased to meet Rosenberg and made no

79 Ludwig Rosenberg, a trade union official in the Weimar Republic, lived in Britain 1933–46. He had headed the foreign department of the D.G.B. (the trade union federation) and became vice-chairman in 1959 and chairman in 1962.
80 Philip Haley had been with the Control Commission 1947–56, and was First Secretary at the Bonn Embassy 1961–4.
81 Their American style was widely remarked on, and in the 1957 federal election they liked to describe themselves as 'youthful', 'sporting', 'adventurous' and 'adaptable' (see next note). By then Dr Dehler – a Bavarian and Adenauer's first Minister of Justice – had been replaced by an elderly figurehead; Döring was campaign manager.

difficulty whatever although he is a Jew, and one had heard that they were anti-Semitic. Scheel was less attractive than Döring and regarded as a very smooth kind of character, not to be trusted. I should think that probably true of all of them, although the Prime Minister of North Rhine-Westphalia, Steinhoff, whom I met later on, spoke in warm terms about his colleagues and thought the coalition could go on quite happily for a long time. They were all against Adenauer, very strongly and bitterly against him, and this seemed to be the main link between themselves and the Socialists. Altogether it was quite an interesting visit and it will also be interesting to compare what I saw this weekend with what eventually happens in the next election.[82]

Tuesday, 9 October 1956 [the last surviving entry]

I must here say something about the problem of Alf Robens. During the Suez debate he made a speech which was very severely criticised in the press. I did not myself think it was so bad, though it was not good. But undoubtedly the Party took a poor view of it. I even had one letter from a tough miners' M.P., David Griffiths, written in the heat of the moment, and saying that I really must find somebody else to look after foreign affairs.[83] But the worst attack of all came from Cassandra in the *Daily Mirror*, a really cruel one, and this was taken up in the press generally. It is fair to say that the *Manchester Guardian* was also, though much kinder, pretty critical. It would not matter so much if this were an isolated case,

82 These Young Turks had in February 1956 broken their alliance with the C.D.U. in the Land government and made one with the S.P.D. under Fritz Steinhoff – a course leading to eventual success but immediate catastrophe: the F.D.P. in Bonn split, and the C.D.U. won easily in 1957 in the country and in 1958 in the Land. Wolfgang Döring died in 1963, at 42, before the tide turned. Willi Weyer, deputy Land premier and minister of finance in coalition with the S.P.D. in 1956–8, led the Land party in opposition after the defeat. In 1962 he became deputy premier and minister of the interior in a coalition with the C.D.U., which did badly in the 1966 Land election. Offered the same posts in a government with the S.P.D., he declined in July 1966 lest the party be charged with opportunism; he continued in office with the C.D.U. until December, when he accepted the S.P.D. offer and served with them 1966–9. He refused to lead the federal opposition in 1967, against the C.D.U.-S.P.D. 'Grand Coalition' in Bonn; Walter Scheel did so instead. In 1969 Weyer took an active part in the S.P.D.-F.D.P. talks which forged their federal coalition, and especially in the football match which began them; he left politics to head the German Athletic Association. Scheel became Foreign Minister in 1969, and President of the Republic 1974–9.
83 M.P. Rother Valley 1945–70, he became vice-chairman of the trade union group of M.P.s. Robens: 558 H.C. Deb. 172–82.

but for some time now there has been criticism in the Party of his performance in the House. The trouble I think is that he does not give the impression of really having the brains to carry foreign affairs, that he speaks too much in slogans, and does not get really to the heart of the matter. It is fair to say on the other side that his work inside the Party in achieving a greater unity on foreign policy has been excellent. However, the speech in the Suez debate and the attacks in the press brought the matter to a head.

The *Daily Mirror* in particular seemed to be determined to get something done about this. Hugh Cudlipp spoke to me several times, asked what I was going to do. I had complained to him about the Cassandra article but he more or less brushed this aside on the grounds that it was necessary to be cruel in order to be kind. Finally [on Monday 24 September], he had a lunch party at which in addition to Alfred and myself, Kingsley Martin was also present. Hugh sat between me and Alfred and in the middle of lunch after a long talk to him, he turned to me and whispered that Alfred was quite content to give up the job. As for Alfred himself he has undoubtedly been having a very difficult time so far as his family is concerned. . . I heard from Jack Diamond that he was not able to do much of a job for *Forward* because he was never there. Altogether his life does not seem to be properly organised at all.

After the *Forward* dinner [that evening], a dinner that was given for the financial backers of the paper, I drove him to Charing Cross and we had a few minutes conversation, in the course of this he said quite definitely that he did not want me to hold on to him if I thought it was better that he should give up the job. He would be quite content to leave it to me and do whatever I asked him to do. He explained the difficulties he had been through, the family difficulties which I have just mentioned, and also he said that he was not well on the day of the debate. I thanked him very much but was non-committal in what I should do. I said that I thought perhaps one needed somebody on foreign affairs who could give absolutely full time to it, and was not beset by family difficulties. But, I repeat, I did not commit myself. I feel very sorry for him, he has certainly had a rough time and seems to have got into rather a state of nerves. At the Blackpool Conference I ran into Eva his wife, at one point, in a positively hysterical mood; it was in the entrance to the Conference Hall during the debate on foreign affairs, and Alfred had not yet been called. She said something like this. 'I don't know what we are going to do. I think we should get out of this Party. They are treating him so badly.' I calmed her down, and said what was the trouble? She implied it was because he had not been able to speak. (He had tried [earlier in the Conference] to speak in the Suez debate.) Fortunately at that moment the Chairman did call him, and she went away pacified. She does not really help him. She went up to George Brown early in the Conference before the result for the Treasurership was known, and said that she hoped for the sake of the Party that he would not get it. Indeed one of the troubles seems to be that George and Alf seem to be all the time sticking pins into each other. No doubt there is a good deal of rivalry between them. However, the basic thing is, I am afraid, that Alfred has not got the intellectual quality which is needed for this absolutely top level work. I doubt even if he had not got these troubles that he could really have managed the foreign affairs. However, we will see. It may be necessary to keep him there for a time in any event.

At the Conference itself a number of points emerged. There is no need for me to go over the ground as a whole, which was very well reported in the press. But I must say something about Frank Cousins. The first thing that strikes me is how very poor his speeches are. He does not seem really to know what he wants to say. It was much the same when he was on the Executive of the Labour Party. He was continually barging into a discussion without really having thought things out. So it was at the Conference. He only made one speech in support of the return of [a] Labour Government. One could not quite make out whether he wanted to re-echo his T.U.C. speech or to qualify it. Then he chucked in, in order to get a cheer (one suspects), a statement about nationalisation and how he liked the old kind of socialism, etc. But, as I say, intellectually, it seemed to me to be pretty poor stuff. Later on I had a talk with Victor Feather about him, who was extremely interesting.[84] He said that Cousins really wanted to be like his father, an old socialist. And that was about as far as he went. And this certainly seems to come out in his conversation and his speeches all the time. He strikes me as being profoundly ignorant of the real issues either on the economic or the political side. And I doubt if he has any deep-laid plot in mind. He clearly is determined to show himself as different from Deakin as possible. According to Victor, he hated Arthur Deakin, who was always bullying him because he, Cousins, stood up to Arthur.

Another characteristic is his obvious love of and desire for power. Dora first mentioned this to me after a conversation she had with him at a dinner one night. But it is best illustrated by the following story which I heard from John Murray and which I believe to be true. Cousins and Bevan had some discussion during the Conference, in the course of which Cousins said that he did not really mind very much if the T.&G.W. remained at its present strength. It would still be true that the Union, stretching as it did across six major industries, could paralyse the country. Whereupon Nye said, 'If you try to do that Parliament will smash you'.

84 Victor (Lord) Feather (1908–76) was an assistant secretary at the T.U.C. 1947–60, assistant general secretary 1960–9, general secretary 1969–73.

And Cousins turned very aggressively to Nye and said, 'And if you try to do that to us, we shall smash you'.[85] It is all rather silly, and quite irrelevant. And I don't imagine that Cousins will go on talking like that for very long. For I must add that despite these rather discouraging features, he and his wife were extremely friendly to us. And he several times went out of his way to show that he was entirely on my side. He did so in an interview with the *Daily Herald*, and at the T.&G.W. dinner when he referred to this interview he added that if anybody tried to upset the present unity they, meaning the Trade Unions, would knock the daylights out of them. I think there is no doubt that he meant this for Bevan.

Victor said also that fundamentally he was a perfectly honest man. He did not believe that he [Cousins] had ever been a Communist though his wife certainly had.[85] His wife, who is quite an attractive woman, is apparently very ambitious for him and Victor advised strongly that we should not forget this, and should as far as possible keep on friendly terms with her, which would have a big effect on Frank. There should be no particular difficulty about this, because as I say she is quite a pleasant person and easy to talk to. I noticed incidentally she did not drink the loyal toast at the T.&G.W. dinner. This may have been a pure accident but I could not help thinking of her Communist past. At the same time there is no great sign of chips on the shoulders or anything of that sort. She has a son, now doing his National service, who is going to Cambridge, and I don't think she feels particularly proletarian. At the same time she, like Frank, is thinking of her family, her father was the first Labour Mayor of Doncaster.

There are one or two other features of the Conference which are worth mentioning. First the extraordinary absence of any Trade Union leadership, either on the platform or from the hall. This may, of course, have been a good thing. Having got a new leader who was acceptable to them the Trade Unions may, so to speak, have said, well, we will keep in the background. Unfortunately, I am afraid it was not really this but the lack of capacity and the split in their own ranks, on account of the arrival of Cousins. I don't think it mattered this year, perhaps indeed it was a good thing, because it left the field fairly clear for me. But it is important that the group that runs the T.U.C. and ultimately the Labour Party should be re-established, otherwise a very dangerous situation might emerge. In fact the Executive were not defeated on anything during the Conference but the way in which Casasola got back onto the Executive on the Trade

85 Cousins' biographer, who knew both men well, says Bevan thought Cousins' view dangerously 'syndicalist': Goodman (1979), pp. 109, 136, 238–9. (On Communism, *ibid.*, pp. 46–7.)

Union list was clear evidence of lack of co-ordination among the Unions voting.[86]

Another feature of the Conference, alas too familiar, was the extraordinarily poor quality of the speeches from the floor, in [the] sense that most of them were remote from reality, miles and miles from the electorate. Perhaps this was partly because we did not have any very big issues, and nobody was bothering very much, but it depresses one all the same. It seems to be so difficult to get the constituency parties to look at politics realistically. Or perhaps the real problem is to get the right people to attend, and be sent to the Conference as delegates. Of course there are a great mass of them who are not really foolish even at the Conference itself. I could judge this from the number of people who came up to me after my Suez speech and said nice things about it.

I must also record my anxieties about the appalling lack of people with both courage and intelligence. When one looks round at the Executive it is hard to see anybody apart from Jim Griffiths who has both these qualities. Harold Wilson has plenty of intelligence and a little courage, but when one gets beyond him, frankly most of the rest are either just incapable of making good speeches – this is true of the best Trade Union ones – or just entirely lacking in courage, with only one idea, namely to get as many cheers from the Left Wing as possible.

Sam Watson was disappointing. It certainly is a tragedy as he certainly has all the qualities necessary – boundless courage and a first class mind. But he just isn't sufficiently wrapped up in the Labour Party, and he didn't make a success of either of his speeches, although we got away as far as the vote was concerned.

Finally, I am left the problem of Nye. Of course it was to be expected that he would very likely get the Treasurership and there is really nothing new in that.[87] On the other hand, it has pushed him forward, not only in the Executive, but also in the Parliamentary Party. And in view of Alf's failure, of course, everybody is wondering whether we are going to offer him foreign affairs. If it were not for Alf's failure I wouldn't think of it, myself. But we have to think of it. I do not know what we shall do, and I am inclined to wait a moment and see what opinion in the Party is like.[88]

86 R.W. Casasola, general secretary of the fellow-travelling Foundry Workers, had been defeated seven times for the N.E.C., but as runner-up had replaced Cousins who had moved to the General Council. As a sitting member he was re-elected in 1956 and 1957, and then retired.

87 As HG had expected, the N.U.R. and USDAW votes decided the outcome; Bevan won by 3,029,000 to 2,755,000 for Brown and 644,000 for Pannell.

88 HG knew that the appointment would make a reconciliation possible; opinion proved favourable and Robens willing to stand down, so Bevan took over in the new session: HG, pp. 440–1 (and pp. 430–1 on the Conference).

One other episode to record. Norris Chipman of the American Embassy rang me up yesterday, or rather the day before, and began to talk about the Tory criticisms of Dulles. He was referring to a speech by Ted Leather[89] which accused Dulles of double-crossing Eden several times. He, Chipman, thought this must have been authorised by 10 Downing Street. And if so, he thought really I ought to know the truth. Accordingly, he came round to my room in the House yesterday and told me the following. It seems that originally the British Government were very keen on the Aswan Dam and last October were pressing the Americans to hurry up and get it through. They even went so far as to send for somebody from the Embassy to come down to 10 Downing Street and urge him to send a telegram telling Dulles that he must get on with the job. There then followed a period of negotiations with Nasser, concerned particularly with whether the Russians would get any contracts out of the building of the Dam if the Americans financed it. There was also the visit of Gene Black and the International Bank.[90] For some reason or other which was not clear, by May the attitude of both America and Britain had changed, and according to Chipman, at the meeting of NATO Dulles and Selwyn Lloyd agreed that the Dam was off. This was really the important point of his speech because the British Government are implying that the Americans did this all on their own. Chipman says quite emphatically that it was agreed in May that the money should not be given for the Dam. They also decided, however, in May not to tell the Egyptians immediately. The thing drifted on and Dulles finally had to tell the Egyptians because as he explained to me Congress was about to turn the thing down anyhow. The British were annoyed with Dulles for doing it quite so suddenly, but there could be no question of their not being party to the decision which was already made a month or two back.

Editor's note on the Suez ultimatum

[The crisis came to a head while Gaitskell was preoccupied by private grief, for his mother died on 14 October. On the 16th the French suggested that a coming pre-emptive strike by Israel against Egypt could provide the pretext for intervention; on the 24th Britain agreed to take care of the Egyptian air force; on the 29th the Israelis attacked; on the 30th the Anglo-French ultimatum was sent, with a quarter of an hour's

89 Ted (Sir Edwin) Leather, a Canadian, was Conservative M.P. for N. Somerset 1950–64, and Governor of Bermuda 1973–7.
90 In early February, when a $200 million loan was promised (but withdrawn on July 24). Black was the Bank's President.

notice to the Opposition; on the 31st an American resolution was vetoed in the Security Council by Britain and France; at dawn on 5 November the troops landed at Port Said.

In Hungary the climax came simultaneously. On 2 November Imre Nagy's national-communist government proclaimed neutrality and appealed to the U.N.; at dawn on the 4th the Russians began their massive and treacherous attack on Budapest.

Gaitskell's broadcast was in reply to Sir Anthony Eden's the evening before. He hoped that senior Ministers like Butler or Monckton would follow the example of Anthony Nutting, who had resigned on 31 October. But none did so, and there was no Conservative revolt.]

Document No. 20

HG's broadcast on behalf of the Opposition,
Sunday 4 November 1956[91]

GAITSKELL: Good evening.

It has been a tragic, terrible week. Indeed a tragic and terrible day with the news coming in about Hungary. It's been, I think, by far the worst week, for the world and for our country, since 1939. Last Monday evening came the news of the Israeli attack on Egypt. Israel had been threatened and provoked – she was entitled to better guarantees of her security. But there's no denying that the large-scale invasion of Egypt was an act of aggression.

I'm not going to try to apportion the blame – that's really the job of the United Nations. But what should we have done? That's the real question.

The Prime Minister says we couldn't afford to wait – we had to act, he said, immediately, on our own, before the Security Council could decide or do anything. Yet what are the facts? By Tuesday evening, even before the twelve-hour ultimatum to Egypt had expired, the Council had met, reached a clear decision, and been blocked by the Prime Minister's own veto. There was no lack of speed here – the trouble was obstruction – obstruction by Great Britain.

What should we have done? If only we had supported that resolution, and followed it up by proposing that a United Nations police force should see that the resolution was carried out, we could have offered to be part of

91 From a transcription of a recording in Gaitskell Papers, file, P. 106–4; broadcast by the B.B.C. and subsequently published in *The Listener*, 8.11.56. For the Government's efforts to prevent it see *HG*, p. 434, and references there.

the police force ourselves. This wouldn't have been intervening on one side or the other. This wouldn't have been acting on our own, this wouldn't have been an act of aggression. We should have been acting on behalf of the United Nations, with their full authority, and with world opinion behind us. But this is not what happened. Something quite different happened. Having rejected the United Nations resolution we carried out our threats – we went to war with Egypt.

Make no mistake about it – this is war – the bombing, the softening up, the attacks on radio stations, telephone exchanges, railway stations, to be followed, very, very soon now, by the landings and the fighting between ground forces.

We're doing all this alone, except for France. Opposed by the world, in defiance of the world. It is not a police action; there is no law behind it. We have taken the law into our own hands. That's the tragic situation in which we British people find ourselves tonight. We would all have thought it inconceivable a week ago.

Why was it done? The Prime Minister justifies it on these grounds. First of all, he says, to protect British lives and property. But there's been no rescue operation. Instead, to tell the truth, thousands of British civilians, now living in Egypt, have been put in grave danger, because of what we have done.

The Prime Minister says it was to safeguard the Canal, and the free passage through it. What has happened to the Canal? It's blocked, because of what we have done. Was the Canal indeed ever really menaced before we began bombing? I very much doubt it. There's no evidence to show that it was.

I'm afraid the real reason for going to war with Egypt, was different. I've seen the text of the first broadcast of the Allied Command to the Egyptians. This is what it said: in Arabic, of course. 'O Egyptians, why has this befallen you? First, because Abdul Nasser went mad and seized the Suez Canal.' The broadcast was right – it was this which really induced the Prime Minister to decide on invasion.

The Prime Minister has said we were going in to separate the two sides, but you don't separate two armies by bombing airfields and landing troops a hundred miles behind one side only. No, this is a second on-slaught on a country which was already the victim of an attack.

Now a new idea has been put forward. The idea that we are going in to make way for a United Nations force. But nothing was said about this in the ultimatum to Egypt. Nothing was said about this at the Security Council. If this was the Government's plan, why on earth did they not put it forward before? Why did they not propose it, right at the beginning, accepting the rest of the Security Council's resolution, as I suggested earlier? I'll tell you why they didn't do this. If the Prime Minister had agreed to this Britain would not have been able to occupy the Canal; for the idea of the United Nations police force, proposed by Canada yesterday, is quite different. It would not give us control of the Canal, it has another aim – the aim of keeping the Israeli and Arab forces within their own frontiers, of patrolling the borders of Israel and the Arab States – and these are one hundred miles from the Canal.

What are the consequences of all this? A profound shock of dismay and a deep sense of anxiety among millions of people, at home and all over the world. The Assembly, resolutions of the United Nations, messages pouring in from everywhere confirm the general opinion that Britain and France used the attack on Egypt by Israel as a bare-faced excuse to seize the Canal. That they're now doing what they wanted to do in August and September, but were stopped from doing by public opinion at that time.

What are the consequences? We have violated the Charter of the United Nations. In doing so, we have betrayed all that Great Britain has stood for in world affairs. Since the war, at least, we have supported every stand against aggression. We did so in the Korean War, we played our part, and we were absolutely right. This was a case of self-defence, collective defence, allowed under the Charter, endorsed unanimously by the Security Council of the United Nations. But today we stand as the aggressors.

What are the consequences? A deep, deep division in the Commonwealth – only Australia and New Zealand support us. Canada and South Africa have abstained. India, Pakistan, and Ceylon are all against us. This is a very grave consequence. For I believe, as do millions of others, that this Commonwealth of ours was – and could have been – the greatest force for peace and unity in the world. Above all, a bridge between East and West, of incalculable value. That bridge is now almost destroyed.

What are the consequences? I cannot but feel hearing today's heart-breaking news from Hungary, how tragic it is that at the very moment when the whole world should be united in denouncing this flagrant, ruthless, savage aggression by Russia, against a liberty-loving people, I can't help feeling how tragic it is that we, by our criminal folly, should have lost the moral leadership of which we were once so proud.

Here at home the Government policy of war with Egypt has produced terrible heartsearchings – the Archbishop of Canterbury has led a deputation, of all denominations of the Churches, to the Government. The all-party United Nations Association has denounced the policy in strong terms. Men and women in all walks of life of all parties and all faiths have expressed their deep concern. Mr. Nutting, the Minister of State, whose job was specially concerned with United Nations affairs, has resigned from the Government, because he thinks the policy is indefensible.

This is not a Labour Party matter – it touches the whole nation – all those who care for the rule of law in international affairs, and wanted to see it triumph. All those who put their faith and worked for the United Nations and its Charter; who accepted that it wasn't our job, in all these vital issues, to decide for ourselves, but to accept the decisions of the United Nations. All those who care for the good name of our country.

Many of you will be saying, I am sure, now what can we do about it? Many of you who feel just as strongly as I do how terribly wrong this whole policy has been and how terribly dangerous, in the long run, to our own security. I don't think there's any doubt as to what the policy should be now. We should, surely, without qualification, argument or conditions, accept the resolution of the Assembly of the United Nations, calling for an immediate cease-fire. Egypt has already said that she accepts this resolution. There's reason to believe that Israel will accept the cease-fire also. Why should not Britain and France do likewise?

We should do something else. We should also give full support to the new resolution on which we abstained today, for a United Nations force to police the Arab-Israel borders, until a proper peace settlement has been reached.

But make no mistake, this means abandoning the idea which has been at the root of this policy – the idea of trying to solve the Suez Canal problem by force. It means going back to negotiating – to negotiating a settlement on this issue.

I don't believe the present Prime Minister can carry out this policy. I bear him no illwill. We have been personally quite friendly. But his policy this last week has been disastrous. And he is utterly, utterly discredited in the world.

Only one thing can save the reputation and the honour of our country – Parliament must repudiate the Government's policy. The Prime Minister must resign.

The Labour Party cannot alone achieve this. We are a minority in the House of Commons. So, the responsibility rests with those Conservatives who like us are shocked and troubled by what is happening and who want a change. I appeal to them especially. Theirs is a difficult decision, but I want to say to them that our purpose too, in this matter, rises above Party – I give them indeed this pledge. We undertake to support a new Prime Minister, in halting the invasion of Egypt, in ordering the cease-fire, and complying with the decisions and recommendations of the United Nations. In that way only, believe me, can the deep divisions in the country on this matter be closed.

I appeal to those who can bring this about, to act now and save the reputation of our country and the future peace of the world.

Goodnight.

APPENDICES

APPENDIX I

THE ATTLEE GOVERNMENTS 1945–51

(peers in italics)

The Cabinet[1]	A[2]	B[2]	C[2]	D[2]
P.M.	Attlee			
Ld. Pres.	Morrison[3]			*Addison*[4]
Ld. Chanc.	*Jowitt*			
Ld. Pr. Seal	Greenwood[5]	*Addison*		Stokes[6]
Chanc. Exch.	Dalton	Cripps[7]	Gaitskell[8]	
Foreign Sec.	Bevin			Morrison[4]
Home Sec.	Ede			(Ede[3,4])
Agric.	T. Williams			
Colonial Sec.	G. Hall[9]	Creech Jones[10]	Griffiths[11]	
C.R.O.	*Addison*	Noel-Baker[12]	Gordon Walker[13]	
Defence	(P.M.)	*Alexander*[14]	Shinwell[15]	
Education	Wilkinson	Tomlinson[16]		
Labour	Isaacs		Bevan[17]	Robens[18]
Scottish Sec.	Westwood	Woodburn[19]	McNeil[20]	
Bd. of Trade	Cripps	Wilson[21]		Shawcross[22]
Admiralty	Alexander[23]	–	–	–
Air (Sec.)	*Stansgate*[23]	–	–	–
Ch. Duchy Lanc.	–	Dalton[24]	*Alexander*	
Civil Av'n	–	*Pakenham*[25]	–	–
Fuel & P.	Shinwell	–	–	–
Health	Bevan[26]			–
India	*Pethick-Lawrence*[27]	–		–
T. & C. Planning	–	–	Dalton	
War (Sec.)	Lawson[23]	–	–	–[28]

*Former (or later) posts held by
Cabinet members; notes (opposite line to which
they refer)*

1 Includes those IN CAPITALS on this page.
2 Unless specified, July 45 (A), Oct. 47 (B), Feb. 50 (C), Apr. 51 (D).

3 Also LEADER OF THE HOUSE.   4 From Mar. 51.

5 Apr.–Oct. 47: *INMAN*; GREENWOOD M. WITHOUT PORTFOLIO.
6 Had been M. of Works (C). BEVIN was L.P.S. Mar.–Apr. 51.
7 M. of ECON. AFF. Sep. 47; also CHANC. Nov. 47 – Oct. 50.
8 P.S. Fuel & P. May 46, Min. (B); M. of State Ec. Aff. (C); CHANC. Oct. 50.
9 First Lord, Admiralty Oct. 46 – May 51 (as *Vt. Hall*).
10 P.S. Col. Office to Oct. 46.   11 M. of Nat. Insurance (A, B).
12 M. of State, F.O. to Oct. 46; Sec. for Air Oct. 46 – Oct. 47; M. of Fuel & P. (C, D).
13 P.S., C.R.O. (B).
14 From Dec. 46; Oct.–Dec., M. WITHOUT PORTFOLIO.   15 Had been Sec. for War (B).
16 From Feb. 47; had been M. of Works (A).
17 From Jan. 51; Isaacs M. of Pensions (C, D).   18 P.S., Fuel & P. (B, C).
19 P.S., Supply (A).   20 P.S., F.O. to Oct. 46; then M. of State (B).
21 P.S., Works to Mar. 47; then Sec. O'seas Trade. 22 Had been Attorney Gen. (A,B,C).

23 To Oct. 46.

24 From May 48.
25 From May 48 (CAB); and (C), not.   P.S. War, Oct. 46; Ch. Duchy, Apr. 47 –
       May 48; Admiralty (D, from May 51).
26 To Jan. 51.
27 And *EARL of LISTOWEL* Apr. 47 – Jan. 48 (abolished).

28 Dashes indicate office outside Cabinet.

All Under-Secs. are called P.S. (or F.S., for Financial Sec.)

Ministers 1945–1951 listed in Biog. Index, but never in Attlee Cabinets

Barnes	M. of Transport (A, B, C, D).
Belcher	P.S., B.o.T. Jan. 46 – Feb. 49.
Bowden	Whip (C, D).
Brown	P.S., Agric. (B, C); M. of Works (D).
Callaghan	P.S., Transport (B), Admiralty (C, D).
Crawley	P.S., Air (C, D).
De Freitas	P.S., Air (from May 46, A, B); Home Off. (C, D).
Durbin	P.S., Works Mar. 47 – Sep. 48.
Edwards, L. J.	P.S., Health Feb. 47; Sec. O'seas Trade Feb. 49; Ec. Sec. Treasury Oct. 50.
Evans, S.	P.S., Food Mar.–Apr. 50.
Fraser	P.S., Scotland (A, B, C, D).
Freeman	F.S., War Oct. 46; P.S., Supply (B, C).
Hall, W. G.	F.S., Treasury (A, B).
Herbison	P.S., Scotland (C, D).
Hynd	Ch. Duchy to Apr. 47; M. of Pensions Apr.–Oct. 47.
Jay	Ec. Sec. Treasury (B, from Dec. 47); F.S. (C, D).
Key	M. of Works Feb. 47 – Feb. 50.
Lee, F.	P.S., Labour (C, D).
Marquand	Sec. O'seas Trade to May 47; Paymaster Gen. to Jul. 48; M. of Pensions to Jan. 51, then M. of Health.
Mayhew	P.S., F.O. Oct. 46 – Mar. 50.
Smith, E.	P.S., B.o.T. to Jan. 46.
Soskice	Solicitor Gen. to Apr. 51, then Att. Gen.
Stewart	Whip (A); P.S. War (B, C), Supply (D).
Strachey	P.S., Air to May 46, then M. of Food (A, B); Sec. for War (C, D).
Strauss	P.S., Transport (A); M. of Supply (B, C, D).
Summerskill	P.S., Food (A, B); M. of Nat. Insurance (C, D).
Webb	M. of Food (C, D).
Whiteley	Chief Whip (A, B, C, D).
Wilmot	M. of Supply (A).
Wyatt	F.S., War (D).
Younger	P.S., Home Off. (B); M. of State, F.O. (C, D).

APPENDIX II

DOCUMENTS ON DEFENCE POLICY

[The documents that follow indicate Gaitskell's attempts to work out a foreign policy that was both acceptable and practicable, first with his disengagement proposals for Central Europe and then over the most emotive question of all, that of nuclear weapons. In April 1957 he had agreed to a patched-up compromise in the Parliamentary Party over Labour's attitude to testing the H-bomb, so laying himself open to effective attack from Macmillan; over the ensuing year he made great efforts to evolve a more defensible Party position in talks with both his parliamentary colleagues (included here) and the T.U.C. (not included). Bevan almost always stood with him against the unilateralists, who were heavily defeated at the Party Conferences in both years. The Campaign for Nuclear Disarmament indeed sprang directly from their failure at Brighton in 1957. The third document shows his own views at the moment when they were least popular and most widely misrepresented in the Party.]

Document No. 21

Disengagement: its origins and purpose

a. HG to Crossman, 28 May 1958 (origins)[1]

As I understood from you the other evening that letters would be forwarded, I am writing now in reply to yours of the 7th May with which you sent me the memorandum on defence policy. I enclose my comments on this. Perhaps the next move after this might be conversation rather than a further exchange of documents.

There is one other thing which I feel I must mention. In your review of Dean Acheson's book in the New Statesman, you ascribe my ideas on

1 From Papers, file P.148.

disengagement as due to the pressure of public opinion here or, as you put it, in another paragraph, 'the pressure of Party politics.' I really cannot accept this, any more than I can accept the phrase 'conversion to disengagement'.

The disengagement proposals with which I have become associated were worked out in the autumn of 1956 and sprung [sic] directly from the impact made upon me by the Polish revolt and the Hungarian revolution. This seemed to me to change the situation in three ways:

First, it made it obvious that the communist regimes in Eastern Europe were extremely unpopular and that the chance that disengagement would be followed by successful communist subversion in Germany was obviously remote.

Secondly, they brought out very clearly the danger that a further rising in East Germany might provoke intervention from West Germany.

Thirdly, they showed vividly how much trouble the Russians were having from the satellite states.

With these points in mind, the plan for disengagement was advanced covering not only Germany but the three major satellite states as well. It really is absurd to speak as though this was the same as the kind of plan for a 'neutral disarmed Germany' put forward during the discussion on German disarmament. I would not defend even now a plan for disengagement and neutralisation applying to Germany alone because I would think it too much to the advantage of the Soviet Union.

As for the pressure of Party politics, I am not aware that anybody at any time except possibly Denis Healey urged me to adopt such a plan.

Incidentally, I had an interesting talk with George Kennan the other day about Acheson. His explanation of Acheson's attitude today was in fact that Acheson had always been exactly the same. He had always been fiercely anti-communist, much more so than the other Democratic leaders. Indeed, I gather that there was an anti-communist campaign in the State Department while Acheson was still Secretary. The impression we have of him over here because of his intervention in the Hiss case is apparently by no means a correct one.[2]

Yours sincerely,

H.G.

2 Acheson, who was bitterly attacked and traduced by Senator McCarthy, had said after Hiss's conviction that he would not turn his back on his former associate. Crossman reviewed his *Power and Diplomacy* in the *New Statesman*, 17.5.58.

b. HG at Chatham House, 23 October 1957 (purpose)[3]

The Rt. Hon. Hugh Gaitskell M.P. then addressed the Group on his proposals for disengagement. He pointed out that they were not his original views but a crystallization of several proposals from different sources, and that he had made no attempt to work them out in great detail.

1. The object of the proposals was to increase the possibility of helping the States of Eastern Europe in their struggle for independence; to make possible the reunification of Germany; and to give the West a degree of flexibility in policy, the lack of which was a major disadvantage in its negotiations with the Soviet Union.

2. The proposals took into account (a) the dangers of neutralising Germany *alone*, which would be a standing invitation to infiltration and intrigue. This danger, however, seemed considerably diminished by recent events in Poland and Hungary. (b) The virtual impossibility of Russia agreeing to German reunification so long as Germany remained a member of NATO.

3. The proposals involved:
    (a) The withdrawal of NATO forces from West Germany and of Soviet forces from East Germany, Hungary, Poland and Czechoslovakia. The States thus evacuated would maintain their own national forces at a level to be determined by international agreement. Any return of NATO or Soviet forces to the territory of the States thus evacuated would be deemed an infringement of the agreement.
    (b) The frontiers of the four States concerned to be guaranteed by a firm security pact between the Great Powers.
    (c) The reunification of Germany on the basis of free elections.

4. These proposals would *not* involve the breaking up of NATO, nor the withdrawal of U.S. and U.K. forces from the mainland of Europe. Both were essential for the maintenance of West European morale.

3 To a study group at the Royal Institute of International Affairs: from Papers, P.107–3. The report, agreed by Gaitskell, was drafted by Michael Howard (later Regius Professor of History at Oxford). These proposals were often linked with those put forward by Adam Rapacki, the Polish Foreign Minister, at the U.N. General Assembly on 3 October 1957 and later in Warsaw on 15 February 1958. He advocated a nuclear-free zone in the same Central European countries (except Hungary). On 4 November, to meet Western objections, he modified his plan by suggesting its introduction in two stages, good faith on both sides in the first stage being the precondition for continuing into the second.

5. A certain loss of military efficiency must be accepted but this would be more than offset by the withdrawal of Soviet forces to the frontier of the U.S.S.R. and the liberation of the East European satellite States.

6. The existing situation had potentially explosive possibilities. If a new rising occurred in East Germany an intervention by West German forces could not be ruled out. The existence of this danger might incline the U.S.S.R. to favour neutralization.

7. The deterioration in the East/West relations during the past eighteen months made it improbable that these proposals would meet with agreement in the near future. This did not affect their long term desirability nor the usefulness of putting them forward.

8. In subsequent discussions Mr. Gaitskell made the following points:

(a) Germany would be allowed, within the general framework of limitations referred to in 3(a) above, to develop her own armaments industry.

(b) The entire plan would have to be approved by all NATO powers and put forward as a joint proposal.

(c) The proposed withdrawal of NATO forces would leave the Baltic Sound no less well protected than it was at present, and would increase the distance which Russian forces would have to traverse to seize it.

(d) There need be no breach in the unity of Western Europe; and the proposal would facilitate the inclusion of East European States in trade agreements.

(e) Provision of early-warning installations could be written into the pact. Arrangements for rapid military intervention in the event of a breach of the agreement could be made either openly or privately.

(f) The intense unpopularity of Communism in both East and West Europe made the danger of subversion in the four evacuated States very remote.

Document No. 22

Defence Questions: talks among eight senior Labour M.P.s on 17, 19 and 25 March 1958[4]

1. The three questions with which we were principally concerned were

(a) The use of 'tactical' nuclear weapons.

(b) Should we consider giving up nuclear weapons ourselves if, by so doing, other countries, except U.S.A. and U.S.S.R. also remained without them?

(c) Could we give any kind of pledge not to use nuclear weapons first?

2. It became clear in the course of discussion that we must be careful to distinguish when we were referring to action by the British Government alone and when we were describing what we hoped the West as a whole might do.

3. So far as (a) is concerned there was general agreement that the West *as a whole* could not give up any idea of using tactical nuclear weapons – and using them if need be before the Russians did – unless and until the Russian superiority in conventional forces ceased to exist. We could not allow the Russians to sweep over the continent with 200 conventional divisons against which we could put only, say, 20–25. We should have to use nuclear weapons with limited explosive effects to prevent this advance – dropping bombs or firing rockets at "bottle necks", i.e., junctions, marshalling yards, river crossings, etc. It was said that 1 kiloton explosives or less would be available before long though it was admitted that the number of these tactical weapons available at present was probably small – except for large atom bombs – say – 10-20 kilotons.

The West, as a whole therefore, could not possibly give a pledge not to use nuclear weapons first because this would appear to be an open invitation to the Russians to aggression with overwhelming conventional forces.

But over *Britain's* policy there was a difference of opinion. A minority considered that while the Americans would have to be ready to use tactical nuclear weapons, Britain should concentrate on building up her

4 This summary by HG (from Papers, P.148) was sent on 11 April to the general secretaries of the T.U.C. and the Party, and the 8 M.P.s: Brown, Healey and Strachey from the majority wing; Bevan, Crossman and Ungoed-Thomas from the minority; the leader, and the deputy leader Griffiths. It is reported briefly in *HG*, pp. 495–6. Emphasis in original.

conventional forces. The same would apply to other European members of N.A.T.O. In our case, however, it was especially important because we might need conventional forces for use outside Europe – and at present we had not enough.

The majority, however, did not consider that it made sense for the American forces, alone in N.A.T.O., to have and be ready to use these tactical weapons while the rest of N.A.T.O. had only conventional arms. If there was to be a war in Europe N.A.T.O. forces as a whole would have to be in a position to use nuclear tactical weapons.[5]

4. *Comment*

(a) This last question of the role of Britain in N.A.T.O., and whether or not on *military* grounds the correct balance between 'conventional' and 'nuclear' forces exists, and what each member country by agreement with the others and the Supreme Commander should do is largely a technical (or economic) matter and must be *sharply* distinguished from the question of principle as to whether on *political* grounds and regardless of *N.A.T.O.*, Britain should renounce the use of nuclear weapons in any form. This latter question surely cannot be considered in terms of *tactical* weapons only. As far as *political* arguments go, it must be a matter of whether or not we give up *all* nuclear weapons.

It is, of course, *not* the view of the Party that we should do this and it was not supported by anyone at the meetings.

(b) So far as the *technical* issue is concerned, some further clarification is still needed. For example, do we say that while we must be ready to use tactical weapons we are content for the United States to "keep the key" of the warheads – as they do at present? Or do we think that other members of N.A.T.O. should be allowed these weapons without restriction?

Again, do we say that Britain must not only be ready to use these weapons but must also manufacture her own? Obviously, we make the atom bomb now but are we to produce the "Matadors", "Corporals", "Long Johns"[6] etc. and the smaller bombs? Personally, I think it is difficult for us to reach any wise decision on this – or for that matter on missile manufacturing policy – while we are in Opposition. We do not know enough about the alternatives and their cost.

---

5 To everyone's surprise, Bevan had changed back and again supported the majority view: Crossman's diary, 19.3.58, 2.4.58, 12.2.60. See *HG*, p. 495.
6 A mistake for 'Honest Johns', another U.S. missile.

5. It became apparent that the *second* question could be interpreted in two quite distinct ways. First, there was the idea that we might give up nuclear weapons as part of some international agreement whereby all the rest of the world, apart from Russia, and America, gave these up. There was no support for this idea on the grounds[7]

(i) that such an agreement was valueless without full international controls;

(ii) that if such controls were possible and accepted by all other nations, there was really no reason why America and Russia should not accept them too;

(iii) that while it might be possible to prevent *manufacture* of nuclear weapons outside America and Russia, it was very hard indeed – assuming no controls in America and Russia – to see how you could prevent these countries from in fact arming their allies with these weapons.

(iv) that this would increase "polarization" since other countries would be far more dependent for their protection on America or Russia and have – so to speak – to shelter behind them.

6. The second interpretation was that Britain should renounce nuclear weapons – use and manufacture – if France and Germany did the same. The argument on this followed much the same lines as that on tactical nuclear weapons with the same minority and majority views.

7. On the third question it followed from the previous discussions that in the opinion of the majority there could be no question of a pledge on the part of the West not to use tactical weapons first. There was, however, general agreement that Britain should state that, in her opinion, the policy of the West in the event of armed conflict should be to try

(i) to limit and localize the conflict as far as possible;

(ii) to end the war by negotiation and agreement – without either side winning – rather than to win it by any and every means.

(iii) never to use more force or fire power than was required to contain the attack.

(iv) to avoid the use of weapons which poisoned the atmosphere over great stretches of territory;

7 Gaitskell adopted that idea later: below, p. 639 n. But in public he was very careful, notably at the 1958 Scarborough Conference, to retain the option of taking up the non-nuclear club policy: *HG*, p. 498; *LPCR*, 1958, p. 222.

(v) while accepting the need for smaller nuclear weapons as a deterrent not only against nuclear but also against a large scale conventional attack, to treat the H. bomb as primarily a deterrent against attacks by H. bomb and in any event, never to contemplate its use until every other method of defence had been exhausted.

It was felt that to go further than this in any pledge about the use of the H. bomb was open to the following objections:

(a) That *at present* the lack of small scale nuclear weapons still leaves us too dependent on the H. bomb as a deterrent against a major conventional attack.

(b) The distinction between nuclear and thermo-nuclear explosions from the point of view of destructive power is not absolute. It may be possible to explode a large atom bomb with as much destructive power as a small H. bomb. It appears that there will be an almost infinite gradation of explosive power with an 'overlap' between 'nuclear' and 'thermo-nuclear' explosions.

(c) To give a pledge that we would never use *thermo-nuclear* weapons first would be misunderstood by the public who would think we meant the pledge to apply to *all* nuclear weapons. Our political opponents would certainly give this impression, and when we tried to clear it up there would be general confusion or at best a sense of 'let down'.

(d) In order to clear up the confusion we should, in any event, have *sharply to emphasise* our readiness to use and reliance upon *nuclear tactical weapons*. Politically, this emphasis would open up divisions in the Party.

(e) Since the case for Britain having the H. bomb is almost wholly our desire to have some deterrent of our own in case America goes isolationist (or breaks off the alliance in consequence of a diplomatic conflict with us), we have to consider any pledge we make in the light of this possibility. If in such a situation we had no tactical nuclear weapons of our own we might have to rely on H. bombs as our only deterrent against conventional attack by Russia; in these conditions a promise never to use them first might invite an attack.

Document 23

*Labour and Defence Policy: HG's Memorandum on
the Deterrent, 13.4.60. (Final version)*[8]

PRIVATE AND CONFIDENTIAL

DEFENCE POLICY

(1) Our supreme aims are:-

 (a) The maintenance of peace:

 (b) The preservation of our own freedom and independence.

(2) The only really sure and satisfactory way of achieving these is through a comprehensive multilateral disarmament agreement with effective international controls.

(3) The pursuit of such an agreement must, therefore, always be paramount and our attention always concentrated upon it. I do not discuss it further here only because our policy on it is in the main both clear and generally accepted, although modifications on points of detail may be needed from time to time.

(4) A comprehensive multilateral disarmament agreement is, however, by no means certain, and, in any event, will probably not be concluded for many years. Pending this, we are obliged as a responsible party, to consider defence policy.

(5) In doing so, it is necessary to distinguish clearly between policy for Britain on the one hand and policy for the West as a whole on the other. A British Government can determine the first but only influence the second – and not always even that.

(6) It has been accepted Party policy for at least the last twelve years that the NATO Alliance of America, Britain and Western Europe is essential, that the Alliance must have sufficient forces, – nuclear and conventional – to provide a Western deterrent – in other words, to retaliate or resist as

8 This memorandum to the Parliamentary Committee was redrafted after Blue Streak was cancelled. The original draft was written when that decision was expected but not yet announced; it was sent to several trade union leaders: Sir Vincent Tewson the T.U.C. general secretary, and Alan Birch (USDAW), William Carron (A.E.U) and Ron Smith (U.P.W.). The differences are shown below, p. 640; they were slight in paras. 8, 9, 14 and 20, substantial in paras. 21–5.

the case may be in the event of a Soviet attack, and that Britain's defence forces must be sufficient for her to play her proper part in this Alliance as well as carrying other commitments outside Europe. We also supported the production by Britain of her own A. and H. bombs, together with bombers capable of delivering them. We did so for political reasons – chiefly the desire not to be too dependent on the U.S.A. and to give added weight to our counsels in world affairs.

(7) Various minority elements in the Party have, however, always been opposed to all or some of this policy.

(8) There are those who urge that we should disarm unilaterally. They usually imply (whether the policy be that of Britain or of the West as a whole) that our example would be followed by others, so that in effect all-round disarmament would be achieved. There is, however, no reason to suppose that this would happen. If such a degree of mutual confidence existed between the great powers, as is implied by this theory of all-round disarmament by example, we should have been able long ago to reach a comprehensive multilateral disarmament agreement with controls. In fact, without controls – which really require an agreement for their establishment, it is doubtful whether mere unilateral declarations on one side or the other would be believed.

(9) In so far as unilateral disarmament is proposed for Britain alone, it is often based on the desire to contract out. It is held that we should withdraw from our Alliances, become neutral and have "nothing to do with the arms race". Usually this is associated with a vague though violent distaste for nuclear weapons. While this policy is supported by the high-minded through the doctrine of example, it is popular with others for purely escapist or beatnik[9] reasons, and with others, again, because they are fellow-travellers, if not avowed Communists.

(10) The case against "neutralism" for Britain is that it is dangerous to peace and unlikely to lead to disarmament. The so-called neutrals – Sweden and Switzerland – are in fact quite heavily armed and are now considering more seriously than any other non-nuclear power the production of their own nuclear weapons.[10]

(11) Moreover, our withdrawal from NATO would have one of two consequences. It might be followed by the break-up of the Alliance and the end of U.S. support for Western Europe. In that event, the Soviet

9 The 'beatniks', who were usually pacifist and anti-American, were unkempt youthful imitators of a vaguely anarchist fashionable life-style imported from the U.S.A.

10 Twenty years later both countries were still without them.

Union would be able to dictate its own terms and secure at little or no cost an extension of its influence and domination over the whole of Europe.

Alternatively, our withdrawal from NATO would simply mean that the U.S.A. would more and more come to regard Western Germany as her strongest and most reliable ally and be correspondingly influenced by her in determining policy. Britain would lose all power to influence events without any certainty that should war break out we would be able to escape it.

(12) For these reasons we cannot possibly adopt the policy of unilateral disarmament and/or neutralism. Incidentally, if we were to do so I believe we should condemn ourselves to a further and far greater electoral defeat.

(13) Assuming then that we remain in NATO and that, pending multilateral disarmament, we believe in effective defence, what defence policy should we follow? In part, this must be based on our NATO commitments, and, therefore, settled in consultation with our allies. In part, it must depend on what other defence commitments, existing or possible, we feel it necessary to accept. The final decision must, of course, be consistent with the kind of total defence expenditure figure which is thought to be reasonable. Much of the discussion of these questions is bound to be technical in character. We may be able to convict the Government of muddle, incompetence and waste, of giving us poor value for money, of being unable to establish a modern defence set-up in which the rivalries of the different services are properly subordinated to the needs of the nation. But in all this it is unlikely that any great issue of principle will arise.

(14) A serious controversy tends to be linked only to the question of whether, how far and in what form, we should have our own independent nuclear weapons. Moreover, even this ought not to give rise to passionate feelings. For so long as we remain in NATO, even if we have no nuclear weapons of our own, we are enjoying the shelter of American nuclear weapons. We are thus fully implicated in nuclear policy and in the guilt, which, in the eyes of some, this is thought to involve. Nevertheless, although the argument is presented on this basis that we remain in NATO and therefore in any event enjoy the protection of the Western deterrent, the emotion which it conjures up is undoubtedly associated with the wider and far more fundamental issues dealt with in paragraphs 7–12 above.

(15) The controversy at this stage becomes very confused. At least three distinct questions are muddled up.

(16) There is *first* the question of whether or not the British defence budget involves too much expenditure on nuclear weapons and too little on conventional forces. Parallel with this is the question whether the balance in the NATO forces is similarly tilted too heavily toward nuclear and away from conventional arms. On both points we have generally taken the line that there has been and is excessive reliance upon nuclear to the neglect of conventional weapons. So far as NATO is concerned, while we have accepted the need for both strategic and tactical weapons, we have argued that the resistance to being the first to use either are [*sic*] so great that we ought to plan so as to avoid this decision as long as we possibly can. This means in turn making more of an effort to contain a conventional attack with conventional forces.

In the case of British policy we have argued that both for our role in NATO and for other purposes, it would be more sensible for us to have more conventional and fewer nuclear arms.

(17) In proposing, however, that the balance should be shifted towards conventional and away from nuclear arms, we encounter two obstacles.

In Britain, at least, any increase in the *number* of conventional troops is limited to what can be raised voluntarily. For we are not, in present conditions, prepared to reintroduce conscription. And it seems to be this rather than money which would soon become the "bottleneck". Secondly, it is not clear exactly what expenditure on nuclear weapons is to be cut to achieve what expansion in conventional weapons.

(18) A *second* and quite distinct issue is whether we retain our existing independent deterrent and means of delivery (H. and A. bombs and V. bombers) or whether we unilaterally destroy them or pass them on to NATO or the U.S.A. The case for their retention is, of course, the same as the case for their production in the first instance, namely, that we thereby enjoy a greater degree of independence from the U.S.A. and have the prestige and political advantages of belonging to the nuclear club. It is difficult to believe that without nuclear weapons of our own, we would enjoy quite the same respect from the Russians or the same opportunity of influencing American policy – or be able to do as much effective bridge building between the two major powers.

(19) It is hard to see what the argument is for giving up these weapons unilaterally. They exist already and the cost of continuing to have them must be negligible. We should not give them up and the political advantage we gain from them without some important compensating advantage. We have decided that such an advantage would exist if thereby we could establish the non-nuclear club, covering all countries except

America and Russia.[11] Is there some other possibly more limited advantage which nevertheless could justify us in abandoning these weapons? It is for those who believe this to try and make the case. But it has not yet been made out.

(20) The *third* issue concerns our *future* nuclear policy. For it seems to be generally accepted that our existing nuclear weapons and means of delivery will within 5–7 years cease to be an effective deterrent, because they will not be able to penetrate the Soviet defences. Do we therefore try to have our own successor? And exactly what do we mean by this?

There seem to be at least four possibilities. *First* we might decide to *produce* our own missile adding on our own war head. This will give us maximum independence of the U.S.A. but would also involve heavy expense without even the certainty of success – as missile technology becomes more and more complicated. The Government seem to have abandoned this. In my opinion we should pretty well rule this out. The lesson of Blue Streak is surely the fact that you cannot go in for the rocket race without making expensive mistakes which we cannot afford.

(21) *Secondly*, we might *procure* the missile from the U.S.A. while adding our own nuclear war heads. This should certainly be much cheaper. If the Americans attached no strings to the sale of the missile, there is a case for this and it seems hard to rule it out altogether.

(22) *Thirdly*, we might make some arrangement for sharing production and/or control of the nuclear weapons with the European members of NATO. This needs further exposition and discussion.

(23) *Fourthly*, we could abandon the attempt even to possess any new nuclear weapon which is wholly under our control, or that of the European members of NATO and leave the supply and control of all nuclear weapons to America.

(24) These are all hypothetical questions involving a balance of pros and cons whose exact significance it is very hard to assess in Opposition. We need to bear in mind not only cost, independence and military issues but also the stopping of the spread of nuclear weapons – even if our full plan for the non-nuclear club cannot be adopted. If we can possibly avoid a detailed commitment at this stage it would be much more sensible.

(25) To sum up – so far

    (1) Our paramount aim if [*sic*] still comprehensive multilateral disarmament with effective international controls.

11 Labour adopted that policy in June 1959: *HG*, Ch. 18–ii.

(2) In the absence of this, we must play our part in NATO which must possess the means of deterring a Soviet attack.

(3) We should press that NATO policy should rely more on conventional and less on nuclear arms; similarly we should urge that the balance in the British budget should be shifted in the same direction within the limits set by our policy of not reintroducing conscription.

(4) We should be prepared to give up our *existing* nuclear weapons – as a means of forming the non-nuclear club and so stopping the spread of nuclear weapons.

(5) As regards the future, we should not develop the *production* of our own missile, but consider the three alternatives:

  (a) buying from the U.S.A. and adding our war heads,
  (b) sharing in some sense with the European members of NATO,
  (c) leaving it to the U.S.A. to supply and control all nuclear weapons – though reserving the veto on any to be used from our territory or by our forces.

13th April, 1960.

[The original differed from the final version as follows:
Para. 8 – omits last sentence. Para. 9 – omits 'or beatnik'. Para. 14 – 'if' for 'so long as'. Para. 20 – line 6, 'four' for 'three'; omits last two sentences. Para. 21 – last sentence read 'And, provided that the Americans attach no strings to the sale of the missile, this seems therefore to be obviously preferable.' Para. 22 – omitted. Para. 23 – read '*Thirdly*, if the cost of purchase from the U.S.A. is very high or if the American Government attach strings (e.g. apply to missiles like Polaris or Skybolt the same controls as now apply to Thor) so that we have no real independence, we could nevertheless accept this and thus in effect abandon the attempt even to possess any new nuclear weapon which is wholly under our own control.' Para. 24 – after first sentence, read, 'As far as one can see at present, however, the second course appears to be the sensible one to follow, i.e., not to develop our own missiles any further but to procure the most appropriate one from the U.S.A. (assuming the purchase is not too costly and without strings) to which we add our own warhead. The onus seems to be on those who disagree with this course, either because they propose that we should produce our own missile or because they believe that we should not have such weapons of our own at all, to put forward and establish a contrary point of view. It may be held that the latter course

is desirable as a way of stopping the spread of nuclear weapons even if our plan of the non-nuclear club cannot be adopted. But the exact reasons for this are not clear'. Para. 25 – 'so far' omitted; from sub-para. (5), after 'our own missile', to read 'but rather favour the purchase of the most appropriate types from the U.S.A. and add our own nuclear warheads – providing the cost is not too high and no strings are attached. (6). The policy of continuing in this way to *possess* our own independent nuclear missile should be dropped only if it is regarded as too expensive or if other compensating advantages not so far explained are thereby secured. (7). Lack of precise knowledge makes it impossible for us to take absolutely firm decisions committing a future Labour Government under (5) and (6). But, equally, the information so far available does not justify us in a decision to oppose the idea of an independent deterrent of our own.']

DOCUMENTS ON THE COMMON MARKET

[Editor's Note to Appendix III]

[Three documents are included to illustrate the evolution of Gaitskell's views on the Common Market issue during 1962. (Emphasis in originals.)

The first, sent in May to friendly trade union leaders as a brief for them to use at their union conferences, shows – in its tone rather than its specific statements – that his own private sympathies then leaned towards British entry if the terms were right.

The second, an address to Commonwealth parliamentarians in July and subsequent answers to their questions, brings out his attitude to the respective importance of Commonwealth and European ties, his feelings about British obligations to the Commonwealth and, conversely, his assumption that its reactions would set political limits to the British Government's freedom of action: a view which was to prove mistaken but which had greatly influenced his own tactical approach up to that summer.

The third, a long memorandum sent in December to President Kennedy, explains and justifies his opposition to a policy which had the keen support of the American Administration with which he hoped to work closely on becoming Prime Minister.]

Document No. 24

European Common Market. Resolutions 315–322.
Brief for Trade Union Leaders. [1]

The policy of the Party, overwhelmingly endorsed by our annual conference last year, is that we should not at this stage commit ourselves either to going in *unconditionally* or staying out unconditionally.

---

1 This memorandum, requested by Fred Hayday of the N.U.G.M.W. on 7 May 1962 as a brief for union conferences, went to him, his colleague Jack Cooper, Bill Webber of the T.S.S.A. and other union leaders. It is from Papers, file P.163–2.

If we were to say that we would go in whatever the conditions, this would amount to admitting that we would not mind even if the Commonwealth were to be destroyed. If, on the other hand, we were to say however favourable the conditions, we would *not* go in, we would be ignoring the dangers to us of remaining outside the European Community even though they had met our requirements.

The Party has gone further than this however. It has laid down specifically five conditions as follows:

1. The interests of British agriculture must be safeguarded.
2. The interests of the Commonwealth must be safeguarded.
3. The interest of our partners in the European Free Trade Area must be safeguarded.[2]
4. We must remain free to conduct our own foreign policy as at present.
5. We must be free to introduce whatever measures of socialist economic planning we consider necessary for the welfare of Britain.

So far as the general argument is concerned, *it must be emphasised from the start that by not going in we do not prevent the Common Market from coming into existence*. It already exists and will remain. Our choice is simply whether, since it exists, we go into it or stay out of it. There are dangers in both courses which cannot be ignored.

If we stay out of it, we run the risk of becoming nothing more than a little island off Europe. We shall be dwarfed politically by the Six, particularly if, as is likely to happen in our absence, they form themselves into a Federal State.

In particular, there is the danger that in our absence, Germany would come to dominate such a State. There are also economic dangers. How would the products of the engineering industries fare in a European market where we would have to face higher tariffs against our goods than those of the countries inside the Common Market?[3] There are however also dangers in going in without proper safeguards. We do not want the Commonwealth to break up. We regard it as a valuable multi-racial association. Nor do we want the countries of the Commonwealth to be penalised economically. While we cannot hope to enjoy a preferential system within the Commonwealth and in Europe at the same time, nevertheless we want to retain, as far as possible, our markets in the Commonwealth. We do not, of course, want British agriculture to revert to the depression of the pre-war days. We are also completely committed to going in only with the agreement of the E.F.T.A. countries. This is why

2 The first three were the government's conditions also. On EFTA see below, pp. 651, 664.
3 An argument for use by Bill Carron at the A.E.U. conference.

we have insisted in the Labour Party on the fulfilment of our five conditions.

In fact, we believe that our policy is the only sensible and rational one. It would be a mistake to buy a pig in a poke, we cannot really rationally make up our minds on this vital issue until we know the conditions which have been negotiated. The Labour Party is not committed to going in nor is it committed to staying out.

Most of the resolutions are very wide of the mark and almost certainly inspired by Communists. The Communists naturally oppose our going into the Common Market because they believe it would strengthen the democratic forces of the West.[4] They are right in this sense that if we do not go in as I have said earlier on, there could be rather grave political consequences. By going in, on the other hand, we could prevent the formation of a tight, inward-looking federation and insist that it remains a looser outward-looking affair.

The argument that foreign labour will be allowed in with far lower living standards is greatly exaggerated. The T.U.C. has no great fears of this. The fact is that in the last few years, standards of living in Europe have risen sharply so that in Germany they are virtually as high as our own and not far off in France, Holland and Belgium. Only in Southern Italy can one really say that there is much difference. So far as Social benefits are concerned, these are now on a larger scale on the Continent than they are in Britain. In any case, there are safeguards about the entry of foreign labour which can only come when jobs are available.

It is certainly nonsense to say British foreign policy would be determined by French and German votes. There is nothing whatever in the Rome Treaty as it stands which carries any political commitment whatever. If in the course of the negotiations some kind of federalism were to be set up, then this would be a strong argument for not going in but it is exceedingly unlikely. It is also gravely misleading to suggest that we shall not be able to conduct our own economic policies. In point of fact, France has more public ownership than we have today, and there is certainly nothing in the Rome Treaty which would prevent us from carrying out a policy of nationalisation. The commitments are in fact, confined to the field of foreign trade, but such commitments are inevitable in such a treaty – which regulates trade with other countries.

Finally, the Socialist Democratic Parties of Western Europe who are in the Common Market are very, very anxious indeed that we should join. They do not share any of the fears expressed in these resolutions. On the contrary, they believe that the burying of old animosities between France and Germany and the getting closer together of the peoples of Europe, is

4 Had HG expected to end up opposing entry into the E.E.C., he would not have stressed the Communist influence in that camp.

a step in the right direction, internationalistic in its approach, and getting away from the narrow nationalism of the past.

To sum up: although there are undoubtedly circumstances in which we should not go in if our conditions are not fulfilled, nevertheless, if they are fulfilled, there is little or nothing to fear and great benefits may well result.[5]

Document No. 25

HG's Commonwealth Parliamentary Association speech on the Common Market[6]

MR GAITSKELL: Mr Chairman, Ladies and Gentlemen, I am going to talk about the attitude of the Labour Party to the Common Market problem. Of course, there are some people who regard the case either for or against as so overwhelming that that concludes the matter as far as they are concerned. There are some people both in the Labour Party and in the Conservative Party who, for instance, are confirmed in their views that the only possible future for Britain must be in Europe and, therefore, would go in, whatever the conditions might be. There are not many of them but there are a few. Most of them do not admit it but I think there are some [who] think that way. Equally, there are undoubtedly a number of people who take the opposite view and who are so completely opposed to the idea that, however favourable the conditions, they would not go in just because they dislike Europe or because they feel any conditions are bound to damage the Commonwealth and they do not want to damage the Commonwealth. The Labour Party officially does not take either of these extreme views. In our opinion the case for or against going in is a much more evenly balanced one. We take the view it is more evenly balanced than the view the Government themselves take for reasons I will explain in a moment. That is why our decision as to whether we support or oppose entry will turn entirely on the conditions negotiated. If the case appeared to us to be overwhelmingly for, clearly you would not bother so much about the conditions and that would be equally so if the case appeared to be overwhelmingly against. We think this is an evenly balanced thing.

5 While this paper argues formally (like HG's speech at the Brighton Conference on 3 October) for remaining uncommitted, its whole emotional tone – particularly the last five paragraphs – is as favourable to entry as that of the speech was opposed.

6 He gave this private talk on 12 July 1962. Transcript in his Papers, file P.167B.

We also think a great deal of nonsense has been and is being talked both about the case for and against and I would like to take two particular points where I think much popular discussion is quite wrong. The first is about the economic pros and cons.

It is not my business to attack the Government in this room but I personally disagree with the view which lies behind the Government's attitude or the attitude of many Ministers that there is an overwhelming economic case for going in. Time after time we have had from Government spokesmen statements which imply that all will be well if we go in and equally the situation will be terrible if we stay out. I do not question for one moment the sincerity of the people who hold that view. There are a few in our own Party who hold it but I personally do not hold that view, nor do the majority of our Party. I must say, too, that I do not know of any outstanding economist – and by 'economist' I mean an academic economist who makes his living out of economics and research into economics – who believes that the case for going in is a very strong one. Most of those I know and whose judgment I would trust regard it as very evenly balanced – 50:50. I must emphasise that because I assume you think the economic case is taken for granted and in my view it should not be. In my opinion two people, Sir Donald MacDougall and Professor Meade, have come out quite plainly on this statement. The former has worked for two different Governments and is now deputy head of the planning machine appointed by this present Government, and Professor Meade, one of the most objectively-minded people who is personally in favour of going in on political grounds, nevertheless dismisses the economic argument as being [not?] a very clear-cut one.

It is perfectly easy to seek to show why the thing is not as clear-cut as you might suppose. You cannot say it is more than a hunch either way as to whether there is more to be said for going in or staying out. If people were to ask me 'Would you rather be in or out on purely economic grounds?' in the long run I should say, 'Yes, I would rather be in' but in the short run we are going to run into a lot of trouble which has not been appreciated yet but which is going to occur during the first three or four years of entry. If we go in on bad terms that trouble will be all the greater. That is one thing which is important.

On the other side I must say the arguments of those who are opposed to the Common Market seem to me to be grossly exaggerated. It is frequently said by the left-wingers in the political spectrum that if we go in we will really lose our own independence; we are going to be dominated by Dr. Adenauer and President de Gaulle; we will cease to count at all; we will not be free to conduct our own internal affairs and so on. All sorts of arguments and excuses are put forward. There is as little in this as in the supposed economic argument for going in because as the Treaty of Rome stands today there is no political commitment except for the very vague phrase in the preamble about being in favour of greater unity, or something of that kind. There is no specific commitment on defence or on foreign policy. The only commitments are those relating to the economic and commercial parts of the Treaty of Rome. It is purely an economic and commercial Treaty. So one must dismiss these things.

Going a little further with the political argument I would personally look at it like this as I think it is the most important question since I believe the economic argument to be very evenly balanced: we have to ask ourselves what the probabilities are if we go in or do not go in, recognising that whether we do or do not this thing has come to s[t]ay. Whether you and I like it or not the thing is there. In many ways I cannot help regretting it has been created although I see the advantage of Franco/German understanding is very important. Nevertheless, I confess that at times I doubt whether the whole thing is worth-while; I am not an enthusiastic European in that sense. But it is there, it is going to stay there and we have got to take account of it. Therefore, we have to say to ourselves, assuming this has to be decided on political grounds, 'Is it better that we should be in or out?' What have we to balance? There will be discussions, no doubt, in time as to the formation of closer integration although at the moment we are not committed to any particular political set-up. Closer integration may take the form of some kind of federal arrangement, such as direct elections to a Western European Parliament controlling [an] executive, or it may simply take the form of closer collaboration between governments on what I would call a confederal basis. However, we are not committed to accepting any of these things and therefore it is fair to say if we go in at least we can wield very much greater influence, exercising a veto where we wish to on any developments, political developments, of this sort. This is a powerful argument. If, on the other hand, we were to stay out then many of us feel the probability is that Little Europe – because it would almost certainly be confined to the Six for I doubt if the others would go in except, possibly, Ireland – would form a much closer political association.[7]

Do we, then, want to be a country outside what will become more probably than if we went in fairly soon a more or less integrated political unity? I think our attitude to that is influenced by two things. First of all, what is there for us outside it? This again turns on what is going to happen in the Commonwealth. One has to raise these questions in the privacy of

7 'The others' who had applied were Ireland, Denmark and Norway.

this room because it is in the back of the minds particularly of those who are strongly pro-Europe. If we felt certain the Commonwealth was going to continue and not only continue but grow closer together so that there would be more joint action on the political as well as on the economic field and that by not going in we should also preserve that other special relationship we have with the United States, this obviously would be a tremendous argument for staying out. On the other hand, supposing the Commonwealth is really gradually going to fall apart – if the ties are going to get weaker, if the African members of the Commonwealth are coming closer together, if India is drifting apart from us and if Australia and New Zealand are perhaps going to look more and more towards the United States, and that applies to Canada, too – so that we in ten or twenty years' time are just a little island off Europe and nothing more, we are bound to say, 'We had better be in this, too'. This is the particular problem which faces us because it is very much a matter of judgment what is going to happen in the next ten years or so if we do not go in.

Again, if we do go in, as I implied earlier on, can we not influence this Europe? Can we not somehow or other see to it that they do not develop into a tight little group of six nations but instead into a looser association with a more international outlook? I say frankly that, although I know there are obviously very powerful arguments for countries which are neighbours and which have also fought a great many wars getting closer together, the world is a very small place today and that a particular grouping within one Continent is not going to be the answer or the solution to all the international problems. Therefore, I would say it is important we should try to prevent too tight an association, that we should use our influence to create low external tariffs, a forward-looking outlook, strong support for the U.N. and all that kind of thing. This all adds up to a political case for going in, going in to prevent something which might be bad from developing, while at the same time fulfilling our function as a nation in a way we can feel fairly happy about.

I would add to that what I personally feel very strongly: if that is the case for going in then it is a case that only stands, in my view, if we can go in without destroying our Commonwealth links. If in the process of going in there was to be a dreadful row and the Commonwealth countries felt they were being betrayed by us, particularly those dependent upon us economically, and that in consequence Britain had made her choice and was going into Europe, they would probably say, 'This is the end of the Commonwealth' and that would weaken our capacity for influencing Europe in the way we want to influence it. Therefore, we in the Labour Party do attach very great importance to the conditions of entry and we are not ashamed to say we are accused of sitting on the fence. In my opinion it is the only rational and sensible thing to do. It was notable in the debate we had just before Whitsun that more and more speakers, whatever their party, did really support this line so my colleague George Brown, in winding up, was able to crack a joke and say the fence was probably sagging with the weight of people climbing on to the fence! And there is no doubt this is the case.

Now what are the conditions? We have been specific about this and have laid down five conditions; three of them are essentially the same as those of the Conservative Party, although we might interpret them differently, and there are two others to which we attach particular importance for other reasons. One of them, we say, is the right to continue to have our own independent foreign policy. We do not mean that you can have a foreign policy without regard to other nations; that is absurd. What we mean by that is that we should not be any less free than we are today. This is really another way of saying if there were to be some additional political commitment whereby the foreign policy of Britain were decided by a majority or qualified majority vote of the members of the Common Market this would be a reason for which we would emphatically reject it. I do not believe the Labour Party in those circumstances would accept it, nor do I think the Conservative Party would, either. Nor do I think the country would. We have emphasised this to show we are not going to be committed politically at this stage. What happens in ten or twenty years is another matter and depends on developments I have already referred to which may or may not take place.

Secondly, we have said we must be free to carry out the kind of economic planning in Britain which a Labour Government would regard as necessary for the welfare of the country. Now in the main I think – although there will be some disagreement in the Party on this, perhaps, but it is not always easy to be sure – the Treaty of Rome does not inhibit us from doing the sort of planning we would want to do. There is certainly no question at all of any restraint on our policy if we desire to extend the frontier of public ownership, of introducing controls of one kind or another except in so far as these concern foreign trade. The Treaty of Rome is principally about tariffs and also about certain consequential things. For instance, there is a very elaborate code laid down to secure that competition within the Common Market is genuinely fair, and this involves certain restraints upon members. This is sometimes held to mean that this means we cannot plan as we wish. I do not think so. An international commercial agreement is just as much to our advantage if we can stop people breaking the rules as it is to them. Therefore, I do not think that is really going to prevent what I would regard as economic planning.

One question, for instance, comes up. We are confronted in this country with a good deal of local unemployment, particularly in Scotland. Perhaps you heard something about the possibility of that yesterday. Both Labour Governments and Conservative Governments have used certain devices for attempting to steer industry into these areas. This involved subsidies to the particular area, loans and things of that kind. It has been felt that the Common Market would prevent us from doing this but my interpretation is that it would not.

The only thing in this field which worries me a certain amount is the obligation not to impose restrictions on the movement of capital. We could be confronted with a balance of payments crisis which would rapidly develop into an exchange crisis. We had one, for instance, last year. And then any government would wish to apply restrictions on the movement of capital even within the Common Market. You are allowed to do that in the case of balance of payments crises. It is a rather elaborate arrangement but you could be stopped from doing this and told 'You must not do it' on a qualified majority vote of the Council of Ministers. If you did not obtain enough votes it would mean you would be in trouble. That is one anxiety. In the case of an exchange crisis, not associated with a balance of payments crisis but a flight of capital, the position is less satisfactory because the Commission has the right to tell you to stop imposing restrictions. In practice I do not believe this is going to matter a great deal. I am certain any government, faced with this problem, would do what it felt was necessary in order to sustain the value of the pound and prevent devaluation unless they wanted it, in which case the others would have to lump it.

Nevertheless, if you take the letter of the Treaty as it stands – this is a complication which leads me to throw in something I should have done earlier on but it can be hung conveniently on this point – in our view the voting arrangements resulting from our entry into the Common Market are of the highest importance because, as you know, there are a number of things for which a unanimous decision is necessary. That means the British Government has to agree to them; therefore, it is free to disagree and they cannot happen if the British Government disagrees. However, there are also a number of cases where the decision of the Council of Ministers is taken on a qualified majority vote. A qualified majority at the moment is a two-thirds majority which leaves France with her votes, plus Belgium, in a position to veto. That is to say, it is one large and one small country. Now if Norway and Denmark come in with us – and I attach importance to that – then the Labour Party would like to see a veto in the hands of ourselves and at any rate the two Scandinavian states. However, if it is a two-thirds majority we would need more than that because of the increased number of votes. Therefore, this business is very important for us and one of our worries is that nothing has been done about it and, in a sense, cannot be negotiated until we know who is coming in.

That brings me to the third point, not in order of importance, I would say, and that is we have obligations to the other E.F.T.A. countries, obligations which are very specific. The Government is committed on this and is committed not to go in until their legitimate interests are satisfied; this means those who want to come in must be able to come in with us. Coming in means different things according to whether the country is neutral or not. In the case of Norway and Denmark they want full membership, as we do, but in the case of Sweden, Switzerland and Austria, the neutrals, that is not so. They do not want full membership; they all want associate membership. This is complicated because there are two senses to this word. However, they want to be economic members; they want to be within the Customs Union. There has been a great deal of trouble about this, not from the British Government but from the American Government which appears to be very opposed to the neutrals coming in and particularly to Sweden coming in. They are prepared to swallow Switzerland and Austria but not Sweden because she is neutral and they think this is not good at all. I think personally this is idiotic and have said so. I have good reason for believing that if Sweden did not come in Norway and Denmark would not come in, either, and therefore our position in the Common Market would be very much weaker because we normally work with these Scandinavian States. There we are; that is our third condition – that the E.F.T.A. countries must be satisfied.

Fourthly, there is the question of British agriculture. Here in principle there is no difference between ourselves and the Government, and it is a matter of seeing how the detailed arrangements affect British agriculture and whether they are adequately safeguarded. I take the view that I do not regard this as likely to be the gravest difficulty because British agriculture is very much in the same position as is agriculture in the Common Market countries. It is highly protectionist both in Europe and here and we think British agriculture could be introduced into this protectionist ring. However, there are certain things – for instance, horticulture in particular – which are likely to be adversely affected and some of the small dairy farms as well.

My fifth and last point, and the most important one of all, is the Commonwealth with which you are particularly concerned. One has to break this thing down and I will do it very briefly. There are several different Commonwealth problems. One of them is the problem of tropical products. Now I think this ought to be a relatively easy one to solve because it is hardly conceivable that we can be expected to accept in respect of Commonwealth countries any worse conditions than those available to the former French colonial territories in Africa; if these countries produce the same products as the African members of the Commonwealth it seems fairly certain that that problem will be solved. At the moment, however, it is held up by an argument between the Six and the associated territories, the associated members. There is the possibility – and I would be very interested to hear your views about this – that African countries will not wish to participate in this sense, but you know the position would be that you would be able to have free entry of these tropical products into Europe and that at the same time you would protect your industries, always providing there was no discrimination in the protection as between the different European countries; and, further, there is the aid fund which would be available for such territories. I think it is fair to say that in so far as we are concerned we would not wish to see this as involving any particular political strings or anything of that kind. Of course, it is for countries like Nigeria and Ghana to decide for themselves as to whether they wish to come in on those terms. I personally think the whole concept of associated territories in this sense is out-of-date and I wish the Six would get rid of it. I think a special arrangement, with the implication in some way that these former colonial territories are in a dependent status upon the Common Market, can be very wrong and misleading and very dangerous as well. It is fair to say we would let in free tropical products and have a fund to aid underdeveloped territories but as I have said I think it is a pity that the actual concept of association has been introduced. If they were starting now I do not think the French would do it; this had begun before their own colonies had gained their independence. That is one problem.

There is secondly the problem of manufactured goods from Western European countries; this is the one thing which has so far been negotiated and presumably accepted by the British Government, subject to the position as a whole being satisfactory. There is to be a transitional period. After that the Common Market tariff applies against Canadian manu-factured goods in full but there is quite a long transitional period.

Problem No. 3 is the manufactured goods from the Asian, African and underdeveloped countries generally. We take the view in the Labour Party that it is essential that Europe should throw open its markets to the manufactured goods of these countries although we recognise that you probably have to do the thing gradually because many of our industries are going to be greatly affected by this. Nevertheless, we do attach enormous importance to the fact that the West as a whole must take a much more responsible line about this because I cannot see how African and Asian countries can carry through the development they have got to carry through if there is no outlet for their manufactured goods. Therefore, you have got to negotiate this. At the moment we do not seem to have got very far, only the promise that if Britain goes in then the Common Market will negotiate about this. The Government is not satisfied with this, nor would I be; there must be something firmer and clearer. We feel in the case of textiles that although we take a lot of textiles from underdeveloped countries the European markets are ready to do so now and they might throw open their markets a good deal more.

Then there are the raw materials. Six or seven products are not on the free list – products like aluminium, pulp, leather, lead, zinc and so on – and we would like them to be on the free list. We do not know what is going to happen as far as they are concerned.

Finally, there are the temperate agricultural products from Canada, New Zealand and Australia which present the toughest problem and I would only say this: although you rightly said I am not concerned with the details of the negotiations I think we would lay great stress on one thing. That is, are the arrangements to be negotiated to be of a purely temporary character so that after the transitional period is over the Commonwealth countries concerned are treated just like any other country not in the Commonwealth, or is there to be some permanent arrangement giving reasonable opportunities for these products to be sold under fair conditions in Britain and in Europe? This, I think, will be one of the great sticking points. It is at the moment a sticking point for the British Government and I hope it will remain so. I think it is likely to be a sticking point for those countries themselves.

That brings me to my last point. We follow these negotiations; we have had debates and have put a number of points to the Government in the debates; we have raised the various issues we think we ought to have raised and we shall continue to do that. It may be we shall have another debate before the Recess begins but we shall be very greatly influenced – that is, so far as our Party is concerned – by the attitude of the Prime Ministers' Conference. I do not know exactly what they will be discussing; maybe the discussions will go slowly so that the timing will be wrong and all the British Government will be able to do will be to say, 'This is as far as we have got. Is this all right? This is what we are trying to get'. Therefore, you may have to have another Prime Ministers' Conference. Alternatively, they may have an outline agreement by the end of July or soon afterwards and be able to say, 'Is this all right?' We shall be very much influenced by that and so will opinion in Britain generally. If at this Conference the Prime Ministers say on the one side, 'We are not over-enthusiastic about this but we are prepared to take it; we think the agreement is reasonable; we see, on balance, certain advantages and on balance, although we are not enthusiastic, we will accept it' the Labour Party would be very much influenced by that and would say, 'All right, that is their view. The Commonwealth is satisfied and, subject to other things, we would be disposed to say 'All right'. If, however, at the Commonwealth Prime Ministers' Conference there is a hell of a row and if Mr Menzies and Mr Nehru – who do not always work together in harmony – both say, 'This is intolerable, we are not having this and it means the end of the Commonwealth if you go ahead with it' then I am certain we would come out against it and I do not think any British Government would dare go ahead with it. This is very, very important indeed, and it is as well that the Commonwealth Governments should know the power they have to influence British opinion. I think that power is very great indeed.

Let me say this about British opinion, and I end with this one expression of regret. This is a frightfully difficult issue – let us be clear about this – and it is a very complex issue and British opinion is not clear about it. A little time ago the gallup poll suggested people were in favour of going in; they were more in favour of going in than against. This position has been reversed by the last one. This is not surprising; opinion can easily swing one way or another because this is not a thing on which the majority of the population here feel strongly either way. Small elements on both sides feel passionately about it but the majority of the population are much too confused about it and you might get a big swing of opinion one way or the other. For this reason I repeat that the attitude of the Commonwealth is going to be extremely important.

This is a very difficult problem and I have only one regret about it. I think it is a pity that the Government have at times appeared to be quite so enthusiastic. I realise their dilemma because if they did not show any enthusiasm with the Six in their negotiations the Six may have said, 'We are not going on' but by showing this enthusiasm they have given the impression too frequently that they were suppliants, this is a 'must' for us, we have to go in. This is not true. We do not have to go in. There are difficulties and problems either way. I only wish they had, despite the difficulties, taken it rather more slowly and made it plain this was not just the matter of a suppliant meekly coming along and saying, 'Please let us into the club with the others' which calls for the answer, 'If you join the club you must accept the rules'. This is what I regret; I think it has somewhat weakened our bargaining position when dealing with the Continental countries. I also think it has given a misleading impression to

Britain as a whole. However, this is my personal view and I can only end with this sentiment: on balance, if we can get the right terms, all right. I think this will be O.K. so long as the Commonwealth is preserved. Political arguments have been put forward and if I were asked, 'Would you rather be in or out?' on those terms I would rather be in. If, on the other hand, the negotiations are such that it means the end of the Commonwealth – and I repeat none of us can be sure whether it is going to last but few of us here want to take any steps which would hasten its decline and demise – we are opposed to it. Therefore, I would prefer to see the negotiations prolonged, and do not let us assume it will be a disaster if they are. There is too much of an inclination to say it will be a disaster if things break down. We are overshadowed by the fear of a breakdown in these negotiations but I do not think this will happen. There is just as much pressure in Europe for our going in as there is on our side, and I think, therefore, it is up to us to stand out for the terms which will make our entry tolerable.
(*Applause*).

THE CHAIRMAN:[8] . . . Mr Gaitskell has made the same promise as Mr Ted Heath that if there are any questions he will be pleased to answer them . . .

MR N. J. KING (New Zealand): I would like to ask Mr Gaitskell how great will be the effect of food prices on the British housewife, the British consumer, owing to the fact that at the moment you are getting cheap Commonwealth supplies. May I say at the outset that New Zealand sends 91 lbs. out of every 100 lbs. of butter into the United Kingdom, 94 lbs. of mutton and lamb and 94 lbs. of cheese. So there is a tremendous advantage not only to New Zealand but to the United Kingdom in having your food supplied by us; if there is going to be a tariff and equalising levies within the Common Market which will shut out our supplies not just for the transitional period but for the time afterwards it will affect your food prices. I wonder whether that has been fully recognised by the United Kingdom Government? Also, has British opinion been taken into account?

MR GAITSKELL: I would say – of course, I do not speak for the United Kingdom Government – that as far as British opinion is concerned I cannot honestly say that, taking the cost of living index and spreading it out, the rise over a period of years will have a shattering effect. I think individual prices will make people pay a lot more and someone, discussing this swing of the gallup poll, said to me, 'I think it is entirely

8 Here and below a few phrases from the Chairman are omitted.

because Ted Heath in that broadcast frankly admitted prices were going to go up and this has put a lot of people off'. Therefore, it may be more significant than politicians have implied so far. Secondly, it is really up to the Commonwealth Governments to see in the negotiations that they put forward permanent proposals which will secure that they are not squeezed out by more expensive products from Europe. There are certain proposals which the Australians have been putting forward, presumably with the assent of New Zealand. I do not know exactly what stage they have reached but there are possibly to be arrangements that the butter position, for instance, will not be very different from the present situation which is largely governed by quotas which would prevent a sharp increase in prices. The third thing is that what exactly does turn out depends on the prices fixed by the Common Market, by the Commission themselves, for these different products. If they fix high target or guide prices, with a correspondingly high levy, there will be a much greater rise in living costs. I cannot help feeling, though, that they would be aware of the competition from America and would put some limit on it. But it turns on you people, on the Commonwealth Governments, saying to the British Government, 'Look here, we are deeply concerned about this. This is what we want and will you press our point of view?' This is one of the key points in the whole thing. Are you going to get satisfactory permanent arrangements, not necessarily as good as they are now but a reasonable compromise which gives you a reasonable prospect for the future?

MR S. R. PAGON M.H.R. (Malaya): Could Mr Gaitskell give us a brief résumé of the clauses of the Treaty of Rome?

MR GAITSKELL: Not brief! (*Laughter*) . . . You know, the basic problem is that you would have to accept the complete reverse of the preferential system. It is a preferential system of free trade for all the European products, with a duty imposed on everything from outside. It is an extension of Imperial preferences to Europe, with the Commonwealth in the position it was in before. The agricultural position is much more complicated because there are special cases; it is a planned protectionist system and there are within that a lot of other things governing, for instance, the movement of labour, the right to establish businesses and so on. The essence of it is this Customs Union.

MR L. S. REID, D.F.C., M.P. (Victoria): Taking into consideration the various points for and against, do you think perhaps the timing is perhaps not opportune at this juncture? Would it not be better if this decision was put off for twelve months or two years?

MR GAITSKELL: The argument for going ahead is that the Common Market exists; it has a timetable of its own, a common external tariff is being set up and protection within the Common Market is gradually being demolished. With every year that goes by this is becoming a more complete affair. Therefore, the Government would probably say, 'If we leave this any longer we are going to be up against a more difficult situation'. Against that, however, as I said in my concluding remarks, if it were a choice of either accepting bad terms or breaking off altogether or simply continuing to negotiate until we got better terms and that meant deferring the decision for a year, I would unhesitatingly say that is what I would do.

MR S. C. MAHARAJ M.H.R. (Trinidad and Tobago): Mr Chairman, I want to ask two questions. In view of the possible entry of Britain into the Common Market before a general election, would the Leader of the Opposition in the House consider there should be something in order to allow Members on both sides of the House to have a free vote one way or the other on the question of the Common Market? It seems to me there is a considerable amount of sympathy for the Commonwealth in this country. The second question is this: in view of the statement that the economic case seems to be 50:50, in view of the fact that all the Commonwealth countries – particularly countries such as Canada and Australia – seem to have fought the last war chiefly on the assumption that they would have the leadership of Great Britain in the world and that there will be a certain amount of surrendering of sovereignty by Britain to the European Common Market, and in view of the fact that we heard yesterday there might be a freezing of exports up to a certain point from these places into the Common Market and of the planning of pan-African unity, will he consider that, taking the surrounding circumstances into consideration, the United Kingdom is taking a lead in the breaking-up of the Commonwealth of Nations?

MR GAITSKELL: On the question of the free vote I do not know that I would mind very much if the Conservative Party were prepared to accept it but I do not think there is the slightest chance they will do so. I will put it this way which may comfort you a little: I think the Government has to carry with it the support of its own backbenchers; it can afford a minor but not a major revolt. It is also under attack from the Opposition whilst it is in the middle of a great Commonwealth row. I would have thought it is very probable that somehow or other the Government is going to obtain the views of the Conservative Party Members of Parliament before it reaches its decision. How it does this mysterious operation is for them to decide. We shall certainly have to take the view of our own Labour

Members of Parliament. Indeed, we were recently discussing the procedure involved here in case this came up during the Recess and the possible need to recall, if Parliament is not recalled, the Members of Parliament so that they can be present and discuss these things. So in that sense I think the influence of Members is probably a great deal greater than appears. I would not have thought it was easy for the Government to be very dictatorial about this. It has got to think in terms that people do feel very strongly about this. I am not prepared to say the British Government is breaking up the Commonwealth. I might have to say that if they wanted us to go in under very bad terms but one has to face the fact that this is a real problem, and I hope I have not given the impression that it is not real. It is very real indeed. I think the economic case has been grossly exaggerated. I said I thought that on balance if you offered me the choice on its own, would we be in or out, I would say, 'Yes, I think we would do better to be in'. From the technical argument point of view we would lose in some markets and gain in others. The problem of investment would be a very important one. Investment would tend to go more to Europe. But politically I think any British Government would have to face the problem, 'What are we going to do?' This powerful thing is growing up next door to us. After all, something like 200 million people have formed themselves into a State which could be decidedly awkward in all sorts of ways if we were outside it.[9] What is the impact going to be on our relations with America if we do not go in? Are they going to squeeze us out and deal with these people alone? You cannot ignore the possibility of this. So it is not fair to denounce the Government as though it was a plain act of treachery on their part. It is a very difficult decision but I repeat that we certainly regard ourselves as the Opposition which is in some respects the watchdog of the Commonwealth. I think if you can get the right terms it would not be right to say it means the break-up of the Commonwealth because, with the right terms, this will be much more a purely economic affair. It will mean lower external tariffs. I do not think any of us, leaving out the particular problems of New Zealand and Australia, would say that the system of Imperial preferences is entirely sacrosanct. Many Commonwealth countries have diminished their impact and have all frequently said they are anxious to protect their own industries. After all, the Ottawa Agreement was only in 1932 and I have never taken the view that it depends on this. It is the political implications or the political consequences of economic decisions I would worry about. As far as Canada is concerned, the question of their manufactured goods has

9 Of course, they had not formed a state – as he had himself insisted in the fifth paragraph of this talk. Here and elsewhere in this discussion he caused confusion by casually using the present tense when anticipating possible future developments. (On recalling the P.L.P. – above, this page – see *HG*, p. 720.)

greatly affected our relationship; of course they do not like it and they have complained, but if this was all there was to it I do not think anyone would worry frightfully. It is the political implications, though, we have to watch and the danger that an agreement will be reached which is thought in the Commonwealth to imply – and there is very real danger of this – that the British are abandoning the Commonwealth. This, I think, would be disastrous and I know from talks I have had with Commonwealth people that there is quite a lot of feeling that is so. This comes from an exaggerated pro-European feeling generated, I am sorry to say, by some of the Ministers in the present Government, and if I were in the Common-wealth I would resent that and think it has gone too far.

MR L. R. CROUSE, M.P. (Canada): Regarding what you have said about competition from these 200 million people, would not the British have the same competition from these 200 million people whether they were inside or outside the Common Market?

MR GAITSKELL: I was not referring to competition; I was referring to the ultimate impact of this. At the moment we are a country of at least equal, and most of us say greater, significance with either France, Germany or Italy and with the Commonwealth we exercise quite an influence in the world. Now if the Commonwealth is going to disappear on the one side and these other countries together are going to consist of 200 million people, what is going to be left of Britain on her own? This is quite a problem we cannot entirely ignore. I want to have the best of both worlds, and I am not ashamed to say so, by having a type of federal state developing in Europe and keeping the Commonwealth within it.[10]

MR CROUSE: But Britain has never been on her own; she has all the rest of the Commonwealth faithfully and loyally behind her.

MR GAITSKELL: That is, of course, true if you mean – and I would be the first to agree you have said so in no uncertain terms – that in two world wars Canada and Australia have always been with us. That is true but it is not true that we are a federal state. We are not part of one state and we are not, even, all in the same alliance. Australia [sic] and Canada are; Australia and New Zealand are not; India is neutral and most of the Commonwealth countries are, too. I think that is reasonable. No-one attaches more importance to the Commonwealth than I do but do not let us get illusions about it. It is not a customs union, or a military alliance,

10 As he consistently opposed any federal development in Europe, he probably said or meant 'confederal' here; but not in the sense that it could override national decisions, which he rejected (Document 26 below, para. 51).

and it is not now, I regret, entirely a community of democracies. We have to face this. You have not got democracy in Pakistan today, and certainly you cannot assume you are going to have a replica of our parliamentary democracy in Africa. It would be silly to expect it. Tanganyika is doing jolly well but it is pretty much a one-party affair and it may have to be for a time. So I think the Commonwealth has a great deal to do in the world. It can do a lot by helping to solve racial problems and it can be an influence for democracy, despite the fact that we are not all democracies today. It can also be a very powerful influence if we work together in the United Nations. All these things are possible but that is all. It is not the same thing as a new state which is what we are [*sic*: may be?] confronted with in Western Europe, and we have to ask ourselves, 'What is our position going to be?' I only raise the issue, are you so sure that in ten or twenty years' time the Commonwealth will be there? Any fair-minded person must ask himself that question.

THE HON. R. S. MAHER, M.L.A. (Speaker) (New South Wales): In view of the extraordinarily complicated constitutional nature of the organisation envisaged by the Rome Treaty, we have got one set of voting rules in the Assembly where an absolute majority prevails and a different system of voting in the Council where they are prepared to accept a qualified majority, whatever that phrase might mean, weighted by certain other factors, whatever that might mean. Do you think in the case of economic stringency or political emergency that the spirit rather than the letter of the Treaty of Rome would be observed?

MR GAITSKELL: I think it would be fair. This is a very difficult point to judge but in all fairness from my experience of international negotiations – which, unhappily, is some way away now because we have been in opposition for so long – I would say that even in bodies where there is a unanimous rule there is always a good deal of opinion and talk. You want to have a re-think; you try and persuade people to accept the general view. I think the same sort of thing would probably apply in anything of importance although we are worried about this voting system, I repeat, and I certainly would stand out – and it will be a very important point in the discussions – for a veto in the hands of ourselves plus the two Scandinavian States. That may mean a three-quarters majority is necessary instead of a two-thirds majority. France may feel the same because she probably likes to have her veto with Belgium. I would guess that the thing will be affected by a desire to avoid a major row. One accepts legal obligations and whatever may be accepted in this way in the letter. First of all, however, the letter is not always absolutely clear and, secondly, in the last resort this is not such an emergency as to make it impossible, what-

ever the letter, for withdrawal to take place. Federations have grown up
in the past and civil war has been involved. We are not in that state. It
would be a tremendous upheaval and one would hope if we were to go in
it would never happen. But speaking within the privacy of these four walls
one cannot rule out, unhappily, that this country or some other country
under a new government might decide we just cannot go on; supposing
the worst fears of people are realised and we become a depressed area off
Europe there would be a tremendous urge to get out of it. I do not think
that is likely to happen but to avoid that I think the other countries would
lean over backwards, and the spirit is likely to be just as important as the
letter.

Document No. 26

Gaitskell's Memorandum to President Kennedy, 11 December 1962 [11]

PRIVATE AND CONFIDENTIAL

Memorandum by the Rt. Hon.
Hugh Gaitskell, M.P.

1. Until 1961 no serious or important body of opinion in Britain urged or
believed that we should enter the Common Market. [12] It was regarded as
impossible, since it would mean the complete abandonment of our
Commonwealth trade policy and its replacement with a system which
discriminated against instead of in favour of Commonwealth products.

2. The Conservative Government had been firmly against the idea and
had said so through a series of Ministerial statements of which I quote
only two:

> *Mr. Macmillan, 26th November, 1956.*
>
> 'I do not believe that this House would ever agree to our entering
> arrangements which, as a matter of principle, would prevent our
> treating the great range of imports from the Commonwealth at
> least as favourably as those from the European countries. So this

11 From Papers, P.118–5; the emphasis is his, and the date is that of the covering
letter to the American Ambassador. Kennedy asked George Ball (see note 15
below) to draft a reply, but HG died before it was ready: G. Ball, *The
Discipline of Power* (Bodley Head, 1968), p. 85.
12 The Liberal Party did.

objection, even if there were no other, would be quite fatal to any proposal that the U.K. should seek to take part in a European Common Market by joining a Customs Union.'

Mr. Maudling, 12th February, 1959.

'I cannot conceive that any Government of this country would put forward a proposition which would involve the abandonment of Commonwealth free entry. It would be wrong for us and for the whole free world to adopt a policy of new duties on foodstuffs and raw materials many of which come from underdeveloped countries, at present entering a major market duty-free.'

3. This attitude was fully supported by the Opposition. There was no Party difference whatever. I myself in the Godkin Lectures[13] at Harvard in 1957 made our attitude perfectly plain – our fears for the Commonwealth if we went into Europe, our opposition to the reactionary attitude of some West European Governments, our objection to the 'third force' idea and our desire to build an Atlantic rather than a European community.

4. When, therefore, in July, 1961, the British Government decided to apply for entry it came as a complete surprise to British public opinion, although the shock was tempered by reports in the newspapers which had been put out for some weeks beforehand.

5.   I do not know exactly what caused the change of front. It is frequently said that it was pressure from the United States Government (which I know is not the case); it might have been simply the realisation that the E.E.C. was going ahead; but no doubt the economic crisis of 1961 had a big influence, because it created a deep feeling of depression and disillusionment among Ministers with their existing policy; it is also sometimes suggested that the Prime Minister was personally attracted by the idea of a great historic change of this kind and believed that it might have electoral advantages for his Party.

6. The decision, however, was announced in the most cautious manner. Here are Mr. Macmillan's words on the 31st July, 1961:

'Negotiations must, therefore, be held in order to establish the conditions on which we might join. In order to enter into these negotiations it is necessary, under the Treaty, to make formal application to join the Community, although the ultimate decision whether to join or not must depend on the result of the negotiations.'

13 Published as *The Challenge of Coexistence* (Methuen, 1957); p. 59–62.

It was *not* a decision to join but to start negotiations to see whether we *could* join. Moreover, three conditions were clearly laid down by the Government.

(a) British agriculture was to be safeguarded.

(b) Our links with the Commonwealth were to be fully maintained.

(c) Our pledges to EFTA must be fulfilled.

7. The attitude of the Opposition was a little stiffer but not really very different. We did not oppose the Government's application. But we underlined the three conditions: we said that the terms must be broadly acceptable to a Conference of Commonwealth Prime Ministers; and we added two other conditions – that we should be free to carry out economic planning and to maintain, as at present, our own foreign policy.

8. It is important to realise, therefore, that from the start not only the Opposition but the Government as well were *not* in favour of '*going in and trying to get the best possible conditions*'; but only for '*going in if certain conditions were fulfilled*'. This meant:

(i) that if the conditions were *not* met, we should *not* go in;

(ii) that we did not accept that there was any overriding case for our entry – since, otherwise, it would have been pointless to have laid down conditions.

9. It may be said that in reality the Government had decided to go in whatever the terms and that they only laid down conditions in order to make their new policy acceptable to their Party. I do not know whether this is the case; it is certainly true that without explicit conditions the application would not have been acceptable at that time to the Conservative Party or the country generally. As for the Opposition, we certainly took the conditions very seriously and always meant to stand by them. There were two reasons for this attitude. First, I myself and my leading colleagues all happened to believe and still believe that the arguments of principle were fairly evenly balanced for and against and that the balance would be tipped in favour of our entry only if our conditions were fulfilled. Secondly, this policy of making our final judgment depend on the conditions was the only one which could have been accepted by the Party as a whole. If I had urged unconditional entry (thus going even further than the Government) there would have been bitter opposition from a large minority which was basically hostile to our entry. If I had urged outright opposition whatever the terms, this would also have been bitterly opposed by another, though smaller, minority, who were basically enthusiastic about our entry. In either case, there

would have been a major split in the Party, which, following the great dispute on defence which had only recently been successfully concluded, would have been fatal to our prospects. Both minorities, however, were willing to accept that the issue must be allowed to depend on the terms, nor was there any real disagreement about what the terms must be.

10. Why, then, were these particular conditions laid down? The general answer is that we believed and believe that to join the E.E.C. without them would be the greater evil both for Britain and the Commonwealth – and, so some of us would hold, for the free world. More specifically, these were our reasons.

11. In agriculture we have a system of guaranteed prices, deficiency payments and production grants which has made our farming community both efficient and prosperous. The E.E.C. countries do not have this system. They do not provide the same security. Their farmers are obliged to depend more upon the free play of the market, although they are aided by powerful protection barriers. Naturally, we were concerned lest our entry into the E.E.C. might, through a complete change of policy, seriously damage our agriculture – as well as putting up food prices to consumers.

12. With the Commonwealth countries we have for 30 years deliberately encouraged trade through reciprocal tariff preferences. We recognise that entry into the E.E.C. could not be consistent with the maintenance in full of such a system. But if it were to be scrapped and replaced by the reverse – a preference system with Western Europe – without special arrangements, exceptions or compensations for the Commonwealth, this could both force us to pay more for our imports of food and damage other members of the Commonwealth and so weaken our links with them that the Commonwealth itself would suffer irreparable harm. That we could not have. It would be too high a price to pay. Hence our conditions that there had to be proper safeguards here.

13. As for EFTA, there is a solemn pledge – to maintain the Association "until satisfactory arrangements have been worked out . . . to meet the various legitimate interests of all members of EFTA, and thus enable them all to participate from the same date in an integrated European Market". There is nothing surprising about this, that the countries of EFTA should stand together. Apart from the moral obligation thereby involved, it was our conviction that those countries with many of which Britain has especially close ties, must be allowed in with us, even though some, because they were neutral, would not wish for more than associate membership.

14. As for the other two conditions which the Labour Party added, the first concerned with economic planning was introduced, not because we wished to exempt ourselves from basic agreements on tariffs and trade, but mainly because some parts of the Treaty of Rome could be interpreted in ways which might clash with a policy of full employment. In particular, we were anxious lest the free movement of capital might play havoc with the value of sterling – always a matter of concern to a British Government; and, secondly, we were worried lest the rules of the E.E.C. would deter us from giving special help in areas of higher unemployment. [14]

15. The second condition – that we should maintain as at present our own independent foreign policy – has been described as unnecessary, because there is nothing in the Treaty of Rome which touches upon it. But we have been told often enough of the great political significance of the E.E.C. Indeed, many statesmen in the Six and in other countries have put this forward as the major argument of Britain's entry. It was, therefore, impossible to ignore it and it would have been dishonest not to make clear where we stood on it. The condition is sometimes misunderstood. Of course, no country is completely independent in the conduct of its foreign policy. But there is, nevertheless, a difference between deciding your own policy and proclaiming it as you think fit, and either having no foreign policy at all because you are part of a larger state, or accepting that your foreign policy should be decided on the basis of a majority vote of a Council of Ministers. This condition means in so many words that we could not accept, as a result of our entry into E.E.C. either a European federation or a supra-national system applied to foreign policy. While, obviously, no Party or Government can commit itself ten, twenty and fifty years ahead, we wanted it made plain that our entry into E.E.C. would carry with it no commitment whatever to any political institutional change.

16. These five conditions, however, should not be looked upon as simply negative – safeguards to ward off dangers. Taken together they greatly affect the kind of European Community into which we would be entering. It would, for example, be a larger not a smaller Europe, for the whole of EFTA would be included. It would involve the forging of new links without the severing of old ones; for the Commonwealth tie would be preserved no less than the ties with the former French colonies. And this, in turn, would profoundly affect the attitude of the community, which would certainly be outward-looking, concerning itself with world problems

14 The same concerns he had always felt at the Treasury, about giving up controls shielding the British economy from international pressures for deflation or devaluation. Cf. above, pp. 115–17, 127–8, 149–50, 175, 650.

and accepting world responsibilities. For the same reasons, its external tariffs would be low, its commercial policy based not merely or mainly on the desire to expand trade between its members as to develop trade in the world as a whole. Finally, any political association would be loose. If there were attempts at harmonising foreign policy, these would not be pressed too far. Each country would be free as now to put its own point of view both in the Western alliances and on the world stage.

17. In short, by laying down these conditions we, in effect, sketched the kind of Europe we wanted to see. It would not be a single state or a new military bloc, but an association of neighbours, each maintaining close links with other friends, not seeking to impose a rigid uniformity upon one another, still less to build a new European nationalism, but co-operating with each other both for mutual benefit and, even more important, in a common search for world solutions which are relevant to the problems of today. If the entry of Britain could be combined with a sure and certain advance along this path, then indeed we held it to be of great value. But the conditions were vital. For they alone could guarantee the sureness and certainty of the advance.

18. It is sometimes said that these conditions were 'impossible', that indeed we only put them forward so as to have an excuse for not supporting entry. But three of the five conditions were Government pledges as well as Opposition conditions. And the argument chiefly used against the other two is not that they are 'impossible' but that they are unnecessary. The fact is that when these conditions were put forward at the start of the negotiations, no one dreamt of saying they were impossible. It is only recently, since it appeared that the Six were not prepared to concede them, that this kind of comment has become fashionable. That the acceptance of the conditions would mean a very different Community than that of the Six alone is true enough. But, after all, Britain was going to make immense changes in her commercial policies. Was it so unreasonable to ask the Six, if they wanted us in, to make adjustments as well?

19. To begin with the prospects did not seem too bad. Mr. Heath's opening statement in October, 1961, put forward what seemed to us quite firm proposals. And right up to midsummer 1962 we remained reasonably hopeful. I myself expected that the terms would be such as to prove broadly acceptable to the Commonwealth Prime Ministers and that my task would be to persuade my Party to accept them because they were by and large in accordance with our own conditions. I did not think it would be easy to handle the extreme anti-marketeers, but I was prepared to do it as being the only course consistent with the line we had followed.

20. To prepare the way we organised a series of discussions within our Party on the kind of conditions which would be acceptable – especially as far as the Commonwealth was concerned. To help us in this I had a private talk with Mr. Menzies, the Australian Prime Minister. I asked him what his 'sticking points' were. He said, 'If you mean the difference between me saying "Well, we're not enthusiastic, but we'll take it" and "Not on your bloody life"? – that will depend on whether the special arrangements for us are permanent or just transitional'.

21. This seemed to us reasonable and not unduly optimistic. Similarly, we considered that if the Asian Commonwealth countries lost their preferences in the British market, this would be at least made up for them at once by the removal of barriers in Europe. We assume[d], in fact, that as part of the terms of entry Europe would be ready to share with us the 'burden' of accepting imports of cheap Asian manufactures. On agriculture, we expected a half-way house between our system and the continental one. On EFTA, it did not really seem to us (despite what George Ball had said to me in Washington) that there should be any serious trouble. [15]

22. We were, therefore, bitterly disappointed and indeed astonished at the provisional agreements reached at the beginning of August. It became clear that the British Government had swallowed the whole E.E.C. policy both on tariffs and on agriculture and had obtained virtually no offsetting concessions in exchange. Britain would reverse preferences, adopt a variable import levy system on major foodstuffs, abandon our system of deficiency payments for agriculture and pay into the Community fund the proceeds of any import levies. These precise arrangements were to begin to operate from the moment of our entry into the Community and be carried through remorselessly stage by stage until the whole process was completed by 1970. The fact that in some cases the speed of the change was to be slower at first and faster as 1970 approached was no real alleviation. In return for this Mr. Heath obtained almost nothing but vague assurances as to what might be done in the future. Special consideration for New Zealand – which might mean anything or nothing; an attempt to negotiate world commodity agreements, but no one knew what they would contain or whether they would ever be made; India, Pakistan and Ceylon, struggling with their appalling develop-

15 George Ball, once Jean Monnet's representative in the United States, was Under-Secretary of the Treasury for Economic Affairs until November 1961 when he became Under-Secretary of State. He was a passionate advocate of European federalism, and Gaitskell had warned his American friends against Ball's influence: *HG*, p. 744. (See above, pp. 651, 661 n., and below, para. 37).

ment problems, received little more than a promise of a comprehensive trade agreement by the end of 1966 – a poor return for the definite removal of preference in the British market; for the countries of the Commonwealth which refused on political grounds the status of A.O.T.s, there were to be further negotiations, but, meanwhile, they too would face discrimination against their products in Britain.[16]

23. I do not see how it can be seriously argued that these agreements in any way fulfilled either the Government's pledges or the Labour Party's conditions. Nor, indeed, have even the strongest pro-market people in our Party ever suggested this. Had such terms been announced at the beginning of negotiations, they would have been rejected out of hand by the British people. They were in glaring contrast to what was originally proposed by Mr. Heath himself and to what most of us hoped would be agreed.

24. It was perfectly clear that if these were indeed the final terms there was no change [sic: chance] whatever that the Labour Party would accept them. I pointed this out, early in August, to Roy Jenkins, the leader of the 'Pro-Market' minority who happens to be one of my closest personal friends. He did not demur. My deputy, George Brown, also agreed.

25. There remained, however, the possibility (the White Paper describing the negotiations was not clear on this point) that the Government would not regard the terms as in any way binding and would simply report them to the Commonwealth Prime Ministers' Conference in September without commendation or commitment.

26. Unfortunately, this was not at all the line they followed. On the contrary, they created the impression both to the Press and to the Prime Ministers – as was reported day after day during the Conference, that while much had still to be negotiated, they could not reopen the August agreements and that they were determined to enter the E.E.C., if necessary on these terms, whatever the Prime Ministers said. They used very heavily at that time the 'inevitability technique'. 'We are going in anyhow; you may as well make the best of it'. This was, of course, a complete change from the previous lines of 'only if the terms are right', 'we shall decide only after we have heard the Prime Ministers' views; 'the agreements are purely provisional (and therefore can be reopened)'.

27. The reaction of the Prime Ministers both to the terms themselves and to the Government's declaration was sharp, clear and almost entirely hostile. Only two of them accepted the terms – Dr. Williams of Trinidad

16 A.O.Ts: Associated Overseas Territories.

who told me it was because he had no use for the Commonwealth and intensely disliked the U.S.A and therefore preferred us to be tied up with Europe, and Sir Roy Welensky who, of course, represents only a handful of white settlers in Rhodesia. The others were in varying degrees bitterly opposed. Indeed, there has never been a Prime Ministers' Conference – normally a very friendly and polite affair, where there has been so much anger and bad blood and none which did so much damage to the Commonwealth. Many of those present went away sadly concluding that, despite the smooth words of the communique, Britain was ditching the Commonwealth and they must make their plans accordingly.

28. None of this, however, deflected the Government from the new line on which they had clearly decided in August. Indeed, it seemed pretty certain that they were shortly to launch a major propaganda campaign in favour of Britain's entry on broadly any terms – leading up to the General Election. The emphasis was being shifted not only away from the con- ditions (which were barely mentioned in a pro-Market pamphlet by the Prime Minister issued at that time) but also towards the political implica- tions which had hitherto been kept in the background. Nevertheless, on this there remained the greatest confusion and contradictions which none of the Government's statements were able, or perhaps calculated, to dispel.

29. This was the background to the Party Conferences at the beginning of October. Faced with what had happened, there was only one possible line for us in the Labour Party to take – to make it plain that we stood by our five conditions with all that they implied, that the terms so far negotiated could not possibly be regarded as fulfilling either these conditions or the Government's pledges and that the Government must go back and negotiate and secure terms consistent with those conditions or else we would be bound to oppose Britain's entry.

30. On this our Party was virtually unanimous. There were, of course, differences of emphasis. I myself was criticised by some for the tone of hostility which I was alleged to have displayed to "Europe". I do not accept this at all. But, of course, I was spelling out the case against unconditional entry and deliberately rousing the Party against what the Government had done and issuing what might be called a "mobilisation" warning in view of what seemed to be an inevitable major clash with the Government.

31. The Tories at their conference which followed ours did exactly what I had predicted, dropped almost all talk about terms and swept the delegates – always obedient – into support for our entry. There is good

reason to think, however, that this enthusiasm was by no means echoed in the rank and file.

32. Since then there has been something of a change. The resumed negotiations at Brussels have proved far more difficult than the Government had led everyone to assume, while at the same time there is at home a growing realisation of how bad the terms so far agreed already are. What will happen now is hard to predict. In fact [*sic*: part?], it will turn on whether the Six are prepared to meet the British case, in part on whether the British Government will accept really bad terms and try to get them accepted at home, or whether they will find it necessary to break off the talks because they dare not do this.

33. If the final terms are as bad as now seems likely, then it is inevitable that we shall oppose them. This does not mean, of course, that the General Election when it comes will necessarily be fought exclusively on them. This is probably unlikely, for the simple reason that people are interested in other things besides the Common Market. Nor does it mean that I should threaten to repudiate any agreements reached. I have been very careful to say nothing on that. There are circumstances in which I might feel obliged to do so – that is true – but obviously, one would not dream of taking such a grave step without the most careful weighing up of all the possible consequences. [17]

34. I am told that in the United States it is thought that our policy on the Common Market has been followed for purely party political reasons, that we decided to oppose because we thought this would enable us to win the Election. Such motives are not in my view always dishonourable. But the allegation in this case is utterly false. On the contrary, until August I had always assumed and said that we should not have an election on the Common Market. I took the view that either the Government would obtain sufficiently good terms to justify us in supporting them or that the terms would be too bad for them to proceed at all. [18] On this I was wrong – and it is this – their decision to go ahead despite the fact that the terms were in flagrant breach of their pledges and therefore quite unacceptable

17 A pledge to repudiate, demanded by the Labour Left, would probably force a general election since the Six might refuse to let Britain join without one. It would do great harm to Britain's relations with her neighbours. On Gaitskell's attitude to it, *HG*, pp. 741–2.
18 He had often said so: to the House in early August 1961; to Alastair Hetherington (editor of the *Guardian* and a Fleet Street ally of HG) in November; to Roy Jenkins in May 1962; to the Commonwealth M.P.s in July; to the Australian Labour leader Arthur Calwell in August 1962: *HG*, pp. 781, 721 (and above, pp. 654, 657). He thus hoped his tactical dilemma would be resolved for him.

to us – which has brought this whole matter into the arena of party politics in Britain.

35. This completes my story of our policy, why we followed it in these last months and how we stand today. But I would like in the final section of this long paper to say something about the really basic issues of Britain's entry or non-entry. For I suspect that this is the source of any differences that there are between us.

36. The impression has been created over here that your Administration and you personally are passionately keen on our entry, that you would regard it as a major step towards Western unity and that, equally, it would be a disaster if we do not join. Will you allow me to probe these questions with you.

37. First, however, I would like to refer to one matter of presentation. Nothing could be worse for Anglo-American relations than the feeling here that America is trying to force Britain into Europe because she does not think we are 'any good' outside it. The Acheson line is a real bomb under the alliance, well calculated to break it, not cement it. [19] I beg you to realise this. Equally, nothing could be worse for relations between France, Germany, Britain and the U.S.A. than for it to be thought that you were suggesting that Britain should enter in order to keep the new Community on the right lines – which, as I found last week, is interpreted in France as meaning that we will run it for you! When all this is combined with hints that because of the attitude of the Labour Party to the Common Market, you might help the present Government to win the next Election or make it difficult for us if we were to win, it is all a bit unsatisfactory. Of course, I know you will treat such rumours with the contempt which they deserve but unhappily this is what the British Press has been reporting from Washington – and I fear it may have come to some extent from Government circles.

38. As I think you know, Mr. President, no one has fought harder than I against neutralism and anti-Americanism. More than once I have staked my whole career on this. I beg you to understand that nothing is more calculated to stimulate them than the kind of attitude in Washington to which I have just referred. The British people can be wooed by friendship and won by argument. But they do not respond well to being kicked around. All my adult life I have believed in the necessity for Anglo-American friendship. For the past 20 years – up hill and down dale – I have defended the Western alliance. But that friendship and that alliance

19 Acheson had aroused anger in Britain by saying at West Point on 5 December that she 'had lost an empire and not yet found a role'.

cannot survive on the basis of threats and pressures. This is all the more true when the occasion for them is a tremendous complex issue such as the relations between Britain, Europe and the Commonwealth on which we may be pardoned for thinking that America is not always the best judge. I know, of course, that you yourself have been most careful not to say a word in public that suggests that you are intervening in our affairs. But your successful use of the Press – which I greatly admire – has one grave disadvantage, as soon as it becomes generally known – that what the Press reports is far too frequently supposed to be inspired by you and your Cabinet. Please forgive me for writing so frankly. I do so only to avoid the possibility of misunderstanding and presuming still on the happy relations I have had with you.

39. And now for the substance of the problem. I imagine you may say, if you have read all this, that you understand the way in which we laid down conditions regarding our entry into the Common Market, that you appreciate our view that the conditions have not been fulfilled, but that you had hoped we might judge the terms less harshly. It is obvious that how one judges the terms is bound to be affected by how one evaluates the basic arguments for and against Britain's entry. The more enthusiastic one is, the worse the terms which would be acceptable. The more hostile one is, the more one would be inclined to reject any terms – even quite good ones. I have tried on this to take the middle road. But I appreciate that some account of our attitude on the basic argument – for or against entry in contrast with what I believe to be yours – is called for.

40. Any rational approach to this problem must be based on a comparison – a comparison of the consequences of our entry with the consequences of our non-entry. First, there is the economic aspect. I shall not spend much time on this partly because it is really a technical matter and partly because I can hardly suppose that your desire for our entry rests to any extent on this. It is clearly our affair. And in so far as U.S. economic interests are concerned, they are, I imagine, likely to be adversely rather than favourably affected by Britain's entry.

41. I content myself accordingly with these few comments. I know that many Americans think it will be greatly to our economic advantage to enter. They are, if I may say so, dazzled by the mystique of 'the large market' – projecting what they believe to be the secret of American prosperity on to Europe. There is something, but not a great deal, in this argument; in any case, it is only one consideration out of many. On the whole, taking the many into account, I have always regarded the economic pros and cons as fairly evenly balanced – recognising that there are difficult matters of judgment here on which it is hard to be at all certain.

This happens also to be the view of the economists whose judgment I must [*sic*: ? most] respect. Moreover, if we accept, with the United States Administration, the urgent need to reduce trade barriers everywhere, it seems to me that the economic significance of the E.E.C. Customs Union can be greatly exaggerated. If, for example, through negotiations resulting from the U.S. Trade Bill, the E.E.C. general tariff is to be no higher than say 5–10 per cent, it is really impossible to ascribe to it very devastating consequences either for good or for ill. And is it not clear that both European and world prosperity is going to depend far more on wider agreements which are not bound up with Britain's entry – world commodity agreements to check the dangerous fall in raw material prices, international financial co-operation, aid for underdeveloped countries on a world not a local basis?

42. These are surely the really vital economic tasks that lie before us. To this I would add my conviction that the future efficiency of British industry depends far less on entry into the Common Market and far more on what we do at home. Because there happens to have been a rapid rate of growth in Europe in the last few years, it is often assumed first that this is due to the Common Market and, secondly, that in some mysterious way we should, by joining, share it. Neither assumption proves, on examination, to [be] wholly valid. At the most one can say that there is perhaps something in the argument – but it is little more than 'hunch'.

43. So I come to the political issue. Again, one has to balance what happens if we go in against what happens if we stay out.

44. There is first the question of Western European political unity as such. It is usually taken for granted that this is a good thing. We all pay tribute to it. If in its absence there was a danger of conflict and even war between the West European States, obviously this would be an overwhelming argument. But there seems to me to be no such danger. It is no doubt desirable that Western Germany should be somehow or other firmly embraced in a Western alliance – and, probably, Western European unity helps to achieve this. Of course, this unity would also be good if it resulted in a new, more powerful State which in practice gave enthusiastic and practical support to the Western Alliance and the policies of the other members. There is, however, no guarantee that this will happen.

45. But then we come to the second argument – that this result is just what Britain's entry will achieve. We must go in, it is said, because our influence will keep the new Europe on the right lines, firmly tied in with the Western Alliance, following policies agreeable to the United States.

46. But how exactly is this going to happen? It is far from clear. The

Treaty of Rome carries no specific political commitment. So it is assumed there will be some other political change. What?

47. Some think and talk in terms of a new Federal State. This without doubt underlines the main political case both for the so-called unity and for Britain's entry. But the fact is that both the British Government and still more, the Opposition are pledged against Federation. Both want Britain to continue to have her own foreign policy and both see Federation as the end of the Commonwealth. There is no question that British opinion is a long, long way from accepting entry into a Federal European state.

48. But it is not only Britain which opposes it. The present French Government is no less hostile. The French Prime Minister said to me last week 'not at any rate for 20 years'. The French Foreign Secretary said 'not for 50 years'![20] So long as de Gaulle is in power – and possibly afterwards – whether Britain goes in or stays out – there will not be a Federal Western European State.

49. Suppose, however, I am wrong or suppose the de Gaulle era is over and Federation does become a reality, what then? I must admit personally to the gravest doubts whether Britain should enter such a federation. These doubts do not spring from a conservative old-fashioned jingoism. While it is pardonable to view with some qualms the disappearance of one's country as an independent nation and while you will surely not be surprised that such a prospect should generate a good deal of emotion, yet the grounds for my apprehension are more rational than that. Certainly they do not derive from any hostility to internationalism. If I really believed that this step would lead to, and was necessary for, the establishment of a world government, which alone would guarantee peace, I should welcome it. But I am in no way convinced that this is so.

50. The truth is that no one can really say what exactly the consequences of a new European state on international relations would be. To predict the foreign policy of the new state would be the wildest speculation. But the idea that it will necessarily be just what the British or the Americans want seems to be [me?] to have no basis in reality. I should myself say that if the federation is to overcome the powerful separatist forces which will certainly be at work, then it will have to be supported by the development of a new European nationalism or patriotism. Thus the change would be rather a transformation from one nationalism to another than a switch to some newer and higher international order. I believe too that a new

20 HG had just visited Paris and talked to both Georges Pompidou the Prime Minister and Maurice Couve de Murville the Foreign Minister.

powerful European state may well seek to become that 'third force' after which, as I think mistakenly, some Europeans have long hankered.

It is highly probable that the new state would insist on having its own powerful armoury of up-to-date nuclear weapons. It is possible that far from leading to a strengthening of the western alliance, it would prove a most unstable influence on world affairs.

51. What about confederation? – in the sense of majority decisions being taken by a Committee of Ministers. Is this any more likely or, if it were to exist, any more attractive. Surely not. One really cannot see France, Germany or Britain allowing their policy on Berlin or NATO bases being decided in this way. And if there were to be majority decisions, why assume they would be welcome to the U.S.A.? Would, for example, such a decision be more or less likely to favour U.S. bases in Europe?

52. At any rate, I conclude that in practice all that is likely to happen in the way of political union at present is more talking, with or without Britain, in a vague attempt to reach a common foreign and defence policy. But, again, is there any real reason to think that agreement is more likely because of such talks? And, again, if it is achieved will it be what the U.S.A. wants? Is not the real truth that the differences in the Western alliance spring partly from basic clashes of interest, partly from suspicions and lack of confidence, and partly from personalities? Why should any of these be removed by our entry?

53. I cannot help feeling some times that the very natural desire of America to deal with one instead of 15 partners leads her to overlook the question of what sort of single partner she would get.

54. I do not pretend to be sure about all this. But I am convinced that the tendency to assume that if Britain enters the E.E.C. somehow magically the political difficulties in the Western Alliance will vanish is simply not justified by any rational analysis.

55. And supposing we do not join? Will this be so terrible? If my argument is sound, we shall not be losing anything of great value. Nor, I believe, shall we be putting any new strain on the alliance. On the other hand, Britain would almost certainly develop especially close relations with the E.E.C. All her European commitments would be maintained. She would be certain to trade with the E.E.C. on a larger scale – and, of course, her cultural ties with continental Europe would be as strong as ever. It might be that at a later stage negotiations – perhaps this time between the whole of EFTA and the EEC could be resumed. Meanwhile, given low tariffs – which all agree to be necessary – there is no special reason to fear economic friction between the two groups.

56. But what of the bogey of a new unstable and reactionary state of a little Europe? Will this not now come into existence and with dangerous consequences? I do not believe so. As I have already said, the French have no desire for it. The disappearance of Adenauer will not make it any more likely.

If this produces any significant change it will probably be to isolate the French a little more in NATO. Is this such a bad thing?

57. I do not want you to conclude from this that I am opposed in principle to our entry into E.E.C. It is simply that I do not see it in any way as a black and white issue. On balance, given the terms which we have laid down, we should most certainly go in, though one should not expect any very significant changes politically if we did so. But if because we cannot get the right terms, we stay out, this in turn will not be disastrous or even dangerous. The only thing that might make it so it [sic] too much talk to that effect.

58. I venture to suggest that while Britain and the Six must continue to try to negotiate the right terms, we should all of us now be at least contemplating alternatives. I have reason to think that the French would be much more willing to contemplate these in the economic field now than they were a few years ago. And I sometimes wonder whether if they were relieved from the obvious fear and dislike of our entry into E.E.C., they might not prove far more amenable on political issues.

59. Finally, would it not be as well to bring into the foreground of international discussions now the real economic problems – reduction of *world* trade barriers – establishment of *world* commodity agreement – a new look at the Aid problem – and a more radical approach to international monetary co-operation. These are the really urgent economic problems. Should we not get on with trying to solve them?

60. As for the really urgent political problems, these lie almost wholly in the field of East-West relations – too big a subject to touch on here, but one which is not likely to be greatly affected by the Common Market and all that.

61. Perhaps we should begin to take a rather more relaxed view of the strains and stresses within the Western Alliance. These are a nuisance, but I have the feeling that a period of less emphasis on them with all the tensions thus created would do no harm. Too much intervention and 'pushing around' can create more trouble than it is worth. In its absence I do not believe that the alliance will crumble. There is enough self interest to keep it together. And even if it is far from perfect there is no reason to fear that it will be too weak to do its job.

To sum up our position.

(1) Until 1961, it was not seriously supposed in Britain that we would or even could enter the Common Market.

(2) When the Government applied for entry they laid down three conditions. The Opposition did likewise, adding two more of their own – which, however, are usually criticised as unnecessary. No one suggested at the time that those conditions were impossible.

(3) The fact that we laid down conditions meant that neither the Government nor the Opposition considered that there was any overriding case for Britain's entry, but rather that the arguments for and against were [sufficiently?] evenly balanced in principle for them to be tilted in favour only by the fulfilment of the conditions.

(4) In the view of the Opposition the provisional agreements announced in August – which especially concerned the Commonwealth – cannot possibly be regarded as fulfilling the conditions. The agreements were bitterly attacked by the Commonwealth Prime Ministers at the Conference in September.

(5) While no final judgment is possible until the negotiations are concluded, the Labour Party has declared that the Government must obtain better terms – terms which do fulfil both their own and the Opposition's conditions. Otherwise, they would be obliged to oppose the agreement. This does not carry any commitment to repudiate the agreements.

(6) Since October the conduct of the negotiations does not suggest that the Six are likely to make any substantial concessions.

(7) While the Labour Party still considers that the best solution will be to go in on the right terms, they do not consider that breakdown will be disastrous.

(8) In the circumstances, it would be as well while continuing the negotiations to consider alternatives in case agreement proves impossible.

December 1962.

[Four days after sending the memorandum to Kennedy, Gaitskell entered hospital. He was discharged for Christmas, was readmitted on 4 January, and died on 18 January 1963 of systemic lupus erythematosus, an uncommon and obscure disease of the tissues.]

APPENDIX IV

CHRONOLOGICAL LIST OF DOCUMENTS

BIOGRAPHICAL NOTES

(All members of the Royal Family appear under that heading. M.P.s are Labour unless specified.)

Abbott, Douglas (b. 1899) Canadian Lib. Min. of Defence 1945, Finance 1946–54; Supreme Court 1954–73.

Acheson, Dean (1893–1971) U.S. lawyer; Democrat; Sec. of State 1949–53.

Acland, Sir Richard (b. 1906) Lib. M.P. for Barnstaple (Devon) 1935. Founded Common Wealth, 1942. This socialist party challenged the wartime coalition at by-elections and won three seats, holding one in 1945 when Acland lost at Putney. He held Gravesend for Labour 1947–55; on his election see p. 49 and n.

Addison, Viscount (1869–1951) M.P. (Lib.) 1910–22, (Labour) 1929–31, 1934–5. Several offices 1914–21, 1929–31, and as Leader of the House of Lords 1945–51 when he was Attlee's confidant.

Adenauer, Konrad (1876–1967) Lord Mayor of Cologne 1917–33 (removed by the Nazis) and 1945 (installed and removed by the British). C.D.U. leader and Chancellor 1949–63, and an uncompromising cold warrior.

Allen, Arthur (b. 1887) Trade union official (Boot & Shoe Operatives). M.P. Bosworth (Leics.) 1945–59. HG's P.P.S. 1950–9.

Alsop, Joseph (b. 1910) Prominent U.S. columnist, mainly on the *New York Herald Tribune* 1932–58.

Armstrong, William (Lord; 1915–80) Principal Private Sec. to successive Chancellors of the Exchequer 1949–53. Joint Perm. Sec. of the Treasury 1962–8, of the Civil Service Dept. (Head of the Service) 1968–74. Chairman, Midland Bank from 1975.

Ashton, (Sir) Hubert (1898–1979) With Burmah Oil Company 1922–45. Married HG's sister Dorothy 1927. Cons. M.P. Chelmsford (Essex) 1950–64, P.P.S. to R.A. Butler 1951–7, Church Estates Comm. 1957–72. President of Essex Co. Cricket Club 1948–70, of MCC 1961 (committee, 1947–64).

Astor, David (b. 1912) Son of 2nd Viscount Astor, owner of *The Observer*. Its foreign editor 1946–8, and editor 1948–75.

Attlee, Clement R. (Earl; 1883–1967) M.P. Stepney (Limehouse) 1922–50, Walthamstow W. 1950–5. Various offices 1924, 1930–1 and (in

· Cabinet) 1940–5. Deputy P.M. 1942–5, P.M. 1945–51. Dep. Leader of L.P. 1931–5, Leader 1935–55.

Bacon, Alice (Baroness) M.P. Leeds N.E. 1945–55, S.E. 1955–70. Min. of State, Home Office 1964–7, Education 1967–70. N.E.C. 1941–70.

Balogh, Dr Thomas (Lord; b. Budapest, 1905) Economist, who knew HG before the war (once lived in same house). Fellow of Balliol Coll. Oxford 1945–73. Adviser to L.P., esp. to Wilson before and during his premiership. Min. of State for Energy 1974–5.

Beaverbrook, Lord (1879–1964) (Sir) Max Aitken, a Canadian, built up the *Express* group of newspapers. Was a Cons. M.P., and a Minister briefly in the First World War and for most of the Second. Promoter of Empire Free Trade, violently against Britain entering the E.E.C.

Ben-Gurion, David (1886–1973) b. Poland, founding father of Israel. Sec.-gen. of the Histadruth (Jewish T.U.s) 1921–35, Chairman Jewish Agency for Palestine 1935–48, leader of Mapai (the Israeli Labour Party) till 1963, P.M. and Min. of Defence 1948–53, 1955–63.

Benn, Anthony Wedgwood (b. 1925) M.P. Bristol S.E. 1950–60 and, after a long struggle to renounce his inherited peerage, since 1963. P.M.G. 1964–6, Min. of Technology 1966–70, Sec. State for Industry 1974–5, Energy 1975–9. N.E.C. 1959–60 and since 1962. P.C. 1970–4, Jan.–Nov. 1981. Stood for Dep. Leader 1971, 1981; for Leader 1976, 1980.

Berry, H.V. (Sir Vaughan; 1891–1979) Founder of XYZ in 1932. Regional Comm. at Hamburg 1946–9, U.K. delegate to Ruhr Authority 1949–50, on Iron & Steel Corp. 1950–3.

Berry, Lady Pamela. Daughter of F.E. Smith, Earl of Birkenhead. Married Michael Berry (Lord Hartwell), son of the 1st Lord Camrose (proprietor of the *Daily Telegraph*), who became its Ed.-in-Chief in 1954.

Bevan, Aneurin (1897–1960) M.P. Ebbw Vale (Mon.) 1929–60. Min. of Health 1945–51, of Labour Jan.–April 1951. Expelled from L.P. with Cripps 1939; rejoined, threatened with expulsion 1944 and 1955. N.E.C. 1944–54; (as Treasurer) 1956–60. P.C. 1952–4 (resigned), 1955–8. Stood against Morrison for Dep. Leader 1952, against Griffiths 1956; against HG for Treasurer 1954 and 1955, and for Leader 1955. Parl. spokesman on colonies Jan. 1956, on foreign affairs from Nov. 1956. Elected Treasurer 1956 (against Brown); Dep. Leader 1959 (unop.).

Bevin, Ernest (1881–1951) Gen. Sec. T.&G.W.U. 1921–40, on Gen. Council 1925–40, the leading trade unionist of his day. M.P. Wandsworth C. 1940–50, Woolwich E. 1950–1. Min. of Labour 1940–5, Foreign Sec. 1945–51 (March), Lord Privy Seal for a month.

Birch, (Sir) Alan (1909–61) Gen. Sec. of USDAW and on Gen. Council, 1949–61.

Bissell, Richard M. jr. (b. 1909) U.S. economist, assistant E.C.A. administrator 1948–51. Joined C.I.A., became dep. director for plans, resigned 1962 after the Bay of Pigs invasion of Cuba.

Black, Eugene (b. 1898) U.S. banker, Chase Nat. Bank, N.Y. 1933–47. U.S. exec. director of the World Bank 1947–9, its pres. 1949–53.

Boothby, Sir Robert (Lord; b. 1900) Cons. M.P. Aberdeenshire E. 1924–58. P.P.S. to Churchill 1926–9, junior office 1940–1. Council of Europe 1949–57.

Bowden, Bert (Lord Aylestone; b. 1905) M.P. Leicester S. 1945–50, S.W. 1950–67. Whip 1949, Deputy 1951, Chief Whip 1955–64. Lord Pres. & Leader of the House 1964–6, Commonwealth Sec. 1966–7. Chairman I.T.A. 1967–75. Leader of SDP peers, 1981.

Bowles, Chester (b. 1901) U.S. businessman; Democrat. Price Administrator 1943–6, War Production Board 1946–9; Gov. of Connecticut 1949–51, Congressman 1959–60; Amb. to India 1951–3, 1963–9; Under Sec. of State 1961, Special Rep. (Amb.) for Asia, Africa and Latin America, 1961–3.

Bowman, (Sir) James (1895–1978) Sec. Northumberland miners 1935–49, T.U.C. Gen. Council 1946–50. Chairman N. Div. Coal Board 1950–5, N.C.B. 1956–61 (member 1955–6).

Bowra, (Sir) Maurice (1898–1971) Classical scholar, close friend of both Gaitskell brothers from their undergraduate days. Fellow of Wadham Coll. Oxford 1922–38, Warden 1938–70; Vice-Chancellor, Oxford Univ. 1951–4, Pres. British Academy 1958–62.

Braddock, Mrs Bessie (1899–1970) Liverpool Council 1930–61, and wife of its leader. M.P. Liverpool Exchange 1945–70. Ex-C.P.; became strong anti-Bevanite; easily overcame constituency opposition 1955. N.E.C. 1947–8, 1958–69.

Brandt, Willi (b. 1913) Mayor of West Berlin 1957–66. Chairman of S.P.D. in Berlin 1958–63, in W. Germany from 1964. Foreign Min. 1966–9, Chancellor 1969–74.

Brentano, Heinrich von (1904–64) A founder of the C.D.U., its parl. leader 1949–55, 1961–4. Foreign Min. 1955–61.

Bridges, Sir Edward (Lord; 1892–1969) Sec. to the Cabinet 1938–46. Perm. Sec. of the Treasury 1945–56. Son of Robert Bridges, Poet Laureate.

Brook, (Sir) Robin (b. 1908) Banker, wartime colleague of HG on Dalton's staff in Min. of Econ. Warfare. Director, Bank of England, 1946–9; chairman or pres., London Chamber of Commerce, 1966–72.

Brown, George (Lord George-Brown; b. 1914) M.P. Belper (Derbyshire) 1945–70, chairman T.U. group of M.P.s 1955–64. Parl. Sec. Agric. 1947–51; Min. of Works 1951; spokesman on defence 1956–61; then on home affairs. P.C. 1955–8, 1959–60. First Sec. (Econ. Affairs)

1964–6, Foreign Sec. 1966–8. Dep. Leader of L.P. 1960–70 (contested 1960, 1961, 1962); stood against Wilson for Leader 1963. Joined SDP.

Bulganin, Marshal Nikolai (1895–1975) Soviet Defence Min. 1947–9, 1953–5; Deputy P.M. 1938–41, 1949–55; P.M. 1955–8. Politburo/ Praesidium 1948–58, ousted for opposing Khrushchev with the 'Anti-Party Group' in 1957. Chairman, Stavropol Econ. Region, 1958–62.

Butler, Richard Austen ('RAB'; Lord Butler; 1902–82) Cons. M.P. Saffron Walden (Essex) 1929–65. Min. of Education 1941–5, of Labour 1945; Chanc. of Exchequer 1951–5, Leader of the House 1955–61 (mainly as Lord Privy Seal), Home Sec. 1957–62, First Sec. (Central Africa) 1962–3, Foreign Sec. 1963–4. Thought likely P.M., 1957 and 1963. Master of Trinity Coll. Cambridge, 1965–78.

Callaghan, L. James (b. 1912) M.P. Cardiff S. 1945–50, S.E. since 1950; Parl. Sec. Transport 1947–50, Admiralty 1950–1. P.C. 1951–64, 1970–4; colonial spokesman, 1956–61; Shadow Chancellor 1961–4. Chanc. of Exchequer 1964–7, Home Sec. 1967–70; Foreign Sec. 1974–6, P.M. 1976–9. N.E.C. 1957–62, 1963–7; Treasurer 1967–76; stood for Dep. Leader 1960, for Leader 1963. Leader 1976–80.

Castle, Barbara. M.P. Blackburn 1945–79. P.P.S. to Cripps and Wilson; leader of Labour's M.E.P.s since 1979. N.E.C. 1950–79. Stood for Dep. Leader 1961. Min. of Overseas Devel. 1964–5, Transport 1965–8, First Sec. (Employment) 1968–70, Social Services Sec. 1974–6. P.C. 1970–1, 1972.

Churchill, Randolph (1911–1968) Journalist; lost 6 parl. contests; Cons. M.P. Preston 1940–5, unop. under wartime truce. Son of Sir Winston Churchill.

Churchill, (Sir) Winston (1874–1965) M.P. (Cons.) 1900–04, 1924–64; (Lib.) 1904–22. In Lib. Cabinet 1908–15, Coalition 1919–22, Cons. 1924–9, 1939–40. P.M. (Nat. Govt.) 1940–5, (Cons.) 1951–5. Led Cons. party 1940–55.

Citrine, Walter (Lord; 1887–1983) Gen. Sec. T.U.C. 1926–46. On N.C.B. 1946–7; chairman, B.E.A. May 1947–57.

Clark, William (b. 1916) *Observer* journalist; pub. relations adviser to Eden as P.M. 1955–6, resigned over Suez. Director of Inst. of Overseas Devel. 1960–8. World Bank 1968–80, Dir. of Information 1973, Vice Pres. External Rels. 1974–80.

Cooper, Jack (Lord; b. 1908) N.U.G.M.W. district sec. 1944–61, Gen. Sec. & Treasurer 1962–73. M.P. Deptford 1950–1, P.P.S. to Gordon Walker. N.E.C. 1953–7, Gen. Council 1959–73.

Cousins, Frank (b. 1904) ass. gen. sec. T.&G.W.U. 1955–6, on N.E.C. Gen. Sec., and on Gen. Council 1956–64, 1966–8. M.P. Nuneaton (Warwickshire) 1965–6, Min. of Technology 1964–6.

Cripps, Sir Stafford (1889–1952) M.P. Bristol E. 1931–50, S.E. 1950–2. Solicitor-Gen. 1930–1. P.C. 1931–5. Led Soc. League 1932–7 (dissolved). N.E.C. 1934–5 (resigned), 1937–9. Expelled from L.P. 1939, rejoined 1945. Amb. to U.S.S.R. 1940–2, Lord Privy Seal & Leader of the House 1942, Min. of Aircraft Production 1942–5. Pres. B.o.T. 1945–7, Chanc. of Exchequer and Min. of Econ. Affairs 1947–50.

Crosland, Anthony (1918–77) M.P. Gloucestershire S. 1950–5, Grimsby 1959–77; author of *The Future of Socialism*, 1956; close friend of HG. Econ. Sec. to Treasury 1964–5; Cabinet 1965–70, 1974–7 (Education, B.o.T., Local Govt., Environment, Foreign Sec.). P.C. 1970–4. Stood for Dep. Leader 1972, and for Leader 1976.

Crossman, Richard (1907–74) With HG at Winchester. Psychological warfare specialist, journalist. M.P. Coventry E. 1945–74. On Palestine Commission 1946, became leading critic of Bevin's foreign policy and prominent Bevanite, reconciled with HG 1955, broke with him 1960. N.E.C., 1952–67. Min. of Housing 1964–6, Lord Pres. and Leader of House 1966–8, Health & Social Security Sec. 1968–70. Ed., *New Statesman* 1970–2. Author, *Diaries of a Cabinet Minister*, 1975–7; *Backbench Diaries*, 1981.

Cudlipp, Hugh (Lord; b. 1913) Ed., *Sunday Pictorial* 1937–40, 1946–9; Ed. Director of it and of *Daily Mirror* 1952–63; chairman Daily Mirror Newspapers 1963–8, I.P.C. 1968–73.

Dalton, Hugh (Lord; 1887–1962) M.P. Camberwell (Peckham) 1924–9, Bishop Auckland (Durham) 1929–31, 1935–59. Under-Sec. F.O. 1929–31, Min. of Econ. Warfare 1940–2, Pres. B.o.T. 1942–5, Chanc. of Exchequer 1945–7, of Duchy 1948–50, Min. of Planning 1950–1. P.C. 1925–9, 1935–40, 1951–5 (resigned). N.E.C. 1926–7, 1928–52. HG's original political patron.

Deakin, Arthur (1890–1955) Dockers' union official 1919, in T.&G.W.U. 1922; ass. gen. sec. 1935, acting gen. sec. 1940, Gen. Sec. (succeeding Bevin) and on Gen. Council, 1945–55; its most powerful member and a violent anti-Bevanite.

Diamond, Jack (Lord; b. 1907) M.P. Manchester (Blackley) 1945–51, Gloucester 1957–70. Chief Sec., Treasury 1964–70 (Cabinet, 1968). Treasurer of many Labour organisations. Joined SDP.

Donnelly, Desmond (1920–74) Journalist; Common Wealth candidate 1945. M.P. Pembrokeshire 1950–70 (lost). Early Bevanite, broke 1954; resigned Lab. whip over E. of Suez withdrawal 1968, sat as Ind. 1968–70, became Cons. 1971.

Douglass, Harry (Lord; 1902–78) T.U. member of N.E.C. 1948–53; Gen. Sec. Iron & Steel Trades Confed., and on Gen. Council 1953–67 (chairman Econ. C'ttee 1962–7).

Driberg, Tom (1905–76; Lord Bradwell 1976) Beaverbrook journalist and Bevanite. M.P. Maldon, Essex (Ind.) 1942–5, (Lab.) 1945–55, and Barking 1959–74. N.E.C. 1949–72.

Dulles, John Foster (1888–1959) U.S. lawyer. At Hague Peace Conf. 1906, on Reparation Comm. 1919, at San Francisco conf. 1945. Republican Senator, New York 1949–52. Sec. of State 1953–9.

Durbin, Evan (1906–48; drowned in swimming accident) Economist; L.S.E. lecturer until war; HG's closest friend, and fought the seat next to his (Gillingham) in 1935. Inspired many groups advising the L.P. on econ. policy. Author, *The Politics of Democratic Socialism*, 1940. Attlee's personal assistant in the war; M.P. Edmonton 1945–8; Parl. Sec. Works 1947–8.

Eccles, Sir David (Viscount; b. 1904) with HG at Winchester and New College. Cons. M.P. Chippenham (Wilts.) 1943–62. Min. of Works 1951–4, of Education 1954–7 and 1959–62, Pres. B.o.T. 1957–9; Paymaster Gen. 1970–3.

Ede, James Chuter (1882–1965; Lord Chuter-Ede, 1964) Schoolmaster. Surrey Co. Council 1914–49. M.P. Mitcham 1923, S. Shields 1929–31, 1935–64; Parl. Sec. Education 1940–5, co-author of Butler's 1944 Act; Home Sec. 1945–51, Leader of the House 1951. P.C. 1951–5.

Eden, Sir Anthony (Earl of Avon; 1897–1977) Cons. M.P. Warwick & Leamington 1923–57. Foreign Sec. 1935–8, 1940–5, 1951–5; Dominions 1939–40, War 1940; Leader of the House 1942–5. P.M. 1955–7.

Edwards, Ebby (1884–1961) Pres. (1931–2) and Gen. Sec. Miners Fed. (1932–46); on Gen. Council 1931–46; labour director of NCB 1946–53. M.P. Morpeth 1929–31.

Edwards, L. John (1904–59) Gen. Sec. Post Office Engineering U. 1938–47. M.P. Blackburn 1945–50, Brighouse & Spenborough 1950–60. P.P.S. to Cripps; Parl. Sec. Health 1947–9, B.o.T. 1949–50, Econ. Sec. to Treasury (succeeding HG) 1950–1.

Eisenhower, Dwight D. (1890–1969) U.S. General; C.-in-C. N. Africa 1942, Europe 1943–5. Army Chief of Staff 1945–8; NATO Supreme Commander 1950–2. President of the U.S. 1953–61.

Elath, Eliahu (b. 1903) Israeli Amb. to U.S. 1948–50, to U.K. 1952–9; had many Labour contacts. Pres. emeritus, Hebrew University.

Evans, Stanley (1898–1970) A very independent Labour M.P. A business-man who, on becoming Parl. Sec. Min. of Food (1950), at once denounced 'featherbedding farmers' and resigned. M.P. Wednesbury 1945–56; abstained in two divisions on Suez (as P.L.P. standing orders allowed); asked by local L.P. to resign seat, did so; they selected John Stonehouse.

Fergusson, Sir Donald (1891–1963) Private sec. to successive Chancellors

1920–36. Perm. Sec. at Agric. 1936–45, at Fuel & Power 1945–52 (with HG, 1947–50).

Finletter, Thomas K. (1893–1980) U.S. lawyer; Democrat. Head of E.C.A. mission to U.K. 1948–9, Sec. of Air Force 1950–3, Amb. to NATO 1961–5.

Fleming, Anne (d. 1981) Prominent Society hostess, married to Ian Fleming the creator of James Bond, and previously (1945–52) to Esmond Harmsworth, 2nd Viscount Rothermere, owner of the *Daily Mail* and chairman of Associated Newspapers 1932–71.

Foot, Michael (b. 1913) M.P. Plymouth (Devonport) 1945–55, Ebbw Vale (Mon.) since 1960 – succeeding Bevan, whose life he wrote. Editor and manager of *Tribune* for many years, one of HG's most persistent critics. Employment Sec. 1974–6; Lord Pres., Leader of the House and Deputy P.M. 1976–9. N.E.C. 1947–50 and since 1972. P.C. 1970–4. Stood for Dep. Leader 1970, 1971, 1972; elected 1976. Stood for Leader 1976. Leader since 1980.

Foster, William Chapman (Bill; b. 1897) U.S. businessman; Democrat. In E.C.A. as deputy Special Rep. 1948–9, Dep. Administrator 1949–50, Administrator 1950–1; Dep. Sec. of Defense 1951–3; Director, Arms Control & Disarmament Agency 1961–9.

Franks, Sir Oliver (Lord; b. 1905) Prof. of philosophy; wartime civil servant, Perm. Sec. Min. of Supply 1945–6; Provost of Queen's Coll. Oxford 1946–8, of Worcester Coll. Oxford 1962–76. Amb. to U.S. 1948–52. Chairman of Lloyds Bank 1953–75, and of many committees on public policy.

Fraser, Tom (b. 1911) Miner, M.P. Hamilton (Lanark) 1943–67. U. Sec. Scotland 1945–51, Min. of Transport 1964–5. P.C. 1955–64. Chairman N. of Scotland Hydro-electric Board 1967–73.

Freeman, John (b. 1915) M.P. Watford 1945–55, retired. Fin. Sec. or Parl. Sec. War 1946–7, Supply 1947–51, resigned with Bevan. On *New Statesman* staff 1951–60, Ed. 1961–5. High Comm. to India 1965–8, Amb. to U.S. 1969–71. Chairman, London Weekend Television since 1971 (and I.T.N. 1976–81).

Fyfe, Sir D. Maxwell, *see* Kilmuir.

Gaitskell, (Sir) Arthur (Hugh's older brother, b. 1900) Manager, Sudan Plantations, Gezira scheme 1945–52. Colonial Devel. Corp. 1954–73, retired.

Gaitskell, Dora (Baroness) Née Creditor; married Hugh G. 1937; cr. Baroness Gaitskell of Egremont after his death; several times U.K. delegate to U.N. or ECOSOC.

Gaitskell, Hugh (1906–63) Father in I.C.S., Burma. Ed. Winchester and New Coll. Oxford. Taught economics to Notts miners (extra-mural), and at U.C.L. 1928–39; in Vienna 1933–4. Fought Chatham 1935, adopted for Leeds S. 1937. Wartime civil servant in Min. of Econ. Warfare and B.o.T.; personal assistant to Dalton (M.E.W. and Min. of Mines), 1940–2. M.P. Leeds S., 1945–63. Parl. Sec. Fuel & Power 1946–7, Min. 1947–50 (temp. in Treasury, summer 1949); Min. of State for Econ. Affairs 1950, Chanc. of Exchequer 1950–1. P.C. 1951–5, Treasurer of L.P. 1954–6, Leader 1955–63.

Gaulle, General Charles de (1890–1970) Under-Sec. for War 1940, Free French leader; headed provisional governments in Algiers and Paris, 1943–6, resigned; led Rassemblement du Peuple Français 1947–53; recalled as Prime Minister, May 1958; President of the Republic, 1959; re-elected 1965; resigned 1969.

Geddes, Charles (Lord Geddes of Epsom; b. 1897) Gen. Sec. of Union of Post Office Workers, and on Gen. Council, 1946–57.

Godson, Joseph P. (b. Poland 1913) Publicity officer for U.S. trade unions 1940–50, U.S. Foreign Service (Ottawa, London, Belgrade) from 1950. Labor Attaché in U.K. 1952–9 and close friend of Sam Watson, whose daughter married his son.

Gooch, Edwin (1889–1964) Pres. Nat. U. of Agric. Workers 1928–64. M.P. Norfolk N. 1945–64. N.E.C. 1946–61.

Gordon Walker, Patrick (Lord; 1907–80) Univ. teacher. M.P. Smethwick 1945–64 (lost), Leyton 1966–70. Morrison's P.P.S. 1946; Commonwealth U. Sec. 1947–50, Sec. 1950–1; from 1959 HG's 'chief of staff'. P.C. 1957–64. Foreign Sec. 1964–5 (lost Leyton by-election); Min. without Portfolio Jan.–Aug. 1967, Education Sec. 1967–8.

Greenwood, Anthony (Lord; 1911–82) Son of Arthur Greenwood, Treasurer and Dep. Leader of L.P. M.P. Heywood & Radcliffe 1946–50, Rossendale (Lancs.) 1950–70. N.E.C. 1954–70. P.C. 1951, 1955–60, resigned. Stood for Leader against HG, 1961. Colonial Sec. 1964–5, Min. Overseas Devel. 1965–6, Housing & Local Govt. 1966–70.

Griffiths, James (1890–1975) Miner. M.P. Llanelly 1936–70. Min. of Nat. Insurance 1945–50, Sec. for Colonies 1950–1, for Wales 1964–6. N.E.C. 1939–40, 1941–56; P.C. (top of poll) 1951–5; Dep. Leader 1956–9.

Gromyko, Andrei (b. 1909) Soviet Amb. to U.S. 1943–6, U.N. 1946–8, U.K. 1952–3; Deputy Foreign Min. 1946–52, 1953–7; Foreign Min. since 1957, in Politburo since 1973. Deputy P.M., 1983.

Gruenther, Alfred M. (b. 1899) U.S. general. Eisenhower's chief of staff 1951–3, and his successor as NATO Supreme Commander 1953–6; retired.

Haley, Sir William (b. 1901) Former man. director of the *Manchester Guardian*, Reuters and the Press Assoc.; and Ed.-in-chief at the B.B.C.; its Director-Gen. 1944–52; Ed. of *The Times*, 1952–66, later chairman.

Hall, (Sir) Robert (Lord Roberthall; b. Australia 1901) Economist;
Fellow of Trinity Coll. Oxford 1927–50, Min. of Supply 1939–46;
B.o.T. 1946–7, Director Econ. Sec. Cab. Office 1947–53, Econ.
Adviser to H.M.G. 1953–61. Principal, Hertford Coll. Oxford
1964–7. Among the economists whose advice HG valued most.

Hall, William Glenvil (1887–1962) Lawyer. M.P. Portsmouth C. 1929–
31, Colne Valley (Yorks.) 1939–63. Stood for Party Treasurer 1943.
Fin. Sec. Treasury 1945–50; chairman of P.L.P. 1950–1; P.C. 1951–5.

Harriman, Averell (b. 1891) Wealthy U.S. Democrat. Amb. to U.S.S.R.
1943–6, to U.K. 1946; Sec. of Commerce 1946–8; E.C.A. Special
Rep. in Europe 1948–50, Special Ass. to President 1950–1, Director
Mutual Security Agency 1952–3. Gov. of New York 1954–8, sought
Pres. nomination 1956. Amb. at large 1961, 1965–9.

Healey, Denis (b. 1917) International Sec. of the L.P. 1946–52. M.P.
Leeds S.E. or E. since 1952. Defence Sec. 1964–70, Chanc. of
Exchequer 1974–9. N.E.C. 1970–5. P.C. 1959–64, 1970–4, 1979–
Stood for Leader 1976, 1980. Dep. Leader since 1980.

Herbison, Margaret (Peggy) Teacher. M.P. N. Lanark 1945–70. U. Sec.
Scotland 1950–1, Min. of Pensions 1964–7, and Soc. Security 1966–7.
N.E.C. 1948–68.

Horner, Arthur (1894–1968) Gen. Sec. N.U.M. 1946–59; the most
powerful post ever held by a member of the Communist Party.

Houghton, Douglas (Lord; b. 1898) Civil Servant. Sec. Inland Revenue
Staff Fed. 1922–60, T.U.C. Gen. Council 1952–60. M.P. Sowerby
(Yorks.) 1949–74. Chanc. of the Duchy 1964–6, Min. without
Portfolio 1966–7. P.C. 1960–4, 1970. Chairman P.L.P. 1967–74.

Hynd, John (1902–71) N.U.R. official. M.P. Sheffield (Attercliffe)
1944–70. Chanc. of the Duchy (resp. for Germany) 1945–7; Min. of
Pensions 1947. Later chairman of P.L.P. foreign affairs c'ttee.

Hyndley, Viscount (1883–1963) Commercial adviser to Mines Dept.
1918–42; Controller-gen., Min. of Fuel & Power 1942–5; Chairman
N.C.B. 1946–51.

Jacobson, Sydney (Lord; b. 1904) Pol. editor, *D. Mirror* 1952–62; Ed.,
D. Herald 1962–4, *Sun* 1964–5. Ed. director, I.P.C. Newspapers
1968–74.

James, Eric (Lord James of Rusholme; b. 1909) High Master of
Manchester Grammar School 1945–62. Vice-Chancellor of York
University 1962–73.

Jay, Douglas (b. 1907) Economist and journalist, pre-war friend of HG.
Dalton's personal assistant at B.o.T. 1943–5. M.P. Battersea N.
since 1946. Econ. Sec. to Treasury 1947–50, Fin. Sec. 1950–1; Pres.
B.o.T. 1964–7. P.C. 1963–4.

Jebb, (Sir) Gladwyn (Lord Gladwyn; b. 1900) With HG on Dalton's staff in Min. of Econ. Warfare 1940–2 (as F.O. rep.). Amb. to U.N. 1950–4, to France 1954–60. Vice-Chairman, European Movement; Lib. Dep. Leader in Lords.

Jenkins, Roy (b. 1920) M.P. Southwark 1948–50, Birmingham (Stechford) 1950–76. Close friend of HG, but led Labour supporters of E.E.C. entry 1962. Min. of Aviation 1964–5 (not Cab.); Home Sec. 1965–7, 1974–6; Chanc. of Exchequer 1967–70. Dep. Leader 1970–2, resigned over E.E.C.; P.C. 1973–4; stood for Leader 1976. Pres., E.E.C. Commission 1977–81. M.P. Glasgow (Hillhead), and Leader of SDP, 1982–.

Jones, W. Ernest (1895–1973) Sec. Yorkshire miners 1939–54; N.U.M. Vice-pres. 1950, Pres. 1954–60; T.U.C. Gen. Council 1950–60.

Khrushchev, Nikita S. (1894–1971) First Sec. of the Soviet C.P. 1953–64, and also P.M. 1958–64 when he was ousted.

Kilmuir, Viscount (Earl 1962; formerly Sir David Maxwell Fyfe; 1900–67) Cons. M.P. Liverpool (W. Derby) 1935–54; Solicitor Gen. 1942–5, Attorney Gen. 1945, Dep. Prosecutor at Nuremberg; Home Sec. 1951–4, Lord Chancellor 1954–62.

King, Cecil Harmsworth (b. 1901) Nephew of Lord Northcliffe, the first of the press lords. Chairman of Mirror Group 1951–63, and of I.P.C. 1963–8 when he was ousted, as he had been installed, by a boardroom coup. Director, Bank of England 1965–8. Kept Cabinet list for a National Govt. in his desk for convenience, as he frequently wished to promote or relegate its prospective members.

Lawther, (Sir) Will (1889–1976) Miner. President, N.U.M. 1940–54; T.U.C. Gen. Council 1935–54. M.P. Barnard Castle (Durham) 1929–31.

Lee, Fred (Lord Lee of Newton; b. 1906) A.E.U. M.P. Manchester (Hulme) 1945–50 (Cripps' P.P.S. 1948) and Newton (Lancs.) 1950–74. Parl. Sec. Min. of Labour 1950–1. Stood for Dep. Leader as Wilson's ally against HG, 1960. P.C. 1959–64. Min. of Power 1964–6, Colonial Sec. 1966–7, Chanc. of Duchy 1967–9.

Lee, Jennie (Baroness Lee of Asheridge) M.P. N. Lanark 1929–31, and candidate (for I.L.P.) 1935; Cannock (Staffs) 1945–70 (lost). Married Aneurin Bevan 1934. N.E.C. 1958–70. Min. of State, Education (Min. for the Arts) 1967–70.

Lennox-Boyd, Alan (Viscount Boyd of Merton; 1904–83) Cons. M.P. 1931–60; Min. of State Colonies 1951–2, Transport 1952–4; Colonial Sec. 1954–9, then in business (Guinness, I.C.I.).

Leslie, S.C. ('Clem'; 1898–1980; Australian) Head of Information Div., H.M. Treasury 1945–59.

Lippmann, Walter (1889–1974) Perhaps the most influential and distinguished U.S. commentator on world affairs, of which his experience went back to the First World War; mainly in *The New Republic*, *New York World*, *New York Herald Tribune*.

Lloyd, Selwyn (Lord Selwyn-Lloyd; 1904–78) Cons. M.P. Wirral 1945–76. Min. of State, F.O. 1951–4; Min. of Supply 1954–5; Defence 1955; Foreign Sec. 1955–60; Chanc. of Exchequer 1960–2, dismissed in 'July massacre'; Lord Privy Seal and Leader of the House 1963–4; Speaker 1971–6.

Longford, Earl and Countess of, *see* Pakenham.

Macleod, Iain (1913–70) Cons. M.P. Enfield W. 1950–70; Min. of Health 1952–5, of Labour 1955–9, Colonial Sec. 1959–61; Party chairman, Leader of the House, and Chanc. of the Duchy 1961–3; of the Exchequer, 1970.

Macmillan, Harold (b. 1894) Publisher. Cons. M.P. Stockton 1924–9, 1931–45 (persistent rebel 1930s); Bromley 1945–64. Min.: N. Africa 1942–5, Air 1945, Housing & Local Govt. 1951–4, Defence 1954–5, Foreign Sec. 1955, Chanc. of Exchequer 1955–7, P.M. 1957–63. Chancellor, Oxford U. since 1960. Chairman Macmillans 1963–74, pres. since 1974.

McNeil, Hector (1907–55) Journalist. M.P. Greenock 1941–55. U. Sec. F.O. 1945–6, Min. of State 1946–50; Sec. for Scotland 1950–1.

Makins, Sir Roger (Lord Sherfield; b. 1904) Diplomat. Dep. Under Sec. F.O. 1948–52. Amb. to U.S. 1953–6. Joint Perm. Sec., Treasury 1956–9.

Malenkov, Georgi M. (b. 1902) Soviet P.M. 1953–5, Min. of Power Stations 1955–7, ousted from Praesidium with 'Anti-Party Group' of Khrushchev's opponents, managed a remote power station 1957–63, retired.

Malik, Yakov (1906–80) Soviet diplomat. Amb. to Japan 1942–5, to U.N. 1948–52 and 1968–76, to U.K. 1953–60; in Moscow meanwhile.

Manley, Norman (1893–1969) Founded People's National Party (of Jamaica) 1938. Chief or Prime Minister 1955–62, led Opposition 1962–9.

Mann, Mrs Jean (1890–1964) M.P. Coatbridge (and Airdrie, Lanarkshire) 1945–59. N.E.C. 1953–8.

Marquand, Hilary (1901–72) M.P. Cardiff E. 1945–50, Middlesbrough E. 1950–62. Sec. Overseas Trade 1945–7, Paymaster Gen. 1947–8, Min. of Pensions 1948–51, of Health 1951.

Martin, Basil Kingsley (1877–1969) Edited the *New Statesman* 1930–60 (ed. director 1961–2) with very great journalistic acumen and very little political sense. (After urging resistance to Hitler until September 1938, it became the first British paper to propose ceding him the Sudetenland.)

Maudling, Reginald (1917–79) Cons. M.P. Barnet (Herts) 1950–79. Econ. Sec. Treasury 1952–5, Min. of Supply 1955–7, Paymaster Gen. 1957–9, Pres. B.o.T. 1959–61, Colonial Sec. 1961–2, Chanc. of Exchequer 1962–4, Home Sec. 1970–2.

Mayhew, Christopher (Lord; b. 1915) With HG on Dalton's staff at Min. of Econ. Warfare. M.P. Norfolk S. 1945–50, Woolwich E. (succeeding Bevin) 1951–74. Morrison's P.P.S. 1945–6; Under Sec. F.O. 1946–50; Min. of Defence (Navy) 1964–6, resigned. Joined Liberals July 1974, stood for Bath Oct. 1974 and 1979.

Menzies, (Sir) Robert (1894–1978) Australian Lib. P.M. 1939–41, 1949–66; led Opp., 1943–9.

Mikardo, Ian (b. 1908) Industrial consultant. M.P. Reading 1945–59 (S., 1950–5), Poplar 1964–74, Tower Hamlets (Bethnal Green & Bow) since 1974. N.E.C. 1950–9, 1960–78. Chairman of P.L.P. March–Nov. 1974.

Mikoyan, Anastas I. (1895–1978) Armenian; the most durable of Soviet leaders; Central Committee of the C.P.S.U. from 1923, Praesidium 1952–66; Min. for Supply, Food or Trade between 1926 and 1955, Deputy P.M. 1955–64.

Mintoff, Dom (b. 1916) Leader of Malta's Labour Party since 1949; P.M. 1955–8 and since 1971; led Opposition 1962–71.

Mollet, Guy (1905–75) Led French Socialist party 1946–69. P.M. 1956–7, responsible for Suez. Facilitated de Gaulle's return to power 1958, broke with him 1959.

Molotov, V.M. (b. 1890) Soviet Foreign Min. 1939–49, 1953–6; Min. of State Control 1956–7; ousted with 'Anti-Party Group'; Amb. to Outer Mongolia 1957–60. Out of C.P.S.U., 1962.

Monckton, Sir Walter (Viscount; 1891–1965) King Edward VIII's chief adviser. Cons. M.P. Bristol W. 1951–7; Min. of Labour 1951–5, of Defence 1955–6 (sought move, because he opposed Suez); Paymaster Gen. 1956–7. Chairman, Comm. on C. African Fed. constitution, 1960.

Monnet, Jean (1888–1979) Proposed Anglo-French union 1940. Chief promoter of movement for united Europe, and chairman of action committee 1956–75. Architect of French econ. planning 1944, first Commissioner of the Plan; proposed Eur. Coal & Steel Community (the Schuman Plan) to French Foreign Min. Robert Schuman 1950; was its president 1952–3.

Montgomery, Field Marshal Viscount (of Alamein; 1887–1976) After major commands in N. Africa, Italy and France, was C.I.G.S. 1946–8.

Morrison, Herbert (Lord M. of Lambeth; 1888–1965) M.P. Hackney S. 1923–4, 1929–31, 1935–45; Lewisham E. 1945–51, S. 1951–9. Sec.

London L.P. 1915–47, Treasurer 1945–62; Leader of L.C.C. 1934–40. Min. of Transport 1929–31, Supply 1940, Home Sec. 1940–5; Deputy P.M., Lord Pres. and Leader of the House 1945–51; Foreign Sec. March–Oct. 1951. N.E.C. 1920, 1922–43, 1944–52 and (as Dep. Leader) 1953–5. P.C. 1935–40. Stood for Treasurer of L.P. against Arthur Greenwood, 1943; for Leader against Attlee and Greenwood 1935, and against HG and Bevan 1955. Dep. Leader, 1945–55.

Mountbatten, Admiral of the Fleet Earl (of Burma; 1900–79) Second cousin of the Queen. Supreme Commander S.E. Asia 1943–6; last Viceroy of India 1947 & Gov.-Gen. 1947–8; C.-in-C. Mediterranean 1952–4; First Sea Lord 1955–9; chairman Chiefs of Staff C'ttee 1959–65; assassinated by the Irish Republican Army.

Murphy, (Sir) Leslie (b. 1915) Private sec. to HG as Min. of Fuel & Power. Went into business 1952 (oil, merchant banking); dep. chairman, Nat. Enterprise board 1975–7, chairman 1977–9. Prominent member of SDP.

Murphy, Robert D. (1894–1978) U.S. businessman and diplomat. Arranged N. Africa landings with the French, 1942, became pol. adviser to U.S. commanders there and in Europe; then Amb. to Japan, senior State Dept. official; Dep. Under Sec. of State 1953–9.

Noel-Baker, Philip (Lord; 1889–1982) Disarmament expert (Nobel Peace Prize 1959). M.P. Coventry 1929–31, Derby 1936–70 (S. 1950–70). P.P.S. to Henderson, Foreign Sec. 1929–31. Parl. Sec. 1942–5; Min. of State F.O. 1945–6; Sec. Air 1946–7; Commonwealth Sec. (in Cabinet) 1947–50; Min. Fuel & Power (not Cab.) 1950–1. N.E.C. 1937–48; P.C. 1936–40, 1951–9.

Norstad, Lauris (b. 1907) U.S. Air Force general. Deputy (Air) to NATO Supreme Commander, 1953; Supreme Commander, 1956–62; retired (business).

Padley, Walter (b. 1916) I.L.P. Nat. Council 1940–6; later a Bevanite. M.P. Ogmore (Glam.) 1950–79; Min. of State, F.O. 1964–7. Pres. of USDAW 1948–64. N.E.C. 1956–79.

Pakenham, Frank (Earl of Longford; b. 1905) Shared HG's undergraduate lodgings. Univ. teacher; Conservative, Labour in 1930s, stood for Oxford 1945. Married Elizabeth Harman, undergraduate friend of HG, who stood for Oxford 1950; writer. As Lord Pakenham, U. Sec. War 1946–7, Min. of Civil Aviation 1948–51 (in Cab. till 1950), First Lord Admiralty 1951; as Lord Longford, Colonial Sec. 1965–6, Lord Privy Seal 1964–5, 1966–8, resigned.

Pannell, Charles (Lord; 1902–80) Engineer, A.E.U. M.P. Leeds W. 1949–74; hon. sec. T.U. Group of M.P.s 1953–62. Stood for Treasurer of L.P. 1956. Min. of Works 1964–6.

Pearson, Lester ('Mike'; 1897–1972) Canadian Min. of External Affairs 1948–57 (Nobel Peace Prize, 1957); led Liberal Opposition 1958–63; P.M. 1963–8.

Phillips, Morgan (1902–63) Research sec. of L.P. 1942; Gen. Sec. 1944–62.

Pineau, Christian (b. 1916) French trade unionist, Resistance leader, and Socialist deputy 1945–58. Foreign Min. 1956–8.

Plowden, Sir Edwin (Lord; b. 1907) Chief Planning Officer in Treasury 1947–53. Chairman, Atomic Energy Authority 1954–9; later, of Tube Investments.

Robens, Alfred (Lord; b. 1910) M.P. Wansbeck, Northumberland 1945–50, Blyth 1950–60. HG's Parl. Sec. at Fuel & Power 1947–51, Min. of Labour April–Oct. 1951. P.C. 1951–60; shadow Foreign Sec. 1955–6. Chairman of N.C.B. 1961–71, of Vickers Ltd. since 1971.

Roberthall, Lord, *see* Hall, Sir Robert.

Robertson, Norman (1904–68) Canadian Under-Sec. External Affairs 1941–6, 1958–64; Sec. to the Cabinet 1949–52; High Comm. in U.K. 1946–9, 1952–6; Amb. to U.S. 1957–8.

Rowan, Sir Leslie (1908–72) Private Sec. to Churchill 1941–5, Attlee 1945–7; Econ. Minister in Washington 1949–51; head of Overseas Finance Div. in Treasury 1951–8, retired.

Royal Family:
Queen Elizabeth II, b. 1926, Queen since 1952; m. 1947 Prince Philip, Duke of Edinburgh (b. 1921). Sister, Princess Margaret, Countess of Snowdon, b. 1930, m. 1960–78 Antony Armstrong-Jones, cr. Earl of Snowdon. Father, King George VI, 1895–1952, King from 1936; m. 1923 (as Duke of York) Lady Elizabeth Bowes-Lyon (b. 1900), now Queen Elizabeth the Queen Mother.

Russell, Bertrand, O.M. (3rd Earl Russell; 1872–1970) Famous as a mathematician, philosopher, political writer and (at most times) pacifist.

Salisbury, 5th Marquis of (1893–1972) As Visc. Cranborne was Cons. M.P. S. Dorset 1929–41; U. Sec. at F.O. 1935–8, resigned with Eden whom he is said to have persuaded. Peer 1941, succ. as Marquis 1947; Cons. leader in Lords 1942–57, as Dominions Sec., Lord Privy Seal, or (1952–7) Lord President; resigned over Cyprus.

Sandys, Duncan (Lord Duncan-Sandys; b. 1908) Married Churchill's daughter Diana. Cons. M.P. Norwood 1935–45, Streatham 1950–74; founded European Movement, 1947. Min. of Works 1944–5, Supply 1951–4, Housing and Local Govt. 1954–7, Defence 1957–9, Aviation 1959–60, Commonwealth Sec. 1960–4 (and Colonial Sec. 1962–4).

Shawcross, Sir Hartley (Lord; b. 1902) M.P. St. Helens 1945–58. Attorney

Gen. 1945–51, Pres. B.o.T. April–Oct. 1951. On Monckton Comm. on C. African Fed., 1960. Now a cross-bencher.

Shinwell, Emanuel (Lord; b. 1884) M.P. Linlithgow 1922–4, 1928–31; Durham (Seaham) 1935–50, (Easington) 1950–70. Parl. Sec. Mines 1924, 1930–1; Min. of Fuel & Power (in Cabinet) 1945–7, Sec. for War (not Cab.) 1947–50, for Defence 1950–1. N.E.C., 1940–51; P.C. 1923, 1937–9, 1951–5; chairman of P.L.P. 1964–7.

Silverman, Sydney (1895–1968) Solicitor. M.P. Nelson & Colne (Lancs.) 1935–68. Prominent left-winger, esp. in V.F.S. after 1958; his main parl. cause was ending the death penalty. N.E.C. 1956–7.

Smith, Ellis (1896–1969) M.P. Stoke 1935–66 (S. from 1950). Gen. Pres. United Patternmakers Ass. 1946–58. Parl. Sec. B.o.T. 1945–6.

Snyder, John W. (b. 1884) U.S. banker (from Missouri, President Truman's home state). Held several federal financial posts; Truman's Sec. of the Treasury, 1946–53.

Soskice, Sir Frank (Lord Stow Hill; 1902–79) M.P. Birkenhead E. 1945–50, Sheffield (Neepsend) 1950–5, Newport 1956–66. Solicitor Gen. 1945–51, Attorney Gen. April–Oct. 1951, Home Sec. 1964–5, Lord Privy Seal 1965–6. P.C. 1952–5, 1956–64.

Spender, (Sir) Percy (b. 1897) Former Australian Treasurer (Finance Min.); Min. of External Affairs 1949–51, Amb. to U.S. 1951–8.

Stevenson, Adlai E. (1900–65) Eisenhower's Democratic opponent for President of U.S. both 1952 and 1956 (when Harriman contested the nomination with ex-President Truman's support); a hero to liberal intellectuals on both sides of the Atlantic. Gov. of Illinois 1949–53; did not obtain nomination in 1960, but became Kennedy's Amb. to the U.N. 1961–5, when he died suddenly in a London street.

Stewart, Michael (Lord; b. 1906) M.P. Fulham 1945–79. U. Sec. War 1947–51, Supply 1951. P.C. 1960–4. Education Sec. 1964–5, Foreign Sec. 1965–6, 1968–70, First Sec. (Econ. Affs.) 1966–8.

Stokes, Richard R. (1897–1957) Ipswich manufacturer, and its M.P. 1938–57. Min. of Works 1950–1, of Materials (and Lord Privy Seal) 1951. P.C. 1951–2, 1955–6; defence spokesman 1955–6.

Strachey, John (1901–63) M.P. Birmingham (Aston) 1929–31; Dundee 1945–63 (W. from 1950). Left L.P. Feb. 1931 to join Mosley's New Party; left it July 1931, and became leading C.P. propagandist (never a member) until 1939. Author; Parl. Sec. Air 1945–6; Min. of Food 1946–50, Sec. for War 1950–1. A defence spokesman 1955–61.

Strauss, G. Russell (Lord; b. 1901, son of Cons. M.P.) M.P. Lambeth (N.) 1929–31, 1934–50; (Vauxhall) 1950–79. Expelled from L.P. with Cripps 1939, but quickly rejoined. Min. of Supply 1947–51 (not in Cabinet). Father of the House 1974–9.

Street, Sir Arthur (1892–1951) Perm. Sec. Air Ministry 1939–45; in Germany 1945–6; dep. chairman N.C.B. 1946–51.

Summerskill, Dr Edith (Baroness; 1901–80) M.P. Fulham W. 1938–55, Warrington 1955–61. Parl. Sec. Food 1940–50, Min. of Nat. Insurance 1950–1. N.E.C. 1944–58; P.C. 1951–7, 1958–9.

Tewson, (Sir) Vincent (1898–1981) ass. gen. sec. T.U.C. 1931–46; Gen. Sec. 1946–60.

Tiffin, Arthue E. ('Jock'; 1896–1955) ass. gen. sec. T.&G.W.U. 1948–55; Gen. Sec. June–Dec. 1955. N.E.C. 1949–55, Gen. Council 1955.

Tomlinson, George (1890–1952) Cotton weaver; Lancs. County Council 1931–52; M.P. Farnworth (Lancs.) 1938–52; Parl. Sec. Min. of Labour 1941–5, Min. of Works 1945–7, of Education 1947–51.

Truman, Harry S. (1884–1972) Farmer; judge; Democratic Senator from Missouri 1934–44; Vice-Pres. of U.S. 1945, President 1945–53.

Tyerman, Donald (1908–81) Once HG's co-examiner before the war. Journalist on the *Observer* and *The Times*; Ed. *The Economist* 1956–65.

Ungoed-Thomas, Sir Lynn (1904–72) M.P. Llandaff & Barry (Glam.) 1945–50, Leicester N.E. 1950–62. Solicitor Gen. 1951; judge, 1962.

Walston, Harry (Lord; b. 1912) Wealthy farmer who fought E. Anglian seats, as Lib. 1945 and four times for Labour in 1950s. An under-sec. 1964–7, and later chairman of the E. Anglian Rural Planning Commission. Joined SDP.

Warbey, William (1903–80) Adult ed. tutor. M.P. Luton 1945–50; Notts. 1953–66 (Broxtowe 1953–5, then Ashfield); among the few left-wingers asked to resign by his local Party.

Watson, Sam (1898–1967) Sec. of Durham miners 1936–63, and HG's closest T.U. ally. Refused all offers to enter politics or move to London. N.E.C. 1941–63.

Webb, James (b. 1906) U.S. industrialist; Democrat. Director, Bureau of the Budget 1946–9; Under Sec. of State 1949–52; Dir. Nat. Aeronautic and Space Admin. 1961–8.

Webb, Maurice (1904–56) *D. Herald* journalist 1935–44. M.P. Bradford C. 1945–55; chairman of P.L.P. 1946–50. Min. of Food 1950–1.

Webber, (Sir) William (1901–82) Ass. gen. sec. of T.S.S.A. 1949–53, Gen. Sec. 1953–62. N.E.C. 1949–53, Gen. Council 1953–62. On N.C.B. 1962–7.

Welensky, Sir Roy (b. 1907) S. Rhodesian: engine-driver, trade unionist and boxing champion. Deputy P.M. of C. African Federation 1953–6, P.M. 1956–63.

Whiteley, William (1882–1955) Miner. M.P. Blaydon (Durham) 1922–31, 1935–55. Whip 1927, Chief Whip 1942–55.

Wigg, George (Lord; b. 1900) Regular Army 1919–37, 1940–6. M.P.
Dudley 1945–67; Shinwell's P.P.S. Military specialist. Paymaster
Gen. 1964–7, resp. for security. Since 1957, various posts regulating
forms of gambling.

Williamson, (Sir) Tom (Lord; 1897–1983) Gen. Sec. N.U.G.M.W.
1946–61. N.E.C. 1940–7, Gen. Council 1947–62. M.P. Brigg (Lincs.)
1945–8; director, *D. Herald*, 1953–62.

Wilmot, John (Lord; 1895–1964) M.P. Fulham E. (winning a famous
by-election) 1933–5, Lambeth (Kennington) 1939–45, Deptford
1945–50. N.E.C. 1940–1. Dalton's P.P.S. 1940–4. Parl. Sec. Supply
1944–5, Minister 1945–7. Went into business.

Wilson, (Sir) Harold (b. 1916) Economist. M.P. Ormskirk (Lancs.)
1945–50, Huyton since 1950. Director Econ. and Statistics, Min. of
Fuel & Power during war. Parl. Sec. Works 1945–7, Sec. Overseas
Trade 1947, Pres. B.o.T. 1947–51, resigned. N.E.C. 1952–63; P.C.
1953–63. Shadow Chancellor 1955–61, Shadow Foreign Sec. 1961–
3. Stood against HG for Leader 1960, against Brown for Deputy
1962. Leader 1963–76; of Opposition, 1963–4, 1970–4; P.M. 1964–
70, 1974–6, resigned.

Woodburn, Arthur (1890–1978) Engineering administrator. Scottish Sec.
of L.P. 1931–9. M.P. Clackmannan & E. Stirling 1939–70. Parl. Sec.
Supply 1945–7; Sec. for Scotland 1947–50.

Wyatt, Woodrow (b. 1918) M.P. Birmingham (Aston) 1945–55, Bosworth
(Leics.) 1959–70. Under-Sec. War 1951. Journalist; in original Keep
Left group, but broke with Bevanites 1951.

Younger, (Sir) Kenneth (1908–76) M.P. Grimsby 1945–59. Under Sec.
Home Office 1947–50; Min. of State F.O. 1950–1. P.C. 1955–7.

Zilliacus, Konni (1894–1967) Son of a Finnish father and Scots-American
mother, born in Japan, ed. U.K. and U.S.; League of Nations
official 1919–39 where HG knew him well at Geneva in 1935. M.P.
Gateshead 1945–50, Manchester (Gorton) 1955–67. Expelled from
L.P. 1949 as fellow-traveller, back 1952, suspended briefly 1962.

SELECT BIBLIOGRAPHY

Particulars of publication are given in the first footnote where a book is cited in one chapter only; those listed below appear in more than one.

Chester, Sir Norman, *The Nationalisation of British Industry 1945–51* (H.M. Stationery Office, 1975).

Dalton, Hugh, *High Tide and After* (Memoirs III: Muller, 1962).

Donoughue, Bernard and Jones, G.W., *Herbert Morrison: Portrait of a Politician* (Weidenfeld & Nicolson, 1973).

Eden, Anthony, Earl of Avon, *Full Circle* (Cassell, 1960).

Foot, Michael, *Aneurin Bevan 1945–1960* (Davis-Poynter, 1973).

Gardner, Richard N., *Sterling-Dollar Diplomacy* (OUP, 1956; new ed., McGraw Hill, N.Y., 1969).

Goodman, Geoffrey, *The Awkward Warrior: Frank Cousins, His Life and Times* (Davis-Poynter, 1979).

Hunter, Leslie, *The Road to Brighton Pier* (Arthur Barker, 1959).

Macmillan, Harold, *At the End of the Day* (Memoirs VI; Macmillan, 1973).

Pincher, Chapman, *Inside Story* (Sidgwick & Jackson, 1979 ed.).

Schlesinger, Arthur M. junior, *A Thousand Days: John F. Kennedy in the White House* (André Deutsch, 1965).

Williams, Francis, *A Prime Minister Remembers* (Heinemann, 1961).

Williams, Philip M., *Hugh Gaitskell: A Political Biography* (Cape, 1979).

INDEX

Using the Index: Organisations indexed by their initials come *first* under the relevant letter, e.g. AEU before Abadan. Titles are normally those used during the period of the diary. All members of the Royal Family appear under that heading. Source footnotes and Appendix I are not indexed. Reference to offices held includes shadow posts.